Advances in Network Information Theory

DIMACS

Series in Discrete Mathematics and Theoretical Computer Science

Volume 66

Advances in Network Information Theory

DIMACS Workshop
Network Information Theory
March 17-19, 2003
Piscataway, New Jersey

Piyush Gupta
Gerhard Kramer
Adriaan J. van Wijngaarden
Editors

Center for Discrete Mathematics
and Theoretical Computer Science
A consortium of Rutgers University, Princeton University,
AT&T Labs–Research, Bell Labs (Lucent Technologies),
NEC Laboratories America, and Telcordia Technologies
(with partners at Avaya Labs, IBM Research, and Microsoft Research)

American Mathematical Society

This DIMACS volume presents the proceedings from the workshop Network Information Theory held at the DIMACS Center, Rutgers University, March 17–19, 2003.

2000 *Mathematics Subject Classification.* Primary 94A15, 94A17, 94A40, 94A05, 94A29, 94A24, 94B35, 94-06.

Library of Congress Cataloging-in-Publication Data

Advances in network information theory: DIMACS Workshop Network Information Theory, March 17–19, 2003, Piscataway, New Jersey / Piyush Gupta, Gerhard Kramer, Adriaan J. van Wijngaarden, editors.

p. cm. — (DIMACS series in discrete mathematics and theoretical computer science ; v. 66)

Includes bibliographical references.

ISBN 0-8218-3467-3 (alk.paper)

1. Computer networks–Congresses. 2. Information theory–Congresses. I. Gupta, Piyush, 1971– II. Kramer, Gerhard, 1970– III. Van Wijngaarden, Adriaan J., 1968– IV. Series.

TK5105.5.A335 2004
004.6–dc22 2004051900

∞ The paper used in this book is acid-free and falls within the guidelines
established to ensure permanence and durability.
Visit the AMS home page at http://www.ams.org/

10 9 8 7 6 5 4 3 2 1 09 08 07 06 05 04

Contents

Part III. Information Theory for Sources and Channels

Part IV. Coding

Foreword

This DIMACS volume on "Network Information Theory" is a collection of refereed contributions written by leading researchers in the area of information theory. The articles focus on problems concerning efficient and reliable communication in multi-terminal settings. The articles were developed from the DIMACS Workshop on Network Information Theory held at Rutgers University, Piscataway, NJ, on March 17-19, 2003. This workshop was part of the 2001–2004 Special Focus on Computational Information Theory and Coding, which aims to explore interconnections among coding theory, theoretical computer science, information theory, and related areas of computer science and mathematics. It addresses some of the challenges for the next 50 years—in particular, wireless communication, magnetic/optical storage, the role of signal processing in networks, network information theory, and the creation of quantum information theory.

We would like to express our appreciation to Piyush Gupta, Gerhard Kramer and Adriaan J. van Wijngaarden for organizing this successful workshop and for editing this volume. We extend our thanks to Robert Calderbank, Chris Rose, Amin Shokrollahi, Emina Soljanin and Sergio Verdú for their efforts as Special Focus organizers.

The Special Focus was made possible by funding from the National Science Foundation and the New Jersey Commission on Science and Technology. We would also like to express our appreciation to the DIMACS partners at Rutgers University, Princeton University, AT&T Labs, Bell Labs, NEC Laboratories America, and Telcordia Technologies, and to our affiliate partners at Avaya Labs, IBM Research and Microsoft Research for their support of this and other DIMACS programs.

Fred S. Roberts
DIMACS Director

Robert Tarjan
Co-Director for Princeton

Preface

This volume on network information theory focuses on efficient and reliable communication in multi-terminal settings. This field has recently attracted renewed attention due to fast-growing applications such as the Internet, wireless cellular and LAN data services, ad hoc networks and sensor networks. As these networks mature, the need for good transmission strategies and codes becomes more acute. Recent advances in the area have revived interest in codes for networks, e.g., codes for efficient routing and codes for multiple antenna wireless channels. This volume aims to contribute to the understanding of better models of networks, to the creation of new ways of coding, and to making existing coding techniques practical.

The articles collected here are first-rate refereed constributions on network information theory by leading researchers in the area. The volume developed from the DIMACS Workshop on Network Information Theory that was held at Rutgers University, Piscataway, NJ on March 17–19, 2003. This event was part of a series of workshops being organized under the auspices of the "DIMACS 2001–2004 Special Focus on Computational Information Theory and Coding," which is a program funded by the National Science Foundation and the New Jersey Commission on Science and Technology. The workshop consisted of 27 invited presentations, and there were 132 registered participants, many of them from the local institutions: Rutgers, AT&T Research, Princeton, Bell Labs, Brooklyn Polytechnic, but also several from Ann Arbor, Berkeley, CalTech, Cornell, Maryland, MIT, UCLA, UCSD, UIUC, Yale, as well as from Canada, Denmark, Germany, Israel, The Netherlands, Sweden and Switzerland.

The volume is divided into four main parts. The first part, "Information Theory for Sources," concentrates on network source coding problems. The contribution by A. Faridi, K. Sayrafian-Pour, M. Alasti and A. Ephremides shows how source coding, and especially multiple-description source coding, can be used to improve the performance of parallel routing algorithms. The contribution by S.A. Savari introduces a new graph entropy called the "interchange entropy," which can be expected to become important for network problems where ordering of events and concurrency are studied. The contribution by P. Viswanath studies the difficult problem of lossy multiterminal source coding, and finds new solutions for a class of Gaussian sources and distortion measures. The contribution by F.M.J. Willems and T. Kalker looks at several new data-hiding problems that are practically motivated, and provides their solutions.

The second part of the volume contains contributions on "Information Theory for Channels" where now the channels, rather than the sources, are central to the problem. The contribution by A.S. Cohen and R. Zamir considers the celebrated dirty paper coding problem, and presents a class of channels for which the capacity loss with causal side information as compared to the no-interference case is unbounded. The contribution by R.J. La and V. Anantharam considers a multiaccess channel where the users can form coalitions to try to jam the other users, and employs concepts from both information theory and game theory. The contribution by X. Liu and R. Srikant studies the sum timing capacity for discrete-time queues, and the impact of scheduling disciplines on eavesdropping. The contribution by S. Raj, E. Telatar and D. Tse develops interconnections between information theory for multiaccess channels and job scheduling for multiprocessor queues. The contribution by D. Tuninetti and S. Shamai considers fading broadcast channels and explains some of the subtleties of the existing rate regions. The contribution by L.-L. Xie and P.R. Kumar discusses fundamental issues concerning the architecture of future wireless networks. Finally, the contribution by W. Yu gives a complete characterization of the worst-case noise for Gaussian vector broadcast channels.

The third part includes contributions that address both source and channel coding, and is named "Information Theory for Sources and Channels." The contribution by J. Barros and S.D. Servetto gives a comprehensive solution to a problem that includes multiterminal source coding, conferencing and channel coding. The contribution by M. Effros, M. Médard, T. Ho, S. Ray, D. Karger, R. Koetter and B. Hassibi treats source, channel and network coding in a common framework by using random linear coding arguments. The contribution by M. Gastpar develops a cut-set bound for networks that utilizes the Wyner-Ziv rate-distortion function, and further gives scaling laws for Gaussian sensor networks. The contribution of S.S. Pradhan and K. Ramchandran derives several theorems on the functional duality between source and channel coding.

The fourth part, entitled "Coding," is concerned with more practical issues than the first three categories. The first contribution, by G. Caire, S. Shamai and S. Verdú, describes a noiseless data compression algorithm that employs low-density parity-check codes and the Burrows-Wheeler block sorting transform. The contribution by S.N. Diggavi, N. Al-Dhahir and A.R. Calderbank constructs space-time codes that have a high-diversity code embedded within them. The contribution by E. Erkip, A. Sendonaris, A. Stefanov and B. Aazhang develops coding strategies that take advantage of user cooperation to reduce the frame error rate. The contribution by E. Soljanin, R. Liu and P. Spasojevic analyzes the performance of hybrid automatic repeat request schemes and practical codes. The contribution by J.K. Wolf presents an information-theoretic approach to bit-stuffing, a coding technique commonly used in networks, and shows how bit-stuffing can be modified to yield rates equal to the capacity.

It is a great pleasure to acknowledge Fred Roberts, DIMACS Director, for creating and maintaining the excellent infrastructure for the workshop and Robert Calderbank, Chris Rose, Amin Shokrollahi, Emina Soljanin and Sergio Verdú for organizing the Special Focus on Computational Information Theory and Coding. We are grateful to Alexander Barg and Mel Janowitz, DIMACS Associate Directors, and to Linda Casals, Sarah Donnelly, Jessica Herold, Christine Houck and Maria Mercado of DIMACS for their assistance during the workshop organization, and to Luann Cole, Christine Thivierge and Shirley Hill of the American Mathematical Society for their assistance in the preparation of this volume. We are indebted to the National Science Foundation and the New Jersey Commission on Science and Technology for their financial support of the workshop and the American Mathematical Society for publishing this volume. Finally, we wish to thank the authors for their outstanding contributions and their cooperation in the reviewing process.

Piyush Gupta, Gerhard Kramer, and Adriaan J. van Wijngaarden

Part I

Information Theory for Sources

DIMACS Series in Discrete Mathematics
and Theoretical Computer Science
Volume **66**, 2004

Source Coding and Parallel Routing

A. Faridi, K. Sayrafian-Pour, M. Alasti, and A. Ephremides

ABSTRACT. We consider a simple communication network model and focus on a single source-destination pair to exploit the interconnection between Source Coding and Parallel Routing. We consider a Distortion Measure that combines signal reconstruction fidelity with network delay and we pose the problem of minimizing this Measure by jointly choosing the Encoder Parameters and the Routing Parameters. We look at single-description coding as well as multiple-description coding and we perform numerical optimization that yields interesting design trade-offs that are insightful and can be exploited in more realistic environments.

1. Introduction

It is recognized that in Communication Networks the inherent coupling and dependence among the layers of traditional architectures provides opportunities for significant performance improvement by exploiting these interactions selectively.

In this paper we demonstrate this principle by focusing on the interaction between Source Coding (traditionally a layer 6 issue with physical layer connections) and Routing (a layer 3 issue). In particular we observe that in networks, often, packets are duplicated and routed over separate paths to their common destination to increase the chance of timely delivery and to provide protection against packet loss and long delays. This practice is called parallel routing and obviously results in increasing the offered load to the network.

At the same time we know that compression techniques can reduce packet length. So a natural question is how to choose the source encoding parameters in conjunction with the routing parameters so as to minimize a suitable distortion measure that incorporates both the quality of the signal reconstruction as well as its delay.

In particular if multiple description coding is used the possibility arises naturally that each description follows a different path to the destination, thereby

Key words and phrases. Source coding, multiple description coding, parallel routing, end-to-end distortion, delay-sensitive traffic.

This work was supported in part by NSF Grant No. AN10205330 and ONR Grant No. N000140310007. Prepared through collaborative participation in the Collaborative Technology Alliance for Communications & Networks sponsored by the U.S. Army Research Laboratory under Cooperative Agreement DAAD19-01-2-0011.

The material is based upon work supported by NASA under award No. NCC8-235.

combining the idea of protection through redundancy with the need to reduce the traffic load.

Finally choosing the packet length itself (or, more accurately, the source encoding rate or "symbol"-length) along with designing the multiple description coding and choosing the routing parameters goes even further in exploiting the observed interrelationships.

In this paper we study precisely this problem in the simplest of settings and identify and analyze the underlying trade-offs. More complicated and realistic models can be naturally studied along similar lines in the future.

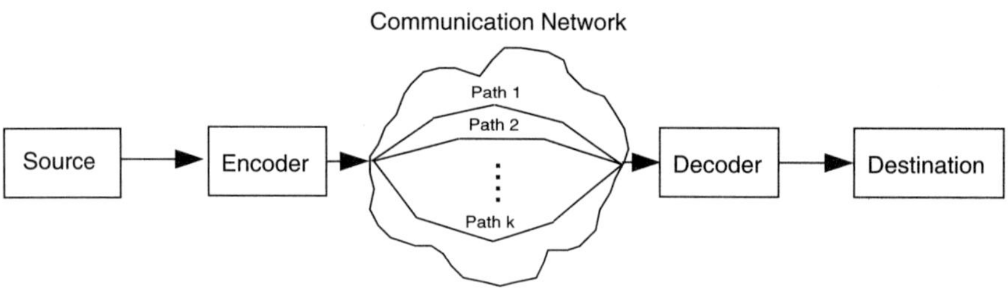

FIGURE 1. System Diagram

Consider the simple diagram shown in Figure 1 that consists of a source-destination pair, a source encoding-decoding module and a communication network that delivers packets from the source to the destination. If the source is delay-sensitive (e.g. real time voice or video), then any delay incurred by packets transiting the network could decrease the perceived quality at the receiver.

A distortion function is a mathematical performance measure that indicates the amount of degradation in the quality of the decoded information. The delay budget that each packet can afford is determined by the application. For example for Voice over IP (VoIP), a network delay of more than 50 msec creates unacceptable quality or equivalently high distortion.

Normally, each source symbol is compressed and appropriately transformed to a single codeword by the encoder before entering the network. This coding scheme is referred to as Single Description Coding (SDC). The coded symbols (i.e. packets) usually follow a single path determined by the network to reach to the destination. A path usually consists of several segments or communication links that connect nodes in a network. Since each node could experience congestion, there is a chance that a particular packet will be excessively delayed or even be dropped from the transmission queue.

As mentioned before, parallel transmission reduces the chance of packet loss when congestion occurs in a network; however, the excess bit rate introduced by the extra copies creates additional traffic that in effect contributes to congestion and thus increases the probability of packet loss.

A Multiple Description Coder (MDC) also transforms the sequence of source symbols into several parallel data streams; however, no excess bit rate over a single description coder is used. Therefore, the source traffic can potentially adjust itself to the state of the network without being a contributing factor to congestion [**A01**].

Achievable rate-distortion region for a Double Description Coder (DDC) and a Gaussian source has been studied in [**O80**], [**E82**]. In [**A01**], it was shown that for a simple network that consists of two parallel communication links, using an optimized DDC amounts to significant reduction in distortion compared to SDC. In this paper, we include multiple routing into the optimization process and consider the effects of this cross-layer interaction into the average end-to-end distortion.

The general modeling and assumptions are described next. Then, in Section 3, we provide analytical and numerical results for the SDC case. Section 4 considers a simplified double description coding system and provides the numerical results for the behavior of the end-to-end average distortion. Section 5 compares the results obtained for SDC and DDC systems. Finally, conclusions and suggestions for future works are provided in Section 6.

2. General Modeling and Assumptions

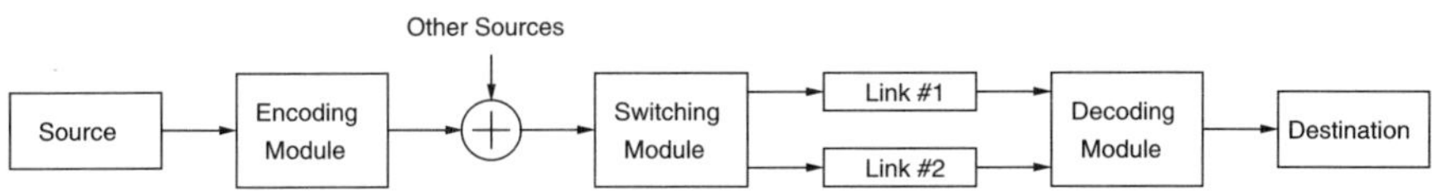

FIGURE 2. General System Model

To better focus on the interrelationships of the source coding and routing parameters, we consider the simple setting shown in Figure 2 along with the following simplifying assumptions.

1. The source is memoryless, loss-tolerant, and delay-sensitive (the symbols can tolerate a delay of up to Δ seconds)
2. The source generates i.i.d., zero mean, unit variance, Gaussian symbols.
3. Two classes of encoding-decoding schemes (i.e., SDC and DDC) are considered.
4. The length of the output codewords (i.e. packets) of each encoder follows an exponential distribution. This assumption greatly simplifies the analysis of the problem.
5. The decoding module drops the packets that have experienced a delay exceeding Δ seconds and replaces them with "null" symbols.
6. The output of the encoding module is added to the traffic coming from other similar (i.e., with the same packet length distribution) independent sources. These traffic streams are coming from different paths in the network. According to the Palm-Khintchin theorem [**R92**] this type of aggregate traffic converges to a Poisson point process. Moreover, the packets of this aggregate traffic will follow an exponential distribution similar to that of the encoder outputs.
7. The switching module will determine how the aggregate traffic is distributed among different paths.
8. The network consists of two disjoint, noise-free communication links with capacities C_i, $i = 1, 2$.
9. Each communication link is modelled by a First Come First Serve (i.e. FCFS) single server queue.

It should be noted that since we will be dealing with the rate distortion function in this paper, the most practical choice for the packet length distributions would be one that complies with the codewords of the encoders that can achieve the rate-distortion function. To approach the rate-distortion limits, one needs to employ a vector quantizer with a sufficiently large block length (encode n symbols at a time). If n is large enough the block lengths will approach a constant in the limit according to AEP (Asymptotic Equipartition Property). The case of constant packet lengths was studied in [**A01**] where it is shown that the general behavior observed under exponential packet length distribution is similar to that of a deterministic distribution. This justifies the use of assumption (4).

It should also be noted that large block lengths will result in long delays. Since delay is a crucial component of the distortion function we will choose, we need to implicitly assume that the transmission rates are sufficiently fast so that "long" packets in number of bits are not "long" with respect to time.

Details regarding the operation of the system with SDC or DDC are considered next in sections 3 and 4.

3. System with Single Description Coding

In this case (SDC), the source symbols are encoded with an average rate of R bits/symbol. The codewords generated by the encoder are added to the traffic coming from other similar and independent sources in the network. The aggregate traffic forms a Poisson process with rate λ packets/sec and an exponential packet length distribution with average length R bits/packet. This traffic is routed to the first queue with probability $q_1 = q$ and to the second queue with probability $q_2 = 1 - q$. Figure 3 represents the system model that will be analyzed in the rest of this section.

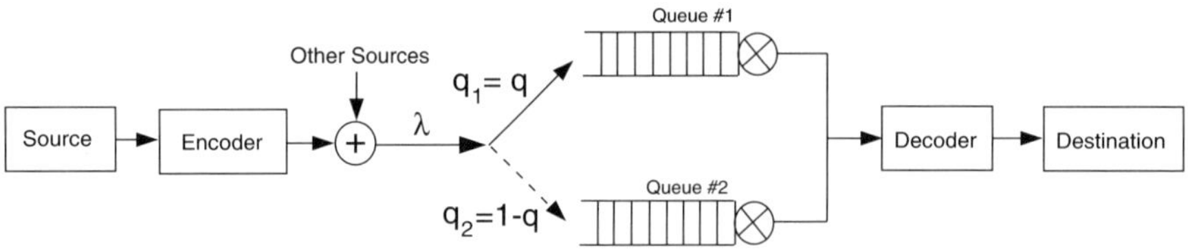

FIGURE 3. SDC System Model

3.1. Average End-to-End Distortion for SDC.

Let T be a random variable indicating the total delay that a packet experiences before reaching its destination. If D represents the achieved mean square error (MSE) distortion for an i.i.d. zero mean, unit variance Gaussian source, based on [**C91**] and on our concept of delay-based distortion, we have

$$D = \begin{cases} 2^{-2R} & \text{if} \quad T \leq \Delta \\ 1 & \text{if} \quad T > \Delta \end{cases}$$

The end-to-end average distortion, therefore, can be written as

$$\overline{D} = 2^{-2R} P[T \leq \Delta] + P[T > \Delta] \tag{3.1}$$

In order to easily compute the probabilities for packet delay, it is assumed that the length of the transmitted codewords follow an exponential distribution and so the service time for each queue (i.e. 'τ_i' $i = 1, 2$) is an exponential random variable. Packet arrival and service rates for each single queue are

$$\lambda_i = q_i \lambda, \ \mu_i = \frac{C_i}{R}, \ i = 1, 2$$

Therefore, the loading factor for each queue is given by

$$\rho_i = \min\left(\frac{q_i \lambda R}{C_i}, 1\right), \ i = 1, 2$$

The distribution of the system delay for an $M/M/1$ queue is known to be [**W89**] given by

$$F_{T_i}(t) = \left(1 - e^{-\mu_i (1-\rho_i) t}\right) u(t), \ i = 1, 2$$

where 'T_i', $i = 1, 2$ is a random variable indicating the total delay of a typical packet that is routed to queue 'i' $i = 1, 2$ and u(t) is the unit step function. If T is a random variable indicating the total delay of a typical packet, then we have

$$P[T > \Delta] = \sum_{i=1}^{2} q_i (1 - F_{T_i}(\Delta)) = \sum_{i=1}^{2} q_i e^{-\mu_i (1-\rho_i)\Delta} \ u(t) \tag{3.2}$$

Minimizing the average distortion in this case is equivalent to minimizing the delay probability expression of Eq 3.2.

3.2. Jointly Optimal SDC with Fixed Average Encoding Rate. If the average encoding rate (R) is fixed, then the average end-to-end distortion is only a function of the multiplexing ratio (q). Define q^* to be the optimal multiplexing ratio, in other words

$$q^* = \arg\min \ \overline{D}(q)$$

Then define

$$q_1^* = q^* \ , \ q_2^* = 1 - q^*$$

$$\rho_i^* = \min\left(\frac{q_i^* \lambda R}{C_i}, 1\right) \ i = 1, 2$$

Figure 4 demonstrates the achieved end-to-end distortion (i.e. $\overline{D}(q)$) for $q = 0.5$ and $q = q^*$ for a given set of parameters ($R = 6$ bits/symbol, $\Delta = 50$ msec, $C_1 = C_2 = 1000$ bits/sec). The variations in q^*, ρ_1^* and ρ_2^* for various arrival rates λ have been displayed in Figure 5 . For $\lambda \leq 316$, the value of q^* is indeed 0.5 and the curve for $\overline{D}(q^*)$ is identical to $\overline{D}(0.5)$. When $\lambda > 316$, $\overline{D}(q^*)$ is clearly less than $\overline{D}(0.5)$. To illustrate this phenomenon, it is instructive to consider the behaviors of q^*, ρ_1^* and ρ_2^* for various arrival rate values. At $\lambda = 316^+$, $\rho_2^* = 1$ and ρ_1^* jumps to 0.76. This means that the second queue is severely back-logged and all arrivals to this queue will be increasingly delayed. In the mean time q^* is adjusting itself so that ρ_1^* is kept at 0.76; and therefore, the first queue is operating under a stable condition. In effect, what is happening is that the router is sacrificing a portion of the traffic in order to enable the remaining packets to maintain an acceptable delay.

In other words, at some arrival rate (λ), instead of having two equally congested queues, the multiplexer reduces the amount of distortion by avoiding congestion in one queue and dumping the excess traffic into the second queue. The point that this event occurs (i.e., $\lambda = 316$) is clearly a function of the parameters R, Δ and C. This phenomenon has been analytically explained in Appendix A.

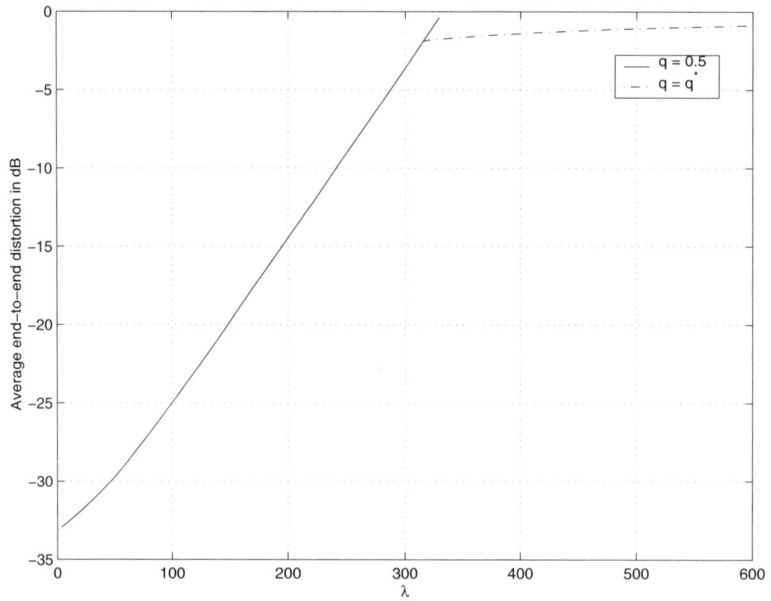

FIGURE 4. Average End-to-End Distortion for SDC, $C_1 = C_2 = C = 1000$ bits/sec, $R = 6$ bits, $\Delta = 50$ msec

Figures 6 and 7 display the same results in case of $C_1 = 1.4C$ and $C_2 = 0.6C$. Under this unbalanced set of capacity values, using q^* yields considerable gain in the achieved distortion compared to the case of $q = 0.5$. By observing the variation of q^* in Figure 7, one can identify three regions for the system behavior. Region 1 suggests that up to a certain load, all packets should be routed to the faster link (e.g. C_1). In region 2, both links are used for packet transmission and q^* is gradually decreased until $\lambda \approx 300$, at which point we enter region 3 where q^* decreases further so that ρ_1^* is maintained around 0.8 and $\rho_2^* = 1$. This situation is similar to that observed for the case where $C_1 = C_2$.

3.3. Jointly Optimal SDC with Optimal Average Encoding Rate. So far, we have performed the optimization over the multiplexing ratio q. Another parameter that can affect both the coding segment as well as the network segment is R. From the coding point of view, R determines the average codeword length; therefore, higher R results in higher resolution for the codewords and thus, less distortion is expected at the decoder. On the other hand, R is the average packet length which means that higher R results in longer packets or equivalently longer delay; and therefore, higher distortion for a delay sensitive source.

This tradeoff points to the possibility of the existence of an optimal R that minimizes the average end-to-end distortion for such delay sensitive sources. In

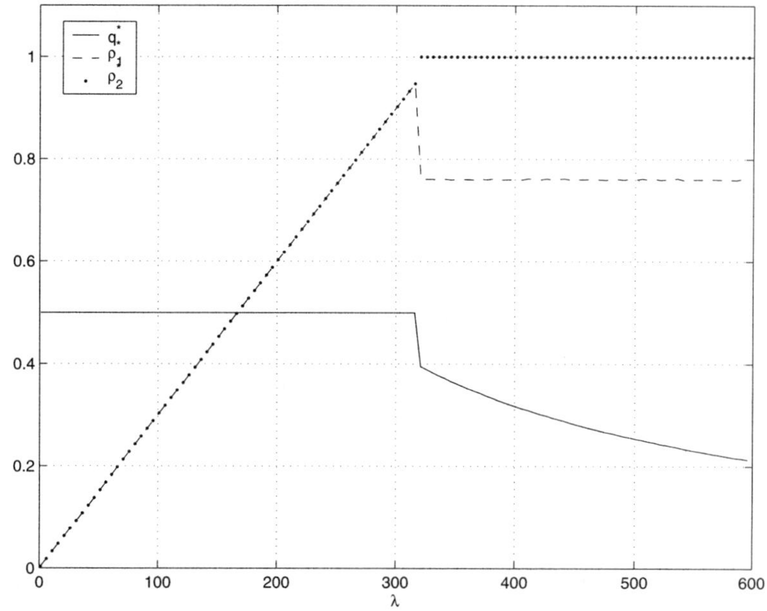

FIGURE 5. Optimal Network Parameters for SDC, $C_1 = C_2 = C = 1000$ bits/sec, $R = 6$ bits, $\Delta = 50$ msec

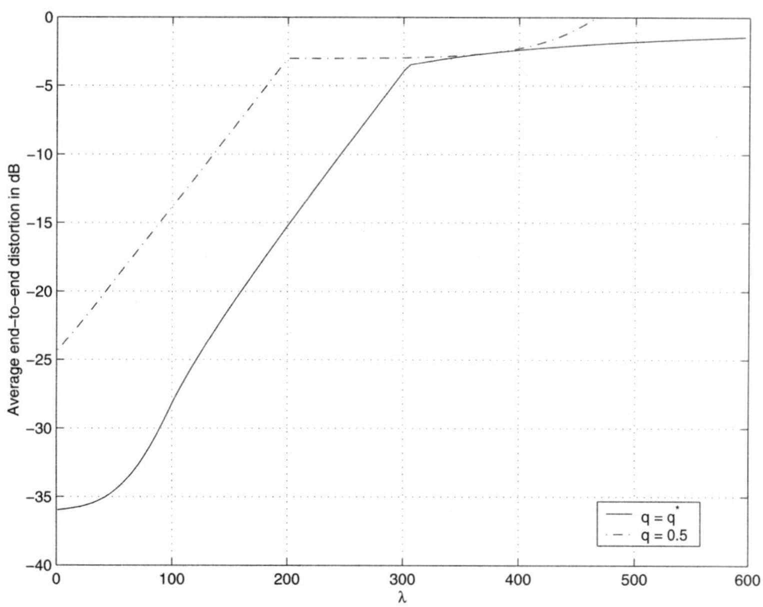

FIGURE 6. Average End-to-End Distortion for SDC, $C_1 = 1400$ bits/sec, $C_2 = 600$ bits/sec, $R = 6$ bits, $\Delta = 50$ msec

this section, we reformulate our problem to find this optimal average rate (i.e. R^*) for any given network load. In other words, we have

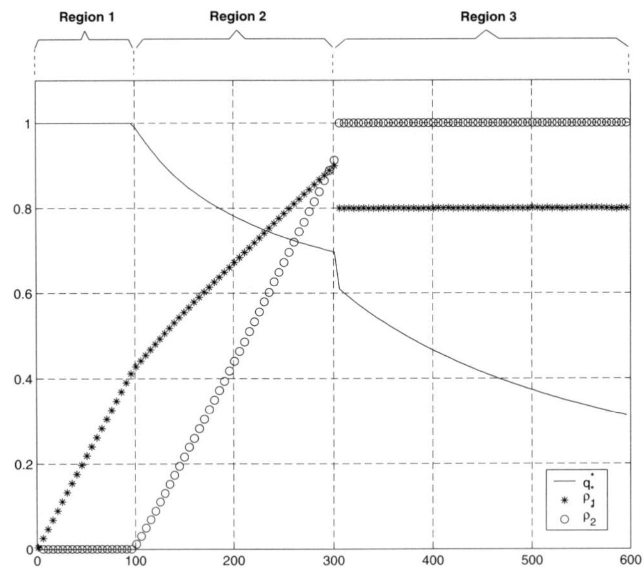

FIGURE 7. Optimal Network Parameters for SDC, $C_1 = 1400$ bits/sec $C_2 = 600$ bits/sec, $R = 6$ bits, $\Delta = 50$ msec

$$(q^*, R^*) = \arg\min \overline{D}(q, R)$$

The expected distortion and delay probability are calculated as in Eq 3.1 and Eq 3.2 respectively. The average end-to-end distortion and the value of R^* that minimizes the distortion are demonstrated in Figures 8 and 9 for $C_1 = C_2 = 1000$ bits/sec and $\Delta = 50$ msec. The optimal value for q turns out to be $q^* = 0.5$. Note that for $\lambda \approx 0$ value of R^* is 6.006.

For the case where $C_1 = 1400$ bits/sec, $C_2 = 600$ bits/sec, and $\Delta = 50$ msec, the average end-to-end distortion, R^* and q^* have been displayed in Figures 10, 11 and 12 respectively. Comparing Figure 10 to Figure 6 shows how optimizing the rate can result in a smaller distortion. Note that in Figure 10 the results are plotted for a wider range of values of λ.

For small values of λ, $q^* = 1$; therefore, all packets are routed to the link with the higher capacity. When λ increases, the multiplexing ratio starts to decrease to allow packets to utilize both links. At the same time R is decreasing to compensate for the occurring queueing delay.

Also as seen in Figure 12, asymptotic behavior of q^* points to a system with balanced load. At high values of the arrival rate $\rho_1 = \rho_2$ or equivalently

$$q^* = \frac{C_1}{C_1 + C_2}$$

Note that both queues are stable for all values of λ. This asymptotic behavior was not observed when we considered a fixed value for R. In that case, at high

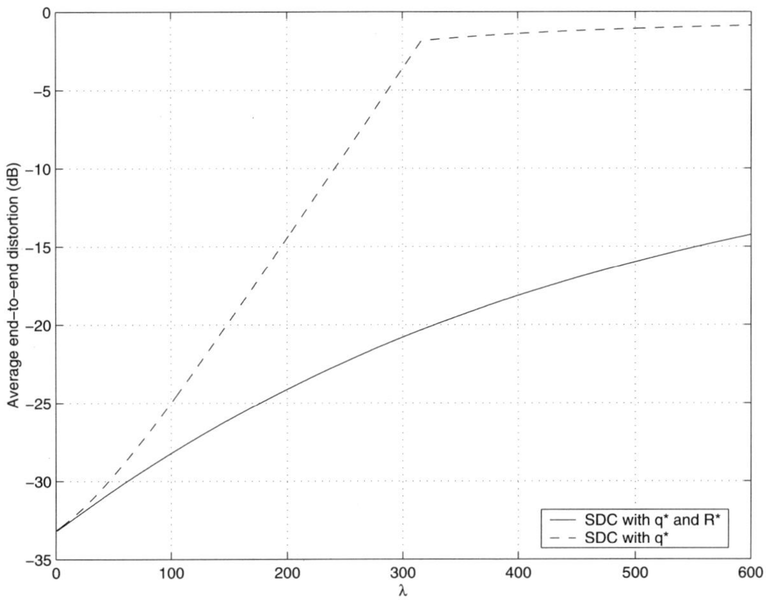

FIGURE 8. Improvement achieved by optimizing R in SDC system, $C_1 = C_2 = 1000$ bits/sec, $\Delta = 50$ msec

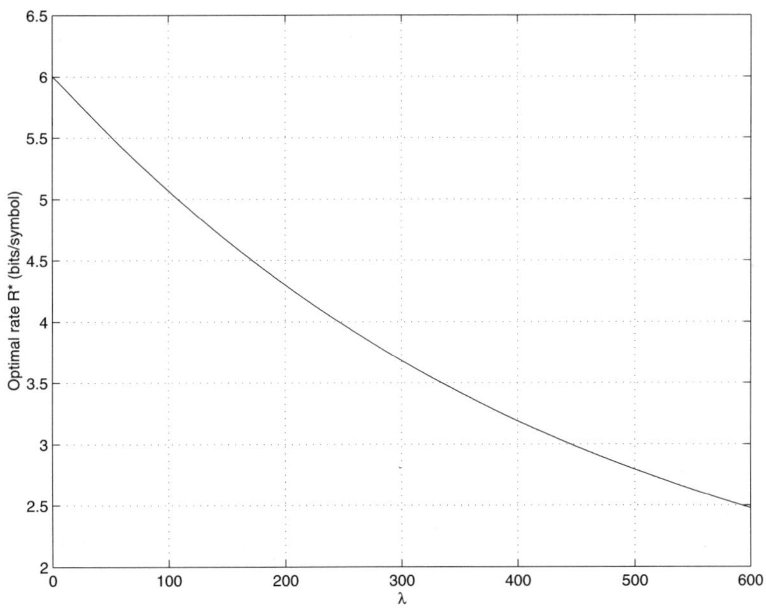

FIGURE 9. Optimal rate (R^*) in SDC, $C_1 = C_2 = 1000$ bits/sec, $\Delta = 50$ msec

arrival rates, one queue would become severely congested (i.e. unstable) and smaller description of the source would use the second queue to reach the destination.

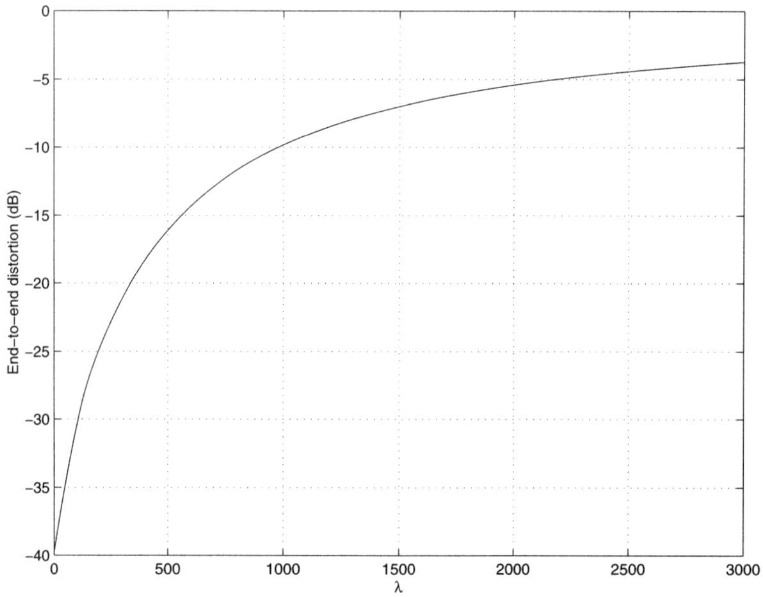

FIGURE 10. Optimized end-to-end distortion in SDC with $C_1 \neq C_2$, $C_1 = 1400$, $C_2 = 600$ bits/sec, $\Delta = 50$ msec

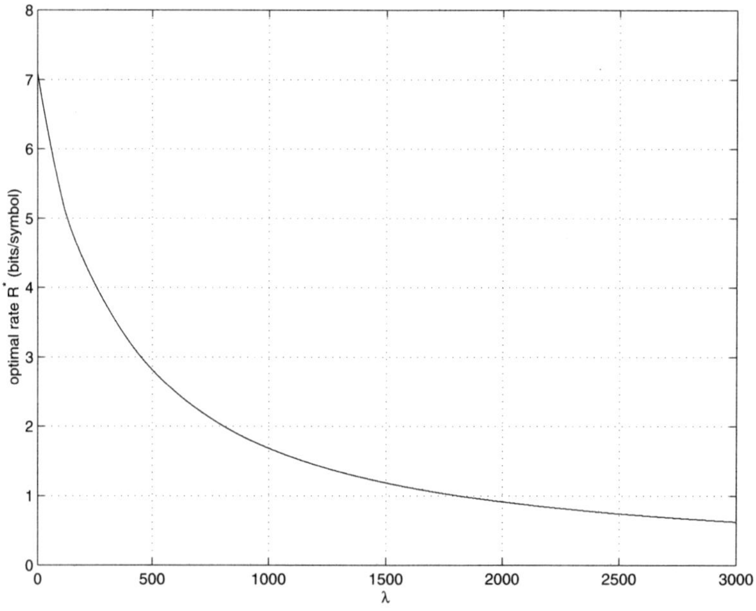

FIGURE 11. Optimal rate R^* in SDC with $C_1 \neq C_2$, $C_1 = 1400$, $C_2 = 600$ bits/sec, $\Delta = 50$ msec

4. Systems with Double Description Coding

In this case (DDC), the source information is encoded by two side-encoders ($i = 1, 2$) (Hereafter, referred to as simply encoders) as shown in Figure 13. The

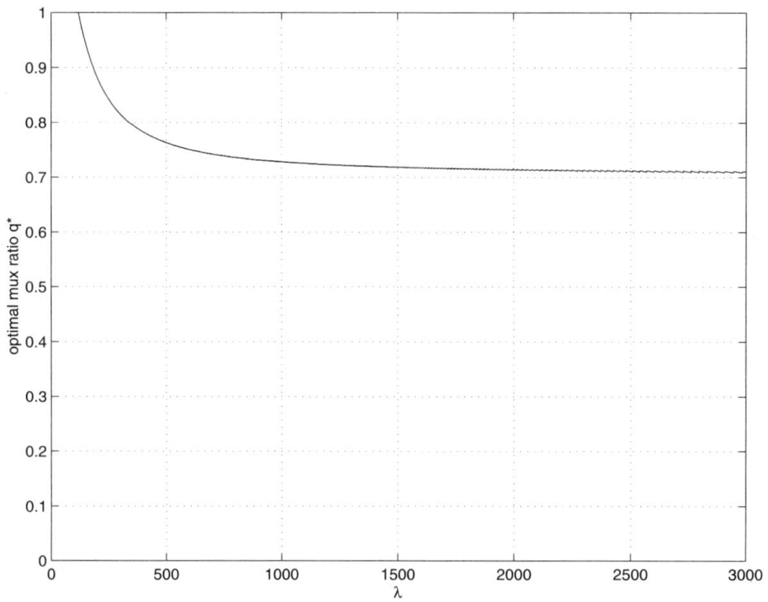

FIGURE 12. Optimal q^* in SDC with $C_1 \neq C_2$, $C_1 = 1400$, $C_2 = 600$ bits/sec, $\Delta = 50$ msec

codeword length generated by encoder i follows an exponential distribution with average of R_i bits such that $R_1 + R_2 = R$. It is assumed that the traffic generated by other sources having the same distribution are added to the traffic generated by encoder i. The aggregate traffic is also assumed to be a Poisson process with rate λ. In this system, the output of encoder i goes to queue i with probability q. However, the two descriptions of the same sample are not routed to the same path. This last assumption suggests a dependance between the traffic in the two queues. However, considering the large traffic from "other sources" that is added to the output of the two encoders, we can assume that the arrival processes to the two queues are independent from each other. This means that the traffic entering queue i is a Poisson process with rate $\lambda_i = \lambda$ $(i = 1, 2)$.

4.1. Average End-to-End Distortion for DDC. Let T^i $(i = 1, 2)$ be the total delay experienced by the output packets of encoder 'i'. If D_{DDC} represents the achieved MSE distortion, then for an i.i.d., zero mean, unit variance Gaussian source, based on [**O80**] and on our concept of delay-based distortion, we have

$$D_{\text{DDC}} = \begin{cases} d_0 = 2^{-2(R_1+R_2)} \frac{1}{1-[\max(0,(\sqrt{\Pi}-\sqrt{\Lambda}))]^2} & \text{if } T^1 \leq \Delta, T^2 \leq \Delta \\ d_1 = 2^{-2R_1(1-\delta_1)} & \text{if } T^1 \leq \Delta,\ T^2 > \Delta \\ d_2 = 2^{-2R_2(1-\delta_2)} & \text{if } T^1 > \Delta,\ T^2 \leq \Delta \\ 1 & \text{if } T^1 > \Delta,\ T^2 > \Delta \end{cases}$$

where

$$0 \leq \delta_1, \delta_2 < 1$$

$$\Pi = (1 - d_1)(1 - d_2) \text{ and } \Lambda = d_1 d_2 - 2^{-2(R_1+R_2)}$$

Here, δ_i $(i = 1, 2)$ signifies the amount of redundancy in each side-encoder. Low values of δ_i (i.e. $\delta_i \approx 0$) indicate good individual descriptions that jointly contribute little extra information beyond one alone. On the other hand, high values of δ_i (i.e. $\delta_i \approx 1$) indicate independent descriptions that are not individually good; however, jointly they can achieve the same amount of distortion as in the case of SDC.

The end-to-end average distortion can be written as

$$\overline{D}_{\text{DDC}} = d_0 P\left[\, T^1 \leq \Delta,\ T^2 \leq \Delta \,\right] + d_1 P\left[\, T^1 \leq \Delta,\ T^2 > \Delta \,\right] + d_2 P\left[\, T^1 > \Delta,\ T^2 \leq \Delta \,\right] + P\left[\, T^1 > \Delta,\ T^2 > \Delta \,\right] \tag{4.1}$$

As observed in Figure 13, all variables that can affect the average end-to-end distortion have been classified into two groups. Group 1 consists of parameters that are basically coding related while group 2 consists of those specified by the network. The quantity δ_i $(i = 1, 2)$ signifies the amount of redundancy in the encoder i, $\alpha = R_1/(R_1 + R_2)$ is the rate ratio, q is the multiplexing ratio, and $\gamma = C_1/(C_1 + C_2)$ is the capacity ratio of the two links that are carrying traffic. The average end-to-end distortion is affected by the coding parameters as well as by the network related parameters.

In [**A01**], the significance of using DDC in reducing the average end-to-end distortion with optimal values for coding parameters has been investigated. It is interesting to point out that further gain can be achieved by considering the network parameters in the optimization process.

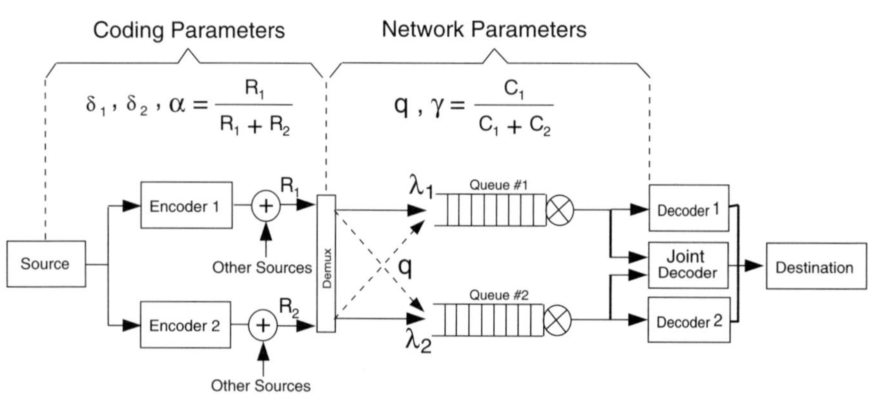

FIGURE 13. DDC System Model

Suppose $C_1 + C_2 = 2C$, $q_1 = q$, $q_2 = 1 - q$, and note that $R_1 + R_2 = R$ and $\lambda_1 = \lambda_2 = \lambda$. If μ_i^j $(i, j = 1, 2)$ represents the service rate of queue i for output packets of encoder j, then we have

$$\mu_i^j = \frac{C_i}{R_j} \; i, j = 1, 2$$

If μ_i $(i = 1, 2)$ is the average service rate for queue i, then

$$\mu_1 = \frac{C_1}{qR_1 + (1-q)R_2} \; , \; \mu_2 = \frac{C_2}{(1-q)R_1 + qR_2}$$

And

$$\rho_1 = \min\left(\frac{\lambda[qR_1 + (1-q)R_2]}{C_1}, 1\right) \; , \; \rho_2 = \min\left(\frac{\lambda[(1-q)R_1 + qR_2]}{C_2}, 1\right)$$

For the exponential packet length assumption, if τ_i $(i = 1, 2)$ is the average service time for queue i, then

$$f_{\tau_i}(t) = \left[q_i \mu_i^1 e^{-\mu_i^1 t} + (1-q_i)\mu_i^2 e^{-\mu_i^2 t}\right] u(t) \; i = 1, 2$$

Taking the Laplace-Stieltjes transform of the above we obtain

$$\hat{F}_{\tau_i}(s) = \frac{q_i \mu_i^1}{s + \mu_i^1} + \frac{(1-q_i)\mu_i^2}{s + \mu_i^2} \; i = 1, 2$$

Using the Pollaczek-Khinchin formula, the Laplace-Stieltjes transform of the distribution of average packet waiting time in queue i (i.e. $\hat{F}_{W_i}(s)$) becomes

$$\hat{F}_{W_i}(s) = \frac{(1-\rho_i)s}{s - \lambda_i + \lambda_i \hat{F}_{\tau_i}(s)} \; i = 1, 2 \tag{4.2}$$

If T_i^j $(i, j = 1, 2)$ represents the random variable denoting the time it takes for the output packet of encoder j to reach the destination through queue i, we have

$$\hat{F}_{T_i^j}(s) = \hat{F}_{W_i}(s) \times \hat{F}_{\tau_i^j}(s) \; i, j = 1, 2 \tag{4.3}$$

where τ_i^j is a r.v. indicating the service time of packets of encoder j in queue i, and

$$\hat{F}_{\tau_i^j}(s) = \frac{\mu_i^j}{s + \mu_i^j} \; i, j = 1, 2 \tag{4.4}$$

Replacing Eq 4.2 and 4.4 in Eq 4.3 and simplifying, we finally get

$$\hat{F}_{T_i^j}(s) = \frac{\mu_i^j(1-\rho_i)(s + \mu_i^{3-j})}{s^2 + (\mu_i^1 + \mu_i^2 - \lambda_i)s + \mu_i^1\mu_i^2 - \lambda_i[(1-q_i)\mu_i^1 + q_i\mu_i^2]} \; i, j = 1, 2$$

The delay probability $P[T_i^j > \Delta]$ for $i, j = 1, 2$ can be derived from the above equation. For the total delay that the output packets of encoder j experience before reaching the destination we have

$$P[T^j > \Delta] = q_j P[T_1^j > \Delta] + (1-q_j)P[T_2^j > \Delta] \; j = 1, 2$$

Having the above probabilities, the average end-to-end distortion for the multiple description coding system can be easily obtained.

4.2. Jointly Optimal DDC with Fixed Average Encoding Rate. If the average encoding rate (R) is fixed, the average end-to-end distortion is a function of rate ratio (α), the encoder redundancies (δ_1, δ_2) and the multiplexing ratio (q). Define the optimal parameters $(\alpha^*, \delta_1^*, \delta_2^*, q^*)$ as

$$(\alpha^*, \delta_1^*, \delta_2^*, q^*) = \arg\min \ \overline{D}(\alpha, \delta_1, \delta_2, q)$$

The curves $\overline{D}(\alpha^*, \delta_1^*, \delta_2^*, 0.5)$ and $\overline{D}(\alpha^*, \delta_1^*, \delta_2^*, q^*)$ for the case when $\gamma = 0.5$, $C = 1000$ bits/sec, $R = 6$ bits/symbol, and $\Delta = 50$ msec have been displayed in Figure 14. To differentiate between the two, hereafter we refer to the case where $(\alpha = \alpha^*, \delta_1 = \delta_1^*, \delta_2 = \delta_2^*, q = 0.5)$ as simply optimal DDC and the case where $(\alpha = \alpha^*, \delta_1 = \delta_1^*, \delta_2 = \delta_2^*, q = q^*)$ as jointly optimal DDC. This reflects the fact that in optimal DDC only coding parameters have been optimized to yield the best distortion while in the jointly optimal DDC all system parameters (i.e. coding as well as network) have been appropriately optimized. As seen in Figure 14, up until the point $\lambda \approx 300$, the two curves overlap, after which using q^* makes a considerable contribution towards lowering the distortion. Figures 15 and 16 display the variation of network parameters (i.e. q^*, ρ_1^*, ρ_2^*) and coding parameters (i.e. $\alpha^*, \delta_1^*, \delta_2^*$), respectively. We observe that for $\lambda < 300$, the optimal value of rate ratio (α^*) is 0.5. Since the packet lengths for both encoders have the same distribution (Exponential), the optimal solution is independent of the multiplexing ratio (q). So, without loss of generality, for $\lambda < 300$, we choose $q^* = 0$. For $\lambda > 300$, q^* is indeed zero; forcing packets of encoder 'i' to be routed to queue i ($i = 1, 2$). Therefore, as observed in Figure 15, we can take $q^* = 0$ regardless of the value of λ. We use this observation in the next section to simplify our optimization process.

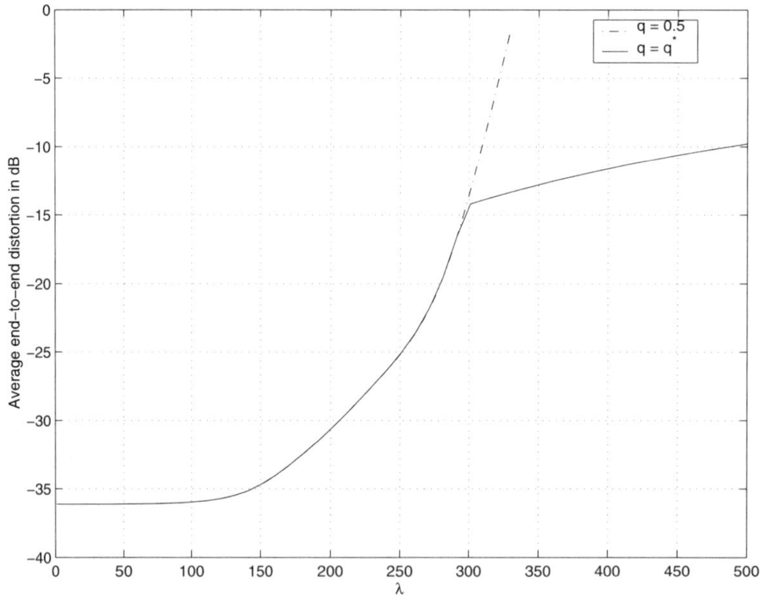

FIGURE 14. $C_1 = C_2 = C = 1000$ bits/sec, $R = 6$ bits, $\Delta = 50$ msec

For $\lambda > 300$, many packets in the optimal DDC system will reach the deadline Δ while still waiting in the queue and few packets in their entirety will reach the

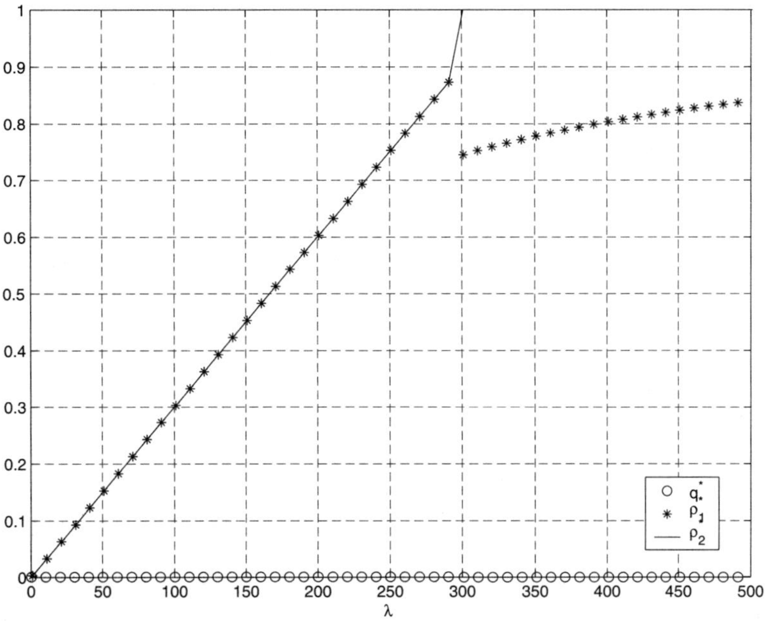

FIGURE 15. $C_1 = C_2 = C = 1000$ bits/sec, $R = 6$ bits, $\Delta = 50$ msec

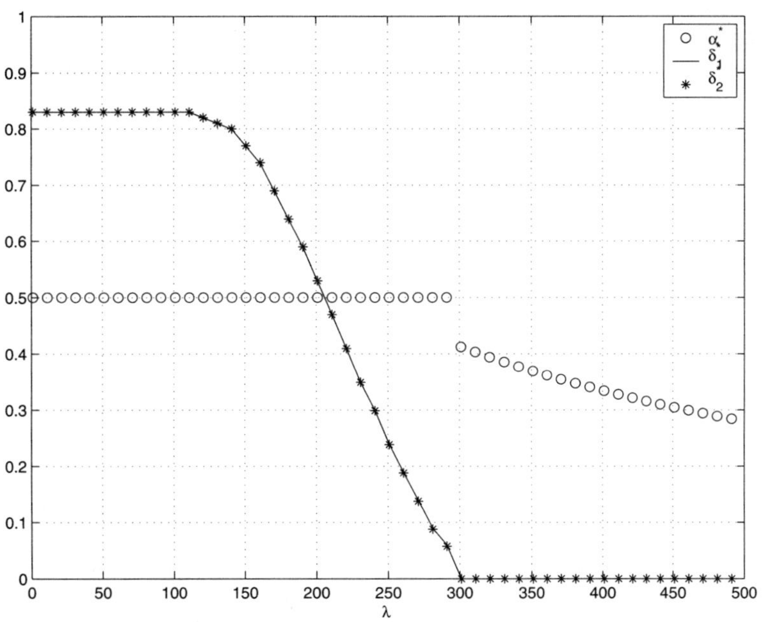

FIGURE 16. $C_1 = C_2 = C = 1000$ bits/sec, $R = 6$ bits, $\Delta = 50$ msec

destination. However, in the jointly optimal DDC system, the rate ratio (i.e. α^*) is reduced to compensate for the occurring traffic congestion. Since $q^* = 0$, all descriptions that are generated by encoder 1 are routed to one queue and will most likely meet the deadline. While almost all codewords in the other queue will most likely expire before reaching to the destination. In essence, this situation points to the following fact. For the distortion function we have chosen, it is better to have a small portion of information about each individual symbol (as in the jointly optimal DDC system) than to have the whole information for a small portion of the packet stream (as in the case of a simple optimal DDC).

4.3. Jointly Optimal DDC with Optimal Average Encoding Rate. Another parameter that can affect distortion is R. Similar to the SDC, a tradeoff between delay and distortion also exists in this case. This tradeoff points to the possibility of the existence of an optimal R that minimizes the average end-to-end distortion for such delay sensitive sources.

An interesting observation in the previous section was the value of q^* for the optimal DDC system (i.e. $q^* = 0$). This means that packets from the encoder i are routed directly to path i ($i = 1, 2$). We will use this observation and take $q = 0$ in order to simplify our optimization process in this section. For $C_1 = C_2 = C$ and $\lambda_1 = \lambda_2 = \lambda$, the network consists of two identical queues with identical and independent arrival processes. Due to this symmetry, we expect $R_1^* = R_2^* = R^*/2$ and $\delta_1^* = \delta_2^* = \delta^*$. Therefore, the optimization problem in this case is

$$(\delta^*, R^*) = \arg\min\ \overline{D}(\delta, R)$$

The optimal average end-to-end distortion is demonstrated in Figure 17 for $C_1 = C_2 = 1000$ bits/sec, and $\Delta = 50$ msec. As shown in this figure, R^* contributes in lowering the overall distortion for all values of λ. The optimal encoding rate R^* is shown in Figure 18, where similar to the SDC case, we can see that R^* is finite at $\lambda = 0$, and that it decreases with λ.

Note that there is a discontinuity in R^* as is depicted in Figure 18. To explain this behavior more clearly, let's define the parameter δ_0 to be the value of δ that minimizes d_0. In other words

$$\delta_0 = \arg\min\ d_0(\delta)$$

Note that δ_0 is a function of R. Since d_1 and d_2 are monotonically increasing with δ and d_0 is minimized at δ_0, the optimal value of distortion happens at $\delta^* \leq \delta_0$. The value of δ_0 at the optimal rate R^* can be calculated as follows [**A01**]

$$\delta_0 = \frac{1}{R^*} \log_2 \left(\frac{2^{R^*} + 2^{-R^*}}{2} \right)$$

Using Eq 4.1, it is clear that if $P[T^1 \leq \Delta, T^2 \leq \Delta] = 1$, then $\delta^* = \delta_0$. Figure 19 shows the value of δ^* as well as δ_0. As we can see in this figure, for small λ's, where we expect to have smaller delay probabilities, the value of δ^* is significantly lower than δ_0, which seems counterintuitive. To explain this behavior, we take a look at the optimal delay probability ($P[T > \Delta] = P[T^1 > \Delta] = P[T^2 > \Delta]$) as shown in Figure 20.

Note that the discontinuity occurs for R^*, δ^*, and $P[T > \Delta]$ at $\lambda \approx 90$. For $\lambda < 90$ the optimization process chooses to increase the encoding rate as much as possible at a cost of getting a higher delay probability, which in turn decreases the chance of receiving both descriptions on time and thus relies mostly on receiving only one description and thus chooses a small value for δ^* to get better values for d_1 and d_2. When $\lambda > 90$, the optimal solution would be one that decreases R^* to an extent that results in a small delay probability and thus increases the chance of both descriptions' on-time arrival at the destination. Therefore as can be seen in Figure 19, the value of δ^* is very close to the value of δ_0.

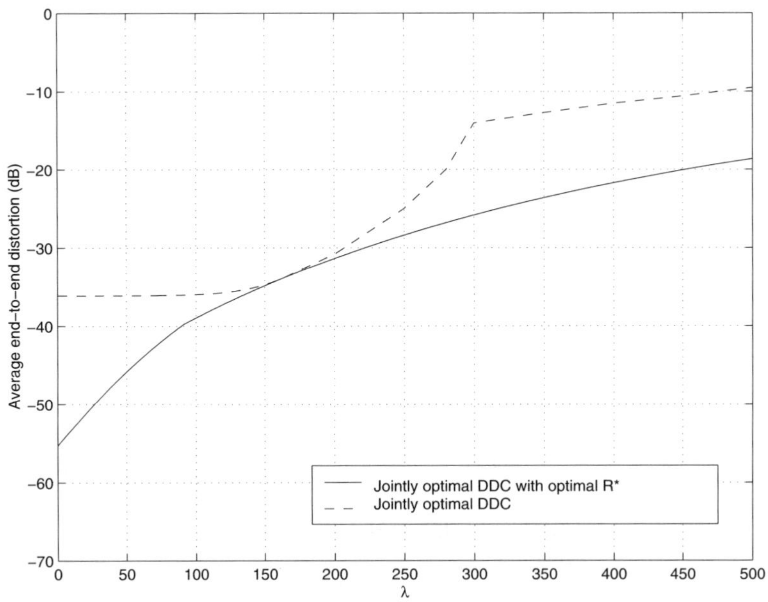

FIGURE 17. Improvement achieved by optimizing R in jointly optimal DDC system, $C_1 = C_2 = 1000$ bits/sec, $\Delta = 50$ msec

5. Comparison of the SDC and the DDC Systems

So far, we have considered all parameters that directly affect the end-to-end average distortion for a simple system consisting of two routes. Two general classes of coding schemes were considered and in each case a joint optimization problem to minimize the average end-to-end distortion was solved. In this section, we would like to quantify and compare the results obtained in the previous sections.

Assume that $C_1 = C_2 = 1000$ bits/sec, and $\Delta = 50$ msec. Figure 21 displays the performance of both systems (SDC and DDC) with and without optimal encoding rate. As observed, the DDC system with optimal rate outperforms all other systems. Similarly, the SDC system with non-optimal rate has the highest distortion. In comparing the SDC system with optimal rate to the DDC system with non-optimal rate, it is interesting to note that there exists a λ (i.e. $\lambda \approx 270$) beyond which the SDC system with optimal rate outperforms the DDC with non-optimal rate. This is because in a system with optimal encoding rate, the chance for packets to miss their deadlines is much smaller compared to a system without optimal encoding rate.

Knowing the results in Figure 21, and given the cost and complexity of implementing a particular approach, better decisions can be made to design a system. For example, if the maximum acceptable average distortion for an application is -20 dB, then the arrival rate in an SDC system with fixed (i.e. non-optimal) rate is limited to 150 packets/sec. However, in the DDC system with fixed rate, the arrival

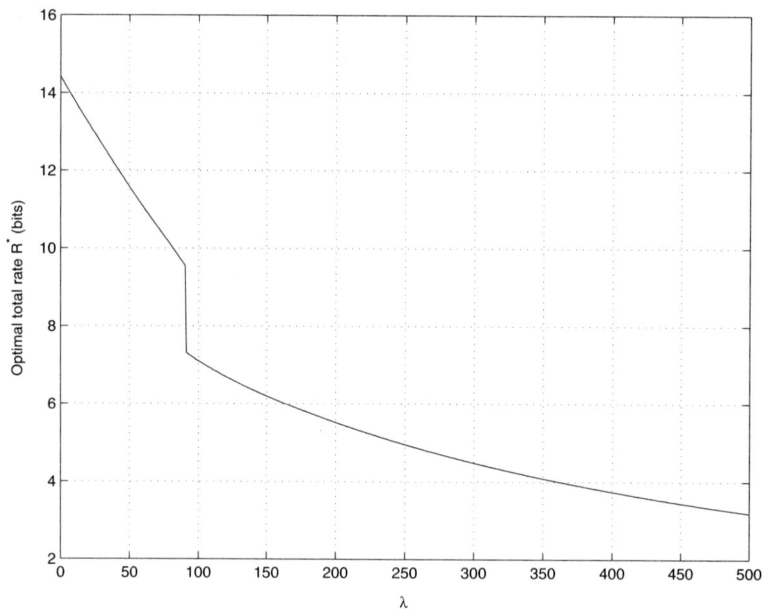

FIGURE 18. Optimal rate R^* in DDC system, $C_1 = C_2 = 1000$ bits/sec, $\Delta = 50$ msec

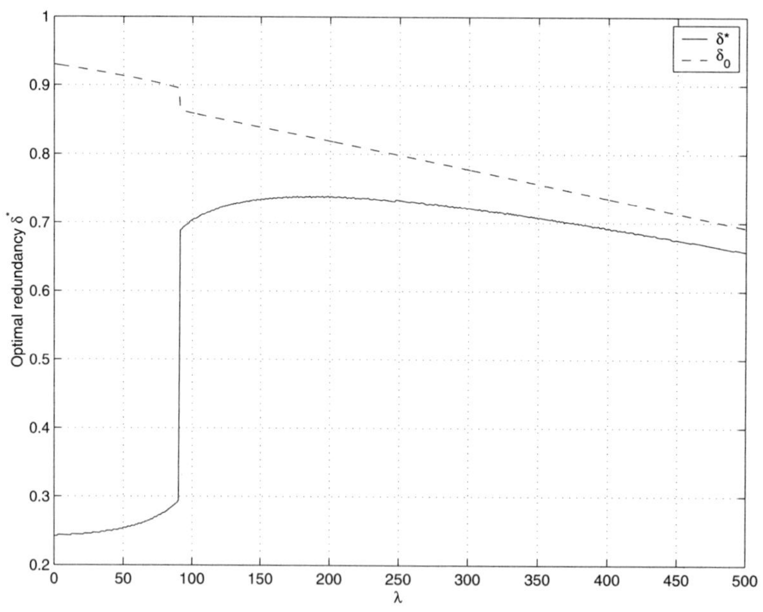

FIGURE 19. Optimal $\delta^* = \delta_1^* = \delta_2^*$ and δ_0 in DDC system, $C_1 = C_2 = 1000$ bits/sec, $\Delta = 50$ msec

rate can be increased up to 280 packets/sec for the same amount of distortion. The effect of optimal routing appears at $\lambda > 320$ for SDC and at $\lambda > 300$ for DDC.

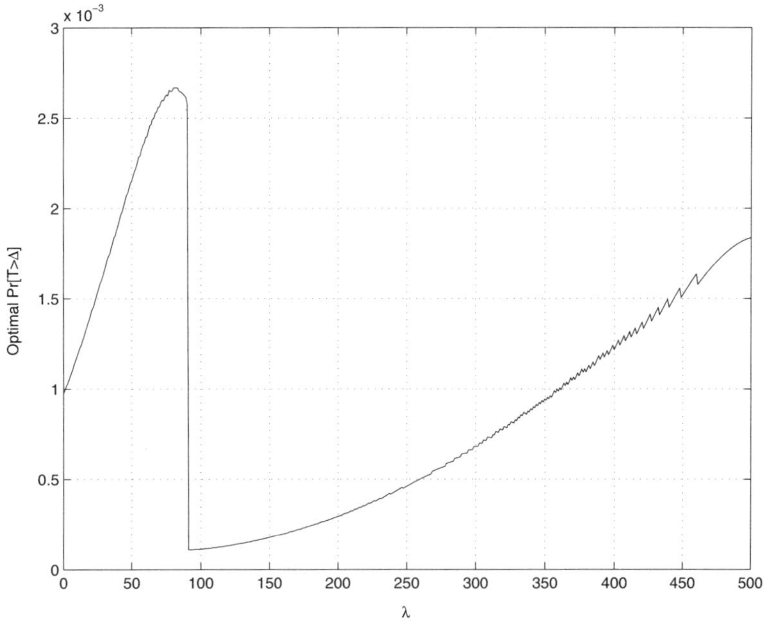

FIGURE 20. Optimal $P[T > \Delta]$ in DDC system, $C_1 = C_2 = 1000$ bits/sec, $\Delta = 50$ msec

The optimal routing reduces the sensitivity of the average distortion to network load. Similarly, in order to keep the distortion below −20dB, the arrival rate of the SDC system with optimal rate should be less than 330 packets/sec, and for a DDC system with optimal encoding rate, the arrival rate can go up to 450 packets/sec.

It was shown in [**A01**] that the DDC system achieves a better performance than the SDC system (without optimizing q and R). As it can be seen in Figure 21 a similar result holds in this paper. More specifically, with optimal routing and fixed encoding rate, the DDC system is still superior to the SDC system. Similarly, with optimal encoding rate, the DDC system outperforms the SDC system.

6. Conclusion and Future Work

We have presented a joint optimization problem that considers the effects of both coding and network parameters in minimizing the achieved distortion. In essence, we have provided an illustration of a cross-layer interaction that vividly contributes to the bridging between Networks and Information Theory. Our analysis shows that a smart encoding scheme (such as Multiple Description Coding) along with a smart routing protocol can significantly contribute to lower the achieved distortion. Additional improvement can be expected if the switching module is intelligent enough to drop packets that have passed their deadline.

We have outlined a trade-off between packet delay and average distortion. The average distortion is a decreasing function of the encoding rate; however, the encoding rate, which translates to packet length, in turn, determines the delay experienced by a packet. Higher encoding rates results in larger packet delays. In this paper, we have shown that there exists an optimal value for the encoding rate that significantly impacts the achieved distortion.

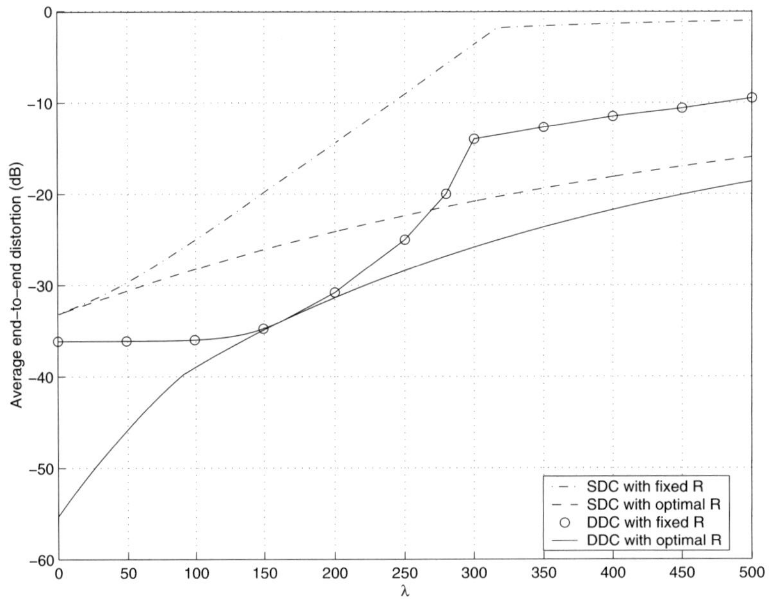

FIGURE 21. Comparison of SDC and DDC with fixed R, $C_1 = C_2 = 1000$ bits/sec, $\Delta = 50$ msec

To obtain our results, we have assumed the source to be memory-less and Guassian; and we used the rate-distortion bounds obtained by Ozarow [**O80**]. For a general memory-less source, explicit inner and outer bounds for the multiple description rate-distortion region have been found in [**Z99**]. These bounds maintain the form provided by Ozarow; therefore, our analysis is also applicable for any memory-less source.

Further studies need to be done to find the applicability of the results obtained in this paper in more realistic and complex networks (e.g., multi-hop). Moreover, we only studied the case of double description coding. The problem addressed in this paper can be generalized for more than two encoders (i.e. Multiple Description Coding). The achievable rate-distortion bounds for such encoders have been found in [**V03**].

Appendix A

The average end-to-end distortion in SDC is equal to

$$\overline{D} = 2^{-2R} + \left(1 - 2^{-2R}\right) P[T > \Delta]$$

Therefore,

$$\min\left(\overline{D}\right) = 2^{-2R} + \left(1 - 2^{-2R}\right) \min\left(P[T > \Delta]\right)$$

However,

$$\min\left(P[T>\Delta]\right)=\min\begin{cases} f(q)=e^{-\mu\Delta}\left[qe^{q\rho\mu\Delta}+(1-q)e^{(1-q)\rho\mu\Delta}\right] & \text{if } \rho_1,\rho_2<1 \\ g(q)=qe^{-\mu\Delta}e^{q\rho\mu\Delta}+(1-q) & \text{if } \rho_1<1,\rho_2=1 \\ g(1-q)=(1-q)e^{-\mu\Delta}e^{(1-q)\rho\mu\Delta}+q & \text{if } \rho_1=1,\rho_2<1 \\ 1 & \text{if } \rho_1=\rho_2=1 \end{cases}$$

where

$$\mu=\frac{C}{R},\ \rho=\frac{\lambda}{\mu}$$

It can be easily verified that $f(.)$ is a convex function of q, and also $f(q)=f(1-q)$. Therefore we have

$$f(q)=\frac{1}{2}f(q)+\frac{1}{2}f(1-q)\geq f\left(\frac{1}{2}q+\frac{1}{2}(1-q)\right)=f\left(\frac{1}{2}\right)=e^{-\mu\Delta}e^{\mu\rho\Delta/2}$$

For $\rho_1,\rho_2<1$ and $q^*=0.5$, we obtain

$$\rho_1^*=\rho_2^*=\frac{R}{2C}\lambda$$

For the case where $\rho_1<1$ and $\rho_2=1$, to minimize $P[T>\Delta]$, the following equation needs to be solved.

$$\frac{dg(q)}{dq}=e^{-\mu\Delta}e^{q\rho\mu\Delta}\left[1+q\rho\mu\Delta\right]-1=0$$

For given values of Δ, C and R, if $\rho_1=q\rho$, the above equation can be written in the following form.

$$e^{-\mu\Delta}e^{\rho_1\mu\Delta}\left[1+\rho_1\mu\Delta\right]-1=0$$

By solving the above equation, we obtain a fixed value for ρ_1 irrespective of the arrival rate (λ). This behavior was observed in Figure 4. For $C=1000 bits/sec$, $R=6$ bits/symbol and $\Delta=50$ msec, we obtain $\rho_1^*=q^*\frac{\lambda R}{C}\approx 0.76$, and

$$q^*\approx\frac{0.76C}{R\lambda}=\frac{126.7}{\lambda}$$

Also, we can derive the following statement for $g(q^*)$.

$$g(q^*)=q^*e^{-\mu\Delta}e^{q^*\rho\mu\Delta}+(1-q^*)=1-q^*\frac{q^*\lambda\Delta}{1+q^*\lambda\Delta}\approx 1-\frac{109.4}{\lambda}$$

The transition point happens at the λ where $f(q^*)=g(q^*)$, i.e.,

$$e^{-\mu\Delta}e^{\lambda\Delta/2}=1-\frac{109.4}{\lambda}$$

Considering that $\mu=\frac{C}{R}=166.7$ and $\Delta=50$ msec, by solving the above equation $\lambda=316$, and $q^*=0.4$ are obtained.

References

[A01] M. Alasti, K. Sayrafian-Pour, A. Ephremides, and N. Farvardin, "Multiple description coding in networks with congestion problems", *IEEE Trans. Inform. Theory*, vol. 47, no. 3, Mar. 2001, pp. 891–903.

[C91] T. M. Cover, and J. A. Thomas, *Elements of Information Theory*, John Wiley & Sons, Inc., New York, NY, 1991

[E82] A. A. El Gamal, and T. Cover , "Achievable rates for multiple descriptions", *IEEE Trans. Inform. Theory*, vol. 28, Nov 1982, pp. 851–857.

[O80] L. Ozarow, "On a source coding problem with two channels and three receivers", *Bell Syst. Tech. J.*, vol. 59, no. 10, Dec 1980, pp. 84–91.

[R92] S. Resnick, *Adventures in Stochastic Processes.*, Cambridge, MA: Birkhäuser,1992.

[V03] R. Venkataramani, G. Kramer, and V.K. Goyal, "Multiple description coding with many channels", *IEEE Trans. Inform. Theory*, vol. 49, no. 9, Sept. 2003, pp. 2106–2114.

[W89] R. W. Wolff, *Stochastic Modeling and the Theory of queues*, Prentice Hall 1989.

[Z99] R. Zamir, "Gaussian codes and Shannon bounds for multiple descriptions", *IEEE Trans. Inform. Theory*, vol. 45, no. 7, Nov 1999, pp. 2629–2636.

Electrical & Computer Engineering Department, University of Maryland, College Park, Maryland 20740

E-mail address: azadeh@glue.umd.edu

Electrical & Computer Engineering Department, University of Maryland, College Park, Maryland 20740

E-mail address: kamrans@eng.umd.edu

Current address: Wireless Communications Technologies Group, National Institute of Standard and Technology, 100 Bureau Drive Stop 8920, Gaithersburg, MD 20899-8920

E-mail address: ksayrafian@nist.gov

Electrical & Computer Engineering Department, University of Maryland, College Park, Maryland 20740

E-mail address: mehdi@eng.umd.edu

Electrical & Computer Engineering Department, University of Maryland, College Park, Maryland 20740

E-mail address: tony@eng.umd.edu

The views and conclusions contained in this document are those of the authors and should not be interpreted as representing the official policies, either expressed or implied, of the Army Research Laboratory or the U.S. Government.

Any opinions findings, and conclusions or recommendations expressed in this material are those of the author(s) and do not necessarily reflect the views of the National Aeronautics and Space Administration.

DIMACS Series in Discrete Mathematics
and Theoretical Computer Science
Volume **66**, 2004

Compressing a Representation of Events in a Concurrent System

Serap A. Savari

ABSTRACT. Network infomation theory traditionally studies communication problems involving many senders and receivers. Using different connotations of the word "network" we begin to explore an alternate type of network information theory problem in which relationships among letters in the source alphabet are exploited to achieve gains in compression. This *semantic* rate distortion problem is motivated by work in computer science in the areas of concurrency, program profiling, and compression of executable code, and leads to a new generalization of Kolmogorov complexity and a new graph entropy called the *interchange entropy.* We provide some of the basic properties of the interchange entropy.

1. Introduction

Information theory [**1, 2**] studies systems which communicate or manipulate information and seeks quantitative measures of the capacity of these systems to process information. Shortly after Shannon's 1948 pioneering paper, he began in [**3**] to contemplate a "lattice" theory of information aimed at investigating communication problems with a number of information sources operating simultaneously. This idea has been developed considerably since 1950 and is now called "network" information theory.

There are many connotations of the word "network." The 1989 edition of the *Oxford English Dictionary* provides well over a page of possible definitions. The two meanings which appear to be closest for traditional network information theory are

- a broadcasting system consisting of a series of transmitters capable of being linked together and
- calculation of the currents flowing in the various meshes of a network

In this paper, we will be interested in linking information theory to two different definitions of "network" from the Oxford English Dictionary. These are

- a representation of interconnected events, processes, etc. used in the study of work efficiency and

Key words and phrases. Data compression, concurrent processes, executable code, semantics, trace theory, renewal theory, graph entropy.

- to link (computers) together to make possible one or more of several functions, as the transfer of data, the sharing of processing capability or workloads, and accessibility from many locations.

The first motivation for the "network information theory" problem we will be describing below comes from a recent prize-winning paper [**4**] in the area of computing systems. The temporal ordering of events in a sequential process is well modeled by the string of symbols over some alphabet. The author of [**4**] applies a lossless data compression algorithm known as SEQUITUR [**5**] to the the sequence of events that occur while a computer program runs and uses the hierarchical structure inferred by the algorithm to better understand the program's dynamic behavior and improve its performance. The implicit assumption in using lossless data compression for this application is that there is a well-defined total ordering of event occurrences.

Concurrency is a fundamental concept in computer science which is concerned with the study of systems involving multiple processes. Multiprocessor configurations, distributed systems and communication networks are examples are systems consisting of a collection of distinct processes which communicate with one another but are also partly autonomous. The concept of ordering of events for these concurrent systems is more complex than that of sequential centralized systems [**6**]. Here certain events are allowed to occur independently while others must happen in a predetermined order. In other words, there is a *partial ordering* of events rather than a total ordering [**7**].

Trace theory [**8**]-[**10**] is an approach to generalizing the notion of a string in order to model the executions of concurrent processes. The idea is to provide the sequential observer of a concurrent system with a set of atomic actions together with a labeled and undirected *dependence relation* or *noncommutation graph* indicating which actions can be performed independently or concurrently. For a noncommutation graph G with vertex set V we say that two words are *congruent* or *equivalent* if one can be transformed into the other by a sequence of steps each of which consists of interchanging two consecutive letters that are nonadjacent vertices in G. For example, if the noncommutation graph G is given by a—b—c—d, then the two words $dabac$ and $abdca$ are equivalent through the transformation $dabac \equiv_G adbac \equiv_G adbca \equiv_G abdca$. To generalize lossless data compression to concurrent systems, [**11**] introduces a compression problem where it is only necessary to reproduce a string which is equivalent to the original string. That paper describes some compression schemes for the congruence class of a string that in the best cases can be exponentially more succinct than a grammar-based compression (see, e.g., [**12**]) of the corresponding string. In this paper, we initiate a study of this compression problem from an information theoretic perspective.

There are two special cases of the dependence relation which are standard in information theory. When G is the complete graph on the vertex set V, i.e., when there is an edge connecting every pair of vertices, every word over V is congruent only to itself. At the other extreme, if G is the empty graph on the vertex set, i.e., if no two vertices are adjacent, then two words are congruent if and only if the number of occurrences of each symbol in V is the same for both words. Here the equivalence classes on words are frequently called *type classes* [**13**, p.280]. When G is neither the complete graph nor the empty graph on the vertex set V, the vertex set forms a partially commutative alphabet. Mazurkiewicz [**8**] introduced the label *trace* to denote a congruence class of words because they represent traces of processes, i.e., the sequence of states traversed by the process from initialization to termination, in nonsequential systems. Because the word trace has numerous connotations, we will introduce the terminology *interchange class* to refer to an equivalence class of words.

This compression problem also appears in the compression of executable code [**14**]. Executable code or program "binaries" are files whose content must be interpreted by a program or hardware processor which knows exactly how the data inside the file is formatted in order to utilize it. One of the techniques given in [**14**] for this compression application is "instruction rescheduling," in which instructions can be reordered if the decompressed program is execution-isomorphic to the original. Note that [**14**] claims to exploit the syntax and semantics of executable code to achieve better compression. One of the definitions of the word *semantic* given in *Webster's Third New International Dictionary* (1966) is "the study of the relations of a sign to its referent and to other signs within a system." In explaining the notion of measurement of information, Shannon [**2**, p.213] states that "often the messages to be transmitted have meaning: they describe or relate to real or conceivable events." In the computer science literature, particularly in the study of programming languages and information processing, the term *semantics* refers to the meaning or behavior of a program or process when executed by computers (see, e.g., [**15**], [**16**, p.577]). Since words in the same congruence class are equivalent or have the same meaning, this compression problem exploits known semantic relationships and can consequently be viewed as a topic in "semantic" information theory.

We propose a new generalization of Kolmogorov-Chaitin complexity (see, e.g., [**17**]) called the *interchange complexity* and use a version of the subadditive ergodic theorem [**18**] to provide sufficient conditions on probabilistic sources so that an extension of the asymptotic equipartition property [**1**], [**19**] to interchange classes holds. We name the average number of bits per symbol needed to represent an interchange class the *interchange entropy*. The interchange entropy is a functional on a graph with a probability distribution on its vertex set. For memoryless sources there are two earlier graph entropies which have received considerable attention. The first of these was introduced by Körner in [**20**] and has subsequently been found to have applications in network information theory, characterization of perfect graphs, and lower bounds on perfect hashing, Boolean formulae size and sorting. The survey article [**21**] reviews many of the properties of Körner's graph entropy, and our discussion of some of the characteristics of the interchange entropy is strongly influenced by Section 3 of this article. Chromatic entropy was defined by Boppana in connection with certain parallel-computing models in [**22**] and demonstrated in [**23**] to be linked to the expected number of bits required by a transmitter to convey information to a receiver who has some related data. As we will see, the interchange entropy has some properties in common with these other graph entropies. We shall also investigate some universal compression schemes for this problem and demonstrate that we can asymptotically achieve the interchange entropy for a large collection of dependence alphabets.

2. The Interchange Complexity and the Interchange Entropy

The asymptotic equipartition property states that most long sequences from a discrete and finite alphabet ergodic source are typical in the sense that their mean self-information per symbol is close to the entropy of the source. This result implies that the average number of bits per symbol required to losslessly encode the output of an ergodic source is asymptotically bounded from below by the binary entropy of the source. In order to find a counterpart for this lossy compression problem, we begin by considering the least amount of information about an individual string that must be described in order to reproduce another string within the same interchange class. This discussion fall into the framework of algorithmic information theory (see, e.g., [**26**] and [**17**]). For a finite length string x over the vertex set V, let $C(x)$ denote the Kolmogorov complexity of x and refer to [**17**, §2.1, p. 107] for the basic properties of $C(x)$. Let V^* be the set of all finite words from V and $|V|$ denote the cardinality of V. We define the *interchange complexity* of $x \in V^*$ with respect to a noncommutation graph G with vertex set V by

$$C_\iota(G,x) \;=\; \min\{C(y) \mid y \in V^*,\; y \equiv_G x\}.$$

$C_\iota(G,x)$ is the length of the shortest program for a universal computer that will print out a word y which is congruent to x with respect to the noncommutation graph G.

We will make use of the following result [**25**], which is one way to characterize the equivalence of two strings with respect to a noncommutation graph G.

THEOREM 2.1 (Perrin (1985)). *For any subset A of the vertex set V and any word w over V, let $\pi_A(w)$ denote the projection of w onto A which is obtained by deleting from w all symbols which are not in A. The necessary and sufficient conditions for two words w and x to be congruent is that they are in the same type class and that $\pi_{\{u,v\}}(w) = \pi_{\{u,v\}}(x)$ for all pairs of symbols $u,\ v \in V$ which are adjacent in G.*

Continuing our earlier example, suppose our noncommutation graph G is given by a—b—c—d and we wish to characterize the interchange class containing the word *dabac*. The "edge projections" are $\pi_{\{a,b\}}(dabac) = aba$, $\pi_{\{b,c\}}(dabac) = bc$, and $\pi_{\{c,d\}}(dabac) = dc$. The interchange class containing *dabac* are all words with the same type class and the same three edge projections, i.e., the set of words $\{abadc,\ abdac,\ abdca,\ adbac,\ adbca,\ dabac,\ dabca\}$.

Since Theorem 2.1 specifies the necessary and sufficient conditions for two words to be congruent with respect to a non-commutation graph G, we have that the interchange class containing a string can be completely determined by any element of the interchange class which can be used to provide the type class and edge projections. Conversely, given the type class and edge projections of an interchange class, it is possible to use a knowledge of these to produce a word in the interchange class for a noncommutation graph G as follows. If G is the empty graph, then it is straightforward to use the type class to reconstruct a word consistent with the type. If G is not the empty graph, we use the type class to determine the number of appearances of any symbol which commutes with every other symbol in V. We are left with the symbols appearing in the edge projections. The leftmost symbol in each projection is initially a possibility for the next symbol in our word. In our example, the leftmost symbol in the three projections are a, b, and d. If there are any two symbols, say u and v, among these which do not commute, then the projection onto edge $\{u, v\}$ determines which symbol appears first in the projection, and the other is removed from the set of possible next symbols. This procedure is iterated until the set of possible next symbols contains no pair of symbols which are adjacent in G. Any symbol from this set can be chosen as the next letter. Persisting with our example, since symbols a and b do not commute, from the first edge projection we see that the first appearance of a b in a word comes after the first appearance of an a; hence, the first symbol of a word in the interchange class must begin with either an a or a d. If symbol u is chosen, then the leftmost u is removed from every edge projection onto u and its neighbors in G. This algorithm is repeated until every edge projection is empty. It follows that we can also view $C_\iota(G, x)$ as the length, to within $O(1)$, of the shortest program for a universal computer that will determine the interchange class containing x.

Suppose that we have words $u, v, w, x \in V^*$ with $u \equiv_G w$ and $v \equiv_G x$. Then it is easily seen that the words uv and wx formed by respectively appending v to u and x to w satisfies $uv \equiv_G wx$. Therefore, the interchange complexity is *almost subadditive.* In particular, to bound $C_\iota(G, uv)$ from above, we follow [**17**, p.102] and observe that one way to produce a string equivalent to uv is to use a shortest program p to find a string w equivalent to u, a shortest program q to construct a string x congruent to v, a means to schedule the two programs to produce w followed by x, and an identification of the programs p and q. Using this encoding technique we find that

$$C_\iota(G, uv) \;\le\; C_\iota(G, u) + C_\iota(G, v) + 2\log_2(\min(C_\iota(G, u), C_\iota(G, v))) + 0(1). \tag{2.1}$$

Let $l(u)$ denote the length of word $u \in V^*$. We have that $C_\iota(G, u) \le C(u),\ u \in V^*$ and $C(u) \le l(u)\log_2|V| + 2\log_2|V| + c$ for some constant c independent of u and V [**17**, p.107]. Hence, (2.1) implies that

$$C_\iota(G, uv) \;\le\; C_\iota(G, u) + C_\iota(G, v) + 2\log_2(\min(l(u), l(v))) + 0(1). \tag{2.2}$$

For a word $u_1 \ldots u_n$ with $u_i \in V,\ i \in \{1, \ldots, n\}$, we consider the behavior of $n^{-1}C_\iota(G, u_1u_2\ldots u_n)$ for large n. We can directly employ the following result [**27**].

THEOREM 2.2 (De Bruijn-Erdös (1952)). *Suppose ϕ is a positive and nondecreasing function that satisfies*

$$\int_1^\infty \frac{\phi(t)}{t^2} < \infty.$$

If $\{x_n\}$ satisfies the relaxed subadditivity relation

$$x_{n+m} \;\le\; x_n + x_m + \phi(n+m),\ \frac{n}{2} \le m \le 2n$$

then as $n \to \infty$, x_n/n converges to $\gamma = \inf_{m\ge1} x_m/m$.

Hence (2.2) and Theorem 2.2 imply that the asymptotic per symbol information content needed to convey a word equivalent to the original bound is well-defined. More specifically, we have

PROPOSITION 2.3. *For any word $u_1 \ldots u_n$ with $u_i \in V,\ i \in \{1, 2, \ldots, n\}$, we have that n approaches infinity, $n^{-1}C_\iota(G, u_1\ldots u_n)$ converges to*

$$\inf_{m\ge1} m^{-1}C_\iota(G, u_1\ldots u_m).$$

We next wish to find a probabilistic version of Proposition 2.3. The appropriate frame of reference is subadditive ergodic theory. We will utilize the following theorem [**18**] (see also [**28**, §5.2]).

THEOREM 2.4 (Derriennic (1983)). *Let $X_{m,n}$ and $A_{m,n}$, $m \le n$, be two sequences of random variables with the following properties:*

1. $X_{0,n} \le X_{0,m} + X_{m,n} + A_{m,n}$.
2. $X_{m,n}$ *is stationary, i.e., for every* $k \ge 1$ *the distribution of* $X_{m,m+k}$ *is independent of* m, *and ergodic.*
3. $E[X_{0,1}] < \infty$ *and for each* n, $E[X_{0,n}] \ge c_0 n$ *with* $c_0 > -\infty$.
4. $A_{m,n} \ge 0$ *and* $\lim_{n\to\infty} E[A_{0,n}/n] = 0$.

Then

$$\lim_{n\to\infty} \frac{X_{0,n}}{n} = \lim_{n\to\infty} \frac{E[X_{0,n}]}{n} = \inf_{m\ge 1} \frac{E[X_{0,m}]}{m} \quad \textit{almost surely.}$$

We will apply Theorem 2.4 to the output of two very broad categories of sources. A discrete source is said to be stationary if its probabilistic specification is independent of a time origin and ergodic if it cannot be separated into two or more different persisting modes of behavior. A more precise definition of a discrete, stationary, and ergodic source can be found in [**29**, §3.5]. A unifilar Markov source with finite alphabet V and finite set of states Σ is defined by specifying for each state $s \in \Sigma$ and letter $v \in V$

1. the probability $p_{s,v}$ that the source emits v from state s;
2. the unique next state $S[s, v]$ after v is output from state s.

Given any initial state $s_0 \in \Sigma$, these rules inductively specify both the probability $P(\sigma|s_0)$ that any given source string $\sigma \in V^*$ is emitted and the resulting state $S[s_0, \sigma]$ after σ is output. For the null string $\emptyset$ and each state $s \in \Sigma$, our convention is that $P(\emptyset|s) = 1$. We assume that the source has a single recurrent class of states; i.e., for each pair of states s and r, there is a non-null string $\sigma \in V^*$ such that $P(\sigma|s) > 0$ and $S[s, \sigma] = r$. The class of unifilar Markov sources is fairly general and includes, for each $l \ge 1$, the group of sources for which each output depends statistically only on the l previous output symbols. We have the following result.

THEOREM 2.5 (A.E.P. for interchange classes). *Let U_1, U_2, ... be the random output of a finite alphabet, discrete, stationary, and ergodic source or of a finite state and finite alphabet unifilar Markov source. Then*

$$\lim_{n\to\infty} \frac{C_\iota(G, U_1U_2\ldots U_n)}{n} = \lim_{n\to\infty} \frac{E[C_\iota(G, U_1U_2\ldots U_n)]}{n} = \inf_{m\ge 1} \frac{E[C_\iota(G, U_1U_2\ldots U_m)]}{m}$$

almost surely.

PROOF. We first consider the case where U_1, U_2, ... is the random output of a finite alphabet, discrete, stationary, and ergodic source. In this case, we set $X_{m,n} = C_\iota(G, U_{m+1}U_{m+2}\ldots U_n)$ and $A_{m,n} = 2\log_2(n-m) + O(1)$ and employ (2.2) and Theorem 2.4.

Next we assume a finite state and finite alphabet unifilar Markov source. Let s_0 denote the initial state of the source. We rewrite the random output of the source $U_1U_2\ldots U_n$ as the unique concatenation of random strings $\Psi_1\Psi_2\ldots\Psi_k\omega$ with $\Psi_i \in V^*$, $l(\Psi_i) \ge 1$, $i \in \{1, \ldots, k\}$, and $\omega \in V^*$ satisfying the following properties:

1. $S[s_0, \Psi_i] = s_0, \quad i \in \{1, \ldots, k\}$.
2. For each $i \in \{1, \ldots, k\}$, there is no proper prefix σ of Ψ_i with $S[s_0, \sigma] = s_0$.
3. If $l(\omega) \geq 1$, then for each non-null prefix σ of ω including the string ω itself we have $S[s_0, \sigma] \neq s_0$.

Let

$$\begin{aligned} X_{m,n} &= C_\iota(G, \Psi_{m+1}\Psi_{m+2}\ldots\Psi_n) \\ \text{and } A_{m,n} &= 2\log_2(l(\Psi_{m+1}\Psi_{m+2}\ldots\Psi_n)) + O(1) \end{aligned}$$

and consider the conditions of Theorem 2.4. Property 1 holds by (2.2). The random strings $\{\Psi_i,\ i \geq 1\}$ are independent and identically distributed and therefore Property 2 holds. To bound $E[X_{0,1}]$ from above, we observe that

(2.3)
$$E[C_\iota(G, \Psi_1)] \leq E[C(\Psi_1)] \leq E[l(\Psi_1)\log_2|V| + 0(1)] = E[l(\Psi_1)]\log_2|V| + 0(1).$$

Let π_{s_0} denote the steady-state probability that the source is in state s_0. Since we assume that the source has a single recurrent class of states, $\pi_{s_0} > 0$. It is known (see, e.g., [**30**, Proposition 3.3.1]) that

$$E[l(\Psi_1)] = 1/\pi_{s_0}. \tag{2.4}$$

Property 3 follows from (2.3), (2.4), and the fact that $X_{0,n} > 0$ for all n. To establish Property 4, observe that

$$\begin{aligned} E\left(\frac{A_{0,n}}{n}\right) &= E\left(\frac{2\log_2(l(\Psi_1\Psi_2\ldots\Psi_n)) + O(1)}{n}\right) \\ &\leq \frac{1}{n}\left(2\log_2 E[l(\Psi_1\Psi_2\ldots\Psi_n)] + O(1)\right), \text{ by Jensen's inequality} \\ &= \frac{1}{n}\left(2\log_2\left(\frac{n}{\pi_{s_0}}\right) + 0(1)\right), \text{ by (2.4).} \end{aligned}$$

It follows from the four properties that

(2.5)
$$\lim_{k\to\infty}\frac{C_\iota(G, \Psi_1\Psi_2\ldots\Psi_k)}{k} = \lim_{k\to\infty}\frac{E[C_\iota(G, \Psi_1\Psi_2\ldots\Psi_k)]}{k} = \inf_{l\geq 1}\frac{E[C_\iota(G, \Psi_1\Psi_2\ldots\Psi_l)]}{l}$$

almost surely.

Next we wish to consider the behavior of

$$\frac{C_\iota(G, \Psi_1\Psi_2\ldots\Psi_k)}{l(\Psi_1) + l(\Psi_2) + \cdots + l(\Psi_k)}$$

for large k. Observe that

(2.6)
$$\frac{C_\iota(G, \Psi_1\Psi_2\ldots\Psi_k)}{l(\Psi_1) + l(\Psi_2) + \cdots + l(\Psi_k)} = \frac{C_\iota(G, \Psi_1\Psi_2\ldots\Psi_k)}{k}\cdot\frac{k}{l(\Psi_1) + l(\Psi_2) + \cdots + l(\Psi_k)}.$$

By the strong law of large numbers [**30**, §4.3] we have that with probability 1,

$$\lim_{k\to\infty}\frac{k}{l(\Psi_1) + l(\Psi_2) + \cdots + l(\Psi_k)} = \pi_{s_0}. \tag{2.7}$$

It follows from (2.5)-(2.7) that with probability 1,

$$
\text{(2.8)}\quad \lim_{k\to\infty}\frac{C_\iota(G,\Psi_1\Psi_2\ldots\Psi_k)}{l(\Psi_1)+l(\Psi_2)+\cdots+l(\Psi_k)} = \lim_{k\to\infty}\pi_{s_0}\cdot\frac{E[C_\iota(G,\Psi_1\Psi_2\ldots\Psi_k)]}{k} = \inf_{l\geq 1}\pi_{s_0}\cdot\frac{E[C_\iota(G,\Psi_1\Psi_2\ldots\Psi_l)]}{l}.
$$

We have seen in Proposition 2.3 that for any word $u_1\ldots u_n$ with $u_i\in V$, $i\in\{1,2,\ldots,n\}$, has the property that n approaches infinity, $n^{-1}C_\iota(G,u_1\ldots u_n)$ converges to $\inf_{m\geq 1} m^{-1}C_\iota(G,u_1\ldots u_m)$. This is true in particular for words which are output from our unifilar Markov source. Since a random output leaves the source in state s_0 infinitely often with probability 1 and (2.8) governs the asymptotic behavior of $n^{-1}C_\iota(G,U_1U_2\ldots U_n)$ in these cases, Proposition 2.3 and (2.8) imply the theorem. □

Unless otherwise specified, we assume hereafter that we have probabilistic sources P in which the random variables $n^{-1}C_\iota(G,U_1\ldots U_n)$ converge almost surely or in probability to $\lim_{n\to\infty} n^{-1}E[C_\iota(G,U_1\ldots U_n)]$. We name the latter expression the *interchange entropy* and denote it by $H_\iota(G,P)$. Just as the asymptotic equipartition property for strings leads to a notion of typical sequences which all have about the same probability and together constitute the possible outputs of the source with high probability (see, e.g., [**29**, §3.1] or [**13**, Ch. 3]), Theorem 2.5 provides a comparable concept of typical interchange classes. Most long strings require close to $H_\iota(G,P)$ bits per symbol to describe an equivalent string with respect to the noncommutation graph G. It follows that the typical sequences of length n fall into approximately $2^{nH_\iota(G,P)}$ typical interchange classes.

It is generally considered to be difficult to determine or even bound the limiting constants obtained by a subadditivity argument (see, e.g., [**31**, p.3] or [**28**, pp.114,116]). For our problem, there are two straightforward approaches to bounding $H_\iota(G,P)$ from above. The first of these is to simply reproduce the exact source output string. For a discrete, ergodic source with finite alphabet and entropy $H(P)$, it is known (see, e.g., [**32**]) that $n^{-1}C(U_1\ldots U_n)$ converges to $H(P)$ with probability 1. This procedure is optimal when G is the complete graph on V. Another approach is to count the number of interchange classes for a particular string length and allocate a fixed-length codeword to each interchange class. More precisely, we can assign an alphabetic ordering to the elements of the vertex set, follow [**13**, p.152] and use the program "Generate, in lexicographic order, all alphabetically minimal elements of the interchange classes of length n. Of these words, print the ith word." The moment generating function for the number of interchange classes for words of a given length was shown in [**24**, Ch. II] to be equal to the inverse of the Möbius polynomial corresponding to a function of G. Recently a formula for the dominant term in the asymptotic expansion of the number of traces was provided in [**33**]. In the special case where G is the empty graph, it is well known [**13**, p.280] that the number of type classes of length n for a vertex set V with cardinality $|V|$ is at most $(n+1)^{|V|}$. Hence, if G is the empty graph, then $H_\iota(G,P)=0$ for all probability distributions P. The Körner graph entropy and chromatic entropy are also known to be $H(P)$ when G is the complete graph on the vertex set and 0 when G is the empty graph on the vertex set.

The characterization of interchange classes by type class and edge projections provided in Theorem 2.1 implies that the interchange entropy is *monotonic*, *subadditive*, and for memoryless sources satisfies two special cases of *additivity under vertex substitution*. Let E denote the edge set of a graph.

PROPOSITION 2.6 (Monotonicity). *If F and G are two graphs on the same vertex set and the respective edge sets satisfy $E(F) \subseteq E(G)$, then for any word x we have $C_\iota(F, x) \leq C_\iota(G, x)$. Hence, for any probability distribution P we have $H_\iota(F, P) \leq H_\iota(G, P)$.*

PROOF. The interchange class of any word w under G is contained in its interchange class under F. □

The Körner graph entropy and chromatic entropy are also known to be monotonic.

PROPOSITION 2.7 (Subadditivity). *Let F and G be two graphs on the same vertex set V and define $F \cup G$ to be the graph on V with edge set $E(F) \cup E(G)$. For any word x, we have that $C_\iota(F \cup G, x) \leq C_\iota(F, x) + C_\iota(G, x) + O(1)$. Therefore, for any fixed probability distribution P we have $H_\iota(F \cup G, P) \leq H_\iota(F, P) + H_\iota(G, P)$.*

PROOF. We have seen in Theorem 2.1 and the discussion following the theorem statement that an interchange class for a string can be determined completely by its type class and edge projections and that it is possible to use the type class and edge projections to obtain a word in the interchange class. To prove Proposition 2.7 observe that the type of any word is independent of the noncommutation graph. The edge projections under $F \cup G$ are the union of the edge projections under F with the edge projections under G. Therefore, the following encoding scheme leads to the proposition. We optimally encode the interchange classes of a word both with respect to the noncommutation graph F and the noncommutation graph G, decode the results to obtain the edge projections under F and under G, and finally use the combination of type class and edge projections for $F \cup G$ to reconstruct a word in the congruence class under $F \cup G$. □

The Körner graph entropy is also subadditive.

The concept of *substitution* of a graph F for a vertex v in a disjoint graph G is described in [**21**, §3]. The idea is that v and the edges in G with v as an endpoint are removed and every vertex of F is connected to those vertices of G that were adjacent to v. This notion can be extended to a property of Körner graph entropy known as "additivity of substitution." The concept does not hold in general for the interchange entropy, but there are two special cases which apply. The first one is concerned with graphs consisting of more than one connected component.

PROPOSITION 2.8. *Let the subgraphs G_j denote disjoint components of the graph G; i.e., there is no edge in $E(G)$ with one endpoint in $V(G_j)$ and the other in $V(G_l)$ for $j \neq l$. For a memoryless source with probability distribution P on $V(G)$ define the probability distributions*

$$P_j(x) = P(x)[P(V(G_j))]^{-1}, \; x \in V(G_j). \tag{2.9}$$

Then $H_\iota(G, P) = \sum_j P(V(G_j))H_\iota(G_j, P_j)$.

PROOF. The edge projections of G can be partitioned into those corresponding to G_1, those corresponding to G_2, and so on. The projection of source output symbols onto G_j is a memoryless process with symbol probabilities given by the conditional probability (2.9). Furthermore, since the original process is memoryless, if the lengths λ_1, λ_2, ... of the strings corresponding to the projections onto G_1, G_2, etc. are known, there is no additional correlation among the different projections. Hence, the problem may be decomposed into compressing λ_1 symbols from graph G_1 with vertex set $V(G_1)$ and probability distribution P_1, λ_2 symbols from graph G_2 with vertex set $V(G_2)$ and probability distribution P_2, and so forth. For each j, as λ_j approaches infinity, the number of bits per symbol required to represent the projection onto G_j is $H_\iota(G_j, P_j)$ with probability 1. Furthermore, as the original string length n approaches infinity it follows from the strong law of large numbers that for each j the fraction λ_j/n of symbols belonging to $V(G_j)$ approaches $P(V(G_j))$ almost surely (see, e.g., [**34**, §1.8] or [**13**, §12.2]). The result follows by combining these observations. □

We next show an example illustrating that Proposition 2.8 fails in general to hold for the output of sources with memory. Suppose that $V = \{a, b, c, d\}$, $G = a\text{—}b \quad c\text{—}d$, and the source is an order-1 Markov chain with $P(c|a) = P(d|b) = 1$, $P(a|c) = P(b|c) = P(a|d) = P(b|d) = 0.5$. Assume that the first symbol is equally likely to be an a or a b. In other words, the source outputs *two* symbols at a time independently with half being ac and the other half being bd. It is easy to verify that the entropy of the original source is 0.5 bits per symbol. Next suppose $F = a\text{—}b \quad c \quad d$. In order to represent a word congruent to the source output with respect to F we need to precisely characterize the projection of the string onto the subalphabet $\{a, b\}$. Note that this projection looks like the output of a binary, memoryless source with $P(a) = P(b) = 0.5$. Since half of the symbols from the original string appear in the projection, it follows that $H_\iota(F, P) = 0.5$ bits per symbol. Therefore Proposition 2.6 implies that $H_\iota(G, P) = 0.5$ bits per symbol. Let $G_1 = a\text{—}b$ and $G_2 = c\text{—}d$. Observe that $H_\iota(G, P) \neq P(V(G_1))H_\iota(G_1, P_1) + P(V(G_2))H_\iota(G_2, P_2) = 1$ bit per symbol. The reason that Proposition 2.8 is invalid in this case is that the projection of source output symbols onto G_2 is perfectly correlated with the projection of source output symbols onto G_1 in that it can be obtained by replacing each a with a c and each b with a d.

We next consider a second example of additivity of substitution for the interchange entropy assuming the original source string is the output of a memoryless source.

PROPOSITION 2.9. *Let F be a graph consisting of two vertices x and y and an edge connecting them, let G be a graph with vertex set disjoint from F, and let v be a vertex of G. Form the graph $G_{v\leftarrow F}$ by deleting v and joining both vertices of F to those vertices of G which were adjacent to v. For a memoryless sources with probability distribution $P_{v\leftarrow F}$ on $V(G_{v\leftarrow F})$, we define two auxiliary memoryless sources, one over $V(G)$ with probability distribution P and the other over $V(F)$ with probability distribution Q as follows*

$$(2.10)\qquad \begin{aligned} P(u) &= \begin{cases} P_{v\leftarrow F}(u), & u \in V(G) - \{v\} \\ P_{v\leftarrow F}(x) + P_{v\leftarrow F}(y), & u = v \end{cases} \\ Q(x) &= \frac{P_{v\leftarrow F}(x)}{P(v)} \\ Q(y) &= \frac{P_{v\leftarrow F}(y)}{P(v)} \end{aligned}$$

Then $H_\iota(G_{v\leftarrow F}, P_{v\leftarrow F}) = H_\iota(G,P) + P(v)H(Q)$.

PROOF. There are two cases to consider. Suppose first that v commutes with every other symbol in G. Form the graph G_1 from the graph G by deleting vertex v, and define the probability distribution P_1 over $V(G_1)$ by $P_1(u) = P(u)/(1-P(v))$. By Proposition 2.8 we have

$$\begin{aligned}(2.11)\qquad H_\iota(G_{v\leftarrow F}, P_{v\leftarrow F}) &= (1 - P_{v\leftarrow F}(x) - P_{v\leftarrow F}(y))H_\iota(G_1, P_1) \\ &\quad + (P_{v\leftarrow F}(x) + P_{v\leftarrow F}(y))H_\iota(F, Q) \\ &= (1 - P(v))H_\iota(G_1, P_1) + P(v)H(Q),\end{aligned}$$

using (2.10) and the fact that F is a complete graph on two vertices, which results in the interchange entropy for a memoryless source being equal to its entropy. By another application of Proposition 2.8,

$$(2.12)\quad H_\iota(G,P) = (1-P(v))H_\iota(G_1,P_1) + P(v)\cdot 0 = (1-P(v))H_\iota(G_1,P_1),$$

since the interchange entropy of a graph consisting of a single node is zero. Hence, for this case the result follows from (2.11) and (2.12).

Next suppose that there is at least one other vertex $u \in V(G)$ which is adjacent to v in G. Then in $G_{v\leftarrow F}$ the projections onto the edges $\{u,x\}$, $\{u,y\}$, and $\{x,y\}$ can be deduced from the projection onto the subalphabet $\{u,x,y\}$ and vice versa. The projection onto the subalphabet $\{u,x,y\}$ is equivalent to the combination of the projection onto edge $\{x,y\}$ and the string on the alphabet $\{u,v\}$ obtained by replacing every x and y in the projection onto $\{u,x,y\}$ by v. This argument holds for each vertex adjacent to v in G. Since the probability distribution $P_{v\leftarrow F}$ is for a memoryless source it follows that given the number λ of symbols x and y in the original string, the projection onto edge $\{x,y\}$ is uncorrelated with the string formed by replacing the λ x's and y's in the original string by v's. Hence, the problem is equivalent to compressing n symbols over a memoryless source on $V(G)$ with probability distribution P, exactly λ of which are v's, and λ symbols over a memoryless source on $V(F)$ with probability distribution Q. By the strong law of large numbers, as the original string length approaches infinity, λ/n approaches $P(v)$ almost surely, the number of bits per symbol required to represent the string over $V(G)$ is $H_\iota(G,P)$ with probability 1, and the number of bits per symbol needed to specify the string over $V(F)$ is $H(Q)$ almost surely. □

For discrete memoryless sources, we can obtain the exact expression for $H_\iota(G,P)$ in the case where G is a complete k-partite graph $K_{m_1,m_2,\ldots,m_k}$. We will prove the following result in the next section.

THEOREM 2.10. *Assume a discrete, memoryless source with probability distribution P on vertex set V. Suppose V is of the form $V = V_1 \cup V_2 \cup \cdots \cup V_k$ with $|V_i| = m_i$, $i \in \{1,2,\ldots,k\}$ and label the elements of V_i as $v_{i,j}$, $i \in \{1,2,\ldots,k\}$, $j \in \{1,2,\ldots,m_i\}$. For our complete k-partite graph $K_{m_1,m_2,\ldots,m_k}$ there is an edge corresponding to every pair of vertices $\{v_{i,j}, v_{l,n}\}$, $v_{i,j} \in V_i$, $v_{l,n} \in V_l$, $l \neq i$, and no two vertices from the same subset V_i are adjacent for any $i \in \{1,2,\ldots,k\}$. Define $Q_i = \sum_{j=1}^{m_i} P(v_{i,j})$, $i \in \{1,2,\ldots,k\}$. Then*

$$H_\iota(K_{m_1,m_2,\ldots,m_k}, P) =$$

$$H(P) - \sum_{S=2}^{\infty} \log_2(S) \sum_{i:m_i \geq 2} (1 - Q_i) \left({Q_i}^S - \sum_{j=1}^{m_i} \left(\frac{P(v_{i,j})}{1 - Q_i + P(v_{i,j})} \right)^S \right).$$

Theorem 2.10 leads to the following property of the interchange entropy for the output from a discrete, memoryless source.

COROLLARY 2.11. *Assume a discrete, memoryless source with probability distribution P on vertex set $V(G)$. If G is not the complete graph on $V(G)$, then $H_\iota(G, P) < H(P)$.*

PROOF. The complete graph on $|V|$ vertices has $|V| \cdot (|V| - 1)/2$ edges. Any subgraph with $|V| \cdot (|V| - 1)/2 - 1$ edges can be expressed as a complete-$(|V| - 1)$ partite graph $K_{1,1,\ldots,1,2}$, and it follows from Theorem 2.10 that a memoryless source with probability distribution P on the vertex set satisfies $H_\iota(K_{1,1,\ldots,1,2}, P) < H(P)$. Since our graph G is not the complete graph on $V(G)$, we have that $E(G) \subseteq E(K_{1,1,\ldots,1,2}, P)$ for some complete-$(|V(G)| - 1)$ partite graph. The result follows from an application of Proposition 2.6. □

The example following Proposition 2.8 illustrates that it is possible for a source with memory to satisfy $H_\iota(G, P) = H(P)$ even when the dependence relation G is not the complete graph on $V(G)$.

We conclude with an example to illustrate some of the results in this section. Suppose our noncommutation graph G is a—b—c and $P(a) = P(b) = P(c) = 1/3$. A simple upper bound for $H_\iota(G, P)$ is $H_\iota(G, P) \leq H(P) = \log_2 3 \approx 1.58496$. Define the graphs $F_1 = a$—b c, $F_2 = a$ b—c, $F_3 = c$—a b. By symmetry, $H_\iota(F_1, P) = H_\iota(F_2, P) = H_\iota(F_3, P)$. It follows from Proposition 2.8 that $H_\iota(F_1, P) = \frac{2}{3} \cdot 1 + \frac{1}{3} \cdot 0 = \frac{2}{3}$. Since $G = F_1 \cup F_2$, Proposition 2.7 implies that $H_\iota(G, P) \leq H_\iota(F_1, P) + H_\iota(F_2, P) = 4/3 \approx 1.33333$. Therefore, for this source and dependence relation a compression scheme consisting of encoding the two edge projections and having the decoder use the edge projections to reconstruct a word in the equivalence class would require fewer bits per symbol on average than losslessly compressing the entire string. Since $F_1 \subset G$ and $F_2 \subset G$, we have by Proposition 2.6 that $H_\iota(G, P) \geq H_\iota(F_1, P) \approx 0.66667$. Another lower bound on $H_\iota(G, P)$ follows from the fact that the complete graph on the vertex set is $G \cup F_3$. Therefore, by subadditivity, $H(P) \leq H_\iota(G, P) + H_\iota(F_3, P)$ and so $H_\iota(G, P) \geq \log_2 3 - 2/3 \approx 0.91830$. Since G is a complete bipartite graph, Theorem 2.10 implies that $H_\iota(G, P) = \log_2 3 - \frac{1}{3} \sum_{S=2}^{\infty} [(\frac{2}{3})^S - 2(\frac{1}{2})^S] \log_2(S) \approx 1.27645$.

The paper [**35**] discusses some universal compression schemes for this problem and establishes that these schemes asymptotically attain the interchange entropy for the output of a discrete, memoryless source and a large collection of dependence alphabets.

3. Proof of Theorem 2.10

PROOF. We can uniquely segment the data string into a sequence of variable-length phrases corresponding to maximal runs of symbols from a vertex subset V_i. In other words, if the symbols in a phrase are all from V_i, then the symbols in the next phrase are all from V_j for some $j \neq i$. The projections onto the subalphabets consisting of the various edges can be determined by the sequence of type classes associated with the phrases and also can be used to specify this sequence of type classes. Hence it follows from Theorem 2.1 that the sequence of type classes corresponding to the phrases is the minimal information required to perfectly reconstruct the interchange class containing a string.For a memoryless source, this sequence of type classes forms an ergodic Markov chain, and therefore $H_\iota(K_{m_1,m_2,\ldots,m_k}, P)$ can be found using an analysis based on the theory of semi-Markov processes (see, e.g., [**34**, §5.7]). Let $U_1, U_2, \ldots, U_n$ denote a random string of length n. We can identify epochs $1 = M_1 < M_2 < \ldots$ for which the symbols $U_{M_l}, U_{M_l+1}, \ldots, U_{M_{l+1}-1}$ constitute the lth phrase, $l \geq 1$. Let $T_l = M_{l+1} - M_l$, $l \geq 1$, denote the number of symbols in the lth phrase and Υ_l, $l \geq 1$, represent the index $i \in \{1, 2, \ldots, k\}$ corresponding to the subset of vertices V_i which are represented in the lth phrase. Let R_l denote the self-information corresponding to the type class associated with phrase l. If $\Upsilon_l = i$ and there are exactly $n_{i,j}$ appearances of symbol $v_{i,j}$, $j \in \{1, \ldots, m_i\}$ in phrase l, then $T_l = \sum_{j=1}^{m_i} n_{i,j}$ and

$$R_l = -\sum_{j=1}^{m_i} n_{i,j} \log_2 P(v_{i,j}) - \log_2 \binom{n_{i,1} + \cdots + n_{i,m_i}}{n_{i,1},\ \ldots,\ n_{i,m_i}}.$$

We will see shortly that steady-state distributions for Υ_l and the type class given the value of Υ_l exist. It follows that steady-state distributions for T_l and R_l also exist. Let $L(n) = \sup\{l : M_{l+1} \leq n + 1\}$ denote the number of complete phrases by symbol n. We can then bound the average self-information per symbol from below by $\sum_{l=1}^{L(n)} R_l / \sum_{l=1}^{L(n)+1} T_l$ and from above by $\sum_{l=1}^{L(n)+1} R_l / \sum_{l=1}^{L(n)} T_l$. In the limit as $n \to \infty$ the upper and lower bounds both approach

$$H_\iota(K_{m_1,m_2,\ldots,m_k}, P) = \lim_{L\to\infty} \frac{L^{-1}\sum_{l=1}^{L} R_l}{L^{-1}\sum_{l=1}^{L} T_l} = \frac{\lim_{l\to\infty} E[R_l]}{\lim_{l\to\infty} E[T_l]} \tag{3.1}$$

almost surely. An alternate way to think about the information contained in the phrases is discussed in [**35**]. That approach emphasizes the transition probabilities from one phrase to the next, and it is established in [**35**] that these two formulations lead mathematically to the same result.

Let q_i denote the steady-state probability that $\Upsilon_l = i$. Given that phrase $l - 1$ satisfies $\Upsilon_{l-1} = j$, we have by definition that $\Upsilon_l \neq j$. Since the original process is memoryless, we have that $\text{Prob}[\Upsilon_l = i \mid \Upsilon_{l-1} = j] = (1 - Q_j)^{-1} Q_i$, $i \in \{1, \ldots, k\}$, $i \neq j$. It is straightforward to verify that

$$q_i = \frac{Q_i(1 - Q_i)}{\sum_{j=1}^{k} Q_j(1 - Q_j)}, \qquad i \in \{1, \ldots, k\}. \tag{3.2}$$

We next describe the probability distribution of the type class for a phrase given the subset of vertices V_i which are represented in the lth phrase. For this purpose, we consider an auxiliary memoryless source on the alphabet $\{v_{i,j},\ j \in \{1, \ldots, m_i\}\}$ together with the extra symbol $v_i{}^*$ and assume that the probability of symbol $v_i{}^*$ is $1 - Q_i$ and the probability of symbol $v_{i,j}$ is $P(v_{i,j})$, $j \in \{1, \ldots, m_i\}$. Let $N_{i,j}$ be the random variable denoting the number of appearances of symbol $v_{i,j}$ before the first appearance of symbol $v_i{}^*$ in the auxiliary process. We have that if $\Upsilon_l = i$, the probability of the phrase is determined by the probabilities for the output of the auxiliary source with the added constraint that $\sum_{j=1}^{m_i} N_{i,j} \geq 1$. We have that for

$n_{i,1} \geq 0,\ n_{i,2} \geq 0,\ \dots\ , n_{i,m_i} \geq 0,$

$$\text{Prob}(N_{i,1} = n_{i,1},\ N_{i,2} = n_{i,2},\ \dots, N_{i,m_i} = n_{i,m_i} \mid V_l = i) \quad = \quad (1 - Q_i) \cdot \binom{n_{i,1} + \cdots + n_{i,m_i}}{n_{i,1},\ \dots,\ n_{i,m_i}} \prod_{m=1}^{m_i} [P(v_{i,m})]^{n_{i,m}},$$

and hence,

$$\text{Prob}(N_{i,1} = n_{i,1},\ N_{i,2} = n_{i,2},\ \dots, N_{i,m_i} = n_{i,m_i} \mid V_l = i,\ \sum_{j=1}^{m_i} N_{i,j} \geq 1) \quad = \quad \frac{1 - Q_i}{Q_i} \cdot \binom{n_{i,1} + \cdots + n_{i,m_i}}{n_{i,1},\ \dots,\ n_{i,m_i}} \prod_{m=1}^{m_i} [P(v_{i,m})]^{n_{i,m}},\ \sum_{m=1}^{m_i} n_{i,m} \geq 1.$$

In order to determine the interchange entropy of this process, we need to find $\lim_{l \to \infty} E[T_l]$ and $\lim_{l \to \infty} E[R_l]$. We first evaluate $E[T_l \mid \Upsilon_l = i]$ and $E[R_l \mid \Upsilon_l = i]$. We have that

$$E[T_l \mid \Upsilon_l = i] \ = \ E\left(\sum_{j=1}^{m_i} N_{i,j} \,\middle|\, \sum_{j=1}^{m_i} N_{i,j} \geq 1\right) \tag{3.3}$$

$$E[R_l \mid \Upsilon_l = i] \quad = \quad E\left(-\sum_{j=1}^{m_i} N_{i,j} \log_2 P(v_{i,j}) - \log_2 \binom{N_{i,1} + \cdots + N_{i,m_i}}{N_{i,1},\ \dots,\ N_{i,m_i}} \,\middle|\, \sum_{j=1}^{m_i} N_{i,j} \geq 1\right). \tag{3.4}$$

Observe that

$$E\left(\sum_{j=1}^{m_i} N_{i,j}\right) \ = \ Q_i \cdot E\left(\sum_{j=1}^{m_i} N_{i,j} \,\middle|\, \sum_{j=1}^{m_i} N_{i,j} \geq 1\right) \tag{3.5}$$

and

$$E\left(-\sum_{j=1}^{m_i} N_{i,j} \log_2 P(v_{i,j}) - \log_2 \binom{N_{i,1} + \cdots + N_{i,m_i}}{N_{i,1},\ \dots,\ N_{i,m_i}}\right) \ = \ Q_i \cdot E\left(-\sum_{j=1}^{m_i} N_{i,j} \log_2 P(v_{i,j}) - \log_2 \binom{N_{i,1} + \cdots + N_{i,m_i}}{N_{i,1},\ \dots,\ N_{i,m_i}} \,\middle|\, \sum_{j=1}^{m_i} N_{i,j} \geq 1\right). \tag{3.6}$$

We first find $E[N_{i,j}]$. For $l \in \{2,\ 3,\ \dots\}$, $n_1 \in \{0,\ 1,\ 2,\ \dots\}$, $x_m \geq 0$, $m \in \{2,\ \dots,\ l\}$, $\sum_{m=2}^{l} x_m < 1$, we define

$$\sigma_l(n_1,\ x_2,\ \dots,\ x_l) \ = \ \sum_{n_2=0}^{\infty} \cdots \sum_{n_l=0}^{\infty} \binom{n_1 + \cdots + n_l}{n_1,\ \dots,\ n_l} \prod_{m=2}^{l} {x_m}^{n_m}.$$

Observe that

$$\sigma_l(0,\ x_2,\ \dots,\ x_l) \ = \ \sum_{S=0}^{\infty} \left(\sum_{m=2}^{l} x_m\right)^S \ = \ \frac{1}{1 - \sum_{m=2}^{l} x_m}. \tag{3.7}$$

The following simple identity on multinomial numbers is well-known (see, e.g., [**36**, p.100]) and easy to verify. Assume $n_1, \ldots, n_l \in \{0,\ 1,\ 2,\ \ldots\}$. Then

(3.8)

$$\binom{n_1+\cdots+n_l}{n_1,\ \ldots,\ n_l} = \sum_{m=1}^{l} \binom{n_1+\cdots+n_{m-1}+(n_m-1)+n_{m+1}+\cdots+n_l}{n_1,\ \ldots,\ n_{m-1},\ n_m-1,\ n_{m+1},\ \ldots,\ n_l},$$

where the mth term in the summation is zero if $n_m = 0$. It follows from (3.8) that for $n_1 \geq 1$

(3.9) $\sigma_l(n_1,\ x_2,\ \ldots,\ x_l)$

$$\begin{aligned} &= \sum_{m=1}^{l} \binom{n_1+\cdots+n_{m-1}+(n_m-1)+n_{m+1}+\cdots+n_l}{n_1,\ \ldots,\ n_{m-1},\ n_m-1,\ n_{m+1},\ \ldots,\ n_l} \prod_{\mu=2}^{l} x_\mu{}^{n_\mu} \\ &= \sigma_l(n_1-1,\ x_2,\ \ldots,\ x_l) + \sum_{m=2}^{l} x_m \cdot \sigma_l(n_1,\ x_2,\ \ldots,\ x_l). \end{aligned}$$

By (3.7), (3.9), and induction on n_1 it follows that

(3.10)
$$\begin{aligned} \sigma_l(n_1,\ x_2,\ \ldots,\ x_l) &= \sum_{n_2=0}^{\infty} \cdots \sum_{n_l=0}^{\infty} \binom{n_1+\cdots+n_l}{n_1,\ \ldots,\ n_l} \prod_{m=2}^{l} x_m{}^{n_m} \\ &= \frac{1}{\left(1-\sum_{m=2}^{l} x_m\right)^{n_1+1}}. \end{aligned}$$

We have that for $n \in \{0,\ 1,\ 2, \ldots\}$,

(3.11)

$$\begin{aligned} \mathrm{Prob}[N_{i,j}=n] &= \sum_{m=0}^{\infty} \mathrm{Prob}[N_{i,j}=n,\ \sum_{l\neq j} N_{i,l}=m] \\ &= \sum_{m=0}^{\infty} \binom{m+n}{n} P(v_{i,j})^n (Q_i - P(v_{i,j}))^m (1-Q_i) \\ &= \frac{1-Q_i}{1-Q_i+P(v_{i,j})} \left(\frac{P(v_{i,j})}{1-Q_i+P(v_{i,j})}\right)^n, \quad \text{using (3.10).} \end{aligned}$$

The preceding equation, (3.2), (3.3) and (3.5) imply that

(3.12)
$$\begin{aligned} E[N_{i,j}] &= \frac{P(v_{i,j})}{1-Q_i} \\ E[T_l \mid \Upsilon_l = i] &= \frac{1}{1-Q_i} \end{aligned}$$

(3.13)
$$\lim_{l\to\infty} E[T_l] = \sum_{i=1}^{k} q_i E[T_l \mid \Upsilon_l = i] = \frac{1}{\sum_{j=1}^{k} Q_j(1-Q_j)}.$$

We next simplify $E\left(\log_2\binom{N_{i,1}+\cdots+N_{i,m_i}}{N_{i,1},\ \ldots,\ N_{i,m_i}}\right)$. We have

(3.14)

$$
\begin{aligned}
&E\left(\log_2\binom{N_{i,1}+\cdots+N_{i,m_i}}{N_{i,1},\ \ldots,\ N_{i,m_i}}\right)\\
&= \sum_{n_{i,1}=0}^{\infty}\cdots\sum_{n_{i,m_i}=0}^{\infty}\binom{n_{i,1}+\cdots+n_{i,m_i}}{n_{i,1},\ \ldots,\ n_{i,m_i}}\cdot\left((1-Q_i)\prod_{m=1}^{m_i}[P(v_{i,m})]^{n_{i,m}}\right)\\
&\qquad\cdot\log_2\binom{n_{i,1}+\cdots+n_{i,m_i}}{n_{i,1},\ \ldots,\ n_{i,m_i}}\\
&= (1-Q_i)\sum_{S=0}^{\infty}\log_2(S!)\\
&\qquad\sum_{\substack{n_{i,1},\ldots,n_{i,m_i}\geq 0\\ n_{i,1}+\cdots+n_{i,m_i}=S}}\binom{S}{n_{i,1},\ \ldots,\ n_{i,m_i}}\prod_{m=1}^{m_i}[P(v_{i,m})]^{n_{i,m}}\\
&\quad-(1-Q_i)\sum_{j=1}^{m_i}\sum_{n_{i,1}=0}^{\infty}\cdots\sum_{n_{i,m_i}=0}^{\infty}[P(v_{i,j})]^{n_{i,j}}\log_2(n_{i,j}!)\\
&\qquad\cdot\binom{n_{i,1}+\cdots+n_{i,m_i}}{n_{i,1},\ \ldots,\ n_{i,m_i}}\prod_{\substack{m=1\\ m\neq j}}^{m_i}[P(v_{i,m})]^{n_{i,m}}\\
&= (1-Q_i)\sum_{S=0}^{\infty}[P(v_{i,1})+\cdots+P(v_{i,m_i})]^S\log_2(S!)\\
&\quad-(1-Q_i)\sum_{j=1}^{m_i}\sum_{n_{i,j}=0}^{\infty}[P(v_{i,j})]^{n_{i,j}}\log_2(n_{i,j}!)\cdot\frac{1}{(1-Q_i+P(v_{i,j}))^{n_{i,j}+1}},\\
&\hfill\text{using (3.10)}\\
&= (1-Q_i)\sum_{S=0}^{\infty}{Q_i}^S\log_2(S!)-(1-Q_i)\sum_{j=1}^{m_i}\sum_{S=0}^{\infty}\frac{[P(v_{i,j})]^S}{(1-Q_i+P(v_{i,j}))^{S+1}}\log_2(S!)\\
&= \sum_{S=1}^{\infty}\log_2(S)\sum_{n=S}^{\infty}(1-Q_i)\left({Q_i}^n-\sum_{j=1}^{m_i}\frac{[P(v_{i,j})]^n}{(1-Q_i+P(v_{i,j}))^{n+1}}\right)\\
&= \sum_{S=1}^{\infty}\left({Q_i}^S-\sum_{j=1}^{m_i}\left(\frac{P(v_{i,j})}{1-Q_i+P(v_{i,j})}\right)^S\right)\log_2(S).
\end{aligned}
$$

Combining (3.2), (3.4), (3.6), (3.12), and (3.14), we find that

$$
\begin{aligned}
E[R_l \mid \Upsilon_l = i] \;=\; &\frac{-\sum_{j=1}^{m_i}P(v_{i,j})\log_2 P(v_{i,j})}{Q_i(1-Q_i)}\\
&-\frac{1}{Q_i}\sum_{S=1}^{\infty}\left({Q_i}^S-\sum_{j=1}^{m_i}\left(\frac{P(v_{i,j})}{1-Q_i+P(v_{i,j})}\right)^S\right)\log_2(S)
\end{aligned}
$$

$$(3.15) \qquad \lim_{l\to\infty} E[R_l] = \sum_{i=1}^{k} q_i E[R_l \mid \Upsilon_l = i]$$

$$= \frac{H(P) - \sum_{i=1}^{k}(1-Q_i)\sum_{S=1}^{\infty}\left(Q_i{}^S - \sum_{j=1}^{m_i}\left(\frac{P(v_{i,j})}{1-Q_i+P(v_{i,j})}\right)^S\right)\log_2(S)}{\sum_{j=1}^{k} Q_j(1-Q_j)}.$$

The theorem follows from the combination of (3.1), (3.13), and (3.15). □

Acknowledgment

The author would like to thank K. Etessami, R. Alur, S. Guha, M. Yannakakis, and S. Chaudhuri for formulating and suggesting the problem of compressing partial orders, for helpful discussions, and for providing two drafts of [**11**]. K. Etessami's comments on a number of preliminary versions of [**37**] led to significant improvements. The author is also grateful to an anonymous reviewer of [**35**] for pointing out the paper [**14**].

References

[1] C. E. Shannon, "A mathematical theory of communication," *Bell System Tech. J.* 27, 379-423, pp. 623–656, 1948.
[2] C. E. Shannon, "Information theory," in *Claude Elwood Shannon Collected Papers* edited by N. J. A. Sloane and A. D. Wyner, IEEE Press, New York 1993.
[3] C. E. Shannon, "The lattice theory of information," in *Claude Elwood Shannon Collected Papers* edited by N. J. A. Sloane and A. D. Wyner, IEEE Press, New York 1993.
[4] J. Larus, "Whole program paths," *ACM SIGPLAN Conf. Prog. Lang. Des. Implem.*, pp. 259–269, Atlanta, GA, May 1999.
[5] C. G. Nevill-Manning and I. H. Witten, "Linear-time, incremental hierarchy inference for compression," *Proc. 1997 IEEE Data Comp. Conf.*, pp. 3–11, Snowbird, UT, March 1997.
[6] L. Lamport, "Time, clocks, and the ordering of events in a distributed system," *Comm. ACM* 21, pp. 558–565, 1978.
[7] V. R. Pratt, "Modelling concurrency with partial orders," *Int. J. Parallel Prog.* 15(1), pp. 33–71, 1985.
[8] A. Mazurkiewicz, "Concurrent program schemes and their interpretations," DAIMI Rep. PB 78, Aarhus University, Aarhus, 1977.
[9] A. Mazurkiewicz, "Trace theory," in W. Brauer et. al., ed., *Petri Nets, Applications and Relationship to other Models of Concurrency*, Lecture Notes in Computer Science 255, pp. 279–324, Springer, Berlin, 1987.
[10] V. Diekert and Y. Métivier, "Partial commutation and traces," in G. Rozenberg and A. Salomaa, ed., *Handbook on Formal Languages: Beyond Words*, Volume III, pp. 457–534, Springer, Berlin, 1997.
[11] R. Alur, S. Chaudhuri, K. Etessami, S. Guha and M. Yannakakis, "Compression of partially ordered strings," *Proc. of the 15th International Conference on Concurrency Theory*, Marseille, France, Sept. 2003.
[12] J. C. Kieffer and E. Yang, "Grammar-based codes: a new class of universal lossless source codes," *IEEE Trans. Inform. Theory*, vol. 46, pp. 737–754, 2000.
[13] T. M. Cover and J. A. Thomas, *Elements of Information Theory*, Wiley, New York 1991.
[14] M. Drinić and D. Kirovski, "PPMexe: PPM for compressing software," *Proc. 1997 IEEE Data Comp. Conf.*, pp. 192–201, Snowbird, UT, March 2002.
[15] J. van Leeuwen, "Preface," in J. van Leeuwen, *Handbook of Theoretical Computer Science. Volume B: Formal Methods and Semantics*, v-vi, MIT Press, Cambridge, 1987.
[16] P. D. Mosses, "Denotational Semantics," in J. van Leeuwen, *Handbook of Theoretical Computer Science. Volume B: Formal Methods and Semantics*, pp. 577–631, MIT Press, Cambridge, 1987.

[17] M. Li and P. Vitányi, *An Introduction to Kolmogorov Complexity and Its Applications*, Second Edition, Springer, New York, 1997.
[18] Y. Derriennic, "Un théorème ergodique presque sous-additif," *Ann. Prob.* 11, pp. 669–677, 1983.
[19] B. McMillan, "The basic theorems of information theory," *Ann. Math. Stat.* 24, pp. 196–219, 1953.
[20] J. Körner, "Coding of an information source having ambiguous alphabet and the entropy of graphs," in *Proc. 6th Prague Conf. on Information Theory*, pp. 411–425, 1973.
[21] G. Simonyi, "Graph entropy: a survey," in L. Lovász, P. Seymour, and W. Cook, ed., *DIMACS Volume 20 on Special Year on Combinatorial Optimization*, pp. 399–441, 1995.
[22] R. B. Boppana, "Optimal separation between concurrent-write parallel machines," in *Proc. 21st Ann. ACM Symp. Theory Comp.*, pp. 320–326, 1989.
[23] N. Alon and A. Orlitsky, "Source coding and graph entropies," *IEEE Trans. Inform. Theory*, vol. 42, pp. 1329–1339, 1996.
[24] P. Cartier and D. Foata, *Problèmes combinatoires de commutation et réarrangements*, Lecture Notes in Mathematics 85, Springer, Berlin, 1969.
[25] D. Perrin, "Words over a partially commutative alphabet," in A. Apostolico and Z. Galil, ed., *Combinatorial Algorithms on Words*, NATO ASI Series, Volume F12, pp. 329–340, Springer, Berlin, 1985.
[26] A. N. Kolmogorov, "Logical basis for information theory and probability theory," *IEEE Trans. Inform. Theory* IT-14, pp. 662–664, 1968.
[27] N. G. DeBruijn and P. Erdös, "Some linear and some quadratic recursion formulas I," *Indag. Math.* 13, pp. 374–382, 1952.
[28] W. Szpankowski, *Average Case Analysis of Algorithms on Sequences*, Wiley, New York, 2001.
[29] R. G. Gallager, *Information Theory and Reliable Communication*, Wiley, New York 1968.
[30] S. M. Ross, *Stochastic Processes*, Wiley, New York, 1983.
[31] J. M. Steele, *Probability Theory and Combinatorial Optimization*, SIAM, Philadelphia, 1997.
[32] S. K. Leung-Yan-Cheong and T. M. Cover, "Some equivalences between Shannon entropy and Kolmogorov complexity," *IEEE Trans. Inform. Theory* IT-24, pp. 331–338, 1978.
[33] M. Goldwurm and M. Santini, "Clique polynomials have a unique root of smallest modulus," *Information Processing Letters* 75(3), pp. 127–132, 2000.
[34] R. G. Gallager, *Discrete Stochastic Processes*, Kluwer, Boston 1996.
[35] S. A. Savari, "On Compressing Interchange Classes of Events in a Concurrent System," *Proc. of IEEE Data Compression Conference*, Snowbird, Utah, March 2003.
[36] N. L. Biggs, *Discrete Mathematics*, Clarendon Press, Oxford 1985.
[37] S. A. Savari, "Concurrent Processes and the Interchange Entropy," *Proc. of IEEE International Symposium on Information Theory*, Yokohama, Japan, July 2003.

E-mail address: `savari@eecs.umich.edu`

COMPUTING SCIENCES RESEARCH CENTER, BELL LABS, LUCENT TECHNOLOGIES, MURRAY HILL, NJ 07974

Current address: Department of Electrical Engineering and Computer Science, The University of Michigan, Ann Arbor, MI 48109

DIMACS Series in Discrete Mathematics
and Theoretical Computer Science
Volume **66**, 2004

Sum Rate of a Class of Multiterminal Gaussian Source Coding Problems

Pramod Viswanath

ABSTRACT. We study a class of multiterminal Gaussian source coding problems with quadratic distortion constraints by considering a multiple antenna broadcast channel that serves as a *test* channel. This study allows a representation of a class of coding strategies for the source coding problem in terms of strategies for the multiple antenna broadcast channel. Finally, we conclude with a characterization of the sum rate for a specific class of quadratic distortion constraints.

1. Introduction

Consider the following canonical multiterminal encoding problem of a *memoryless* Gaussian source. At any instant, we let $\mathbf{n} \stackrel{\text{def}}{=} (n_1, \ldots, n_N)$ be the (vector) source of i.i.d. zero mean, unit variance Gaussian random variables and consider

$$\mathbf{x} = H^t \mathbf{n}. \tag{1.1}$$

Here H^t is a $K \times N$ matrix and hence $\mathbf{x} = (x_1, \ldots, x_K)$ is a jointly Gaussian vector. There are K terminals observing distinct components of the source $\mathbf{x}$, i.e., terminal i has access to x_i. The problem is for each terminal to encode its observation *separately* and convey the encoded message to a *common* receiver. The receiver uses these messages $(m_1, \ldots, m_K)$ to jointly estimate the original random variables $n_1, \ldots, n_N$. This is schematically represented in Fig. 1. The goal is to characterize the smallest possible rates of encoding for the terminals such that a constraint on the distortion between the data vector $\mathbf{n}$ and the reconstruction $\hat{\mathbf{n}}$ is met.

The general multiterminal lossy source coding problem is an open problem. Several partial solutions are known; a general achievable region is in [**13**], a distortion constraint on only one of the sources is tackled in [**1**]. Even the multiterminal Gaussian source coding problem with a quadratic distortion function has not been solved. Two Gaussian sources with separate mean squared distortions are addressed in [**15**] where some parts of the achievable region are shown to be tight. Specifically,

1991 *Mathematics Subject Classification.* Primary 94A05, 94A14; Secondary 94B60.
Key words and phrases. Broadcast Channel, Correlated Gaussian Source Coding, Multiple antennas, Multiterminal Source Coding.
This research was supported in part by NSF CAREER CCR 0237549 and NSF ITR 0085929.

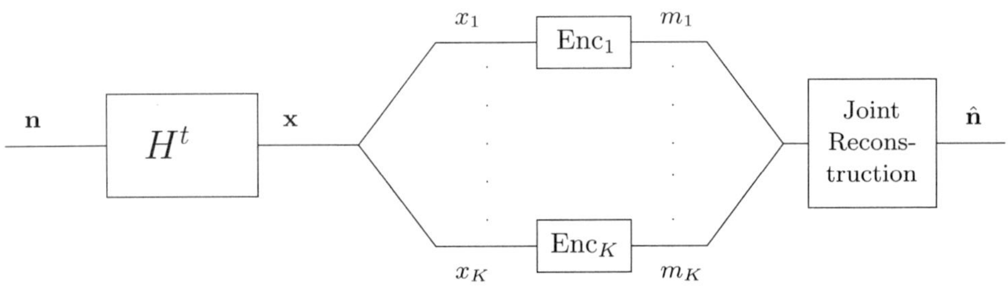

FIGURE 1. A canonical Gaussian multiterminal source coding problem.

the sum rate is not yet characterized for any nontrivial distortion measure (the high resolution case for separate mean squared distortions is addressed in [**31**]).

One of the reasons for absence of a complete solution to the Gaussian multiterminal source coding problem is the lack of a simple parameterization of known achievable schemes (defined via auxiliary random variables). In this paper we propose a *test* channel to provide a parameterization of a class of achievable schemes for the source coding problem: the multiple antenna broadcast channel. This allows us to associate a class of achievable schemes for the multiterminal source coding problem with ones for the broadcast channel. As a byproduct of this association, we can characterize the sum rate of the multiterminal Gaussian encoding as in Fig. 1 with a class of specific quadratic distortion functions.

The proposed test broadcast channel models the downlink of a wireless system with N antennas at the base station and K users with a single antenna at each receiver. The channel is memoryless and focusing on one particular time instant, denote the received symbol at receiver j by y_j and $\mathbf{y} \stackrel{\text{def}}{=} (y_1, \dots, y_K)^t$. They are related by:

$$\mathbf{y} = H^t \mathbf{x}_{\text{dl}} + \mathbf{z} \,. \tag{1.2}$$

Here H is the fixed $N \times K$ matrix (from (1.1)) with H^t_{ij} entry denoting the (flat fading) channel gain from the ith antenna to the jth user, assumed to be known at both the transmitter and receivers. $\mathbf{x}_{\text{dl}}$ is the vector input to the antenna array with an average total power constraint of P. The noise $\mathbf{z} = (z_1, \dots, z_K)$ with z_j Gaussian with zero mean and unit variance. Each user j has access only to the received symbol y_j.

The sum capacity of this nondegraded broadcast channel has been recently addressed in [**26, 30, 23**]. The main result of [**26**] is Theorem 1 which characterizes the sum capacity of this broadcast channel to be

$$C_{\text{sum}} \stackrel{\text{def}}{=} \sup_{D \succeq 0,\ \text{diagonal},\ \text{tr}[D] \leq P} \log\det\left(I + HDH^t\right). \tag{1.3}$$

Let us denote D^* as an optimizing diagonal matrix above. Observe that different choices of P lead to different diagonal matrices D^*. Now consider the quadratic distortion measure

$$d(\mathbf{n}, \hat{\mathbf{n}}) = \frac{1}{N} (\mathbf{n} - \hat{\mathbf{n}})^t \left(I + HD^* H^t\right) (\mathbf{n} - \hat{\mathbf{n}}) . \tag{1.4}$$

Using the association with the test broadcast channel, we can conclude the following, which holds for all P.

THEOREM 1.1. *The sum rate of the rate distortion region of the multiterminal encoding of the source* $\mathbf{x}$ *in* (1.1) *with the distortion function in* (1.4), *and an average distortion no more than 1, is equal to* C_{sum}, *the sum capacity of the broadcast channel in* (1.2).

The forward part of the proof relies on the identification of the appropriate *test* broadcast channel. Several works have suggested the potential of a broadcast channel to serve as a "dual" or "test channel" for multiterminal source coding. The similarity in achievability techniques for the deterministic broadcast channel (solved in [**10**]) and lossless multiterminal source coding (solved by Slepian and Wolf [**19**]) was explored in Section 3 of [**5**]. Similarities (and correspondences) between source and channel coding problems with side information have been pointed out in [**7, 16**]. More recently, [**17**] has extended these observations to multiterminal problems with one side cooperation.

Our main contribution is the identification of a specific broadcast channel, in particular the multiple antenna broadcast channel, as a candidate test channel which then allows us to parameterize a class of achievable schemes for the multiterminal source coding problem. Here our use of the "test" channel is only to the extent of *identifying* a suitable encoding strategy for the multiterminal source coding problem. A deeper use of the test broadcast channel to construct an *actual* coding scheme along the lines of the point to point channel and source coding results in Chapters 2.1 and 2.2 of [**8**] is studied in [**27**].

We begin with a description of an achievable region for a general multiterminal source coding problem in Section 2. We introduce the multiple antenna broadcast channel in Section 3 and summarize the main components of the characterization (in [**26**]) of its sum capacity. This will lead us to explicitly compute an achievable rate tuple for the multiterminal Gaussian source coding problem. In Section 4 we identify a simple quadratic distortion measure for which the achievable sum rate is a lower bound to any scheme meeting the distortion constraint. The converse uses a point to point source coding result by letting the encoders cooperate, completing the proof of Theorem 1.1. Section 5 discusses special cases and generalizations of the source coding problem in Fig. 1 and the corresponding extensions of the sum rate characterization in Theorem 1.1.

Finally a note about notation in the paper. We use lower case letters for scalars (both deterministic and random ones), lower case and bold face for vectors and upper case for matrices. The exceptions are the number of sources (antennas) denoted by N, the number of observations to be encoded (users) denoted by K and the power constraint P. Realizations of random variables are denoted by type face. The superscript $*$ denotes the object to be the optimizing argument of a contextually germane problem. We write $\mathcal{N}(\mu, Q)$ to denote a jointly Gaussian random vector with mean μ and covariance Q. All logarithms are natural. $A \succeq 0$ denotes that A is a positive semidefinite matrix.

2. An Achievable Rate Region

We describe an achievable rate region based on a random binning technique developed by Slepian and Wolf [**19**]. While the description of this region for two sources is in various places in the literature (see [**13**] and Section 4 in [**15**] for example), our description serves two purposes: it demonstrates that the simple and natural extension of the two sources result to multiple sources demonstrates interesting combinatorial properties and second, it develops notation and the language to present our main result. While the description here will be for sources with discrete alphabets, the extension to continuous alphabets has been done in the literature ([**15**]).

We begin with correlated sources $x_1, \ldots, x_K$ (generated via $\mathbf{n}$ as in Figure 1) that have to be separately encoded. The receiver arrives at the joint estimates $\hat{x}_1, \ldots, \hat{x}_K$ and has to meet an average distortion constraint of no more than 1. The distortion measure is denoted by $d(\mathbf{n}, \hat{\mathbf{n}})$. An achievable rate region is defined through the (auxiliary) random variables $u_1, \ldots, u_K$, the joint distribution (with the sources) of which, satisfies the Markov property:

$$\mathtt{P}\left[u_i = \mathtt{u_i},\ i = 1 \ldots K \mid x_i = \mathtt{x_i},\ i = 1 \ldots K\right] = \Pi_{i=1}^{K} \mathtt{P}\left[u_i = \mathtt{u_i} \mid x_i = \mathtt{x_i}\right]. \tag{2.1}$$

Further, we require there exist a deterministic function $g : \mathbf{u} \mapsto \hat{\mathbf{x}}$ such that $\mathtt{E}\left[d(\mathbf{x}, \hat{\mathbf{x}})\right] \leq 1$. Then the tuple of rates $(R_1, \ldots, R_K)$ satisfying the following constraints is achievable:

$$\sum_{i \in S} R_i > f(S) \stackrel{\text{def}}{=} I\left(u_S \,;\, x_S \mid u_{S^c}\right), \quad \forall S \subseteq \{1, \ldots, K\}. \tag{2.2}$$

Here we have denoted $u_S = (u_i,\ i \in S)$ and S^c as the complement of the set S in $\{1, \ldots, K\}$. The interpretation for the auxiliary random variables is that u_i is the encoded message of x_i which are losslessly conveyed to the receiver (possible due to the result of Slepian and Wolf) and the receiver constructs $\hat{\mathbf{x}}$ from $\mathbf{u}$. We summarize the encoding operation briefly (along the lines of the summary in Section 3 of [**5**]) with the random variables involved $(\mathbf{x}, \mathbf{u}, \hat{\mathbf{x}})$ having finite alphabets.

- *Random Binning*: Fix $\epsilon > 0$ and generate $2^{nI(u_i \,;\, x_i) + n\epsilon}$ length n vector u_i's according to the law $\mathtt{P}[u_i]$ independently and bin them randomly in 2^{nR_i} bins. This operation is done independently for each $i = 1 \ldots K$. The bin numbers are the messages encoded by the transmitters. The encoding operation is as follows and done separately at each encoder. Encoder i picks the first n length codeword among the binned u_i's which is jointly typical with the (length n) observation x_i (there is at least one with high probability). The message conveyed is the bin number in which the jointly typical u_i lies.
- *Markov Lemma*: Now, we claim that the $u_1, \ldots, u_K$ picked by the encoders separately are actually jointly typical with high probability. To see this, observe that the observations $x_1, \ldots, x_K$ are themselves jointly typical with high probability, and by construction x_i is jointly typical with u_i for each $i = 1 \ldots K$. The Markov property in (2.1) ensures that $\mathbf{x}$ and $\mathbf{u}$ are all jointly typical.
- *Reconstruction*: The receiver has access to the messages, namely the K bin numbers. We would like to recover the u_i's the transmitters picked. By construction, there is at least one set of jointly typical u_i's in the bins

specified. With high probability there is no more than one set if

$$\sum_{i\in S}\left(I\left(u_i\,;\,x_i\right)-R_i\right)^+<\sum_{i\in S}h\left(u_i\right)-h\left(u_S\mid u_{S^c}\right),\tag{2.3}$$

for every $S\subseteq\{1,\ldots,K\}$. The idea is that for every subset S we do not want to allow any u_i tuples in S that are jointly typical conditioned on a typical u_j tuple from the complement of S. Here we used the notation of $(x)^+$ to be zero if $x<0$ and x otherwise. Also, h is the differential entropy function and for discrete alphabets, the differential entropy function is replaced by discrete entropy. Once the u_i's are reliably recovered by the receiver, it then constructs the $\hat{\mathbf{x}}$ as a deterministic function of the u_i's.

- *An Equivalent Representation*: We have arrived at the conditions in (2.3) that allow the multiterminal encoding scheme described to work. Under the Markov conditions in (2.1), we make the following claim, proved at the end of this section.

PROPOSITION 2.1. The region of rates defined in (2.2) and in (2.3) are the same.

Our focus in this paper is on the sum rate and to arrive at an achievable sum rate we would like to see which of the inequalities in (2.2) bite. Consider the following properties of the set function f for all $S,T\subseteq\{1,\ldots,K\}$. We have $f\left(\phi\right)\overset{\text{def}}{=}0$.

PROPOSITION 2.2.

$$f\left(S\cup\{t\}\right)\ \ge\ f\left(S\right),\ \forall t\in\{1,\ldots,K\},\tag{2.4}$$

$$f\left(S\cup T\right)+f\left(S\cap T\right)\ \ge\ f\left(S\right)+f\left(T\right).\tag{2.5}$$

Proof (2.4) follows from the chain rule of mutual information: For $t\notin S$, we have

$$\begin{aligned}f\left(S\cup\{t\}\right)&=I\left(u_S\,;\,x_tx_S\mid u_{S^c}\right)+I\left(u_t\,;\,x_tx_S\mid u_{(S\cup\{t\})^c}\right),\\&\ge I\left(u_S\,;\,x_S\mid u_{S^c}\right),\\&=f\left(S\right).\end{aligned}$$

The supermodularity property in (2.5) requires the use of the property (2.1). In particular, (2.1) implies that

$$\mathsf{P}\left[u_S=\mathtt{u}_S,\mid x_S=\mathtt{x}_S,u_{S^c}=\mathtt{u}_{S^c}\right]=\Pi_{i\in S}\mathsf{P}\left[u_i=\mathtt{u}_\mathtt{i}\mid x_i=\mathtt{x}_\mathtt{i}\right],$$

and we can write

$$h\left(u_S\mid x_S,u_{S^c}\right)=\sum_{i\in S}h\left(u_i\mid x_i\right).\tag{2.6}$$

Now we rewrite $f(S)$ as, using (2.6)

$$f\left(S\right)=h\left(u_S\mid u_{S^c}\right)-\sum_{i\in S}h\left(u_i\mid x_i\right),\tag{2.7}$$

$$=h\left(\mathbf{u}\right)-h\left(u_{S^c}\right)-\sum_{i\in S}h\left(u_i\mid x_i\right).\tag{2.8}$$

It follows from (2.8) that we have shown (2.5) if

$$\begin{aligned} h\left(u_{S^c}\right)+h\left(u_{T^c}\right) &\geq h\left(u_{(S\cup T)^c}\right)+h\left(u_{(S\cap T)^c}\right), \text{ or} \\ h\left(u_{S^c-T^c} \mid u_{S^c\cap T^c}\right) &\geq h\left(u_{S^c-T^c} \mid u_{T^c}\right), \end{aligned}$$

which is true since conditioning cannot increase the entropy. This completes the proof of Prop. 2.2. □

A polyhedron such as the one in (2.2) with the *rank* function f satisfying the properties in Prop. 2.2 is called a *contra-polymatroid.* A generic reference to the class of polyhedrons called *matroids* is [**29**] and an application to information theory is in [**22, 11**] where achievable regions of the multiple access channel are shown to be *polymatroids.* An important property of contra-polymatroids is summarized in Lemma 3.3 of [**22**]: the characterization of its vertices. For π a permutation on the set $\{1,\ldots,K\}$, let

$$b_i^{(\pi)} \stackrel{\text{def}}{=} f\left(\{\pi_1,\pi_2,\ldots,\pi_i\}\right)-f\left(\{\pi_1,\pi_2,\ldots,\pi_{i-1}\}\right),\ i=1\ldots K,$$

and $\mathbf{b}^{(\pi)}=\left(b_1^{(\pi)},\ldots,b_K^{(\pi)}\right)$. Then the $K!$ points $\left\{\mathbf{b}^{(\pi)},\ \pi \text{ a permutation}\right\}$, are the vertices of (and hence belong to) the contra-polymatroid (2.2). We use this result to conclude that all the constraints in (2.2) are tight and in particular a sum rate of

$$R_{\text{sum}}=I\left(u_i,\ i=1\ldots K\ ;\ x_i,\ i=1\ldots K\right), \tag{2.9}$$

is achievable.

Proof of Prop 2.1: We fix $S\subseteq\{1,\ldots,K\}$ and see from (2.7) that

$$f(S)=\sum_{i\in S} I\left(u_i\ ;\ x_i\right)-\sum_{i\in S} h\left(u_i\right)+h\left(u_S \mid u_{S^c}\right).$$

Comparing (2.2) and (2.3) in the light of the equation above (and observing that $R_i\leq I(u_i\,;\,x_i)$ in the boundary of the region in (2.3)), we conclude the proof of the proposition. □

From now, we specialize and take the observations $x_1,\ldots,x_K$ to be jointly Gaussian as in (1.1). We use an appropriate "test" broadcast channel to construct the auxiliary random variables $u_1,\ldots,u_K$ satisfying the property (2.1) and to evaluate the corresponding sum rate (2.9). This is done in the next section.

3. Multiple Antenna Broadcast Channel

Consider the multiple antenna broadcast channel in (1.2). For $N>1$, this is a vector Gaussian broadcast channel, and unlike the scalar Gaussian broadcast channel ($N=1$), it is in general not degraded and the capacity region is unknown. Recent works [**26, 30, 23**] have addressed the sum capacity of this channel. We begin with a summary of the key components of our characterization (in [**26**]) of the sum capacity of this channel.

3.1. Forward Part. The best known achievable region for the general broadcast channel is due to Marton ([**14**], Theorem 5 in [**5**]). While the result in these references is for two users alone, a simple and natural extension to the multiple user case is the following. We fix auxiliary random variables $u_1,\ldots,u_K$ that are jointly distributed with the input $\mathbf{x}_{\text{dl}}$. Then the rate tuple $(R_1, \dots, R_K)$ is achievable if it satisfies the following constraints, $\forall S = \{s_1, \dots, s_k\} \subseteq \{1, \dots, K\}$:

$$\sum_{i \in S} R_i < \sum_{i \in S} (I(u_i \,;\, y_i) - I(u_{s_1} \,;\, u_{s_2} \,;\, \cdots \,;\, u_{s_k}). \tag{3.1}$$

Here we have used the notation of *symmetric* mutual information to be

$$I(u_{s_1} \,;\, u_{s_2} \,;\, \cdots \,;\, u_{s_k}) \stackrel{\text{def}}{=} \sum_{i=1}^{k} h(u_{s_i}) - h(u_{s_1}, \dots, u_{s_k}). \tag{3.2}$$

In [**26**] we identified a rich class of inputs (auxiliary random variables) for the multiple antenna broadcast channel in (1.2) with the corresponding achievable rate tuple that is easily computable. The strategy involves a bank of linear transmit filters along with a *precoding* scheme built on a result of Costa [**4**]. Consider the scalar point-to-point channel:

$$y = x + s + z$$

where s, z are independent Gaussian noise with s known to the transmitter but not to the receiver and z known to no one. Costa showed that the capacity of this channel is the same as that of the AWGN channel $y = x + z$, i.e. having the side information on s at the transmitter is as powerful as knowing s both at the transmitter *and* the receiver. We let the input signal be

$$\mathbf{x}_{\text{dl}} = \sum_{i=1}^{K} \tilde{x}_i \mathbf{v}_i, \tag{3.3}$$

where $\tilde{x}_1, \dots, \tilde{x}_K$ are zero mean, unit variance Gaussian.The N dimensional vectors $\mathbf{v}_1, \dots, \mathbf{v}_K$ are such that the square of their l_2 norms sum to P. The idea here is that $\tilde{x}_i$ is the message intended for user i and direction $\mathbf{v}_i$ (and has power $\|\mathbf{v}_i\|^2$). We can apply Costa precoding to improve the performance of simple linear transmit beamforming strategies. The received signal at user k is:

$$y_k = \tilde{x}_k \mathbf{h}_k^t \mathbf{v}_k + \sum_{j>k} \tilde{x}_j \mathbf{h}_k^t \mathbf{v}_j + \sum_{j<k} \tilde{x}_j \mathbf{h}_k^t \mathbf{v}_j + z_k$$

Here we have written $H = [\mathbf{h}_1, \dots, \mathbf{h}_K]$. We perform Costa precoding for each user k, encoding the information in $\tilde{x}_k$ treating the interference $\sum_{j>k} \sqrt{q_j} \tilde{x}_j \mathbf{h}_k^t \mathbf{v}_j$ from users $k+1, \dots, K$ as side information s known at the transmitter and the interference from the other users as Gaussian noise. With this strategy, the achievable rate tuple is

$$R_i = \log\left(1 + \frac{(\mathbf{h}_i^t \mathbf{v}_i)^2}{1 + \sum_{j=1}^{i-1} (\mathbf{h}_i^t \mathbf{v}_j)^2}\right), \quad i = 1, \dots, K.$$

This can also be cast in terms of the Marton strategy by considering the following choice of the auxiliary random variables (by using the auxiliary random variable prescribed in [**4**]):

$$u_i \stackrel{\text{def}}{=} \mathbf{h}_i^t \mathbf{v}_i \, \tilde{x}_i + \frac{(\mathbf{h}_i^t \mathbf{v}_i)^2}{1 + \sum_{j=1}^{i-1} (\mathbf{h}_i^t \mathbf{v}_j)^2} \sum_{j=i+1}^{k} \mathbf{h}_i^t \mathbf{v}_j \, \tilde{x}_j, \; i = 1 \dots K. \tag{3.4}$$

The conceptual connection between Marton's and Costa's result is that they are both based on a random binning encoding technique.

By maximizing over all transmit vectors $\mathbf{v}_1, \ldots, \mathbf{v}_K$ (subject to the sum of their l_2 norm squared equal to P) we showed in Section 2 of [**26**] that the achievable sum rate is equal to C_{sum} defined in (1.3)

$$\sup_{D \succeq 0,\ \text{diagonal},\ \operatorname{tr}[D] \leq P} \log\det\left(I + HDH^t\right). \tag{3.5}$$

Let us denote the auxiliary random variables that achieve the sum rate in (3.5) by $u_1^*, \ldots, u_K^*$, i.e.,

$$C_{\text{sum}} = \sum_{i=1}^{K} I\left(u_i^* \,;\, y_i^*\right) - I\left(u_1^* \,;\, u_2^* \,;\, \cdots \,;\, u_K^*\right). \tag{3.6}$$

Here we have denoted y_i^* as the signal by user i with the optimal input $\mathbf{x}_{\text{dl}}^*$.

3.2. Converse. In [**26**] the converse statement that the sum rate in (3.5) cannot be exceeded by any strategy is done by creating a point to point channel by letting the users cooperate (this vector Gaussian channel is in (1.2)). Now, the capacity region of a broadcast channel depends only on the marginal channels from the transmitter to the users separately (Theorem 14.6.1 in [**6**]) and in the multiple antenna channel we can choose any joint distribution on $\mathbf{z}$ retaining the marginal distributions of the components to be Gaussian with zero mean and unit variance. Thus, to obtain an upper bound on the sum rate of (1.2), we can choose a joint distribution on $\mathbf{z}$ in the point to point channel that we have created that minimizes the benefit of the cooperation by the users while ensuring that $z_1, \ldots, z_K$ are marginally zero mean Gaussian with variance no more than 1. In Section 3 of [**26**] we focus on the choice of $\mathbf{z}$ to be jointly Gaussian with the covariance

$$\frac{1}{\lambda^*} H^t \left(I + HD^*H^t\right)^{-1} H. \tag{3.7}$$

Here we have denoted D^* to be the optimizing argument and λ^* as the Kuhn-Tucker coefficient (Chapter 28 in [**18**]) corresponding to the power constraint in (3.5). With this choice, the point to point channel formed by the cooperating receivers can be written as

$$\mathbf{y} = H^t \left(\mathbf{x}_{\text{dl}} + \tilde{\mathbf{z}}\right), \tag{3.8}$$

where

$$\tilde{\mathbf{z}} \sim \mathcal{N}\left(0, \frac{1}{\lambda^*}\left(I + HD^*H^t\right)^{-1}\right). \tag{3.9}$$

The capacity is given by

$$C_{\text{p-p}} = \max_{\operatorname{tr}[\Sigma_x] \leq P} I\left(\mathbf{x}_{\text{dl}} \,;\, \mathbf{y}\right), \tag{3.10}$$

where $\mathbf{x}_{\text{dl}} \sim \mathcal{N}(0, \Sigma_x)$. In Section 3.3 of [**26**] we show the following results, validating the specific choice (in (3.7)) of coloring of the noise.

1. The diagonal entries of the covariance matrix in (3.7) are less than or equal to unity. Hence this choice preserves the marginal distributions of the noise.
2. The point to point channel in (3.8) and the broadcast channel (1.2) share the following quantities.

(a) The optimal input covariance for the point to point channel in (3.10) is the same as that induced on $\mathbf{x}_{\text{dl}}$ by the optimal choice of transmit filters $\mathbf{v}_1, \dots, \mathbf{v}_K$ (and hence deciding the powers of the users signals) in the Marton (or equivalently Costa precoding) strategy for the broadcast channel.

(b) The capacity of the point to point channel where the users cooperate (denoted by $C_{\text{p-p}}$) is equal to the sum rate C_{sum} (in (3.5)). In other words,

$$C_{\text{sum}} = \min_{\mathbf{z} \sim \mathcal{N}(0,\Sigma_z),\ (\Sigma_z)_{ii} \leq 1}\ \max_{\mathbf{x}_{\text{dl}} \sim \mathcal{N}(0,\Sigma_x),\ \text{tr}[\Sigma_x] \leq P} I\left(\mathbf{x}_{\text{dl}}\ ;\ \mathbf{y}\right), \tag{3.11}$$

and the choice of Σ_z in (3.9) is a solution to the minimization problem here.

(c) The Kuhn-Tucker coefficient corresponding to the constraint on the total power in the maximization of (3.10) can be taken to be λ^*, i.e., the Kuhn-Tucker coefficients corresponding to the power constraints in (3.10) and (3.5) are equal.

3.3. Joint Distribution of $\mathbf{x}_{\text{dl}}$ and $\mathbf{y}$. The optimal input distribution on $\mathbf{x}_{\text{dl}}$ is somewhat hard to see from the optimization using the Marton strategy, but is easy to calculate from the point to point channel of (3.8). Continuing from (3.10) and using the observation that the Kuhn-Tucker coefficient corresponding to the power constraint is λ^*, we can calculate the covariance of $\mathbf{x}^*_{\text{dl}}$ (the optimal input) to be the *waterfilling* solution:

$$\Sigma_x = \frac{I}{\lambda^*} - \frac{1}{\lambda^*}\left(I + HD^*H^t\right)^{-1}. \tag{3.12}$$

The corresponding distribution of the output $\mathbf{y}^*$ is

$$\mathbf{y}^* \sim \mathcal{N}\left(0, \frac{1}{\lambda^*}H^tH\right). \tag{3.13}$$

The joint distribution is given via (3.8).

3.4. Markov Property. We have not explicitly constructed the auxiliary random variables $u_1^*, \dots, u_K^*$ in the Marton strategy and only identified their structure (in (3.4)) through the transmit filters $\mathbf{v}_1, \dots, \mathbf{v}_K$ that optimize the sum rate. In [**26**], the proof that the optimal sum rate with this class of Marton strategies (in (3.6)) is equal to the expression of (3.5) is through a *reciprocal* multiple access channel which sheds further insight into the structure of the optimizing $\mathbf{v}_i$.Here we focus on a Markov property satisfied by the optimal auxiliary random variables. Since the achievable sum rate with the Marton strategy (using the optimal auxiliary random variables, see (3.6)) is equal to the capacity of the point to point channel of (3.8), we can write

$$I\left(\mathbf{x}^*_{\text{dl}}\ ;\ \mathbf{y}^*\right) = \sum_{i=1}^{K} I\left(u_i^*\ ;\ y_i^*\right) - I\left(u_1^*\ ;\ u_2^*\ ;\ \cdots\ ;\ u_K^*\right). \tag{3.14}$$

We also have

$$I\left(\mathbf{x}^*_{\text{dl}}\ ;\ \mathbf{y}^*\right) = I\left(u_1^*, \dots, u_K^*\ ;\ \mathbf{y}^*\right). \tag{3.15}$$

(3.15) follows by the relation between $\mathbf{u}$ and $\mathbf{x}_{\text{dl}}$ defined through (3.3) and (3.4) and the Markov chain $\mathbf{u} \to \mathbf{x}_{\text{dl}}^* \to \mathbf{y}$. Now we can expand $I\left(u_1^*, \ldots, u_K^* \,;\, \mathbf{y}^*\right)$ by the chain rule of mutual information as

$$\begin{aligned}
&= \sum_{i=1}^{K} I\left(u_i^* \,;\, \mathbf{y}^* \mid u_1^*, u_2^*, \ldots, u_{i-1}^*\right), \\
&= \sum_{i=1}^{K} I\left(u_i^* \,;\, \mathbf{y}^*, u_1^*, u_2^*, \ldots, u_{i-1}^*\right) - \sum_{i=2}^{K} I\left(u_i^* \,;\, u_1^*, u_2^*, \ldots, u_{i-1}^*\right), \\
&= \sum_{i=1}^{K} I\left(u_i^* \,;\, \mathbf{y}^*, u_1^*, u_2^*, \ldots, u_{i-1}^*\right) \\
&\qquad - \sum_{i=2}^{K} h\left(u_i\right) + h\left(u_1^*, \ldots, u_{i-1}^*\right) - h\left(u_1^*, \ldots, u_i^*\right), \qquad (3.16) \\
&= \sum_{i=1}^{K} I\left(u_i^* \,;\, \mathbf{y}^*, u_1^*, u_2^*, \ldots, u_{i-1}^*\right) - I\left(u_1^* \,;\, u_2^* \,;\, \cdots \,;\, u_K^*\right), \qquad (3.17)
\end{aligned}$$

where the last step followed by a telescoping of the second summation in (3.16). Comparing (3.14) and (3.17), we arrive at

$$I\left(u_i^* \,;\, y_1^*, \ldots, y_{i-1}^*, y_{i+1}^*, \ldots, y_K^*, u_1, \ldots, u_{i-1}^* \mid y_i^*\right) = 0, \quad \forall i = 1 \ldots K,$$

and hence at the Markov properties for $i = 1 \ldots K$:

$$\mathsf{P}\left[u_i^* = \mathtt{u}_i \mid y_j^* = \mathtt{y}_j, u_k^* = \mathtt{u}_k,\ j = 1 \ldots K,\ k = 1 \ldots i-1\right] = \mathsf{P}\left[u_i^* = \mathtt{u}_i \mid y_i^* = \mathtt{y}_i\right].$$

Finally, we can conclude that

$$\mathsf{P}\left[u_i^* = \mathtt{u}_\mathtt{i},\ i = 1 \ldots K \mid y_i^* = \mathtt{y}_\mathtt{i},\ i = 1 \ldots K\right] = \Pi_{i=1}^{K} \mathsf{P}\left[u_i^* = \mathtt{u}_\mathtt{i} \mid y_i^* = \mathtt{y}_\mathtt{i}\right]. \qquad (3.18)$$

3.5. An achievable rate tuple for Gaussian source coding. We first summarize the joint distribution between the various random variables associated with the multiple antenna broadcast channel.

$$\tilde{\mathbf{x}} \sim \mathcal{N}\left(0, I\right) \text{ and } \tilde{\mathbf{z}} \sim \mathcal{N}\left(0, \frac{1}{\lambda^*}\left(I + HD^*H^t\right)^{-1}\right)$$

are independent and all the other variables are derived from these two. In particular, we have

$$\mathbf{x}_{\text{dl}}^* \text{ and } \mathbf{u}^* \text{ are derived from } \tilde{\mathbf{x}} \text{ via (3.3) and (3.4),}$$

and

$$\mathbf{y}^* = H^t\tilde{\mathbf{y}} \text{ where } \tilde{\mathbf{y}} = \mathbf{x}_{\text{dl}}^* + \tilde{\mathbf{z}}.$$

Now we scale $\tilde{\mathbf{x}}$ and $\tilde{\mathbf{z}}$ by $\sqrt{\lambda^*}$ and consider the following correspondence between the multiterminal source coding and broadcast channel parameters.

1. We identify the (scaled) optimal *channel output* $\mathbf{y}^*$ with the *source observations* $\mathbf{x}$. We first observe that the alphabet sizes match and further from (3.13) and (1.1) that the distributions are the same ($\mathcal{N}\left(0, H^tH\right)$).
2. We identify the (scaled) optimal *channel input* $\mathbf{x}_{\text{dl}}^*$ with the *source reconstruction* $\hat{\mathbf{n}}$. Again, observe that the alphabet sizes match (they are both N dimensional vectors).

3. We associate the (scaled) $\tilde{\mathbf{y}}$ with the *sources* $\mathbf{n}$, observing that they have the same distribution ($\mathcal{N}(0, I)$).
4. Finally we identify the (scaled) optimal *channel auxiliary variables* $\mathbf{u}^*$ with the *source auxiliary variables* $\mathbf{u}$.

With this correspondence, the Markov property in (3.18) allows us to exactly derive the property required by auxiliary random variables and source observations in (2.1). Using the (scaled) optimal input, output and auxiliary random variables in the Marton strategy for the broadcast channel, we have arrived at a strategy for the multiterminal Gaussian source coding problem in Fig. 1.

Here we have only considered sum capacity achieving inputs to the multiple antenna broadcast channel. We find in Appendix A where we find that the class of achievable schemes for the multiterminal source coding problem is not increased by considering Gaussian inputs.

4. Sum Rate for a Specific Distortion Measure

We can evaluate the sum rate achieved and the distortion caused by this scheme with the distortion measure as in (1.4). Scaling $\mathbf{u}$ and $\mathbf{x}$ by the same number $(\sqrt{\lambda^*})$ does not alter the mutual information between them and the sum rate achieved (see (2.9)) is equal to the sum capacity of the multiple antenna broadcast channel, the expression in (3.5). The relationship between the source and reconstruction (from the correspondence with the broadcast channel variables) is

$$\mathbf{n} = \hat{\mathbf{n}} - \sqrt{\lambda^*}\tilde{\mathbf{z}}$$

where we recollect $\tilde{\mathbf{z}} \sim \mathcal{N}\left(0, \frac{1}{\lambda^*}\left(I + HD^*H^t\right)^{-1}\right)$. The factor of $\sqrt{\lambda^*}$ is due to the scaling operation before the correspondence. The average distortion caused is

$$\mathsf{E}\left[d\left(\mathbf{n}, \hat{\mathbf{n}}\right)\right] = \frac{\lambda^*}{N}\mathsf{E}\left[\tilde{\mathbf{z}}^t\left(I + HD^*H^t\right)\tilde{\mathbf{z}}\right] = 1.$$

A lower bound on the sum rate of any encoding scheme that meets the distortion is obtained via the rate distortion function of the point to point source coding problem where the encoders all cooperate. This lower bound is given by

$$\min_{\mathsf{P}[\hat{\mathbf{n}}|\mathbf{n}]} \quad I\left(\mathbf{n}\,;\,\hat{\mathbf{n}}\right), \tag{4.1}$$

subject to the constraints

$$\mathbf{n} \sim \mathcal{N}\left(0, I\right) \text{ and } \mathsf{E}\left[\left(\mathbf{n} - \hat{\mathbf{n}}\right)^t\left(I + HD^*H^t\right)\left(\mathbf{n} - \hat{\mathbf{n}}\right)\right] \le N. \tag{4.2}$$

This is an instance of the classical (vector) Gaussian source coding problem with a quadratic distortion function and the value in (4.1) is evaluated to be

$$\log\det\left(I + HD^*H^t\right). \tag{4.3}$$

An alternative approach to see this is to use the results of [**9**] where the authors construct for every point to point source coding problem with a "desired" optimal test channel, a distortion function that achieves it. Here, to obtain the rate distortion value of (4.3), we want the test channel to be

$$\mathbf{n} \sim \mathcal{N}\left(0, I\right), \text{ and } \mathbf{n} = \hat{\mathbf{n}} + \mathcal{N}\left(0, \left(I + HD^*H^t\right)^{-1}\right).$$

Using the result of [**9**], the corresponding distortion function is of the form

$$d\left(\mathbf{n}, \hat{\mathbf{n}}\right) = -\log\mathsf{P}\left[\mathbf{n} \mid \hat{\mathbf{n}}\right]$$

which is the same as the distortion function we have here (in (4.2)). This shows the result claimed in Theorem 1.1.

5. Discussion

We have characterized the sum rate of the multiterminal Gaussian source coding problem for a class of distortion measures. While this is restrictive (the problem with a general quadratic (or otherwise) distortion measure is still open), this is the first instance in the literature of such a solution. To understand the result better, we discuss various aspects of the solution in this section.

5.1. Distortion constraint. In the statement of our main result (Theorem 1.1) we specified the average distortion to be less than or equal to 1. If instead we change the average distortion constraint to some positive number c, how does the sum rate required change? To see this, let us first look at the vector point to point Gaussian source coding result. With the Gaussian source $\mathbf{n} \sim \mathcal{N}(0, I)$ and a quadratic distortion measure (for some $A \succ 0$)

$$\frac{1}{N} (\mathbf{n} - \hat{\mathbf{n}})^t A (\mathbf{n} - \hat{\mathbf{n}})$$

and an average distortion constraint of c we have the rate distortion function equal to

$$R = (\log \det A - N \log c)^+ .$$

Thus if we scale the distortion constraint by a factor $a > 1$ then the rate required decreases by an amount $N \log a$. However, if the distortion constraint is larger than the "variance" of the source, then we do not need to encode the source at all and the rate is zero. The multiterminal case shows a similar behavior and we summarize this in the following.

PROPOSITION 5.1. For the source in (1.1) and distortion measure in (1.4) and an average distortion constraint of c, the sum rate is equal to

$$(C_{\text{sum}} - N \log c)^+ .$$

With a change in allowed distortion from 1 to c, the sum rate is reduced by an amount $N \log c$, while remaining nonnegative.

Proof The converse part involves a point to point (vector) Gaussian source coding problem and the difference of $N \log c$ in the rate distortion function follows just as in the vector Gaussian example above (with $A = I + HD^* H^t$). For the forward part, we maintain the correspondence as in Section 3 with a somewhat different scaling. We scale $\tilde{\mathbf{x}}$ by $\sqrt{\lambda^*}$ as before but scale $\tilde{\mathbf{z}}$ by $\sqrt{c\lambda^*}$. Now the relation between $\mathbf{x}$ and the reconstruction $\hat{\mathbf{n}}$ is

$$\mathbf{x} = H^t \mathbf{n} \text{ and } \mathbf{n} = \hat{\mathbf{n}} + \sqrt{c\lambda^*} \tilde{\mathbf{z}}.$$

The sum rate achieved is $I(\mathbf{n}\,;\,\hat{\mathbf{n}})$ which evaluates to C_{sum} reduced by an amount $N \log c$. Further, the average distortion caused is

$$\mathsf{E}\left[d(\mathbf{n}, \hat{\mathbf{n}})\right] = \frac{c\lambda^*}{N} \mathsf{E}\left[\tilde{\mathbf{z}}^t \left(I + HD^* H^t\right) \tilde{\mathbf{z}}\right] = c.$$

□

5.2. Class of Distortion Measures. Let us fix the source observations through the matrix H. Our focus has been on a quadratic distortion function of the type in (1.4). The key parameter D^* is the optimizing diagonal matrix in (1.3). However, the power constraint in the broadcast channel (denoted by P), is a parameter we can vary thus varying D^*. Thus for every fixed source observations (i.e., fixed H) we have characterized the sum rate for a class of distortion measures parameterized by P.

Now suppose we fix the source observation statistics through the covariance H^tH. Then we observe that multiplying H by an orthogonal matrix from the left does not change the observation statistics. On the other hand, for every fixed P, the corresponding D^* also does not change if H is multiplied by the left with an orthogonal matrix. Thus, the class of distortion measures for which we have a characterization of the sum rate is now parameterized by P and Q, an $N \times N$ orthogonal matrix:

$$d(\mathbf{n}, \hat{\mathbf{n}}) = \frac{1}{N} (\mathbf{n} - \hat{\mathbf{n}})^t \left(I + QHD^*H^tQ^t\right) (\mathbf{n} - \hat{\mathbf{n}}). \tag{5.1}$$

5.3. Class of Sources. In the previous subsection, we fixed the source statistics and focused on the class of distortion measures for which our characterization holds. We can ask a dual question by fixing the distortion measure and asking what class of source statistics have we characterized the multiterminal sum rate of. In particular, consider the canonical distortion measure:

$$d(\mathbf{n}, \hat{\mathbf{n}}) = c\,(\mathbf{n} - \hat{\mathbf{n}})^t (\mathbf{n} - \hat{\mathbf{n}}), \tag{5.2}$$

for some positive constant c. What class of source observation statistics (parameterized through H) have we covered in our sum rate characterization? It is particularly simple to identify a subset of this class: the class of WBE (Welch Bound Equality) matrices characterizes via,

$$H^tH \text{ has unit diagonal entries and } HH^t = \frac{\operatorname{tr}\left[HH^t\right]}{N}.$$

WBE matrices were defined by Welch [**28**] in the context of sequences with small correlation among themselves. Their application in the context of communication theory (in particular, as the spreading sequences of the users in DS-CDMA (direct sequence code division multiple access) system) is brought out in [**24, 25**]. For a WBE matrix H we have

$$\operatorname{tr}[D] = \operatorname{tr}\left[HDH^t\right].$$

Since $\log\det$ is concave in the cone of positive definite matrices (see [**20**] for an application of this idea),

$$\max_{D \succeq 0,\text{diagonal and } \operatorname{tr}[D] \le P} \log\det\left(I + HDH^t\right)$$

is maximized at $D^* = \frac{P}{N}I$. Hence the distortion constraint in (1.4) simplifies to that in (5.2).

5.4. Vector Observations. In this section, we look to generalize the problem posed in Fig. 1, where each terminal has access to only a *scalar* observation while the source itself is N dimensional. Consider the following generalization of the problem formulation. As before the source is $\mathbf{n} \sim \mathcal{N}(0, I)$ but terminal i has access to an M_i dimensional observation vector $\mathbf{x}_i$:

$$\mathbf{x}_i = H_i^t \mathbf{n}, \quad i = 1 \dots K. \tag{5.3}$$

Here H_i^t is a $M_i \times N$ dimensional matrix. The receiver is joint as usual and attempts to get a reconstruction $\hat{\mathbf{n}}$ of the source $\mathbf{n}$ meeting a suitable distortion constraint.

Following the proof of the case of scalar observation at each terminal, the natural test channel here is the multiple antenna broadcast channel with multiple *receive antennas*, M_i number of them at receiver i. The received signal by user i, denoted by $\mathbf{y}_i$ is

$$\mathbf{y}_i = H_i^t \mathbf{x}_{\mathrm{dl}} + \mathbf{z}_i. \tag{5.4}$$

The sum capacity of the multiple antenna broadcast channel as presented in [**26**] was limited to single receive antennas at the users, but the technique allows a simple and natural generalization with multiple receive antennas at the users. This extension is shown in [**21**]. This natural extension of the result in the broadcast channel allows us to extend our main result (Theorem 1.1) to the vector observation case with the same relative ease. Here we state this extension skipping the details of the proof. We fix $P > 0$ the power constraint for the broadcast channel of (5.4), the sum capacity of which is given by (the main result of [**21**])

$$C \stackrel{\text{def}}{=} \max_{\Sigma_1, \dots, \Sigma_K \succeq 0, \ \sum_{i=1}^K \operatorname{tr}[\Sigma_i] \leq P} \log\det\left(I + \sum_{i=1}^K H_i \Sigma_i H_i^t\right). \tag{5.5}$$

This is the extension of the single receive antenna result in (1.3). Consider the distortion measure

$$d(\mathbf{n}, \hat{\mathbf{n}}) = \frac{1}{N} (\mathbf{n} - \hat{\mathbf{n}})^t \left(I + \sum_{i=1}^K H_i \Sigma_i^* H_i^t\right)^{-1} (\mathbf{n} - \hat{\mathbf{n}}), \tag{5.6}$$

parameterized by P. We have denoted the optimizing arguments in (5.5) by $\Sigma_1^*, \dots, \Sigma_K^*$. The extension of Theorem 1.1 is the following, which holds for all P.

THEOREM 5.1. *The sum rate of the Gaussian multiterminal source coding problem in* (5.3) *with the distortion function in* (5.6) *and an average distortion constraint of 1 is equal to C, the sum capacity (in* (5.5)*) of the multiple antenna broadcast channel in* (5.4).

6. Acknowledgements

P. Viswanath thanks S. Pradhan, K. Ramchandran, D. Tse, H. Wang and W. Yu for stimulating discussions on this topic.

Appendix A. Gaussian Inputs to the Multiple Antenna Broadcast Channel

The connection between the multiple antenna broadcast channel and the multiterminal source coding problem is via the following key observation: the auxiliary random variables achieving the sum capacity of the broadcast channel (denoted by

$u_1^*, \dots, u_K^*$) satisfies a Markov property with the corresponding channel outputs (denoted by $y_1^*, \dots, y_K^*$) in (3.18):

$$\text{(A.1)} \quad \mathsf{P}\left[u_i^* = \mathtt{u_i},\ i = 1 \dots K \mid y_i^* = \mathtt{y_i},\ i = 1 \dots K\right] = \Pi_{i=1}^K \mathsf{P}\left[u_i^* = \mathtt{u_i} \mid y_i^* = \mathtt{y_i}\right].$$

The relation between the auxiliary random variables $\mathbf{u}$ and the channel outputs $\mathbf{y}$ is through the input $\mathbf{x}_{\text{dl}}$ and the noise $\mathbf{z}$. However, both the source distribution and distortion measure are determined only by the components of the broadcast channel $(\mathbf{y}, H, \mathbf{x}_{\text{dl}}, \mathbf{z})$ in (1.2):

$$\mathbf{y} = H^t \mathbf{x}_{\text{dl}} + \mathbf{z},$$

and not on the actual structure of the auxiliary random variables. So far, we have considered only a specific class of channel inputs $\mathbf{x}_{\text{dl}}$: those that achieve the sum capacity of the broadcast channel. In this section, we look at an arbitrary jointly Gaussian input $\mathbf{x}_{\text{dl}}$ (still subject to the overall transmit power constraint) to the fixed downlink channel H and see if we can increase the class of achievable schemes for the corresponding multiterminal source coding problem.

Let us consider the channel input $\mathbf{x}_{\text{dl}}$ of the form: $\mathbf{x}_{\text{dl}} \sim \mathcal{N}(0, \Sigma_x)$. Can we find the auxiliary random variables $u_1, \dots, u_K$ and the correlated noise $\mathbf{z}$ such that the Markov property in (A.1) holds? We show below that we can (this approach was taken independently in [**30**] to characterize the sum capacity of the multiple antenna broadcast channel with a different proof technique). However, we will see that the corresponding noise correlation (for which the Markov property of (A.1) holds) is such that the generated pair, source distribution and distortion measure, is still contained in the class given in Theorem 1.1. In other words, looking at a general Gaussian input to a fixed multiple antenna broadcast channel does not allow us to extend the class of achievable schemes for the multiterminal source coding problem.

To choose the noise correlation, we adopt the same strategy as that in the converse of the sum capacity (c.f. Section 3.2): look for the noise correlation that minimizes the capacity of the point-to-point channel formed by allowing all the users to cooperate. If we can achieve the capacity of the point-to-point channel with this worst case noise using a Costa coding strategy, i.e., with appropriately defined auxiliary random variables $u_1, \dots, u_K$,

$$\text{(A.2)} \qquad I(u_1, \dots, u_K) = \min_{\mathbf{z} \sim \mathcal{N}(0, \Sigma_z),\ (\Sigma_z)_{ii} \le 1} I(\mathbf{x}_{\text{dl}}\ ;\ \mathbf{y}),$$

then we have identified a potential extension of Theorem 1.1, via the correspondence of Section 3.5. In (A.2), the channel input is fixed to be of the form $\mathbf{x}_{\text{dl}} \sim \mathcal{N}(0, \Sigma_x)$. To make the input interesting, let us assume that the kernels of Σ_x and H^t are identical. (If $\text{Ker}(\Sigma_x)$ is larger than $\text{Ker}(H^t)$, then we can choose a different H (without affecting the channel output $\mathbf{y}$ and hence the optimization problem in the right side of (A.2)) whose transpose has the same kernel as that of Σ_x. On the other hand, only the image of H^t plays a role in the eventual distribution of $\mathbf{y}$ and thus there is no loss in generality in assuming that $\text{Ker}(\Sigma_x)$ is no smaller than that of H^t.)

First consider the following map from the jointly Gaussian channel inputs (parameterized via the covariance Σ_x) to the mutual information with the worst case noise:

$$\text{(A.3)} \qquad \Sigma_x :\mapsto \min_{\mathbf{z} \sim \mathcal{N}(0, \Sigma_z),\ (\Sigma_z)_{ii} \le 1} I(\mathbf{x}_{\text{dl}}\ ;\ \mathbf{y}).$$

Our first observation is that this map is concave (on the cone of positive semidefinite matrices). This follows from the fact that for any fixed Σ_z the mutual information is concave in Σ_x and then observing that the pointwise infimum of a collection of concave functions (parameterized here by the noise covariance Σ_z) is still concave. Hence there exists a positive semidefinite matrix Q (that depends on both Σ_x and the channel H) such that

$$\Sigma_x = \operatorname{argmax}_{\Sigma \succeq 0: \mathbf{x}_{\text{dl}} \sim \mathcal{N}(0,\Sigma),\ \operatorname{tr}[Q\Sigma] \le P} \min_{\mathbf{z} \sim \mathcal{N}(0,\Sigma_z),\ (\Sigma_z)_{ii} \le 1} I(\mathbf{x}_{\text{dl}}\ ;\ \mathbf{y}). \tag{A.4}$$

A modern reference on the properties of convex functions on the cone of positive semidefinite matrices is Section 4 of [**2**]. In particular, this provides a justification for (A.4) and further to see that

$$\text{the kernel of } Q \subseteq \text{ the kernel of } \Sigma_x. \tag{A.5}$$

Thus we can write the expression on the right side of (A.2) as

$$\max_{\Sigma \succeq 0: \mathbf{x}_{\text{dl}} \sim \mathcal{N}(0,\Sigma),\ \operatorname{tr}[Q\Sigma] \le P} \ \min_{\mathbf{z} \sim \mathcal{N}(0,\Sigma_z),\ (\Sigma_z)_{ii} \le 1} I(\mathbf{x}_{\text{dl}}\ ;\ \mathbf{y}). \tag{A.6}$$

The similarity of this expression to that in (3.11) can be seen by the following correspondence:

$$\hat{\mathbf{x}} := Q^{\frac{1}{2}} \mathbf{x}_{\text{dl}}, \quad \text{and} \quad \hat{H} \text{ is chosen such that } \hat{H}^t Q^{\frac{1}{2}} \mathbf{x} = H^t \mathbf{x}, \ \ \forall \mathbf{x}. \tag{A.7}$$

This can be achieved since the kernel of Q is contained in that of H^t. Here we have written $Q^{\frac{1}{2}}$ to have the same eigenvectors as that of Q but with eigenvalues square roots of the former ones. The distribution of $\mathbf{y}$ is invariant to this change of variable and hence we rewrite the optimization problem in (A.6) as

$$\max_{\Sigma \succeq 0: \hat{\mathbf{x}} \sim \mathcal{N}(0,\Sigma),\ \operatorname{tr}[\Sigma] \le P} \ \min_{\mathbf{z} \sim \mathcal{N}(0,\Sigma_z),\ (\Sigma_z)_{ii} \le 1} I\left(\hat{\mathbf{x}}\ ;\ \mathbf{y} = \hat{H}^t \hat{\mathbf{x}} + \mathbf{z}\right). \tag{A.8}$$

This problem is identical to the one solved in the sum capacity characterization and an optimal noise correlation (as in (3.9)) is

$$\tilde{\mathbf{z}} \sim \mathcal{N}\left(0, \frac{1}{\lambda^*}\left(I + \hat{H}\hat{D}^* \hat{H}^t\right)^{-1}\right). \tag{A.9}$$

An optimal channel output is (as in (3.13))

$$\mathbf{y}^* \sim \mathcal{N}\left(0, \frac{1}{\lambda^*} \hat{H}^t \hat{H}\right). \tag{A.10}$$

We can write the optimal input as (c.f. (3.3))

$$\hat{\mathbf{x}} = \sum_{i=1}^{K} \tilde{x}_i \hat{\mathbf{v}}_i, \tag{A.11}$$

As before $\tilde{x}_1, \dots, \tilde{x}_K$ are i.i.d. and $\mathcal{N}(0,1)$. Previously we had focused on a specific collection of transmit vectors $\mathbf{v}_1, \dots, \mathbf{v}_K$ (those that achieve the sum capacity of the channel H), but now we have the transmit vectors to achieve the sum capacity of the channel $\hat{H}$. With this identification of the optimal arguments in (A.8), we can revert to the original optimization problem (c.f. (A.6)) and identify the optimal input as

$$\mathbf{x}_{\text{dl}} := Q^{-\frac{1}{2}} \hat{\mathbf{x}} = \sum_{i=1}^{K} \tilde{x}_i Q^{-\frac{1}{2}} \hat{\mathbf{v}}_i. \tag{A.12}$$

Here $Q^{-\frac{1}{2}}$ refers to a matrix with the same eigenvectors as those of Q but with inverted positive eigenvalues. The equality in (A.12) follows from the fact that $\hat{\mathbf{v}}_i, i = 1 \ldots K$ are perpendicular to the kernel of Q (c.f. (A.5)). Further more, by construction we must have $\sum_{i=1}^{K} Q^{-\frac{1}{2}}\hat{\mathbf{v}}_i\hat{\mathbf{v}}_i^t Q^{-\frac{1}{2}} = \Sigma_x$. We continue to pick the auxiliary random variables $u_1, \ldots, u_K$ exactly as in (3.4) (with $Q^{-\frac{1}{2}}\hat{\mathbf{v}}_i$ replacing $\mathbf{v}_i$). With these associations (i.e., the auxiliary random variables, the channel input and the channel noise correlation) and the relation to an associated broadcast channel (with channel matrix $\hat{H}$) we have shown the validity of (A.2).

The first step in our proposed extension of Theorem 1.1 is complete and we can consider the correspondence to a multiterminal source coding problem as in Section 3.5. We see that the source distribution and distortion measure generated using the channel H and input Σ_x are identical to those generated via the broadcast channel $\hat{H}$ and its sum capacity achieving input. Thus, this approach does not permit an extension beyond the class of achievable schemes already identified for the multiterminal source coding problem.

References

[1] T. Berger and R. Yeung, "Multiterminal source encoding with one distortion criterion", *IEEE Trans. Inform. Theory*, vol. 35(2), Mar. 1989, pp. 228-236.

[2] S. Boyd and L. Vandenberghe, "Convex Optimization", *course reader for EE364 (Stanford) / EE236B (UCLA)*.

[3] G. Caire and S. Shamai, "On the Achievable throughput in Multiple Antenna Gaussian Broadcast Channel", to appear in *IEEE Trans. Inform. Theory*, 2003.

[4] M. H. M. Costa, "Writing on dirty paper", *IEEE Trans. Inform. Theory*, pp. 439–441, May 1983.

[5] T. M. Cover, "Comments on broadcast channels", *IEEE Trans. Information Theory*, vol. 44(6), Oct. 1998, pp. 2524-2530.

[6] T. M. Cover and J. Thomas, *Elements of Information Theory*, John Wiley, 1991.

[7] T. M. Cover and M. Chiang, "Duality between channel and source coding problems with side information", *IEEE Trans. Information Theory*, pp. 1629-1638, vol. 48(6), June 2002.

[8] I. Csiszar and J. Korner, *Information Theory: Coding Theorems for Discrete Memoryless Systems*, Akademiai Kiado, Jan. 1997.

[9] M. Gastpar, B. Rimoldi and M. Vetterli, "To code, or not to code: Lossy Source-Channel Communication Revisited", *IEEE Trans. Information Theory*, vol. 49(5), pp. 1147-1158, May 2003.

[10] S. I. Gelfand, "Capacity of one broadcast channel", *Probl. Peredachi Inform.*, vol. 13(3), pp. 106-108, Sept. 1977.

[11] S. Hanly and D. Tse, "Multi-Access Fading Channels: Part II: Delay-Limited Capacities", *IEEE Trans. Inform. Theory*, vol. 44, No. 7, Nov. 1998, pp. 2816-2831.

[12] N. Jindal, S. Vishwanath and A. Goldsmith, "On the duality between multiple access and broadcast channels", *Annual Allerton Conference*, 2001.

[13] A. H. Kaspi and T. Berger, "Rate distortion for correlated sources with partially separated encoders", *IEEE Trans. Inform. Theory*, vol. 28, pp. 824-840, Nov. 1982.

[14] K. Marton, "A coding theorem for the discrete memoryless broadcast channel", *IEEE Trans. Inform. Theory*, pp. 306–311, May 1979.

[15] Y. Oohama, "Gaussian multiterminal source coding", *IEEE Trans. Inform. Theory*, vol. 43(6), pp. 1912-1932, Nov. 1997.

[16] S. S. Pradhan, J. Chou and K. Ramachandran, "Duality between source and channel coding with side information", *UCB/ERL Technical Memo. M0/34*, Dec. 2001.

[17] S. S. Pradhan and K. Ramachandran, "On functional duality in MIMO source and channel coding problems having one-sided collaboration", *ITW 2002*, Bangalore India, Oct. 20-25, 2002.

[18] R. T. Rockafellar, *Convex Analysis*, Princeton University Press, Princeton, 1970.

[19] D. Slepian and J. K. Wolf, "Noiseless coding of correlated information sources", *IEEE Trans. Inform. Theory,*, vol. 19, pp. 471-480, July 1973.

[20] E. Telatar, "Capacity of the Multiple antenna Gaussian channel", *European Transactions on Telecommunications*, vol. 10(6), pp. 585-595, Nov/Dec 1999.

[21] D. Tse and P. Viswanath, "On the capacity of the multiple antenna broadcast channel", to appear in *DIMACS Series in Discrete Mathematics and Theoretical Computer Science*, 2003.

[22] D. Tse and S. Hanly, "Multi-Access Fading Channels: Part I: Polymatroid Structure, Optimal Resource Allocation and Throughput Capacities", *IEEE Trans. Inform. Theory*, vol. 44(7), Nov. 1998, pp. 2796-2815.

[23] S. Vishwanath, N. Jindal, and A. Goldsmith, "On the Capacity of Multiple Input Multiple Output Broadcast Channels", *International Conference on Communications*, 2002.

[24] P. Viswanath, V. Anantharam and D. Tse, "Optimal Sequences, Power Control and Capacity of Spread-Spectrum systems with Linear MMSE Multiuser Receivers", *IEEE Trans. Inform. Theory*, Sept. 1999, vol. 45, no. 6, pp.1968-1983

[25] P. Viswanath and V. Anantharam, "Optimal Sequences and Sum Capacity of Synchronous CDMA Systems", *IEEE Trans. Inform. Theory*, Sept. 1999, vol. 45, No.6, pp. 1984-1991.

[26] P. Viswanath and D. Tse, "Sum capacity of the multiple antenna Gaussian broadcast channel", *IEEE Trans. Inform. Theory*, vol. 49, No. 8, pp. 1912-1921, Aug. 2003.

[27] H. Wang and P. Viswanath, "Fixed Binning Schemes for Channel and Source Coding Problems: An Operational Duality", submitted to *IEEE Trans. Inform. Theory*, Sept. 2003.

[28] L. R. Welch, "Lower bounds on the maximum cross correlation of signals", *IEEE Trans. Inform. Theory*, vol. IT-20, pp. 397-399, May 1974.

[29] D. J. A. Welsh, *Matroid theory*, Academic Press, London, 1976.

[30] W. Yu, and J. Cioffi, "Sum Capacity of Gaussian Vector Broadcast Channels", submitted to *IEEE Trans. Inform. Theory*, Nov. 2001.

[31] R. Zamir and T. Berger, "Multiterminal source coding with high resolution", *IEEE Trans. Inform. Theory*, vol 45(1), Jan. 1999, pp. 106–117.

DEPARTMENT OF ECE, UNIVERSITY OF ILLINOIS AT URBANA-CHAMPAIGN.
E-mail address: pramodv@uiuc.edu

DIMACS Series in Discrete Mathematics
and Theoretical Computer Science
Volume **66**, 2004

Coding Theorems for Reversible Embedding

Frans M.J. Willems and Ton Kalker

ABSTRACT. We consider embedding of messages (data-hiding) into i.i.d. host sequences. As in Fridrich et al. [2002] we focus on the case where reconstruction of the host sequence from the composite sequence is required. We study the balance between embedding rate and embedding distortion. First we determine the distortion-rate region corresponding to this setup. Then we generalize this result in two directions. (A) The reversible embedding setup is not robust. Therefore we also consider reconstruction based on the output sequence of a discrete memoryless channel whose input is the composite sequence. We also determine the distortion-rate region for this setup. (B) Then we consider the case where only partial reconstruction of the host sequence is required. We determine the possible trade-offs here between embedding rate, distortion between source sequence and composite sequence (embedding distortion), and distortion between source sequence and restoration sequence (restoration distortion), i.e. the distortion-rate region.
All achievability proofs in this paper are based on the Gelfand-Pinsker [1980] achievability proof. Converses are omitted.

1. Introduction

In 1999 it was observed that data-hiding (embedding) is closely related to the information-theoretical concept of "channels with side-information". E.g. Chen [**C00**], Chen and Wornell [**CW00**], and Moulin and O'Sullivan [**MoS03**] realized that in the Gaussian case there is a close connection between data embedding and Costa's result "writing on dirty paper" [**C83**]. The achievability proof in the Costa paper is a consequence of the proof of Gelfand and Pinsker [**GP80**]. The Gelfand-Pinsker result can be regarded as an information-theoretical follow-up of the "memories with defects" paper by Kuznetsov and Tsybakov [**KT77**]. Heegard and El Gamal [**HeG83**] studied codes based on the Gelfand-Pinsker result for computer memories with defects. Coding theorems for data embedding situations appeared in Chen [**C00**] (specialized to the Gaussian case), Moulin and O'Sullivan [**MoS03**], Barron [**B00**], Barron, Chen, and Wornell [**BCW03**], and Willems [**W00**]. In all these papers the trade-off between embedding rate and embedding distortion is investigated (standard embedding). In the present paper we will focus on data

Key words and phrases. Data embedding, data hiding, channels with side information, information theory.

embedding schemes that are *reversible*. These schemes satisfy the additional requirement that the decoder should be able to reconstruct the host sequence. A good overview of the history and the state-of-the-art of reversible data embedding can be found in Fridrich, Goljan, and Du [**FGD02**]. Reversible data embedding schemes are important in cases where no degradation of the original host signal is allowed. This is for example true for medical imagery, military imagery, and multimedia archives of valuable original works.

In [**KW02**], [**WK02**], and [**KW03**] we have determined the fundamental limits of several (partially) reversible embedding setups. The objective of the current paper is to present these results in a unified way. It is demonstrated here that all our achievability proofs are extensions of the Gelfand-Pinsker achievability proof.

The paper is organized as follows. In the next section we consider the Gelfand-Pinsker channel with side-information since its achievability proof forms the basis of all our achievability proofs. We start in Section 3 with standard noise-free embedding. This "classical" embedding method is not reversible. We study this case for comparison only. The first section dealing with reversible embedding is Section 4 in which the rate-distortion region for the basic setup is determined. In this section we assume that the composite sequence is observed by the decoder (noise-free). In Section 5 we study the robust version of this reversible setup. We assume there that the composite sequence is degraded by transmitting it via a discrete memoryless channel. Looking at the output of this channel the decoder should be able to reconstruct the host sequence and the embedded message. In Section 6 we generalize the basic reversible embedding setup in another direction. We require on partial reconstruction of the host sequence there. It is assumed that the composite sequence is noise-free accessible by the decoder. Section 7 concludes the paper.

2. The Gelfand-Pinsker Coding Theorem

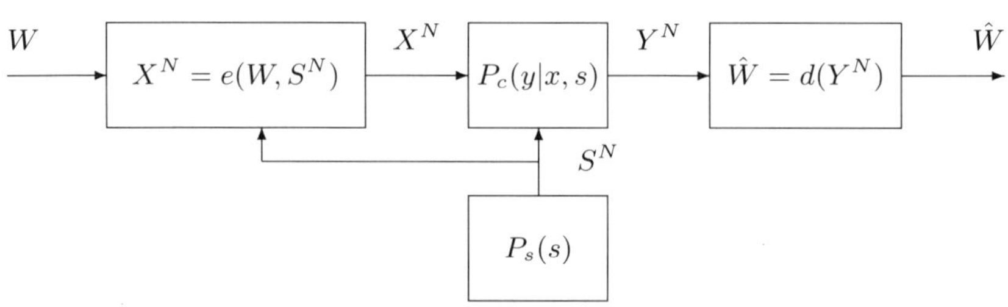

FIGURE 1. The Gelfand-Pinsker side-information channel.

2.1. System description, statement of result. The characteristic of the Gelfand-Pinsker [**GP80**] setup (see Figure 1) is that the transmitter has knowledge of the sequence of channel states that will occur during a block of N transmissions prior to these transmissions. For such a block of transmissions a message source produces one out of M possible message indices. Message index $w \in \{1, 2, \cdots, M\}$ occurs with probability $\Pr\{W = w\} = 1/M$. This message index is conveyed from the transmitter to the receiver in these N transmissions.

The channel $\{\mathcal{X} \times \mathcal{S}, P_c(y|x, s), \mathcal{Y}\}$ is memoryless. It has input alphabet $\mathcal{X}$, output alphabet $\mathcal{Y}$, and state alphabet $\mathcal{S}$, all these alphabets are finite. Given an input symbol $x \in \mathcal{X}$ and a channel state $s \in \mathcal{S}$, the output symbol $y \in \mathcal{Y}$ occurs with probability $P_c(y|x,s)$. The state sequence $s^N = (s_1, s_2, \cdots, s_N)$ is assumed to be generated at random. Sequence $s^N \in \mathcal{S}^N$ occurs with probability $\Pr\{S^N = s^N\} = \Pi_{n=1}^N P_s(s_n)$, therefore the state sequence is i.i.d. and its distribution is $\{P_s(s), s \in \mathcal{S}\}$.

The transmitter (encoder) produces the sequence of channel inputs $x^N = (x_1, x_2, \cdots, x_N)$ based on the message index w that is to be transmitted and the state sequence s^N, we write $X^N = e(W, S^N)$. The receiver (decoder) observes the sequence of channel outputs $y^N = (y_1, y_2, \cdots, y_N)$ and forms an estimate $\hat{w}$ of the transmitted message index, thus $\hat{W} = d(Y^N)$.

The performance of the system is determined by its error probability $P_{\mathcal{E}} = \Pr\{\hat{W} \neq W\}$ and its transmission rate $R = \frac{1}{N}\log_2(M)$. We assume throughout this manuscript that the base of the logarithm is 2, therefore rates, entropies, and mutual informations are expressed in bits.

The Gelfand-Pinsker capacity C_{GP} is the largest ρ such that for all $\epsilon > 0$ there exist for all large enough N encoders and decoders with $R \geq \rho - \epsilon$ and $P_{\mathcal{E}} \leq \epsilon$.

THEOREM 2.1. *(Gelfand and Pinsker [**GP80**]) The capacity*

$$C_{GP} = \max_{P_t(u,x|s)} I(U;Y) - I(U;S). \tag{2.1}$$

The maximum is over all test-channels $\{\mathcal{S},\ P_t(u,x|s), \mathcal{U} \times \mathcal{X}\}$ with input alphabet $\mathcal{S}$, output alphabets $\mathcal{U}$ and $\mathcal{X}$, and transition probability matrix $P_t(u,x|s)$. The joint distribution of S, U, X, and Y is given by $P(s,u,x,y) = P_s(s)P_t(u,x|s)P_c(y|x,s)$. The cardinality $|\mathcal{U}|$ of the auxiliary alphabet need not be larger than $|\mathcal{S}| + |\mathcal{X}|$.

2.2. Achievability proof. We will only give a brief outline of the achievability proof here. Our proof is along the lines of the Gelfand-Pinsker proof [**GP80**]. Details can be found in appendix A.

(a) First fix a test-channel $P_t(u,x|s)$. This determines the joint distribution $P(s,u,x,y) = P_s(s)P_t(u,x|s)P_c(y|x,s)$. Assume that the corresponding $I(U;Y) - I(U;S) > 0$. If a test-channel with $I(U;Y) - I(U;S) > 0$ does not exist, $C_{\text{GP}} = 0$. Fix an $0 < \eta < 1$. Consider sets $\mathcal{T}_\eta^N(\cdot)$ of (strongly) typical sequences, see (A.1) and (A.3), and a reverse set $\mathcal{R}_\gamma^N(\cdot)$ of typical sequences as defined in (A.9).

For each message index $w \in \{1, \cdots, 2^{NR}\}$, generate 2^{NR_u} sequences u^N at random according to $P(u) = \sum_{s,x} P_s(s)P_t(u,x|s)$ and give these sequences the label w.

(b) The encoder observes the state sequence s^N. If $s^N \notin \mathcal{T}_\eta^N(S)$ an error is declared by the encoder and we say that an error event E_1 (of the first kind) occurred. It can be shown that for all N large enough $\Pr\{E_1\} \leq \eta$.

(c) Assume that the complement E_1^c of E_1 occurred, thus $s^N \in \mathcal{T}_\eta^N(S)$. When the message index w is to be transmitted, the encoder chooses a sequence u^N with label w such that $u^N \in \mathcal{T}_\eta^N(U|s^N)$. If such a sequence was not generated the encoder declares an error and we say that an error event E_2 (of the second kind) occurred. It can be shown that $\Pr\{E_2|E_1^c\} \leq \eta$ for N large enough if

$$R_u = (1+\eta)^2 H(U) - (1-\eta)^2 H(U|S) + 2\eta. \tag{2.2}$$

(d) The input sequence x^N results from applying the "channel" $P(x|u,s) = P_t(u,x|s)/\sum_x P_t(u,x|s)$ to u^N and s^N. The resulting x^N is transmitted over the side-information channel, the channel with transition probability matrix $P_c(y|x,s)$. The output of this channel is the sequence y^N. Assume that the complementary events E_1^c and E_2^c occurred. Then by (A.5) the pair $(s^N, u^N) \in \mathcal{T}^N_{(1+\eta)^2-1}(S,U)$. We say that an error event E_3 (of the third kind) occurred when the channel output sequence $y^N \notin \mathcal{T}^N_{(1+\eta)^2-1}(Y|s^N, u^N)$. It can be shown that $\Pr\{E_3|E_1^c, E_2^c\} \leq \eta$ for all large enough N.

(e) The decoder, upon receiving y^N, finds the unique sequence u^N such that $u^N \in \mathcal{R}^N_\zeta(U|y^N)$ where $\zeta \triangleq (1+\eta)^4/(1-\eta)^2 - 1$. If such a unique sequence u^N is not found the decoder declares an error and we say that an error event E_4 (of the fourth kind) occurred. If we assume that the complementary events E_1^c, E_2^c, and E_3^c occurred, the transmitted sequence $u^N \in \mathcal{R}^N_\zeta(U|y^N)$. It can be shown that

$$R + R_u = (1-\zeta)H(U) - (1+\zeta)^2 H(U|Y) - \eta \tag{2.3}$$

implies that $\Pr\{E_4|E_1^c, E_2^c, E_3^c\} \leq \eta$ for all N large enough. The estimated message index $\hat{w}$ is the label of the decoded sequence u^N. If also E_4 did not occur the decoded message index $\hat{w}$ is equal to w.

(f) It can be shown that for all N large enough the total error probability

$$\Pr\{E_1 \cup E_2 \cup E_3 \cup E_4\} \leq 4\eta, \tag{2.4}$$

while, by (2.2) and (2.3), the rate satisfies

$$\begin{aligned} R &= (1-\zeta)H(U) - (1+\zeta)^2 H(U|Y) - \eta \\ &\quad -(1+\eta)^2 H(U) + (1-\eta)^2 H(U|S) - 2\eta \\ &= I(U;Y) - I(U;S) - \delta(\eta), \end{aligned} \tag{2.5}$$

where $\lim_{\eta \downarrow 0} \delta(\eta) = 0$.

So far we have shown that, *averaged over the ensemble of generated auxiliary codewords*, the probability $\Pr\{E_1 \cup E_2 \cup E_3 \cup E_4\} \leq 4\eta$. This however implies that there are encoders and decoders that actually achieve $\Pr\{E_1 \cup E_2 \cup E_3 \cup E_4\} \leq 4\eta$ and thus also $P_\mathcal{E} \leq 4\eta$.

If we now let $\eta \downarrow 0$ then also $\delta(\eta) \downarrow 0$ and we may conclude that

$$\rho = I(U;Y) - I(U;S) \tag{2.6}$$

is achievable. Maximizing over all test channel $P_t(u, x|s)$ yields that C_{GP} is achievable.

2.3. Some observations. From the previous subsection we know that for $0 < \eta < 1$ and N large enough, there are codes with $R = I(U;Y) - I(U;S) + \delta(\eta)$ that achieve $\Pr\{E_1 \cup E_2 \cup E_3 \cup E_4\} \leq 4\eta$. Note also that $\lim_{\eta \downarrow 0} \delta(\eta) = 0$. Consider such a code.

(a) With probability not smaller than $1 - 4\eta$ the state sequence $s^N \in \mathcal{T}^N_\eta(S)$ and the auxiliary sequence u^N is conditionally typical with the state sequence s^N, i.e. $u^N \in \mathcal{T}^N_\eta(U|s^N)$. Therefore the joint composition of (s^N, u^N) is close to $P(s,u) = \sum_x P_s(s)P_t(u,x|s)$, see (A.5). Consider a matrix $\{D_{su}(s,u), s \in \mathcal{S}, u \in \mathcal{U}\}$ with non-negative components, and let $\sum_{s,u} P(u,s)D_{su}(s,u) < \infty$, then we can write

$$\begin{aligned} \frac{1}{N}\sum_{n=1,N} D_{su}(s_n,u_n) &= \frac{1}{N}\sum_{s,u} \#(s,u|s^N,u^N)D_{su}(s,u) \\ &\leq (1+\eta)^2 \sum_{s,u} P(s,u)D_{su}(s,u) \\ &\leq \sum_{s,u} P(s,u)D_{su}(s,u) + 3\eta d_{\max}, \end{aligned} \tag{2.7}$$

where also $d_{\max} \stackrel{\Delta}{=} \max_{s,u:P(s,u)>0} D_{su}(s,u) < \infty$. Now suppose that the encoder, when E_1 or E_2 occurred, chooses the auxiliary sequence u^N that minimizes $\sum_{n=1,N} D_{su}(s_n,u_n)$. Then we obtain from (2.7) the following upper bound

$$\begin{aligned} \overline{D_{su}} &= \sum_w \sum_{s^N} \frac{1}{M} \Pr\{S^N = s^N\} \frac{1}{N} \sum_{n=1,N} D_{su}(s_n, u_n(w,s^N)) \\ &\leq \Pr\{E_1^c \cap E_2^c) \left(\sum_{s,u} P(s,u)D_{su}(s,u) + 3\eta d_{\max} \right) + \Pr\{E_1 \cup E_2) d_{\max} \\ &\leq \sum_{s,u} P(s,u)D_{su}(s,u) + 7\eta d_{\max}. \end{aligned} \tag{2.8}$$

Here $u_n(w,s^N)$ is the n-th component of u^N.

(b) Moreover observe that as an "intermediate" result the decoder recovers the auxiliary sequence u^N if the event $E_1 \cup E_2 \cup E_3 \cup E_4$ does not occur i.e. with probability not smaller than $1 - 4\eta$ for N large enough.

Both results (a) and (b) will be used in the achievability proofs for several embedding situations that we will investigate in the next sections.

3. Standard Noise-Free Embedding

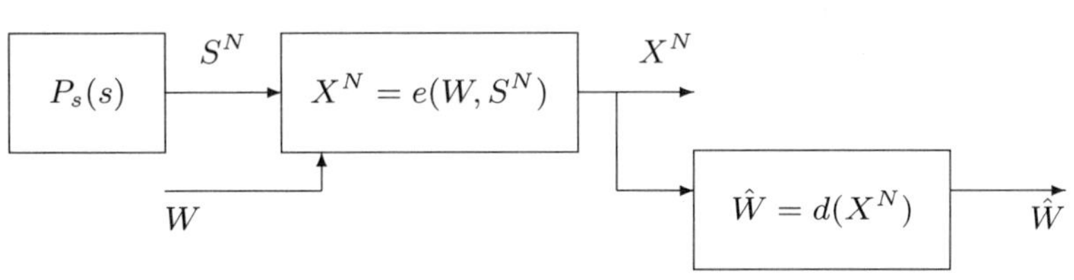

FIGURE 2. The standard noise-free embedding situation.

3.1. System description, statement of result. Standard noise-free embedding was first investigated by Chen [**C00**] and Barron [**B00**]. In [**WvD01**] codes were studied for the standard noise-free case for gray-scale symbols and squared error distortion. These authors considered the situation depicted in Figure 2. The objective there is to embed as much information in an i.i.d. host sequence as possible, without changing this sequence too much, i.e. without increasing the distortion between the source sequence and the composite sequence too much. We model this system as follows.

A message source produces one out of M possible message indices. Message index $w \in \{1, 2, \cdots, M\}$ occurs with probability $\Pr\{W = w\} = 1/M$. This message index is embedded in a host sequence $s^N = (s_1, s_2, \cdots, s_N)$ consisting of N symbols from the finite alphabet $\mathcal{S}$. The host sequence is assumed to be generated at random. Sequence $s^N \in \mathcal{S}^N$ occurs with probability $\Pr\{S^N = s^N\} = \Pi_{n=1}^{N} P_s(s_n)$, therefore the host sequence is i.i.d. and its distribution is $\{P_s(s), s \in \mathcal{S}\}$.

The encoder produces the composite sequence $x^N = (x_1, x_2, \cdots, x_N)$ based on the message index w that must be embedded and the host sequence s^N, we write $X^N = e(W, S^N)$. The symbols $x_n, n = 1, N$, from the composite sequence assume values from the finite alphabet $\mathcal{X}$. The decoder observes the composite sequence x^N and forms an estimate $\hat{w}$ of the embedded message index, thus $\hat{W} = d(X^N)$.

The performance of the system is determined by its error probability $P_{\mathcal{E}} = \Pr\{\hat{W} \neq W\}$, its embedding rate $R_e = \frac{1}{N}\log_2(M)$, and the average embedding distortion

$$\overline{D^e_{sx}} = \sum_w \sum_{s^N} \frac{1}{M} \Pr\{S^N = s^N\} \frac{1}{N} \sum_{n=1,N} D^e_{sx}(s_n, e_n(w, s^N)), \tag{3.1}$$

where $e_n(w, s^N)$ is the n-th component of $e(w, s^N)$ and $D^e_{sx}(s, x)$ is the embedding distortion between symbols $s \in \mathcal{S}$ and $x \in \mathcal{X}$. Without loss of generality we assume that the components of $D^e_{sx}(\cdot, \cdot)$ are non-negative.

We say that a distortion-rate pair (Δ_{sx}, ρ_e) is achievable in the standard noise-free case if for all $\epsilon > 0$ there exist for all large enough N encoders and decoders with

$$\begin{aligned} R_e &\geq \rho_e - \epsilon, \\ \overline{D^e_{sx}} &\leq \Delta_{sx} + \epsilon, \text{ and} \\ P_{\mathcal{E}} = \Pr\{\hat{W} \neq W\} &\leq \epsilon. \end{aligned} \tag{3.2}$$

Here we restrict ourselves to rates $\rho_e \geq 0$ and finite distortions Δ_{sx}. It makes no sense to consider rates smaller than zero, and allowing infinite distortion is essentially the same as no distortion constraint. The set of all achievable distortion-rate pairs in the standard noise-free embedding case is denoted by $\mathcal{G}_{\text{snf}}$. The capacity-distortion function $C_{\text{snf}}(\Delta)$ is defined as $C_{\text{snf}}(\Delta) \stackrel{\Delta}{=} \max\{\Delta : (\Delta, \rho) \in \mathcal{G}_{\text{snf}}\}$.

THEOREM 3.1. *(Chen* [**C00**] *and Barron* [**B00**]*) The achievable region in the standard noise-free embedding case is given by*

$$\begin{aligned} \mathcal{G}_{snf} = \{(\Delta_{sx}, \rho_e) \quad &: \quad \Delta_{sx} \geq \sum_{s,x} P(s,x) D^e_{sx}(s,x), \\ &0 \leq \rho_e \leq H(X|S), \\ &\text{where } P(s,x) = P_s(s)P_t(x|s) \text{ for some } P_t(x|s)\}. \end{aligned} \tag{3.3}$$

Therefore the capacity-distortion function

$$C_{snf}(\Delta) = \max_{P_t(x|s): \sum_{s,x} P_s(s) P_t(x|s) D^e_{sx}(s,x) \leq \Delta} H(X|S). \tag{3.4}$$

The test-channel $\{\mathcal{S}, P_t(x|s), \mathcal{X}\}$ has input alphabet $\mathcal{S}$, output alphabet $\mathcal{X}$, and transition probability matrix $P_t(x|s)$.

3.2. Achievable region. Fix a test-channel $\{\mathcal{S}, P_t(x|s), \mathcal{X}\}$ with $H(X|S) > 0$. If such a test-channel does not exist, only distortion-rate pairs $(\Delta_{sx}, 0)$ must be shown to be achievable which is trivial. Let $0 < \eta < 1$. The definition of achievability implies that $\sum_{s,x} P_s(s)\, P_t(x|s) D^e_{sx}(s,x) < \infty$. The achievability proof now follows directly from the Gelfand-Pinsker achievability proof in Section 2.2

and observation (a) in Section 2.3. Note that the host sequence plays the role of the state sequence here. Also observe that $Y \equiv X$ since our "channel" is noise-free. Finally substitute X for the auxiliary random variable U, thus $U = X$ and $D_{su}(s,u) = D^e_{sx}(s,u), s \in \mathcal{S}, u \in \mathcal{X}$. Then from the arguments in Section 2.3 we may conclude that there exists a code with error probability $P_{\mathcal{E}} \leq 4\eta$, and embedding rate and average embedding distortion satisfying

$$\begin{aligned} R_e &= I(U;Y) - I(U;S) - \delta(\eta) = H(X|S) - \delta(\eta), \\ \overline{D^e_{sx}} &\leq \sum_{s,u} P(s,u) D_{su}(s,u) + 7\eta d_{\max} \\ &= \sum_{s,x} P_s(s) P_t(x|s) D^e_{sx}(s,x) + 7\eta d_{\max}, \end{aligned} \tag{3.5}$$

for all N large enough. Here $d_{\max} \triangleq \max_{s,x:P(s,x)>0} D^e_{sx}(s,x)$. The achievability proof is complete if we let $\eta \downarrow 0$.

4. Reversible Noise-Free Embedding

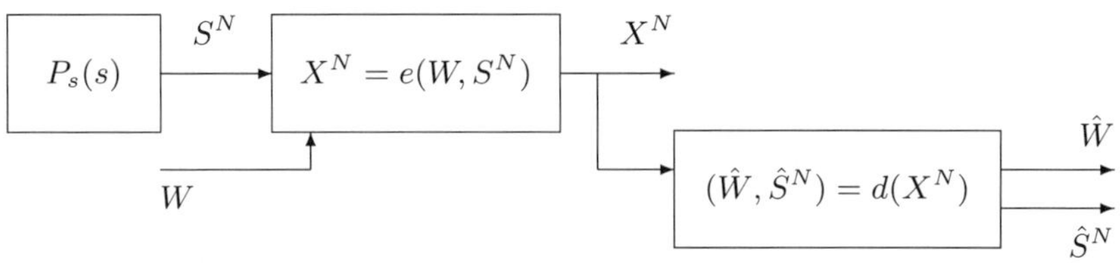

FIGURE 3. The reversible noise-free embedding situation.

4.1. System description, statement of result. Reversible embedding situations were considered recently by Fridrich, Goljan, and Du [**FGD02**]. Their setup is similar to the standard noise-free setup. There is again a balance between embedding rate and embedding distortion, but it in addition to the message the decoder should reconstruct the host sequence after having received the composite sequence, see Figure 3. Although actual embedding methods were discussed in [**FGD02**], the capacity-distortion function for reversible noise-free embedding was determined a little later in [**KW02**] by the authors. Coding techniques based on [**KW02**] were discussed in [**MKW02**]. We first describe the reversible noise-free embedding model and then state the result of [**KW02**].

As before the message source produces M possible message indices. Index $w \in \{1, 2, \cdots, M\}$ occurs with probability $\Pr\{W = w\} = 1/M$. This message index is embedded in host sequence $s^N = (s_1, s_2, \cdots, s_N)$ consisting of symbols from the finite alphabet $\mathcal{S}$. Sequence $s^N \in \mathcal{S}^N$ occurs with probability $\Pr\{S^N = s^N\} = \Pi_{n=1}^N P_s(s_n)$, therefore the host sequence is i.i.d. with distribution $\{P_s(s), s \in \mathcal{S}\}$.

The encoder produces the composite sequence $x^N = (x_1, x_2, \cdots, x_N)$ based on the message index w that is to be embedded and host sequence s^N, we write $X^N = e(W, S^N)$. The symbols $x_n, n = 1, N$, are in the finite alphabet $\mathcal{X}$. The decoder observes the composite sequence x^N and forms an estimate $\hat{w}$ of the embedded message index, and an estimate $\hat{s}^N$ of the host sequence hence $(\hat{W}, \hat{S}^N) = d(X^N)$.

The performance of the reversible noise-free embedding system is determined by the error probability $P_{\mathcal{E}} = \Pr\{\hat{W} \neq W \cup \hat{S}^N \neq S^N\}$, its embedding rate $R_e =$

$\frac{1}{N}\log_2(M)$, and the average embedding distortion

$$\overline{D^e_{sx}} = \sum_w \sum_{s^N} \frac{1}{M} \Pr\{S^N = s^N\} \frac{1}{N} \sum_{n=1,N} D^e_{sx}(s_n, e_n(w, s^N)). \tag{4.1}$$

We again say that a distortion-rate pair (Δ_{sx}, ρ_e) (for $\Delta_{sx} < \infty$ and $\rho_e \geq 0$) is achievable in the reversible noise-free case if for all $\epsilon > 0$ there exist for all large enough N encoders and decoders with

$$\begin{aligned} R_e &\geq \rho_e - \epsilon, \\ \overline{D^e_{sx}} &\leq \Delta_{sx} + \epsilon, \text{ and} \\ P_{\mathcal{E}} = \Pr\{\hat{W} \neq W \cup \hat{S}^N \neq S^N\} &\leq \epsilon. \end{aligned} \tag{4.2}$$

The set of all achievable distortion-rate pairs in the reversible noise-free embedding case is denoted by $\mathcal{G}_{\text{rnf}}$. The capacity-distortion function $C_{\text{rnf}}(\Delta)$ is defined as $C_{\text{rnf}}(\Delta) \stackrel{\Delta}{=} \max\{\Delta : (\Delta, \rho) \in \mathcal{G}_{\text{rnf}}\}$.

THEOREM 4.1. *(Kalker and Willems* [**KW02**]*) The achievable region in the reversible noise-free embedding case is given by*

$$\begin{aligned} \mathcal{G}_{rnf} = \{(\Delta_{sx}, \rho_e) \quad : \quad & \Delta_{sx} \geq \sum_{s,x} P(s,x) D^e_{sx}(s,x), \\ & 0 \leq \rho_e \leq H(X) - H(S), \\ & \textit{where } P(s,x) = P_s(s)P_t(x|s) \textit{ for some } P_t(x|s)\}. \end{aligned} \tag{4.3}$$

Therefore the capacity-distortion function

$$C_{rnf}(\Delta) = \max_{P_t(x|s): \sum_{s,x} P_s(s) P_t(x|s) D^e_{sx}(s,x) \leq \Delta} H(X) - H(S). \tag{4.4}$$

Test-channel $\{\mathcal{S}, P_t(x|s), \mathcal{X}\}$ has input alphabet $\mathcal{S}$, output alphabet $\mathcal{X}$, and transition probability matrix $P_t(x|s)$.

4.2. Achievability proof. We start by fixing a test-channel $\{\mathcal{S}, P_t(x|s), \mathcal{X}\}$ for which $H(X) - H(S) > 0$ and an $0 < \eta < 1$. We assume that $\sum_{s,x} P_s(s)P_t(x|s)$ $D^e_{sx}(s,x) < \infty$. The achievability proof now follows again from the Gelfand-Pinsker achievability proof in Section 2.2 and observations (a) and (b) in Section 2.3. The host sequence plays the role of the state sequence. Note that $Y \equiv X$ since the channel is noise-free. We now substitute (S, X) for the auxiliary random variable U, thus $U = (S, X)$ and $D_{su}(s, (s', x)) = D^e_{sx}(s, x)$ if $s = s'$ for $s \in \mathcal{S}$, $x \in \mathcal{X}$. From the arguments in Section 2.3 we may conclude that there exists a code with embedding rate and embedding distortion satisfying

$$\begin{aligned} R_e &= I(U;Y) - I(U;S) - \delta(\eta) = H(X) - H(S) - \delta(\eta), \\ \overline{D^e_{sx}} &\leq \sum_{s,u} P(s,u) D_{su}(s,u) + 7\eta d_{\max} \\ &= \sum_{s,x} P_s(s) P_t(x|s) D^e_{sx}(s,x) + 7\eta d_{\max}, \end{aligned} \tag{4.5}$$

for all N large enough. Here $d_{\max} \stackrel{\Delta}{=} \max_{s,x:P(s,x)>0} D^e_{sx}(s,x)$. Moreover from observation (b) in Section 2.3 we may conclude that the decoder recovers $u^N = (s^N, x^N)$ if $E_1 \cup E_2 \cup E_3 \cup E_4$ does not occur. This implies that also s^N is reconstructed and hence $P_{\mathcal{E}} \leq 4\eta$ for all N large enough. The achievability proof for test-channels with $H(X) - H(S) > 0$ is complete if we let $\eta \downarrow 0$.

Let $(d,0) \in \mathcal{G}_{\text{rnf}}$ be the distortion-rate pair with minimal distortion d. This distortion-rate pair corresponds to a test channel having $\rho = H(X) - H(S) = 0$. Since $\mathcal{G}_{\text{rnf}}$ can be shown to be closed and convex, also the distortion-rate pair $(d,0)$ should be achievable (if there is a test channel with $\rho = H(X) - H(S) > 0$ and $\Delta_{sx} < \infty$).

5. Reversible and Robust Embedding

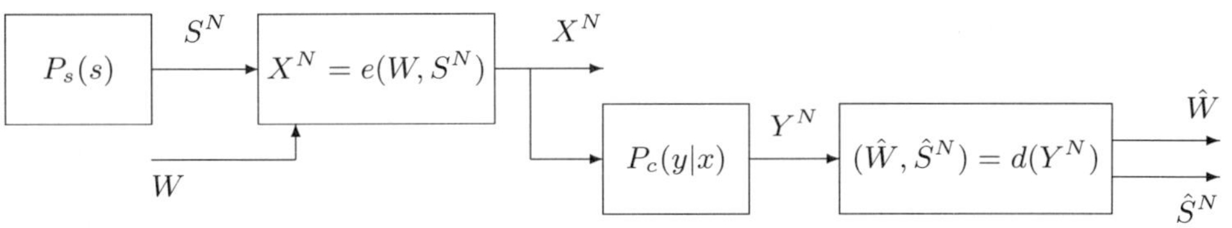

FIGURE 4. The reversible and robust embedding situation.

5.1. System description, statement of result. Reversible noise-free embedding has the disadvantage that it is not robust against errors that may occur in the composite sequence. Therefore in [**KW03**] the authors considered a modification of the reversible noise-free embedding configuration in Figure 3 in which the composite sequence is transmitted over a discrete memoryless channel, before being observed by the decoder that extracts the host sequence and the embedded message index, see Figure 4. For this model the authors could determine the capacity-distortion region. We first describe the reversible and robust embedding model and then state the result of [**KW03**].

We mainly describe the differences with the reversible noise-free embedding situation. There is also a message source and a source that produces the host sequence. The message index w is embedded in host sequence s^N. The encoder produces the composite sequence x^N based on the message index w that is to be embedded and host sequence s^N, i.e. $X^N = e(W, S^N)$. The composite sequence x^N is now transmitted over the channel $\{\mathcal{X}, P_c(y|x), \mathcal{Y}\}$. This channel is memoryless. It has input alphabet $\mathcal{X}$, output alphabet $\mathcal{Y}$, both finite. Given an input symbol $x \in \mathcal{X}$, the output symbol $y \in \mathcal{Y}$ occurs with probability $P_c(y|x)$. The decoder observes the channel output sequence $y^N = (y_1, y_2, \cdots, y_N)$ and forms an estimate $\hat{w}$ of the embedded message index, and estimate $\hat{s}^N$ of the host sequence thus $(\hat{W}, \hat{S}^N) = d(Y^N)$.

The performance of the reversible embedding system is determined by the error probability $P_{\mathcal{E}} = \Pr\{\hat{W} \neq W \cup \hat{S}^N \neq S^N\}$, its embedding rate $R_e = \frac{1}{N}\log_2(M)$, and the average embedding distortion

$$\overline{D^e_{sx}} = \sum_w \sum_{s^N} \frac{1}{M} \Pr\{S^N = s^N\} \frac{1}{N} \sum_{n=1,N} D^e_{sx}(s_n, e_n(w, s^N)). \tag{5.1}$$

A distortion-rate pair (Δ_{sx}, ρ_e) with $\Delta_{sx} < \infty$ and $\rho_e \geq 0$ is achievable in the robust and reversible case if for all $\epsilon > 0$ there exist for all large enough N encoders and decoders with

$$\begin{aligned} R_e &\geq \rho_e - \epsilon, \\ \overline{D^e_{sx}} &\leq \Delta_{sx} + \epsilon, \text{ and} \\ P_{\mathcal{E}} = \Pr\{\hat{W} \neq W \cup \hat{S}^N \neq S^N\} &\leq \epsilon. \end{aligned} \tag{5.2}$$

The set of all achievable distortion-rate pairs in the reversible and robust embedding case is denoted by $\mathcal{G}_{\rm rr}$. The capacity-distortion function $C_{\rm rr}(\Delta)$ is defined as $C_{\rm rr}(\Delta) \stackrel{\Delta}{=} \max\{\Delta : (\Delta, \rho) \in \mathcal{G}_{\rm rr}\}$.

THEOREM 5.1. *(Kalker and Willems* **[KW03]***) The achievable region in the reversible and robust embedding case is given by*

$$\begin{aligned} \mathcal{G}_{rr} = \{(\Delta_{sx}, \rho_e) \quad : \quad & \Delta_{sx} \geq \sum_{s,x} P(s,x) D^e_{sx}(s,x), \\ & 0 \leq \rho_e \leq I(X;Y) - H(S), \\ & \textit{where } P(s,x,y) = P_s(s)P_t(x|s)P_c(y|x) \textit{ for some } P_t(x|s)\}. \end{aligned} \tag{5.3}$$

Therefore the capacity-distortion function

$$C_{rr}(\Delta) = \max_{P_t(x|s): \sum_{s,x} P_s(s)P_t(x|s)D^e_{sx}(s,x) \leq \Delta} I(X;Y) - H(S). \tag{5.4}$$

Test-channel $\{\mathcal{S},\ P_t(x|s),\ \mathcal{X}\}$ *has input alphabet* $\mathcal{S}$, *output alphabet* $\mathcal{X}$, *and transition probability matrix* $P_t(x|s)$.

5.2. Achievability proof. Fix a test-channel $\{\mathcal{S}, P_t(x|s), \mathcal{X}\}$ and $0 < \eta < 1$. We assume that $\sum_{s,x} P_s(s)P_t(x|s)D^e_{sx}(s,x) < \infty$. The achievability proof follows again from the Gelfand-Pinsker achievability proof in Section 2.2 and observations (a) and (b) in Section 2.3. The host sequence plays the role of the state sequence. Substitute (S, X) for the auxiliary random variable U again, thus $U = (S, X)$ and $D_{su}(s, (s', x)) = D^e_{sx}(s, x)$ if $s = s'$ for $s \in \mathcal{S}$, $x \in \mathcal{X}$. Note that $(S, X) - X - Y$ form a Markov chain. The arguments in Section 2.3 imply that there exists a code with embedding rate and embedding distortion such that

$$\begin{aligned} R_e &= I(U;Y) - I(U;S) - \delta(\eta) = I(X;Y) - H(S) - \delta(\eta), \\ \overline{D^e_{sx}} &\leq \sum_{s,u} P(s,u) D_{su}(s,u) + 7\eta d_{\rm max} \\ &= \sum_{s,x} P_s(s)P_t(x|s)D^e_{sx}(s,x) + 7\eta d_{\rm max}, \end{aligned} \tag{5.5}$$

for all N large enough. Here $d_{\rm max} \stackrel{\Delta}{=} \max_{s,x:P(s,x)>0} D^e_{sx}(s,x)$. Moreover from observation (b) in Section 2.3 we may conclude that the decoder recovers $u^N = (s^N, x^N)$ and hence s^N if $E_1 \cup E_2 \cup E_3 \cup E_4$ does not occur. Hence $P_{\mathcal{E}} \leq 4\eta$ for all N large enough. The achievability part of theorem 5.1 for pairs with $I(X;Y) - H(S) > 0$ is complete if we let $\eta \downarrow 0$.

Distortion-rate pairs having $I(X;Y) - H(S) = 0$ are achievable by the fact that $\mathcal{G}_{\rm rr}$ is closed and convex.

6. Partially Reversible Noise-Free Embedding

6.1. System description, statement of result. Another disadvantage of reversible noise-free embedding is that the requirement that the host sequence must be reconstructed in addition to the message index has a strong negative effect on the

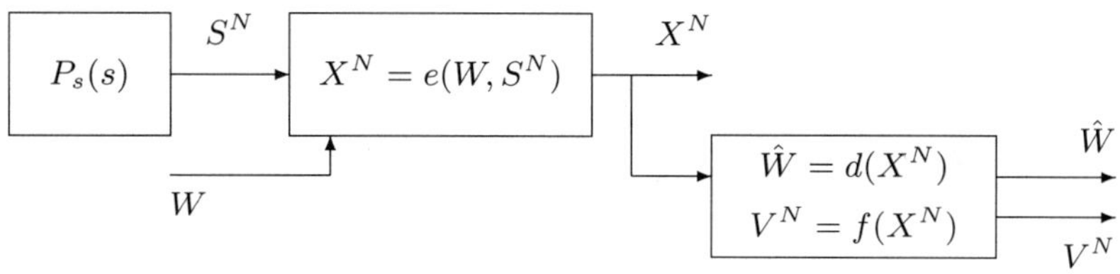

FIGURE 5. The partially reversible noise-free embedding situation.

embedding rate. In [**WK02**] the authors studied a reversible embedding situation where only partial reconstruction of the host sequence was required, see Figure 5. Note that this setup is not robust.

There is a message source and a source that produces the host sequence. Message index w is embedded in host sequence s^N. The encoder produces the composite sequence x^N based on the message index w that is to be embedded and host sequence s^N, i.e. $X^N = e(W, S^N)$. The composite sequence x^N is now observed by the decoder that forms an estimate $\hat{w}$ of the embedded message index, and a restoration sequence $v^N = (v_1, v_2, \cdots, v_N) \in \mathcal{V}^N$ that is close to the host sequence s^N. We write $\hat{W} = d(X^N)$ and $V^N = f(X^N)$. We assume that the alphabet $\mathcal{V}$ is finite.

The performance of the partially reversible noise-free embedding system is determined by the error probability $P_\mathcal{E} = \Pr\{\hat{W} \neq W\}$, its embedding rate $R_e = \frac{1}{N}\log_2(M)$, the average embedding distortion

$$\overline{D^e_{sx}} = \sum_w \sum_{s^N} \frac{1}{M} \Pr\{S^N = s^N\} \frac{1}{N} \sum_{n=1,N} D^e_{sx}(s_n, e_n(w, s^N)), \tag{6.1}$$

and the average restoration distortion

$$\overline{D^r_{sv}} = \sum_w \sum_{s^N} \frac{1}{M} \Pr\{S^N = s^N\} \frac{1}{N} \sum_{n=1,N} D^r_{sv}(s_n, f_n(e(w, s^N))), \tag{6.2}$$

where $f_n(x^N)$ is the n-th component of $f(x^N)$ and $D^r_{sv}(s, x)$ is the restoration distortion between symbols $s \in \mathcal{S}$ and $v \in \mathcal{V}$. Without loss of generality we assume that the components of $D^r_{sv}(\cdot, \cdot)$ are non-negative. We assume also that all components are finite however.

A distortion-rate triple $(\Delta_{sx}, \Delta_{sv}, \rho_e)$ is achievable in the partially reversible noise-free case if for all $\epsilon > 0$ there exist for all large enough N encoders and decoders with

$$\begin{aligned} R_e &\geq \rho_e - \epsilon, \\ \overline{D^e_{sx}} &\leq \Delta_{sx} + \epsilon, \\ \overline{D^r_{sv}} &\leq \Delta_{sv} + \epsilon, \text{ and} \\ P_\mathcal{E} = \Pr\{\hat{W} \neq W\} &\leq \epsilon. \end{aligned} \tag{6.3}$$

The set of all achievable distortion-rate triples in the partially reversible noise-free embedding case is denoted by $\mathcal{G}_{\text{prnf}}$.

THEOREM 6.1. *(Willems and Kalker* [**WK02**]*). The achievable region in the partially reversible noise-free embedding case is given by*

$$\mathcal{G}_{prnf} = \{(\Delta_{sx}, \Delta_{sv}, \rho_e) : \Delta_{sx} \geq \sum_{s,x} P(s,x) D^e_{sx}(s,x),$$

$$\Delta_{sv} \geq \sum_{s,v} P(s,v) D^r_{sv}(s,v),$$

$$0 \leq \rho_e \leq H(X) - I(S;X,V),$$

$$\text{where } P(s,x,v) = P_s(s)P_t(x,v|s) \text{ for some } P_t(x,v|s)\}. \tag{6.4}$$

(6.5)

Test-channel $\{\mathcal{S},\ P_t(x,v|s),\ \mathcal{X}\times\mathcal{V}\}$ *has input alphabet* $\mathcal{S}$, *output alphabets* $\mathcal{X}$ *and* $\mathcal{V}$, *and transition probability matrix* $P_t(x,v|s)$.

6.2. Achievability proof. Fix a test-channel $\{\mathcal{S}, P_t(x,v|s), \mathcal{X}\times\mathcal{V}\}$ and an η such that $0 < \eta < 1$. Assume that $H(X) - I(S;X,V) > 0$. By the definition of achievability we may assume that $\sum_{s,x,v} P_s(s)P_t(x,v|s)D^e_{sx}(s,x) < \infty$ and $\sum_{s,x,v} P_s(s)P_t(x,v|s)D^r_{sv}(s,v) < \infty$. The achievability part of theorem 6.1 now follows directly from the Gelfand-Pinsker proof in Section 2.2 and the two observations in Section 2.3. The host sequence plays the role of the state sequence. Also observe that $Y \equiv X$, the channel is noise-free. Finally substitute (V,X) for the auxiliary random variable U, thus $U = (V,X)$. Now define the matrices $D'_{su}(\cdot,\cdot)$ and $D''_{su}(\cdot,\cdot)$:

$$\begin{aligned} D'_{su}(s,(v,x)) &= D^e_{sx}(s,x) \text{ and} \\ D''_{su}(s,(v,x)) &= D^r_{sv}(s,v) \text{ for } s\in\mathcal{S}, x\in\mathcal{X}, v\in\mathcal{V}. \end{aligned} \tag{6.6}$$

The arguments in Section 2.3 imply that there exists a code with embedding rate and embedding distortion such that $P_{\mathcal{E}} \leq 4\eta$ and

$$\begin{aligned} R_e &= I(U;Y) - I(U;S) - \delta(\eta) = H(X) - I(S;X,V) - \delta(\eta), \\ \overline{D^e_{sx}} = \overline{D'_{su}} &\leq \sum_{s,u} P(s,u)D'_{su}(s,u) + 7\eta d'_{\max} \\ &= \sum_{s,x} P_s(s)P_t(x|s)D^e_{sx}(s,x) + 7\eta d'_{\max}, \end{aligned} \tag{6.7}$$

for all N large enough. Here $d'_{\max} \stackrel{\Delta}{=} \max_{s,x:P(s,x)>0} D^e_{sx}(s,x)$. Moreover from observation (b) in Section 2.3 we may conclude that the decoder recovers $u^N = (v^N, x^N)$ if $E_1 \cup E_2 \cup E_3 \cup E_4$ does not occur. We can now write

$$\begin{aligned} \overline{D^r_{sv}} &\leq \Pr\{E_1\cup E_2\cup E_3\cup E_4\}\overline{D''_{su}} + (1-\Pr\{E_1\cup E_2\cup E_3\cup E_4\})d''_{\max} \\ &\leq \sum_{s,u} P_s(s)P_t(u|s)D''_{su}(s,u) + 7\eta d''_{\max} + 4\eta d''_{\max} \\ &\leq \sum_{s,v} P_s(s)P_t(v|s)D^r_{sv}(s,v) + 11\eta d''_{\max} \end{aligned} \tag{6.8}$$

for all N large enough. Now $d''_{\max} \stackrel{\Delta}{=} \max_{s,v} D^r_{sv}(s,v)$. The achievability part of theorem 6.1 for triples with $H(X) - I(S;XV) > 0$ follows if we let $\eta \downarrow 0$. Note that by convexity and closed-ness of $\mathcal{G}_{\text{prnf}}$ triples with $H(X) - I(S;XV) = 0$ are achievable.

7. Concluding remarks

The reader may have observed that actually there is a section missing in this paper. We can not give results on partially reversible and robust embedding here. Although it is possible to prove the achievability of a (reasonable) distortion-rate region for this setup we cannot prove the corresponding converse and therefore we omit this "result". The region that we have in mind is actually very similar to the region that is mentioned in Sutivong et al. [**SCCK02**] (see also [**SCC01**]) for channels with state information available to the transmitter whose task it is to send the states and a message to the receiver. In the setup of Sutivong et al. embedding distortion does not play a role, however in our setup it is an essential parameter.

In both the reversible and robust case considered in Section 5, and the partially reversible noise-free case that was subject of Section 6 it makes sense to consider the zero-rate case. In the reversible and robust case this leads to an expression for the smallest possible distortion that can be obtained if we want to transmit an i.i.d. sequence over a discrete memoryless channel by changing it into a channel codeword. This instance of joint source-channel coding shows that reliable transmission is possible also when channel codewords are only slightly different from the source sequences that need to be transmitted to the receiver. In the zero-rate partially reversible noise-free case the composite sequence is close to the host sequence (measured by the embedding distortion) but from this composite sequence a restoration sequence can be derived which is in general even closer to the host sequence (if the restoration distortion and embedding distortion measures are identical). Such a system is actually a scalar quantizer in which a vector quantizer is hidden [**WK02**]. Theorem 6.1 shows what embedding (scalar) distortion and restoration (vector) distortions are jointly achievable.

Appendix A. Details Gelfand-Pinsker achievability proof

This proof is based on strong typicality, see e.g. Cover and Thomas [**CT91**], pp. 370-372. Fix a $0 < \gamma < 1$ and a block-length N.

(a) Consider random variables A and B with finite alphabets $\mathcal{A}$ and $\mathcal{B}$ and joint distribution $\{P(a,b), a \in \mathcal{A}, b \in \mathcal{B}\}$. The marginal distribution of A is $\{P(a), a \in \mathcal{A}\}$, the marginal distribution of B is $\{P(b), b \in \mathcal{B}\}$. First consider the set $\mathcal{T}_\gamma^N(A)$ of typical a-sequences $a^N \in \mathcal{A}^N$ defined by

$$(1-\gamma)NP(a) \leq \#(a|a^N) \leq (1+\gamma)NP(a), \tag{A.1}$$

for all $a \in \mathcal{A}$, where $\#(a|a^N)$ denotes the number of occurrences of a in a^N. Then, by the weak law of large numbers,

$$\lim_{N\to\infty} \sum_{a^N \in \mathcal{T}_\gamma^N(A)} P(a^N) = 1. \tag{A.2}$$

For the conditional probability of b given a with $P(a) > 0$ we can write $P(b|a) = P(a,b)/P(a)$ for $a \in \mathcal{A}, b \in \mathcal{B}$. Next consider for each $a^N \in \mathcal{A}^N$ the set $\mathcal{T}_\gamma^N(B|a^N)$ of b-sequences $b^N \in \mathcal{B}^N$ conditionally typical with a^N, i.e. sequences that satisfy

$$(1-\gamma)\#(a|a^N)P(b|a) \leq \#(a,b|a^N,b^N) \leq (1+\gamma)\#(a|a^N)P(b|a), \tag{A.3}$$

for all $a \in \mathcal{A}, b \in \mathcal{B}$. Again by the weak law of large numbers, for all $a^N \in \mathcal{T}_\gamma^N(A)$,

$$\lim_{N\to\infty} \sum_{b^N \in \mathcal{T}_\gamma^N(B|a^N)} P(b^N|a^N) = 1. \tag{A.4}$$

Note that for all $b^N \in \mathcal{T}_\gamma^N(B|a^N)$ with $a^N \in \mathcal{T}_\gamma^N(A)$ the composition $\#(a,b|a^N,b^N)$ satisfies for all $a \in \mathcal{A}, b \in \mathcal{B}$

$$(1-\gamma)^2 NP(a,b) \le \#(a,b|a^N,b^N) \le (1+\gamma)^2 NP(a,b), \tag{A.5}$$

which implies that $(a^N,b^N) \in \mathcal{T}_{(1+\gamma)^2-1}^N(A,B)$. From (A.4) and (A.5) we obtain that, for all N large enough, the size of the set $\mathcal{T}_\gamma^N(B|a^N)$ for $a^N \in \mathcal{T}_\gamma^N(A)$ is lower bounded by

$$|\mathcal{T}_\gamma^N(B|a^N)| \ge 2^{N[(1-\gamma)^2 H(B|A)-\gamma]}. \tag{A.6}$$

Furthermore, if $b^N \in \mathcal{T}_\gamma^N(B|a^N)$ for $a^N \in \mathcal{T}_\gamma^N(A)$, the composition $\#(b|b^N)$ is such that for all $b \in \mathcal{B}$

$$(1-\gamma)^2 NP(b) \le \#(b|b^N) \le (1+\gamma)^2 NP(b). \tag{A.7}$$

If we now define $Q(a^N) \triangleq \sum_{b^N \in \mathcal{T}_\gamma^N(B|a^N)} P(b^N)$ this leads to

$$Q(a^N) \ge 2^{-N[(1+\gamma)^2 H(B)-(1-\gamma)^2 H(B|A)+\gamma]} \tag{A.8}$$

for N large enough.

Next we define for each $b^N \in \mathcal{B}^N$ the "reverse" set

$$\mathcal{R}_\gamma^N(A|b^N) \triangleq \{a^N \in \mathcal{T}_\gamma^N(A) \text{ such that } b^N \in \mathcal{T}_\gamma^N(B|a^N)\}, \tag{A.9}$$

then the size of the set $\mathcal{R}_\gamma^N(A|b^N)$ is upper bounded by

$$|\mathcal{R}_\gamma^N(A|b^N)| \le 2^{N(1+\gamma)^2 H(A|B)}. \tag{A.10}$$

If we now define $Q(b^N) \triangleq \sum_{a^N \in \mathcal{R}_\gamma^N(A|b^N)} P(a^N)$ this leads to

$$Q(b^N) \le 2^{-N[(1-\gamma)H(A)-(1+\gamma)^2 H(A|B)]}. \tag{A.11}$$

(b) When the encoder receives a state sequence $s^N \notin \mathcal{T}_\eta^N(S)$, an error event E_1 of the first kind occurs. By (A.2) however $\Pr\{E_1\} \le \eta$ for all N large enough.

(c) An error event E_2 of the second kind occurs if among the 2^{NR_u} sequences u^N that were generated at random, and that have label w, there is no sequence in $\mathcal{T}_\gamma^N(U|s^N)$. By event E_1^c the state sequence $s^N \in \mathcal{T}_\eta^N(S)$. Now for large enough N

$$\begin{aligned}
\Pr\{E_2|s^N \in \mathcal{T}_\eta^N(S)\} &= (1-Q(s^N))^{2^{NR_u}} \\
&= 2^{2^{NR_u}\log_2(1-Q(s^N))} \\
&\le 2^{-2^{NR_u}Q(s^N)/\ln(2)} \\
&\le 2^{-2^{NR_u}2^{-N[(1+\eta)^2 H(U)-(1-\eta)^2 H(U|S)+\eta]}/\ln(2)} = \exp(-2^{N\eta})
\end{aligned} \tag{A.12}$$

if $R_u = (1+\eta)^2 H(U) - (1-\eta)^2 H(U|S) + 2\eta$. Note that the last inequality follows from (A.8). From (A.12) we can conclude that also $\Pr\{E_2|E_1^c\} \le \eta$ for all N large enough.

(d) An error event of the third kind occurs if $y^N \notin \mathcal{T}_{(1+\eta)^2-1}^N(Y|s^N,u^N)$. It follows from (A.4) and the fact that $(s^N,u^N) \in \mathcal{T}_{(1+\eta)^2-1}^N(S,U)$ that $\Pr\{E_3|E_1^c,E_2^c\} \le \eta$ for all large enough N.

(e) First note that the occurrence of the complementary events E_1^c, E_2^c, and E_3^c implies that

$$NP(s,u,y)(1-2\eta-\eta^2)^2 \leq \#(s,u,y|s^N,u^N,y^N) \leq NP(s,u,y)(1+\eta)^4. \tag{A.13}$$

Since $(1-\eta)^2 NP(u) \leq \#(u|u^N) \leq (1+\eta)^2 NP(u)$ for $u \in \mathcal{U}$ we obtain

(A.14)
$$\frac{(1-2\eta-\eta^2)^2}{(1+\eta)^2}\#(u|u^N)P(y|u) \leq \#(u,y|u^N,y^N) \leq \frac{(1+\eta)^4}{(1-\eta)^2}\#(u|u^N)P(y|u),$$

and it can be checked that $y^N \in \mathcal{T}_\zeta^N(Y|u^N)$ for $\zeta \triangleq (1+\eta)^4/(1-\eta)^2 - 1$. Moreover $u^N \in \mathcal{T}_{(1+\eta)^2-1}^N(U) \subseteq \mathcal{T}_\zeta^N(U)$. Hence $u^N \in \mathcal{R}_\zeta^N(U|y^N)$. Event E_4 occurs when among the other $2^{N(R+R_u)} - 1$ auxiliary sequences there is at least one sequence $\tilde{u}^N \neq u^N$ that is in the reverse set $\mathcal{R}_\zeta^N(U|y^N)$. Now we can write

$$\begin{aligned} \Pr\{E_4|y^N \in \mathcal{T}_\zeta^N(Y)\} &\leq (2^{N(R+R_u)}-1)Q(y^N) \\ &\leq 2^{N(R+R_u)}2^{-N[(1-\zeta)H(U)-(1+\zeta)^2H(U|Y)]} = 2^{-N\eta} \end{aligned} \tag{A.15}$$

if $R+R_u = (1-\zeta)H(U)-(1+\zeta)^2H(U|Y)-\eta$. Note that the first inequality in (A.15) comes from the union bound, the second follows from (A.11).

(f) For the total error probability we can write

$$\begin{aligned} &\Pr\{E_1 \cup E_2 \cup E_3 \cup E_4\} \\ &= \Pr\{E_1\} + \Pr\{E_1^c, E_2\} + \Pr\{E_1^c, E_2^c, E_3\} + \Pr\{E_1^c, E_2^c, E_3^c, E_4\} \\ &\leq \Pr\{E_1\} + \Pr\{E_2|E_1^c\} + \Pr\{E_3|E_1^c, E_2^c\} + \Pr\{E_4|E_1^c, E_2^c, E_3^c\} \leq 4\eta, \end{aligned} \tag{A.16}$$

for all N large enough.

References

[B00] R.J. Barron, *Systematic Hybrid Analog/Digital Signal Coding,* Ph.D. dissertation, Massachusetts Inst. of Techn., June 2000.

[BCW03] R.J. Barron, B. Chen, G.W. Wornell, "The duality between information embedding and source coding with side information and some applications," *IEEE Trans. Inform. Theory,* vol. IT-49, pp. 1159-1180, May 2003.

[C00] B. Chen, *Design and Analysis of Digital Watermarking, Information Embedding, and Data Hiding Systems,* Ph.D. dissertation, Massachusetts Inst. of Techn., June 2000.

[CW00] B. Chen and G.W. Wornell, "Quantization index modulation: A class of provably good methods for digital watermarking and information embedding," *IEEE Trans. Inform. Theory,* vol. IT-47, pp. 1423-1443, May 2001.

[C83] M.H.M. Costa, "Writing on dirty paper," *IEEE Trans. Inform. Theory,* vol. IT-29, pp. 439-441, May 1983.

[CT91] T.M. Cover and J.A. Thomas, *Elements of Information Theory.* Wiley, New York, 1991.

[FGD02] J. Fridrich, M. Goljan, and R. Du, "Lossless data embedding for all image formats," *Proc. SPIE, Security and Watermarking of imedia Contents,* San Jose, California, 2002.

[GP80] S. Gelfand and M. Pinsker, "Coding for a channel with random parameters", *Problems of Control and Information Theory,* vol. 9, pp. 19-31, 1980.

[HeG83] C. Heegard and A. El Gamal, "On the capacity of computer memory with defects," *IEEE Trans. Inform. Theory,* vol. IT-29, pp. 731-739, September 1983.

[KW02] T. Kalker and F.M.J. Willems, "Capacity bounds and constructions for reversible data-hiding," *Proc. Int. Conf. DSP,* Santorini, Greece, July 1-3, 2002.

[KW03] T. Kalker and F.M.J. Willems, "Capacity bounds and code constructions for reversible data-hiding," *IS & T / SPIE's 15th Ann. Symp. Electronic Imaging,* January 20-24, 2003. Santa Clara, California. CDROM.

[MKW02] D. Maas, T. Kalker, and F. Willems, "Code construction for recursive reversible data-hiding," *Multimedia and Security Workshop at ACM Multimedia 2002,* December 1-6, 2002, Juan-les-Pins, France. CDROM.

[MoS03] P. Moulin and J.A. O'Sullivan, "Information-theoretic analysis of information hiding," *IEEE Trans. Inform. Theory,* vol. IT-49, pp. 563- 593, Mar. 2003.

[SCC01] A. Sutivong, T.M. Cover, and M. Chiang, "Trade-off between message and state information rates," *Proc. ISIT 2001,* Washington DC, June 24 - 29, 2001, p. 303.

[SCCK02] A. Sutivong, T.M. Cover, M. Chiang, and Young-Han Kim, "Rate vs. distortion trade-off for channels with state information," *Proc. ISIT 2002,* Lausanne, Switzerland, June 30 - July 5, 2002, p. 226.

[KT77] A.V. Kuznetsov and B.S. Tsybakov,"Coding in a memory with defective cells," translated from *Prob. Peredach. Inform.*, vol. 10, no. 2, pp. 52-60, April-June 1974.

[WvD01] F.M.J. Willems and M. van Dijk, "Codes for embedding information in grayscale signals," *Proceedings 39th Allerton Conference*, October 1-3, 2001, Monticello, Illinois.

[WK02] F.M.J. Willems and T. Kalker, "Methods for reversible embedding," *Proc. 40th Annual Allerton Conference on Communication, Control, and Computing,* Allerton House, Monticello, Illinois, Oct. 2-4, 2002. CDROM.

[W00] F.M.J. Willems, "An informationtheoretical approach to information embedding," *Proc. 21st Symp. Inform. and Comm. Theory in the Benelux,* May 25-26, 2000, Wassenaar, Werkgemeenschap voor Informatie- en Communicatietheorie, Enschede, pp. 255 - 260.

Eindhoven University of Technology, Eindhoven, The Netherlands. Also Philips Research Laboratories, Eindhoven.

E-mail address: `f.m.j.willems@tue.nl`

Philips Research Laboratories, Eindhoven, The Netherlands. Also Eindhoven University of Technology, Eindhoven.

E-mail address: `ton.kalker@ieee.org`

Part II

Information Theory for Channels

DIMACS Series in Discrete Mathematics
and Theoretical Computer Science
Volume **66**, 2004

Unbounded Loss in Writing on Dirty Paper is Possible

Aaron S. Cohen and Ram Zamir

ABSTRACT. For a generalization of Costa's writing on dirty paper with irregular additive noise distribution, we show that the loss between the zero-interference capacity and the causal side information capacity can be arbitrarily large. This contrasts to the Gaussian noise case, where the capacity loss is zero or at most 1/4 bit for the non-causal and causal side information cases, respectively. This also contrasts to the bounded loss in the "dual" problem of rate distortion with side information.

1. Introduction

We consider a generalization of Costa's writing on dirty paper [**Cos83**], in which a channel has two independent sources of additive noise. The first source, S^n, is known to the transmitter and is referred to as "side information" or "interference". The second source, Z^n, is not directly known to any part of the communication system. The input X^n and the output Y^n are related as $Y^n = X^n + S^n + Z^n$.

Here, we fix constants α and L and a set $A_z \subset \{1, \dots, L\}$. The noise sources are i.i.d. with Z_i uniformly distributed over A_z and S_i uniformly distributed over $\{1, \dots, L\}$, which refer to as "strong interference". Each input symbol X_i is restricted to $\{1, \dots, \alpha\}$. All arithmetic is done modulo L with results in $\{1, \dots, L\}$.

We write the capacity of this channel as $C_{\mathrm{C}}(\alpha, L, A_z)$ or $C_{\mathrm{NC}}(\alpha, L, A_z)$ depending on whether the transmitter side information can be used causally (i.e., X_k can depend only on $S_1, \dots, S_k$) or non-causally (i.e., the input sequence X^n depends on the entire side information sequence S^n). The causal version is sometimes referred to as "writing on dirty tape". Our main result compares the causal case to the zero-interference case, where the output is given by $Y^n = X^n + Z^n$ and the capacity is denoted by $C_{\mathrm{ZI}}(\alpha, L, A_z)$. The zero-interference case is equivalent to both the transmitter and receiver having access to the side information (either causally or non-causally). See Section 2 for the definitions of the capacities.

THEOREM 1.1. *The capacity loss between the zero-interference case and the causal side information case is potentially unbounded. That is, for any* $\Delta > 0$,

---

1991 *Mathematics Subject Classification.* Primary 94A24; 05A99.

Key words and phrases. Channels with Side Information, Rate Loss, Capacity.

A. Cohen supported in part by the National Science Foundation under Grant DMS-0074276.

R. Zamir supported in part by the Israel Science Foundation.

there exists a modulo-additive noise channel with parameters α, L, and A_z such that $C_{ZI}(\alpha, L, A_z) - C_C(\alpha, L, A_z) > \Delta$.

This result contrasts with the uniform bound on the rate loss per degree of freedom in the Wyner-Ziv problem, relative to common fidelity criteria such as the rth-power distortion measure [**Zam96, Zam02**]. Duality between such rate distortion with side information problems and communication with side information problems like writing on dirty paper has been the subject of several recent research efforts [**CC02, BCW03, PCR03**]. The two results may seem in conflict if one views the channel input constraint in Theorem 1.1 as a peak amplitude constraint, which corresponds to an l_∞ norm based measure in the rate-distortion problem.

This result also contrasts with Costa's writing on dirty paper result [**Cos83**] of no loss for Gaussian noise and side information and a power constraint, albeit for the non-causal case. For the causal version of Costa's problem, the loss is bounded by the shaping gain (at most 1/4 bit) [**ESZ00, ESZ02**]. We also see the importance of the necessary conditions of no loss (in the non-causal case) for generalized writing on dirty paper [**CL02**]. The unboundedness of the loss in the non-causal case is addressed in [**CZ03b**]. In the remainder of this paper, we prove Theorem 1.1.

2. Capacities

The capacity is the largest rate at which reliable communication is achievable. For example, a rate R is achievable in the zero-interference case if we can construct sequences (as $n = 1, 2, \dots$) of rate R, blocklength n encoders, $f_n : \{1, \dots, 2^{nR}\} \mapsto \{1, \dots, \alpha\}^n$, and decoders, $g_n : \{1, \dots, L\}^n \mapsto \{1, \dots, 2^{nR}\}$, such that $\Pr(g_n(f_n(W) + Z^n) \neq W) \to 0$ as $n \to \infty$ for W uniformly distributed on $\{1, \dots, 2^{nR}\}$. For the causal side information case, a blocklength-n encoder consists of a sequence (as $k = 1, \dots, k$) of functions,

$$\{f_{n,k} : \{1, \dots, 2^{nR}\} \times \{1, \dots, L\}^k \mapsto \{1, \dots, \alpha\}, 1 \leq k \leq n\}, \tag{2.1}$$

where $f_{n,k}$ produces the kth input X_k from the entire message W and the first k side information values. The capacity for the causal side information case is otherwise the same as for the zero-interference case.

2.1. Zero-Interference. In this case, the capacity is given by

$$C_{\mathrm{ZI}}(\alpha, L, A_z) = \max_{P_X} I(X; X + Z), \tag{2.2}$$

where the maximum is over all distributions on $\{1, \dots, \alpha\}$ and the random variable Z is independent of X and uniformly distributed over A_z. Here, $I(X;Y)$ is the mutual information between random variables X and Y, which can be written as a difference of entropies, $I(X;Y) = H(X) - H(X|Y)$. The entropy of a random variable X with distribution P is defined by $H(X) = -E[\log P(X)] = -\sum_x P(x) \log P(x)$.

We now give a condition on A_z that results in the maximum possible capacity.

LEMMA 2.1. *If A_z satisfies*

$$|z_1 - z_2| \geq \alpha, \quad \forall z_1, z_2 \in A_z, \; z_1 \neq z_2, \tag{2.3}$$

then $C_{ZI}(\alpha, L, A_z) = \log \alpha$.

PROOF. First, note that $C_{\mathrm{ZI}}(\alpha, L, A_z) \leq \log \alpha$ since the transmitter can send one of α values at each time (also since $I(X;Z) \leq H(X) \leq \log \alpha$). However, the decoder can exactly recover any transmitted sequence since the values in A_z are separated by at least α. More technically, if we let P_X be uniform over $\{1,\ldots,\alpha\}$, then (2.3) implies that $\Pr(X+Z=j)$ is $\frac{1}{\alpha|A_z|}$ for $\alpha|A_z|$ values of j. Thus, the mutual information of interest, which can be written $I(X;X+Z)=H(X+Z)-H(X+Z|X)=H(X+Z)-H(Z)$, is $\log\alpha|A_z|-\log|A_z|=\log\alpha$. □

2.2. Causal Side Information. In [**Sha58**], Shannon developed a general formula for capacity with causal side information. This formula involves maximizing over distributions of functions from the side information space to the input space (here, this would be functions from $\{1,\ldots,L\}$ to $\{1,\ldots,\alpha\}$, and there are α^L such functions). In [**ESZ00, ESZ02**], the capacity optimization is simplified for the important case of additive noise and strong interference (e.g., for S uniform over $\{1,\ldots,L\}$). By further imposing a hard input constraint, we see that

$$C_{\mathrm{C}}(\alpha,L,A_z)=\log L-\min_{t:\{1,\ldots,L\}\to\{1,\ldots,\alpha\}} H(t(S)+S+Z). \tag{2.4}$$

This formula only requires an optimization over the α^L functions $t(\cdot)$ from the side information space to the input space, *not* the distributions over such functions.

3. Lower Bounding The Loss

In this section, we prove Theorem 1.1 by lower bounding the difference between the zero-interference capacity and the causal capacity. In Section 3.1, we develop a general lower bound on the entropy of $t(S)+S+Z$. We refer to this random variable as the *effective noise* and denote its probability mass function (PMF) by $\boldsymbol{p}^{\mathrm{eff}}=\boldsymbol{p}^{\mathrm{eff}}(t(\cdot),A_z,L)$. This distribution can be expressed in terms of the sets

$$C_j=\{1\le s\le L\,:\,j-t(s)-s\in A_z\},\quad \forall 1\le j\le L. \tag{3.1}$$

The set C_j consists of the side information values s that contribute to the distribution of the effective noise at j since $s\in C_j$ implies that $t(s)+s+z=j$ for some $z\in A_z$. Indeed, since S is uniformly distributed over $\{1,\ldots,L\}$ and Z is uniformly distributed over A_z, we have that

$$p_j^{\mathrm{eff}}=\Pr(t(S)+S+Z=j)=\frac{|C_j|}{L|A_z|},\quad \forall 1\le j\le L. \tag{3.2}$$

In Section 3.2, we upper bound the number of sets C_j that can be large (and hence the number of values of p_j^{eff} that can be large) using the size of the intersection of A_z with a shifted version of itself. In Section 3.3, we construct a set A_z that satisfies (2.3) yet has a small self intersection. In Section 3.4, we complete the proof by combining the previous steps.

3.1. Majorization Bound on Entropy. We first consider the points in the PMF of the effective noise that are relatively large. For $0\le\beta\le L$, define the set

$$J(\beta,t,A_z,L)=\left\{j\,:\,p_j^{\mathrm{eff}}\ge\beta/L\right\}. \tag{3.3}$$

Clearly, we must have $|J(\beta,t,A_z,L)|\le L/\beta$. The next lemma uses a majorization argument assuming that, for some $\beta<\alpha$, we have $|J(\beta,t,A_z,L)|\le L/\alpha$.

LEMMA 3.1. *For any $\beta<\alpha$ with $|J(\beta,t,A_z,L)|\le L/\alpha$,*

$$H(t(S)+S+Z)\ge|J(\beta,t,A_z,L)|\frac{\alpha}{L}\log\frac{L}{\alpha}+\left(1-|J(\beta,t,A_z,L)|\frac{\alpha}{L}\right)\log\frac{L}{\beta}. \tag{3.4}$$

PROOF. For simplicity we write J for $J(\beta, t, A_z, L)$ during the course of the proof. Consider the PMF $\boldsymbol{p}^*$ on the L-dimensional simplex defined as

$$\boldsymbol{p}^* = \Big[\underbrace{\frac{\alpha}{L}, \frac{\alpha}{L}, \ldots, \frac{\alpha}{L}}_{|J| \text{ times}}, \underbrace{\frac{\beta}{L}, \frac{\beta}{L}, \ldots, \frac{\beta}{L}}_{\left\lfloor \frac{L-|J|\alpha}{\beta} \right\rfloor \text{ times}}, \xi, 0, \ldots, 0\Big], \tag{3.5}$$

where $\xi \leq \beta/L$ is chosen so that $\sum_{j=1}^{L} p_j^* = 1$. The PMF $\boldsymbol{p}^*$ majorizes the PMF $\boldsymbol{p}^{\text{eff}}$, written $\boldsymbol{p}^{\text{eff}} \prec \boldsymbol{p}^*$; see **[MO79]** for the definition of majorization and the results below. To see this, first note that $p_j^{\text{eff}} \leq \frac{\alpha}{L}$ since $|C_j| \leq \alpha |A_z|$ for all j; see (3.1) and (3.2). Thus, the sum of the largest $k \leq |J|$ components of $\boldsymbol{p}^{\text{eff}}$ cannot exceed $\frac{k\alpha}{L}$. Next, from the definition of $J(\beta, t, A_z, L)$ note that only $|J|$ components of $\boldsymbol{p}^{\text{eff}}$ can exceed $\frac{\beta}{L}$. Thus, the sum of the largest $k > |J|$ components cannot exceed $\frac{|J|\alpha + (k-|J|)\beta}{L}$ or 1, whichever is smaller. These two properties insure that the sum of the largest k components of $\boldsymbol{p}^{\text{eff}}$ cannot exceed the sum of the largest k components of $\boldsymbol{p}^*$, which is precisely the definition of majorization. Since entropy is Schur-concave, we can conclude that $H(\boldsymbol{p}^{\text{eff}}) \geq H(\boldsymbol{p}^*)$. We complete the proof by lower bounding the entropy of $\boldsymbol{p}^*$

$$H(\boldsymbol{p}^*) = |J| \frac{\alpha}{L} \log \frac{L}{\alpha} + \left\lfloor \frac{L - |J|\alpha}{\beta} \right\rfloor \frac{\beta}{L} \log \frac{L}{\beta} + \xi \log \frac{1}{\xi} \tag{3.6}$$

$$\geq |J| \frac{\alpha}{L} \log \frac{L}{\alpha} + \left(1 - |J| \frac{\alpha}{L}\right) \log \frac{L}{\beta}. \tag{3.7}$$

□

3.2. Combinatorial Bound on Effective Noise Distribution. We next define a function related to the auto-correlation of the actual noise distribution,

$$M(n, A_z) = |A_z \cap (A_z + n)|. \tag{3.8}$$

Here, $A_z + n = \{a + n : a \in A_z\}$. We upper bound $|J(\beta, t, A_z, L)|$ using

$$M^*(A_z) = \max_{n \neq 0} M(n, A_z). \tag{3.9}$$

LEMMA 3.2. *For any β with $\sqrt{\alpha M^*(A_z) L / |A_z|^2} < \beta < \alpha$ and for all functions $t(\cdot)$,*

$$|J(\beta, t, A_z, L)| \leq \frac{\beta |A_z| - \alpha M^*(A_z)}{\frac{(\beta |A_z|)^2}{L} - \alpha M^*(A_z)}. \tag{3.10}$$

PROOF. We shall again write J for $J(\beta, t, A_z, L)$ in this proof. The intersection of two C_j's can be written as

$$C_j \cap C_{j'} = \{1 \leq s \leq L \,:\, j - s - t(s) \in A_z \cap (A_z + j - j')\}; \tag{3.11}$$

compare with (3.1). This follows since $s \in C_j \cap C_{j'}$ only if $j - s - t(s) \in A_z$ *and* $j' - s - t(s) \in A_z$, and the latter is equivalent to $j - s - t(s) \in (A_z + j - j')$. Since the function $t(\cdot)$ only takes on α different values, we can bound the size of the intersection by

$$|C_j \cap C_{j'}| \leq \alpha M^*(A_z), \;\; \forall j \neq j'; \tag{3.12}$$

see (3.8), (3.9), and (3.11). We also see that

$$|C_j| \geq \beta |A_z|, \quad \forall j \in J; \tag{3.13}$$

see (3.2) and (3.3). We use these bounds to give a combinatorial proof of the lemma.

Let us define $\gamma(s) = |\{j \in J \,:\, s \in C_j\}|$ and $\bar{\gamma} = L^{-1}\sum_{s=1}^{L}\gamma(s)$. That is, $\gamma(s)$ is the number of members of J for which s contributes to the PMF of the effective noise. We first observe that $\sum_{s=1}^{L}\gamma(s) = \sum_{j\in J}|C_j|$, since both sums are counting the same objects. Thus, the average value can be lower bounded using

$$\bar{\gamma} = L^{-1}\sum_{s=1}^{L}\gamma(s) = L^{-1}\sum_{j\in J}|C_j| \geq \frac{\beta|J||A_z|}{L}, \tag{3.14}$$

where we have used (3.13) above. A similar counting argument for pairs of elements gives $\sum_{s=1}^{L}\binom{\gamma(s)}{2} = \sum_{j\neq j'\in J}|C_j \cap C_{j'}|$. Therefore,

$$\frac{\bar{\gamma}(\bar{\gamma}-1)}{2} \leq L^{-1}\sum_{s=1}^{L}\binom{\gamma(s)}{2} = L^{-1}\sum_{j\neq j'\in J}|C_j \cap C_{j'}| \leq \binom{|J|}{2}\frac{\alpha M^*(A_z)}{L}, \tag{3.15}$$

where the first bound follows from Jensen's inequality since $x(x-1)/2$ is convex in x and the second bound follows by (3.12) since there are $\binom{|J|}{2}$ pairs of elements in the set J. The combination of the bounds (3.14) and (3.15) under the condition given in the lemma gives (3.10), and the proof is complete. □

3.3. Construction of A_z Using Arithmetic Differences. We next construct a set A_z and give an upper bound on $M^*(A_z)$ for this A_z. The main idea is to find a set A_z in which (2.3) is satisfied (so that $C_{\mathrm{ZI}}(\alpha, A_z, L)$ is large) and yet the maximum autocorrelation $M^*(A_z)$ is small (so that $C_{\mathrm{C}}(\alpha, A_z, L)$ is small). Before giving our construction, we consider some other possibilities. The set cannot be periodic, since $M^*(A_z)$ would then be large. For example, if $A_z = \{\alpha, 2\alpha, \ldots, \lfloor L/\alpha \rfloor \alpha\}$, then $M^*(A_z) \geq |A_z| - 1$ which is practically the maximum value. Another possibility could be to let A_z be a subset of the exponential series $\{2^k; k = 1, 2, \ldots\}$, which results in the minimal $M^*(A_z) = 1$. However, the size of any such set grows as $\log L$ and the denominator (3.10) would not grow to infinity. A final possibility could be to find a set A_z so that $M(n, A_z) = 1$ for *all* non-zero n, while the size of A_z grows as $\sqrt{L}$. Such a set (known as a planar difference set) exists for all $L = p^k + 1$, where p is a prime and k is an integer [**BJL99**]. A planar difference set minimizes $M^*(A_z)$ for fixed L and $|A_z|$, but does not necessarily satisfy (2.3); see [**CZ03b**] for the use of difference sets in this problem.

To construct our A_z, we let $L = (2\alpha - 1)^2$ and let

$$A_z = \left\{\sum_{k=1}^{j}\alpha + k - 1 \,:\, 0 \leq j < 2\alpha - 1\right\}. \tag{3.16}$$

For example, if $\alpha = 3$, then $A_z = \{3, 7, 12, 18, 25\}$. We refer to this A_z as an *arithmetic difference sequence* since the difference between the jth and $(j+1)$st points in A_z is $\alpha + j - 1$. We thus see that (2.3) is satisfied. Note that for every $z \in A_z \cap (A_z + n)$, there exists integers j_1 and j_2 such that either n or $L - n$ can be represented as $\sum_{k=j_1+1}^{j_2}\alpha + k - 1 = (j_2 - j_1)(2\alpha + j_1 + j_2 - 1)/2$. In other words, the size of $A_z \cap (A_z + n)$ is related to the number of factorizations of n and $L - n$.

Let $d(n)$ be the number of factors of n (e.g., $d(4) = 3$, $d(5) = 2$, $d(6) = 4$). This reasoning gives the following result.

LEMMA 3.3. *For any α, if $L = (2\alpha - 1)^2$ and A_z is defined as in (3.16), then*

$$M(n, A_z) \leq \frac{d(n) + d(L-n)}{2}, \forall 1 \leq n \leq L. \tag{3.17}$$

Consequently, $M^*(A_z) \leq \max_{1 \leq n \leq L} d(n)$.

The final step is to bound the growth of $M^*(A_z)$ as a function of α. (Note that it is necessary to let α grow to infinity in order for the loss to become unbounded.) A sufficient bound on the growth is given by the following number theoretic result on the number of divisors.

LEMMA 3.4. [**HW79**, Theorem 315] *For any $\delta > 0$, $\lim_{n\to\infty} d(n)/n^\delta = 0$.*

3.4. Combining the Bounds. For any β and A_z such that the conditions in Lemmas 3.1 and 3.2 are satisfied, we see that

$$C_{\mathrm{ZI}}(\alpha, L, A_z) - C_{\mathrm{C}}(\alpha, L, A_z) \geq \max_{t(\cdot)} \left(1 - |J(\beta, t, A_z, L)| \frac{\alpha}{L}\right) \log \frac{\alpha}{\beta} \tag{3.18}$$

$$\geq \left(1 - \frac{\beta|A_z| - \alpha M^*(A_z)}{\frac{(\beta|A_z|)^2}{L} - \alpha M^*(A_z)} \frac{\alpha}{L}\right) \log \frac{\alpha}{\beta} \tag{3.19}$$

where (3.18) follows by Lemma 3.1 and (3.19) follows by Lemma 3.2. So far, we have not used the arithmetic difference sequence A_z. For this A_z, we can write the relevant parameters as functions of α. In particular, we have that $L = (2\alpha - 1)^2$, $|A_z| = (2\alpha - 1) = \sqrt{L}$, and that (from Lemmas 3.3 and 3.4) $M^*(A_z) = o(\alpha^{2\delta})$ for any positive δ. Thus, for any $1/2 < \lambda < 1$, let $\beta = \alpha^\lambda$ and the bound becomes

$$C_{\mathrm{ZI}}(\alpha, L, A_z) - C_{\mathrm{C}}(\alpha, L, A_z)$$

$$\geq \left(1 - \frac{\alpha^\lambda(2\alpha - 1) - \alpha M^*(A_z)}{\alpha^{2\lambda} - \alpha M^*(A_z)} \frac{\alpha}{(2\alpha-1)^2}\right)(1-\lambda)\log\alpha \tag{3.20}$$

$$= (1-\lambda)\log\alpha + o(\log\alpha), \tag{3.21}$$

where the asymptotics follow since $M^*(A_z)$ is $o\left(\alpha^{2\lambda-1}\right)$ and $o\left(\alpha^\lambda\right)$ for all $\lambda > 1/2$. Thus, the big fraction grows as $\alpha^{-\lambda}$ which tends to zero as α grows to infinity. This completes the proof of the theorem since we can choose α arbitrarily large.

4. Conclusions

We have shown that the the capacity with causal side information at the transmitter can be arbitrarily smaller than the capacity with side information at both the transmitter and receiver. Indeed, for the arithmetic difference sequence A_z (3.16), we have asymptotically upper bounded $C_{\mathrm{C}}(\alpha, L, A_z)/C_{\mathrm{ZI}}(\alpha, L, A_z)$ by $1/2$.

In [**CZ03a, CZ03b**], we strengthen these results in several ways. First, we extend the capacity analysis to the non-causal case. In particular, we show that the non-causal capacity is given by

$$C_{\mathrm{NC}}(\alpha, L, A_z) = \max_{P_V} \left(H(V) - \min_{t:\{1,\ldots,L\}\to\{1,\ldots,\alpha\}} H(t(V) + V + Z)\right), \tag{4.1}$$

where the maximum is over distributions of the random variable V, which takes value on the set $\{1, \ldots, L\}$. Note that the right hand side of (4.1) is equal to the causal capacity (2.4) when P_V is uniform over $\{1, \ldots, L\}$. Second, we show that if A_z is a difference set, then the non-causal capacity is at most 2 bits/channel use, while the zero-interference capacity is at least $\log \alpha - 1$ bits/channel use for any constraint set of size α. The minus one results from the fact that (2.3) is not satisfied all of the time. Thus, the rate loss can be arbitrarily large in the non-causal case as well. Furthermore, for both causal and non-causal cases, the ratio of capacity with side information to zero-interference capacity can be arbitrarily small. Finally, we would like to generalize our results to continuous alphabets and expected input constraints.

Acknowledgments

The authors would like to thank Uri Erez, Dave Forney, Aaron Hoffman, Ishai Ilani, and Simon Litsyn for helpful comments and suggestions.

References

[BCW03] R. J. Barron, B. Chen, and G. W. Wornell, "The duality between information embedding and source coding with side information and some applications", *IEEE Trans. Inform. Theory*, vol. 49, no. 5, pp. 1159–1180, May 2003.

[BJL99] T. Beth, D. Jungnickel, and H. Lenz, *Design theory*, 2nd ed., vol. 1, Cambridge University Press, 1999.

[CC02] M. Chiang and T. M. Cover, "Duality between channel capacity and rate distortion with two-sided state information", *IEEE Trans. Inform. Theory*, vol. 48, no. 6, 1629–1638, June 2002.

[CL02] A. S. Cohen and A. Lapidoth, "Generalized writing on dirty paper", in *Proc. Int'l. Symposium on Inform. Theory*, Lausanne, Switzerland, June 2002, p. 227.

[Cos83] M. H. M. Costa, "Writing on dirty paper", *IEEE Trans. Inform. Theory*, vol. 29, no. 3, 1983, pp. 439–441.

[CZ03a] A. S. Cohen and R. Zamir, "The rate loss in writing on dirty paper", in preparation, 2003.

[CZ03b] A. S. Cohen and R. Zamir, "Writing on dirty paper in the presence of difference set noise", in *Proc. Allerton Conf. on Comm., Control and Computing*, 2003.

[ESZ00] U. Erez, S. Shamai, and R. Zamir, "Capacity and lattice-strategies for cancelling known interference", in *Proc. Int'l Symposium on Inform. Theory and its Applications*, Honolulu, HI, 2000, pp. 681–684.

[ESZ02] U. Erez, S. Shamai, and R. Zamir, "Capacity and lattice-strategies for cancelling known interference", submitted to *IEEE Trans. Inform. Theory*, 2002.

[HW79] G. H. Hardy and E. M. Wright, *An introduction to the theory of numbers*, 5th ed., Oxford, Clarendon, 1979.

[MO79] A. W. Marshall and I. Olkin, *Inequalities: Theory of majorization and its applications*, Academic Press, New York, 1979.

[PCR03] S. S. Pradhan, J. Chou, and K. Ramchandran, "Duality between source coding and channel coding and it extension to the side information case", *IEEE Trans. Inform. Theory*, vol. 49, no. 5, May 2003, pp. 1181–1203.

[Sha58] C. E. Shannon, "Channels with side information at the transmitter", *IBM Journal of Research and Development*, 1958, pp. 289–293.

[Zam96] R. Zamir, "The rate loss in the Wyner-Ziv problem", *IEEE Trans. Inform. Theory*, vol. 42, no. 6, 1992, pp. 2073–2084.

[Zam02] R. Zamir, "The half a bit loss of robust source/channel codebooks", in *Proc. Inform. Theory Workshop*, Bangalore, India, Oct. 2002, p. 123.

Division of Applied Mathematics, Brown University, Providence, Rhode Island 02912, United States

E-mail address: acohen@dam.brown.edu

Research Laboratory for Electronics, Massachusetts Institute of Technology, Cambridge, Massachusetts 02139, United States

Current address: Department of Electrical Engineering, Tel Aviv University, Ramat Aviv 69978, Israel

E-mail address: zamir@eng.tau.ac.il

DIMACS Series in Discrete Mathematics
and Theoretical Computer Science
Volume **66**, 2004

A Game-theoretic Look at the Gaussian Multiaccess Channel

Richard J. La and Venkat Anantharam

ABSTRACT. We study the issue of how to fairly allocate communication rate among the users of a Gaussian multiaccess channel. All users are assumed to value rate equally and each is assumed to have no limit on its desired rate. We adopt a cooperative game-theoretic viewpoint, i.e. it is assumed that the users can potentially form coalitions off line to threaten other users with jamming the channel, using this as an argument for deserving a larger share of the rate. To determine the characteristic function of the game, we first determine the capacity region of the Gaussian multiaccess arbitrarily varying channel, with an operational meaning of capacity somewhat modified from the usual one, which is more appropriate to our context and permits time sharing. We then propose a solution concept for the game through a set of natural fairness axioms and prove that there exists a unique fair allocation that satisfies the axioms. Moreover, we demonstrate that the unique allocation is always feasible and lies in the core of the game. It is also shown to possess some intuitively natural qualitative properties as the signal to noise ratio varies.

1. Introduction

There has been a resurgence of interest in multiuser information theory. Major driving forces behind this are the growth of networking, the increasing penetration of wireless local access (including multiple antenna techniques), and the drive to develop sensor networks using ad hoc wireless networking technology.

Apart from playing an obvious role in meeting the technical challenges needed to develop and deploy such systems, we believe that information theory can also help to provide insight into the important social choice issues that arise from this networking explosion. By this we mean aspects of multiple agent interaction that are normally studied in the economics literature, such as fairness, incentive compatibility, mechanism design, pricing, revenue maximization, budget balance, etc. [**3, 7**]. When the system is modeled as having a single objective, which may be shared by the agents or imposed from above, some of these issues disappear, and such problems fall within the traditional domain of optimization theory. There is a well established body of such work in the information-theoretic literature. However, much less attention has been paid to the study of situations where the individual agents may have objectives that are in conflict with each other.

Key words and phrases. Cooperative game theory, Gaussian multiaccess channel, arbitrarily varying channel.

The first author was supported in part by the Minta Martin Award from the University of Maryland.

The second author was supported by DARPA Grants F30602-00-2-0538 and N66001-00-C-8062, and by ONR Grant N00014-1-0637.

In this paper we make a start on the discussion of such issues by considering one of the most basic multiuser information theory models : the Gaussian multiaccess channel. We view the channel from the point of view of the users and ask : what is a fair way for the users to choose an operating point in the capacity region? The answer, of course, depends on what one means by "fair". To this end we adopt the viewpoint of cooperative game theory. First of all, we assume that all users value rate equally and each user has no intrinsic limit on its desired rate. We envision subsets of the users as being able to form contracts off line that enable them to act as coalitions; such a coalition of users can threaten the others with using its power to jam the shared channel and can implicitly demand a larger share of the resource as a payoff to avoid the execution of such a threat. Cooperative game theory addresses this by defining a notion called the "characteristic function" : this associates to each subset of the players (users) a number which is the largest payoff that they are guaranteed even if all the other players form a coalition to work against them. A fair allocation may then be roughly defined as one that is compatible with the characteristic function (precise definitions are given later – what we mean is that the allocation should lie in the core of the game) and satisfies some natural set of fairness axioms. Our goal in this paper is to carry out this cooperative game-theoretic program for the Gaussian multiaccess channel.

There are several aspects that we need to address. First, we need to determine the characteristic function of the game, and for this we need to solve a version of the Gaussian multiaccess arbitrarily varying channel problem. This problem has been known to the community for some time and the major bottleneck to its solution is the ability, in the traditional formulation, of the jammer to use a very skewed power distribution in its jamming sequence, preventing the use of time sharing. In our context it is natural to think of all users as aligned to a common underlying time frame, so we are able to finesse this problem by working with an alternative operational meaning of capacity region (which reduces to the usual definition in the absence of a jammer). This development is carried out in Section 2. Secondly, we need to propose a natural set of fairness axioms for the problem. We do this, with the notion of envy-freeness, in Section 4, after a quick introduction to standard cooperative game-theoretic concepts in Section 3. Finally, we need to demonstrate the existence and uniqueness of a rate allocation that is both compatible with the characteristic function (in the core) and feasible – *i.e.,* it is in the capacity region. We do this in Section 5. We make some concluding remarks in Section 6. Some simple inequalities that we use in the proof are gathered in an Appendix.

2. Capacity region of Gaussian multiaccess arbitrarily varying channel

We first discuss the standard power constrained Gaussian multiaccess channel with an alternative operational interpretation of capacity that yields a capacity region identical to the original one. The reason for doing this will become apparent when we turn to the analysis of the version of the Gaussian multiaccess arbitrarily varying channel that is necessary for us to set up the game-theoretic formulation of the problem we are interested in.

2.1. A mildly different look at the usual Gaussian multiaccess channel. Consider a Gaussian multiple access channel with I users and let $\mathcal{I} = \{1, \ldots, I\}$ denote the set of users. A *coding scheme* at block length n for this channel is a collection of sequences of codes $\{\mathcal{C}_i(k), k \geq 1\}$, one for each user, where $\mathcal{C}_i(k) \; : \; M_i(k) \mapsto \mathbf{R}^n$. Here $(M_i(k), k \geq 1)$ is a sequence of positive integers. The coding scheme is assumed to be common knowledge to all users and to the receiver. The coding scheme is said to satisfy power constraints $\underline{\Gamma} = (\Gamma_1, \dots, \Gamma_I)$ if for each $i \in \mathcal{I}$, each $k \geq 1$, and each $m \in M_i(k)$ we have

$$\sum_{j=1}^{n} x_j^2 \leq n\Gamma_i$$

where $\underline{x} = (x_1, \dots, x_n) = \mathcal{C}_i(k)(m)$ is the codeword corresponding to message m of user i in block k. We denote a coding scheme at block length n by $\mathcal{C}^{(n)}$.

Let

$$\rho_i = \liminf_K \frac{\sum_{k=1}^{K} \log M_i(k)}{nK}$$

where the logarithm is to base 2, and let $\underline{\rho}$ denote $(\rho_1, \dots, \rho_I)$. We call $\underline{\rho}$ the rate vector of the coding scheme $\mathcal{C}^{(n)}$.

Each user i uses its sequence of codebooks in the coding scheme to encode a sequence of messages block by block, being allowed to send one of $M_i(k)$ messages in block k. Suppose user i sends message $m_i(k)$ in block k. The received vector in block k is

$$\underline{y} = \sum_{i=1}^{I} \underline{x}_i(k) + \underline{z}(k)$$

where $\underline{x}_i(k) = (x_1, \dots, x_n) = \mathcal{C}_i(k)(m_i(k))$ is the codeword corresponding to message $m_i(k)$ of user i in block k and $\underline{z} = (z_1, \dots, z_n)$ is a sequence of independent Gaussian random variables of mean zero and variance σ^2. A decoding scheme for the given coding scheme is a sequence $(d(k), k \geq 1)$ where $d(k) : \mathbf{R}^n \mapsto [M_1(k)] \times \dots \times [M_I(k)] \cup \{*\}$. Here $[M_i(k)]$ denotes the set $\{1, \dots, M_i(k)\}$. The probability of error of the decoding scheme in block k is defined as

$$e(k) = P(d(k)(\underline{y}) \neq (m_1(k), \dots, m_I(k))$$

where $\underline{y}$ is the received vector in block k corresponding to the users having transmitted messages $m_i(k)$ in block k and the choices of messages in the message sets of the individual users assumed to be uniformly distributed. The probability of error of the decoding scheme is defined as $e = \sup_{k \geq 1} e(k)$. Finally, for the given coding scheme at block length n, $\mathcal{C}^{(n)}$, let $e(\mathcal{C}^{(n)})$ denote the infimum of the probability of error over all decoding schemes for that coding scheme.

We say coding is achievable at rate vector $\underline{R} = (R_1, \dots, R_I)$ if there is a sequence of coding schemes $(\mathcal{C}^{(n)}, n \geq 1)$ such that both $e(\mathcal{C}^{(n)}) \to 0$ as $n \to \infty$ and $\liminf_n \underline{\rho}(\mathcal{C}^{(n)}) \geq \underline{R}$. The capacity region of the Gaussian multiaccess channel with I users satisfying power constraints $\underline{\Gamma}$ is defined as the closure of all achievable rate vectors.

THEOREM 2.1. *The capacity region of the Gaussian multiaccess channel as defined in the preceding paragraphs is identical to the capacity region of the channel as it is usually defined.*

PROOF. The usual definition of coding at block length n differs from our definition precisely in that it presumes a coding scheme where each user uses the same code in each block, *i.e.*, $M_i(k) \equiv M_i$ and $\mathcal{C}_i(k) \equiv \mathcal{C}_i$ for each $k \geq 1$, and also requires that the same decoding rule be used in each block, *i.e.*, $d(k) \equiv d$ for each $k \geq 1$. One then has $e(k) = e$ for each $k \geq 1$ and the rate vector of the code becomes $\underline{\rho} = (\rho_1, \dots, \rho_I)$ with $\rho_i = \frac{\log M_i}{n}$. Also, in the usual case, one has exactly the same definition for the concept of coding being achievable at rate $\underline{R}$ as we have, only that one has already restricted to coding schemes using the same set of codebooks in each block.

It follows then that the capacity region of a Gaussian multiaccess channel, as we have defined it, is no smaller than the capacity region as usually defined. For the converse, suppose we are given a sequence of coding schemes in our sense, $(\mathcal{C}^{(n)}, n \geq 1)$, such that both $e(\mathcal{C}^{(n)}) \to 0$ as $n \to \infty$ and $\liminf_n \underline{\rho}(\mathcal{C}^{(n)}) \geq \underline{R}$. Then, for any $\delta > 0$, for all sufficiently large n we have $\underline{\rho}(\mathcal{C}^{(n)}) \geq \underline{\bar{R}}$ where $\underline{\bar{R}} = (\bar{R}_1, \dots, \bar{R}_I)$ with $\bar{R}_i = (R_i - \delta)^+$. Given $\epsilon > 0$, however small, we then also have, for all sufficiently large n, that for every block $k \geq 1$ of the coding scheme $\mathcal{C}^{(n)}$ there is a decoding rule for the associated family of codes $\mathcal{C}_i^{(n)}(k), 1 \leq i \leq \mathcal{I}$, resulting in average probability of error at most ϵ. By applying Fano's inequality in the usual way we then conclude that for any subset $\mathcal{J} \subseteq \mathcal{I}$ of users we have

$$\sum_{i \in \mathcal{J}} \frac{1}{n} \log M_i^{(n)}(k) \leq \frac{1}{2} \log(1 + \frac{\sum_{i \in \mathcal{J}} P_i}{\sigma^2}) + D\epsilon$$

where D is a fixed constant that does not depend on n, k, δ or ϵ. From this we conclude that

$$\sum_{i \in \mathcal{J}} \bar{R}_i \leq \frac{1}{2} \log(1 + \frac{\sum_{i \in \mathcal{J}} P_i}{\sigma^2}) + D\epsilon \,.$$

Since this holds for every $\delta > 0$ and every $\epsilon > 0$, we conclude that the capacity region of the channel in our sense is identical to the capacity region of the channel as it is usually defined. □

2.2. A fresh look at the Gaussian multiaccess arbitrarily varying channel. We next turn to study the Gaussian multiaccess channel where a subset of the users form a coalition attempting to limit the ability of the other users to communicate. We call these users the jamming users, while the remaining users are called the communicating users. Assume, for notational convenience, that the jamming users are users $J + 1 \leq i \leq I$, so that the communicating users are users $1 \leq i \leq J$. We assume that communication takes places with all users using codes at block length n to determine their input into the channel. We may then describe the overall communication system via a coding scheme with notation essentially as above, while noting the following crucial difference : since the jamming users are no longer participating in the communication process, we assume that the inputs to the channel of the jamming users are private knowledge to the coalition of jammers. The sequences of codes of the communicating users are assumed to be common knowledge to all users and to the receiver. The communicating users should be able to communicate irrespective of the jamming strategy of the jamming users. With this in mind we may set up the problem as follows :

Since the jamming users do not wish to communicate, we do not ascribe a set of messages to such users, but rather use the notation $\underline{s}_i(k)$ for the input to the channel of the jamming user i, $J + 1 \leq i \leq I$, in the block k. Thus a coding scheme $\mathcal{C}^{(n)}$ at block length n for a Gaussian multiaccess channel with I users where users $J + 1 \leq i \leq I$ are the jamming users is a collection of sequences of codes $\{\mathcal{C}_i(k), k \geq 1\}$, one for each communicating user, $1 \leq i \leq J$, where $\mathcal{C}_i(k) \; : \; M_i(k) \mapsto \mathbf{R}^n$ and a collection of sequences $(\underline{s}_i(k), k \geq 1)$, one for each jamming user i, $J+1 \leq i \leq I$, where $\underline{s}_i(k) \in \mathbf{R}^n$. The coding scheme is said to satisfy power constraints $\underline{\Gamma} = (\Gamma_1, \dots, \Gamma_I)$ if for each $1 \leq i \leq J$, each $k \geq 1$, and each $m \in M_i(k)$ we have

$$\sum_{j=1}^{n} x_j^2 \leq n\Gamma_i$$

where $\underline{x} = (x_1, \ldots, x_n) = C_i(k)(m)$ is the codeword corresponding to message m of user i in block k, and further, for each $J + 1 \leq i \leq I$ and each $k \geq 1$ we have

$$\sum_{j=1}^{n} s_{ij}(k)^2 \leq n\Gamma_i$$

where $\underline{s}_i(k) = (s_{i1}(k), \ldots, s_{in}(k))$ is the input to the channel of jamming user i. Let

$$\rho_i = \liminf_K \frac{\sum_{k=1}^K \log M_i(k)}{nK}, \quad 1 \leq i \leq J,$$

where the logarithm is to base 2, and let $\underline{\rho}$ denote $(\rho_1, \ldots, \rho_J)$. We call $\underline{\rho}$ the rate vector of the block coding scheme $\mathcal{C}^{(n)}$.

Suppose communicating user i, $1 \leq i \leq J$, sends message $m_i(k)$ in block k. The received vector in block k is

$$\underline{y} = \sum_{i=1}^{J} \underline{x}_i(k) + \sum_{i=J+1}^{I} \underline{s}_i(k) + \underline{z}(k)$$

where $\underline{x}_i(k) = (x_1, \ldots, x_n) = C_i(k)(m_i(k))$ is the codeword corresponding to message $m_i(k)$ of communicating user i in block k, and $\underline{z} = (z_1, \ldots, z_n)$ is a sequence of independent Gaussian random variables of mean zero and variance σ^2. A decoding scheme for the given coding scheme is a sequence $(d(k), k \geq 1)$ where $d(k) : \mathbf{R}^n \mapsto [M_1(k)] \times \ldots \times [M_J(k)] \cup \{*\}$. The probability of error of the decoding scheme in block k is defined as

$$e(k) = \sup_{\{\underline{s}_i(k), J+1 \leq i \leq I\}} P(d(k)(\underline{y}) \neq (m_1(k), \ldots, m_I(k))$$

where $\underline{y}$ is the received vector in block k corresponding to the communicating users having transmitted messages $m_i(k)$ in block k and the choices of messages of the communicating users in the individual message sets assumed to be uniformly distributed. The probability of error of the decoding scheme is defined as $e = \sup_{k \geq 1} e(k)$. Finally, for the given coding scheme at block length n, $\mathcal{C}^{(n)}$, let $e(\mathcal{C}^{(n)})$ denote the infimum of the probability of error over all decoding schemes for that coding scheme.

We say coding is achievable at rate vector $\underline{R} = (R_1, \ldots, R_J)$ if there is a sequence of coding schemes $(\mathcal{C}^{(n)}, n \geq 1)$ such that both $e(\mathcal{C}^{(n)}) \to 0$ as $n \to \infty$ and $\liminf_n \underline{\rho}(\mathcal{C}^{(n)}) \geq \underline{R}$. The capacity region of the Gaussian multiaccess channel with I users where users $J + 1 \leq i \leq I$ are jamming users, and satisfying power constraints $\underline{\Gamma}$, is defined as the closure of all achievable rate vectors.

THEOREM 2.2. *The capacity region of the Gaussian multiaccess channel with I users where users $J + 1 \leq i \leq I$ are jamming users, and satisfying power constraints $\underline{\Gamma}$, is a convex set.*

PROOF. Suppose coding is achievable at rate vectors $\underline{R}_0$ and $\underline{R}_1$, where $\underline{R}_0 = (R_1^0, \ldots, R_J^0)$ and $\underline{R}_1 = (R_1^1, \ldots, R_J^1)$, and let $\lambda \in (0, 1)$. We will show that coding is achievable at rate vector $\underline{R}_\lambda$, where $\underline{R}_\lambda = \lambda \underline{R}_1 + (1 - \lambda)\underline{R}_0$. Choose integers $(l_n, n \geq 1)$ such that $\frac{l_n}{n} \to \lambda$ and consider the sequence of coding schemes where the one at block length n is constructed by repeatedly interlacing l_n blocks of the coding scheme at block length n in the sequence that verifies the achievability of $\underline{R}_1$ with $n - l_n$ blocks of the coding scheme at block length n in the sequence that verifies the achievability of $\underline{R}_0$. □

THEOREM 2.3. *The capacity region of the Gaussian multiaccess channel with I users where users $J+1 \leq i \leq I$ are jamming users, and satisfying power constraints $\underline{\Gamma}$ is*

$$\{(R_1, \ldots, R_J) \ : \ R_i = 0 \ \text{for all } 1 \leq i \leq J \text{ such that } \Gamma_i \leq \Lambda \text{ and} \quad \sum_{i \in A} R_i \leq C(\sum_{i \in \hat{A}} \Gamma_i, \Lambda + \sigma^2) \ \text{for all } A \subseteq [J] \ \} \tag{1}$$

where Λ denotes $(\sum_{i=J+1}^{I} \sqrt{\Gamma_i})^2$, $C(\Gamma, \Sigma)$ denotes $\frac{1}{2}\log(1+\frac{\Gamma}{\Sigma})$, $[J]$ denotes $\{1, \ldots, J\}$, and for $A \subseteq [J]$, $\hat{A}$ denotes $\{i \in A \ : \ \Gamma_i > \Lambda\}$.

PROOF. *Proof of the converse* : Since the jamming users are acting as a single coalition we can think of them as a single agent, which we will call the combined jammer. This combined jammer is power limited to Λ, as can be seen from the fact that the jamming users can coherently combine their jamming vectors.

Let $1 \leq i \leq J$ be such that $\Gamma_i \leq \Lambda$. Consider any sequence $(\mathcal{C}^{(n)}, n \geq 1)$ of coding schemes for which $\limsup_n \sup_{k \geq 1} M_i^{(n)}(k) \geq 2$. We claim that $\limsup_n e(\mathcal{C}^{(n)}) \geq \frac{1}{4}$. This proves that no vector of rates $\underline{R} = (R_1, \ldots, R_J)$ with $R_i > 0$ is achievable. Hence the capacity region of the channel is contained in the set of vectors of rates where $R_i = 0$ for all $1 \leq i \leq J$ such that $\Gamma_i \leq \Lambda$.

The proof of this follows Blackwell's argument, which was also used in [**1**] (see the beginning of the Appendix on page 23 of [**1**]). Given any $n_0 > 0$ there is $n > n_0$ and at least one block k with $M_i^{(n)}(k) \geq 2$. We now consider the family of jamming strategies for the combined jammer, indexed by $M_i^{(n)}(k)$, with strategy m being to use as jamming sequence (in block k, which is all we are interested in) the codeword $\mathcal{C}_i^{(n)}(k)(m)$ of user i corresponding to his message m. We think of the combined jammer as choosing one of these strategies uniformly at random. Then, for any decoding rule in block k, the error probability in block k for decoding the message of user i, averaged over equiprobable messages and averaged over the strategies of the jammer is at least $\frac{1}{4}$ (in fact very close to $\frac{1}{2}$ if $M_i^{(n)}(k)$ is large) because any decoding rule that is correct when the message is m and the jamming strategy is $\tilde{m}$ $(m \neq \tilde{m})$ is wrong when the message is $\tilde{m}$ and the jamming strategy is m. This means that the jammer has a strategy whose probability of error for decoding the message of user i, averaged over equiprobable messages, is at least $\frac{1}{4}$. This being true in block k, and since the error probability of a coding scheme is given by the supremum of the error probability over its blocks, we have $e(\mathcal{C}^{(n)}) \geq \frac{1}{4}$. Since given arbitrary $n_0 > 0$ there is $n > n_0$ for which this is true, we have $\limsup_n e(\mathcal{C}^{(n)}) \geq \frac{1}{4}$.

Next consider a sequence of coding schemes where for all sufficiently large n we have $M_i^{(n)}(k) = 1$ for all $k \geq 1$ and for all $1 \leq i \leq J$ such that $\Gamma_i \leq \Lambda$. Given $\tilde{\Lambda} < \Lambda$ consider the strategy of the combined jammer for the coding scheme at block length n which is to pick a jamming sequence whose components are independent Gaussian random variables of mean zero and variance $\tilde{\Lambda}$ and to use the same jamming sequence in each block. The probability that the jamming sequence does not meet the power constraint goes to zero as $n \to \infty$. In any block of the coding scheme at block length n the average probability of error, averaged over equiprobable messages and the randomly chosen jamming sequence, is bounded above by the sum of the probability that the randomly chosen jamming sequence does not meet the power constraint and the maximum over jamming sequences that do meet the power constraint of the average probability of error, averaged over equiprobable messages. Since this goes to zero as $n \to \infty$ it must be the case that in each block the rate vectors asymptotically satisfy the capacity constraints for a Gaussian multiaccess channel with noise power $\tilde{\Lambda} + \sigma^2$. We may now let $\tilde{\Lambda} \to \Lambda$ to complete the proof of the converse.

Proof of achievability :

We first need to verify that everything in the paper of Csiszar and Narayan goes through with the following noise model : instead of the noise vector $\underline{V} = (V_1, \ldots, V_n)$ in a block having i.i.d Gaussian coordinates, it is modeled as

$$\underline{V} = \underline{W} + \underline{U}_1 + \ldots + \underline{U}_L$$

where $\underline{W} = (W_1, \ldots, W_n)$ has i.i.d Gaussian coordinates, $\underline{W}, \underline{U}_1, \ldots, \underline{U}_L$ are independent, and each $\underline{U}_l$ is chosen uniformly at random from a sphere in $\mathbf{R}^n$ of fixed radius.

Let $\underline{R} = (R_1, \ldots, R_J)$ be a corner point of the rate region given in the theorem. To clarify what this means let us assume, for notational convenience, that $\Gamma_i > \Lambda$ for $1 \leq i \leq K$ and $\Gamma_i \leq \Lambda$ for $K + 1 \leq i \leq J$ and let us consider the corner point corresponding to the decoding order : decode user 1, followed by user 2, and so on ending with user K. By this we mean the rate vector $\underline{R} = (R_1, \ldots, R_J)$ with

$$\begin{aligned}
R_1 &= C(\Gamma_1, \sum_{i=2}^{K} \Gamma_i + \Lambda + \sigma^2) \\
R_2 &= C(\Gamma_2, \sum_{i=3}^{K} \Gamma_i + \Lambda + \sigma^2) \\
&\vdots \\
R_K &= C(\Gamma_K, \Lambda + \sigma^2) \\
R_i &= 0 \text{ for } K + 1 \leq i \leq J .
\end{aligned}$$

Fix $\delta > 0$ with $\delta < \min_{1 \leq i \leq K} R_i$. We will demonstrate the achievability of the rate vector $\underline{\bar{R}}$ where $\underline{\bar{R}} = (\bar{R}_1, \ldots, \bar{R}_J)$ with $\bar{R}_i = (R_i - \delta)$ for $1 \leq i \leq K$ and $\bar{R}_i = 0$ for $K + 1 \leq i \leq J$. From the result on the convexity of the capacity region that we have proved earlier, on letting $\delta \to 0$, this will complete the proof.

We will show the existence of a sequence of coding schemes that verify the achievability of $\underline{\bar{R}}$ by a random coding argument. The coding schemes that we will show the existence of will be coding schemes in the usual sense, *i.e.,* they will be constant in each block. Thus we focus on any one block of the coding scheme to be constructed at block length n and drop the notation for the specific block under consideration.

Following Csiszar and Narayan, we change the normalization of power so that the additive Gaussian noise in the channel has mean zero and variance $\frac{\sigma^2}{n}$ in each coordinate and so that each codeword of each communicating user i and the jamming sequence of each jamming user i have norm at most $\sqrt{\Gamma_i}$ respectively.

Suppose user 1 chooses a random codebook $\mathcal{C}_1$ as follows : he first picks $M_1 = 2^{n\bar{R}_1}$ independent vectors in $\mathbf{R}^n$, each uniformly distributed on the sphere of radius 1, call them $\underline{z}_{11}, \ldots, \underline{z}_{1M_1}$. These are scaled by $\sqrt{\Gamma_1}$ to give the codewords $\underline{x}_{1i_1} = \sqrt{\Gamma_1} \underline{z}_{1i_1}, 1 \leq i_i \leq M_1$. Users 2 through K choose their random codebooks by an analogous procedure.

The average probability of error of maximum likelihood decoding for user K, assuming that users 1 through $K - 1$ have already been correctly decoded, when the jamming users use jamming sequences $\underline{s}_i$, $J + 1 \leq i \leq I$ and users $K + 1 \leq i \leq J$ send the zero vector, is given by

$$\bar{e}_K(\underline{s}) = \frac{1}{M_K} \sum_{i_K=1}^{M_K} P(\|\underline{x}_{Ki_K} + \sum_{i=J+1}^{I} \underline{s}_i + \underline{W} - \underline{x}_{Kj_K}\|^2 \leq \| \sum_{i=J+1}^{I} \underline{s}_i + \underline{W}\|^2$$
$$\text{for some } j_K \neq i_K) .$$

This should be thought of as a random variable, which is a function of the realization of the random codebook $\mathcal{C}_K$ as well as $\underline{s} = (\underline{s}_i, J+1 \leq i \leq I)$. Here $\underline{W} = (W_1, \ldots, W_n)$ with coordinates that are i.i.d. Gaussian with mean zero and variance $\frac{\sigma^2}{n}$.

Fix $1 \leq k < K$. The average probability of error of maximum likelihood decoding for user k, assuming that users 1 through $k-1$ (this set is empty if $k = 1$) have already been correctly decoded, when the jamming users use jamming sequences $\underline{s}_i$, $J+1 \leq i \leq I$ and users $K+1 \leq i \leq J$ send the zero vector is given by

$$\bar{e}_k(\underline{s}) = \frac{1}{M_k} \sum_{i_k=1}^{M_k} P(\|\underline{x}_{ki_k} + \sum_{l=k+1}^{K} \underline{x}_{li_l} + \sum_{i=J+1}^{I} \underline{s}_i + \underline{W} - \underline{x}_{kj_k}\|^2$$
$$\leq \| \sum_{l=k+1}^{K} \underline{x}_{li_l} + \sum_{i=J+1}^{I} \underline{s}_i + \underline{W}\|^2 \text{ for some } j_k \neq i_k) .$$

Here i_l for $k+1 \leq l \leq K$ are thought of as random, uniformly distributed on $[M_l]$ respectively. Also, $\bar{e}_k(\underline{s})$ is thought of as a random variable which is a function of the realizations of the random codebooks $\mathcal{C}_k$ through to $\mathcal{C}_K$ as well as of $\underline{s} = (\underline{s}_i, J+1 \leq i \leq I)$.

For each $1 \leq k \leq K$, let $\bar{e}_k$ denote $\sup_{\underline{s}} \bar{e}_k(\underline{s})$. Again these are thought of as random variables dependent on the realization of the random codebooks.

We now consider the expectations of each of these quantities, taken over the distribution of the random codebooks. Consider first the expectation of $\bar{e}_K$. On the event that the random codebook $\mathcal{C}_K$ is derived from scaling a set of unit norm vectors that satisfy the conditions of Lemma 1 of Csiszar and Narayan, $\bar{e}_K$ is pointwise dominated by γ_n for some $\gamma_n \to 0$ as $n \to \infty$. Further, the complement of this event has probability bounded above by τ_n for some $\tau_n \to 0$ as $n \to \infty$. Hence the expectation of $\bar{e}_K$ is bounded above by some α_n where $\alpha_n \to 0$ as $n \to \infty$.

Next consider any $1 \leq k < K$. On the event that the codebook $\mathcal{C}_k$ is derived from scaling a set of unit norm vectors that satisfy the conditions of Lemma 1 of Csiszar and Narayan, $\bar{e}_k$ is pointwise dominated by γ_n for some $\gamma_n \to 0$ as $n \to \infty$, where in making this claim we appeal to the extension of the results in Csiszar and Narayan to noise models which are of the extended type discussed above, the salient point being that we now treat the entire vector $\sum_{l=k+1}^{K} \underline{x}_{li_l} + \underline{W}$ as a noise vector (where we recall that for each $k+1 \leq l \leq K$ we think of i_l as a random variable drawn uniformly at random from $[M_l]$). As before the complement of this event has probability bounded above by τ_n for some $\tau_n \to 0$ as $n \to \infty$. Hence the expectation of $\bar{e}_k$ is bounded above by some α_n where $\alpha_n \to 0$ as $n \to \infty$.

We may therefore find realizations of the codebooks $\mathcal{C}_k, 1 \leq k \leq K$ such that for these realizations each of the quantities $\bar{e}_k, 1 \leq k \leq K$ is bounded above by α_n, where $\alpha_n \to 0$ as $n \to \infty$. This completes the proof. □

3. Cooperative games

In Section 2 we have characterized the capacity region of a Gaussian multiaccess channel when a subset of users form a coalition of jamming users. The formation of such coalitions will depend on the offered rates to each individual user by proposed coalitions. In other words, a user will join a coalition of communicating users only if it feels that it is getting a fair share of the available rate based on its perception. A natural question that arises in such a scenario is how these users should allocate the available rate among themselves, given the possibility of forming different coalitions among themselves. Providing a plausible answer to this question for the Gaussian multiaccess channel is the main aim of this paper. We approach this question via cooperative game theory. In this section we therefore first briefly review the language of cooperative game theory [**5**].

Let $\mathcal{I} = \{1, 2, \cdots, I\}$ be the set of players. The problem is to decide how to allocate some fungible quantity between the users (in our case this quantity is communication rate), which we will call value. A key assumption is that all the users have a shared notion of value. A non-empty subset of $\mathcal{I}$ is called a coalition. The basic mathematical object that describes the game between the players is its *characteristic function*. This is a function v defined on the subsets of $\mathcal{I}$, which associates to each $S \subset \mathcal{I}$ the maximum value that the players in S can acquire from the game regardless of what the players in $\mathcal{I} \setminus S$ do. Namely, the players in S, acting as a coalition, can guarantee themselves as a group the value $v(S)$ even if the players in $\mathcal{I} \setminus S$, acting as a coalition, work to minimize the total value achieved by the players in S.

In the Gaussian multiaccess channel viewed as a game, $v(S)$ for a subset of users $S \subseteq \mathcal{I}$ is seen, from Theorem 2.3, to be

$$v(S) = C(\Gamma_{\hat{S}}, \Lambda_{\mathcal{I}\setminus S} + \sigma^2) \tag{2}$$

where $\Lambda_{\mathcal{I}\setminus S} = (\sum_{i\in\mathcal{I}\setminus S} \sqrt{\Gamma_i})^2$, $\hat{S} = \{i \in S \mid \Gamma_i > \Lambda_{\mathcal{I}\setminus S}\}$, and $\Gamma_{\hat{S}} = \sum_{i\in\hat{S}} \Gamma_i$.

It is generally assumed that the characteristic function should satisfy the following two properties :

(i) The value of characteristic function for an empty set is zero, *i.e.*, $v(\emptyset) = 0$.
(ii) Suppose that S and T are two disjoint coalitions, *i.e.*, $S \cap T = \emptyset$. Then,

$$v(S) + v(T) \leq v(S \cup T) \qquad \text{(superadditivity)} \tag{3}$$

In our case, these properties are apparent. The truth of the second property is most easily seen from the obvious fact that the sum of the sum rates achievable by two disjoint coalitions of users each acting separately when its complementary set of users acts to jam it is no bigger than the sum rate that can be achieved when both these sets of users group together to form a single coalition whose complement is then acting to jam it.

An imputation for an I-person game v is a vector $x = (x_1, \cdots, x_I)$ that satisfies (i) $\sum_{i\in\mathcal{I}} x_i = v(\mathcal{I})$, and (ii) $x_i \geq v(\{i\})$ for all $i \in \mathcal{I}$. One can argue that any proposed allocation of value among the users that is not an imputation is unreasonable. This is because, first of all there is no point in leaving some value unallocated so the first condition had better be satisfied, and second, if some user is given an allocation that is less than what he/she could get by acting unilaterally even when everybody else forms a coalition to work against him/her, this user will not be satisfied with the proposed allocation.

We say that an imputation x dominates another imputation y through a coalition S if (i) $x_i > y_i$ for all $i \in S$, and (ii) $\sum_{i\in S} x_i \leq v(S)$. Also, we say that x dominates y if there exists some coalition S such that x dominates y through S. One can argue that any proposed allocation of value among the users that is dominated by another allocation is unreasonable. This is because if the proposed allocation (necessarily an imputation), say y, is dominated by some other imputation, say x, through a subset of users S, then the users in S will find it to their advantage to disregard the proposed allocation, since they can act as a coalition to guarantee each of them a strictly better allocation even when the users in $\mathcal{I} \setminus S$ work as a coalition against them.

The set of all undominated imputations is called the *core* of the game, denoted by $C(v)$. With the axioms we have assumed on the characteristic function, one can show that $C(v)$ is given by the set of imputations that satisfy $\sum_{i\in S} x_i \geq v(S)$ for all $S \subset \mathcal{I}$. Also, what we have argued so far suggests that any proposed allocation of value among the users must lie in the core of the game if it is to be considered reasonable.

Here it is necessary, unfortunately, to point out a key problem with cooperative game theory : there are examples of games where the core can be empty. Such games would then seem to have no reasonable solution. On the other hand, in many examples the core is nonempty and for such games (of which, as we will prove, the Gaussian multiaccess game is one) the core provides a natural starting point in the search for reasonable solutions. However, for most games, including the one we are interested in, the core has more than one element. Thus one needs some additional natural set of axioms to further restrict the set of reasonable solutions. We will carry out this program for our game in the next two sections. To end this section, we mention another very popular axiomatic approach to the search for a notion of solution for a cooperative game, due to Shapley. Our purpose in describing the Shapley approach is only for completeness : axiom (a3) in the axiomatic formulation below is not natural for the class of games we consider, since there is no natural way in which the sums of the characteristic functions of two of our games is physically relevant. Indeed, the Shapley value also suffers from another problem, in that it can result in an allocation that is not in the core, as we will later show it does in our game. Nevertheless, being such a popular concept, it merits some discussion.

Let π be a permutation of the set of players $\mathcal{I}$. Then, we denote by πv the new game u such that, for all $S = \{i_1, \cdots, i_s\} \subseteq \mathcal{I}$, $u(\{\pi(i_1), \pi(i_2), \cdots, \pi(i_s)\}) = v(S)$. Clearly, this new game is the game v with the roles of the players interchanged by the permutation π.

Shapley proposed to study an allocation of value $\phi[v]$ in game v that satisfies the following set of axioms:

a1. Additive partition of the value of the game: $\sum_{i\in\mathcal{I}} \phi_i[v] = v(\mathcal{I})$.
a2. Invariance under permutation: for any permutation π and $i \in \mathcal{I}$, $\phi_{\pi(i)}[\pi v] = \phi_i[v]$.
a3. If u and v are any two games, $\phi_i[u + v] = \phi_i[u] + \phi_i[v]$.

He showed that there is a unique function ϕ defined on all games that satisfies the axioms above. It is given by

$$\phi_i[v] = \sum_{T\subset\mathcal{I}, i\in T} \frac{(t-1)!(I-t)!}{I!} \left(v(T) - v(T - \{i\})\right) , \tag{4}$$

where $t = |T|$. This allocation is called the *Shapley value* of the game.

4. An envy-free allocation of rate

In the preceding section we have already implicitly introduced our notion of the Gaussian multiaccess game through definition of its characteristic function, given in equation (2). Communication rate plays the role of value in our game, and the maximum value that a coalition of users can get even when the other users work as a coalition against them is the maximum sum capacity of the corresponding Gaussian multiaccess arbitrarily varying channel, whose capacity region we characterized in Theorem 2.3.

In this section we first discuss the core of our game. The core can be immediately written down as the set of allocations satisfying a set of linear inequalities determined from the characteristic function, as was mentioned in Section 3 – all this uses is that the characteristic function of our game is superadditive. The most important point for us is that the core contains all feasible imputations, as demonstrated in subsection 4.1. We then propose a natural set of fairness axioms which we will work with in Section 5 to propose an allocation in the game that is uniquely defined as the one satisfying our axioms and will turn out to be both feasible and in the core. This is done in subsection 4.2. Finally in subsection 4.3 we briefly return to the Shapley value and give a simple example of a Gaussian multiaccess game where the Shapley value is neither feasible nor in the core.

4.1. The core of a Gaussian multiaccess game. Recall that the capacity region for a Gaussian multiaccess channel, which can be thought of as the capacity region corresponding to the game when all the users form a single communicating coalition, is given by the set of rate vectors satisfying

$$\sum_{i\in A} R_i \leq \quad C(\Gamma_A, \sigma^2) \qquad \text{for all } A \subseteq \mathcal{I} \ . \tag{5}$$

We denote the set of rate vectors $\underline{R}$ that satisfy (5) by $\mathcal{C}$. The main result about the core of our game that interests us is the following :

PROPOSITION 1. *The core of the game* $C(v)$ *contains* $\{\underline{R} \in \mathcal{C} \mid \sum_{i\in\mathcal{I}} R_i = C(\Gamma_{\mathcal{I}}, \sigma^2)\}$.

PROOF. We show that if $\underline{R}$ belongs to the capacity region and $\sum_{i\in\mathcal{I}} R_i = C(\Gamma_{\mathcal{I}}, \sigma^2)$, then for all $S \subseteq \mathcal{I}$,

$$\sum_{i\in S} R_i \geq C(\Gamma_S, \lambda_{\mathcal{I}\setminus S} + \sigma^2) \geq v(S) \ .$$

This can be easily shown from the following:

$$\begin{aligned} \sum_{i\in S} R_i &= C(\Gamma_{\mathcal{I}}, \sigma^2) - \sum_{j\in\mathcal{I}\setminus S} R_j \\ &\geq C(\Gamma_{\mathcal{I}}, \sigma^2) - C(\Gamma_{\mathcal{I}\setminus S}, \sigma^2) \\ &= C(\Gamma_S, \lambda_{\mathcal{I}\setminus S} + \sigma^2) \ , \end{aligned}$$

where the inequality follows from the capacity constraint in (5) with $A = \mathcal{I} \setminus S$. □

One sees from this result that the core of our game is not empty. In fact, *all* imputations in $\mathcal{C}$ belong to the core, and so it is also the case that the core is not unique. Therefore, to arrive at a reasonable allocation that serves as a solution for the game, we need to propose a natural system of axioms that one can argue the allocation should satisfy. This allocation should, of course, also be feasible for it to make sense. We now turn to this issue.

4.2. Fair allocation. We now propose an axiomatic system to define a fair allocation in our game. The first two axioms of Shapley (axioms a1 and a2) which require efficiency and invariance under permutation respectively, are both natural requirements : there is no point in leaving some rate unallocated, and any solution concept that yields different values for the same player if they are labelled differently is hardly natural. Hence, we impose the following two axioms:

(f1) Efficiency or Pareto optimality: $\sum_{i\in\mathcal{I}} \psi_i(v) = C(\Gamma_{\mathcal{I}}, \sigma^2)$.
(f2) Invariance under permutation: for any permutation π and $i\in\mathcal{I}$, $\psi_i(v) = \psi_{\pi(i)}(\pi v)$, where πv is the permuted game.

To these, we add a third axiom based on the notion of envy [**2**].[1] The second axiom of Shapley states that two users with the same power constraint should receive the same rate. Now suppose that we take two users i and j such that $\Gamma_i > \Gamma_j$. Then, clearly user i can act as if its power constraint were also Γ_j instead of Γ_i by not consuming all of its power constraint. Let this new game with user i's power constraint reduced to Γ_j be

[1]The definition of envy is slightly modified in our context from the reference.

denoted by $v^{i,j}$. We say that user i envies user j if $\psi_j(v) \neq \psi_i(v^{i,j})$, and we measure it by the difference $\psi_j(v) - \psi_i(v^{i,j})$. Based on this definition of envy we impose the following fairness constraint:

(f3) Fairness (or envy-free allocation)

$$\sum_{\{j \neq i | \Gamma_j \leq \Gamma_i\}} \psi_j(v) - \psi_i(v^{i,j}) = \sum_{\{j \neq i | \Gamma_j < \Gamma_i\}} \psi_j(v) - \psi_i(v^{i,j}) = 0 \text{ for all } i \in \mathcal{I},$$

where the first equality is a consequence of axiom (f2).

We will show in the following section that axiom (f3) is equivalent to the stronger requirement that for all i and j such that $\Gamma_i > \Gamma_j$

$$\psi_j(v) - \psi_i(v^{i,j}) = 0 . \tag{6}$$

Also in that section we will show that there is a unique allocation satisfying our axioms and this allocation is feasible and in the core.

4.3. About the Shapley value. To end this section we briefly discuss the popular concept of Shapley value, even though we have argued that the axiom system underlying this concept is not appropriate for our game. We give an example of a Gaussian multiaccess game where the Shapley value is not feasible and does not lie in the core.

Consider the following example: there are three users with $\Gamma_1 = 10.1, \Gamma_2 = 10$, and $\Gamma_3 = 1$. The noise power is given by $\sigma^2 = 10$. In this example, from (4), the Shapley value of user 3 is

$$\begin{aligned}\phi_3[v] &= \frac{1}{3}\left(v(\{3\}) - v(\emptyset)\right) + \frac{1}{6}\left((v(\{1,3\}) - v(\{1\})) + (v(\{2,3\}) - v(\{2\}))\right) \\ &\quad + \frac{1}{3}\left(v(\{1,2,3\}) - v(\{1,2\})\right) \\ &= \frac{1}{3}(0-0) + \frac{1}{6}((C(10.1,20) - 0) + (0-0)) + \frac{1}{3}(C(21.1,10) - C(20.1,11)) \\ &= 0.07206 .\end{aligned}$$

However, the rate of user 3 cannot be larger than $C(\Gamma_3, \sigma^2) = C(1, 10) = 0.06875$ from the capacity constraint in (5). Therefore, the Shapley value of this game does not belong to $\mathcal{C}$.

In addition, one can see that the Shapley value of the game does not belong to the core of the game by realizing that $\phi_1[v] + \phi_2[v] = C(21.1, 10) - \phi_1[v] < C(20.1, 11) = v(\{1, 2\})$.

5. Existence, uniqueness and properties of a fair allocation

In this section we first show that there exists a unique function ψ, defined on all games, which satisfies axioms (f1) - (f3) in Section 4.2, and then prove that the unique allocation always lies in the capacity region, *i.e.,* it is feasible. Since the allocation is efficient it then follows from Proposition 1 that it is also in the core. Without loss of generality we assume that users are ordered by decreasing power constraint Γ_i throughout the rest of this paper.

5.1. Existence of a fair allocation.

THEOREM 5.1. *There exists a unique rate allocation that satisfies axioms (f1) through (f3).*

PROOF. Consider the following rate allocation: for all $i \in \mathcal{I}$

$$\varphi_i(v) = \frac{C(i\Gamma_i + \sum_{j=i+1}^{I} \Gamma_j, \sigma^2) - \sum_{j=i+1}^{I} \varphi_j(v)}{i} . \tag{7}$$

One can see that such an allocation can be easily computed recursively, starting with user I. Axiom (f1) is trivially satisfied by construction. Suppose that there are two users i and $i+1$ such that $\Gamma_i = \Gamma_{i+1}$. We show that $\varphi_i(v) = \varphi_{i+1}(v)$. In order to show this we prove that for all $k = 1, \cdots, I-1$,

$$\varphi_k(v) - \varphi_{k+1}(v) = \frac{C(k\Gamma_k + \sum_{j=k+1}^{I} \Gamma_j, \sigma^2) - C(k\Gamma_{k+1} + \sum_{j=k+1}^{I} \Gamma_j, \sigma^2)}{k} . \tag{8}$$

This can be proved by showing that the sum of the right-hand side of (8) and $\varphi_{k+1}(v)$ from (7) equals $\varphi_k(v)$, and the details are provided in [**4**]. From (8) one can see that if $\Gamma_i = \Gamma_{i+1}$, then $\varphi_i(v) - \varphi_{i+1}(v) = 0$. Hence, this proves that the allocation given by (7) satisfies axiom (f2).

In order to show that axiom (f3) is satisfied, we first prove the following Lemma.

LEMMA 1. *For all i and j such that $\Gamma_i > \Gamma_j$, $\varphi_i(v^{i,j}) = \varphi_j(v)$.*

PROOF. This can be easily shown from

$$\begin{aligned}
\varphi_i(v^{i,j}) &= \frac{C(j\Gamma_j + \sum_{k=j+1}^{I} \Gamma_k, \sigma^2) - \sum_{k=j+1}^{I} \varphi_k(v^{i,j})}{j} \\
&= \frac{C(j\Gamma_j + \sum_{k=j+1}^{I} \Gamma_k, \sigma^2) - \sum_{k=j+1}^{I} \varphi_k(v)}{j} \\
&= \varphi_j(v) ,
\end{aligned}$$

where the first equality is a consequence of axiom (f2), and the second equality follows because for all $k > j$, $\varphi_k(v) = \varphi_k(v^{i,j})$, *i.e.*, the rates of users $k > j$ are not affected by the replacement of power constraint of user i by that of user j as can be seen from (7). □

Now axiom (f3) holds trivially from

$$\sum_{\{j>i|\Gamma_j<\Gamma_i\}} (\varphi_j(v) - \varphi_i(v^{i,j})) = \sum_{\{j>i|\Gamma_j<\Gamma_i\}} (0) = 0 .$$

Note that, combined with Lemma 1, axiom (f3) implies the stronger condition given in (6) under $\varphi(\cdot)$.

5.2. Uniqueness of the fair allocation. We now prove the uniqueness of rate allocation that satisfies axioms (f1) - (f3). For $i = 2, \cdots, I$, let $u^{i,j}, j < i$, be the game where the power constraints of the users are given by $\tilde{\Gamma}_k$

$$\tilde{\Gamma}_k = \begin{cases} \Gamma_i & j \le k \le i \\ \Gamma_k & \text{otherwise} \end{cases} .$$

Let $i = I$. From the fairness constraint in axiom (f3), we have $\psi_{I-1}(u^{I,I-1}) = \psi_I(v) = \psi_I(u^{I,I-1})$. Starting with $j = I-1$ repeatedly applying the fairness requirement to user $j-1$ in game $u^{I,j}$ with decreasing j, $j = 2, \cdots, I-1$, yields

$$\psi_{j-1}(u^{I,j-1}) = \psi_j(u^{I,j-1}) = \cdots = \psi_{I-1}(u^{I,I-1}) = \psi_I(v) ,$$

which, for $j = 2$, gives us $\psi_I(v) = \frac{C(I\cdot\Gamma_I, \sigma^2)}{I}$ from axiom (f2) since all users have the same power constraint Γ_I in game $u^{I,1}$. Following similar steps with $v^{j,I}$, $j = 1, \cdots, I-1$, also leads to $\psi_j(v^{j,I}) = \psi_I(v) = \frac{C(I\cdot\Gamma_I, \sigma^2)}{I}$.

Decrease i by one, *i.e.*, let $i = I-1$. Following the above argument starting with $j = i$ and successively applying the fairness requirement to $u^{i,j-1}$ with decreasing j yields

$$\psi_i(v) = \frac{1}{i}\left(C(i\Gamma_i + \sum_{k=i+1}^{I} \Gamma_k, \sigma^2) - \sum_{k=i+1}^{I} \psi_k(v) \right) = \varphi_i(v)\,. \tag{9}$$

Repeating this procedure after decrementing i by one until $i = 1$ leads to (9) for all $i = 1, \cdots, I$. This completes the proof. □

5.3. On the structure of the fair allocation. We now provide an intuitive way of understanding the structure of the fair allocation whose existence and uniqueness was demonstrated in the last two subsections. Consider the following scenario. Initially all users start with the same power constraint Γ_I, where each user receives a rate of $\frac{C(I\cdot\Gamma_I,\sigma^2)}{I}$. Now suppose that user $I-1$ decides to unilaterally increase its power constraint to Γ_{I-1}. Then, since user $I-1$ was willing to pay the price of increasing its power constraint (assuming that it finds this decision beneficial), the increase in the total rate, namely $C(\Gamma_{I-1} + (I-1)\cdot\Gamma_I, \sigma^2) - C(I\Gamma_I, \sigma^2)$, should be assigned to user $I-1$, while the rates of the other users remain the same. Suppose now user $I-2$ pays the price to increase its power constraint to Γ_{I-1}. Then, the gain enjoyed by user $I-1$ before should be shared with user $I-2$ as well. More specifically, the increase in the total rate $C(2\Gamma_{I-1} + (I-2)\cdot\Gamma_I, \sigma^2) - C(I\Gamma_I, \sigma^2)$, should be equally shared by users $I-2$ and $I-1$. Similar arguments can be made when another user unilaterally changes its power constraint. The rate allocation in (7) is a generalization of the allocation scheme resulting from this thought process.

5.4. Feasibility and reasonableness of the fair allocation. We now demonstrate that the rate allocation $\varphi(v)$ lies in the capacity region, i.e. it feasible, and then show that it is in the core of the game.

THEOREM 5.2. *The rate allocation given by (7) lies in the capacity region, i.e., for all* $S \subseteq \mathcal{I}$, $\sum_{i\in S}\varphi_i(v) \le C\left(\sum_{i\in S}\Gamma_i, \sigma^2\right)$.

PROOF. Before we prove the theorem we note that several simple inequalities will be used in the proof, all of which can be obtained from the strict concavity of log function. These are gathered in the Appendix.

We prove the theorem by induction. If there is only one user, the theorem is true. Now suppose that the theorem holds for any set of k users, $k = 1, \cdots, K$. We now show that the theorem is true for any set of $K+1$ users.

Let $\mathcal{I}^{K+1} = \{1, \cdots, K+1\}$ be the set of users and denote the game by v. We let $S^j = \mathcal{I}^{K+1} \setminus \{j\}$, where $j \in \mathcal{I}^{K+1}$, and denote the game only with the users in S^j by v^j. In order to prove that theorem holds with $\mathcal{I}^{K+1}$, it suffices to show that, for all $j \in \mathcal{I}^{K+1}$

$$\varphi_i(v^j) > \varphi_i(v),\ i \neq j\,. \tag{10}$$

Eq. (10) tells us that when a new user enters the game, the rate of the existing users strictly decreases. Therefore, from the induction hypothesis, for all strict subsets S of $\mathcal{I}^{K+1}$ we will have $\sum_{i\in S}\varphi_i(v) < C\left(\sum_{i\in S}\Gamma_i, \sigma^2\right) = \sum_{i\in S}\varphi_i(v^S)$, where v^S is the game only with users in S. Thus, the theorem will follow.

We consider the following three cases: (1) $\Gamma_j = \Gamma_{K+1}$, (2) $\Gamma_j = \Gamma_1$, and (3) $\Gamma_1 < \Gamma_j < \Gamma_{K+1}$.

case (1). $\Gamma_j = \Gamma_{K+1}$: In this case, from axiom (f2), without loss of generality we assume that $j = K+1$. First, from (7) and (8)

$$\begin{aligned}\varphi_K(v) &= \varphi_{K+1}(v) + (\varphi_K(v) - \varphi_{K+1}(v)) \\ &= \frac{C((K+1)\Gamma_{K+1}, \sigma^2)}{K+1} + \frac{C(KP_K + \Gamma_{K+1}, \sigma^2) - C((K+1)\Gamma_{K+1}, \sigma^2)}{K} \\ &= \frac{C(KP_K + \Gamma_{K+1}, \sigma^2)}{K} - \frac{C((K+1)\Gamma_{K+1}, \sigma^2)}{K(K+1)}\end{aligned}$$

$$\begin{aligned}&\varphi_K(v^{K+1}) - \varphi_K(v) \\ &= \frac{1}{K}\left(C(K\cdot\Gamma_K, \sigma^2) - C(K\cdot\Gamma_K + \Gamma_{K+1}, \sigma^2) + \frac{1}{K+1}C((K+1)\Gamma_{K+1}, \sigma^2)\right) \\ &\geq \frac{1}{K}\left(\frac{1}{K+1}C((K+1)\Gamma_{K+1}, \sigma^2) - \left(C((K+1)\Gamma_{K+1}, \sigma^2) - C(K\Gamma_{K+1}, \sigma^2)\right)\right) \\ &> 0\,,\end{aligned}$$

where the first inequality follows from (16) (with $x = K\cdot\Gamma_{k+1}, y = K\cdot\Gamma_k$, and $z = \Gamma_{k+1}$), and the second inequality from (17) (with $x = \Gamma_{k+1}$, and $z = 0$). From (8) and (19), one can show that for all $i = 1, \cdots, K-1$,

$$\begin{aligned}\varphi_i(v) - \varphi_{i+1}(v) &= \frac{1}{i}\left(C(i\Gamma_i + \sum_{j=i+1}^{K+1}\Gamma_j, \sigma^2) - C(i\Gamma_{i+1} + \sum_{j=i+1}^{K+1}\Gamma_j, \sigma^2)\right) \\ &\leq \frac{1}{i}\left(C(i\Gamma_i + \sum_{j=i+1}^{K}\Gamma_j, \sigma^2) - C(i\Gamma_{i+1} + \sum_{j=i+1}^{K}\Gamma_j, \sigma^2)\right) \\ &= \varphi_i(v^{K+1}) - \varphi_{i+1}(v^{K+1})\end{aligned}$$

where the equality holds only if $\Gamma_i = \Gamma_{i+1}$. Eq. (10) now follows from the above two inequalities.

case (2). $\Gamma_j = \Gamma_1$: again, from axiom (f2), without loss of generality we assume that $j = 1$. This case follows directly from (8) and (18) because, for all $i = 2, \cdots, K$,

$$\varphi_i(v) - \varphi_{i+1}(v) = \frac{1}{i}\left(C(i\Gamma_i + \sum_{k=i+1}^{K+1}\Gamma_k, \sigma^2) - C(i\Gamma_{i+1} + \sum_{k=i+1}^{K+1}\Gamma_k, \sigma^2)\right)$$

$$\leq \frac{1}{i-1}\left(C((i-1)\Gamma_i + \sum_{k=i+1}^{K+1}\Gamma_k, \sigma^2) - C((i-1)\Gamma_{i+1} + \sum_{k=i+1}^{K+1}\Gamma_k, \sigma^2)\right) \tag{11}$$

$$= \varphi_i(v^1) - \varphi_{i+1}(v^1)\,.$$

and $\varphi_{K+1}(v) = \frac{1}{K+1}C((K+1)\Gamma_{K+1}, \sigma^2) < \frac{1}{K}C(K\Gamma_{K+1}, \sigma^2) = \varphi_{K+1}(v^1)$.

case (3). $\Gamma_1 < \Gamma_j < \Gamma_{K+1}$: Similarly as in (11), we have for all $i = j+1, \cdots, K$,

$$\varphi_i(v) - \varphi_{i+1}(v) \leq \varphi_i(v^j) - \varphi_{i+1}(v^j) \text{ and } \varphi_{K+1}(v) < \varphi_{K+1}(v^j)\,. \tag{12}$$

We first show that, for all $\Gamma_j \in [\Gamma_{j+1}, \Gamma_{j-1}]$

$$\varphi_{j-1}(v) - \varphi_{j+1}(v) \leq \varphi_{j-1}(v^j) - \varphi_{j+1}(v^j)\,. \tag{13}$$

Suppose that $\Gamma_{j-1} = \Gamma_{j+1}$. Then, (13) is trivially true from axiom (f2). Hence, we assume that $\Gamma_{j-1} > \Gamma_{j+1}$. One can see from (7) that $\varphi_{j-1}(v) - \varphi_{j+1}(v)$ is strictly decreasing in

Γ_j over the range $[\Gamma_{j+1},\ \Gamma_{j-1}]$. For more details, see [**4**]. Hence, it suffices to show that (13) is true with $\Gamma_j = \Gamma_{j+1}$ as follows:

$$\begin{aligned}
&\varphi_{j-1}(v) - \varphi_{j+1}(v) = \varphi_{j-1}(v) - \varphi_j(v) \\
&\quad = \frac{1}{j-1}\left(C((j-1)\Gamma_{j-1} + \sum_{k=j}^{K+1} \Gamma_k, \sigma^2) - C((j-1)\Gamma_j + \sum_{k=j}^{K+1} \Gamma_k, \sigma^2) \right) \\
&\quad < \frac{1}{j-1}\left(C((j-1)\Gamma_{j-1} + \sum_{k=j+1}^{K+1} \Gamma_k, \sigma^2) - C((j-1)\Gamma_{j+1} + \sum_{k=j+1}^{K+1} \Gamma_k, \sigma^2) \right) \\
&\quad = \varphi_{j-1}(v^j) - \varphi_{j+1}(v^j)\,,
\end{aligned}$$

where the inequality follows from (19).

Now we show that for all $i = 1, \cdots, j-2$,

$$\varphi_i(v) - \varphi_{i+1}(v) \leq \varphi_i(v^j) - \varphi_{i+1}(v^j)\,. \tag{14}$$

This follows trivially because

$$\begin{aligned}
&\varphi_i(v) - \varphi_{i+1}(v) \\
&\quad = \frac{1}{i}\left(C(i \cdot \Gamma_i + \sum_{k=i+1}^{I} \Gamma_k, \sigma^2) - C(i \cdot \Gamma_{i+1} + \sum_{k=i+1}^{I} \Gamma_k, \sigma^2) \right) \\
&\quad \leq \frac{1}{i}\left(C(i \cdot \Gamma_i + \sum_{k=i+1, k\neq j}^{I} \Gamma_k, \sigma^2) - C(i \cdot \Gamma_{i+1} + \sum_{k=i+1, k\neq j}^{I} \Gamma_k, \sigma^2) \right) \\
&\quad = \varphi_i(v^j) - \varphi_{i+1}(v^j)\,,
\end{aligned}$$

where the inequality is true from (19). Eq. (10) now follows from (12) - (14). □

THEOREM 5.3. *The rate allocation $\varphi(v)$ is in the core of the game.*

PROOF. This is a simple consequence of the fact that the core contains all imputations that are in $\mathcal{C}$ and $\varphi(v)$ is an imputation (from axiom (f1)) and lies in $\mathcal{C}$ from Theorem 5.2. □

5.5. Qualitative properties of the fair allocation. Finally, we investigate how the allocation $\varphi(v)$ changes as one varies the noise power σ^2. In order to make the dependence on σ^2 explicit we denote by $\varphi^\sigma(v)$ the rate allocation given the noise power σ^2.

THEOREM 5.4. *The rate allocation $\varphi^\sigma(v)$ satisfies the following: for all $i, j \in \mathcal{I}$ such that $\Gamma_j > \Gamma_i$*

(1) $\frac{\varphi_j^\sigma(v)}{\varphi_i^\sigma(v)}$ *is strictly increasing in $\sigma, \sigma > 0$.*
(2) $\lim_{\sigma^2 \downarrow 0} \frac{\varphi_j^\sigma(v)}{\varphi_i^\sigma(v)} = 1$.
(3) $\lim_{\sigma^2 \uparrow \infty} \frac{\varphi_j^\sigma(v)}{\varphi_i^\sigma(v)} = \frac{\Gamma_j}{\Gamma_i}$.

From (1) - (3) for any i and j such that $\Gamma_j \geq \Gamma_i$, we have

$$1 \leq \frac{\varphi_j(v)}{\varphi_i(v)} \leq \frac{\Gamma_j}{\Gamma_i}\,.$$

PROOF. The first property can be proved by showing that for all $k = 1, \cdots, I-1$, and $\epsilon > 0$,

$$\frac{\varphi_k^{\sigma+\epsilon}(v) - \varphi_{k+1}^{\sigma+\epsilon}(v)}{\varphi_k^{\sigma}(v) - \varphi_{k+1}^{\sigma}(v)} \geq \frac{\varphi_{k+1}^{\sigma+\epsilon}(v) - \varphi_{k+2}^{\sigma+\epsilon}(v)}{\varphi_{k+1}^{\sigma}(v) - \varphi_{k+2}^{\sigma}(v)} \tag{15}$$

where Γ_{I+1} and $\varphi_{I+1}^{\sigma}(v)$ are defined to be zero. The manipulations required to prove this are standard, so, in the interest of meeting the page count constraint, they are left to the reader. If necessary, see [**4**] for the details.

We now prove that $\lim_{\sigma^2 \downarrow 0} \frac{\varphi_j^{\sigma}(v)}{\varphi_i^{\sigma}(v)} = 1$. In order to show this, it suffices to show that, for all $k = 1, \cdots, I-1$, $\frac{\varphi_k^{\sigma}(v) - \varphi_{k+1}^{\sigma}(v)}{\varphi_I^{\sigma}(v)} \to 0$ as $\sigma \downarrow 0$. This can be easily shown as follows. From (7) $\varphi_I^{\sigma}(v) = \frac{C(I \cdot \Gamma_I, \sigma^2)}{I} \to \infty$ as $\sigma \downarrow 0$. On the other hand, from (8)

$$\begin{aligned}
\varphi_k^{\sigma}(v) - \varphi_{k+1}^{\sigma}(v) &= \frac{C(k\Gamma_k + \sum_{j=k+1}^{I} \Gamma_j, \sigma^2) - C(k\Gamma_{k+1} + \sum_{j=k+1}^{I} \Gamma_j, \sigma^2)}{k} \\
&= \frac{C(k(\Gamma_k - \Gamma_{k+1}), \sigma^2 + k\Gamma_{k+1} + \sum_{j=k+1}^{I} \Gamma_j)}{k} \\
&\to \frac{C(k(\Gamma_k - \Gamma_{k+1}), k\Gamma_{k+1} + \sum_{j=k+1}^{I} \Gamma_j)}{k} \qquad \text{as } \sigma \downarrow 0\,.
\end{aligned}$$

Thus, the difference $\varphi_k^{\sigma}(v) - \varphi_{k+1}^{\sigma}(v)$ is decreasing in σ and $\lim_{\sigma \downarrow 0} \left(\varphi_k^{\sigma}(v) - \varphi_{k+1}^{\sigma}(v)\right)$ is finite for all $k = 1, \cdots, I-1$, whereas $\lim_{\sigma \downarrow 0} \varphi_I^{\sigma}(v) = \infty$. Therefore, $\frac{\varphi_k^{\sigma}(v)}{\varphi_I^{\sigma}(v)} \downarrow 1$ as $\sigma \downarrow 0$ for all $k = 1, \cdots, I$.

To prove the last property we show that for all $k = 1, \cdots, I-1$,[2]

$$\frac{\varphi_k^{\sigma}(v) - \varphi_{k+1}^{\sigma}(v)}{\varphi_{k+1}^{\sigma}(v) - \varphi_{k+2}^{\sigma}(v)} \to \frac{\Gamma_k - \Gamma_{k+1}}{\Gamma_{k+1} - \Gamma_{k+2}} \qquad \text{as } \sigma \uparrow \infty\,.$$

The rest can be easily proved from that $\frac{d}{dx}\log(1+x) = \frac{1}{(1+x)\ln 2}$.[3] From (8)

$$\begin{aligned}
\frac{\varphi_k^{\sigma}(v) - \varphi_{k+1}^{\sigma}(v)}{\varphi_{k+1}^{\sigma}(v) - \varphi_{k+2}^{\sigma}(v)} &= \frac{(k+1) \cdot C\Big(k(\Gamma_k - \Gamma_{k+1}), \sigma^2 + k \cdot \Gamma_{k+1} + \sum_{j=k+1}^{I} \Gamma_j\Big)}{k \cdot C\Big((k+1)(\Gamma_{k+1} - \Gamma_{k+2}), \sigma^2 + (k+1)\Gamma_{k+2} + \sum_{j=k+2}^{I} \Gamma_j\Big)} \\
&\to \frac{\Gamma_k - \Gamma_{k+1}}{\Gamma_{k+1} - \Gamma_{k+2}} \qquad \text{as } \sigma \uparrow \infty \text{ by L'Hôpital's rule}
\end{aligned}$$

This completes the proof of the theorem. □

Theorem 5.4 tells us that when the signal-to-noise-ratio (SNR) is high for all users, their rates are roughly the same, while when the SNR is low, their rates are approximately proportional to their power constraints. In the two users case when the noise power is very small, *i.e.*, high SNR, the constraint that $R_1 + R_2 \leq C\left(\Gamma_1 + \Gamma_2, \sigma^2\right)$ becomes the dominant constraint. Hence, the allocation is mostly governed by this constraint and both users receive roughly the same rate. On the other hand, if the power constraints of the two users are quite different and the noise power is high, *i.e.*, low SNR, then the constraint on the rate of the user with smaller power constraint becomes more active. Therefore, the rate allocation is close to the intersection of these two constraints. Similar intuition carries over

---

[2]Here we assume that $\Gamma_{k+1} > \Gamma_{k+2}$.

[3]Recall that the logarithm is to base 2 in this paper.

to multiple user cases. Thus, in conclusion, we have also demonstrated some pleasing and natural properties of the fair rate allocation as the noise power varies.

6. Concluding remarks

We have studied the issue of how to fairly allocate communication rate among the users of a Gaussian multiaccess channel. We adopted a cooperative game-theoretic viewpoint which presumed the ability to make contracts offline based on threat strategies and the potential formation of coalitions. Contributions of the paper included (i) determining the capacity region of the Gaussian multiaccess arbitrarily varying channel (albeit with an alternative operational definition of capacity which avoids the main technical difficulty of the usual approach); (ii) determining the characteristic function of the Gaussian multiaccess game; (iii) proposing a natural set of axioms that a fair allocation should satisfy; (iv) proving the existence and uniqueness of a fair allocation that satisfies these axioms; (v) demonstrating that this fair allocation is feasible and reasonable, in the sense that it lies in the core of the game; and finally (vi) demonstrating some nice qualitative properties of the fair allocation as the noise power varies. We also briefly touched upon the Shapley value as a solution concept, even though we argued that the axioms underlying this concept are not natural for our game.

Our main motivation for undertaking this study was to explore the intersection of the two rich fields of cooperative game theory and information theory. We believe that investigations in this intersection can have a valuable role to play in bringing information-theoretic ideas to bear on the social choice issues that arise in multiuser communication systems where the agents might have diverse objectives.

7. Appendix

Here we gather some simple inequalities which the reader will have no trouble verifying in a few minutes.

- If $y \geq x \geq 0$ and $z > 0$, then
$$C(x+z,\sigma^2) - C(x,\sigma^2) \geq C(y+z,\sigma^2) - C(y,\sigma^2)\,, \tag{16}$$
and the equality holds only if $y = x$.
- If $x > 0$ and $z \geq 0$, then
$$C((k+1)x+z,\sigma^2) > (k+1)\left(C((k+1)x+z,\sigma^2) - C(kx+z,\sigma^2)\right) \tag{17}$$
where $k \in \mathcal{N} = \{1, 2, \cdots\}$.
- If $y \geq x \geq 0$ and $z \geq 0$, then for $k = 2, 3, \cdots$,
$$\begin{aligned} &\frac{1}{k}\left(C(ky+z,\sigma^2) - C(kx+z,\sigma^2)\right) \\ &\quad \leq \frac{1}{k-1}\left(C((k-1)y+z,\sigma^2) - C((k-1)x+z,\sigma^2)\right) \end{aligned} \tag{18}$$
and the equality holds only if $x = y$.
- If $z_1 > z_2 \geq 0$ and $y \geq x \geq 0$, then for all $k \in \mathcal{N}$
$$C(ky+z_1,\sigma^2) - C(kx+z_1,\sigma^2) \leq C(ky+z_2,\sigma^2) - C(kx+z_2,\sigma^2)\,, \tag{19}$$
and the equality holds only if $y = x$.
- If $y > x \geq 0$ and $z \geq 0$, then
$$\begin{aligned} &C(ky+z,\sigma^2) - C(kx+z,\sigma^2) \\ &> k\left(C((k-1)y+y+z,\sigma^2) - C((k-1)y+x+z,\sigma^2)\right)\,. \end{aligned} \tag{20}$$

References

[1] I. Csiszár and P. Narayan, "Capacity of the Gaussian Arbitrarily Varying Channel", *IEEE Trans. Inform. Theory*, vol. 37, no. 1, pp. 18–26, Jan. 1991.

[2] A. Feldman and A. Kirman, "Fairness and Envy", *The American Economic Review*, Vol. 64(6), pp. 995-1005, Dec. 1974.

[3] Vijay Krishna, "Auction Theory", Academic Press, San Diego, 2002.

[4] R. J. La and V. Anantharam "A Game-theoretic look at the Gaussian multiaccess channel", *ISR Technical Report, University of Maryland*, 2003.

[5] G. Owen, "Game Theory", 3rd ed., Academic Press, 1995.

[6] L. S. Shapley, "A value for n-person games", in *Classics in Game Theory, edited by K. W. Tucker*, Princeton University Press, Princeton, 1997.

[7] H. R. Varian, "Microeconomic Analysis", Norton, W. W. and Company, Inc., New York, 1992.

DEPARTMENT OF ELECTRICAL AND COMPUTER ENGINEERING, UNIVERSITY OF MARYLAND, COLLEGE PARK, MD 20742

E-mail address: hyongla@eng.umd.edu

DEPARTMENT OF ELECTRICAL ENGINEERING AND COMPUTER SCIENCES, UNIVERSITY OF CALIFORNIA, BERKELEY, CA 94720

E-mail address: ananth@eecs.berkeley.edu

DIMACS Series in Discrete Mathematics
and Theoretical Computer Science
Volume **66**, 2004

Bounds on the Sum Timing Capacity of Single-server Queues with Multiple Input and Output Terminals

Xin Liu and R. Srikant

ABSTRACT. We consider an exponential server queue accessed by many different flows. It is assumed that the source and destination information of each flow is available in the packet. We compute upper and lower bounds on the sum timing capacity of this channel. We derive asymptotically tight lower and upper bounds on the sum timing capacity for discrete-time queues with general service-time distributions. We also discuss the role of the scheduling discipline at the server on the amount of uncertainty in the information obtained by an eavesdropper who only observes the packet but not the timing between the packets.

1. Introduction

In [**AV96**], the authors analyze the timing capacity of continuous-time $\cdot/G/1$ queues. They show that, when the service time distribution is exponential, the timing capacity is e^{-1} nats per average transmission time, which is the lowest among all service time distributions. In other words, if the service rate is μB nats/sec and each packet contains B nats, then the timing capacity of the exponential server is $e^{-1}\mu$ nats/sec. To achieve this timing capacity, the input process is a Poisson process with rate $e^{-1}\mu$.

In this paper, we consider an exponential server queue accessed by many different flows. It is assumed that the source and destination information of each flow is available in the packet header. We study the amount of timing information that can be sent through the system. Timing information is the amount of information conveyed through packets timing. Specifically, the sender encodes information into the time intervals of packets sent to the server and the receiver decodes information by observing the inter-departure times of packets. First, we consider the situation where there are two flows. We are interested in sending information in the inter-packet timing of one flow, while the the other flow behaves as interference traffic. We obtain a lower bound on the timing capacity. In this paper, when we refer to the timing capacity of multiple flows, we mean the *sum* timing capacity instead of the capacity region. We then calculate lower and upper bounds on the sum timing capacity of multiple flows. We also study the system in the presence of an

Research supported by DARPA through grant F30602-00-2-0542 and AFOSR through URI grant F49620-01-1-0365.

eavesdropper and the effects of scheduling policies at the server on the amount of additional uncertainty in the information observed by the eavesdropper as compared to the uncertainty at the intended receiver.

In data networks such as the Internet, information in the packet header is used to distinguish flows from different sources and to different destinations, and thus, to facilitate routing. Given that packets naturally contain information in their headers to distinguish between various flows, the problem we consider in this paper is one of computing the sum timing capacity of many flows traversing a single server. Consider the following example. A protocol reserves B nats in each packet header for address, and thus can distinguish up to $N = e^B$ flows. Suppose that N such flows are queued at a server which processes μ packets per second. Our results show that, for an exponential server queue in continuous-time or for general service-time queues in discrete-time, the sum timing capacity of the N flows is asymptotically close to μB nats per second as $N \to \infty$. Of course, one can achieve this capacity by sending the information in the usual manner, i.e., in the packet contents than in the timing. Thus, it raises the question as to whether there is any advantage to transmitting information in the timing between packets.

One possible advantage could be that the timing information may be covert. Typically, for billing/traffic-monitoring reasons, routers (especially those at the edges of a network) record the contents of the packets of some or all of the packets that traverse the network. However, they do not typically measure the timing (inter-arrival times) between packets. From a timing channel point of view, the router can be viewed as an eavesdropper who has access to only packet header information. Thus, the channel model here is similar to the Wyner's wiretap channel [**Wyn75**]. A natural question is the following: how much timing information can the router extract by just looking at the packet header information of a sequence of packets?

For example, suppose that there are two flows, say RED and GREEN flows, traversing a router and the router records the following sequence of 15 packets going through it: a RED packet, followed by 2 GREEN packets, followed by another RED packet, followed by 10 GREEN packets, and finally a RED packet again. After this packet sequence is recorded at the router, suppose that the network operator obtains information that the RED and GREEN flows have been conveying information through timing and also gains access to the timing code book of both flows. Then, it may be possible to obtain some of the timing information that was conveyed through the queue as follows: it is likely that the timing between the second and third RED packets is larger than the timing between the first and second RED packets since the number of GREEN packets in between the second and third RED packets is larger than the number of GREEN packets in between the first and second RED packets. Thus, it is of interest to quantify the amount of covert information that one can convey using timing when flow identification is available at the eavesdropper. We also study the effects of service disciplines at the router on the additional uncertainty at the eavesdropper.

2. Main Results

We start by studying the timing capacity of a flow which shares a single server with one other flow, which we call the *interference flow*. The existence of interference traffic results in additional randomness (in addition to the randomness due to the service times) in the departure times of packets. We then study the case where multiple input and multiple output flows share the same server. To obtain a bound on the timing capacity in the case of multiple flows, we consider one flow at a time and treat all the other flows together as interference traffic.

2.1. Interference Traffic. Suppose that a sender controls the input process of flow 0 to the server. The server is shared with another flow, denoted by flow I, the interference flow. The sender cannot control or detect the arrivals of the interference packets, and vice-versa. The service discipline is FIFO.

It is interesting to note that, if the service times of flow 0's packets are deterministic, then the sender can achieve infinite timing capacity, regardless the existence of the uncontrollable interference traffic. The reason is that despite the presence of the interference traffic, if the total arrival rate is less than the server's service rate, the steady-state probability that a packet belonging to flow 0 sees an empty queue upon arrival is non-zero, and thus, with a positive probability, the decoder can extract timing information without any randomness. For the ease of argument, assume that the service time of a packet from the interference flow is continuous distributed and assume that the steady state distribution exists. One simple strategy to achieve the infinite capacity is to transmit M packets with the same inter-arrival times. The inter-arrival times should be large enough so that the probability of an arrival finding no packets in the queue is positive. Because the service time of an interference packet is chosen from a continuous distribution, the probability of any two packets have the same *non-zero* waiting time is zero. Given any $\epsilon > 0$, let M be large enough so that the probability that at least three packets (which may not be consecutive) from flow 0 incur zero waiting times in the queue is greater than $1 - \epsilon$. Given the departure times of packet i and packet j, $1 \leq i < j \leq M$, we can estimate the inter-arrival time as the difference of the departure times of packets i and j divided by $(j-i)$. With M packets, we obtain total $M(M-1)/2$ estimates of the inter-arrival time. Since at least three packets have departed without incurring waiting in the queue, there are at least two estimated inter-departure times that are exactly equal to the corresponding inter-arrival time of two packets. Therefore, the decoder can measure the inter-arrival time exactly with probability 1, and thus, receive an infinite amount of information.

From now on, we assume that the service times of packets from both flows 0 and I are i.i.d. (independent and identically distributed) random variables with an exponential distribution unless explicitly stated otherwise. The arrival process of flow I is a Poisson process with rate λ_I. The variables A_i and D_i denote the inter-arrival and inter-departure times of the ith packet of flow 0, as shown in Figure 1. In the figure, the solid lines with arrows indicate the arrivals and departures of flow 0's packets and the dashed lines with arrows indicate the arrivals and departures of interference packets. Let $\hat{W}_i$ be the *effective idling time* of the server, i.e., $\hat{W}_i$ is the elapsed time between the departure of the $(i-1)$th packet and the arrival of the ith packet of flow 0. In other words, $\hat{W}_i$ is the idling time of the server from the viewpoint of flow 0. We can write

$$\hat{W}_i = \max\left\{0, \sum_{j=1}^{i} A_j - \sum_{j=0}^{i-1} D_j\right\},$$

where $D_0 = 0$ if the queue is initially empty and D_0 is the system time when packet 0 from flow 0 departs if the queue is initially in equilibrium.

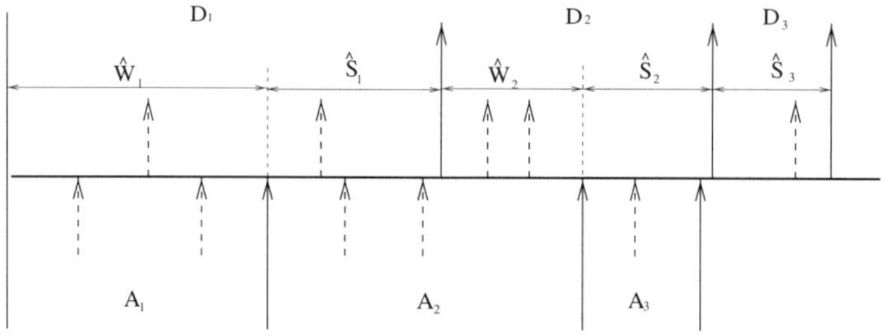

FIGURE 1. Illustration of inter-arrival, inter-departure, and effective service times.

We define $\hat{S}_i$ to be the *effective* service time of the ith packet, which is the time elapsed between the later of the arrival of the ith packet and the departure of the $(i-1)$th packet, and the departure of the ith packet. Let n_i be the number of *effective* interference packets for the ith packet of flow 0. To elaborate, if the ith packet arrives before the departure of the $(i-1)$th packet, n_i is the number of packets from the interference traffic that arrived during A_i. If the ith packet arrives after the departure of the $(i-1)$th packet, n_i is the number of interference packets in the system when the ith packet arrives. In other words, the ith packet from flow 0 has to wait for n_i interference packets to be served after the departure of the $(i-1)$th packet. In Figure 1, $n_1 = 1$, $n_2 = 0$, and $n_3 = 1$. In other words, $\hat{S}_i$ is the sum of the service time of the ith packet and that of the n_i interference packets, as shown in Figure 1.

The interference traffic affects the timing information conveyed by flow 0 packets by increasing the randomness of the effective service time. The $\cdot/M/1$ queue studied in [**AV96**] can be considered as a special case where $n_i \equiv 0$. From the viewpoint of flow 0, packets from the interference traffic that depart when there is no flow 0 packet in the queue do not cause any distortion on the timing, and thus, need not be considered. In Figure 1, the first, third, and fourth interference packets do not have any effect on the departure times of flow 0 packets while the second interference packet does.

PROPOSITION 1. The timing capacity of flow 0 with rate λ_0, denoted by $C(\lambda_0)$, satisfies

$$C(\lambda_0) \geq \lambda_0 \log \frac{\mu - \lambda_I}{\lambda_0}. \tag{2.1}$$

PROOF. Let the input process of flow 0 be a Poisson process with rate λ_0 and independent of the arrival process of interference traffic. Thus, the input process of the server is Poisson with rate $\lambda_0 + \lambda_I$. Assume that the queue is initially in equilibrium. Burke's theorem for an $M/M/1$ queue (e.g, p. 218 in [**BG87**]) states that the output process is Poisson with rate $\lambda_0 + \lambda_I$ in steady state. Because the service discipline is FIFO, each output packet belongs to flow 0 with probability $\lambda_0/(\lambda_0 + \lambda_I)$ independently. Thus, the output process of flow 0 is a Poisson process with rate λ_0. Let $\bar{D}^n = \{D_0, D_1, \cdots, D_n\}$.

We obtain a lower bound on the mutual information between the inter-arrival and inter-departure times of flow 0 in a manner similar to the arguments in [**AV96**] by noting that the effective service time and the effective idling time of the server play the role of the service time and idling time in the single-flow $\cdot/M/1$ queue.

However, we only obtain a lower bound on the capacity since the effective service times of the packets are not independent. We provide the argument below for completeness:

$$I(A^n; \bar{D}^n) = h(\bar{D}^n) - h(\bar{D}^n|A^n),$$

where

$$\begin{aligned} h(\bar{D}^n|A^n) &= \sum_{i=1}^{n} h(D_i|A^n, \bar{D}^{i-1}) + h(D_0) \\ &\overset{(1)}{=} \sum_{i=1}^{n} h(D_i|A^n, \bar{D}^{i-1}, \hat{W}_i) + h(D_0) \\ &\leq \sum_{i=1}^{n} h(\hat{W}_i + \hat{S}_i|\hat{W}_i) + h(D_0) \\ &= \sum_{i=1}^{n} h(\hat{S}_i|\hat{W}_i) + h(D_0) \\ &\leq \sum_{i=1}^{n} h(\hat{S}_i) + h(D_0) \\ &\overset{(2)}{=} \sum_{i=1}^{n} \left(\log \frac{1}{\mu - \lambda_I} + 1\right) + h(D_0), \end{aligned}$$

where (1) holds because $\hat{W}_i$ is a deterministic function of $(A^n, \bar{D}^{i-1})$, and the two inequalities hold because conditioning decreases entropy. Note that in the special case where $\lambda_I = 0$, both inequalities hold with equality because $(A^n, \bar{D}^{i-1}) \to \hat{W}_i \to D_i$ is a Markov chain and $\hat{S}_i = S_i$ is independent of $\hat{W}_i$. Last, (2) holds because the $\hat{S}_i$s are exponentially distributed with mean $1/(\mu - \lambda_I)$ as shown in Lemma 2.1 below. Further, we have

$$h(\bar{D}^n) = \sum_{i=1}^{n} \left(\log \frac{1}{\lambda_0} + 1\right) + h(D_0|D^n),$$

where D_is are independent and exponentially distributed with mean $1/\lambda_0$ because the output process of flow 0 is Poisson with rate λ_0. Since

$$\lim_{n\to\infty} \frac{1}{n} I(D_0; D^n) = 0,$$

we have

$$\lim_{n\to\infty} \frac{\lambda_0}{n} I(A^n; \bar{D}^n) \geq \lambda_0 \log \frac{\mu - \lambda_I}{\lambda_0}.$$

One way to prove that a lower bound on the mutual information is a lower bound on the capacity is to take the approach in [**VH94**]; i.e., to show that for some input process, the inf-information rate is greater than the lower bound. We can do this along the lines of the proof of Theorem 7 in [**AV96**]. Because the effective service times, S_is, are not independent, we cannot directly apply the result of Theorem 7 in [**AV96**]. However, examining the proof of Theorem 7 in [**AV96**], we note that the theorem holds when $\sum_{i=1}^{n} D_i/n$ converges in probability to $1/\lambda_0$ and $\sum_{i=1}^{n} \hat{S}_i/n$ converges in probability to $1/(\mu - \lambda_I)$. The first convergence holds because the output process of flow 0 is a Poisson process with rate λ_0, and the second one is shown in Lemma 2.1. □

LEMMA 2.1. *The effective service time, $\hat{S}_i$, is exponentially distributed with mean $1/(\mu - \lambda_I)$, and $\sum_{i=1}^n \hat{S}_i/n$ converges in probability to $E(\hat{S}_i)$.*

PROOF. Let q_0 be the probability a packet belongs to flow 0, i.e., $q_0 = \lambda_0/(\lambda_0 + \lambda_I)$. Let $\rho = (\lambda_0 + \lambda_I)/\mu$. Because flow 0 and flow I generate independent Poisson arrivals with rate λ_0 and λ_I, a packet belongs to flow 0 with probability q_0, and it is independent of previous packets. Let $\pi(j)$ be the steady state probability that there are j packets in the queue (both waiting and in service) when the ith packet arrives and $p(k|j)$ be the probability that $n_i = k$ given that there are j packets in the queue (both waiting and in service) when the ith packet arrives. We have

$$\begin{aligned}
P(n_i = k) &= \sum_{j=k}^{\infty} \pi(j)p(k|j) \\
&= (1-\rho)\rho^k(1-q_0)^k + \sum_{j=k+1}^{\infty} (1-\rho)\rho^j(1-q_0)^k q_0 \\
&= \rho^k(1-q_0)^k(1-\rho(1-q_0)) \\
&= \left(\frac{\lambda_I}{\mu}\right)^k \left(1 - \frac{\lambda_I}{\mu}\right), \quad k = 0, 1, 2, \cdots.
\end{aligned}$$

In other words, $n_i + 1$ is a geometrically distributed random variable with mean $\mu/(\mu - \lambda_I)$, and thus

$$E(\hat{S}_i) = E\left(\sum_{k=1}^{n_i+1} S_k\right) = \frac{1}{\mu}E(n_i + 1) = \frac{1}{\mu - \lambda_I}.$$

Next, we show that the correlation between the effective service times of packets that are far apart is sufficiently small and thus, one can apply Chebychev's inequality as in the standard proofs of the weak law of large numbers to prove the rest of the lemma. To this end, let

$$g(i) = \{k : \text{the } i\text{th and } k\text{th packets of flow 0 belong to the same busy period}\}.$$

In other words, $g(i)$ is the set of all packets which were served in the same busy period as packet i. For any $\delta > 0$, there exists $N > 0$, such that $P(j \in g(i)) \leq \delta$ if $|i - j| \geq N$. Let B_i be the duration of the busy period that contains packet i. Now,

$$E\left[\left(\sum_{i=1}^n \hat{S}_i\right)^2\right] = \sum_{i=1}^n E\left[\hat{S}_i \sum_{j=1}^n \hat{S}_j \mathbf{1}\{j \in g(i)\}\right] + \sum_{i=1}^n E\left[\hat{S}_i \sum_{j=1}^n \hat{S}_j \mathbf{1}\{j \notin g(i)\}\right].$$

We have

$$\sum_{i=1}^n E\left[\hat{S}_i \sum_{j=1}^n \hat{S}_j \mathbf{1}\{j \in g(i)\}\right] \leq \sum_{i=1}^n E(\hat{S}_i B_i) \leq nE(B_1^2),$$

and

$$\begin{aligned}
&E\left[\hat{S}_i \sum_{j=1}^{n} \hat{S}_j \mathbf{1}\{j \notin g(i)\}\right] \\
&= E\left[\hat{S}_i \sum_{j:|i-j|<N} \hat{S}_j \mathbf{1}\{j \notin g(i)\}\right] + E\left[\hat{S}_i \sum_{j:|i-j|\geq N} \hat{S}_j \mathbf{1}\{j \notin g(i)\}\right] \\
&\leq (2N-1)E(B_1^2) + E\left[\hat{S}_i \sum_{j:|i-j|\geq N} \hat{S}_j \mathbf{1}\{j \notin g(i)\}\right].
\end{aligned}$$

For $|i-j| \geq N$, we have

$$\begin{aligned}
&E\left[\hat{S}_i \hat{S}_j \mathbf{1}\{j \notin g(i)\}\right] \\
&= \sum_{k_1=0}^{\infty}\sum_{k_2=0}^{\infty}\left[\left(\sum_{i_1=1}^{k_1+1} S_{i_1}\right)\left(\sum_{i_2=1}^{k_2+1} S'_{i_2}\right) P(n_i = k_1, n_j = k_2 | j \notin g(i)) P(j \notin g(i))\right] \\
&\overset{(1)}{=} \sum_{k_1=0}^{\infty}\sum_{k_2=0}^{\infty}\left[\left(\sum_{i_1=1}^{k_1+1} S_{i_1}\right)\left(\sum_{i_2=1}^{k_2+1} S'_{i_2}\right) P(n_i = k_1 | j \notin g(i))\right. \\
&\qquad \left. \times P(n_j = k_2 | j \notin g(i)) P(j \notin g(i))\right] \\
&\leq \sum_{k_1=0}^{\infty}\sum_{k_2=0}^{\infty}\left[\left(\sum_{i_1=1}^{k_1+1} S_{i_1}\right)\left(\sum_{i_2=1}^{k_2+1} S'_{i_2}\right) \frac{P(n_i = k_1)}{1-\delta} P(n_j = k_2)\right] \\
&= \frac{E(S_i)E(S_j)}{1-\delta},
\end{aligned}$$

where S_{i_1} (S'_{i_2}) is the service time of a packet that is counted in $\hat{S}_i$ ($\hat{S}_j$), and (1) holds because n_i and n_j are independent given $j \notin g(i)$. Thus,

$$\sigma^2(n) = \frac{1}{n^2}\left(E\left[\left(\sum_{i=1}^{n}\hat{S}_i\right)^2\right] - E^2\left[\left(\sum_{i=1}^{n}\hat{S}_i\right)\right]\right) \leq \frac{2NE(B_1^2)}{n} + \frac{\delta}{1-\delta}E^2(S_1).$$

Because $E(B_1^2)$, the second moment of a busy period of an $M/M/1$ queue, is finite (see e.g., p. 214, (5.142) in [**Kle75**]) when $\lambda_0 + \lambda_I < \mu$, and δ is chosen arbitrarily, we have

$$\lim_{n\to\infty} \sigma^2(n) = 0.$$

By Chebychev's inequality,

$$P\left(\left|\frac{1}{n}\sum_{i=1}^{n}\hat{S}_i - \frac{1}{\mu-\lambda_I}\right| \geq \epsilon\right) \leq \frac{\sigma^2(n)}{\epsilon^2}.$$

Thus, $n^{-1}\sum_{i=1}^{n}\hat{S}_i$ converges in probability to $1/(\mu-\lambda_I)$. □

So far we have provided a lower bound on the timing capacity of a flow in the presence of independent Poisson interference traffic when the service time distribution is exponential. Further, the derivation of the lower bound indicates that the bound is achieved when the input process is a Poisson process, independent of the interference traffic and service times. From the point of view of flow 0, the server behaves *as if* it allocates just enough service to flow I to accommodate its traffic, i.e., the interference traffic gets a service rate of λ_I and flow 0 gets a service rate of $\mu - \lambda_I$. We next use the results of this section to study the timing capacity of multiple flows.

2.2. Multiple Input and Multiple Output Terminals. Let us consider a system where multiple flows share the same server. Information is encoded in the inter-arrival times of packets from the same flow. Assume that the service times of packets from all flows are i.i.d. (independent and identically distributed) random variables with an exponential distribution. From the viewpoint of any one flow, all packets from other flows behave as interference traffic. Suppose each flow i, $i = 1, 2, \ldots, N$, generates packets according to an independent Poisson process with rate λ_i, where $\sum_i \lambda_i < \mu$. Following the proofs in Prop. 1, we can show that $R_L(\lambda_1, \cdots, \lambda_N)$ is a lower bound on the timing capacity, where

$$R_L(\lambda_1, \cdots, \lambda_N) = \sum_{i=1}^{N} \lambda_i \log \frac{\mu - \sum_{j \neq i} \lambda_j}{\lambda_i}.$$

LEMMA 2.2. *The timing capacity of the N-flow system satisfies*

$$C(\lambda_1, \cdots, \lambda_N) \geq R_L(\lambda_1, \cdots, \lambda_N) \geq \left(\sum_{i=1}^{N} \lambda_i \right) \log \frac{\mu}{\sum_{i=1}^{N} \lambda_i}.$$

Further, for a fixed $\sum_{i=1}^{N} \lambda_i$, the lower bound $R_L(\lambda_1, \cdots, \lambda_N)$ is maximized when $\lambda_i = \lambda_j$ for all i and j.

PROOF. First, let $N = 2$. Because one flow treats the other flow as interference, the lower bound on the capacity is

$$R_L(\lambda_1, \lambda_2) = \lambda_1 \log \frac{\mu - \lambda_2}{\lambda_1} + \lambda_2 \log \frac{\mu - \lambda_1}{\lambda_2}.$$

The Hessian matrix of R_L is

$$\nabla^2 R_L = \begin{bmatrix} -\frac{1}{\lambda_1} - \frac{\lambda_2}{(\mu-\lambda_1)^2} & -\frac{1}{\mu-\lambda_1} - \frac{1}{\mu-\lambda_2} \\ -\frac{1}{\mu-\lambda_1} - \frac{1}{\mu-\lambda_2} & -\frac{1}{\lambda_2} - \frac{\lambda_1}{(\mu-\lambda_2)^2} \end{bmatrix}.$$

It is easy to see that the Hessian matrix is negative definite, and thus, R_L is a concave function of (λ_1, λ_2). Further, R_L is a symmetric function of (λ_1, λ_2), i.e., $R_L(\lambda_1, \lambda_2) = R_L(\lambda_2, \lambda_1)$. Thus, we have

$$R_L(\lambda_1, \lambda_2) \geq \alpha R_L(\lambda_1 + \lambda_2, 0) + (1 - \alpha) R_L(0, \lambda_1 + \lambda_2) = (\lambda_1 + \lambda_2) \log \frac{\mu}{\lambda_1 + \lambda_2},$$

where $\alpha = \lambda_1/(\lambda_1 + \lambda_2)$. In words, splitting a single flow into two flows increases the timing capacity. By induction, it is easy to see that

$$R_L(\lambda_1, \cdots, \lambda_N) \geq \left(\sum_{i=1}^{N} \lambda_i \right) \log \frac{\mu}{\sum_{i=1}^{N} \lambda_i}.$$

Further, because R_L is symmetric and concave when $N = 2$, we have

$$R_L(\lambda_1, \lambda_2) \leq R_L\left(\frac{\lambda_1 + \lambda_2}{2}, \frac{\lambda_1 + \lambda_2}{2} \right).$$

Thus, the lower bound is maximized when $\lambda_1 = \lambda_2$. Next, we show it holds for all N. Let $\bar{\lambda} = (\sum_{i=1}^N \lambda_i)/N$. Without loss of generality, we assume that $\lambda_1 \geq \lambda_2 \cdots, \geq \lambda_N$. Note that

$$R_L(\lambda_1, \cdots, \lambda_N) = R_L(\lambda_1', \cdots, \lambda_N'),$$

where $(\lambda_1', \cdots, \lambda_N')$ is a permutation of $(\lambda_1, \cdots, \lambda_N)$. We have

$$\begin{aligned}
R_L(\lambda_1, \lambda_2, \cdots, \lambda_{N-1}, \lambda_N) &\leq R_L\left(\frac{\lambda_1 + \lambda_N}{2}, \lambda_2, \cdots, \lambda_{N-1}, \frac{\lambda_1 + \lambda_N}{2}\right) \\
&= R_L\left(\lambda_1^{(1)}, \lambda_2^{(1)}, \cdots, \lambda_{N-1}^{(1)}, \lambda_N^{(1)}\right) \\
&\leq R_L\left(\frac{\lambda_1^{(1)} + \lambda_N^{(1)}}{2}, \lambda_2^{(1)}, \cdots, \lambda_{N-1}^{(1)}, \frac{\lambda_1^{(1)} + \lambda_N^{(1)}}{2}\right) \\
&\vdots \\
&\leq R_L(\bar{\lambda}, \cdots, \bar{\lambda}) \\
&= N\bar{\lambda} \log \frac{\mu - (N-1)\bar{\lambda}}{\bar{\lambda}},
\end{aligned}$$

where $(\lambda_1^{(1)}, \lambda_2^{(1)}, \cdots, \lambda_{N-1}^{(1)}, \lambda_N^{(1)})$ is a permutation of $((\lambda_1 + \lambda_N)/2, \lambda_2, \cdots, \lambda_{N-1}, (\lambda_1 + \lambda_N)/2)$ in decreasing order. In other words, the lower bound is maximized when all flows have the same arrival rates. □

LEMMA 2.3. *Suppose that there are N flows, $N \geq 2$. Then the overall timing capacity of the N flows, C, satisfies*

$$C \geq \frac{N}{N-1}\mu x^*,$$

where x^* satisfies $x^* e^{x^*} = (N-1)e^{-1}$. To achieve the lower bound, the input processes of the N flows are independent Poisson flows with the same rate

$$\lambda^* = \frac{x^*}{1+x^*}\frac{\mu}{N-1}.$$

PROOF. Let the input process of each flow be an independent Poisson process with rate λ such that $N\lambda \leq \mu$. Each flow considers the other flows as interference traffic. By Prop. 1, we have

$$C \geq N\lambda \log \frac{\mu - (N-1)\lambda}{\lambda}, \quad N\lambda \leq \mu.$$

To find the value of λ that maximizes the lower bound, we take derivative of the right-hand side with respect to λ and set it equal to zero. Let

$$x = \frac{(N-1)\lambda}{\mu - (N-1)\lambda}.$$

The lower bound is maximized when $x^* e^{x^*} = (N-1)e^{-1}$, and we have

$$C \geq \frac{N}{N-1}\mu x^*.$$

The optimal arrival rate of each flow is

$$\lambda^* = \frac{x^*}{1+x^*}\frac{\mu}{N-1}.$$

Because xe^x is an increasing function of x, we have $x^* \leq N-1$. Thus, we verify that $\lambda^* \leq \mu/N$. $\square$

PROPOSITION 2. Let C be the sum timing capacity of a server shared by N flows. It satisfies

$$(B-1-\log B)\mu \leq C \leq B\mu, \tag{2.2}$$

where $B = \log N$, $N \geq 3$.

PROOF. Following Lemma 2.3, we have

$$C \geq \frac{N}{N-1}\mu x^*,$$

where x^* satisfies $x^* e^{x^*} = (N-1)e^{-1}$. Note that xe^x is an increasing function of x. Let

$$x_0 = B - 1 - \log B.$$

We have

$$x_0 e^{x_0} = \frac{B-1-\log B}{B} e^{B-1} \leq \frac{N-1}{N} e^{B-1} = (N-1)e^{-1} = x^* e^{x^*},$$

i.e,

$$x^* \geq x_0 = B - 1 - \log B.$$

Thus,

$$C \geq \mu(B - 1 - \log B).$$

Next, we show that the maximum timing capacity is upper bounded by μB. Let $X^n = \{X_1, \cdots, X_n\}$ be the information sent in the contents of the packets, which is received error-free. Let A^n and D^n be the inter-arrival and inter-departure times of packets passing through the server (which may belong to different flows). The total amount of information passing through the server satisfies:

$$\begin{aligned} I(X^n, D^n; X^n, A^n) &= I(D^n; X^n, A^n) + I(X^n; X^n, A^n | D^n) \\ &\overset{(1)}{=} I(D^n; A^n) + I(X^n; X^n), \end{aligned}$$

where (1) holds because X^n contains no additional information regarding D^n other than that in A^n. Thus,

$$C \leq \sup_{X^n, A^n} \frac{\lambda}{n} I(X^n, D^n; X^n, A^n) \leq \frac{\lambda}{n}(I(D^n; A^n) + H(X^n)).$$

From [**AV96**], we know that if $B > 1$ (nat), the maximum information capacity of the channel is μB nats/sec. Thus, $C \leq \mu B$ nats/sec, which concludes the proof. $\square$

We note that the above theorem shows that the ratio of the upper bound to the lower bound goes to one as B becomes large. Thus, the lower bound on the capacity obtained by considering one flow at a time, and treating the rest of the flows as interference to the first flow, is asymptotically tight.

If the service rate is μ packets per second and each packet contains B nats, then the service rate can be expressed as $\hat{\mu} = \mu B$ nats per second. Suppose there are $N = e^B$ flows in the system, then we have the following result.

COROLLARY 1. The sum timing capacity of the N flows satisfies

$$\left(1 - \frac{1}{B} - \frac{\log B}{B}\right) \hat{\mu} \leq C \leq \hat{\mu}, \text{ where } N \geq 3.$$

Note that if the service rate $\hat{\mu}$ is increased proportional with N, which is often the case in a large system, then the timing capacity *per* flow does not vanish. It is well-known in queueing theory that scaling the capacity with the number of flows has the effect of reducing the waiting time in the system; a fact known as the *statistical multiplexing gain*. However, we note that our result does not exploit the statistical multiplexing gain, i.e., it holds independent of whether or not the system capacity is scaled with the number of flows.

The results in this subsection can be applied to any combination of single sender/receiver, multiple senders/receivers. The upper-bound/lower-bound provided in Prop. 2 bounds the sum timing capacity. Note that we do not claim that the Shannon capacity of the single server queue increases (compared to the result in [**AV96**]. The interpretation of the result is that the number of bits needed to distinguish different flows can almost be compensated by the timing information conveyed by these flows. To achieve the capacity lower bound, a random encoding strategy for each flow is to assign codewords that are independent realizations of a Poisson process with rate λ^*, and each flow encodes information independently, as discussed in [**AV96**][1]. Each flow decodes information independently by observing the inter-departure times of the flow. There is no collaboration required among different flows. Further, if there exists Poisson cross-traffic with rate λ_I and the service time distribution is exponential with rate μ, then we obtain the capacity bound simply by replacing μ by $\mu - \lambda_I$ in (2.2). If there are multiple destinations in the system, then marking is necessary to distinguish different flows and route packets to their corresponding destinations. However, if there is a single sender and a single receiver, then marking is not necessary, and thus the result should be be interpreted as trading "marking capacity" for "timing capacity".

Note that the scheme studied in the paper is different from a multi-user case in the traditional sense, e.g., the case studied in Section 3.2.3 in [**Sun99**]. In the multi-user case studied in [**Sun99**], the receiver cannot distinguish between packets from different transmitters. In the current scheme, different flows have different identities and are thus distinguishable. Hence, the result here does not contradict with the result in [**Sun99**].

2.3. Discrete Case. In [**BA98**], the authors study the timing capacity of discrete queues. Their first model assumes single packet arrivals and departures in a time slot and independent service times. In such a model, the geometric distribution plays a role similar to exponential distribution in the continuous case. In other words, when the service time is geometrically distributed, the server has the least timing capacity among all distributions with the same average service time, and to achieve the capacity, the input process is Bernoulli process.

In this section, we consider a discrete single server queue shared by many flows. We assume single packet from each flow arrives in a time slot and single departure in a time slot. The service discipline is FIFO. Packets arrived in the same time slot (from different flows) are queued randomly. The service time of each packet is independent and identically distributed, denoted as S. The following theorem

[1]There are alternative coding schemes, such as the window code in [**Sun99**].

provides bounds on the total timing capacity of such a system for service time distributions with a finite second moment.

PROPOSITION 3. The sum timing capacity of a server shared by N flows satisfies[2]

$$\frac{B-1}{B}\mu\left(B-\log\left(1+\frac{(B-1)\mu^2E(S^2)}{2}\right)\right)\leq C\leq \mu B+1, \tag{2.3}$$

where $\mu = 1/E(S)$. In particular, if the service-time distribution is geometrically distributed, then

$$\mu(B-1)-\mu\log B\leq C\leq \mu B+1.$$

PROOF. As in the continuous-time case, we obtain a lower bound by computing the effective service time. However, it is difficult to precisely characterize the effective service time for a general server queue. To overcome the difficulty, we use the "waiting time + service time" as an upper bound on the effective service time. The intuition is that when the arrival rate is small, the inter-arrival of packets from the same flow is large, and thus the "waiting time + service time" becomes a good upper bound on the effective service time.

We first calculate an upper bound on the average effective service time. In [**BK93**] (p.51), the average waiting time, W, is shown to be:

$$W=(W_r+W_s)/(1-\rho),$$

where $\rho=\lambda/\mu$, W_r is the average remaining service time, and W_s is the average service time of packets that arrive at the same slot, but served before the tagged packet. It is shown that

$$\begin{aligned} W_r &= \frac{E(S^2)-E(S)}{2E(S)}\rho=\frac{E(S^2)}{2E(S)}\rho-\frac{\rho}{2} \\ W_s &= \frac{E(K^2)-E(K)}{2E(K)}E(S), \end{aligned}$$

where S is the service time and K is the total number of packets arrived in a time-slot.

To obtain a lower bound, let the arrivals of each flow be Bernoulli with rate λ_0. The aggregate arrival process is binomial with mean rate $N\lambda_0$, where N is the number of flows. Let $N\lambda_0=(B-1)\mu/B$. We have

$$W_s = \frac{E(K^2)-E(K)}{2E(K)}E(S)=\frac{(N-1)\lambda_0}{2\mu}\leq\frac{\rho}{2},$$

where $\rho = N\lambda_0/\mu$. Thus,

$$W = \frac{W_r+W_s}{1-\rho}\leq\frac{\rho\frac{E(S^2)}{2E(S)}}{1-\rho}=\frac{(B-1)E(S^2)}{2E(S)}.$$

Let $1/\mu'$ be the average effective service time. It satisfies

$$\frac{1}{\mu'}\leq\frac{1}{\mu}+W.$$

[2]For the convenience of argument, the base of the logarithm in this section when we discuss discrete case is 2, and thus the unit of capacity is bits per slot.

We have

$$\mu' \geq \frac{1}{\frac{1}{\mu} + \frac{(B-1)E(S^2)}{2E(S)}} = \frac{\mu}{1 + (B-1)\mu^2 E(S^2)/2}.$$

In [**BA98**], it is shown that the timing capacity of a geometric server has the smallest timing capacity among all service distributions with the same average service time, which is

$$C(\lambda) = h(\lambda) - \frac{\lambda}{\mu} h(\mu),$$

where $h(x) = -x \log x - (1-x)\log(1-x)$. To achieve this timing capacity, the arrival process is Bernoulli process with rate λ.

Following the proofs in [**BA98**], by proving the stability and the convergence of the average effective service time, we have

$$\begin{aligned}
C &\geq N\left(h(\lambda_0) - \frac{\lambda_0}{\mu'} h(\mu')\right) \\
&= -N\lambda_0 \log \lambda_0 - N(1-\lambda_0)\log(1-\lambda_0) + N\lambda_0 \log \mu' + N\lambda_0 \frac{1-\mu'}{\mu'} \log(1-\mu') \\
&= N\lambda_0 \log \frac{\mu'}{\lambda_0} + N\lambda_0 \left[\frac{1-\lambda_0}{\lambda_0} \log \frac{1}{1-\lambda_0} - \frac{1-\mu'}{\mu'} \log \frac{1}{1-\mu'}\right].
\end{aligned}$$

We note that $f(x) = (1/x - 1)\log \frac{1}{1-x}$ is a decreasing function of x, $0 \leq x \leq 1$. Thus, when $\lambda_0 \leq \mu'$,

$$\begin{aligned}
C(N) &\geq N\lambda_0 \log \frac{\mu'}{\lambda_0} \\
&\geq \frac{B-1}{B}\mu \log\left(\frac{\mu}{(1 + (B-1)\mu^2 E(S^2)/2)\lambda_0}\right) \\
&= \frac{B-1}{B}\mu \left(\log \frac{\mu}{\lambda_0} - \log(1 + (B-1)\mu^2 E(S^2)/2)\right) \\
&= \frac{B-1}{B}\mu \left(B + \log \frac{B}{B-1} - \log(1 + (B-1)\mu^2 E(S^2)/2)\right) \\
&\geq \frac{B-1}{B}\mu \left(B - \log(1 + (B-1)\mu^2 E(S^2)/2)\right).
\end{aligned}$$

If $\lambda_0 \geq \mu'$, $N\lambda_0 \log \mu'/\lambda_0 \leq 0$, and thus the lower bound also holds.

The upper bound is clear:

$$\begin{aligned}
\frac{\lambda}{n} I(X^n, A^n; X^n, D^n) &\leq \frac{\lambda}{n} H(X^n, A^n) \leq \frac{\lambda}{n}(H(X^n) + H(A^n)) \\
&\leq \lambda B + h(\lambda) \leq \mu B + 1,
\end{aligned}$$

which completes the proof for the general service time distribution.

If the service time is geometrically distributed with mean $1/\mu$, then

$$E(S^2) = \frac{2(1-\mu)}{\mu^2} + \frac{1}{\mu} \leq \frac{2}{\mu^2}.$$

Substitute it into (2.3), and we have

$$\mu(B-1) - \mu \log B \leq C \leq \mu B + 1,$$

which completes the proof. □

In this section, we obtained asymptotically tight upper and lower bounds for the timing capacity of discrete queues with a general service time distribution. Note that we can also obtain a similar lower bound for continuous queues with general service time distributions as well. However, it is more difficult to find a tight upper bound. Theorem 5 in [**AV96**] provides an upper bound on the timing capacity. Combining with Theorem 9 in [**AV96**], an upper bound on the capacity of the information-bearing queue is

$$\mu B + \mu D(P_S \| e_\mu),$$

where $D(P_S\|e_\mu) \geq 1$ nat. However, the second term is not bounded in general (e.g., in the case where the service time is constant). Thus, we have not been able to obtain an asymptotically tight upper bound.

2.4. Eavesdropper. Consider a system where a sender transmits a private message to a receiver, while an eavesdropper observes the packets passing through the server. The eavesdropper records the sequence and contents of the packets, but not their timings. As noted in Section 1, just by looking at the sequence of packet colors, the eavesdropper obtains some information about the timing between the packets. In what follows, we quantify the amount of the additional uncertainty in the information about the private message received by the eavesdropper (as compared to the uncertainty at the intended receiver). Further, if the eavesdropper is located at the output of the queue, we show that this additional uncertainty is affected by the service discipline used in the queue.

Let us consider the case where there are two flows accessing an exponential server which serves at rate μ packets/sec. Let λ_1 and λ_2 be the data rates (packets-per-second) of flow 1 and flow 2, respectively. Suppose that flow i uses its first n_i packets to transmit timing information, and let $n = n_1 + n_2$. Let A^{n_1} denote the sequence of inter-arrival times of flow 1, T^{n_2} the sequence of inter-arrival times of flow 2. Let D^n be the sequence of inter-departure times of the aggregate flow, S^n the service times of the packets (S_i is the service time of the ith departure), and N^n the sequence of colors of the departing packets, i.e, if $N_k = i$, then the kth departure packet belongs to flow i.

Let

$$R_e = \lim_{n\to\infty} \frac{\lambda_1+\lambda_2}{n} I(A^{n_1}, T^{n_2}; N^n)$$

be the information rate obtained at the eavesdropper, and

$$R_r = \lim_{n\to\infty} \frac{\lambda_1+\lambda_2}{n} I(A^{n_1}, T^{n_2}; N^n, D^n)$$

be the total information rate observed at the receiver, where it is assumed that $\lim_{n\to\infty} n_1/n = \lambda_1/(\lambda_1+\lambda_2)$. Then,

$$R_c = R_r - R_e$$

is the additional uncertainty rate at the eavesdropper as compared to the intended receiver. In this section, we quantify this uncertainty as a function of the service discipline.

We begin by considering the case where the service discipline is FIFO. We note that in this subsection we only consider exponential service time distribution. Let the input processes of flow 1 and flow 2 be Poisson processes with rate λ_1 and λ_2, respectively.

PROPOSITION 4. When the service discipline is FIFO and the input processes of flow 1 and flow 2 are Poisson processes with rate λ_1 and λ_2, respectively, the additional uncertainty rate, R_c, at the eavesdropper is equal to the timing capacity of a single flow with rate $\lambda_1 + \lambda_2$.

PROOF. The information rate at the receiver, R_r, is the transmission rate of a single server queue where each packet has only one bit and the input/output rate is $\lambda_1 + \lambda_2$. In other words,

$$R_r = C(\lambda_1 + \lambda_2) + \lim_{n\to\infty} \frac{H(N^n)}{n}.$$

The information rate at the eavesdropper, R_e, is the information rate conveyed in the packets, which is $\lim_{n\to\infty} H(N^n)/n$. Thus, the additional uncertainty rate, R_c, at the eavesdropper is equal to the timing capacity of a single flow with rate $\lambda_1+\lambda_2$. □

Next, we consider the case where the eavesdropper is located at the output of the queue, i.e., it observes the sequence of departing packets, and a random service discipline is employed by the server, i.e., the server randomly picks a packet in queue to serve. The following proposition shows that the difference in the uncertainty between the intended receiver and the eavesdropper can be increased compared to that of FIFO discipline when the input distribution is Poisson.

PROPOSITION 5. Suppose that the service discipline is random service. The additional sum uncertainty rate at the eavesdropper, R_c, can be made strictly larger than the timing capacity of a single flow with rate $\lambda_1+\lambda_2$, when the input processes of flow 1 and flow 2 are Poisson processes with rate λ_1 and λ_2, respectively.

PROOF. Assume the queue is initially in equilibrium. The input processes from flows 1 and 2 are independent Poisson processes with rate λ_1 and λ_2, respectively. The first n_1 (n_2) in flow 1 (2) are used to convey timing information for flow 1 (2). Let $\tilde{A} = \{\hat{A}_1, \hat{A}_2, \cdots, \hat{A}_n, \hat{A}_{n+1}, \cdots\}$ be the inter-arrival times of the aggregate flow, and $\tilde{N} = \{\hat{N}_1, \hat{N}_2, \cdots, \hat{N}_n, \hat{N}_{n+1}, \cdots\}$ be the ID sequence of the aggregate flow on the arrival. Thus, $\hat{A}_i$s are i.i.d. random variables with an exponential distribution, and $\hat{N}_i$s are i.i.d. random variables with a Bernoulli distribution. At the receiver, we have

$$I(A^{n_1}, T^{n_2}; N^n, \bar{D}^n) = I(\tilde{A}, \tilde{N}; N^n, \bar{D}^n) - I(\tilde{A}, \tilde{N}; N^n, \bar{D}^n | A^{n_1}, T^{n_2}).$$

We also have

$$\begin{aligned} I(\tilde{A}, \tilde{N}; N^n, \bar{D}^n) &= I(\tilde{A}, \tilde{N}; \bar{D}^n) + I(\tilde{A}, \tilde{N}; N^n | \bar{D}^n) \\ &= I(\tilde{A}, \tilde{N}; \bar{D}^n) + H(N^n | \bar{D}^n) - H(N^n | \tilde{A}, \tilde{N}, \bar{D}^n). \end{aligned}$$

Next, we show that $H(N^n|\bar{D}^n) = H(N^n)$ for the random policy, which is equivalent to showing that $I(N^n; \bar{D}^n) = 0$. We have

$$I(N^n; \bar{D}^n) \le I(N^n; \hat{A}^n, S^n, \bar{D}^n) = I(N^n; \hat{A}^n, S^n, D_0).$$

The equality holds because $\bar{D}^n$ can be determined by $(\hat{A}^n, S^n, D_0)$. Now, since $(\hat{A}^n, S^n, D_0)$ cannot give us any information about the identity of a particular packet, $I(N^n; \hat{A}^n, S^n, D_0) = 0$. Thus, $H(N^n|\bar{D}^n) = H(N^n)$. In summary,

$$\begin{aligned} I(A^{n_1}, T^{n_2}; N^n, \bar{D}^n) &= I(\tilde{A}, \tilde{N}; \bar{D}^n) + H(N^n) - H(N^n | \tilde{A}, \tilde{N}, \bar{D}^n) \\ &\quad - I(\tilde{A}, \tilde{N}; N^n, \bar{D}^n | A^{n_1}, T^{n_2}), \end{aligned}$$

where the information rate from the packet header sequence at the eavesdropper is

$$I(N^n; A^{n_1}, T^{n_2}) = H(N^n) - H(N^n|A^{n_1}, T^{n_2}) \leq H(N^n) - H(N^n|\tilde{A}, \tilde{N}).$$

Thus, the additional uncertainty at the eavesdropper is given by

$$\begin{aligned} &I(\tilde{A}, \tilde{N}; \bar{D}^n) + H(N^n|A^{n_1}, T^{n_2}) - H(N^n|\tilde{A}, \tilde{N}, \bar{D}^n) - I(\tilde{A}, \tilde{N}; N^n, \bar{D}^n|A^{n_1}, T^{n_2}) \\ &\quad \geq I(\hat{A}^n; \bar{D}^n) + H(N^n|\tilde{A}, \tilde{N}) - H(N^n|\tilde{A}, \tilde{N}, \bar{D}^n) - I(\tilde{A}, \tilde{N}; N^n, \bar{D}^n|A^{n_1}, T^{n_2}). \end{aligned}$$

Note that $I(\hat{A}^n; \bar{D}^n)$ is the mutual information between the inter-arrivals and inter-departures of a single flow where the input process is Poisson with rate $\lambda_1 + \lambda_2$, and thus

$$\lim_{n\to\infty} \frac{\lambda_1 + \lambda_2}{n} I(\hat{A}^n; \bar{D}^n) = C,$$

where C is the timing capacity of a single flow with rate $\lambda_1 + \lambda_2$.

Next, we show that

$$\lim_{n\to\infty} \frac{1}{n} \left(H(N^n|\tilde{A}, \tilde{N}) - H(N^n|\tilde{A}, \tilde{N}, \bar{D}^n)\right) > 0, \tag{2.4}$$

and

$$\lim_{n\to\infty} \frac{1}{n} I(\tilde{A}, \tilde{N}; N^n, \bar{D}^n|A^{n_1}, T^{n_2}) = 0. \tag{2.5}$$

We have

$$H(N^n|\tilde{A}, \tilde{N}) - H(N^n|\tilde{A}, \tilde{N}, \bar{D}^n) = \sum_{i=1}^{n} I(N_i; \bar{D}^n|\tilde{A}, \tilde{N}, N^{i-1}).$$

For $i \geq 2$, we have

$$\begin{aligned} I(N_i; \bar{D}^n|\tilde{A}, \tilde{N}, N^{i-1}) &\geq I(N_i; D_{i-1}|\tilde{A}, \tilde{N}, \bar{D}^{i-2}, N^{i-1}) \\ &= I(N_i; D_{i-1}|\tilde{A}, \tilde{N}, \bar{D}^{i-2}, N^{i-1}, M_1(i-1), M_2(i-1)), \end{aligned} \tag{2.6}$$

where $M_1(i-1)$ ($M_2(i-1)$) is the number of flow 1 (2) packets in the queue (i.e., packets that are waiting for service) right after the $(i-1)$th packet begins its service. Note that $M_1(i-1)$ and $M_2(i-1)$ are determined by $(\tilde{A}, \tilde{N}, \bar{D}^{i-2}, N^{i-1})$. Thus,

$$\begin{aligned} (2.6) \geq\ & I(N_i; D_{i-1}|\tilde{A}, \tilde{N}, \bar{D}^{i-2}, N^{i-1}, M_1(i-1) = 1, M_2(i-1) = 1) \\ & \times P(M_1(i-1) = 1, M_2(i-1) = 1). \end{aligned}$$

Note that

$$\begin{aligned} &I(N_i; D_{i-1}|\tilde{A}, \tilde{N}, \bar{D}^{i-2}, N^{i-1}, M_1(i-1) = 1, M_2(i-1) = 1) \\ &= I(N_i; S_{i-1} + W_{i-1}|\tilde{A}, \tilde{N}, \bar{D}^{i-2}, N^{i-1}, M_1(i-1) = 1, M_2(i-1) = 1, W_{i-1} = 0) \\ &= I(N_i; S_{i-1}|\tilde{A}, \tilde{N}, \bar{D}^{i-2}, N^{i-1}, M_1(i-1) = 1, M_2(i-1) = 1, W_{i-1} = 0), \end{aligned}$$

where W_{i-1} is the idling time of the server between the departure of the $(i-2)$th packet and the arrival of the $(i-1)$th packet. Because the input process is Poisson, $(M_1(i-1) = 1, M_2(i-1) = 1)$ implies that $(W_{i-1} = 0)$. Let t be the time when the $(i-1)$th packet begins its service. Note that conditioning on $(M_1(i-1) = 1, M_2(i-1) = 1)$, N_i only depends on events that happen after time t. Let

$$\begin{aligned} \tilde{A}' &= \{\hat{A}', \hat{A}_{i+3}, \hat{A}_{i+4}, \cdots\} \\ \tilde{N}' &= \{\hat{N}_{i+2}, \hat{N}_{i+3}, \hat{N}_{i+4}, \cdots\} \end{aligned}$$

be the inter-arrival times and ID sequence of packets arrived after time t, where $\hat{A}'$ is a random variable denoting the time elapsed between t and the first packet arrives after t. Note that $\hat{A}'$ is exponential with mean $1/(\lambda_1+\lambda_2)$. Thus, $\tilde{A}'$ and $\tilde{A}$ have the same distribution, and so do $\tilde{N}'$ and $\tilde{N}$. Note that $\tilde{A}'$ and $\tilde{N}'$ are independent of $(M_1(i-1)=1, M_2(i-1)=1)$. Then, we have

$$\begin{aligned}
& I(N_i; D_{i-1}|\tilde{A}, \tilde{N}, \bar{D}^{i-2}, N^{i-1}, M_1(i-1)=1, M_2(i-1)=1) \\
= \;& I(N_i; S_{i-1}|\tilde{A}', \tilde{N}', M_1(i-1)=1, M_2(i-1)=1) \\
= \;& \int E\left(\log \frac{p(N_i|s_{i-1}, \tilde{a}, \tilde{n}, M_1(i-1)=1, M_2(i-1)=1)}{p(N_i|\tilde{a}, \tilde{n}, M_1(i-1)=1, M_2(i-1)=1)}\right) \mathrm{d}F(s_{i-1}, \tilde{a}, \tilde{n}).
\end{aligned}$$

Now, we show that $I(N_i; S_{i-1}|\tilde{A}', \tilde{N}', M_1(i-1)=1, M_2(i-1)=1)$ is positive. Consider two events that occur with positive probabilities: 1) during the service time of the $(i-1)$th packet, no new packet arrives. 2) during the service time of the $(i-1)$th packet, one new packet arrives. In these two cases, $p(N_i=k|s_{i-1}, \tilde{a}, \tilde{n}, M_1(i-1)=1, M_2(i-1)=1)$ is different. Thus, $p(N_i=k|s_{i-1}, \tilde{a}, \tilde{n}, M_1(i-1)=1, M_2(i-1)=1) \neq p(N_i=k|\tilde{a}, \tilde{n}, M_1(i-1)=1, M_2(i-1)=1)$. Thus, $c_1 =: I(N_i; S_{i-1}|\tilde{A}', \tilde{N}', M_1(i-1)=1, M_2(i-1)=1) > 0$. Further, because $P(M_1(i-1)=1, M_2(i-1)=1)=c_2>0$ and is independent of i in steady state, we have

$$I(N_i; \bar{D}^n|\tilde{A}, \tilde{N}, N^{i-1}) \geq c_1c_2 > 0,$$

and thus (2.4) holds. Intuitively, knowing the departure times help reduce the randomness caused by the random policy at the router conditioning on the knowledge of arrivals.

Next, we show (2.5). We have

$$\begin{aligned}
& I(\bar{D}^n, N^n; \tilde{A}, \tilde{N}|A^{n_1}, T^{n_2}) \\
= \;& I(D_0; \tilde{A}, \tilde{N}|A^{n_1}, T^{n_2}) + \sum_{i=1}^{n} I(D_i, N_i; \tilde{A}, \tilde{N}|A^{n_1}, T^{n_2}, \bar{D}^{i-1}, N^{i-1}) \\
= \;& \sum_{i=1}^{n} I(D_i, N_i; \tilde{A}, \tilde{N}|A^{n_1}, T^{n_2}, \bar{D}^{i-1}, N^{i-1}, 1_{Z_i}),
\end{aligned}$$

where 1_{Z_i} is the indicator function of the event Z_i. Recall that Z_i is the event that the $(i-1)$th packet departs before either n_1 packets arrive from flow 1 or n_2 packets arrive from flow 2. When Z_i happens, $(\tilde{A}, \tilde{N})$ does not contain additional information about (D_i, N_i) conditioning on $(A^{n_1}, T^{n_2}, \bar{D}^{i-1}, N^{i-1})$. Thus,

$$\begin{aligned}
& I(D_i, N_i; \tilde{A}, \tilde{N}|A^{n_1}, T^{n_2}, \bar{D}^{i-1}, N^{i-1}, 1_{Z_i}) \\
= \;& I(D_i, N_i; \tilde{A}, \tilde{N}|A^{n_1}, T^{n_2}, \bar{D}^{i-1}, N^{i-1}, 1_{Z_i}=0)(1-P(Z_i)) \\
\leq \;& \left(I(D_i; \tilde{A}, \tilde{N}|A^{n_1}, T^{n_2}, \bar{D}^{i-1}, N^{i-1}, 1_{Z_i}=0) + H(N_i)\right)(1-P(Z_i)) \\
\leq \;& \left(h(D_i) - h(D_i|\tilde{A}, \tilde{N}, \bar{D}^{i-1}) + H(N_i)\right)(1-P(Z_i)) \\
= \;& (h(D_i) - h(S_i) + 1)(1-P(Z_i)) \\
= \;& \left(\log \frac{\mu}{\lambda_1+\lambda_2} + 1\right)(1-P(Z_i)).
\end{aligned}$$

Since $\sum_{i=1}^{n} n^{-1}(1-P(Z_i))$ converges to 0 as as shown earlier, we have shown (2.5), and thus complete the proof. □

Let the arrival processes of flow 1 and flow 2 be independent Poisson processes. If the service discipline is FIFO or if the eavesdropper is located before the server (i.e., observes the packet headers of the arriving packets), then the additional uncertainty at the eavesdropper (as compared to the uncertainty at the intended receiver) equals the timing capacity of a single flow whose arrival rate is the sum of the arrival rates of the two flows. If the service discipline is random, then this additional uncertainty increases. The intuition is that the eavesdropper does not observe or record departure times. The intended receivers' knowledge of the departure times reduces the randomness introduced by the random service discipline conditioned on the arrival times. Thus, the additional uncertainty at the eavesdropper increases.

Note that it has been shown that for a discrete memoryless channel, if $R_c \leq I(X;Y) - I(X;Z)$, where X is the input random variable, Y and Z are the output random variables observed at the receiver and the eavesdropper respectively, then R_c can be achieved with perfect secrecy [**Wyn75, CK78**]. Perfect secrecy means that the transmitter can reliably send information to the receiver while the information obtained by the eavesdropper is arbitrarily small [**CK78**]. We are not aware of any coding theorems that show this for our model. Thus, an open problem is to check whether the transmitter and the receiver can communicate at rate R_c with perfect secrecy in our timing channel.

Conclusions

In this paper, we first studied the case when a flow shares an exponential server with uncontrolled, independent interference traffic. When the interference traffic is Poisson, we obtained a lower bound on the timing capacity. Further, we derived asymptotically tight lower and upper bounds on the total timing capacity of multiple flows when the service time distribution is exponential. Lower and upper bounds are also calculated for discrete-time queues with a general service time distribution. We also studied the system where an eavesdropper can observe the sequence and contents of the departure packets, but not their timing. We showed that the amount of uncertainty at the eavesdropper is affected by the scheduling discipline at the server.

Acknowledgment

We sincerely thank the reviewers for their thorough reviews and very insightful comments.

References

[AV96] V. Anantharam and S. Verdu, "Bits through queues", *IEEE Trans. Inform. Theory*, vol. 42, no. 1, Jan. 1996, pp. 4–18.

[BA98] A. Bedekar and M. Azizoglu, "The information-theoretic capacity of discrete-time queues", *IEEE Trans. Inform. Theory*, vol. 44, no. 2, Mar. 1998, pp. 446–461.

[BG87] D. Bertsekas and R. Gallager, *Data networks*, Prentice-Hall Inc., 1987.

[BK93] H. Bruneel and B. Kim, *Discrete-time models for communication systems including ATM*, Kluwer Academic Publishers, 1993.

[CK78] I. Csiszar and J. Korner, "Broadcast channels with confidential messages", IEEE Trans. Inform. Theory, vol. 24, no. 3, 1978, pp. 339 –348.

[Kle75] L. Kleinrock, *Queueing systems, volume i: Theory*, vol. I, Wiley Interscience, New York, 1975.

[Sun99] R. Sundaresan, *Coded communication over timing channels*, Ph.D. thesis, Princeton University, 1999.

[VH94] S. Verdu and T. Han, "A general formula for channel capacity", *IEEE Trans. Inform. Theory*, vol. 40, no. 4, July 1994, pp. 1147–1157.

[Wyn75] A. Wyner, "The wire-tap channel", *Bell System Technical Journal*, vol. 54, no. 8, 1975, pp. 1355–1387.

Department of Computer Science, University of California, Davis, CA 95616
E-mail address: liu@cs.ucdavis.edu

Coordinated Science Laboratory, University of Illinois at Urbana-Champaign, Urbana, IL 61801
E-mail address: rsrikant@uiuc.edu

DIMACS Series in Discrete Mathematics
and Theoretical Computer Science
Volume **66**, 2004

Job Scheduling and Multiple Access

Sibi Raj, Emre Telatar, and David Tse

ABSTRACT. We establish an analogy between the additive Gaussian multiple access channel and multi-processor queues. We exploit this analogy to investigate certain problems arising in multiple access information theory. In particular we address the question of minimal average delay for multiple users, each with a finite bit pool, and then a multiple access channel with users arriving according to a Poisson process. In the latter case, we show that the system is stable under all arrival rates, and show that the communication analog of shorter-tasks-faster strategy is close to optimal for high arrival rates.

1. Introduction

A multiple access communication system is comprised of a set of transmitters sending information to a common receiver. Transmitters are driven by independent information sources generating streams of packets; typically this is a bursty stream. Each transmitter encodes the packets it receives in a signal, and the receiver observes a noisy signal that depends on these transmitted signals. The transmitters are uncoordinated except via a "weak" feedback they may get from the receiver.

Information theory views multiple access as a matter of combating noise and interference. The issue of bursty packet arrival is something to be dealt by appropriate source coding. Network theory, on the other hand, views multiple access as a matter of resource allocation and distributed scheduling, taking advantage of the bursty arrival of packets, but ignoring the issues of noise and interference. Neither approach is entirely satisfactory [**Ga**]: By dropping the question of source burstiness, the information theoretic approach makes any meaningful analysis of end-to-end delay impossible, by trivializing the issue of interference and noise, the networking approach takes an oversimplified view of the physical layer.

Our aim here is to present a partially unified view. We will consider a Gaussian multiple access channel with equal power transmitters, and will attempt to say something about average packet delay while keeping to an information theoretic framework. Our method is based on the exploitation of a certain analogy between

1991 *Mathematics Subject Classification.* Primary 94A24, 68M20; Secondary 94A40, 90B36.
Key words and phrases. Packet delay, network information theory.
S. Raj is supported in part by the NCCR-MICS, a center supported by the Swiss National Science Foundation under grant number 5005-67322.
Part of this work was performed in 1995 while both E. Telatar and D. Tse were with AT&T Bell Laboratories, Murray Hill, NJ.

this channel and job scheduling on multi-processor queues. Accordingly, first, we will discuss scheduling.

2. Job Scheduling

Suppose we have n tasks to complete. Task k requires τ_k units of service. To complete these tasks we have m processors; processor k can deliver service at a rate of s_k units of service per unit time. We can assign tasks to processors, and are able to change the assignment at any time. However, at any given time no more than one processor may be assigned to any task. Nor can any processor be assigned to more than one task at any given time. A task is completed when the cumulative service it has received meets its service requirement. We will call such a system a multi-processor queue.

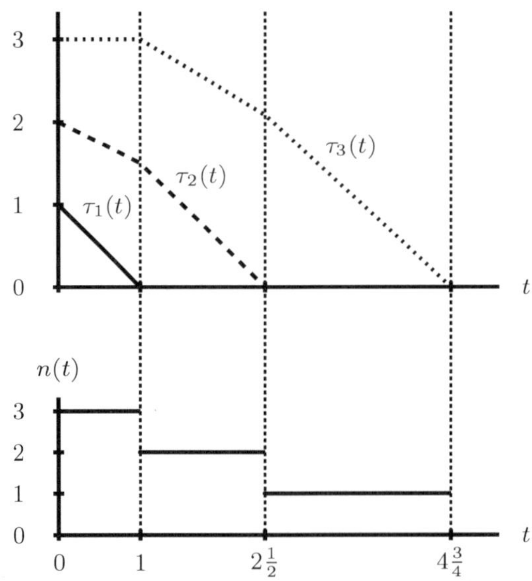

The top graph shows the remaining service requirement $\tau_k(t)$ of each task as a function of elapsed time t. The lower graph shows the number of tasks $n(t)$ still to be completed, again as a function of the elapsed time.

FIGURE 1. Job Scheduling for Example 2.1

EXAMPLE 2.1. Let there be three tasks and two processors ($n = 3$, $m = 2$). Let $\tau_1 = 1$, $\tau_2 = 2$, $\tau_3 = 3$, and $s_1 = 1$, $s_2 = \frac{1}{2}$. We may assign processor 1 to task 1 and processor 2 to task 2 for one unit of time. At the end of this period, task 1 will be completed and task 2 will have a remaining service requirement of $1\frac{1}{2}$ units of service. We can then assign processor 1 to task 2 and processor 2 to task 3 for $1\frac{1}{2}$ units of time. At the end of this period, task 2 will be completed, and task 3 will have $2\frac{1}{4}$ units of service remaining. We can now assign processor 1 to task 3 for $2\frac{1}{4}$ units of time and all tasks will be complete. (See Figure 1.)

2.1. Service Rate Vectors. Suppose we have an infinite collection of processors, with service rates $s_1, s_2, \ldots$. The case of a finite number m of processors can be included in this framework by defining the service rates of all but the first m processors to be zero. Without loss of generality, assume that $s_1 \geq s_2 \geq \cdots$.

Suppose we have n tasks at hand. Clearly, we only need to consider processors 1 through n, since at any given time we cannot use more than n processors and these are the n most powerful processors we have.

By assigning processor k to task k we can deliver a service rate vector of $(s_1, \ldots, s_n)$, where the kth component of this vector is the service rate delivered to the kth task.

By permuting the assignment, for any permutation π of the integers $\{1, \ldots, n\}$, the service rate vector $s_\pi = (s_{\pi(1)}, \ldots, s_{\pi(n)})$ is achievable.

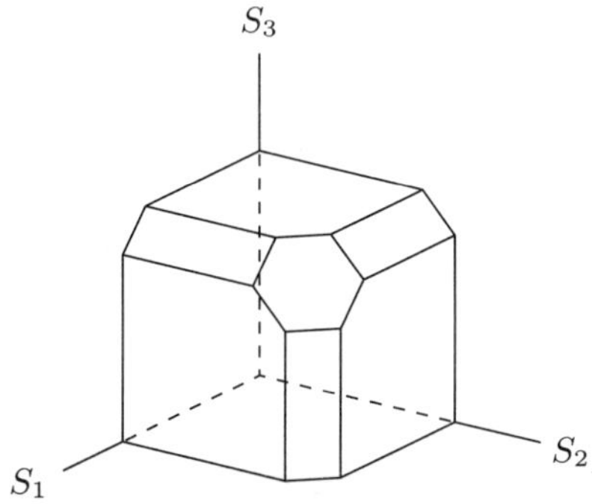

The vertices of the hexagon are those rates achievable by permuting the assignments of tasks to processors. The hexagon itself is achieved by time sharing between its vertices. Any point in the entire region is dominated by some point in the hexagon.

FIGURE 2. Rate region example with $n = 3$.

By moving between these assignments arbitrarily quickly, any convex combination of the rate vectors s_π can be achieved. It is also clear that any rate vector which is dominated in every component by an achievable rate vector is also achievable. Thus the achievable service rate vectors form a polymatroid (see e.g., [**W**, §18.3–4]), and thus are those $(S_1, \ldots, S_n)$ that satisfy

$$\text{for all } I \subset \{1, \ldots, n\}, \qquad \sum_{i \in I} S_i \leq \sum_{k=1}^{|I|} s_k \tag{2.1}$$

(see Figure 2). That one cannot achieve any other service rate vector follows from the form of (2.1): if any of the inequalities is not satisfied, then there is a collection I of tasks which get service at a rate exceeding the sum rate of the $|I|$ fastest processors, a contradiction.

2.2. Service Policies. Given a collection of processors and a set of tasks, the state of the system at time t is completely determined by the remaining service requirement $\tau_k(t)$ of each task k at this time. We will denote the number of uncompleted tasks at this time by $n(t)$, that is, $n(t) = |\{k : \tau_k(t) > 0\}|$.

A service policy P is a function that maps a remaining service requirement vector to an achievable service rate vector. Thus, a policy determines the rate of service offered to each task based on the state of the system.

EXAMPLE 2.2. Suppose there is an infinite number of processors, with service rates $s_1, s_2, \ldots$ and that $s_1 \geq s_2 \geq \cdots$. Consider a policy L that assigns faster processors to the shorter tasks. If the state of the system is $(\tau_1, \ldots, \tau_n)$ and if π is the permutation of the integers $\{1, \dots, n\}$ that orders the tasks in increasing order of service requirement, i.e.,

$$\tau_{\pi(1)} \le \cdots \le \tau_{\pi(n)}$$

then, the policy L will assign to $(\tau_1, \dots, \tau_n)$ the service rate vector

$$(s_{\pi^{-1}(1)}, \dots, s_{\pi^{-1}(n)}).$$

We will call L the "shorter tasks faster" policy. Note that in Example 2.1 we employed this policy.

2.3. Scheduling for the Smallest Sum Completion Time. Again suppose we have an infinite number of processors with rates $s_1, s_2, \dots$ with $s_1 \ge s_2 \ge \cdots$, and n tasks with service requirements $\tau_1, \dots, \tau_n$ with $\tau_1 \le \cdots \le \tau_n$. Let $C_k(\tau_1, \dots, \tau_n; P)$ denote the completion time of task k under a given service policy P. The quantity

$$\bar{C}(\tau_1, \dots, \tau_n; P) = \frac{1}{n} \sum_{k=1}^{n} C_k(\tau_1, \dots, \tau_n; P)$$

is then the average time the tasks spend in the system

We are interested in finding a policy P which minimizes $\bar{C}$. It is clear that the minimization of $\bar{C}$ is equivalent to the minimization of $\sum_k C_k$, the sum completion time. Fortunately for us, this is a well studied problem in scheduling theory. In the scheduling terminology the multi-processor system we have described is known as "uniform machines with preemption" (the adjective "uniform" indicating that the processors differ only in speed), and the following is well known [**Go**] (see, e.g., [**BEP**, p. 171]):

THEOREM 2.3. *Policy L of serving shorter tasks faster minimizes the average completion time.*

REMARK 2.4. Policy L not only minimizes $\sum_{k=1}^{n} C_k$, it also minimizes $\sum_{k=1}^{j} C_k$ for every $j = 1, \dots, n$.

REMARK 2.5. Under policy L, since shorter tasks are served faster, if $\tau_i < \tau_j$, then $\tau_i(t) < \tau_j(t)$ for all time t: there is no 'overtaking.'

REMARK 2.6. Under policy L, if $\tau_i < \tau_j$, then increasing the length of task j does not change C_i: longer tasks do not interfere with the service of shorter ones.

3. The Gaussian Multiple access Channel

We now turn to the Gaussian multiple access channel, and show that results in scheduling theory can be adapted to questions arising in its treatment. Suppose we have n transmitters with equal power P and a single receiver. The signal received at the receiver is the sum of the signals of the transmitters and Gaussian noise:

$$y = \sum_{k=1}^{n} x_k + z \tag{3.1}$$

where y is the received signal, x_k is the signal transmitter by the kth transmitter, and z is a zero mean Gaussian random variable with unit variance. Suppose that transmitter k has a data rate of R_k. Call a data rate vector $(R_1, \dots, R_n)$ achievable if for any prescribed error probability, no matter how small, there exists codes with rates arbitrarily close to the given data rate for each transmitter and a decoding strategy for the receiver such that the error probability is smaller than that prescribed. It is well known (see e.g., [**CT**, §14.3]) that a data rate vector $(R_1, \ldots, R_n)$ is achievable if and only if[1]

$$\text{for all } I \subset \{1, \ldots, n\}, \qquad \sum_{i \in I} R_i \le \frac{1}{2} \log(1 + |I|P). \tag{3.2}$$

For $k = 1, 2, \ldots,$ let

$$\begin{aligned} s_k &= \frac{1}{2}\log(1 + kP) - \frac{1}{2}\log(1 + (k-1)P) \\ &= \frac{1}{2}\log\left(1 + \frac{P}{1 + (k-1)P}\right). \end{aligned} \tag{3.3}$$

Observe that s_k is non-increasing in k and that for $m = 0, 1, \ldots,$

$$\frac{1}{2}\log(1 + mP) = \sum_{k=1}^{m} s_k.$$

Thus, equation (3.2) can be expressed as

$$\text{for all } I \subset \{1, \ldots, n\}, \qquad \sum_{i \in I} R_i \le \sum_{k=1}^{|I|} s_k. \tag{3.4}$$

Comparing equations (2.1) and (3.4) we see that the data rates achievable over an additive Gaussian multiple access channel are the same as the service rates available from a multi-processor server with processor rates given by (3.3). This suggests an analogy between multiple access channels and multi-processor queues. To illustrate the analogy consider the following problem.

3.1. Transmitters with finite bit pools. Suppose there are n users of a Gaussian multiple access system, each user with power P and user k having a message of length τ_k bits to transmit. Note that unlike the usual information theoretic scenario the users do not have a stream of data arriving at a given rate, but each has a fixed pool of bits to send. We want to minimize the average delay of the messages, the delay of a message being the time until the message is decoded by the receiver. From the previous section, we know how to solve this optimization problem: Assume without loss of generality that $\tau_1 \le \cdots \le \tau_n$. Operate at the rate vector $(s_1, \ldots, s_n)$ until the message of user 1 is decoded. By this time a number of bits of the remaining messages will be decoded also. Next operate at the rate vector $(0, s_1, \ldots, s_{n-1})$ until the message of the second user is decoded. Continue in this fashion until all the messages are decoded. The resulting decoding times $C_k(\tau_1, \ldots, \tau_n; L)$ will have the least sum (and arithmetic mean) of all possible decoding schemes. Let $\Sigma(\tau_1, \ldots, \tau_n) = \sum_k C_k(\tau_1, \ldots, \tau_n; L)$ denote this least sum.

From an information theoretic point of view, it is clear that no encoding and decoding scheme can have an average delay less than the one computed via this analogy and policy L; there will not be enough mutual information and Fano's inequality will establish a lower bound on the probability of error. However, it is not clear if the average delay as computed by the analogy can actually be achieved: since the number of bits to be transmitted is finite, the usual machinery of the law of large numbers cannot be brought onto this problem. One can, however, look at the case of each user having a large number of bits.

[1] We measure data rates in this paper in bits, and the logarithms are taken to be base 2.

THEOREM 3.1. *Suppose user k has $\lceil \alpha\tau_k \rceil$ bits to transmit ($k = 1, \dots, n$), where $\alpha > 0$ is a scaling parameter. Then the sum completion time, when normalized by α, can be made arbitrarily close to $\Sigma(\tau_1, \dots, \tau_n)$ by choosing α sufficiently large.*

PROOF. We will show that for any $\epsilon > 0$, there exists a large enough α and an encoding and decoding scheme such that the error probability is no more than ϵ and the normalized sum completion time is within ϵ of $\Sigma(\tau_1, \dots, \tau_n)$.

For $0 \le \delta < 1$, let $\Sigma^{(\delta)}(\tau_1, \dots, \tau_n)$ denote the sum completion time of the tasks when the processor rates are reduced by a factor δ, i.e., when the processor rates are $(1-\delta)s_1, (1-\delta)s_2, \dots$. Note that $\Sigma^{(\delta)} = \Sigma/(1-\delta)$ is a continuous function of δ. Given $\epsilon > 0$, first choose $\delta > 0$ such that

$$\Sigma^{\delta}(\tau_1, \dots, \tau_n) < \Sigma(\tau_1, \dots, \tau_n) + \epsilon.$$

Now consider a multi-processor queue with these reduced rates, and let $C_1, \dots, C_n$ denote the completion times of the tasks, and let $t_1 = C_1$, $t_k = C_k - C_{k-1}$. There are thus n epochs, $[0, C_1)$, $[C_1, C_2)$, $\dots$, $[C_{n-1}, C_n)$ during which the assignment of the processors to tasks are fixed. During the jth epoch, processor 1 is assigned to task j, processor 2 to task $j+1$, etc. Let τ_k^j denote the amount of work done on task k during the jth epoch, $\tau_k^j = t_j(1-\delta)s_{k-j+1}$, $1 \le j \le k \le n$. Choose now β large enough so that for all $1 \le j \le k \le n$,

$$\frac{\lceil \beta\tau_k^j \rceil}{\lfloor \beta t_j \rfloor} < s_{k-j+1}.$$

We can now choose a positive integer M such that there exists n multiple access codes, the jth of blocklength $M\lfloor \beta t_j \rfloor$ and rate vector

$$\left(\frac{\lceil \beta\tau_k^j \rceil}{\lfloor \beta t_j \rfloor} : k = j, \dots, n \right)$$

and each with error probability less than ϵ/n. Choosing $\alpha = M\beta$, we thus have a coding scheme with error probability at most ϵ and normalized sum completion time within ϵ of $\Sigma(\tau_1, \dots, \tau_n)$. □

3.2. Poisson Arrivals to a Gaussian Multi-user System. Suppose that tasks are not all present at the beginning of time, but they arrive one by one. In the language of scheduling theory, the tasks now has 'release dates,' furthermore the policy needs to be 'on line'. Under these circumstances, it is known that the policy L of serving shorter tasks faster does not necessarily minimize the average time tasks spend in the system. Indeed, policy L is not necessarily optimal even in the case when each arriving task demands 1 unit of service.

Nonetheless, it is interesting to examine how policy L behaves in this last situation. Since the service demand of a new arrival is 1, it is necessarily at least as large as the service demands of the tasks already in the system. Thus, if there are n tasks in the system just before an arrival, the new task is assigned the $n+1^{\text{st}}$ processor. It also follows from Remark 2.6 that the completion time of a task is independent of the arrival times of the tasks arriving later. Thus, policy L operates in a "first come fastest served" fashion (see Figure 3). To further illustrate the idea, one may think of the tasks lining up in front of the processors. A new arrival goes to the end of the line and moves to faster processors as tasks before it are completed, until it reaches the fastest processor and departs when its service is finished.

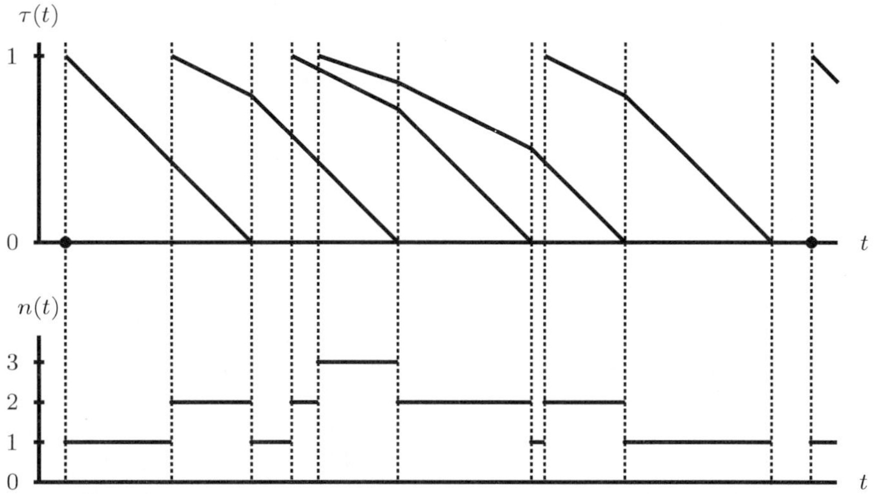

A sample path for a multi-processor queue with tasks arriving according to a renewal process. Here $s_k = 1/k$, $k = 1, 2, \dots$, and each task requires 1 unit of service. The upper curve traces the remaining service requirement of each task as they arrive to the queue. Note that if there are n tasks in the system, the service rate each receives is determined by the temporal ordering of their arrivals; the kth task receives $1/k$ units of service per unit time. The renewal instants for the system, i.e., the instants of arrival to an empty system is marked with a circle in the upper time axis.

FIGURE 3. Sample path with tasks arriving over time

Although we remarked that policy L is not optimal in general, it is possible that it does minimize the expected time tasks spend in the system for some particular arrival processes. In any case, we can reach some conclusions without requiring the optimality of policy L. For example, suppose that the arrival process is a renewal process with rate λ, and that $\sum_{k=1}^{\infty} s_k$ diverges. Then, the overall system will be stable for all finite λ. To see this, consider the amount of work that needs to be done to clear the system. This quantity increases by 1 every time a new task arrives, and decreases at a rate of $\sum_{k=1}^{n} s_k$ when there are n tasks to complete. Since customers arrive at a rate of λ, the rate at which the new work arrives is λ, and the rate at which work is done will exceed the arrival rate when n is large enough. The remaining work thus performs a random walk with negative drift and a boundary at the origin, and hence will enter a compact set around the origin infinitely often.

We can now consider a continuous time Gaussian multiple access channel of single-sided bandwidth W. Let all the transmitters have the same power, and let P be the ratio of a transmitters power to the power of the additive Gaussian noise.

At a time when there are n active transmitters, the capacity region of this channel is again given by (3.4) with

$$s_k = W \log\Big(1 + \frac{P}{1 + (k-1)P}\Big). \tag{3.5}$$

Now suppose that the packets arrive to this system according to a Poisson process. Just as in the analysis of the ALOHA protocol, we will assume that each arriving packet is associated to a different transmitter. This simplifies the analysis, but is less innocent than it looks. In the case of ALOHA this assumption is a pessimistic one, here it is not so: on the one hand it disallows the cooperative scheduling of packets that would have arrived to the same user, on the other hand, by creating more users it increases the total available transmitted power. It is thus neither an optimistic nor a pessimistic assumption.

Suppose each arriving packet has a fixed number Q of bits to be transmitted. We wish to process the packets in analogy with policy L: if an arriving packet finds an empty system it should be transmitted at the rate s_1; if it finds a system with one other packet, it should transmitted at rate s_2 until the first user is decoded, after which it should be transmitted at rate s_1 until it is decoded. In general, an arriving packet that finds $j-1$ packets already in the system should go through transmission rates $s_j, \dots, s_1$ in that order with the transitions occurring at the times when the packets before it are decoded. Note that these times are independent of the later arrivals.

Of course, it is one thing to wish to serve the arriving packets according to a policy which prescribes what rates they should be served at what times, and another thing to be able to come up with an encoding and decoding method that can implement these rates. It is not true that an arbitrary job scheduling policy can be turned into a communication scheme. The remarkable property of policy L is that it is implementable with a small amount of feedback from the receiver. The key enabler is again Remark 2.6: when a new transmission starts, the receiver can inform the transmitter of the decoding times of the transmissions already in progress. The transmitter then knows at which data rates it should communicate at which periods of time, and also when it is to be decoded. Since the transmission rates it sends at are precisely those which allow it to be decoded regarding the existing transmissions as noise, it can be decoded, *and its signal can be subtracted from the received signal, causing no interference to the transmissions scheduled to complete before it.*

Let us illustrate this through an example. Suppose a user finds an empty system. It will then use a code with rate $s_1 = W \log(1 + P)$, which gives it a decoding time of $C_1 = S/s_1$. Suppose a second user arrives at a time $r_1 < C_1$. It is not clear, a priori, that the first user can still be decoded at time C_1 in the presence of the new user. To see how this can be done, split the second user's bits into two parts: a first part consisting of $(C_1 - r_1)s_2$ bits and a second part consisting of the remaining bits. For the duration from r_1 to C_1, let the second user transmit at rate $s_2 = W \log\bigl(1 + \frac{P}{1+P}\bigr)$. At the end of this duration, the first part of the bits of the second user can be decoded by regarding the first user as noise. Once these bits are known, the second user's signal can be canceled from the received signal and the first user can be decoded as well. The second user will now transmit the rest of its bits at rate s_1. Note that s_k is precisely the rate up to which we can decode a user in the presence of $k-1$ others by regarding these other users as noise.

We should note that the discussion above is valid only when Q is relatively large; otherwise, the splitting of the bits may result in the number of messages to be distinguished during a time interval becoming fractional, or the code lengths becoming too short to allow allow efficient encoding. It should be clear, nonetheless, that an argument of the type used in Theorem 3.1 will establish the required asymptotic. A perhaps cleaner argument will use error exponents as done in [**TG**] and obtain the results above as a limiting case.

Figure 4 shows the average delay $\bar{D}$ of a message (i.e., the time elapsed since its arrival till its decoding) as a function of the arrival rate and the signal to noise

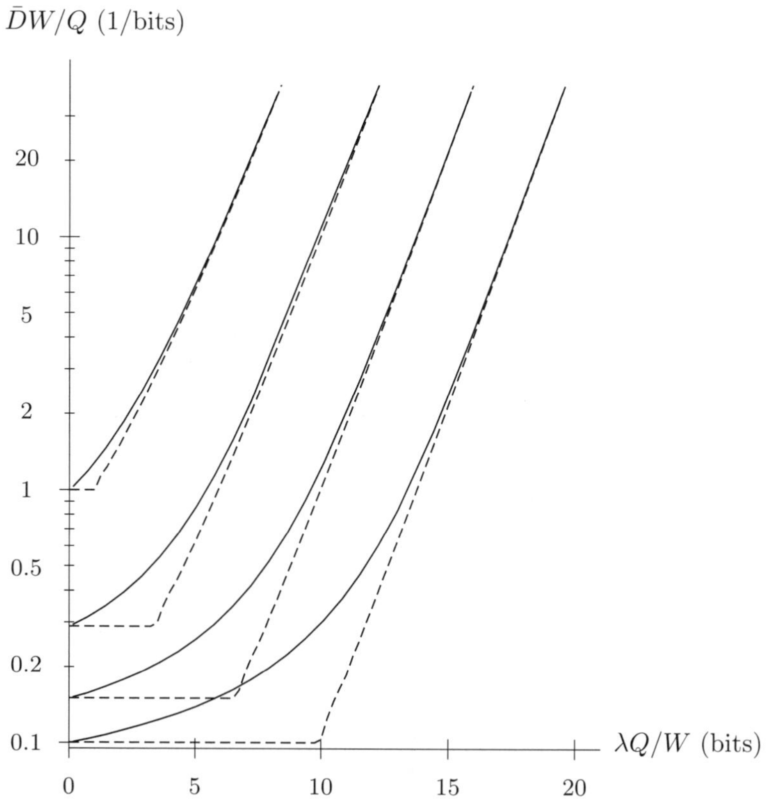

The average delay (solid curves) of a packet at different SNR's versus the arrival rate under policy L. Note that the vertical axis is delay normalized by the bandwidth and also the packet length Q (in bits), and the horizontal axis is the arrival rate (in bits per unit time) normalized by the bandwidth. The curves are for SNR values of $0, 10, 20$ and 30 dBs. Also shown (dashed curves) is a lower bound on average delay for any policy.

FIGURE 4. Average Delay vs. Arrival rate

ratio P. Note the normalizations of the axes in this figure; the horizontal axis is the bit arrival rate per unit bandwidth, and the vertical axes is the delay per bit in units of inverse bandwidth.

Since we do not claim any optimality of policy L, what guarantee is there that there is not some other, more clever, policy that makes the average delay $\bar{D}$ much less than that achievable by L? The next section derives a lower bound to this average delay and indicates that policy L cannot be beaten by much.

3.3. A lower bound on average delay. We will now derive a lower bound on the average delay for any arrival process of rate λ and any service policy. To that end, suppose we have a multiprocessor queue to which unit length tasks arrive at a rate of λ. Suppose we have some service policy, and let p_n denote the long term fraction of time during which there are n tasks in the queue. Thus, the time-average number of tasks in queue is $\bar{N} = \sum_n np_n$. By Little's law, the average time

$\bar{D}$ a task spends in the system satisfies

$$\lambda \bar{D} = \bar{N}. \tag{3.6}$$

Observe now, that since the total service rate cannot exceed $\sigma_n = \sum_{k=1}^{n} s_k$ when there are n tasks in the queue, the long-term average total service rate offered by the system is at most

$$\sum_n p_n \sigma_n.$$

For stability we need $\lambda \le \sum_n p_n \sigma_n$, and thus,

$$\bar{N} \ge \inf\Big\{\sum_n n p_n : \sum_n p_n \sigma_n \ge \lambda\Big\},$$

or equivalently,

$$\begin{aligned}\lambda &\le \sup\Big\{\sum_n p_n \sigma_n : \sum_n n p_n \le \bar{N}\Big\}\\ &= \sup\big\{E\big[\sigma_N\big] : E[N] \le \bar{N}\big\},\end{aligned}$$

where the supremum is over all non-negative integer valued random variables N. Let $\sigma : [0,\infty) \to [0,\infty)$ be obtained by linearly interpolating σ_n; $\sigma(x) = \sigma_{\lfloor x \rfloor} + (x - \lfloor x \rfloor)[\sigma_{\lceil x \rceil} - \sigma_{\lfloor x \rfloor}]$. Since $\{s_n : n \ge 1\}$ is a non-increasing, non-negative sequence, σ is a concave, non-decreasing function. Thus, by relaxing the integer restriction on N, and using Jensen's inequality

$$\begin{aligned}\lambda &\le \sup\{E[\sigma(X)] : E[X] \le \bar{N}\}\\ &\le \sup\{\sigma(E[X]) : E[X] \le \bar{N}\}\\ &= \sigma(\bar{N}).\end{aligned}$$

Combined with Little's law (3.6) this yields

$$\bar{D} \ge \sigma^{-1}(\lambda)/\lambda, \tag{3.7}$$

where σ^{-1} is the inverse function of σ. One can check that for an arrival process with constant interarrival times this lower bound is achieved by policy L, so the bound cannot be improved without assuming something more about the arrival process.

Figure 4 shows this lower bound as the dashed curves. It is seen to be tight at high arrival rates, the bound is essentially indistinguishable to the performance of policy L. We thus conclude that policy L, even if it is not optimal, performs quite well in this regime.

4. Remarks

The reader will have noticed that this correspondence is based on the fact that both the multi-processor queue and the multiple access channel are governed by the same formal equation (eqs. (2.1) and (3.4)). We exploit this relationship to adapt problems that are natural in one to the other, and thus obtain novel results in the field of multiple access.

A genuine understanding of multiple access communication requires a combined treatment of bursty sources and noisy channels. Network information theory is difficult enough without further complicating it, but we feel that it is still possible to incorporate some aspects of bursty sources. The approach outlined here is perhaps a little fragile—the results we derive are heavily dependent on, for example, the symmetry between the transmitters—nonetheless, perhaps it can serve as an encouragement for further research.

Acknowledgments

E. Telatar and D. Tse would like to thank S. Hanly, H.-L. Huynh and A. Orlitsky for numerous comments and discussions.

References

[BEP] J. Błażewicz, K. H. Ecker, E. Pesch, G. Schmidt and J. Węglarz, *Scheduling computer and manufacturing processes,* Springer, Berlin, 1996.

[CT] T. Cover and J. Thomas, *Elements of information theory,* Wiley, New York, 1991.

[Ga] R. G. Gallager, "A perspective on multiaccess channels," *IEEE Trans. Inform. Theory,* vol. IT-31, no. 2, pp. 124–142, Mar. 1985.

[Go] T. Gonzalez, "Optimal mean finish time preemptive schedules," Technical report 220, Computer Science Department, Pennsylvania State University, 1977.

[TG] İ. E. Telatar and R. G. Gallager, "Combining queueing theory and information theory for multiaccess," *IEEE Journal on Selected Areas in Communication,* vol. 13, no. 6, pp. 963–969, Aug. 1995.

[W] D. J. A. Welsh, *Matroid theory,* Academic Press, London, 1976.

Laboratory of Information Theory, École Polytechnique Fédérale de Lausanne, CH-1015 Lausanne, Switzerland
E-mail address: bsraj@lth.epfl.ch

Laboratory of Information Theory, École Polytechnique Fédérale de Lausanne, CH-1015 Lausanne, Switzerland
E-mail address: Emre.Telatar@epfl.ch

Department of Electrical Engineering and Computer Science, University of California at Berkeley, Berkeley CA 94720, USA
E-mail address: dtse@eecs.berkeley.edu

DIMACS Series in Discrete Mathematics
and Theoretical Computer Science
Volume **66**, 2004

Fading Gaussian Broadcast Channels with State Information at the Receivers

Daniela Tuninetti and Shlomo Shamai (Shitz)

ABSTRACT. Fading Gaussian broadcast channels, where the instantaneous fading values are known at the receivers but not at the transmitter, are considered. An achievable rate region valid for any fading distribution is derived from Marton's inner bound region and it is shown that stripping at the decoder of the channel with larger single user capacity (the optimal decoding strategy for degraded channels) might incur inherent performance degradations.

1. Introduction and Background

In 1972 Cover posed the problem of characterizing the capacity region of broadcast channels [**Co72**]. A **general two-user memoryless Broadcast Channel** (BC), as illustrated in Fig. 1, is defined by one input alphabet $\mathcal{X}$, two output alphabets $(\mathcal{Y}, \mathcal{Z})$ and a channel transition probability $P_{YZ|X}(y, z|x)$, $(x, y, z) \in \mathcal{X} \times \mathcal{Y} \times \mathcal{Z}$. With *general* BC it is meant that no particular structure is assumed on $P_{YZ|X}$. The transmitter wishes to send a *common message* w_0 to both receivers, a *private message* w_y to receiver-Y and a *private message* w_z to receiver-Z. The three messages are independent and each drawn uniformly from a set $\mathcal{W}_u$, $u \in \{0, y, z\}$. In order to send this triplet, the channel is used n times. The channel output pair (Y_i, Z_i) at time $i = 1, \cdots, n$ only depends on the present input X_i but not on the past since the channel has no memory and there is no feedback channel available. The average probability of error at the decoders and the region of ϵ-achievable rate-triplets (R_0, R_y, R_z), where $R_u = \log(|\mathcal{W}_u|)/n$ for $u \in \{0, y, z\}$, are defined as usual [**CT91**]. The capacity region $\mathcal{C}$ is the subset of non-negative rate-triplets (R_0, R_y, R_z) that are ϵ-achievable for all $\epsilon > 0$.

The *single letter* characterization of the capacity region of general BCs is an open problem. A capacity expression is known if the channel from X to Y is *superior* to the channel from X to Z. The ranking of the overall channel $P_{YZ|X}$ is done in terms of a relationship between the two component channels with probability $P_{Y|X} = \sum_z P_{YZ|X}$ and $P_{Z|X} = \sum_y P_{YZ|X}$. In fact, whether the probability of error can be driven to zero or not, only depends on the marginal distributions of the channel transition probability $P_{YZ|X}$ [**Co72**]. In particular, a BC is said to be

---

Key words and phrases. Broadcast channels, ergodic fading, receiver channel state information.

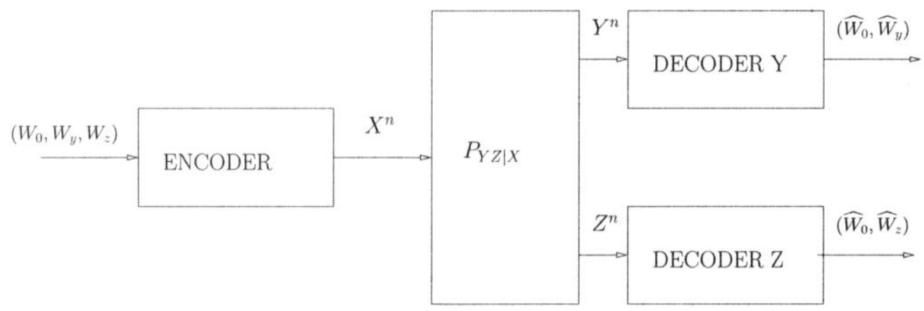

FIGURE 1. A general two-user Broadcast Channel without feedback.

- **stochastically degraded** if

$$P_{Z|X} = \sum_y P_{Y|X}\, \widetilde{P}_{Z|Y} \quad \text{for some} \quad \widetilde{P}_{Z|Y} \tag{1.1}$$

  If the channel transition probability factors as $P_{YZ|X} = P_{Y|X}\, P_{Z|Y}$ then the BC is said to be **physically degraded**.
- **less noisy** if

$$I(V;Z) \le I(V;Y) \quad \text{for all} \quad P_{VXYZ} = P_V P_{X|V} P_{YZ|X} \tag{1.2}$$

- and **more capable** if

$$I(X;Z) \le I(X;Y) \quad \text{for all} \quad P_X \tag{1.3}$$

Clearly, the class of more capable channels includes the class of less noisy channels, which in turns includes the class of degraded channels. These inclusions are strict as shown in [**KM75**].

Bergmans [**Br73**], Gallager [**Ga74**] and Ahlswede and Körner [**AK75**] proved that the capacity region of degraded BCs is the set of rate-triplets

$$\mathcal{C}^{(\mathrm{deg})} = \bigcup_{P_{VXYZ}} \Big\{ (R_0, R_y, R_z) \in \mathbb{R}_+^3 : \begin{array}{rcl} R_0 + R_z & \le & I(V;Z) \\ R_y & \le & I(X;Y|V) \end{array} \quad \text{for} \quad P_{VX} : P_{VXYZ} = P_V P_{X|V} P_{YZ|X} \quad \text{and} \quad |\mathcal{V}| \le |\mathcal{X}| \Big\} \tag{1.4}$$

as was conjectured in Cover's original paper [**Co72**]. Körner and Marton [**KM75**] proved that the capacity region of less noisy BCs is also given by (1.4).

El Gamal [**ElG79**] generalized (1.4) and proved that the capacity region of more capable BCs is the set of rate-triplets

$$(1.5)\quad \mathcal{C}^{(\mathrm{mc})} = \bigcup_{P_{VXYZ}} \Big\{ (R_0, R_y, R_z) \in \mathbb{R}_+^3 : \begin{array}{rcl} R_0 + R_z & \le & I(V;Z) \\ R_y + R_0 + R_z & \le & I(V;Z) + I(X;Y|V) \\ R_y + R_0 + R_z & \le & I(X;Y) \end{array} \text{ for } P_{VX} : P_{VXYZ} = P_V P_{X|V} P_{YZ|X} \text{ and } |\mathcal{V}| \le |\mathcal{X}| + 2 \Big\}$$

Notice that the last sum-rate inequality in (1.5) is immaterial for less noisy and degraded channels because the less noisy condition (1.2) implies that $I(X;Y) = I(V;Y) + I(X;Y|V) \ge I(V;Z) + I(X;Y|V)$. If the channel is degraded, it can be shown that the region (1.5) is equivalent to the region (1.4) [**CK81**, Problem 4 pag. 379].

The capacity region is also known if one of the private messages has rate zero (i.e., the projection of $\mathcal{C}$ onto the (R_0, R_y)-plane or onto the (R_0, R_z)-plane) in the so-called **degraded message set** case [**KM77**]; if the BC has at least one **deterministic component** [**MK79, GP80**] and if the BC is the **sum or product of reversely degraded BCs** [**ElG80**]. A complete list of known results (up to 1998) for BCs can be found in Cover's survey paper [**Co98**].

For a general BC only inner and outer bounds for the capacity region are known. The largest known inner bound, due to Marton [**MK79**, Th. 2], is the set

$$(1.6)\quad \mathcal{I} = \bigcup_{P_{WVUXYZ}} \Big\{ (R_0, R_y, R_z) \in \mathbb{R}_+^3 : \begin{array}{rcl} R_0 & \le & \min\{I(W;Y), I(W;Z)\} \\ R_0 + R_y & \le & I(WU;Y) \\ R_0 + R_z & \le & I(WV;Z) \\ R_0 + R_y + R_z & \le & \min\{I(W;Y), I(W;Z)\} + \\ & & +I(U;Y|W) + I(V;Z|W) - I(U;V|W) \end{array} \text{ for } P_{WUVX} : P_{WVUXYZ} = P_{WUV} P_{X|WUV} P_{YZ|X} \Big\}$$

Notice that the capacity region for more-capable channels is obtained by setting $W = V$ and $U = X$ in (1.6). This implies the more capable capacity region (1.5) is an inner bound for a general BC. We shall use this fact later to determine an achievable region for the general fading Gaussian BC. The same is not true for the degraded region in (1.4) as it is a special case of region (1.5) when the degraded condition (1.1) is satisfied. [1]

[1] Notice that the choice of pairwise independent triplet (W, V, U) in (1.6) gives the so-called "Cover-van der Meulen-Hadjek-Pursley achievable region" [**Co75, VdM75, HP79**]. Moreover, the formulation in (1.6), with the common rate R_0, as in Han and Costa [**HC87**], is internally consistent according to Hadjek and Pursley's definition [**HP79**].

The tightest outer bound without common rate, i.e., $R_0 = 0$, due to Körner and Marton [**MK79**, Th. 5], is the set $\mathcal{O} = \mathcal{O}_y \cap \mathcal{O}_z$ where

$$(1.7) \quad \mathcal{O}_y = \bigcup_{P_{VXYZ}} \Big\{ (R_y, R_z) \in \mathbb{R}_+^2 : \begin{array}{rcl} R_y & \le & I(X;Y) \\ R_z & \le & I(V;Z) \\ R_y + R_z & \le & I(X;Y|V) + I(V;Z) \end{array} \text{ for } P_{VX} : P_{VXYZ} = P_V P_{X|V} P_{YZ|X} \text{ and } |\mathcal{V}| \le |\mathcal{X}| + 2 \Big\}$$

and where $\mathcal{O}_z$ is obtained from (1.7) by reversing the role of the users. Region (1.7) is tight for semi-deterministic BCs [**MK79**]. The "more capable" inner bound region in (1.5) differs from the Körner and Marton outer bound region in (1.7) in that the term $I(X;Y)$ bounds the sum-rate $R_y + R_z$ in the former and only the user-Y rate R_y in the latter.

By removing some of the constraints from (1.7) the outer bound is weakened. In particular, by removing in (1.7) the user-Y rate constraint we obtain

$$(1.8) \quad \mathcal{O}_y^{(\mathrm{deg})} = \bigcup_{P_{VXYZ}} \Big\{ (R_y, R_z) \in \mathbb{R}_+^2 : \begin{array}{rcl} R_z & \le & I(V;Z) \\ R_y + R_z & \le & I(X;Y|V) + I(V;Z) \end{array} \text{ for } P_{VX} : P_{VXYZ} = P_V P_{X|V} P_{YZ|X} \text{ and } |\mathcal{V}| \le |\mathcal{X}| + 2 \Big\}$$

This shows that the "degraded" region is actually an outer bound to the capacity region of a general BC, and not an inner bound as mistakenly assumed in [**Se02**].

After these results from the late '70s, the determination of the capacity region of general BCs has defied many years of research. Recently the *Gaussian* BC problem has regained attention. A BC is Gaussian if $P_{Y|X}$ and $P_{Z|X}$ are both Gaussian. The interest in these BCs stems from the practical importance of such channel models. The capacity region of scalar unfaded Gaussian BCs with Inter Symbol Interference [**EG01**] and the capacity and the outage region of scalar fading Gaussian BCs with perfect state information at the transmitter and at the receivers [**LG01**] are now available. Moreover, the maximum achievable sum-rate for vector Gaussian BCs has been found [**CS03, WC02, VT03, JWG02**] and the full capacity region is discussed in [**Wea02**].

In this work, we are interested primarily in scalar BCs where the information carrying signal is constrained in average power, fades and is corrupted by an additive white Gaussian noise. We assume that the instantaneous channel gains are perfectly known at the receivers but not at the transmitter. Previously, this channel model was considered in [**LTU02**] where an outer bound for a special class of degraded BCs was derived in order to prove the asymptotic optimality of TDMA (Time Division Multiple Access) in the low power regime. Here we are interested in achievable regions valid for general fading Gaussian BCs at any SNR (Signal to Noise Ratio).

The rest of the paper is organized as follows: Section 2 contains the description of the channel models, Section 3 is devoted to the derivation of an inner bound to the the capacity region and Section 4 contains some concluding remarks.

2. Scalar Fading Gaussian Broadcast Channels

We consider complex-valued BCs described by

$$\left\{ \begin{array}{lcl} Y & = & A\,X + N_y \\ Z & = & B\,X + N_z \end{array} \right. \tag{2.1}$$

where A and B are ergodic processes, not necessarily independent, instantaneously known at the corresponding receivers but unknown at the transmitter, $N_u \sim \mathcal{N}(0, N)$ is a proper complex Gaussian process (with zero mean and variance N) representing the additive white noise at receiver $u \in \{y, z\}$ and X is the useful signal subject to the average power constraint $\mathrm{E}[|X|^2] \leq P$. We shall write F-AWGN for "fading Gaussian" BCs and RX-CSI for "receiver channel state information". In order to be consistent with the notation of Section 1, the output of the channel-Y is the pair (Y, A), the output of the channel-Z is the pair (Z, B). The channel input X, as well as the auxiliary random variables (W, U, V), are independent of A and B since the channel is unknown at the transmitter. Without loss of generality, we shall assume that channel-Y has the largest single user capacity for the given power constraint P, i.e., $C_y(P) \geq C_z(P)$ where $C_y(P) = \mathrm{E}_A[\log(1+|A|^2\,P/N)]$ and $C_z(P) = \mathrm{E}_B[\log(1+|B|^2\,P/N)]$. Model (2.1) is relevant, for example, in the study of the down-link of wireless cellular systems with a delay constraint much larger than the fading coherence time and where no feedback channel is available [**Pr95**].

The result we shall present in the following section uses the "more capable" inner bound region in (1.5), originally derived for *discrete memoryless* BCs, for channels with *continuous* alphabets and with *memory*. While dealing with continuous alphabets, the standard argument of fixing partitions on the input and the output alphabets, computing the capacity of the so obtained discrete channel, repeating the same procedure for all possible partitions and then taking as channel capacity the supremum over all partitions holds. When considering fading processes, possibly with memory, we recall that each user decodes optimally based on $\Pr[Y^n, A^n|W_y] = \Pr[A^n]\Pr[Y^n|A^n, W_y]$, where Y^n is the set of the n channel observations, A^n is the set of the n fading realizations and W_y is the user message (to be decoded). From the decoder point of view, the term $\Pr[A^n]$ is irrelevant as it is a common factor and all that matters is $\Pr[Y^n|A^n, W_y] = \sum_{W_z}\Pr[W_z]\prod_{i=1}^n \Pr[Y_i|X_i(W_y, W_z), A_i]$ where the last factorization follows because the noise is assumed white. From this point on-wards anything established for memoryless channels applies.

Channels without fading. If A and B are deterministic constants, the overall channel (2.1) is degraded and its capacity region is

$$\bigcup_{\alpha\in[0,1]} \left\{ \begin{array}{rcl} R_y & \leq & \log\left(1 + \frac{|A|^2\,\alpha\,P}{N}\right) \\ R_0 + R_z & \leq & \log\left(1 + \frac{|B|^2\,(1-\alpha)P}{N+|B|^2\,\alpha\,P}\right) \end{array} \right. \tag{2.2}$$

where, without loss of generality, we have taken $|A|^2 > |B|^2$. If $|A|^2 = |B|^2$ then the capacity region coincides with the TDMA region

$$\mathcal{J}^{(\mathrm{tdma})} = \left\{ 0 \leq \frac{R_y}{C_y(P)} + \frac{R_z}{C_z(P)} \leq 1 \right\} \tag{2.3}$$

since the two channels are statistically equivalent. Rate-points on the convex closure of (2.2) are achieved by (X,V) jointly Gaussian

$$\begin{bmatrix} V \\ X \end{bmatrix} \sim \mathcal{N}\left(\mathbf{0}, P\begin{bmatrix} 1-\alpha & 1-\alpha \\ 1-\alpha & 1 \end{bmatrix}\right) \tag{2.4}$$

for $\alpha \in [0,1]$. In words, the transmitter independently encodes the message w_z into the codeword V and the message w_y into the codeword U. A fraction α of the available power P is assigned to codeword U, intended for user-Y, and a fraction $(1-\alpha)$ to message V, intended for user-Z. The actual signal sent over the channel is the superposition of the two codewords, i.e., $X = U + V$. User-Z (the "weakest" user) decodes its codeword V by treating codeword U as noise, while user-Y (the "strongest" user) first decodes V, strips it from its received signal and finally decodes its own codeword U. For unfaded AWGN BCs, the optimality of (2.4) was shown by Bergmans [**Br74**] by using a proof technique based on the entropy power inequality. Unfortunately, Bergmans's proof technique does not seem to extend to channels with fading.

Fading channels. When A and B in (2.1) are random variables, then the overall channel might not be degraded. Moreover, the direct verification of the less noisy condition (1.2) or of the more capable condition (1.3) might not be easy as it requires to test for all possible joint distributions P_{VX}. Consider the following two examples.

Example 1. Let $B \sim k\,A$ for some constant $k \in \mathbb{C}$ such that $|k| \leq 1$. The overall channel is degraded since the output Z can be written as $Z = k\,Y + \widetilde{N}_z$, where the random variable $\widetilde{N}_z \sim \mathcal{N}(0, N(1-|k|^2))$ represents an extra noise. Hence, any distribution on the pair (V,X) in (1.4) gives a region of achievable rates for this channel. In particular, distribution (2.4) gives the achievable rate region

$$\text{CH} \bigcup_{\alpha\in[0,1]} \left\{ \begin{array}{rcl} R_y & \leq & \mathrm{E}\left[\log\left(1+\dfrac{|A|^2\,\alpha\,P}{N}\right)\right] \\ R_0 + R_z & \leq & \mathrm{E}\left[\log\left(1+\dfrac{|B|^2\,(1-\alpha)P}{N+|B|^2\,\alpha\,P}\right)\right] \end{array} \right. \tag{2.5}$$

where "CH" stands for convex hull. The rate-points on convex closure of (2.5) are achieved by superposition coding and by stripping at the receiver-Y. Fig. 2 shows the achievable region (2.5) as well as the TDMA achievable region (2.3).

Example 2. Let A and B be two random variables with equally likely mass points at $|A|^2 \in \{2, 16\}$ and $|B|^2 \in \{4, 8\}$. The achievable single user rates with Gaussian input, i.e., $X \sim \mathcal{N}(0,P)$, and equally likely binary input, i.e., $\Pr[X = +\sqrt{P}] = \Pr[X = -\sqrt{P}] = 1/2$, are depicted in Fig. 3. For a Gaussian input, the more capable condition $I(X;Y) \leq I(X;Z)$ is verified for any power constraint P, but the channel is not more capable. In fact, for $P/N > 0.17$ and binary input, the mutual information achievable by user-Z is larger than the corresponding mutual information achievable by user-Y. As noticed before, if the channel is not less noisy, then region (1.4) cannot be considered achievable. This subtle point is often overlooked. In [**Se02**] for example, the author states that two superimposed codewords, as in (2.4), can always be decoded by stripping at the receiver with largest single user capacity. This approach implicitly assumes that the condition $C_y(P) \geq C_z(P)$ for the given P guarantees that the overall channel behaves as a degraded channel. Unfortunately this is not true, even in the case when the stronger

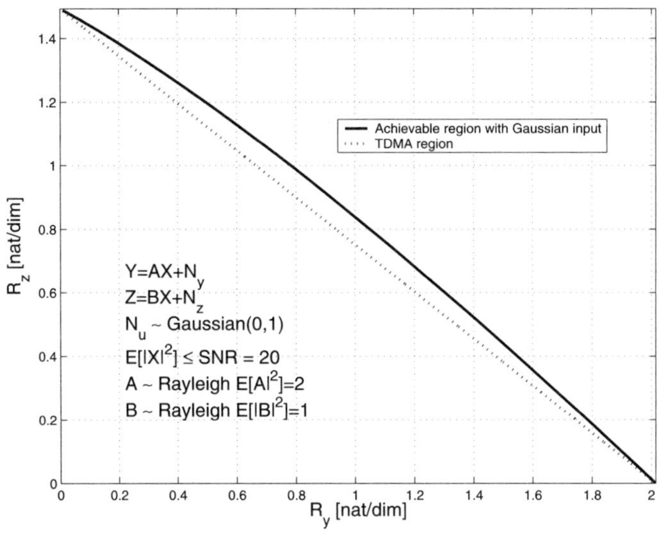

FIGURE 2. Achievable rate region for degraded fading Gaussian BCs with Gaussian input, superposition coding and stripping at the receiver of the user with largest single user capacity.

condition $C_y(x) > C_z(x)$ is met for all $x > 0$. Consider the following reasoning. Rate-pairs in (2.5) are achievable if user-Y can decode first the message intended for user-Z, strip it from its received signal and then decode its own message. This is possible if, for every $\alpha \in [0, 1]$, the rate R_z given in (2.5) satisfies

$$R_z \leq \mathrm{E}\left[\log\left(1 + \frac{|A|^2(1-\alpha)P}{N + |A|^2\alpha P}\right)\right] \tag{2.6}$$

By rewriting (2.6) in terms of single user capacities

$$C_y(P) - C_z(P) \geq C_y(\alpha P) - C_z(\alpha P) \quad \forall \alpha \in [0, 1] \tag{2.7}$$

it appears immediately that the condition for successive cancellation (2.6) is satisfied, for a given power constraint P, if the difference $C_y(\alpha P) - C_z(\alpha P)$ in the interval $\alpha \in [0, 1]$ has its absolute maximum for $\alpha = 1$. If $P = 0.5$ in the current example, then condition (2.7) is not met and successive decoding is not feasible. On the other hand, condition (2.7) is satisfied if $P/N < 0.17$, as it can be seen from Fig. 4 where the difference of the single user capacities is plotted. Notice that successive cancellation can be always performed by the user with largest average fading power gain if P/N is small "enough". In fact, in the low power regime $C_y(P) \simeq \mathrm{E}[|A|^2]\, P/N$ and the condition $C_y(P) \geq C_z(P)$ reads $\mathrm{E}[|A|^2] \geq \mathrm{E}[|B|^2]$.

Interestingly, if (2.7) is satisfied for all $P \geq 0$ then the difference $C_y(P) - C_z(P)$ is a non-decreasing function of P for all $P \geq 0$. In this case the region (2.5) is achievable for every P. The condition of "never decrease" can be expressed in

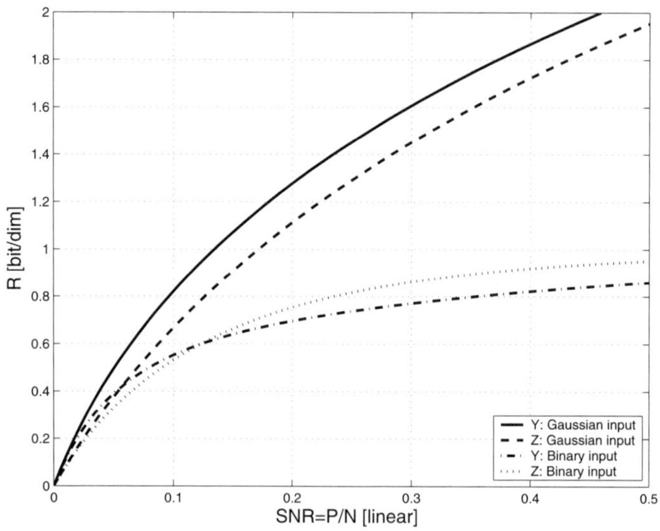

FIGURE 3. Achievable single user rates for the channel of Example 2 with Gaussian input and equally likely binary input.

terms of Stieltjes transform of the fading power pdf [2] as

$$\frac{\mathrm{d}}{\mathrm{d}P}\{C_y(P) - C_z(P)\} \geq 0$$

implies

$$\mathrm{E}_A\left[\frac{1}{N/P + |A|^2}\right] \leq \mathrm{E}_B\left[\frac{1}{N/P + |B|^2}\right] \tag{2.8}$$

where the members on the inequality (2.8) are the Stieltjes transform computed in the point $-N/P$. For example, less noisy channels (1.2) satisfy (by definition) the condition for successive cancellation in (2.7), but the opposite is not true in general.

In the next section we shall derive an inner bound that is valid for any fading distribution, namely we shall make use of the "more capable" region in (1.5).

3. An achievable region

As already pointed out in Section 1, the choice of $W = V$ and $U = X$ in Marton's inner bound region (1.6) gives the more capable capacity region (1.5). Region (1.5) is hence an inner bound for a general BC. By choosing (X, V) jointly

[2]The Stieltjes transform of a random variable X with cumulative distribution function $F_X(x)$ is defined as

$$S_X(z) \triangleq \int \frac{1}{x-z} \mathrm{d}F_X(x)$$

where z has positive imaginary part.

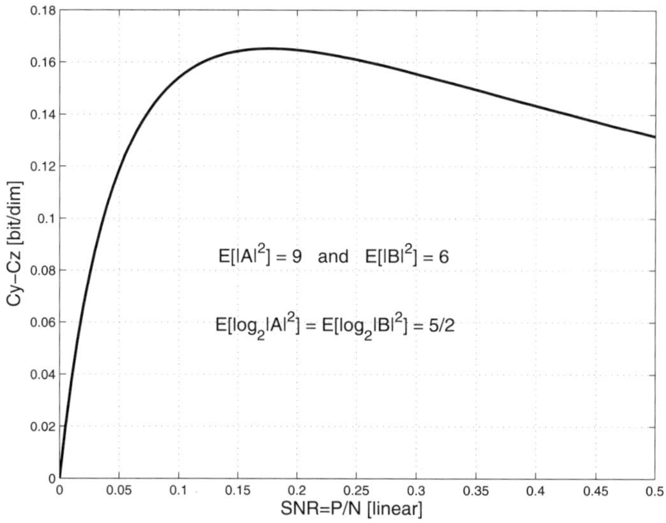

FIGURE 4. Difference of the single user capacities of the component channels of Example 2.

Gaussian as in (2.4), region (1.5) becomes

$$\mathcal{I}_y = \text{CH} \bigcup_{\alpha\in[0,1]} \Big\{ (R_y, R_z) \in \mathbb{R}_+^2 : \tag{3.1}$$
$$\begin{aligned} R_z &\leq \mathrm{E}\left[\log\left(1 + \frac{|B|^2(1-\alpha)P}{N + |B|^2\alpha P}\right)\right] \\ R_y + R_z &\leq \mathrm{E}\left[\log\left(1 + \frac{|B|^2(1-\alpha)P}{N + |B|^2\alpha P}\right)\right] + \mathrm{E}\left[\log\left(1 + |A|^2\frac{\alpha P}{N}\right)\right] \\ R_y + R_z &\leq \mathrm{E}\left[\log\left(1 + |A|^2\frac{P}{N}\right)\right] \equiv C_y(P) \quad \Big\} \end{aligned}$$

We shall refer to region $\mathcal{I}_y$ as the "more-capable-like" region. The subscript "y" stresses the fact that region (3.1) is not symmetric with respect to the two users. The "unbalance" is due to the fact that optimal rate-pairs in (3.1) are achieved by superposition coding and *joint* decoding at the receiver-Y. On the other hand, receiver-Z performs a single user decoding of its message by treating the other user message as noise. When the most stringent sum-rate constraint is $R_y + R_z \leq C_y(P)$, conventional stripping is not feasible. In this case the condition (2.7) for successive decoding is not satisfied and indeed the two superimposed messages must be decoded *jointly*. From the point of view of receiver-Y things are like in a multiple access channel where the users transmit a rate-point on the dominant face of the capacity region different from the vertices.

Fig. 5 shows the achievable region (3.1), the TDMA region (2.3) and the region (2.5) for the channel of Example 2. The rate-pairs for which the constraint $R_y + R_z \leq C_y(P)$ is effective are those on the straight part of the closure of the inner bound region (thick line).

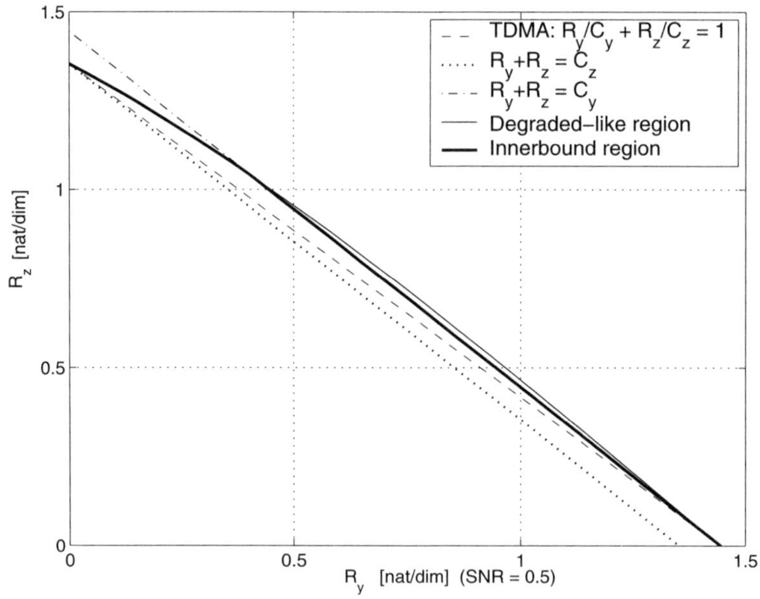

FIGURE 5. Achievable rate region for the fading Gaussian BC of Example 2 with Gaussian input, superposition coding and stripping at the receiver of the user with largest single user capacity.

It is interesting to notice that region (3.1) is completely included in the set

$$\left\{ 0 \leq R_y + R_z \leq C_y(P) = \max\{C_y(P), C_z(P)\} \right\} \tag{3.2}$$

which means that by superposition encoding and joint decoding at the best receiver it is not possible to achieve a sum-rate larger than the largest single user capacity. Moreover, region $\mathcal{I}_y$ coincides with the TDMA region in (2.3) if the two component channels have the same single user capacity.

Since the choice $W = V$ and $U = X$ in (1.6) is arbitrary, larger inner bounds could be found in principle by considering Marton's inner bound region as function of the three auxiliary random variables (W, V, U). Although, with more than one auxiliary random variable, the computation of the convex closure of the achievable set of rates can be done only numerically. Yet, there are other reasons for the choice $W = V$ and $U = X$. It is optimal for more capable channels, for the case of degraded message set case and under the constraint that $V \to W \to U \to X$ forms a Markov chain in this order. Furthermore, the more capable region (1.5), as a general inner bound, differs from Körner-Marton's outer bound region (1.7) in that the sum-rate rate constraint $R_y + R_z \leq I(X;Y)$ in the former is "replaced" by the looser rate constraint $R_y \leq I(X;Y)$ in the latter. Under certain conditions the two bounds might coincide.

Notice that the dual choice $W = U$ and $V = X$, with (U, X) jointly Gaussian, gives the achievable region (3.1) but with the role of the users exchanged. This achievable region is completely included in

$$\left\{ 0 \leq R_y + R_z \leq \min\{C_y(P), C_z(P)\} = C_z(P) \right\}$$

thus giving a region inferior to TDMA. For sake of completeness, we point out that the choice $W = X$ gives the region

$$\left\{ 0 \leq R_0 + R_y + R_z \leq \max_{P_X} \min\{I(X;Y),\, I(X;Z)\} \right\}$$

also included in the TDMA region. Hence, non-trivial enlargements of the "more-capable-like" inner bound region (3.1) require considering more than one auxiliary random variable in Marton's achievable region (1.6).

4. Conclusions

In this work we considered two-user scalar fading Gaussian Broadcast channels with state information available at the receivers only.

We derived an inner bound that is valid for any fading distribution and that has the flavor of the more capable capacity region. We showed that the rate-points on the convex closure of this rate region are achievable by *superposition coding* and *joint decoding* at the receiver with largest single user capacity. Moreover, we showed that stripping at one of the decoders might incur in performance degradation.

However we conjecture that Gaussian input is optimal for fading Gaussian Broadcast channels with state information available at the receivers, we have not been able to rigorously prove it yet.

Acknowledgments

The authors would like to thank Nihar Jindal, Sriram Vishwanath and Syed Ali Jafar for helpful comments, and for spotting an error in our DIMACS presentation, in reference to the optimality of Gaussian inputs.

References

[AK75] R.F. Ahlswede and J. Körner, "Source coding with side information and a converse for degraded broadcast channels," *IEEE Trans. Inform. Theory*, vol. 21, no. 6, 1975, pp. 629–637.

[Br73] P.P. Bergmans, "Random coding theorem for broadcast channels with degraded components," *IEEE Trans. Inform. Theory*, vol. 19, no. 2, 1973, pp. 197–207.

[Br74] P.P. Bergmans, "A simple converse for broadcast channels with additive white Gaussian noise," *IEEE Trans. Inform. Theory*, vol. 20, no. 4, 1974, pp. 279–280.

[CK81] I. Csiszar and J. Korner, "Coding theorems for discrete memoryless systems", Akademiai Kiado, Budapest, 1981.

[Co72] T.M. Cover, "Broadcast channels," *IEEE Trans. Inform. Theory*, vol. 18, no. 1, 1972, pp. 2–14.

[Co75] T.M. Cover, "An achievable rate region for the broadcast channel," *IEEE Trans. Inform. Theory*, vol. 21, 1975, pp. 399–404.

[Co98] T.M. Cover, "Comments on broadcast channel," *IEEE Trans. Inform. Theory*, vol. 44, no. 6, 1998, pp. 2524–2530.

[CS03] G. Caire and S. Shamai, "On the achievable throughput of a multiantenna Gaussian broadcast channel," *IEEE Trans. Inform. Theory*, vol. 49, no. 7, 2004, pp. 1691–1706.

[CT91] T.M. Cover and J. Thomas, *Elements of information theory*, Wiley, New York, 1991.

[EG01] A.J. Goldsmith and M. Effros, "The capacity region of broadcast channels with intersymbol interference and colored Gaussian noise," *IEEE Trans. Inform. Theory*, vol. 47, no. 1, 2001, pp. 219–240.

[ElG79] A.A. El Gamal, "The capacity of a class of broadcast channels," *IEEE Trans. Inform. Theory*, vol. 25, no. 2, 1979, pp. 166–169.

[ElG80] A.A. El Gamal, "Capacity of the product and sum of unmatched broadcast channels", *Probl. Peredac. Inform.*, vol. 16, no. 1, 1980, pp. 3–23.

[Ga74] R. Gallager, "Capacity and coding for degraded broadcast channels," *Probl. Peredac. Inform.*, vol. 10, no. 3, 1974, pp. 3–14.

[GP80] S.I. Gelfand and M.S. Pinsker, "Capacity of a broadcast channel with one deterministic component," *Probl. Peredac. Inform.*, vol. 16, no. 1, 1980, pp. 24–34.

[HC87] T.S. Han and M.H.M. Costa, "Broadcast channels with arbitrarily correlated sources", *IEEE Trans. Inform. Theory*, 1987, pp. 641–650.

[HP79] B.E. Hajek and M.B. Pursley, "Evaluation of an achievable rate region for the broadcast channel," *IEEE Trans. Inform. Theory*, vol. 25, no. 1, 1979, pp. 36–46.

[JWG02] N. Jindal, S. Vishwanath and A.J. Goldsmith, "On the duality of Gaussian multiple-access and broadcast channels," in *Proc. Int'l Symposium on Inform. Theory*, June 2002, p. 500.

[KM75] J. Körner and K. Marton, "A source network problem involving the comparison of two channels", *Trans. Colloquium Inform. Th.*, Keszthely, Hungary, Aug. 1975.

[KM77] J. Körner and K. Marton, "General broadcast channels with degraded message sets," *IEEE Trans. Inform. Theory*, vol. 23, no. 1, 1977, pp. 60–64.

[LG01] L. Li and A.J. Goldsmith, "Capacity and optimal resource allocation for fading broadcast channels. Part I: ergodic capacity. Part II: outage capacity," *IEEE Trans. Inform. Theory* vol. 47, no. 3, 2001, pp. 1083–1127.

[LTU02] A. Lapidoth, I.E. Telatar and R.L. Urbanke, "On wideband broadcast channels", in *Proc. Int'l Symp. on Inform. Theory*, Aug. 1998, p. 188.

[MK79] K. Marton, "A coding theorem for the discrete memoryless broadcast channel," *IEEE Trans. Inform. Theory*, vol. 25, no. 3, 1979, pp. 306–311.

[Pr95] J.G. Proakis, *Digital communications*, 3rd edition, McGraw Hill, New York, 1995.

[Se02] A. Seeger, "Broadcast communication on fading channels using hierarchical coded modulation", *GLOBECOM*, vol. 1, 2002, pp. 92–97.

[VdM75] E.C. van der Meulen, "Random coding theorems for the general discrete memoryless broadcast channel", *IEEE Trans. Inform. Theory*, vol. 21, no. 3, 1975, pp. 180–190.

[VT03] P. Viswanath and D. Tse, "Sum capacity of the vector Gaussian broadcast channel and uplink-downlink duality," *IEEE Trans. Inform. Theory,* vol. 49, no. 8, 2003, pp. 1912–1921.

[Wea02] S. Vishwanath et al., "Capacity bounds for Gaussian vector broadcast channels", DIMACS series, 2002.

[WC02] W. Yu and J.M. Cioffi, "Sum capacity of a Gaussian vector broadcast channel," in *Proc. Int'l Symposium on Inform. Theory*, June 2002, p. 498.

Swiss Federal Institute of Technology in Lausanne (EPFL), Lausanne, Switzerland
E-mail address: daniela.tuninetti@epfl.ch

Technion - Israel Institute of Technology, Haifa, Israel
E-mail address: sshlomo@ee.technion.ac.il

DIMACS Series in Discrete Mathematics
and Theoretical Computer Science
Volume **66**, 2004

Wireless Network Information Theory

Liang-Liang Xie and P. R. Kumar

ABSTRACT. We address the problem of forming a wireless network out of a set of geographically dispersed nodes, each equipped with a radio transceiver. The two questions that we address are: (i) What should be the strategy for transporting information over the wireless network?, and (ii) How much information can possibly be transported?

We present a model of such systems which lends itself to a tractable information theory that is able to shed light on these issues. A key role is played in our model by the distances between nodes, and the attenuation as a function of distance suffered by radio signals. The main quantity we study is the transport capacity which is the supremal distance weighted sum of routes that the network can support. We obtain scaling laws for the growth of the transport capacity as the number of nodes in the network increases, and bound the preconstant involved. There is an interesting dichotomy. When the medium has any absorption or the path loss exponent is greater than 3, then the transport capacity grows linearly, and an order optimal strategy is multihop transport where nodes relay packets after fully decoding them treating all interference as noise. This is in fact the strategy which current protocol development efforts are targeted towards, which is reassuring. However, when there is no absorption at all and the path loss exponent is small, then one can obtain unbounded transport capacity for finite total transmitted power, and even superlinear scaling. A strategy which emerges as of interest is for upstream nodes to coherently cooperate in sending a packet to the next downstream node, and for each node to decode a packet based on all its observations and subtracting out the known interference generated by downstream transmissions.

1. The architecture for information transfer in wireless networks

We consider wireless networks which are to be formed out of groups of geographically dispersed set of nodes each equipped with a radio transceiver.

Please address all correspondence to the second author.

The work of the first author was conducted while he was visiting the Coordinated Science Laboratory, University of Illinois.

This material is based upon work partially supported by USARO under Contract Nos. DAAD19-00-1-0466 and DAAD19-01010-465, DARPA under Contract Nos. N00014-01-1-0576 and F33615-01-C-1905, AFOSR under Contract No. F49620-02-1-0217, DARPA/AFOSR unfer Contract No. F49620-02-1-0325, and NSF under Contract No. NSF ANI 02-21357. Any opinions, findings, and conclusions or recommendations expressed in this publication are those of the authors and do not necessarily reflect the views of the above agencies.

How should information be transferred from sources to destinations in such networks? One possibility is to choose for each pair of source and destination nodes a sequence of nodes forming the path, and then to relay packets from node to node along the path until they reach the destination. At each node along the path, packets can be fully decoded by treating all interference as noise. The digitally regenerated packets are then retransmitted to the next node along the path. This mode of information transfer is the one around which there is much protocol development activity today; let us call it the "multihop node."

The choice of the multihop mode as the method of information transfer creates the need for several protocols to realize it. For example, since one is treating all interfering transmissions as noise, one would like to regulate the number of such interferers in the vicinity of the receiver. This gives rise to the medium access control problem. The currently popular IEEE 802.11 [**1**] MAC protocol addresses (among other things) this issue. As another example, since interference is greater when the power of the interfering transmission is large, there is a social need to regulate the powers of all transmissions and thus be able to spatially reuse the spectrum. This gives rise to the power control problem for ad hoc networks. The protocols COMPOW [**2**] and Cluster POW [**3**] are aimed at this problem. As a third example, since the goal is to relay packets along a string of nodes from source node to destination node, one needs to find such a path from source to destination, and that too when nodes are possibly mobile. This gives rise to the routing problem. The routing protocols DSDV [**4**], AODV [**5**], DSR [**6**], TBRPF, OLSR, ZRP [**7**], STARA [**8**], etc., address this problem.

Thus, we see that the problem of designing wireless networks can be roughly divided into two phases. First one needs to choose the strategy by which nodes equipped with wireless transceivers should cooperate to achieve information transfer. This problem of choosing the overall strategy to adopt is one of choosing the architecture for information transport. Subsequent to the choice of strategy/architecture, there arises the problem of protocol development, where the goal is to realize the architecture that has been adopted.

In this paper, we consider the first question: How should wireless nodes cooperate to achieve information transfer? The multihop mode is only one possibility. There are countless other possibilities, since cooperation over the ether can be done in many strange ways. Just to stretch one's imagination, let us consider the following possibility. Suppose node A is receiving a transmission from node B in the presence of an interfering transmission from node C. Then a node D can help A by transmitting a signal which cancels the interference created by node C at node A's location. This is a form of cooperation which is not possible in wireline networks, but which may be possible (if one knows the channel, etc.) for wireless networks. One can think of this cooperation in the following way. Consider the signal to interference plus noise ratio (SINR) at node A:

$$\text{SINR at node } A \quad = \quad \frac{\gamma_{BA} P_B}{N + \gamma_{CA} P_C}$$

where P_B is the power of node B, and P_c the power of node C, while γ_{BA} and γ_{CA} are the attenuations from B to A, and C to A, respectively. Here, node D attempts to cancel the contribution $\gamma_{CA} P_C$ from the denominator, and thus boost the SINR at node A to $\frac{\gamma_{BA} P_B}{N}$. This is a strange form of cooperation (akin to noise cancelling). Should node D indeed help node A in this way?

As another possibility, suppose (A, B, C) is a route from source A to destination C, and node B is a relay node along the path. Then node B could serve as a relay not by fully decoding packets from node A and then retransmitting the digitally regenerated packets to node C, but simply by amplifying the signal plus noise that is received from node A; see [**9**]. Thus the relaying could be done by "amplifying and forward" rather than "decode and forward." Which is it to be?

As yet another possibility consider a network consisting of nodes $\{A, B, C, D, E, F\}$. Suppose node A is a source and node F is a destination for a certain stream of information. This could be transported in two phases. In the first phase, node A could broadcasts a packet simultaneously to $\{B, C, D, E\}$. In the second phase, nodes $\{B, C, D, E\}$ simultaneously transmit this packet to F. Thus, the node of information transfer is a fan-out, followed by a fan-in; see [**10**]. Should this be how nodes cooperate?

In fact since one is in the wireless would, one need not devote all of the power to any one mode. A node A could spend 30% of its power cancelling the interference created by node B at node C, 20% of its power to relay packets from node D to node F by "amplifying and forwarding," 10% of its power to relay packets from node F to node G, 20% of its power in broadcasting packets of node H to nodes $\{I, J, K, L\}$, etc.

To quote Shakespeare's Hamlet:

> "There are more things in heaven and earth, Horatio, than are dreamt of in your philosophy."

Multihop is clearly not the only strategy for information transfer over wireless networks. What indeed should be the architecture for information transfer in wireless networks?

2. The amount of information that wireless networks can transport

Another utilitarian issue of importance for wireless networks is to determine how much information can be carried over wireless networks. That is, what is the capacity of wireless networks? Since there are many possible source-destination pairs, one needs to talk of a rate vector. For a network with n nodes, there are $n(n-1)$ possible source-destination pairs, and the rate vector is an $n(n-1)$-dimensional vector $R = (R_{12}, R_{13}, \ldots, R_{1n}, R_{21}, R_{23}, \ldots, R_{1n}, \ldots, R_{n1}, R_{n2}, \ldots, R_{n(n-1)})$. The capacity is (the closure of) the set of such feasible rate vectors. This a clearly a subset of a very dimensional space when n is large.

Another issue needs to be kept in mind, and that is that we are not simply interested in the (already complicated) capacity of a single wireless network, but in the class of wireless networks. That is, we are not interested in having an architecture for wireless network 1, another architecture for wireless network 2, etc. What one wants is to say something about a large class of wireless networks of interest to us. That is, we seek some sort of a uniformity result.

So the problem is to deal with the sets of feasible regions for the class of wireless networks of interest to us, where the number of nodes, then locations, channel conditions, etc., may differ. This raises the issue of how one is to measure the capacity of a class wireless networks.

3. The need for an information theory for wireless networks

The two problems noted above, that of determining the appropriate architecture for information transfer among a group of wireless nodes, and that of determining the amount of information that they can transport, both belong to the realm of network information theory.

Indeed, Shannon's contributions in [**11**] are at (at least) two fold. Not only does his theory provide the architecture for information transfer, but also the capacity. For the first issue, the determination that the problems of source coding and channel coding can be separated is of paramount importance, and, in fact, is at the heart of the digital communication revolution. Source coding today is performed by programs such as zip, while channel coding is preformed by network interface cards. For the second problem, he provided, amazingly, a beautifully elegant (what we call today a single letter) characterization of capacity.

Ever since Shannon's work, there has been great interest in generalizing information theory from a single link to a network, and Shannon himself was interested in this. However, while there have been some singular amazing triumphs, by and large the problem of developing a general network information theory has defied a solution. Among the triumphs are the characterization of the capacities of the scalar Gaussian broadcast channel [**12, 13, 14, 15**], the general multiple access channel [**16, 17**], and certain generalizations of source coding to take advantage of dependencies and side information [**18**].

However, almost all other problems have defied a general solution. One such is the three node relay channel, consisting of two nodes a source and a destination with the only complication being that there is one other node, a relay, which is there to assist in the information transfer. In spite of at least three decades of sustained attention, the general case is unsolved, though special cases have been most elegantly characterized [**19**]. So also for the interference channel which features two source-destination pairs (A, B) and (C, D) with the only complication being that A's transmission interferes with D's reception, and C's transmission interferes with B's reception. When the power levels of A and C are moderate, this problem is unsolved.

One can perhaps regard the three node relay problem as the simplest generalization of Shannon's original problem consisting of a source and a destination. When even this problem appears formidable, what possible guidance can information theory provide concerning the architecture for information transport? Indeed, this has been the reason for the "unconsummated union" [**20**] between information theory and the world of networking.

4. The Model

To address this problem, we consider the following model. It should be noted that the distances between nodes will play a key and explicit role in this model.

Consider a two-dimensional plane (or a one-dimensional line) on which are located n nodes. We will suppose that the (Euclidean) distance between any two pair of nodes i and j, denoted ρ_{ij}, is at least a minimum distance ρ_{min}. If $x_i(t)$ is broadcast by node i at time t, then

$$y_j(t) = \sum_{i \neq j} \frac{ce^{-\gamma\rho_{ij}}}{\rho_{ij\delta}} x_i(t) + n_j(t),$$

is received at node j at time t, where $n_j(t)$ is AWGN of variance σ^2. The factor $\frac{ce^{-\gamma\rho_{ij}}}{\rho_{ij}^{\delta}}$ is the attenuation of a signal from node i to node j. The quantity δ will be called the path loss exponent, and $\delta = 1$ (since δ needs to be doubled if one is interested in power) corresponds to the familiar inverse square law in free space. The quantity $\gamma \geq 0$ will be called the absorption constant, and it is generally strictly positive if there is absorption; see [**21, 22**]. Each node is also assumed to have a power constraint P.

It should be noted that at this point, distance has already come in explicitly in two ways. First, we have modeled the distances between nodes, and second, we have modeled attenuation as a function of distance.

The third way distance will explicitly enter our model is through the choice of the performance measure — the transport capacity. Denote by $R = (R_{12}, R_{13}, \ldots, R_{1n}, R_{21}, R_{23}, \ldots, R_{2n}, \ldots, R_{n1}, R_{n2}, \ldots, R_{n(n-1)})$, a feasible rate vector (which is defined in the standard information theoretic manner; see Chapter 14 of [**23**], for instance), and let $\Re$ be the set of feasible rate vectors. Then we study

$$C_T := \sup_{R\in\Re} \sum_{i=1} \sum_{\substack{j=1 \\ j\neq i}}^{n} R_{ij}\rho_{ij},$$

the supremal distance weighted sum of rates. We call this the "transport capacity." It is analogous to the man-miles/year metric used to measure the size of an airline.

We note that rather than studying the entire feasible region $\Re$ which is a subset of a very high dimensional space, we have chosen a much simpler scalar quantity to study.

5. The Results

It turns out, interestingly, that there is a dichotomy. The cases where there is relatively high attenuation and relatively small attenuation differ, and require different architectures for information transport.

When the attenuation is relatively large, then the transport capacity scales linearly in the number of nodes: (Expressions for constants, proofs of the results, as well as other results and more details, can all be found in the full paper [**24**]).

THEOREM 5.1. *When $\gamma > 0$ or $\delta > 3$,*

$$C_T \leq c_1 n.$$

What is interesting about this result is that in many cases one can obtain this order of transport capacity, or nearly this order, by simply using the multihop strategy. It is shown in [**25**] that for n nodes in an area A, the transport capacity is $O(\sqrt{An})$. In fact, when nodes are regularly arranged, say at the sites of an integer lattice, then the order can, in fact, be achieved by multihop transport. Even when nodes are randomly located, a transport capacity of $\Theta\left(\sqrt{\frac{An}{\log n}}\right)$ can be obtained. Keeping in mind that in our model in this paper the area A grows like $\Omega(n)$ since nodes are mutually separated by a minimum distance ρ_{min}, we see that $\Theta(n)$ can be realized by multihop transport when nodes are regularly arranged, while $\Theta\left(\frac{n}{\sqrt{\log n}}\right)$ can be realized when nodes are randomly located. Since $\sqrt{\log n}$ grows slowly in comparison to n we see that the multihop mode of operating a wireless network is nearly order optimal.

Thus, we determine that multihop is an order optimal architecture for information transport in wireless networks when there is relatively large attenuation. This is gratifying since it is, in fact, the architecture towards which current protocol efforts are targeted.

Now let us turn to the relatively low attenuation case. Here a different strategy emerges as interesting, one which we call Coherent Relaying with Interference Subtraction (CRIS). To illustrate CRIS, consider a set of nodes numbered 1, 2, ... , K with 1 being the source node and K the destination node. Node 1 begins by sending packet 1 to node 2 in slot 1. In slot 2 nodes 1 and 2 coherently cooperate to send the packet 1 to node 3. (In slot 2, node 1 also spends a portion of its power to send the next packet, packet 2, to node 2). In slot 3, nodes 1, 2, and 3 coherently cooperate to send the packet 1 to node 4. (Also node 1 spends a portion of its power to send packet 3 to node 2, and nodes 1 and 2 both spend certain portions of their power to send packet 2 to node 3). The scheme continues with upstream nodes coherently cooperating to send the next packet to a downstream node in each slot.

For decoding, assuming correct decoding has occurred in the past (and that the channel state information is known), each node can simply subtract that portion of its received signal which is due to downstream nodes transmitting packets that it has already decoded. Also, each node hears a packet many times when each of its upstream nodes was receiving it. Each node uses all this cumulative information, and subtracts already decoded signals, to decode the current packet of interest.

It turns out that one can actually achieve unbounded transport capacity, and that it can in fact grow superlinearly.

THEOREM 5.2. : *(i) When $\gamma = 0$ and $\delta < \frac{3}{2}$ then even if the entire network's transmission power budget is limited to P_{total}, there are networks where nodes can allocate this power among themselves to achieve unbounded transport capacity, and the order optimal strategy is CRIS.*

: *(ii) When $\gamma = 0$ and $\delta < 1$, then there are networks of nodes arranged along a straight line, i.e., a linear world, where $C_T = \Theta(n^\sigma)$ for $\frac{1}{2} < \sigma < \frac{1}{\delta}$, i.e., superlinear growth is possible, and CRIS is an order optimal strategy.*

We thus see that when attenuation is low, nodes can profitably cooperate among themselves to achieve superlinear growth, and multi-user estimation and coherence can be used to advantage.

The result of Theorem 5.2(i) may also be interesting when viewed in the context of [**26**] which studies the power requirements of communication across large distances.

6. Concluding Remarks

We have sketched the elements of an information theory for wireless networks which sheds light on important issues such as how information ought to be transported over wireless networks, and how much information can be so transported; see [**24**] for full details. A key role is played in our model by distances between nodes, and the attenuation as a function of distance. Another aspect of our studies is that rather than considering the set of feasible rate vectors, we consider the transport capacity, which is simply a scalar. Further, rather than characterize the transport capacity precisely, we study how it grows as the number of nodes increases, i.e., its scaling laws. We characterize the exponent in the scaling law, and since it is also important, we bound the preconstant involved. Through this approach we are able to get to the all important issue of the architecture of information transport in wireless networks. We see that there is a dichotomy. When the medium has absorption (generically always the case when not in free space) or has large enough path loss exponent, the transport capacity grows linearly, and multihop transport with packets fully decoded at each hop, treating interference as noise, is order optimal. This is gratifying since it is the scheme to which current protocol development efforts are targeted. However, when the medium has no absorption and low enough path loss exponent, then relaying by coherent cooperation among upstream nodes to send a packet to the next downstream node, along with decoding by subtracting the known interference from downstream nodes, a strategy we dub CRIS, emerges as of interest. Unlimited transport capacity for fixed finite total transmission power and superlinear scaling are both possible. How to exploit this in the future is an interesting question.

Needless to say, we have only scratched the surface, and much remains to be done.

References

[1] IEEE Protocol 802.11, "Draft standard for wireless LAN: Medium access control (MAC) and physical layer (PHY) specifications." IEEE, July 1996.

[2] S. Narayanaswamy, V. Kawadia, R. S. Sreenivas, and P. R. Kumar, "The compow protocol for power control in ad hoc networks: Theory, architecture, algorithm, implementation, and experimentation." http://black1.csl.uiuc.edu/ prkumar/postscript_files.html#Wireless Networks, May 16 2001.

[3] V. Kawadia and P. R. Kumar, "Power control and clustering in ad hoc networks," in *INFOCOM 2003*, (San Francisco, CA), March 30 - April 3 2003.

[4] C. E. Perkins and P. Bhagwat, "Highly dynamic destination-sequenced distance-vector routing (DSDV) for mobile computers," *Computer Communications Review*, vol. 24, no. 4, pp. 234–244, 1994. (ACM SIGCOMM '94).

[5] C. Perkins, E. Royer, and S. Das, "Ad hoc on demand distance vector (AODV) routing." http://www.ietf.org/internet-drafts/draft-ietf-manet-aodv-03.txt. IETF Internet Draft (work in progress), June 1999.

[6] J. Broch, D. Johnson, and D. Maltz, "The dynamic source routing protocol for mobile ad hoc networks." http://www.ietf.org/internetdrafts/draft-ietf-manet-dsr-01.txt, December 1998. IETF Internet Draft (work in progress).

[7] M. IETF, 2003. http://www.ieft.org/html.charters/manet-charter.html.

[8] P. Gupta and P. R. Kumar, "A system and traffic dependent adaptive routing algorithm for ad hoc networks," in *Proceedings of the 36th IEEE Conference on Decision and Control*, (San Diego, CA), pp. 2375–2380, December 1997.

[9] B. Schein and R. Gallager, "The Gaussian parallel relay network," in *Proc. IEEE Int'l Symp. Information Theory*, Sorrento, Italy, June 25–30, 2000.

[10] M. Gastpar and M. Vetterli, " On the asymptotic capacity of Gaussian relay networks," *Proc. IEEE Int'l Symp. Information Theory*, Lausanne, Switzerland, July 2002.

[11] C. E. Shannon, "A mathematical theory of communication," *Bell Syst. Tech. J.*, vol. 27, pp. 379–423, 1948.

[12] T. Cover, "Broadcast channels," *IEEE Trans. Inform. Theory*, vol. 18, pp. 2–14, 1972.

[13] P. Bergmans, "Random coding theorem for broadcast channels with degraded components," *IEEE Trans. Inform. Theory*, vol. 19, pp. 197–207, 1973.

[14] P. Bergmans, "A simple converse for broadcast channels with additive white Gaussian noise," *IEEE Trans. Inform. Theory*, vol. 20, pp. 279–280, 1974.

[15] T. Cover, "Comments on broadcast channels," *IEEE Trans. Inform. Theory*, vol. 44, pp. 2524–2530, 1998.

[16] R. Ahlswede, "Multi-way communication channels," in *Proceedings of the 2nd Int. Symp. Inform. Theory (Tsahkadsor, Armenian S.S.R.)*, (Prague), pp. 23–52, Publishing House of the Hungarian Academy of Sciences, 1971.

[17] H. Liao, *Multiple access channels.* PhD thesis, University of Hawaii, Honolulu, HA, 1972. Dept of Electrical Engineering.

[18] D. Slepian and J. K. Wolf, "Noiseless coding of correlated information sources," *IEEE Trans. Inform. Theory*, vol. IT-19, pp. 471–480, 1973.

[19] A. El Gamal and T. Cover, "Multiple user information theory," *Proceedings of the IEEE*, vol. 68, pp. 1466–1483, 1980.

[20] A. Ephremides and B. Hajek, "information theory and communication networks: An unconsummated union," *IEEE Transactions on Information Theory*, vol. IT-44, pp. 2416–2434, 1998.

[21] M. Franceschetti, J. Bruck, and L. Schulman, "Microcellular systems, random walks and wave propagation." To appear in *Proceedings of the IEEE Symposium on Antennas and Propagation Society* (IEEE AP-S 2002, San Antonio, TX), June 2002.

[22] M. Franceschetti, J. Bruck, and L. Schulman, "The wandering photon model of wave propagation," technical report, California Institute of Technology, 2003.

[23] T. Cover and J. Thomas, *Elements of Information Theory.* New York: Wiley and Sons, 1991.

[24] L. Xie and P. R. Kumar, "A network information theory for wireless communication: Scaling laws and optimal operation", submitted to *IEEE Trans. Inform. Theory*, Apr. 2002.

[25] P. Gupta and P. R. Kumar, "The capacity of wireless networks," *IEEE Trans. Inform. Theory*, vol. IT-46, pp. 388–404, Mar. 2000.

[26] C. Rose and G. Wright, "Write or radiate? Inscribed Mass and Electromagnetic Channels", Aug. 13, 2003. Preprint. Rutgers University.

Institute of Systems Science, Chinese Academy of Sciences, Beijing 100080, China.

University of Illinois, Coordinated Science Laboratory, 1308 West Main St., Urbana, IL 61801-2307, USA.

E-mail address: `prkumar@uiuc.edu`. Web: `http://black.csl.uiuc.edu/~prkumar`.

DIMACS Series in Discrete Mathematics
and Theoretical Computer Science
Volume **66**, 2004

The Structure of Least-Favorable Noise in Gaussian Vector Broadcast Channels

Wei Yu

ABSTRACT. The sum capacity of the Gaussian vector broadcast channel is the saddle point of a Gaussian mutual information game in which the transmitter maximizes the mutual information by choosing the best transmit covariance matrix subject to a power constraint, and the receiver minimizes the mutual information by choosing a least-favorable noise covariance matrix subject to a diagonal constraint. This result has been established using a decision-feedback equalization approach under the assumption that the least-favorable noise covariance matrix is non-singular. This paper generalizes the above result to the case where the least-favorable noise is singular. In particular, it is shown that the least-favorable noise is not unique, and different least-favorable noise covariance matrices are related to each other by a linear estimation relation.

1. Introduction

A communication model with a single transmitter sending independent information to multiple receivers at the same time is referred to as a broadcast channel. Although the capacity region of a general broadcast channel is still an unsolved problem, recent progress has been made in the special case of the sum capacity of Gaussian vector broadcast channels [**1**] [**2**] [**3**] [**4**]. A Gaussian vector broadcast channel with K receivers can be modeled as follows:

$$\mathbf{Y_i} = H_i\mathbf{X} + \mathbf{Z_i}, \qquad i = 1, \cdots, K \tag{1.1}$$

where $\mathbf{X}$ is a vector-valued transmit signal, $\mathbf{Y_i}$ is the vector-valued receive signal, H_i is the channel matrix, and $\mathbf{Z_i}$ is the additive Gaussian vector noise at receiver i. The solution to the Gaussian vector broadcast channel sum capacity problem is based on two key ideas. First, an achievability result can be obtained using a precoding technique that effectively pre-subtracts multi-user interference at the transmitter. The precoding technique is known as "writing-on-dirty-paper" [**5**]. Second, a converse theorem can be obtained using the idea that the broadcast channel capacity is bounded by a cooperative bound with a least-favorable noise.

Key words and phrases. multi-user information theory, broadcast channel, least-favorable noise, decision-feedback equalization.

This work was supported by the Natural Sciences and Engineering Research Council of Canada and by the Canada Research Chairs program.

The least-favorable-noise converse is based on the following: the sum capacity of the broadcast channel is clearly bounded by the capacity of the vector channel with cooperative receivers: $\max I(\mathbf{X};\mathbf{Y_1}\cdots\mathbf{Y_K})$. Further, Sato [**6**] observed that the sum capacity of a broadcast channel depends only on the marginal distribution of the noises and not on their correlation. This is because receivers of a broadcast channel cannot cooperate. So, they are ignorant of the actual noise correlation. Therefore, the sum capacity of a broadcast channel must be bounded by the minimum mutual information

$$\min_{S_{zz}} \max_{S_{xx}} I(\mathbf{X};\mathbf{Y_1}\cdots\mathbf{Y_K}), \tag{1.2}$$

minimized over all possible joint distributions of the noises. For a Gaussian vector broadcast channel with a convex input constraint, restricting the above minimax problem to joint Gaussian input and noise distributions is without loss of generality. Further, it can be shown that this upper bound is tight.

The achievability of the minimax mutual information expression can be established using several different methods. In [**2**], it is shown that if a decision-feedback equalizer is used as a joint receiver in the broadcast channel, the least-favorable noise would induce a feedforward matrix that is diagonal. In addition, the feedback section can be moved to the transmitter as a precoder. Thus, with a least-favorable noise, no receiver cooperation in a decision-feedback equalizer is necessary and $\min I(\mathbf{X};\mathbf{Y_1}\cdots\mathbf{Y_K})$ is achievable. The above minimum can be further maximized over all possible input distributions. Since min-max is equal to max-min in a convex-concave function, this implies that (1.2) is indeed the sum capacity of a Gaussian vector broadcast channel. However, the proof in [**2**] appears to apply only to least-favorable noise covariances that are non-singular.

In [**3**] and [**4**], a completely different approach is taken. Focusing on sum power constrained channels, [**4**] showed that the precoding region for a Gaussian vector broadcast channel is precisely a "dual" multiple access channel with the transmitter and receivers interchanged. Based on this duality, [**4**] showed that the minimization for the least-favorable noise and the maximization for the dual multiple access channel sum capacity have the same solution. In addition, [**4**] gives an explicit solution for the least-favorable noise. The derivation in [**4**] is most transparent if the least-favorable noise is non-singular. To circumvent the singular noise issue, [**4**] used a sequence of non-singular noise covariance to approximate the singular noise, thus proving the result in full generality. Strictly speaking, however, this solution is not constructive when the least-favorable noise is singular.

The singular noise issue is circumvented in [**3**] using a different technique. Although also based on duality, the treatment in [**3**] involves a transformation of the noise covariance matrix for the broadcast channel to an input cost constraint for the multiple access channel. This approach resolves the singularity issue, but it does not characterize the entire class of least-favorable noise.

It should be noted that the duality approach [**3**] [**4**] applies only to Gaussian vector broadcast channels with a power constraint. The decision-feedback equalization approach [**2**], on the other hand, applies to Gaussian vector broadcast channels with arbitrary convex constraints, and is therefore more general. However, neither approach has explicitly dealt with the issue of singular least-favorable noise so far.

Singular least-favorable noise is not necessarily an unlikely event. In fact, the least-favorable noise is almost always singular in a broadcast channel where the number of receive dimensions is larger than the number of transmit dimensions.

The main purpose of this paper is to give a complete characterization of the least-favorable noise for an arbitrary channel. A combination of the decision-feedback equalization approach and the duality approach is taken. The main results are, first, the decision-feedback equalizer approach can be generalized to the case of singular least-favorable noise. Second, least-favorable noises are not unique, and they can be characterized via a duality between the broadcast channel and the multiple access channel.

2. Decision-Feedback Equalization with Singular Noise

Without loss of generality, consider a Gaussian vector broadcast channel with two receivers $\mathbf{Y} = H\mathbf{X} + Z$, where $H^T = [H_1^T H_2^T]$, $\mathbf{Y}^T = [\mathbf{Y}_1^T \mathbf{Y}_2^T]$ and $\mathbf{Z}^T = [\mathbf{Z}_1^T \mathbf{Z}_2^T]$. The objective of this section is to show that

$$\min_{S_{zz}} \frac{1}{2} \log \frac{|HS_{xx}H^T + S_{zz}|}{|S_{zz}|} \tag{2.1}$$

is achievable even if the minimizing S_{zz} is singular. Recall that the minimization is over all S_{zz} with fixed block diagonal terms. The fixed block diagonals can be assumed to be identity matrices with no loss of generality. This is a generalization of the earlier result in [**2**] where the case for non-singular S_{zz} is solved. The earlier result showed that if S_{zz} satisfies the Karush-Kuhn-Tucker (KKT) condition for the minimization problem

$$S_{zz}^{-1} - (HS_{xx}H^T + S_{zz})^{-1} = \begin{bmatrix} \Psi_1 & 0 \\ 0 & \Psi_2 \end{bmatrix}, \tag{2.2}$$

then there exists a decision-feedback equalizer (DFE) with a diagonal feedforward matrix. When the channel matrix H is full rank, the minimizing noise covariance matrix is always non-singular. However, this is not the case when H has more rows than columns. This situation corresponds to the case where there are more receiver antennas than transmit antennas in the broadcast channel. To extend the achievability result to accommodate singular least-favorable noises, both the KKT condition and the design of the DFE need to be generalized.

The decision-feedback equalizer that is required to accommodate singular noise differs from the conventional structure in one crucial aspect. A conventional DFE never processes more output dimensions than input dimensions. For example, in a channel with two transmit antennas and three receive antennas, a conventional DFE always reduces the two-by-three channel to a two-by-two channel by receiver joint processing. However, in a broadcast channel, receivers cannot cooperate and joint processing is not possible. Thus, a non-trivial generalization of the conventional DFE structure is required.

Without loss of generality, S_{xx} is assumed to be fixed and full-rank. Let $S_{xx} = V\Sigma V^T$ be an eigenvalue decomposition. It is convenient to set $H' = HV\sqrt{\Sigma}M$ to be the effective channel, and let the input covariance matrix be simply an identity matrix. The choice of M will be made later.

Suppose that S_{zz} is a low-rank solution to the minimization problem (2.1). Decompose S_{zz} in the following form:

$$S_{zz} = \begin{bmatrix} U_1 & U_2 \end{bmatrix} \begin{bmatrix} S_{\tilde{z}\tilde{z}} & 0 \\ 0 & 0 \end{bmatrix} \begin{bmatrix} U_1^T \\ U_2^T \end{bmatrix}, \tag{2.3}$$

where $S_{\tilde{z}\tilde{z}}$ is invertible and $[\ U_1\ U_2\ ]$ is an orthonormal matrix. The null space of S_{zz} must be a subspace of the null space of the channel, (because otherwise the capacity would be infinity). Thus, it must be possible to express the channel matrix H' as:

$$H' = U_1 \tilde{H}. \tag{2.4}$$

The minimization problem now becomes

$$\begin{aligned} \min_{S_{\tilde{z}\tilde{z}}} \quad & \frac{1}{2} \log \frac{|\tilde{H}\tilde{H}^T + S_{\tilde{z}\tilde{z}}|}{|S_{\tilde{z}\tilde{z}}|} \\ \text{s.t.} \quad & U_1 S_{\tilde{z}\tilde{z}} U_1^T \text{ has identities on the diagonal.} \end{aligned} \tag{2.5}$$

A necessary condition for the least-favorable noise is

$$S_{\tilde{z}\tilde{z}}^{-1} - (\tilde{H}\tilde{H}^T + S_{\tilde{z}\tilde{z}})^{-1} = U_1^T \begin{bmatrix} \Psi_1 & 0 \\ 0 & \Psi_2 \end{bmatrix} U_1. \tag{2.6}$$

The objective of this section is to show that if the noise covariance matrix satisfies the above condition, then there exists a decision-feedback equalizer whose feedforward matrix is diagonal. The development of decision-feedback equalizer follows that of [**2**]. The difference between the new proof and the original treatment is highlighted here.

The derivation of the decision-feedback equalizer is based on minimum mean-square error (MMSE) estimation. The key observation is that MMSE estimator is not unique when both the channel and the noise are rank deficient. Consider the MMSE estimation of $\mathbf{X}$ given $\mathbf{Y} = H\mathbf{X} + \mathbf{Z}$. The MMSE estimation is a matrix multiplication $\hat{\mathbf{X}} = W\mathbf{Y}$, where W satisfies a normal equation:

$$W S_{yy} = S_{xy}. \tag{2.7}$$

Because both S_{zz} and H are low rank, S_{yy} is also low rank. It is not difficult to verify that

$$W = \tilde{H}^T(\tilde{H}\tilde{H}^T + S_{\tilde{z}\tilde{z}})^{-1}U_1^T + SU_2^T \tag{2.8}$$

satisfies the normal equation for any choice of S. A different DFE can be designed for each choice of S. The rest of the section is devoted to showing that there exists a choice of S (along with a choice of M) that makes the DFE feedforward matrix diagonal.

The first step in the design of a decision-feedback equalizer is noise whitening. Define

$$\hat{H} = S_{\tilde{z}\tilde{z}}^{-\frac{1}{2}} \tilde{H}. \tag{2.9}$$

The MMSE estimator matrix W can be re-written as

$$W = S_{xx}\hat{H}^T(\hat{H}\hat{H}^T + I)^{-1}S_{\tilde{z}\tilde{z}}^{-\frac{1}{2}}U_1^T + SU_2^T \tag{2.10}$$

The structure of the feedforward matrix involves a Cholesky factorization of $R_b = \mathbf{E}[(\mathbf{X} - \hat{\mathbf{X}})(\mathbf{X} - \hat{\mathbf{X}})^T]$. It turns out that R_b is independent of the choice of S. Using the matrix inversion lemma, it can be shown that

$$R_b = (\hat{H}^T\hat{H} + I)^{-1}. \tag{2.11}$$

Further, W can be re-written as follows:

$$W = (\hat{H}^T\hat{H} + I)^{-1}\hat{H}^T S_{\tilde{z}\tilde{z}}^{-\frac{1}{2}} U_1^T + SU_2^T. \tag{2.12}$$

In a decision-feedback equalizer, half of the Cholesky factorization $R_b = G^{-1}\Delta^{-1}G^{-T}$ is placed in the feedback section, and the remaining half is placed in the feedforward section. Thus, the feedforward matrix has the form:

$$F = \Delta^{-1} G^{-T} \hat{H}^T S_{\tilde{z}\tilde{z}}^{-\frac{1}{2}} U_1^T + S' U_2^T . \tag{2.13}$$

The goal of this section is to use the generalized least-favorable noise condition (2.6) to show that F can be made diagonal. Using the matrix inversion lemma,

$$\begin{aligned} U_1^T \begin{bmatrix} \Psi_1 & 0 \\ 0 & \Psi_2 \end{bmatrix} U_1 &= S_{\tilde{z}\tilde{z}}^{-1} - (\tilde{H}\tilde{H}^T + S_{\tilde{z}\tilde{z}})^{-1} \\ &= \hat{H}(I + \hat{H}\hat{H}^T)^{-1}\hat{H}^T . \end{aligned} \tag{2.14}$$

With some algebra (see [**2**] for details), it is possible to prove that, by an appropriate choice of M, the Cholesky factorization of R_b can be made to give:

$$\Delta^{-\frac{1}{2}} G^{-T} \hat{H}^T S_{\tilde{z}\tilde{z}}^{-\frac{1}{2}} = \begin{bmatrix} \sqrt{\Psi_1} & 0 \\ 0 & \sqrt{\Psi_2} \end{bmatrix} . \tag{2.15}$$

Therefore, by choosing

$$S' = \Delta^{-\frac{1}{2}} \begin{bmatrix} \sqrt{\Psi_1} & 0 \\ 0 & \sqrt{\Psi_2} \end{bmatrix} U_2 , \tag{2.16}$$

the feedforward matrix becomes

$$F = \Delta^{-\frac{1}{2}} \begin{bmatrix} \sqrt{\Psi_1} & 0 \\ 0 & \sqrt{\Psi_2} \end{bmatrix} (U_1 U_1^T + U_2 U_2^T) , \tag{2.17}$$

which is diagonal since

$$U_1 U_1^T + U_2 U_2^T = [\, U_1 \; U_1 \,] \begin{bmatrix} U_1^T \\ U_2^T \end{bmatrix} = I . \tag{2.18}$$

To summarize, when the least-favorable noise is singular, it must satisfy a modified KKT condition (2.2). The decision-feedback equalizer structure with the singular noise is not unique. However, among the class of decision-feedback equalizers, there exists one whose feedforward matrix is diagonal. This is true for any fixed S_{xx}. Thus, in a Gaussian vector broadcast channel, the minimum mutual information $I(\mathbf{X}; \mathbf{Y_1}, \mathbf{Y_2})$ is an achievable sum rate, even when the least favorable noise covariance matrix is singular.

3. The Structure of Least-Favorable Noise

3.1. Uplink-Downlink Duality. The previous section shows that whenever the noise covariance matrix satisfies the least-favorable noise condition, (2.2) or (2.6), the mutual information $I(\mathbf{X}; \mathbf{Y})$ is achievable in a broadcast channel even without receiver cooperation. However, it does not give an explicit method to compute the least-favorable noise. Neither (2.2) nor (2.6) appears to have a closed-form solution. Further, although $I(\mathbf{X}; \mathbf{Y})$ is a convex function of S_{zz}, the numerical computation of the least-favorable noise is not necessarily easy, especially when the minimizing noise covariance matrix is singular. Fortunately, there is one important special case for which the computation is easy. This is when the transmit covariance S_{xx} is being maximized at the same time.

Consider a Gaussian vector broadcast channel with a power constraint $\mathrm{tr}(S_{xx}) \leq P$. Sato's outer bound states that the sum capacity is less than $\min \max I(\mathbf{X}; \mathbf{Y})$, where the maximization is over the power constraint and the minimization is over all possible noise correlations. The achievability result in the previous section states that a sum rate of $\max\min I(\mathbf{X};\mathbf{Y})$ is achievable. Since the mutual information is concave in S_{xx} and convex in S_{zz}, the minimization and maximization operations can be interchanged. Thus, the sum capacity of a Gaussian vector broadcast channel is precisely

$$C = \max_{S_{xx}} \min_{S_{zz}} \frac{1}{2} \log \frac{|HS_{xx}H^T + S_{zz}|}{|S_{zz}|}, \tag{3.1}$$

where $\mathrm{tr}(S_{xx}) \le P$ and S_{zz} has fixed diagonal terms. Surprisingly, this minimax problem has a special structure that gives it a particularly simple solution. The new ingredient is the uplink-downlink duality[1].

Uplink-downlink duality refers to the observation that the achievable rate region of a broadcast channel using "writing-on-dirty-paper" precoding is the same as the capacity region of a "dual" multiple access channel with the roles of the input and output terminals interchanged and with a sum power constraint across all input terminals. This duality was established in [**4**] and [**3**]. In this section, a different derivation of duality is given. The main purpose is to illustrate that the minimax problem can be solved efficiently via duality.

To simplify matters, let's first assume that H is square and invertible, and also that the maximizing S_{xx} and the least-favorable S_{zz} are both full rank. Further, assume that each receiver in the broadcast channel is equipped with a single-antenna. The starting point of the new derivation is the KKT condition for the minimax problem (3.1). Because the objective function in (3.1) is concave in S_{xx} and convex in S_{zz}, the KKT condition completely characterizes the saddle point. The KKT condition is:

$$H^T(HS_{xx}H^T + S_{zz})^{-1}H = \lambda I \tag{3.2}$$

$$S_{zz}^{-1} - (HS_{xx}H^T + S_{zz})^{-1} = \Psi \tag{3.3}$$

where λ is the dual variable associated with the power constraint and Ψ is a diagonal matrix of dual variables associated with the diagonal constraint on the noise covariance matrix. Multiplying (3.3) by H^T on the left and H on the right and substituting in (3.2), we obtain

$$H^T S_{zz}^{-1} H = H^T \Psi H + \lambda I. \tag{3.4}$$

The above is equivalent to

$$H(H^T\Psi H + \lambda I)^{-1}H^T = S_{zz}. \tag{3.5}$$

Observe that (3.5) is precisely the KKT condition for a multiple access channel with diagonal matrix Ψ as the transmit covariance matrix and $\mathrm{tr}(\Psi S_{zz}) \le P$ as the input constraint. Since S_{zz} has 1's on the diagonal, the constraint is equivalent to a sum power constraint on Ψ. After a proper scaling of the power constraint, Ψ, λ and S_{zz}, it can be shown that (3.5) is precisely the KKT condition for the following

[1]Uplink-downlink duality can be generalized beyond the power constrained broadcast channels. Duality exists whenever the input constraint is a linear covariance constraint. See [**7**] for a detailed discussion.

optimization problem

$$(3.6)\qquad \begin{aligned} \max_{D} \quad & \frac{1}{2}\log|H^T D H + I| \\ \text{s.t.} \quad & D \text{ is diagonal} \\ & \text{trace}(D) \le P, \\ & D \ge 0, \end{aligned}$$

(where $D = \Psi/\lambda$.) Thus, there is a duality between a multiple access channel and a broadcast channel. The solution to the minimax problem (3.1) can be obtained from the solution to a maximization problem (3.6). Since (3.6) is much easier to solve numerically (see e.g. [**8**] [**9**]), uplink-downlink duality gives an efficient way to solve the minimax problem (3.1).

3.2. Least-Favorable Noise. The duality result suggests that the least favorable noise in the minimax problem can be computed via a multiple access channel. In particular, (3.5) gives an explicit formula for the covariance matrix of the least-favorable noise. This formula has also appeared in both [**3**] and [**4**]. However, (3.5) is derived assuming that the channel matrix H is square and invertible and both the least-favorable noise and the maximizing input covariance matrices are full rank. In the general case, this is not necessarily true. In particular, the maximizing input covariance matrix D of the dual multiple access channel may not have non-zero entries everywhere on its diagonal. When the diagonals of D are all non-zero, the KKT condition for the maximization problem (3.6) ensures that the diagonal terms of $H(H^T\Psi H+\lambda I)^{-1}H^T$ are all 1's. Otherwise, slack variables need to be introduced and $H(H^T\Psi H + \lambda I)^{-1}H^T$ does not necessarily have 1's on its diagonal. Thus, it cannot be a valid choice of the least-favorable noise.

The purpose of the rest of the section is to show that a least-favorable noise covariance can be obtained by adding a positive semi-definite matrix to $H(H^T\Psi H+\lambda I)^{-1}H^T$ so that the sum of the two matrices has 1's on the diagonal. Such a positive semi-definite matrix is not unique, so the least-favorable noise covariance matrix is not unique. In fact, in some cases, the class of least favorable noises can be further enlarged by taking an additional step. Consider the candidate least-favorable noise, re-labeled as $S_{zz}^{(0)}$:

$$(3.7)\qquad S_{zz}^{(0)} = H(H^T\Psi H + \lambda I)^{-1}H^T.$$

It is easy to see that the water-filling input covariance matrix S_{xx} with respect to the channel H and the noise $S_{zz}^{(0)}$ is:

$$(3.8)\qquad S_{xx} = (\lambda I)^{-1} - (H^T\Psi H + \lambda I)^{-1}.$$

Now, S_{xx} may be rank deficient. In this case, the dimension of H must be reduced, and the least-favorable noise must be re-computed using the reduced channel. The re-computed noise covariance could have fewer 1's on its diagonal, thus enlarging the class of positive semi-definite matrices that can be added to its diagonal terms. For the rest of the proof, it is assumed that this channel reduction step has already taken place.

The proof is fairly lengthy. To simplify the algebra, the broadcast channel considered here is assumed to have only a single antenna at each receiver. This special case exhibits the essential features of the least-favorable noise.

The first step of the proof is to verify that even though its diagonals may not be 1's, the candidate noise covariance matrix (3.7) satisfies the least-favorable noise condition. Assuming that channel has already been reduced, S_{zz} can be re-written as

$$S_{zz}^{(0)} = U_1 S_{\tilde{z}\tilde{z}} U_1^T \tag{3.9}$$

where $S_{\tilde{z}\tilde{z}}$ is invertible and columns of U_1 are orthonormal vectors. Further, H can be re-written as

$$H = U_1 \tilde{H}, \tag{3.10}$$

where $\tilde{H}$ is invertible. The strategy is to solve the minimax problem over $S_{\tilde{z}\tilde{z}}$ and to show that the solution is $S_{zz}^{(0)} = H(H^T \Psi H + \lambda I)^{-1} H^T$. The minimax problem is now

$$\begin{aligned} \max_{S_{xx}} \min_{S_{\tilde{z}\tilde{z}}} \quad & \frac{1}{2} \log \frac{|\tilde{H} S_{xx} \tilde{H}^T + S_{\tilde{z}\tilde{z}}|}{|S_{\tilde{z}\tilde{z}}|} \\ \text{s.t.} \quad & \operatorname{tr}(S_{xx}) \leq P \\ & U_1 S_{\tilde{z}\tilde{z}} U_1^T \text{ has } 1'\text{s on diagonal} \\ & S_{xx} \geq 0, \end{aligned} \tag{3.11}$$

The KKT condition of the minimax problem is:

$$\tilde{H}^T (\tilde{H} S_{xx} \tilde{H}^T + S_{\tilde{z}\tilde{z}})^{-1} \tilde{H} = \lambda I \tag{3.12}$$

$$S_{\tilde{z}\tilde{z}}^{-1} - (\tilde{H} S_{xx} \tilde{H}^T + S_{\tilde{z}\tilde{z}})^{-1} = U_1^T \Psi U_1 \tag{3.13}$$

Pre-multiplying the second equation above by $\tilde{H}^T$ and post-multiplying by $\tilde{H}$, it is not difficult to verify that

$$H(H^T \Psi H + \lambda I)^{-1} H^T = U_1 S_{\tilde{z}\tilde{z}} U_1^T = S_{zz}^{(0)}. \tag{3.14}$$

Thus, the candidate $S_{zz}^{(0)}$ satisfies the least-favorable noise condition.

The rest of the proof is devoted to showing that the least-favorable noise condition remains to be satisfied if a positive semi-definite matrix, denoted as S'_{zz}, is added to $S_{zz}^{(0)}$ to makes its diagonal terms 1. The proof is divided into several parts. First, without loss of generality, the rows of H can be re-arranged so that the upper-left sub-matrix of $S_{zz}^{(0)}$ has 1's on its diagonal. This implies that Ψ only has positive entries on its upper-left diagonal, and S'_{zz} has non-zero entries only in the lower-right corner:

$$\Psi = \begin{bmatrix} \Psi' & 0 \\ 0 & 0 \end{bmatrix}, \quad S'_{zz} = \begin{bmatrix} 0 & 0 \\ 0 & S \end{bmatrix}. \tag{3.15}$$

Let n be the number of receivers in the broadcast channel. So, Ψ, S_{zz} and S'_{zz} are $n \times n$ matrices. Let the dimension of Ψ' be $k \times k$. So, the dimension of S is $(n-k) \times (n-k)$. Also, let the rank of $S_{zz}^{(0)}$ be r. Now, observe that $k \geq r$. The reason for this has to do with the channel reduction step mentioned before. Note that from (3.8) the optimal S_{xx} can be expressed as:

$$\begin{aligned} S_{xx} &= (\lambda I)^{-1} - (H^T \Psi H + \lambda I)^{-1} \\ &= (\lambda I)^{-1} H^T \sqrt{\Psi} (I + \sqrt{\Psi} H H^T \sqrt{\Psi})^{-1} \sqrt{\Psi} H (\lambda I)^{-1}. \end{aligned} \tag{3.16}$$

Thus, the rank of S_{xx} is the same as the rank of $H^T \Psi H$. The channel reduction step guarantees that S_{xx} is full rank. This implies that $H^T \Psi H$ must be full rank.

For this to be true, Ψ must have non-zero diagonal entries in at least r' positions, where r' is the rank of H. So, $k \geq r'$. But, after the channel reduction, the rank of H is the same as the rank of $S_{zz}^{(0)}$. This proves that $k \geq r$.

In general, k can be strictly larger than r. Physically, this implies that in a broadcast channel, the number of active receivers can be larger than the number of transmit dimensions. Also note that since the rank of $S_{zz}^{(0)}$ is r and the rank of S'_{zz} is $(n-k)$, the rank of $S_{zz}^{(0)} + S'_{zz}$ is at most $(n-k+r)$, which is not full rank if k is strictly larger than r.

The next step in the proof involves the decomposition of $S_{zz}^{(0)} + S'_{zz}$ along the direction U_1. The strategy is the following. First, find an $n \times (n-k)$ matrix of orthonormal column vectors, denoted as U_2, extending the space spanned by the columns of U_1, such that S'_{zz} can be expressed as:

$$S'_{zz} = \begin{bmatrix} 0 & 0 \\ 0 & S \end{bmatrix} = \begin{bmatrix} U_1 & U_2 \end{bmatrix} \begin{bmatrix} S_{11} & S_{12} \\ S_{21} & S_{22} \end{bmatrix} \begin{bmatrix} U_1^T \\ U_2^T \end{bmatrix}. \tag{3.17}$$

Recall that U_1 contains r column vectors and U_2 contains $n-k$ column vectors. So, $[\ U_1\ U_2\ ]$ contains $n-k+r$ vectors, which do not necessarily span the whole space. (Note that this U_2 may be different from the U_2 in section 2.)

Partition U_1 and U_2 into sub-matrices:

$$U_1 = \begin{bmatrix} u_{11}^T \\ u_{12}^T \end{bmatrix} \qquad U_2 = \begin{bmatrix} u_{21}^T \\ u_{22}^T \end{bmatrix}. \tag{3.18}$$

Two useful facts about S_{ij} and u_{ij} are derived next. First,

$$S_{11} - S_{12} S_{22}^{-1} S_{21} = 0. \tag{3.19}$$

This is because

$$\begin{bmatrix} U_1^T \\ U_2^T \end{bmatrix} \begin{bmatrix} U_1 & U_2 \end{bmatrix} = I, \tag{3.20}$$

so, from (3.17),

$$\begin{bmatrix} S_{11} & S_{12} \\ S_{21} & S_{22} \end{bmatrix} = \begin{bmatrix} u_{11}^T & u_{12}^T \\ u_{21}^T & u_{22}^T \end{bmatrix} \begin{bmatrix} 0 & 0 \\ 0 & S \end{bmatrix} \begin{bmatrix} u_{11} & u_{21} \\ u_{12} & u_{22} \end{bmatrix}. \tag{3.21}$$

This allows S_{ij} to be solved explicitly:

$$S_{11} = u_{12}^T S u_{12} \qquad S_{12} = u_{12}^T S u_{22} \tag{3.22}$$

$$S_{21} = u_{22}^T S u_{12} \qquad S_{22} = u_{22}^T S u_{22}. \tag{3.23}$$

Therefore,

$$S_{12} S_{22}^{-1} S_{21} = u_{12}^T S u_{22} (u_{22}^T S u_{22})^{-1} u_{22}^T S u_{12} = S_{11}, \tag{3.24}$$

thus proving (3.19).

The second useful fact is the following:

$$u_{21} = u_{11} u_{12}^T u_{22}^{-T}. \tag{3.25}$$

The proof is based on (3.17)

$$\begin{bmatrix} 0 & 0 \\ 0 & S \end{bmatrix} = \begin{bmatrix} u_{11} & u_{21} \\ u_{12} & u_{22} \end{bmatrix} \begin{bmatrix} S_{11} & S_{12} \\ S_{21} & S_{22} \end{bmatrix} \begin{bmatrix} u_{11}^T & u_{12}^T \\ u_{21}^T & u_{22}^T \end{bmatrix}. \tag{3.26}$$

Multiply out the right-hand side. Using the fact that the upper-right sub-matrix of the right-hand side is zero, we get

$$0 = u_{11}S_{11}u_{12}^T + u_{21}S_{21}u_{12}^T + u_{11}S_{12}u_{22}^T + u_{21}S_{22}u_{22}^T. \tag{3.27}$$

Substituting in (3.22)–(3.23), the above is equal to

$$0 = (u_{11}u_{12}^T + u_{21}u_{22}^T)S(u_{11}u_{11}^T + u_{22}u_{22}^T). \tag{3.28}$$

Since S is full rank and $(u_{11}u_{11}^T + u_{22}u_{22}^T)$ is full rank, the above implies

$$u_{11}u_{12}^T + u_{21}u_{22}^T = 0, \tag{3.29}$$

thus proving (3.25).

Finally, we are ready to show that $S_{zz}^{(0)} + S'_{zz}$ satisfies the least-favorable noise condition. Starting from (3.13)

$$S_{\tilde{z}\tilde{z}}^{-1} - (\tilde{H}S_{xx}\tilde{H}^T + S_{\tilde{z}\tilde{z}})^{-1} = U_1^T\Psi U_1, \tag{3.30}$$

the objective is to prove that

(3.31)
$$\begin{bmatrix} S_{\tilde{z}\tilde{z}} + S_{11} & S_{12} \\ S_{21} & S_{22} \end{bmatrix}^{-1} - \begin{bmatrix} \tilde{H}S_{xx}\tilde{H}^T + S_{\tilde{z}\tilde{z}} + S_{11} & S_{12} \\ S_{21} & S_{22} \end{bmatrix}^{-1} = \begin{bmatrix} U_1^T \\ U_2^T \end{bmatrix} \Psi \begin{bmatrix} U_1 \; U_2 \end{bmatrix}.$$

The strategy is to simplify the above using Schur's complement formula:

$$\begin{bmatrix} A & B \\ C & D \end{bmatrix}^{-1} = \begin{bmatrix} \Delta_D^{-1} & -\Delta_D^{-1}BD^{-1} \\ -D^{-1}C\Delta_D^{-1} & D^{-1} + D^{-1}C\Delta_D^{-1}BD^{-1} \end{bmatrix}, \tag{3.32}$$

where $\Delta_D = A - BD^{-1}C$. To evaluate the matrix inversions in (3.31), Δ_D^{-1} can be simplified using (3.19):

$$\Delta_D = S_{\tilde{z}\tilde{z}} + S_{11} - S_{12}S_{22}^{-1}S_{21} = S_{\tilde{z}\tilde{z}}. \tag{3.33}$$

Thus, the first matrix inversion in (3.31) is equal to

$$\begin{bmatrix} S_{\tilde{z}\tilde{z}}^{-1} & -S_{\tilde{z}\tilde{z}}^{-1}S_{12}S_{22}^{-1} \\ -S_{22}^{-1}S_{21}S_{\tilde{z}\tilde{z}}^{-1} & S_{22}^{-1} + S_{22}^{-1}S_{21}S_{\tilde{z}\tilde{z}}^{-1}S_{12}S_{22}^{-1} \end{bmatrix}, \tag{3.34}$$

and the second matrix inversion in (3.31) can be expanded similarly:

(3.35)
$$\begin{bmatrix} (\tilde{H}S_{xx}\tilde{H}^T + S_{\tilde{z}\tilde{z}})^{-1} & -(\tilde{H}S_{xx}\tilde{H}^T + S_{\tilde{z}\tilde{z}})^{-1}S_{12}S_{22}^{-1} \\ -S_{22}^{-1}S_{21}(\tilde{H}S_{xx}\tilde{H}^T + S_{\tilde{z}\tilde{z}})^{-1} & S_{22}^{-1} + S_{22}^{-1}S_{21}(\tilde{H}S_{xx}\tilde{H}^T + S_{\tilde{z}\tilde{z}})^{-1}S_{12}S_{22}^{-1} \end{bmatrix}.$$

Now, using (3.30), the difference between the two can now be simplified:

$$\begin{bmatrix} U_1^T\Psi U_1 & -U_1^T\Psi U_1 S_{12}S_{22}^{-1} \\ -S_{22}^{-1}S_{21}U_1^T\Psi U_1 & S_{22}^{-1}S_{21}U_1^T\Psi U_1 S_{12}S_{22}^{-1} \end{bmatrix}. \tag{3.36}$$

To prove (3.31), it remains to show that the above is equal to

$$\begin{bmatrix} U_1^T \\ U_2^T \end{bmatrix} \Psi \begin{bmatrix} U_1 & U_2 \end{bmatrix} = \begin{bmatrix} U_1^T\Psi U_1 & U_1^T\Psi U_2 \\ U_2^T\Psi U_1 & U_2^T\Psi U_2 \end{bmatrix}. \tag{3.37}$$

Comparing (3.36) with (3.37), it is clear that the two are equal if the following holds:

$$\Psi U_2 = -\Psi U_1 S_{12}S_{22}^{-1}. \tag{3.38}$$

Recall that Ψ has non-zero entries only in its upper-left diagonal. So, the left-hand side of (3.38) is

$$\Psi U_2 = \begin{bmatrix} \Psi' & 0 \\ 0 & 0 \end{bmatrix} \begin{bmatrix} u_{21} \\ u_{22} \end{bmatrix} = \Psi' u_{21}. \tag{3.39}$$

The right-hand side of (3.38) is

$$-\Psi U_1 S_{12} S_{22}^{-1} = -\Psi' u_{11} u_{12}^T u_{22}^{-T}. \tag{3.40}$$

By (3.25), the left-hand side is equal to the right-hand side. This establishes the least-favorable noise condition (3.31).

3.3. Linear Estimation Interpretation. The previous section shows that the least-favorable noise in a Gaussian minimax mutual information game is of the type $S_{zz}^{(0)} + S'_{zz}$. Note that adding the term S'_{zz} does not change the mutual information $I(\mathbf{X};\mathbf{Y})$. This can be seen using the following argument. The value of the minimax expression with $(S_{xx}, S_{zz}^{(0)})$ is

$$C = \frac{1}{2}\log\frac{|\tilde{H} S_{xx} \tilde{H}^T + S_{\tilde{z}\tilde{z}}|}{|S_{\tilde{z}\tilde{z}}|}. \tag{3.41}$$

With $(S_{xx}, S_{zz}^{(0)} + S'_{zz})$, the capacity is

$$C = \frac{1}{2}\log\frac{\begin{vmatrix} \tilde{H} S_{xx} \tilde{H}^T + S_{\tilde{z}\tilde{z}} + S_{11} & S_{12} \\ S_{21} & S_{22} \end{vmatrix}}{\begin{vmatrix} S_{\tilde{z}\tilde{z}} + S_{11} & S_{12} \\ S_{21} & S_{22} \end{vmatrix}}. \tag{3.42}$$

Using the relation $S_{11} - S_{12}S_{22}^{-1}S_{21} = 0$ and the Schur's complement formula for the determinant

$$\begin{vmatrix} A & B \\ C & D \end{vmatrix} = |D| \cdot |A - BD^{-1}C|, \tag{3.43}$$

it is not difficult to show that

$$\frac{|S_{22}| \cdot |\tilde{H} S_{xx} \tilde{H}^T + S_{\tilde{z}\tilde{z}} + S_{11} - S_{12}S_{22}^{-1}S_{21}|}{|S_{22}| \cdot |S_{\tilde{z}\tilde{z}} + S_{11} - S_{12}S_{22}^{-1}S_{21}|} = \frac{|\tilde{H} S_{xx} \tilde{H}^T + S_{\tilde{z}\tilde{z}}|}{|S_{\tilde{z}\tilde{z}}|}. \tag{3.44}$$

Therefore the capacity expressions (3.41) and (3.42) have the same value.

In some sense, $S_{zz}^{(0)}$ is the "smallest" possible noise in the class of least-favorable noises. This is because after the channel reduction step, $HS_{xx}H^T$ is strictly positive everywhere in the span of the U_1 space. Thus, for capacity not to become infinity, the noise covariance must also be strictly positive in the space spanned by U_1. Now, $S_{zz}^{(0)}$ is the only noise covariance entirely in the U_1 space that satisfies the KKT condition. Thus, $S_{zz}^{(0)}$ must be the "smallest" noise covariance that satisfies the KKT condition.

$S_{zz}^{(0)}$ is not, of course, the only such noise. The previous section shows that $(S_{xx}, S_{zz}^{(0)} + S'_{zz})$ also satisfies the least-favorable noise condition. However, the previous section did not explicitly prove that S_{xx} is the water-filling covariance matrix for $S_{zz}^{(0)} + S'_{zz}$. But, because the addition of S'_{zz} can only reduce the minimax capacity, the fact that it does not shows that S_{xx} must be the maximizing covariance for $S_{zz}^{(0)} + S'_{zz}$. Thus, the entire class of $(S_{xx}, S_{zz}^{(0)} + S'_{zz})$ are saddle-points of the minimax problem.

The class of least-favorable noises $S_{zz}^{(0)} + S'_{zz}$ has a linear estimation interpretation. Let $\mathbf{Z}^{(0)}$ and $\mathbf{Z}'$ be independent Gaussian noise vectors with covariance matrices $S_{zz}^{(0)}$ and S'_{zz} respectively. Consider an orthogonal transformation $\mathbf{Z}_u^{(0)} = [U_1 U_2]\mathbf{Z}^{(0)}$ and $\mathbf{Z}'_u = [U_1 U_2]\mathbf{Z}'$. These two noise vectors take the form

$$\mathbf{Z}_u^{(0)} = \begin{bmatrix} \mathbf{z}_1^0 \\ 0 \end{bmatrix}, \qquad \mathbf{Z}'_u = \begin{bmatrix} \mathbf{z}'_1 \\ \mathbf{z}'_2 \end{bmatrix}. \tag{3.45}$$

Consider two receivers, one has $\mathbf{Z}_u^{(0)}$ as noise and the other has $\mathbf{Z}_u^{(0)} + \mathbf{Z}'_u$ as noise. Clearly the second receiver cannot do better than the first one. However, the second receiver does as well as the first receiver if the linear estimation of $\mathbf{z}_1^0 + \mathbf{z}'_1$ given $\mathbf{z}'_2$ is exactly $\mathbf{z}'_1$. Since $\mathbf{z}_1^0$ and $\mathbf{z}'_1$ are independent, this condition is equivalent to $\mathbf{E}[\mathbf{z}'_1|\mathbf{z}'_2] = 0$. But, the covariance matrix of $\mathbf{E}[\mathbf{z}'_1|\mathbf{z}'_2]$ is $S_{11} - S_{12}S_{22}^{-1}S_{21}$. Thus, the covariance matrix of the additional noise S'_{zz} must satisfy the condition

$$S_{11} - S_{12}S_{22}^{-1}S_{21} = 0. \tag{3.46}$$

The above argument shows that the entire class of least-favorable noises are related to each other via a linear estimation relation[2]. As the previous section shows, this relation is crucial in the derivation of the least-favorable condition.

4. Conclusions

This paper deals with the least-favorable noise in a Gaussian vector broadcast channel. The least-favorable noise is not necessarily non-singular. The achievability proof for the broadcast channel sum capacity is extended to the case of singular least-favorable noises. The proof is based on the fact that the decision-feedback equalizer is not unique when the noise is singular. Among all possible equalizers, there exists one with a diagonal feedforward matrix.

In the second part of the paper, a new derivation for the duality between the multiple access channel and the broadcast channel is given. The duality relation gives a natural characterization of the entire class of least-favorable noises. The least-favorable noise is not unique, and all least-favorable noises are related to each other by a linear estimation relation.

References

[1] G. Caire and S. Shamai, "On the achievable throughput of a multi-antenna Gaussian broadcast channel," *submitted to IEEE Trans. Inform. Theory*, July 2001.

[2] W. Yu and J. M. Cioffi, "Sum capacity of Gaussian vector broadcast channels," *submitted to IEEE Trans. Inform. Theory*, Nov. 2001,

[3] P. Viswanath and D. Tse, "Sum capacity of the vector Gaussian broadcast channel and downlink-uplink duality," *submitted to IEEE Trans. Inform. Theory*, July 2002.

[4] S. Vishwanath, N. Jindal, and A. Goldsmith, "Duality, achievable rates and sum-rate capacity of Gaussian MIMO broadcast channels," *submitted to IEEE Trans. Inform. Theory*, Aug. 2002.

[5] M. Costa, "Writing on dirty paper," *IEEE Trans. Inform. Theory*, vol. 29, no. 3, pp. 439–441, May 1983.

[6] H. Sato, "An outer bound on the capacity region of broadcast channels," *IEEE Trans. Inform. Theory*, vol. 24, no. 3, pp. 374–377, May 1978.

[7] W. Yu, "Uplink-downlink duality via minimax duality," *Canadian Workshop on Information Theory*, May 2003.

[2] There is a slight subtlety in that, strictly speaking, $\mathbf{Z}'$ needs not be Gaussian. However, this does not affect the sum capacity. See **[10]** for a discussion.

[8] W. Yu, "A dual decomposition approach to the sum power Gaussian vector multiple access channel sum capacity," *Conference on Information Sciences and Systems (CISS)*, March 2003.

[9] S. Vishwanath, R. Wonjong, N. Jindal, S. Jafar, and A. Goldsmith, "Sum power iterative waterfilling for Gaussian vector broadcast channels," *IEEE Int'l Symp. Inform. Theory (ISIT)*, June 2003. Also in *Asilomar Conf.*, Nov. 2002.

[10] S. N. Diggavi and T. M. Cover, "The worst additive noise under a covariance constraint," *IEEE Trans. Inform. Theory*, vol. 47, pp. 3072–3081, Nov. 2001.

ELECTRICAL AND COMPUTER ENGINEERING DEPARTMENT, UNIVERSITY OF TORONTO
Current address: 10 King's College Road, Toronto, Ontario M5S 3G4, Canada
E-mail address: weiyu@comm.utoronto.ca

Part III

Information Theory for Sources and Channels

DIMACS Series in Discrete Mathematics
and Theoretical Computer Science
Volume **66**, 2004

Coding Theorems for the Sensor Reachback Problem with Partially Cooperating Nodes

João Barros and Sergio D. Servetto

ABSTRACT. We consider a multiaccess communication problem, in which multiple encoders cooperate to send correlated data to a far receiver over a multiple access channel. Cooperation among nodes takes two forms: (a) the multiple access channel is rendered virtually collision free by a suitable MAC protocol; (b) nodes can exchange messages to coordinate their channel inputs. This problem arises in a sensor networking context, where sensors are deployed on a field, and the goal is to send back to a remote location the signals picked up by all nodes. In this paper, we give exact conditions on the sources and the channels under which reliable communication is possible in this context. These conditions generalize in a very meaningful way the condition that $\mathcal{H}(X) < C$ (entropy of a source less than channel capacity) for point-to-point channels, and surprisingly, give source/channel separation theorems for this problem as well. To the best of our knowledge, these are the first non-trivial examples involving multiple sources and multiple channels in which separation holds.

1. Introduction

1.1. Challenges in Wireless Sensor Networks. In recent times much has been said about how, once deployed, networks of devices with wireless communication capabilities will affect the way we work, learn, interact, organize, get entertained, fight wars, and recover from disasters. This interest in wireless networks has led to a fair amount of research activity in the areas of mobile and ad-hoc networking, addressing both systems and theory issues. However, wireless *sensor* networks—i.e., networks of tiny, low power, unreliable devices equipped with very limited sensing and communication capabilities, and embedded in the environment—have only recently started to receive some attention.

Sensor networks are very different from any other type of network studied in the past—well accepted and well established statements about properties of other networks that could be considered "close relatives" of sensor networks (such as mobile ad-hoc networks) do not necessarily hold in this context. For example: a

1991 *Mathematics Subject Classification.* Primary 94A24, 94A29, 94A34; Secondary 68P30.
Key words and phrases. Networks, Information Theory, Multiaccess Communication, Source Coding, Rate/Distortion Theory, Discrete Probability.
Work supported by a Fulbright scholarship, and by the National Science Foundation, under awards CCR-0227676, CCR-0238271 (CAREER), CCR-0330059, and ANR-0325556.

key result due to Gupta and Kumar states that, when n non-mobile nodes are optimally placed in a disk of unit area, traffic patterns are optimally assigned, and the range of each transmission is optimally chosen, the total throughput that the network can carry is $O(\sqrt{n})$. As a result, the per-node throughput is only $O(\frac{1}{\sqrt{n}})$, i.e., decays to zero as the number of nodes in the network increases. From this observation one concludes that large-scale networks are probably not feasible, since the larger the network becomes, the lower the amount of information that any one node can communicate to any other. However, in the context of sensor networks, this inference is not correct: when sensors pick up correlated signals (a condition that must be necessarily true whenever we have a large number of nodes sensing a physical process within a confined area), the total amount of information generated by the entire network is not necessarily linear in the number of nodes, and therefore, provided that the amount of data generated by each node decays at least as fast as network throughput does, the network should still have enough capacity to carry these measurements [**22**].

Observations like the one above clearly illustrate how little we know and we understand about sensor networks, and particularly about *large-scale* sensor networks: in that example, we see at work the seemingly bizarre concept that the amount of information that a node in the network generates does depend on how many nodes there are in the network. Work currently under way at Cornell is addressing issues related to fundamental performance limits for large-scale wireless sensor networks. And one of these issues under study is that of moving data *out* of the network, in what we call the *sensor reachback* problem, explained next.

1.2. Cooperative Transmission of Correlated Information over an Array of Independent Channels.

1.2.1. *A Model for the Network.* In this paper we study a set of communication problems related to the transmission of information generated by multiple correlated sources over multiple independent channels. In particular, we make the following assumptions:

- Each source is assigned a separate transmitter and a separate channel.
- Each transmitter uses one encoder, which only observes the outputs of the one source it has been assigned to, and which can send/receive messages to/from other encoders, over independent channels of limited capacity.
- The receiver has access to all the available channels and is allowed to use the correlation between the sources to achieve the best possible reconstruction of the information sent by each of the transmitters.

These assumptions form what we deem to be a reasonable abstraction of the problem of sending the signals picked up by all the sensors all the way back to a common receiver: the nodes pick up correlated information, this information needs to be encoded by each node (possibly after a cooperative step of information exchange among nodes), sent over a multiple access channel for which a suitable MAC protocol ensures virtually collision-free transmission, and decoded at a common node. This model for the communication system is illustrated in Fig. 1.

Under this scenario, our main task is to establish the ultimate information theoretic bounds for reliable communication.

At this point, some clarification seems due in terms of how the conference mechanism works. For this purpose, we feel we could not provide an explanation more clear and intuitive than that given by Willems in [**26**]. Therefore we quote

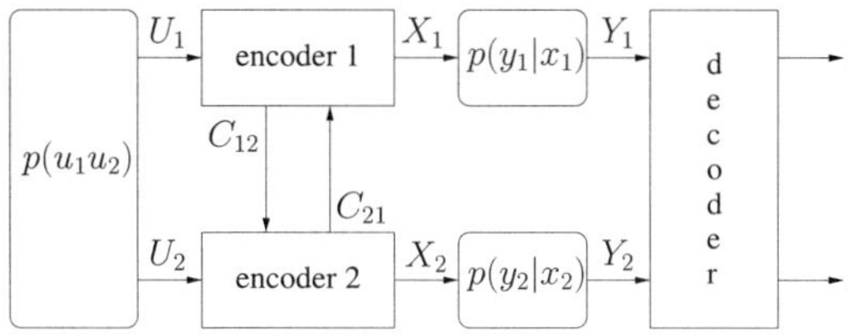

FIGURE 1. A system model for the sensor reachback problem with partially cooperating encoders and independent channels, for the case of 2 sources.

from his paper, where he elaborates on how the encoders can exchange information about their input source messages:

> [...] The main problem in this situation is how to use the communication links (between encoders). One could, e.g., partition each message into equally sized cells and then communicate to the other encoder the number of the cell in which the actual message lies. We can see this as a *pair of simultaneous monologues*, in which functions of the messages are communicated. On the other hand, we can imagine a sort of dialogue between between both encoders; e.g., encoder 1 says: "In transmission 27 I send $X_1 = 2$," and then encoder 2 answers: "In that case I will always send $X_2 = 0$ in transmission 30,31,...,39." Then encoder 1 proceeds: "In transmission 30,31,...,39 I will never send $X_1 = 0$; my message index is between 512 and 1023," and encoder 2 says in the meantime: "My message index is odd." We can see this as a *partially simultaneous dialogue* in which different kids of information can be communicated. Between the two simultaneous monologues and the (partially) simultaneous dialogue there are a lot of other possible communication concepts. The outcome of such a communication process, or *conference*, will be used by the encoders to form their channel input symbols.

A most important point that seems appropriate to emphasize is the fact that channel codewords are functions of the *entire* conference. That is, the encoders first exchange a sequence of messages, and once they have completed their conference process, they choose channel inputs. Clearly, this is a different problem from one in which the computation of codewords and conference messages is interleaved (put a symbol into the channel, get a message from the other encoder, put another symbol, etc.)

1.2.2. *Some Important Questions.* Consider the case illustrated by the block diagram of Fig. 1. The information generated by a pair of correlated sources U_1 and U_2 (with joint probability distribution $p(u_1u_2)$) is to be transmitted over two non-interfering channels. Encoder i ($i = 1, 2$) observes the outputs of its source U_i, and exchanges a series of messages with the other encoder, prior to deciding which codewords X_i to transmit. At the receiving end, the decoder knows the joint distribution $p(u_1u_2)$, and produces the estimates $(\hat{U}_1\hat{U}_2)$, based on that knowledge and the observed channel outputs (Y_1Y_2).

The main question of interest in this work is: *For a given source $p(u_1u_2)$, for a multiple access channel $p(y_1y_2|x_1x_2) = p(y_1|x_1)p(y_2|x_2)$ (each channel $p(y_i|x_i)$*

with capacity C_i), and for channels between encoders 1 and 2 of capacity C_{12} and C_{21}, under what conditions is it possible to reproduce the values of U_1U_2 at a remote receiver with arbitrarily small probability of error?

Clearly, if we were allowed to use a joint encoder, $H(U_1U_2) < C_1 + C_2$ would be a necessary and sufficient condition for reliable communication. Is this also true, when we use a separate encoder for each of the sources? Or do we need to ask for more restrictions? And how does the fact that the encoders can exchange *some* information about their realizations affect such conditions?

Another important question is whether or not there is a separation theorem in this context. In constrast to what Shannon established for point-to-point communication [**9**, Ch. 8.13], in many multi-user problems separating source coding and channel coding does not yield optimal performance. In our case, one could consider compressing the sources first using Slepian-Wolf codes [**24**], and then adding channel coding to overcome the impairments by the channel. Is this strategy optimal? If not, how much do we lose in comparison to an optimal strategy which uses joint source and channel coding?

1.3. Related Work. It is important to relate the previous discussion to the more general case of correlated sources over a *generic* multiple access channel, i.e., one in which simultaneous transmissions do actually interfere with each other.

1.3.1. *On the Capacity of the Multiple Access Channel.* The capacity region for the multiple access channel with non-cooperating encoders is given by the convex hull of the set of points (R_1, R_2) satisfying

$$\begin{aligned} R_1 &< I(X_1;Y|X_2) \\ R_2 &< I(X_2;Y|X_1) \\ R_1 + R_2 &< I(X_1X_2;Y), \end{aligned}$$

for some joint distribution $p_1(x_1)p_2(x_2)$ [**9**, Ch. 14.3]. When cooperation between encoders is allowed, the capacity region is known to take the form

$$\begin{aligned} R_1 &< I(X_1;Y|X_2Z) + C_{12} \\ R_2 &< I(X_2;Y|X_1Z) + C_{21} \\ R_1 + R_2 &< \min\{\, I(X_1X_2;Y|Z) + C_{12} + C_{21},\ I(X_1X_2;Y)\,\}, \end{aligned}$$

for some auxiliary random variable Z such that $|\mathcal{Z}| \leq \min(|\mathcal{X}_1| \cdot |\mathcal{X}_2| + 2, |\mathcal{Y}| + 3)$, and for a joint distribution $p(zx_1x_2y_1y_2) = p(z)p(x_1|z)p(x_2|z)p(y|x_1x_2)$ [**26**]. In both cases, it is assumed that the message sources are independent.

1.3.2. *On the Transmission of Correlated Sources over Multiple Access Channels.* When the sources are no longer independent, computing the capacity region becomes a more complicated matter. For separate encoding of the correlated sources, the Slepian-Wolf theorem provides the achievable compression rates. Clearly, if the Slepian-Wolf rate region intersects the capacity region of the multiple access channel, reliable communication is possible. However, it is possible to show with a simple example that this condition is sufficient, but not necessary. The result which comes closest to a capacity region for this case states that U_1 and U_2 can be communicated reliably if

$$\begin{aligned} H(U_1|U_2) &< I(X_1;Y|X_2U_2) \\ H(U_2|U_1) &< I(X_2;Y|X_1U_1) \\ H(U_1U_2) &< I(X_1X_2;Y), \end{aligned}$$

for some $p(u_1u_2x_1x_2y) = p(u_1u_2)p(x_1|u_1)p(x_2|u_2)p(y|x_1x_2)$ [**8**]. In the same paper, the authors did generalize this region of achievable rates to account for sources (U_1U_2) with a common part $W = f(U_1) = g(U_2)$ (extending the work of [**23**]), but they were not able to prove a converse for the general case of arbitrarily correlated sources. A counterexample was later given to show why the region of achievable rates of [**8**] is not tight [**10**], and so this remains an interesting open problem.

1.3.3. *Cooperative Transmission.* In wireless communications, fading of the signals transmitted due to multipath propagation is one of the major impairments that a communications system has to deal with. A natural way to deal with these impairments is by the use of *diversity*: the transmission of essentially redundant signals over essentially independent channels, which then can be combined at the receiver to average out distortion/noise effects induced by the independent channels [**19**]. Some practical ideas about distributed beamforming that we started studying in [**13, 14**], which triggered our interest in the more information theoretic aspects of the problem that form the core of this paper, fall under the class of *spatial diversity* methods. Among these, the papers of Narula et al. [**18**], Laneman et al. [**16**], and Sendonaris et al. [**20, 21**], most directly influenced our own thinking on this problem.

1.3.4. *In Summary.* The capacity region of the multiple access channel with arbitrarily correlated sources is still unknown. On the other hand, the effects of partial cooperation between encoders was only studied for independent sources. If we eliminate the interference between users (e.g., through orthogonal multiple access), the multiple access channel becomes an array of independent channels. It is thus reasonable to assume that by solving this case, we will gain useful insight towards a complete characterization of the general capacity region. To the best of our knowledge however, other than our previous work [**4**], there are no references to this apparently simpler case (i.e., independent channels).

1.4. Main Contributions and Organization of the Paper.

1.4.1. *Statement of the Main Result.* Our main result is given by the following theorem:

THEOREM 1.1. *Let (U_1U_2) be two correlated sources drawn i.i.d. $\sim p(u_1u_2)$, and sent over two independent channels $(\mathcal{X}_1, p(y_1|x_1), \mathcal{Y}_1)$ and $(\mathcal{X}_2, p(y_2|x_2), \mathcal{Y}_2)$. Assuming that the encoders are connected by links of capacities C_{12} and C_{21}, reliable communication is possible if and only if*

$$H(U_1|U_2) < I(X_1;Y_1) + I(U_1;Z|U_2) \tag{1.1}$$

$$H(U_2|U_1) < I(X_2;Y_2) + I(U_2;Z|U_1) \tag{1.2}$$

$$H(U_1U_2) < I(X_1;Y_1) + I(X_2;Y_2). \tag{1.3}$$

for some auxiliary variable Z such that $I(U_1;Z|U_2) < C_{12}$, $I(U_2;Z|U_1) < C_{21}$, and $|\mathcal{Z}| \leq |\mathcal{U}_1||\mathcal{U}_2|$.

There are a number of interesting remarks we can make about this result, and about what it means.

The first thing to note is that Z is a variable that can be interpreted as the information exchanged by the two encoders. Therefore, by explicitly solving the channel capacity problems for communication between the two encoders and with the far receiver, a simpler (and more intuitive) version of the theorem is obtained:

$$\begin{aligned} H(U_1|U_2) &< C_1 + C_{12} \\ H(U_2|U_1) &< C_2 + C_{21} \\ H(U_1U_2) &< C_1 + C_2, \end{aligned}$$

where C_1, C_2, C_{12}, C_{21} are the capacities of the corresponding channels. Now, from this simpler version, we can see clearly that there is indeed a strict improvement over the conditions obtained in [**4**] for the case of no cooperation. For example, it is easy to see that if $C_{12} > H(U_1|U_2)$, and $C_{21} > H(U_2|U_1)$, then these conditions reduce to the one for the classical point-to-point problem: $H(U_1U_2) < C_1 + C_2$. Any point on the surface of the sum-rate face of the region can be achieved by having encoders send their realization to each other using Slepian-Wolf codes—in this way, both can reconstruct both sources, generate a joint encoding, and then split this encoding in whatever way they choose to. Some of these points are clearly not achievable without cooperation among encoders: e.g., $(R_1, R_2) = (0, H(U_1U_2))$ and $H(U_1|U_2) > 0$, even if $H(U_1U_2)) < I(X_2; Y_2)$. This is illustrated in Fig. 2.

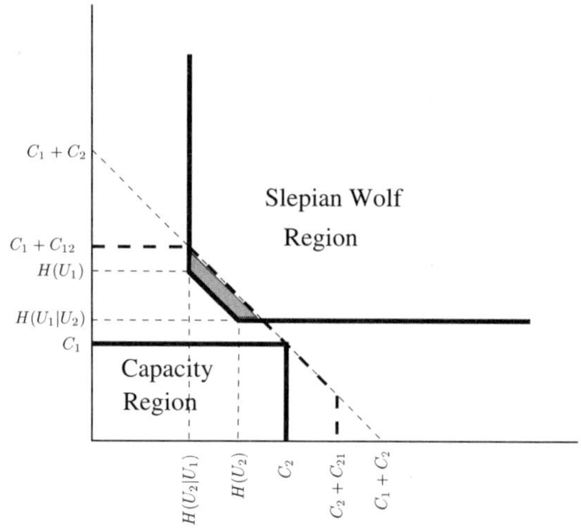

FIGURE 2. To illustrate the effect of cooperation among encoders on the feasibility of establishing reliable communication between the reachback network and the far receiver. This is an example of a situation where without cooperation then reliable communication would be impossible (the standard Slepian-Wolf region and the capacity region for the pair of independent channels do not intersect), but where there are points in the enlarged Slepian-Wolf region (enlarged by the capacity of the conference channels, the shaded portion of the picture) that intersects the capacity region for the pair of independent channels. To achieve these points, it is necessary for the encoder with a bad channel to route some of its data to the joint decoder via the good channel available to the other encoder.

It is also interesting to observe from Fig. 2 that, contrary to what happens with general multiple access channels, in the case of independent channels considered in this work cooperation does *not* lead to an increase in the achievable sum-rate. This suggests a *routing* interpretation[1] for theorem 1.1. If, say, encoder 1 has too much data to send and a channel not good enough (that is, $H(U_1|U_2) > C_1$), and encoder 2 has enough idle capacity (that is, $H(U_2|U_1) < C_2$), then encoder 1 can use Z to route some of its data to the far receiver via encoder 2. The total number of bits that can be sent over the reachback network is still bounded by $I(X_1;Y_1) + I(X_2;Y_2)$. But, provided this constraint is not violated, each encoder can also act as a relay for the other encoder, in this way relaxing the conditions on the minimum amount of data required from each encoder. And the total amount of information that can be exchanged among nodes is given by the capacity of the interconnection network between encoders.

Incidentally, note also that the widely accepted view that "according to the Slepian-Wolf theorem separate encoders can achieve the same compression performance of a joint encoder" is only partially accurate. Indeed, the *total* number of bits required with separate and with joint encoders remains the same. However, for the informal statement above to hold true, the joint decoder needs to receive a minimum amount of information from each encoder, so not any point in the sum-rate region $R_1 + R_2 > H(U_1U_2)$ is achievable without cooperation.[2] The net effect of cooperation is to relax this requirement, to the extent supported by the interconnection network between encoders.

1.4.2. *Relationship to Previous Work.* The sensor reachback problem is closely related to (a) the multiple access channel with correlated sources considered by Cover et al. [**8**], and (b) the multiple access channel with partially cooperating encoders solved by Willems [**26**]. A general problem subsuming these two problems would be a multiple access channel with correlated sources *and* partially cooperating encoders. Our problem is also a special case of this more general problem, since we consider correlated sources, partially cooperating encoders, and a multiple access channel without interference. Fortunately, although for the case considered in [**8**] only a region of achievable rates is known (without a converse), for our model we are able to give an *exact* characterization of the capacity region, converse included.

1.4.3. *On the Separation Principle in Networks.* Unlike the case of most other network source/channel coding problems we are aware of, for this problem we are able to prove that a natural generalization of the joint source/channel coding theorem [**9**, Ch. 8.13] (commonly known as the *separation* theorem) holds. We show that an optimal coding strategy for this problem consists of a cascade of a variant of Slepian-Wolf source codes [**24**] (to account for cooperation among encoders), followed by standard point-to-point channel codes. Therefore, together with our previous results from [**1, 4**] (briefly reviewed in this paper for completeness), we identify an important class of non-trivial network information theory problems, that come up in the context of sensor networks, in which the classical notion of separation between sources and channels holds. The problem of source/channel separation in networks has also been addressed in [**11, 12**], and a source/channel separation theorem for a combination of the Wyner-Ziv and the Gel'fand-Pinsker problems has been established in [**17**].

---

[1]We would like to thank one of the anonymous reviewers of this paper, for pointing out to us that we could simplify our arguments signficantly in terms of this routing property.

[2]Whereas with the benefit of hindsight this might seem obvious, taking the informal statement above literally is a mistake we made in our first steps on this work that slowed us down for a few weeks, by assuming that cooperation would not result in an increase of the capacity region.

1.4.4. *Organization of the Paper.* The rest of this paper is organized as follows. In Section 2 we define our notation. Then, in Section 3, we prove Theorem 1.1. In Section 4 we review our previous results dealing with the case of sending correlated sources over an array of independent channels *without* cooperation among encoders, showing how the conditions of Theorem 1.1 specialize to those in [**4**]. Together with capacity and separation theorems, naturally comes associated a question of tradeoffs between rate and distortion: in Section 5, we present an overview of recent progress we have made towards the solution of the classical Multiterminal Source Coding problem.

2. Definitions and Notation

A *reachback network* consists of two sender nodes and one receiver node. Sender 1 is connected to the receiver via a discrete memoryless channel $(\mathcal{X}_1, p(y_1|x_1), \mathcal{Y}_1)$ and sender 2 via $(\mathcal{X}_2, p(y_2|x_2), \mathcal{Y}_2)$. Senders 1 and 2 are joined by network links of capacity C_{12} and C_{21} with information being exchanged in opposite directions. This setup was illustrated in Fig. 1.

A *conference* among encoders is specified by a set of $2K$ functions

$$\begin{aligned} h_{1k} : \mathcal{U}_1^N \times \mathcal{V}_{21} \times \ldots \times \mathcal{V}_{2(k-1)} &\rightarrow \mathcal{V}_{1k} \\ h_{2k} : \mathcal{U}_2^N \times \mathcal{V}_{11} \times \ldots \times \mathcal{V}_{1(k-1)} &\rightarrow \mathcal{V}_{2k}, \end{aligned}$$

such that the conference message $V_{1k} \in \mathcal{V}_{1k}$ (or $V_{2k} \in \mathcal{V}_{2k}$) of encoder 1 (or encoder 2) at time k depends on the previously received messages V_2^{k-1} (or V_1^{k-1}), plus on the corresponding source message. The conference rates[3] are given by

$$R_{12} = (1/K) \sum_{k=1}^{K} \log |\mathcal{V}_{1k}| \quad \text{and} \quad R_{21} = (1/K) \sum_{k=1}^{K} \log |\mathcal{V}_{2k}|.$$

A conference is said to be (C_{12}, C_{21})-admissible if and only if

$$KR_{12} \leq NC_{12} \quad \text{and} \quad KR_{21} \leq NC_{21}.$$

The *encoders* are two functions:

$$\begin{aligned} f_1 : \mathcal{U}_1^N \times \mathcal{V}_{21} \times \ldots \times \mathcal{V}_{2K} &\rightarrow \mathcal{X}_1^N \\ f_2 : \mathcal{U}_2^N \times \mathcal{V}_{11} \times \ldots \times \mathcal{V}_{1K} &\rightarrow \mathcal{X}_2^N \end{aligned}$$

These functions map a block of N source symbols observed by each encoder, and a block of K messages received from the other encoder, to a block of N channel inputs. The *decoder* is a function

$$g : \mathcal{Y}_1^N \times \mathcal{Y}_2^N \rightarrow \hat{\mathcal{U}}_1^N \times \hat{\mathcal{U}}_2^N.$$

g maps two blocks of channel outputs (one from each channel) into two blocks of reconstructed source sequences.

An $(R_1, R_2, R_{12}, R_{21}, N, K, P_e)$ *code* for this problem is defined by:

- Two encoders f_1,f_2, with $|f_1| = 2^{NR_1}$, $|f_2| = 2^{NR_2}$.
- A decoder g for the two encoders f_1 and f_2.

[3]At first glance, it might seem puzzling that the conference rates are defined in terms of the size of the alphabets as in [**26**], although in our problem the conference messages sent by one encoder and the source values observed by the other encoder are dependent. Note, however, that the definition of the $2K$ encoding functions that characterize the conference is general enough to admit a random binning mechanism that eliminates said statistical dependence. The present definition of the conference rates is therefore perfectly reasonable.

- A (C_{12}, C_{21})-admissible conference of length K and rates R_{12} and R_{21}.
- $\Pr(\hat{U}_1^N \hat{U}_2^N \neq U_1^N U_2^N) \leq P_e$.

Finally, we say that *reliable communication* is possible, meaning that the sources $(U_1 U_2)$ can be sent over this network with arbitrarily small probability of error, if, for sufficiently large blocklength N, there exists a (C_{12}, C_{21})-admissible conference of length K and a $(R_1, R_2, R_{12}, R_{21}, N, K, \epsilon)$ code, for all $\epsilon > 0$.

3. Reachback Capacity with Partially Cooperating Nodes

In this section, our main goal is to prove Theorem 1.1. We start with the achievability part of the proof, which is based on separate source and channel coding. First, we describe the conferencing mechanism, then we give the rate region for distributed source coding. The conditions in the theorem then follow from the intersection of this rate region with the capacity region of the channels.

3.1. A Proof of Achievability based on Cooperative Source Coding. Partition the set $\mathcal{U}_1$ into M_1 cells, indexed by $v_1 \in \{1, \ldots, M_1\}$, such that $v_1(u_1) = c_1$ if u_1 is inside cell c_1. Similarly, partition the set $\mathcal{V}_2$ into M_2 cells, indexed by $v_2 \in \{1, \ldots, M_2\}$, such that $v_2(u_2) = c_2$ if u_2 is inside cell c_2. Upon observing a block U_1^N of source outputs, encoder 1 determines v_1 for each observed value u_1. Similarly, encoder 2 determines v_2 for each observed value u_2 of the source output block U_2^N. Using the conference mechanism encoder 1 can send a block V_1^N to encoder 2 at rate $R_{12} < C_{12}$ and encoder 2 can send a block V_2^N to encoder 1 at rate $R_{21} < C_{21}$.

Next, we show that the rates $R_{12} = H(V_1|U_2)$ and $R_{21} = H(V_2|U_1)$ are sufficient for V_1^N and V_2^N to be exchanged between the encoders with arbitrarily small probability of error. Since $(U_1 U_2)$ are random and $(V_1 V_2)$ are functions of $(U_1 U_2)$, $(V_1 V_2)$ are random as well. The encoders are informed about the joint probability distribution $p(u_1 u_2 v_1 v_2)$, from which they can obtain the marginals $p(u_1 v_2)$ and $p(u_2 v_1)$. Notice that these two distributions can be viewed as two pairs of correlated sources $(U_1 V_2)$ and $(U_2 V_1)$. Since U_2^N is known at encoder 2, it follows from the Slepian-Wolf theorem for $(U_2 V_1)$ that V_1^N can be compressed at rates $R_{12} \geq H(V_1|U_2)$ and still be reconstructed at encoder 2. Similarly, V_2^N can be compressed at rates $R_{21} \geq H(V_2|U_1)$ and still be reconstructed at encoder 1. Thus, provided $H(V_1|U_2) < C_{12}$ and $H(V_2|U_1) < C_{21}$, the conferencing rates

$$\begin{aligned} R_{12} &= H(V_1|U_2) \\ R_{21} &= H(V_2|U_1) \end{aligned}$$

are indeed achievable.

Let now $Z = (V_1 V_2)$. Since $(V_1 V_2)$ are functions of the source random variables $(U_1 U_2)$, Z is also a random variable and a function of $(U_1 U_2)$, which in turn means that $p(u_1 u_2 z) = p(u_1 u_2) p(z|u_1 u_2)$ is a well-defined probability distribution. $H(V_1|U_2)$ can be rewriten as

$$\begin{aligned} H(V_1|U_2) &= H(V_1 V_2|U_2) \\ &= H(V_1 V_2|U_2) - H(V_1 V_2|U_1 U_2) \\ &= I(U_1; V_1 V_2|U_2) \\ &= I(U_1; Z|U_2) \end{aligned}$$

and similarly, $H(V_2|U_1) = I(U_2; Z|U_1)$. Therefore, the conditions $I(U_1; Z|U_2) < C_{12}$ and $I(U_2; Z|U_1) < C_{21}$ are sufficient to show that these conferencing rates can be achieved.

After conferencing, the encoders compress their data using distributed source codes. Let $U_1' = (U_1 Z)$ and $U_2' = (U_2 Z)$. Since U_1 and U_2 are i.i.d. sources, then Z is also i.i.d., and hence U_1' and U_2' are two i.i.d. sources with distribution $p(u_1' u_2') = p(u_1 u_2 z)$. Then, according to the Slepian-Wolf Theorem, the rates

$$\begin{aligned} R_1 &> H(U_1'|U_2') \\ R_2 &> H(U_2'|U_1') \\ R_1 + R_2 &> H(U_1' U_2') \end{aligned}$$

are achievable. Substituting $U_1' = (U_1 Z)$ and $U_2' = (U_2 Z)$, we get

$$\begin{aligned} R_1 &> H(U_1 Z|U_2 Z) &= H(U_1|U_2 Z) \\ R_2 &> H(U_2 Z|U_1 Z) &= H(U_2|U_1 Z) \\ R_1 + R_2 &> H(U_1 U_2 Z) &= H(U_1 U_2). \end{aligned}$$

Adding channel codes separately, we conclude that reliable communication is possible if this rate region intersects the capacity region of the channels. We can write this as

$$\begin{aligned} H(U_1|U_2 Z) &< I(X_1; Y_1) \\ H(U_2|U_1 Z) &< I(X_2; Y_2) \\ H(U_1 U_2) &< I(X_1; Y_1) + I(X_2; Y_2), \end{aligned}$$

or equivalently,

$$\begin{aligned} H(U_1|U_2) &< I(X_1; Y_1) + I(Z; U_1|U_2) \\ H(U_2|U_1) &< I(X_2; Y_2) + I(Z; U_2|U_1) \\ H(U_1 U_2) &< I(X_1; Y_1) + I(X_2; Y_2), \end{aligned}$$

thus proving, together with the previous paragraph, that the rates and conditions of Theorem 1.1 are indeed achievable.

3.2. Converse Proof. The converse part of Theorem 1.1 can be obtained by using the standard proof technique based on Fano's inequality and taking advantage of the two long Markov chains of the form $Y_2 - X_2 - (Z, U_1) - X_1 - Y_1$ and $Y_2 - X_2 - (U_2, Z) - X_1 - Y_1$. Since the complete proof is rather technical and lengthy, we leave details of this proof to Appendix A, where it is established that

$$\begin{aligned} \frac{1}{N} H(U_1^N|U_2^N) &\le \frac{1}{N}\sum_{n=1}^{N} I(X_{1n}; Y_{1n}) + \frac{1}{N}\sum_{n=1}^{N} I(U_{1n}; Z_n|U_{2n}) + \delta(P_e) \\ \frac{1}{N} H(U_2^N|U_1^N) &\le \frac{1}{N}\sum_{n=1}^{N} I(X_{2n}; Y_{2n}) + \frac{1}{N}\sum_{n=1}^{N} I(U_{2n}; Z_n|U_{1n}) + \delta(P_e) \\ \frac{1}{N} H(U_1^N U_2^N) &\le \frac{1}{N}\sum_{n=1}^{N} I(X_{1n}; Y_{1n}) + \frac{1}{N}\sum_{n=1}^{N} I(X_{2n}; Y_{2n}) + \delta(P_e), \end{aligned}$$

and also that

$$\frac{1}{N}\sum_{n=1}^{N} I(U_{1n}; Z_n|U_{2n}) \le C_{12} \qquad \text{and} \qquad \frac{1}{N}\sum_{n=1}^{N} I(U_{2n}; Z_n|U_{1n}) \le C_{21}.$$

Now, from here to the exact form of the conditions in the theorem there is a very short way. First, note that using the standard technique of introducing time-sharing variables (see, e.g., [**9**, pg. 435]), we can replace the averages above by variables with the exact same distribution as prescribed by Theorem 1.1. Note also that by its own definition, $\delta(P_e) \to 0$ as $P_e \to 0$. Finally, note from the achievability proof that $|\mathcal{Z}| \leq |\mathcal{U}_1| \cdot |\mathcal{U}_2| < \infty$ (since Z is made up of partitions of $\mathcal{U}_1$ and $\mathcal{U}_2$). This concludes the proof of Theorem 1.1.

4. A Special Case: Separate Encoders ($C_{12} = C_{21} = 0$)

In this section we show how Theorem 1.1 subsumes one of the main results presented in [**4**]: the capacity region of a reachback network with two correlated sources and no cooperation between encoders, i.e., $C_{12} = C_{21} = 0$. We also review extensions presented in [**4**] for $M \geq 2$ nodes.

4.1. Two Nodes without Conferencing. In [**4**], we established the following theorem:

THEOREM 4.1 (from [**4**]). *A source (U_1U_2) can be communicated reliably over two independent channels $(\mathcal{X}_1, p(y_1|x_1), \mathcal{Y}_1)$ and $(\mathcal{X}_2, p(y_2|x_2), \mathcal{Y}_2)$, if and only if*

$$H(U_1|U_2) < I(X_1;Y_1) \tag{4.1}$$
$$H(U_2|U_1) < I(X_2;Y_2) \tag{4.2}$$
$$H(U_1U_2) < I(X_1;Y_1) + I(X_2;Y_2), \tag{4.3}$$

for some $p(u_1u_2x_1x_2y_1y_2) = p(u_1u_2)p(x_1|u_1)p(x_2|u_2)p(y_1|x_1)p(y_2|x_2)$.

This theorem now follows as a simple corollary to Theorem 1.1, by considering an auxiliary random variable Z with $|\mathcal{Z}| = 1$.

4.2. A Simple Visualization of the Problem. To illustrate the issues involved in this problem consider the rate regions shown in Fig. 3.

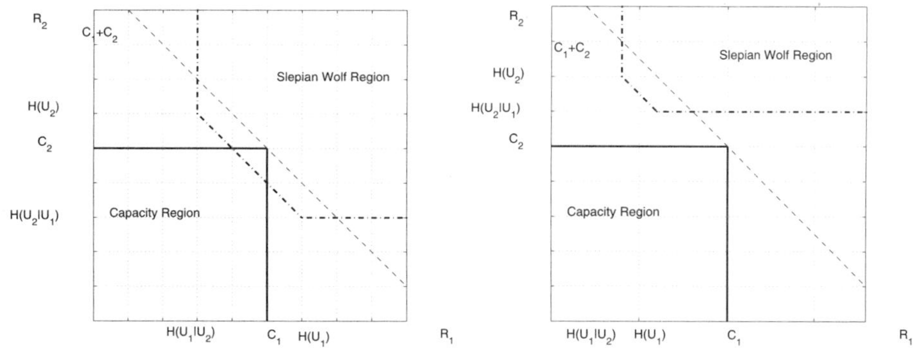

FIGURE 3. Relationship between the Slepian-Wolf region and the capacity region for two independent channels. In the left figure, as $H(U_1|U_2) < C_1$ and $H(U_2|U_1) < C_2$ the two regions intersect and therefore reliable communication is possible. The figure on the right shows the case in which $H(U_2|U_1) > C_2$ and there is no intersection between the two regions.

When the multiple access channel is reduced to two independent channels with capacities C_1 and C_2, its capacity region [**9**, Ch. 14.3] becomes a rectangle with side lengths C_1 and C_2. Also shown is the Slepian-Wolf region of achievable rates for separate encoding of correlated sources, whose limits are defined by $H(U_1)$, $H(U_2)$ and $H(U_1U_2)$. Clearly, $H(U_1U_2) < C_1 + C_2$ is a necessary condition for reliable communication as a consequence of Shannon's joint source and channel coding theorem for point-to-point communication. Assuming that this is the case, consider now the following possibilities:

- $H(U_1) < C_1$ and $H(U_2) < C_2$: The Slepian-Wolf region and the capacity region intersect, so any point (R_1, R_2) in this intersection makes reliable communication possible. Alternatively, we can argue that reliable transmission of U_1 and U_2 is possible even with independent decoders, therefore a joint decoder will also achieve an error-free reconstruction of the source.
- $H(U_1) > C_1$ and $H(U_2) > C_2$: If $H(U_1U_2) < C_1 + C_2$ then there always exists at least one point of intersection between the Slepian-Wolf region and the capacity region, so reliable communication is possible.
- $H(U_1) < C_1$ and $H(U_2) > C_2$ (or vice versa): If $H(U_2|U_1) < C_2$ (or if $H(U_1|U_2) < C_1$) then the two regions will intersect. On the other hand, if $H(U_2|U_1) > C_2$ (or if $H(U_1|U_2) > C_1$), then there are no intersection points, but it is not immediately clear whether reliable communication is possible or not (see Fig. 3), since examples are known in which the intersection between the capacity region of the multiple access channel and the Slepian-Wolf region of the correlated sources is empty and still reliable communication is possible [**8**].

Theorem 4.1 gives a definite answer to this question: in the special case of correlated sources and independent channels an intersection between the capacity region and the Slepian-Wolf rate regions is not only sufficient, but also a necessary condition for reliable communication to be possible.

From this observation we conclude once more that, in the case of independent channels, a two-stage encoder that uses Slepian-Wolf codes to compress the sources to their most efficient representation and then separately adds capacity attaining channel codes, indeed forms an optimal coding strategy—that is, for this reachback network separation continues to hold, even without cooperation.

4.3. Multiple Nodes without Conferencing. For the case of separate encoders, we proved in [**4**] a few more results, which suggest that there are possibly interesting generalizations to Theorem 1.1 worth being studied. One such result deals with an arbitrary number $M > 2$ of sensor nodes, and for this case, we proved the following source/channel separation theorem (with the resulting region illustrated in Fig. 4):

THEOREM 4.2. *A set of correlated sources* $\{U_1, U_2, \ldots, U_M\}$ *can be communicated reliably over independent channels* $(\mathcal{X}_1, p(y_1|x_1), \mathcal{Y}_1)\ldots(\mathcal{X}_M, p(y_M|x_M), \mathcal{Y}_M)$ *if and only if*

$$H(U(S)|U(S^c)) \leq \sum_{i \in S} I(X_i; Y_i),$$

for all subsets $S \subseteq \{1, 2, \ldots, M\}$*, and* $U(S) = \{U_i : i \in S\}$.

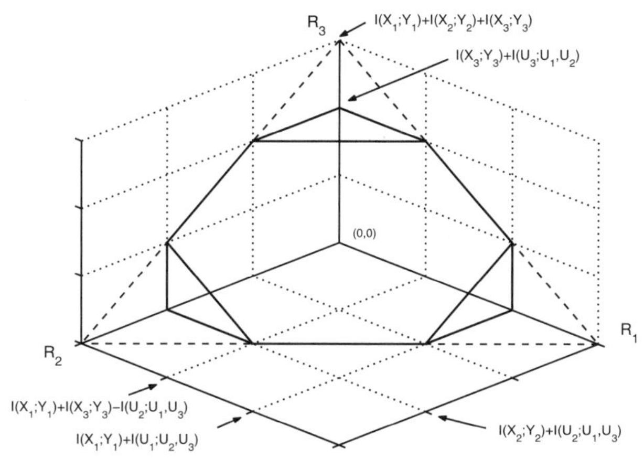

FIGURE 4. The region of achievable rates for three independent channels with correlated inputs. If the sources providing the inputs to the three independent channels were independent, the capacity region would be a parallelipiped with side lengths $I(X_1;Y_1)$, $I(X_2;Y_2)$ and $I(X_3,Y_3)$. As the correlation between the sources increases, the edges of this parallelipiped increase accordingly by the amount of mutual information between the sources. At some point the parallelipiped intersects the plane defined by the equation $R_1 + R_2 + R_3 = I(X_1;Y_1) + I(X_2;Y_2) + I(X_3;Y_3)$. Since this plane represents a necessary condition for reliable communication, the "slice" outside this boundery is not achievable, and so the resulting capacity region becomes a polyhedron.

5. Capacity and Rate/Distortion

After having established source/channel separation theorems for the sensor reachback problem, there is a question that comes up naturally: what if, in a given scenario, it turns out to be impossible to match the rates of an array of Slepian-Wolf encoders to the capacities of the channels? In that case, the best we can hope for is to reconstruct an *approximation* to the original source message. Now, in the point-to-point setup, this is what happens when we have a source X with entropy $H(X) > C$, where C is the capacity of the channel over which it needs to be sent—and in this case, the answer is given by rate-distortion theory [**5**]. Therefore, it is only natural to consider rate-distortion versions of the problems discussed in Sections 3 and 4. In this section, we present a summary of partial results we have obtained on problems of this type.

5.1. The Multiterminal Source Coding Problem. The rate-distortion formulation of the Slepian-Wolf problem, also known as the *Multiterminal Source Coding* problem [**6**], asks for a complete characterization of the achievable rate-distortion tuples of the form (R_1, R_2, D_1, D_2), when two correlated sources are encoded separately as shown in Fig. 5. The known results which come closest to a full description of this rate-distortion region are the inner and outer bounds of Berger and Tung, summarized in the following theorem:

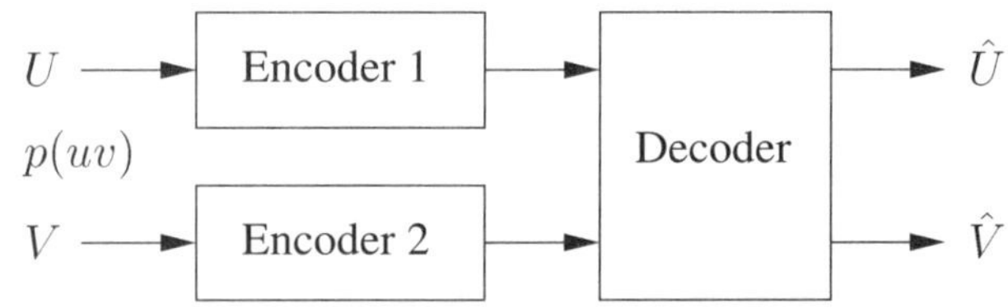

FIGURE 5. System Setup for the Multiterminal Source Coding Problem. Two correlated sources U and V are encoded separately at rates R_1 and R_2. Based on the compressed versions of U and V a joint decoder produces the estimates $\hat{U}$ and $\hat{V}$ with distortions D_1 and D_2, respectively.

THEOREM 5.1 (from [**25**]). *Let (U, V) be drawn i.i.d. $\sim p(uv)$. Let W and Z be two auxiliary random variables, such that there exist $\hat{U}(W, Z)$ and $\hat{V}(W, Z)$, for which $D_1 \geq Ed_U(U, \hat{U})$ and $D_2 \geq Ed_V(V, \hat{V})$. For a given (D_1, D_2), consider the following rate region:*

$$\begin{aligned} R_1 &\geq I(UV; W|Z) \\ R_2 &\geq I(UV; Z|W) \\ R_1 + R_2 &\geq I(UV; WZ). \end{aligned}$$

Then: (a) if $W - U - V - Z$ forms a long Markov chain, rate-distortion codes do exist within *this region of (R_1, R_2) (the BT inner bound); and (b) if $W - U - V$ and $U - V - Z$ only form two short Markov chains (but not the long chain of the inner bound), rate-distortion codes* do not exist outside *this region of (R_1, R_2) (the BT outer bound).*

Notice that in comparison to the two short chain conditions $W - U - V$ and $U - V - Z$ of the outer bound, the long chain $W - U - V - Z$ characterizing the inner bound poses a very significant restriction on the set of auxiliary random variables over which we can minimize the mutual information terms to obtain the boundaries of the rate-distortion region. Consequently, the thus obtained inner bound contains only a subset of the rate-distortion tuples suggested by the outer bound.

To solve this problem, we are required to either provide a better converse, or devise a coding strategy leading to a direct theorem based solely on the two short chain conditions. Our current work is proceeding under the assumption that it will be possible to obtain a direct theorem based on two short chains.

5.2. Time-Sharing of Berger-Yeung Codes. In our first attempt, we focus on a special case of the general multiterminal source coding problem known as the *Berger-Yeung* problem [**7**]. The goal is to determine the region of achievable tuples for multiterminal source coding, but only of the form $(R_1, R_2, D_1, 0)$. The complete solution to this problem is given by the following theorem:

THEOREM 5.2 (from [**7**]). *$(R_1, R_2, D_1, 0)$ is achievable if and only if*

$$\begin{aligned} R_1 &\geq I(U; W|V) \\ R_2 &\geq H(V|W) \\ R_1 + R_2 &\geq H(V) + I(U; W|V), \end{aligned}$$

where W is an auxiliary variable such that $W - U - V$ forms a Markov chain, and there exists a function $\hat{U}(V,W)$ such that $Ed(U,\hat{U}) \leq D_1$.

Our interest in the Berger-Yeung problem is due to the fact that the region for $(R_1, R_2, D_1, 0)$ requires the same constraints on its auxiliary variable as one of the constraints in the Berger-Tung outer bound. Hence, it is only natural to ask what rates can be achieved by time-sharing of the two families of Berger-Yeung codes that give the rate-distortion regions with tuples $(R_1, R_2, D_1, 0)$ and $(R_1, R_2, 0, D_2)$. The answer to this question is given in the following theorem, which we proved in [**3**]:

THEOREM 5.3 (from [**3**]). *(R_1, R_2, D_1, D_2) is achievable by time-sharing of Berger-Yeung codes if and only if*

$$\begin{aligned} R_1 &\geq I(U;VW|Z) \\ R_2 &\geq I(V;UZ|W) \\ R_1 + R_2 &\geq H(UV) - H(U|VW) - H(Z|UV), \end{aligned}$$

where W, Z are auxiliary random variables such that $W - U - V$ and $U - V - Z$ form two Markov chains, and there exist functions $\hat{U}(V,W)$ and $\hat{V}(U,Z)$ such that $Ed(U,\hat{U}) \leq D_1$ and $Ed(V,\hat{V}) \leq D_2$.

Unfortunately, as we show in [**3**], comparing this region against the BT outer bound, we find all faces are strictly inside that region. However, this is the first coding strategy which has been shown to work without requiring the long Markov chain condition $W - U - V - Z$, and hence it does serve the purpose of showing that the restriction imposed by the inner bound is not necessary. Also, due to the difficulty of comparing mutual information expressions defined over different optimization domains, we don't know yet whether there are points or not in this region that are not already contained in the BT inner bound.

5.3. An Informal Notion of Duality. In Theorem 4.1, we established that the cascade of random binning and channel codes is an architecture capable of achieving capacity for a reachback network. Therefore, by relying informally on the idea that capacity and rate-distortion are dual problems (at least in the point-to-point problem), we are led to explore whether a cascade of rate-distortion codes and random binning of blocks of quantization indices could result in an optimal architecture for the multiterminal source coding problem. A coding strategy similar to the one we propose was used first by Wyner and Ziv to prove their result for the rate-distortion problem with side information [**27**]. More recently, a similar strategy has been used in [**28**]. This architecture is illustrated in Fig. 6.

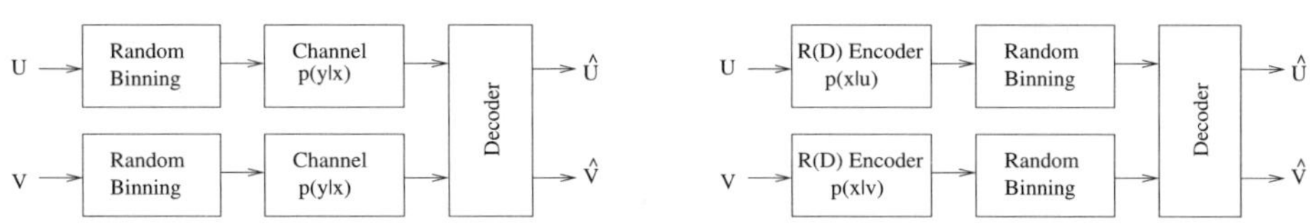

FIGURE 6. Left: optimal architecture for the capacity problem. Right: hypothesized optimal architecture for the rate-distortion problem.

Notice that while the encoder of Berger and Tung performs random binning of reconstruction sequences $\hat{U}^n$ and $\hat{V}^n$, and thus requires the long chain condition $\hat{U}-U-V-\hat{V}$ for typical set decoding of pairs of reconstruction sequences, our encoder maps a source sequence to a quantization index and then performs random binning, *not* on the corresponding reconstruction sequences, but on blocks of quantization indices, or *super-letters*. First, we get a more elegant proof of Berger and Tung's result, because we can apply the Slepian-Wolf theorem directly in the analysis of the decoding mechanism, thus avoiding having to state explicitly all possible error events and upper bounding the corresponding error probabilities. Second, we hope to be able to show that this coding strategy works based solely on the short chain conditions, and not the more restrictive long chain condition.

For this two-stage process (classical quantization followed by random binning), we determined an achievable rate-distortion region given in the following theorem (proved in [**2**]):

THEOREM 5.4 (from [**2**]). *(R_1, R_2, D_1, D_2) is achievable by the two-stage process if and only if*

$$\begin{aligned} R_1 &\geq I(UV; W|Z) \\ R_2 &\geq I(UV; Z|W) \\ R_1 + R_2 &\geq I(UV; WZ), \end{aligned}$$

where (W, Z) is pair of random variables in a class $\mathcal{C}$, in which all pairs satisfy that $W-U-V$ and $U-V-Z$ form a Markov chain; and where there exist functions $\hat{U}(W,Z)$ and $\hat{V}(W,Z)$ such that $D_1 \geq Ed_1(U,\hat{U})$ and $D_2 \geq Ed_2(V,\hat{V})$.

Observe that the rate expressions in Theorem 5.4 match those of the BT outer bound. However, it is still unclear (and currently under investigation) whether the class $\mathcal{C}$ contains *all* possible pairs of short chains. Anyway, this result is interesting in itself for it provides an alternative coding strategy to that of Theorem 5.2, which again does not require the long chain condition, and which gives rate expressions matching those of the BT outer bound.

5.4. On the Problem of Rate/Distortion with Partially Cooperating Encoders. A natural extension for both the classical multiterminal source coding problem, and for our sensor reachback problem with partially cooperating encoders, would be a multiterminal rate-distortion problem in which encoders are allowed to exchange messages over two channels of limited capacity before actually compressing the correlated data. A first step in this direction can be found in [**15**], where results are given for some cases in which one of the encoders gives partial information on its source outputs to the other encoder.

Given the complexity of the classical multiterminal source coding problem, and the fact that this new problem with cooperation contains the classical one as a special case, it seems unlikely to us that we will be able to find a solution for this new rate-distortion problem without solving the classical problem first.

Acknowledgements

The authors would like to acknowledge most useful feedback on this work provided by Professors Toby Berger and Tom Cover, as well as the insightful comments made by the reviewers.

Appendix A. The Converse Proof

A.1. Preliminaries. To develop a converse we start, as is usual, with Fano's inequality. If there is a suitable $(R_1, R_2, R_{12}, R_{21}, N, K, P_e)$-code, then we must have

$$H(U_1^N U_2^N | \hat{U}_1^N \hat{U}_2^N) \le P_e \log\left(|\mathcal{U}_1^N \times \mathcal{U}_2^N - 1|\right) + h(P_e), \tag{A.1}$$

where $h(P_e)$ is the binary entropy function. For convenience, define also

$$\delta(P_e) = \left(P_e \log\left(|\mathcal{U}_1^N \times \mathcal{U}_2^N| - 1\right) + h(P_e)\right)/N.$$

It follows from eqn. (A.1) that

$$\begin{aligned} H(U_1^N U_2^N | Y_1^N Y_2^N) &= H(U_1^N U_2^N | Y_1^N Y_2^N g(Y_1^N Y_2^N)) \\ &= H(U_1^N U_2^N | Y_1^N Y_2^N \hat{U}_1^N \hat{U}_2^N) \\ &\le H(U_1^N U_2^N | \hat{U}_1^N \hat{U}_2^N) \\ &\le N\delta(P_e), \end{aligned}$$

and therefore,

$$H(U_1^N U_2^N | Y_1^N Y_2^N V_1^K V_2^K) \le H(U_1^N U_2^N | Y_1^N Y_2^N) \le N\delta(P_e),$$

and also

$$\begin{aligned} H(U_1^N | Y_1^N Y_2^N V_1^K V_2^K) &\le N\delta(P_e) \\ H(U_2^N | Y_1^N Y_2^N V_1^K V_2^K) &\le N\delta(P_e) \\ H(U_1^N | Y_1^N Y_2^N V_1^K V_2^K U_2^N) &\le N\delta(P_e) \\ H(U_2^N | Y_1^N Y_2^N V_1^K V_2^K U_1^N) &\le N\delta(P_e). \end{aligned}$$

According to the problem statement, we have two long Markov chains in place: $Y_2^N - X_2^N - (V_1^K V_2^K U_1^N) - X_1^N - Y_1^N$ and $Y_2^N - X_2^N - (U_2^N V_1^K V_2^K) - X_1^N - Y_1^N$. These chains (informally referred to as *the long chains* in this section) will prove quite useful in our derivations.

A.2. The Side Faces: Necessity of Equations (1.1) and (1.2). We start by bounding $H(U_1^N)$:

$$\begin{aligned} H(U_1^N) &= I(U_1^N; Y_1^N Y_2^N V_1^K V_2^K U_2^N) + H(U_1^N | Y_1^N Y_2^N V_1^K V_2^K U_2^N) \\ &\le I(U_1^N; Y_1^N Y_2^N V_1^K V_2^K U_2^N) + N\delta(P_e) \\ &= I(U_1^N; U_2^N) + I(U_1^N; Y_1^N Y_2^N V_1^K V_2^K | U_2^N) + N\delta(P_e) \\ &= I(U_1^N; U_2^N) + I(U_1^N; V_1^K V_2^K | U_2^N) + I(U_1^N; Y_1^N Y_2^N | U_2^N V_1^K V_2^K) + N\delta(P_e) \end{aligned}$$

Now, $I(U_1^N; U_2^N)$ and $N\delta(P_e)$ stay the same, and we start with $I(U_1^N; V_1^K V_2^K | U_2^N)$:

$$
\begin{aligned}
& I(U_1^N; V_1^K V_2^K | U_2^N) \\
&= \sum_{n=1}^{N} I(U_{1n}; V_1^K V_2^K | U_2^N U_1^{n-1}) \\
&= \sum_{n=1}^{N} H(U_{1n} | U_2^N U_1^{n-1}) - H(U_{1n} | V_1^K V_2^K U_2^N U_1^{n-1}) \\
&\overset{(a)}{=} \sum_{n=1}^{N} H(U_{1n} | U_{2n}) - H(U_{1n} | V_1^K V_2^K U_{2n}) \\
&= \sum_{n=1}^{N} I(U_{1n}; V_1^K V_2^K | U_{2n}) \\
&= \sum_{n=1}^{N} I(U_{1n}; Z_n | U_{2n})
\end{aligned}
$$

Now, we simplify $I(U_1^N; Y_1^N Y_2^N | U_2^N V_1^K V_2^K)$:

$$
\begin{aligned}
& I(U_1^N; Y_1^N Y_2^N | U_2^N V_1^K V_2^K) \\
&= \sum_{n=1}^{N} I(U_1^N; Y_{1n} Y_{2n} | U_2^N V_1^K V_2^K Y_1^{n-1} Y_2^{n-1}) \\
&\overset{(a)}{=} \sum_{n=1}^{N} I(U_1^N X_{1n}; Y_{1n} Y_{2n} | U_2^N V_1^K V_2^K Y_1^{n-1} Y_2^{n-1} X_{2n}) \\
&= \sum_{n=1}^{N} H(Y_{1n} Y_{2n} | U_2^N V_1^K V_2^K Y_1^{n-1} Y_2^{n-1} X_{2n}) \\
&\qquad - H(Y_{1n} Y_{2n} | U_2^N V_1^K V_2^K Y_1^{n-1} Y_2^{n-1} X_{2n} U_1^N X_{1n}) \\
&\leq \sum_{n=1}^{N} H(Y_{1n} Y_{2n} | U_2^N V_1^K V_2^K X_{2n}) \\
&\qquad - H(Y_{1n} Y_{2n} | U_2^N V_1^K V_2^K Y_1^{n-1} Y_2^{n-1} X_{2n} U_1^N X_{1n}) \\
&\overset{(b)}{=} \sum_{n=1}^{N} H(Y_{1n} Y_{2n} | U_2^N V_1^K V_2^K X_{2n}) - H(Y_{1n} Y_{2n} | U_2^N V_1^K V_2^K X_{2n} U_1^N X_{1n}) \\
&= \sum_{n=1}^{N} I(U_1^N X_{1n}; Y_{1n} Y_{2n} | U_2^N V_1^K V_2^K X_{2n}) \\
&= \sum_{n=1}^{N} I(U_1^N X_{1n}; Y_{1n} | U_2^N V_1^K V_2^K X_{2n}) + \underbrace{I(U_1^N X_{1n}; Y_{2n} | U_2^N V_1^K V_2^K X_{2n} Y_{1n})}_{=0} \\
&\overset{(c)}{=} \sum_{n=1}^{N} I(U_1^N X_{1n}; Y_{1n} | U_2^N V_1^K V_2^K X_{2n})
\end{aligned}
$$

$$
\begin{aligned}
&= \sum_{n=1}^{N} H(Y_{1n}|U_2^N V_1^K V_2^K X_{2n}) - H(Y_{1n}|U_2^N V_1^K V_2^K X_{2n} U_1^N X_{1n}) \\
&= \sum_{n=1}^{N} H(Y_{1n}|U_2^N V_1^K V_2^K X_{2n}) - H(Y_{1n}|V_1^K V_2^K X_{1n}) \\
&\leq \sum_{n=1}^{N} H(Y_{1n}|V_1^K V_2^K) - H(Y_{1n}|V_1^K V_2^K X_{1n}) \\
&= \sum_{n=1}^{N} H(Y_{1n}|V_1^K V_2^K) - H(Y_{1n}|X_{1n}) \\
&\overset{(d)}{\leq} \sum_{n=1}^{N} H(Y_{1n}) - H(Y_{1n}|X_{1n}) \\
&= \sum_{n=1}^{N} I(X_{1n}; Y_{1n})
\end{aligned}
$$

where: (a) follows from the fact that $(U_1^N, V_2^K) \rightsquigarrow X_1^N \rightsquigarrow X_{1n}$ and $(U_2^N, V_1^K) \rightsquigarrow X_2^N \rightsquigarrow X_{2n}$; (b) follows from from the fact that the channels are DMCs, so given $X_{1n}X_{2n}$, $Y_{1n}Y_{2n}$ are independent of anything else, so can drop conditioning terms without changing the entropy; (c) follows from the long chains; and (d) follows from the fact that (V_1^K, V_2^K) are independent of Y_{1n} given X_{1n}.

Combining all of the above, we get that

$$
H(U_1^N) \leq I(U_1^N; U_2^N) + \sum_{n=1}^{N} I(X_{1n}; Y_{1n}) + \sum_{n=1}^{N} I(U_{1n}; Z_n|U_{2n}) + N\delta(P_e),
$$

or equivalently,

$$
\frac{1}{N} H(U_1^N|U_2^N) \leq \frac{1}{N}\sum_{n=1}^{N} I(X_{1n}; Y_{1n}) + \frac{1}{N}\sum_{n=1}^{N} I(U_{1n}; Z_n|U_{2n}) + \delta(P_e).
$$

Symmetric arguments yield

$$
\frac{1}{N} H(U_2^N|U_1^N) \leq \frac{1}{N}\sum_{n=1}^{N} I(X_{2n}; Y_{2n}) + \frac{1}{N}\sum_{n=1}^{N} I(U_{2n}; Z_n|U_{1n}) + \delta(P_e).
$$

A.3. The Sum-Rate Face: Necessity of Equation (1.3). Again, we start by bounding $H(U_1^N U_2^N)$:

$$
\begin{aligned}
H(U_1^N U_2^N) &= I(U_1^N U_2^N; Y_1^N Y_2^N) + H(U_1^N U_2^N | Y_1^N Y_2^N) \\
&\leq I(U_1^N U_2^N; Y_1^N Y_2^N) + N\delta(P_e).
\end{aligned}
$$

Now we need to simplify $I(U_1^N U_2^N; Y_1^N Y_2^N)$. Here we make use of the fact that, from the long chains, it follows that $U_1^N U_2^N - X_1^N X_2^N - X_{1n}X_{2n} - Y_{1n}Y_{2n}$ also forms a Markov chain. So,

$$
\begin{aligned}
&I(U_1^N U_2^N; Y_1^N Y_2^N) \\
&= \sum_{n=1}^{N} I(U_1^N U_2^N; Y_{1n} Y_{2n} | Y_1^{n-1} Y_2^{n-1}) \\
&\leq \sum_{n=1}^{N} I(U_1^N U_2^N; Y_{1n} Y_{2n} | Y_1^{n-1} Y_2^{n-1}) + I(X_{1n} X_{2n}; Y_{1n} Y_{2n} | Y_1^{n-1} Y_2^{n-1} U_1^N U_2^N) \\
&= \sum_{n=1}^{N} I(U_1^N U_2^N X_{1n} X_{2n}; Y_{1n} Y_{2n} | Y_1^{n-1} Y_2^{n-1}) \\
&= \sum_{n=1}^{N} I(X_{1n} X_{2n}; Y_{1n} Y_{2n} | Y_1^{n-1} Y_2^{n-1}) + \underbrace{I(U_1^N U_2^N; Y_{1n} Y_{2n} | Y_1^{n-1} Y_2^{n-1} X_{1n} X_{2n})}_{=0} \\
&\overset{(a)}{=} \sum_{n=1}^{N} I(X_{1n} X_{2n}; Y_{1n} Y_{2n} | Y_1^{n-1} Y_2^{n-1}) \\
&= \sum_{n=1}^{N} H(Y_{1n} Y_{2n} | Y_1^{n-1} Y_2^{n-1}) - H(Y_{1n} Y_{2n} | Y_1^{n-1} Y_2^{n-1} X_{1n} X_{2n}) \\
&\overset{(b)}{=} \sum_{n=1}^{N} H(Y_{1n} Y_{2n} | Y_1^{n-1} Y_2^{n-1}) - H(Y_{1n} Y_{2n} | X_{1n} X_{2n}) \\
&\leq \sum_{n=1}^{N} H(Y_{1n} Y_{2n}) - H(Y_{1n} Y_{2n} | X_{1n} X_{2n}) \\
&\leq \sum_{n=1}^{N} H(Y_{1n}) + H(Y_{2n}) - H(Y_{1n} Y_{2n} | X_{1n} X_{2n}) \\
&= \sum_{n=1}^{N} H(Y_{1n}) + H(Y_{2n}) - H(Y_{1n} | X_{1n}) - H(Y_{2n} | X_{2n}) \\
&= \sum_{n=1}^{N} I(X_{1n}; Y_{1n}) + \sum_{n=1}^{N} I(X_{2n}; Y_{2n}).
\end{aligned}
$$

where: (a) follows from the chain above, and (b) follows from the DMC property.

Therefore, we get that

$$\frac{1}{N} H(U_1^N U_2^N) \leq \frac{1}{N} \sum_{n=1}^{N} I(X_{1n}; Y_{1n}) + \frac{1}{N} \sum_{n=1}^{N} I(X_{2n}; Y_{2n}) + \delta(P_e).$$

A.4. Conditions on the Conference Rates. We now obtain necessary conditions for an admissable conference in terms of the auxiliary random variable Z:

$$\begin{aligned}
NC_{12} &\geq \sum_{k=1}^{K} \log |\mathcal{V}_{1k}| \\
&\geq H(V_1^K) \\
&\geq H(V_1^K | U_2^N) \\
&= H(V_1^K V_2^K | U_2^N) \\
&= H(V_1^K V_2^K | U_2^N) - H(V_1^K V_2^K | U_1^N U_2^N) \\
&= I(V_1^K V_2^K ; U_1^N | U_2^N) \\
&= \sum_{n=1}^{N} I(V_1^K V_2^K ; U_{1n} | U_1^{N-1} U_2^N) \\
&= \sum_{n=1}^{N} H(U_{1n} | U_1^{N-1} U_2^N) - H(U_{1n} | V_1^K V_2^K U_1^{N-1} U_2^N) \\
&= \sum_{n=1}^{N} H(U_{1n} | U_{2n}) - H(U_{1n} | V_1^K V_2^K U_{2n}) \\
&= \sum_{n=1}^{N} I(U_{1n} ; V_1^K V_2^K | U_{2n}) \\
&= \sum_{n=1}^{N} I(U_{1n} ; Z_n | U_{2n}),
\end{aligned}$$

where the first inequality is due to the admissibility condition for conferences, and the rest are standard information theoretic manipulations. Taking the second inequality, a similar argument yields

$$NC_{21} \geq \sum_{n=1}^{N} I(U_{2n}; Z_n | U_{1n}).$$

Thus, the conditions on the conference rates become

$$\frac{1}{N} \sum_{n=1}^{N} I(U_{1n}; Z_n | U_{2n}) \leq C_{12} \quad \text{and} \quad \frac{1}{N} \sum_{n=1}^{N} I(U_{2n}; Z_n | U_{1n}) \leq C_{21}$$

References

[1] J. Barros and S. D. Servetto, "On the Capacity of the Reachback Channel in Wireless Sensor Networks", in *Proc. IEEE Int. Workshop Multimedia Sig. Proc.*, US Virgin Islands, 2002.

[2] J. Barros and S. D. Servetto, "An Inner Bound for the Rate-Distortion Region of the Multiterminal Source Coding Problem", in *Proc. 37th Annual Conf. Inform. Sciences Syst. (CISS)*, Baltimore, MD, 2003.

[3] J. Barros and S. D. Servetto, "On the Rate/Distortion Region for Separate Encoding of Correlated Sources", in *Proc. IEEE Int. Symp. Inform. Theory (ISIT)*, Yokohama, Japan, 2003.

[4] J. Barros and S. D. Servetto, "Reachback Capacity with Non-Interfering Nodes", in *Proc. IEEE Int. Symp. Inform. Theory (ISIT)*, Yokohama, Japan, 2003.

[5] T. Berger, *Rate Distortion Theory: A Mathematical Basis for Data Compression*, Prentice-Hall, Inc., 1971.
[6] T. Berger, *The Information Theory Approach to Communications (G. Longo, ed.)*, Chapter Multiterminal Source Coding, Springer-Verlag, 1978.
[7] T. Berger and R. W. Yeung, "Multiterminal Source Encoding with One Distortion Criterion", *IEEE Trans. Inform. Theory*, vol. 35, no. 2, pp. 228–236, 1989.
[8] T. M. Cover, A. A. El Gamal, and M. Salehi, "Multiple Access Channels with Arbitrarily Correlated Sources", *IEEE Trans. Inform. Theory*, vol. IT-26, no. 6, pp. 648–657, 1980.
[9] T. M. Cover and J. Thomas, *Elements of Information Theory*, John Wiley and Sons, Inc., 1991.
[10] G. Dueck, "A Note on the Multiple Access Channel with Correlated Sources", *IEEE Trans. Inform. Theory*, vol. IT-27, no. 2, pp. 232–235, 1981.
[11] M. Effros, M. Médard, T. Ho, S. Ray, D. Karger, and R. Koetter, "Linear Network Codes: A Unified Framework for Source, Channel, and Network Coding", available from `http://www.mit.edu/people/medard/medard.html`.
[12] M. Gastpar and M. Vetterli, "Source/Channel Communication in Sensor Networks", in *Proc. 2nd International Workshop on Information Processing in Sensor Networks (IPSN)*, Palo Alto, CA, 2003.
[13] A. Hu and S. D. Servetto, "dFSK: *Distributed* Frequency Shift Keying Modulation in Dense Sensor Networks", submitted for publication.
[14] A. Hu and S. D. Servetto, "Asymptotically Optimal Time Synchronization in Dense Sensor Networks", in *Proc. 2nd ACM Workshop on Sensor Networks and Applications (WSNA)*, San Diego, CA, 2003.
[15] A. H. Kaspi and T. Berger, "Rate-Distortion for Correlated Sources with Partially Separated Encoders", *IEEE Trans. Inform. Theory*, vol. IT-28, no. 6, pp. 828–840, 1982.
[16] N. Laneman, D. Tse, and G. W. Wornell, "Cooperative Diversity in Wireless Networks: Efficient Protocols and Outage Behavior", submitted to the *IEEE Trans. Inform. Theory*, Jan. 2002.
[17] N. Merhav and S. Shamai, "On Joint Source-Channel Coding for the Wyner-Ziv Source and the Gel'fand-Pinsker Channel", *IEEE Trans. Inform. Theory*, to appear.
[18] A. Narula, M. D. Trott, and G. W. Wornell, "Performance Limits of Coded Diversity Methods for Transmitter Antenna Arrays", *IEEE Trans. Inform. Theory*, vol. 45, no. 7, pp. 2418–2433, 1999.
[19] J. Proakis, *Digital Communications*, McGraw Hill, 1995.
[20] A. Sendonaris, E. Erkip, and B. Aazhang, "User Cooperation Diversity-Part I: System Description", *IEEE Trans. Commun.*, to appear.
[21] A. Sendonaris, E. Erkip, and B. Aazhang, "User Cooperation Diversity-Part II: Implementation Aspects and Performance Analysis", *IEEE Trans. Commun.*, to appear.
[22] S. D. Servetto, "Quantization with Side Information: Lattice Codes, Asymptotics, and Applications in Sensor Networks", submitted to *IEEE Trans. Inform. Theory*, Mar. 2002, available from `http://cn.ece.cornell.edu/`.
[23] D. Slepian and J. K. Wolf, "A Coding Theorem for Multiple Access Channels with Correlated Sources", *Bell Syst. Tech. J.*, vol. 52, no. 7, pp. 1037–1076, 1973.
[24] D. Slepian and J. K. Wolf, "Noiseless Coding of Correlated Information Sources", *IEEE Trans. Inform. Theory*, vol. IT-19, no. 4, pp. 471–480, 1973.
[25] S.Y. Tung, *Multiterminal Source Coding*, PhD thesis, Cornell University, 1978.
[26] F. M. J. Willems, "The Discrete Memoryless Multiple Access Channel with Partially Cooperating Encoders", *IEEE Trans. Inform. Theory*, vol. 29, no. 3, pp. 441–445, 1983.
[27] A. D. Wyner and J. Ziv, "The Rate-Distortion Function for Source Coding with Side Information at the Decoder", *IEEE Trans. Inform. Theory*, vol. IT-22, no. 1, pp. 1–10, 1976.
[28] R. Zamir and T. Berger, "Multiterminal Source Coding with High Resolution", *IEEE Trans. Inform. Theory*, vol. 45, no. 1, pp. 106–117, 1999.

Institute for Communications Engineering, Munich University of Technology.
Current address: School of Electrical and Computer Engineering, Cornell University.
E-mail address: `joao.barros@ei.tum.de`

School of Electrical and Computer Engineering, Cornell University.
E-mail address: `servetto@ece.cornell.edu`

DIMACS Series in Discrete Mathematics
and Theoretical Computer Science
Volume **66**, 2004

Linear Network Codes: A Unified Framework for Source, Channel, and Network Coding

Michelle Effros, Muriel Médard, Tracey Ho, Siddharth Ray, David Karger,
Ralf Koetter, and Babak Hassibi

ABSTRACT. We examine the issue of separation and code design for network data transmission environments. We demonstrate that source-channel separation holds for several canonical network channel models when the whole network operates over a common finite field. Our approach uses linear codes. This simple, unifying framework allows us to re-establish with economy the optimality of linear codes for single transmitter channels and for Slepian-Wolf source coding. It also enables us to establish the optimality of linear codes for multiple access channels and for erasure broadcast channels. Moreover, we show that source-channel separation holds for these networks. This robustness of separation we show to be strongly predicated on the fact that noise and inputs are independent. The linearity of source, channel, and network coding blurs the delineation between these codes, and thus we explore joint linear design. Finally, we illustrate the fact that design for individual network modules may yield poor results when such modules are concatenated, demonstrating that end-to-end coding is necessary. Thus, we argue, it is the lack of decomposability into canonical network modules, rather than the lack of separation between source and channel coding, that presents major challenges for coding in networks.

1. Introduction

The failure of source-channel separation in networks is often considered to be an impediment in applying information theoretic tools in network settings. A simple multiple access channel from [**CT91**] shows how separation can fail. The channel contains $m \geq 2$ transmitters and a single receiver. The receiver's channel output is the integer sum of the transmitters' binary channel inputs. Since independent, uniformly distributed input signals fail to achieve the maximum mutual information between the transmitted and received signals, direct transmission of dependent source bits over the channel sometimes yields higher achievable transmission rates than Slepian-Wolf source coding followed by multiple access channel coding.

Key words and phrases. Compression, error correction, multiuser information theory, network coding, routing.

This work was supported in part by NSF grant CCR-0220039, a grant from the Lee Center for Advanced Networking, Hewlett-Packard 008542-008, and University of Illinois subaward #02-194.

While this simple example may at first appear to irrefutably establish the failure of source-channel separation in networks, its simplicity is misleading. In particular, note that the alphabet size of the output is dependent on the number of transmitters. Thus, the network lacks a consistent digital framework. Replacing integer addition with binary addition to give a channel with input and output alphabets of the same cardinality yields a communication system for which separation holds.

In this paper, we argue that source-channel separation is more robust than counterexamples may suggest. We assert, however, that separate source and channel code design does not necessarily simplify the design of communication systems for digital networks. The operations of compression and channel coding are conceptual tools rather than necessary components. While modularity, such as that afforded by the separation theorem, is desirable in the design of components, the decomposition of a problem into modular tasks may increase complexity when the decomposition imposes unnecessary constraints.

In addition to examining traditional questions of source-channel separation, we also investigate a variety of other separation assumptions implicit in existing network design techniques. Network coding is an information transmission strategy where nodes of a network are allowed to mix incoming data; a network code is successful if each receiver can deduce from its received data the messages intended for it. By assuming independent data bits and lossless links, the network coding literature and other layered approaches to network design endorse a philosophy where source and channel coding are separated from network coding or routing. Through examples, we demonstrate the fragility of this assumed separation. Even in simple digital networks, neither separate source-network coding strategies nor separate channel-network coding techniques guarantee optimal communication performance.

Our network model requires the same finite alphabet at all nodes and additionally allows noise in the form of erasures.[1] Erasures are assumed to be channel-imposed, irreversible, and independent of the channel input, so that the erasure symbol cannot be used as an additional symbol for coding.

While our examples suggest the robustness of source-channel separation and fragility of source-network and channel-network separation in the resulting systems, we advocate an entirely unified approach, investigating independent, random, linear code design at all nodes of the network. For the examples given, it is not clear, even after the design is completed, what the appropriate decomposition of tasks should be.

We treat two important types of networks in detail: multiple access networks and degraded broadcast networks. For the networks we consider, optimal code construction is particularly simple. We show that random linear codes are sufficient and asymptotically optimal for a wide array of problems. Our approach may be viewed, in the simplest way, as a generalization of information theoretic results known for single-receiver source codes and for single-transmitter, single-receiver channel codes. From the networking perspective, our results bear a different interpretation - compression, channel coding, and routing are not separable functions.

Finally, while the multiple access and broadcast networks considered here are important in their own right, we show that we cannot concatenate them arbitrarily and maintain end-to-end functionality. In effect, there is no separation of large networks into canonical elements. We argue that this lack of separation, rather

[1]While we focus primarily on erasure channels, we also consider additive noise channels.

than the oft-presumed lack of source-channel separation in networks, poses the real challenge in communication system design.

2. Background

The use of random linear transformations in coding receives considerable attention in the literature. For channel coding, Elias [**Eli56**] shows that random linear parity check codes, formed by Bernoulli(1/2) choices for the parity check entries in a systematic code's generator matrix, achieve capacity for the binary erasure channel and the binary symmetric channel. MacKay [**Mac99**] proves that two families of error-correcting codes based on very sparse random parity check matrices – Gallager codes and MacKay-Neal codes (a special case of the former) – when optimally decoded, achieve information rates up to the Shannon limit for channels with symmetric stationery ergodic noise. MacKay also demonstrates empirically, for binary symmetric channels and Gaussian channels, that good decoding performance for these codes can be achieved with a practical sum-product decoding algorithm.

Linear channel coding for network systems has received far less attention. In this work, we consider both multiple access and degraded broadcast channels. In multiple access coding, the model of interest comprises a collection of transmitters sending information to a single receiver. The received signal is the sum of the transmitted signals with the possible inclusion of either erasures or additive noise. While this type of additive interference channel has received considerable attention in the literature (see, for example, [**Ahl71, Lia72, CW79**]) the majority of the work to date considers only the case where the incoming data streams interfere additively in the real field; one notable exception is the work of Poltyrev and Snyder [**PS95**], which treats a modulo-2 multiple access channel without noise in the case where a proper subset of the transmitters sends to the decoder at any given instant. We are unaware of prior work on linear coding for multiple access channels.

In broadcast networks, we consider physically and stochastically degraded channels with both additive noise and erasures. While the degraded broadcast channel is well understood, [**Gal74, Ber73**], we are likewise unaware of any prior work on linear broadcast channel codes.

On the source coding side, Ancheta [**Anc77**] presents universally optimal linear codes for lossless coding of binary sources; he also shows that the rate distortion function of a binary, stationary, memoryless source cannot be achieved by any linear transformation over a binary field into a sequence with rate lower than the entropy of the source. The syndrome-source-coding scheme described by Ancheta uses a linear error correcting code for data compression, treating the source sequence as an error pattern whose syndrome forms the compressed data.

In [**Csi82**], Csiszár generalizes linear source coding techniques to allow linear multiple access source codes that achieve the optimal performance derived by Slepian and Wolf [**SW73**]. Csiszár demonstrates the universality of his proposed linear codes[2] and bounds the corresponding error exponents. These results are generalizable to single or multiple Markov sources.

Addressing the problem of practical encoding and decoding for multiple access source codes, [**PR99, PR00a, PR00b, PR03, RPK00**] introduce the Distributed

[2]In the given fixed-rate coding regime, a universal code is any code that achieves asymptotically negligible error probability on all sources for which the code's rate falls within the source's achievable rate region.

Source Coding Using Syndromes (DISCUS) framework. Schonberg et al. [**SPR02**] note that Csiszár's proof can be used to show that application of LDPC codes in the DISCUS framework approaches the Slepian-Wolf bound for general binary sources; they then demonstrate through simulation that belief propagation decoding works well in practice. Uyematsu proposes a deterministic construction for linear multiple access source codes in [**Uye01**].

Zhao and Effros introduce broadcast system source codes in [**ZE99, ZE00**], presenting design algorithms and performance bounds. We know of no prior work on linear broadcast system source codes.

Network coding is a generalization of routing for transmitting independent bits through lossless networks [**ACLY00**]. Unlike routers, network codes allow nodes of a network to mix their incoming data streams. Koetter and Médard give an algebraic framework in [**KM02**]. Reference [**HKM$^+$03**] considers a randomized approach for independent or linearly correlated sources, while [**JCJ03**] and [**SET03**] give systematic polynomial-time code constructions for independent sources.

3. Preliminaries and Generalizations

Since the focus of our paper is on the relationships between system components and concepts, we give all results in their simplest forms. In particular, we state our results and their corresponding derivations for independent, identically distributed (iid) random processes and focus primarily on binary source and channel alphabets, modified only for the inclusion of the erasure noise model. For simplicity, all code constructions combine random linear encoding with typical set decoding. The definition of the typical set $A_\epsilon^{(n)}$ for a single random sequence $U_1, U_2, \ldots$ drawn iid according to distribution p is

$$A_\epsilon^{(n)} = \left\{ u^n \in \mathcal{U}^n : -\frac{1}{n} \log p(u^n) < H(U) + \epsilon \right\}.$$

Given source alphabet $\mathcal{U}$, $H(U) = -\sum_{u \in \mathcal{U}} p(u) \log p(u)$ is the entropy of iid random process $U_1, U_2, \ldots$. By the Asymptotic Equipartition Property (AEP),

$$|A_\epsilon^{(n)}| \leq 2^{n(H(U)+\epsilon)}$$

and $\Pr(U^n \in A_\epsilon^{(n)}) \to 1$ as $n \to \infty$. We use context to distinguish between distinct typical sets (e.g., $U^n \in A_\epsilon^{(n)}$ and $Z^n \in A_\epsilon^{(n)}$ refer to two distinct typical sets with sizes bounded by $2^{n(H(U)+\epsilon)}$ and $2^{n(H(Z)+\epsilon)}$, respectively). Focusing on linear encoding and typical set decoding allows us to include simple proofs and illuminates the relationships between them.

For readability, we state and prove our results in their simplest forms. We note, however, that all of the results given here generalize widely from the forms that we state explicitly. Some of these generalizations are described below.

- While we focus on the binary alphabet, results generalize to arbitrary finite fields. The requirement that the finite field be the same for all sources, channel codewords, and additive noise processes cannot, however, be relaxed in general. The channel output alphabet is allowed to differ only in the inclusion of erasures. Erasures propagate as erasures when the output of one channel is fed into another channel.
- We state results for iid source and noise random processes; the results generalize to stationary, ergodic processes.

- We use non-systematic codes in channel coding; the results generalize to systematic codes.
- We use source-dependent typical set decoders; many of the results in this paper can be generalized to achieve universal coding performance and improved error exponents using the maximal entropy decoders of Csiszár [**Csi82**].
- We ignore decoder complexity issues; good (sub-optimal) decoders with lower complexity can be derived for many of the systems described here using sparse matrix techniques like those of [**Gal62, Mac99**].
- We give results for the smallest generalizable instances of each network type (e.g., two-receiver broadcast channels and three-receiver broadcast system source codes); our results generalize to larger systems.

4. Single-Transmitter, Single-Receiver Networks

We begin by examining simple forms of some of the prior results described in Section 2. In particular, we give simple new proofs for the linear source and channel coding theorems for single-transmitter, single-receiver networks [**Eli56, Anc77, Csi82**]. These new derivations demonstrate the relationships between these algorithms and random linear network coding techniques. We further provide a linear source coding converse. Finally, we extend the approach to design linear joint source-channel codes for the single-transmitter, single-receiver network.

Random linear source code design for a a single-transmitter, single-receiver network is equivalent to random linear network code design for the same network. We therefore say that a network code accomplishes optimal source coding on a noise-free network if that code can be used to transmit any source with entropy lower than the network capacity with asymptotically negligible error probability.

Shannon's achievability result for lossless source coding demonstrates that for $U_1, U_2, \ldots$ drawn iid from a Bernoulli(p) distribution and any $\epsilon > 0$, there exists a fixed-rate-$(H(U)+\epsilon)$ code for which the probability of decoding error can be made arbitrarily small as the coding dimension n grows without bound. The converse to Shannon's source coding theorem proves that asymptotically negligible error probabilities cannot be achieved with rates lower than $H(U)$. We begin by proving that the expected error probability of a randomly chosen, rate-R, linear source code approaches zero as n grows without bound for any source U with $H(U) < R$. The fixed-rate, linear encoder is independent of the source distribution; we use distribution-dependent typical set decoders for simplicity.

Let a_n be an $\lceil nR \rceil \times n$ matrix with coefficients in the binary field $\mathbb{F}_2$. To use a_n as a linear source code, we define encoder

$$\alpha_n(u^n) = a_n \mathbf{u},$$

for arbitrary source sequence $u^n = \mathbf{u}^t \in (\mathbb{F}_2)^n$. The corresponding decoder is

$$\beta_n(v^{\lceil nR \rceil}) = \begin{cases} u^n & \text{if } u^n \in A_\epsilon^{(n)}, a_n\mathbf{u} = \mathbf{v},\ \nexists \hat{\mathbf{u}}^t \in A_\epsilon^{(n)} \cap \{\mathbf{u}^t\}^c \text{ s.t. } a_n\hat{\mathbf{u}} = \mathbf{v} \\ \hat{U}^n & \text{otherwise,} \end{cases}$$

where $v^{\lceil nR \rceil} = \mathbf{v}^t \in (\mathbb{F}_2)^{\lceil nR \rceil}$ and decoding to $\hat{U}^n$ denotes a random decoder output The error probability for source code a_n is

$$P_e(a_n) = \Pr(\beta_n(\alpha_n(U^n)) \neq U^n).$$

THEOREM 4.1. *Let $U_1, U_2, \ldots, U_n$ be drawn iid according to distribution $p(u)$. Let $\{A_n\}_{n=1}^{\infty}$ be a sequence of rate-R linear source codes with coefficients drawn iid Bernoulli(1/2). For any $R > H(U)$, $EP_e(A_n) \to 0$ as $n \to \infty$.*

PROOF. Let $\mathbf{w}^t \in \mathbb{F}_2^n$ be an arbitrary nonzero vector. Then

$$EP_e^{(n)} = E\Pr(\text{Error} \wedge U^n \notin A_\epsilon^{(n)}) + E\Pr(\text{Error} \wedge U^n \in A_\epsilon^{(n)})$$

$$\leq \epsilon_n + \sum_{u^n, \hat{u}^n \in A_\epsilon^{(n)}} p(u^n) 1(\hat{\mathbf{u}} \neq \mathbf{u}) \Pr(A_n \hat{\mathbf{u}} = A_n \mathbf{u}) \tag{4.1}$$

$$\leq \epsilon_n + \sum_{u^n \in A_\epsilon^{(n)}} p(u^n) 2^{n(H(U)+\epsilon)} \Pr(A_n \mathbf{w} = \mathbf{0}) \tag{4.2}$$

$$\leq \epsilon_n + 2^{n(H(U)+\epsilon)} 2^{-\lceil nR \rceil} \tag{4.3}$$

for some $\epsilon_n \to 0$. Equation (4.1) and the bound on the size of the typical set follow from the AEP. The symmetry represented by the introduction of $\mathbf{w}$ in (4.2) and the bound on the corresponding probability in (4.3) result from the following argument. Let k be the number of ones in an arbitrary $\mathbf{w} \neq \mathbf{0}$. Then each coefficient of vector $A_n \mathbf{w}$ is the sum of k independent Bernoulli(1/2) random variables. Since summing iid Bernoulli(1/2) random variables yields a Bernoulli(1/2) random variable and the rows of A_n are chosen independently, $A_n \mathbf{w}$ is uniformly distributed over its $2^{\lceil nR \rceil}$ possible outcomes. Thus $EP_e^{(n)} \to 0$ as $n \to \infty$ if $R > H(U) + \epsilon$. □

Lemma 4.2 provides a form of converse to Theorem 4.1. While Theorem 4.1 shows that linear source codes are asymptotically optimal, Lemma 4.2 shows that any fixed linear code yields statistically dependent output symbols. An immediate consequence is that linear source codes cannot achieve the entropy bound for non-uniform sources (since achieving the entropy bound would necessarily yield an incompressible data sequence). This result highlights one difference between fixed-rate, asymptotically lossless linear codes and variable-rate, truly lossless algorithms like Huffman and arithmetic codes. Variable-rate schemes can achieve lossless performance for any blocklength and precisely achieve the entropy for dyadic distributions. A compensating advantage of fixed-rate codes becomes clear as we move to linear joint source-channel codes later in this section.

LEMMA 4.2. *Given any $n > 1$, let $p_1, \ldots, p_n$ be non-uniform probability mass functions on the mutually independent random variables $U_1, \ldots, U_n$. Defining $\mathbf{V} = (V_1, \ldots, V_k)^t$ and $\mathbf{U} = (U_1, \ldots, U_n)$, let $\mathbf{V} = a\mathbf{U}$ for an arbitrary $k \times n$ matrix a. If $V_1, V_2, \ldots, V_k$ are mutually independent, then matrix a has at most one non-zero element in each column.*

PROOF. The proof uses the analogue of the Darmois-Skitovich theorem for discrete periodic Abelian groups by Fel'dman [**Fel98**]. Let us proceed by contradiction. Suppose that the jth column of a has non-zero elements in positions i and $\hat{\imath}$ ($\hat{\imath} \neq i$). Then $V_{\hat{\imath}}$ and V_i both experience a non-zero contribution from U_j. In this case, the independence of $V_{\hat{\imath}}$ and V_i requires that p_j be a uniform probability mass function, which gives a contradiction. □

Channel coding can also be viewed as an extension of network coding – in this case to unreliable channels. Prior network coding results that address the issue of robust communication over unreliable channels treat non-ergodic link failures [**KM02, HKM⁺03**]. We here investigate ergodic failures. Random linear code design for an erasure channel is equivalent to random linear network code design for a single-transmitter, single-receiver network with ergodic failures. We say that a network code accomplishes optimal channel coding on the given channel if the network code can be used to transmit, with asymptotically negligible error probability, any source with rate lower than the noisy channel capacity.

For any $n \times \lfloor nR \rfloor$ matrix b_n, we can build a linear channel code with encoder $\gamma(v^{\lfloor nR \rfloor}) = b_n \mathbf{v}$. Let X^n denote the channel input and Y^n denote the corrupted channel output. For the erasure channel, $\mathbf{y}^t = y^n \in \{0, 1, E\}^n$, and we define the decoder as

$$\delta_n(y^n) = \begin{cases} v^{\lfloor nR \rfloor} & \text{if } (b_n\mathbf{v})_i = y_i \text{ for all } i \text{ s.t. } y_i \in \mathbb{F}_2 \\ & \text{and } \nexists \hat{\mathbf{v}} \neq \mathbf{v} \text{ s.t. } (b_n\hat{\mathbf{v}})_i = y_i \text{ for all } i \text{ s.t. } y_i \in \mathbb{F}_2 \\ \hat{V}^{\lfloor nR \rfloor} & \text{otherwise,} \end{cases}$$

where for any $\mathbf{v} \in \mathbb{F}_2^{\lfloor nR \rfloor}$, $(b_n\mathbf{v})_i$ is the ith component of the vector $b_n\mathbf{v}$. Decoding to $\hat{V}^{\lfloor nR \rfloor}$ denotes a random decoder output.

THEOREM 4.3. *Consider an erasure channel with input and output alphabets $\mathbb{F}_2$ and $\{0, 1, E\}$, respectively. The erasure sequence $Z_1, Z_2, \ldots$ is drawn iid according to distribution $q(z)$, where $Z_i = 1$ denotes the erasure event, and $Z_i = 0$ designates a successful transmission. The channel noise is independent of the channel input. Let $\{B_n\}_{n=1}^{\infty}$ describe a sequence of $n \times \lfloor nR \rfloor$ linear channel encoders with elements chosen iid Bernoulli(1/2). If $R < 1 - q(1)$, then $EP_e(B_n) \to 0$ as $n \to \infty$.*

PROOF. For the erasure channel, we can immediately decode Z^n from the received string Y^n. For any $z^n \in \mathbb{F}_2^n$, define $\mathcal{E}(z^n) = \{e^n \in \mathbb{F}_2^n : e_i = z_i \ \forall i \text{ s.t. } z_i = 0\}$. A decoding error occurs if there exists a $\hat{\mathbf{v}} \neq \mathbf{V}$ for which $B_n\mathbf{V} - B_n\hat{\mathbf{v}} = B_n(\mathbf{V} - \hat{\mathbf{v}}) \in \mathcal{E}(Z^n)$, since any such $\hat{\mathbf{v}}$ would be mapped to the same channel output by Z^n. For any z^n with $\sum_{i=1}^n z_i = k$, $|\mathcal{E}(z^n)| = 2^k$. Using the definition of the typical set, $z^n \in A_\epsilon^{(n)}$ implies that $\sum_{i=1}^n z_i \le n(q(1) + \epsilon')$, where $\epsilon' = \epsilon / \log(q(1)/q(0))$. Thus for any fixed $z^n \in A_\epsilon^{(n)}$ and $\mathbf{w}^t \in \mathbb{F}_2^{\lfloor nR \rfloor}$, $\Pr(B_n\mathbf{w} \in \mathcal{E}(z^n)) \le 2^{-n} 2^{n(q(1)+\epsilon')}$ (since $B_n\mathbf{w}$ is uniformly distributed by the argument in the proof of Theorem 4.1), giving

$$\begin{aligned} EP_e^{(n)}(B_n) &= E\Pr(\text{Error} \wedge Z^n \notin A_\epsilon^{(n)}) + E\Pr(\text{Error} \wedge Z^n \in A_\epsilon^{(n)}) \\ &\le \epsilon_n + \sum_{v^{\lfloor nR \rfloor}, \hat{v}^{\lfloor nR \rfloor} \in \mathbb{F}_2^{\lfloor nR \rfloor}} \ \sum_{z^n \in A_\epsilon^{(n)}} p(v^{\lfloor nR \rfloor}) q(z^n) 1(\hat{\mathbf{v}} \neq \mathbf{v}) \\ &\quad \cdot \Pr(B_n(\mathbf{v} - \hat{\mathbf{v}}) \in \mathcal{E}(z^n)) \\ &\le \epsilon_n + \sum_{v^{\lfloor nR \rfloor} \in \mathbb{F}_2^{\lfloor nR \rfloor}} \ \sum_{z^n \in A_\epsilon^{(n)}} p(v^{\lfloor nR \rfloor}) q(z^n) 2^{\lfloor nR \rfloor} 2^{-n} 2^{n(q(1)+\epsilon')} \\ &\le \epsilon_n + 2^{-n(1-q(1)-\epsilon') + \lfloor nR \rfloor} \end{aligned}$$

for some $\epsilon_n \to 0$. The expected error probability decays to zero as n grows without bound provided that $R < 1 - q(1) - \epsilon'$. □

By Shannon's separation theorem, we can achieve optimal communication over the given erasure channel by concatenating optimal source and channel codes. Concatenating the optimal linear source and channel codes of Theorems 4.1 and 4.3 yields an optimal linear source-channel code.

An alternative to separate design and decoding is joint design and decoding. While we call the resulting code a joint source-channel code for historical reason, we note that the code does not perform the separate functions of source and channel coding jointly. Instead, the code maps source sequences to channel inputs in a manner that allows robust communication without any explicit or implicit compression or addition of channel coding redundancy.

Define the joint source-channel code's encoder as $\zeta(u^n) = c_n\mathbf{u}$. Denote the random channel output by Y^n. For any $y^n = \mathbf{y}^t \in \{0,1,E\}^n$ the decoder is defined by

$$\eta_n(y^n) = \begin{cases} u^n & \text{if } (c_n\mathbf{u})_i = y_i \text{ for all } i \text{ s.t. } \ y_i \in \mathbb{F}_2 \\ & \text{and } \nexists \hat{\mathbf{u}} \neq \mathbf{u} \text{ s.t. } (c_n\hat{\mathbf{u}})_i = y_i \text{ for all } i \text{ s.t. } \ y_i \in \mathbb{F}_2 \\ \hat{U}^n & \text{otherwise.} \end{cases}$$

THEOREM 4.4. *Consider the source of Theorem 4.1 and the channel of Theorem 4.3. Let* $\{C_n\}_{n=1}^{\infty}$ *describe a sequence of* $n \times n$ *linear joint source-channel codes with elements chosen iid Bernoulli*$(1/2)$. *If* $H(U) < 1 - q(1)$, *then the expected error probability* $EP_e(C_n) \to 0$ *as* $n \to \infty$.

PROOF. We decode Z^n from the received string Y^n. A decoding error occurs if there exists a $\hat{\mathbf{u}} \neq \mathbf{U}$ for which $C_n(\mathbf{U} - \hat{\mathbf{u}}) \in \mathcal{E}(Z^n)$. Thus

$$\begin{aligned} & EP_e^{(n)}(C_n) \\ = \ & 2\epsilon_n + E\Pr\left(\text{Error} \wedge U^n \in A_\epsilon^{(n)}(p) \wedge Z^n \in A_\epsilon^{(n)}(q)\right) \\ \leq \ & 2\epsilon_n + \sum_{u^n, \hat{u}^n \in A_\epsilon^{(n)}(p)} \ \sum_{z^n \in A_\epsilon^{(n)}(q)} p(u^n)q(z^n)1(\hat{\mathbf{u}} \neq \mathbf{u}) \Pr(C_n(\mathbf{u} - \hat{\mathbf{u}}) \in \mathcal{E}(z^n)) \\ \leq \ & 2\epsilon_n + \sum_{u^n \in A_\epsilon^{(n)}(p)} \ \sum_{z^n \in A_\epsilon^{(n)}(q)} p(u^n)q(z^n)2^{n(H(U)+\epsilon)}2^{-n}2^{n(q(1)+\epsilon')} \\ \leq \ & 2\epsilon_n + 2^{-n(1-q(1)-\epsilon'-H(U)-\epsilon)} \end{aligned}$$

for some $\epsilon_n \to 0$. Here $A_\epsilon^{(n)}(p)$ is the typical set for the source distribution and $A_\epsilon^{(n)}(q)$ is the typical set for the noise. Thus $EP_e^{(n)}(C_n) \to 0$ if $H(U) < 1 - q(1) - \epsilon - \epsilon'$. □

While we focus primarily on the erasure channel model, we note that both the channel coding and joint source-channel coding theorems extend easily to additive noise models.

We begin with the additive noise channel's channel coding theorem. Let a_n be an $\lceil n(1-R) \rceil \times n$ matrix with coefficients in $\mathbb{F}_2$. For channel coding, a_n plays the traditional role of the parity check matrix. Following Csiszár [**Csi82**], however, we interpret a_n as a source code on the noise. For any matrix a_n, we can design an $n \times \lfloor nR \rfloor$ matrix b_n such that b_n has full rank and $a_n b_n = \mathbf{0}$. Matrix b_n plays the role of the generator matrix for the desired channel code. We design b_n to have full rank so that each length-$\lfloor nR \rfloor$ input message maps to a distinct channel codeword. We force $a_n b_n = \mathbf{0}$ so that each codeword is in the null space of a_n.

More precisely, the channel encoder is defined by $\gamma(v^{n-k}) = b_n\mathbf{v}$. The channel output for a random channel input $b_n\mathbf{V}$ is $\mathbf{Y} = b_n\mathbf{V} + \mathbf{Z}$. In decoding the channel output, the receiver first multiplies $\mathbf{Y}$ by a_n to give $a_n\mathbf{Y} = a_n(b_n\mathbf{V} + \mathbf{Z}) = a_n\mathbf{Z}$. The result of this multiplication is a source coded description of the error signal

$\mathbf{Z}$. Thus the decoding procedure involves applying source decoder β_n to $a_n\mathbf{Y}$. The error is decoded correctly with high probability. The receiver then subtracts the error estimate from the received $\mathbf{Y}$ to yield, with high-probability, $b_n\mathbf{V}$. Since b_n has full rank, the receiver can recover $\mathbf{V}$ perfectly from $b_n\mathbf{V}$. Thus the channel code's error probability equals the error probability for the corresponding source code on the error signal Z^n. Given this insight, the channel coding theorem is an immediate extension of the source coding theorem.

THEOREM 4.5. *Consider an additive noise channel with input, output, and noise alphabets all equal to the binary field* $\mathbb{F}_2$. *Let noise* $Z_1, Z_2, \ldots$ *be drawn iid according to distribution* $q(z)$. *The channel noise is independent of the channel input. Let* $\{(B_n, A_n)\}_{n=1}^{\infty}$ *describe a sequence of channel codes. Each* A_n *is an* $\lceil n(1-R)\rceil \times n$ *matrix with elements chosen iid Bernoulli*$(1/2)$. *Each* B_n *is designed to match the corresponding* A_n *as described above. If* $R < 1 - H(Z)$, *then the expected error probability* $EP_e(B_n, A_n) \to 0$ *as* $n \to \infty$.

For any $n \times n$ matrix c_n, we can build a joint source-channel code for the additive noise channel with encoder $\zeta(u^n) = c_n\mathbf{u}$ and decoder

$$\eta_n(y^n) = \begin{cases} u^n & \text{if } u^n \in A_\epsilon^{(n)}(p) \text{ and } \exists z^n \in A_\epsilon^{(n)}(q) \text{ s.t. } c_n\mathbf{u} + \mathbf{z} = \mathbf{y} \\ & \text{and } \nexists(\hat{\mathbf{u}}^n, \hat{\mathbf{z}}^n) \in (A_\epsilon^{(n)}(p) \cap \{\mathbf{u}\}^c) \times A_\epsilon^{(n)}(q) \text{ s.t. } c_n\hat{\mathbf{u}} + \hat{\mathbf{z}} = \mathbf{y} \\ \hat{U}^n & \text{otherwise.} \end{cases}$$

Theorem 4.6 bounds the expected error probability for a randomly chosen linear code C_n.

THEOREM 4.6. *Consider the random source* $U_1, U_2, \ldots$ *drawn iid according to distribution* $p(u)$, *and let* $Z_1, Z_2, \ldots$ *be the channel's random additive noise, where* $Z_1, Z_2, \ldots$ *are drawn iid according to distribution* $q(z)$ *and are independent of the source. Assume that the source, channel input, channel output, and noise alphabets are all equal to the binary field* $\mathbb{F}_2$. *Let* $\{C_n\}_{n=1}^{\infty}$ *describe a sequence of* $n \times n$ *linear joint source-channel codes with elements chosen iid Bernoulli*$(1/2)$. *If* $H(U) < 1 - H(Z)$, *then the expected error probability* $EP_e(C_n) \to 0$ *as* $n \to \infty$.

PROOF. An error occurs if there exists a $\hat{\mathbf{u}}^t \in A_\epsilon^{(n)}(p)$ such that $\hat{\mathbf{u}} \neq \mathbf{U}$ and $C_n(\hat{\mathbf{u}} - \mathbf{U}) \in \{\mathbf{0}\} \cup \{\hat{\mathbf{z}} - \mathbf{Z} : \hat{\mathbf{z}} \in A_\epsilon^{(n)}(q)\}$. For any fixed $\mathbf{u} - \hat{\mathbf{u}} \neq \mathbf{0}$ and randomly chosen C_n, the coefficients of vector $C_n(\mathbf{u} - \hat{\mathbf{u}})$ are sums of fixed numbers of iid Bernoulli$(1/2)$ values. Thus $\Pr(C_n(\hat{\mathbf{u}} - \mathbf{u}) = \mathbf{w}) = 2^{-n}$ for all $\mathbf{w} \in \mathbb{F}_2^n$, and

$$\begin{aligned} EP_e^{(n)}(C_n) &= 2\epsilon_n + E\Pr\left(\text{Error} \wedge U^n \in A_\epsilon^{(n)}(p) \wedge Z^n \in A_\epsilon^{(n)}(q)\right) \\ &\leq 2\epsilon_n + \sum_{(u^n,z^n),(\hat{u}^n,\hat{z}^n) \in A_\epsilon^{(n)}(p) \times A_\epsilon^{(n)}(q)} p(u^n)q(z^n)1(\hat{\mathbf{u}} \neq \mathbf{u}) \\ &\quad \cdot \Pr\left(C_n(\mathbf{u} - \hat{\mathbf{u}}) = \hat{\mathbf{z}} - \mathbf{z}\right) \\ &\leq 2\epsilon_n + \sum_{(u^n,z^n) \in A_\epsilon^{(n)}(p) \times A_\epsilon^{(n)}(q)} p(u^n)q(z^n)2^{n(H(U)+\epsilon)}2^{n(H(Z)+\epsilon)}2^{-n} \\ &\leq 2\epsilon_n + 2^{-n(1-H(Z)-H(U)-2\epsilon)} \end{aligned}$$

for some $\epsilon_n \to 0$. Here $EP_e^{(n)}(C_n) \to 0$ provided that $H(U) < 1 - H(Z) - 2\epsilon$. □

5. Multiple Access Systems

We next generalize to network systems. We begin with a simple re-derivation of the linear multiple access source codes first studied by Csiszár [**Csi82**].

Let each $\lceil nR_1 \rceil \times n$ matrix $a_{1,n}$ and $\lceil nR_2 \rceil \times n$ matrix $a_{2,n}$ define a two-transmitter, linear multiple access source code with encoders $\alpha_{1,n}(u_1^n) = a_{1,n}\mathbf{u}_1$ and $\alpha_{2,n}(u_2^n) = a_{2,n}\mathbf{u}_2$ and decoder

$$\beta_n(v_1^{\lceil nR_1 \rceil}, v_2^{\lceil nR_2 \rceil}) = \begin{cases} (u_1^n, u_2^n) & \text{if } (u_1^n, u_2^n) \in A_\epsilon^{(n)},\ (a_{1,n}\mathbf{u}_1, a_{2,n}\mathbf{u}_2) = (\mathbf{v}_1, \mathbf{v}_2) \\ & \text{and } \nexists(\hat{\mathbf{u}}_1, \hat{\mathbf{u}}_2) \in A_\epsilon^{(n)} \cap \{(\mathbf{u}_1, \mathbf{u}_2)\}^c \text{ s.t.} \\ & (a_{1,n}\hat{\mathbf{u}}_1, a_{2,n}\hat{\mathbf{u}}_2) = (\mathbf{v}_1, \mathbf{v}_2) \\ (\hat{U}_1^n, \hat{U}_2^n) & \text{otherwise.} \end{cases}$$

THEOREM 5.1. *Let $(U_{1,1}, U_{2,1}), (U_{1,2}, U_{2,2}), \ldots$ be drawn iid according to distribution $p(u_1, u_2)$ on $(\mathbb{F}_2)^2$. Choose the sequence $\{(A_{1,n}, A_{2,n})\}_{n=1}^\infty$ of rate-(R_1, R_2) linear multiple-access source codes iid uniform. Then for any rates*

$$R_1 > H(U_1|U_2), \quad R_2 > H(U_2|U_1), \quad R_1 + R_2 > H(U_1, U_2),$$

$EP_e(A_{1,n}, A_{2,n}) \to 0$ as $n \to \infty$.

PROOF. An error occurs if either or both of (U_1^n, U_2^n) is decoded in error. Thus,

$$\begin{aligned}
&EP_e(A_{1,n}, A_{2,n}) \\
&= \epsilon_n + E\Pr(\beta_n(\alpha_{1,n}(U_1^n), \alpha_{2,n}(U_2^n))) \neq (U_1^n, U_2^n) \wedge (U_1^n, U_2^n) \in A_\epsilon^{(n)}) \\
&\leq \epsilon_n + \sum_{(u_1^n, u_2^n) \in A_\epsilon^{(n)}} p(u_1^n, u_2^n) \sum_{\hat{u}_1^n : (\hat{u}_1^n, u_2^n) \in A_\epsilon^{(n)}} 1(\hat{u}_1^n \neq u_1^n) \Pr(A_{1,n}(\mathbf{u}_1 - \hat{\mathbf{u}}_1) = \mathbf{0}) \\
&\quad + \sum_{(u_1^n, u_2^n) \in A_\epsilon^{(n)}} p(u_1^n, u_2^n) \sum_{\hat{u}_2^n : (u_1^n, u_2^n) \in A_\epsilon^{(n)}} 1(\hat{u}_2^n \neq u_2^n) \Pr(A_{2,n}(\mathbf{u}_2 - \hat{\mathbf{u}}_2) = \mathbf{0}) \\
&\quad + \sum_{(u_1^n, u_2^n), (\hat{u}_1^n, \hat{u}_2^n) \in A_\epsilon^{(n)}} p(u_1^n, u_2^n) 1(\hat{u}_1^n \neq u_1^n) 1(\hat{u}_2^n \neq u_2^n) \\
&\qquad \cdot \Pr((A_{1,n}(\mathbf{u}_1 - \hat{\mathbf{u}}_1), A_{2,n}(\mathbf{u}_2 - \hat{\mathbf{u}}_2)) = (\mathbf{0}, \mathbf{0})) \\
&\leq \epsilon_n + 2^{n(H(U_1|U_2)+2\epsilon)} \Pr(A_{1,n}\mathbf{w} = \mathbf{0}) + 2^{n(H(U_2|U_1)+2\epsilon)} \Pr(A_{2,n}\mathbf{w} = \mathbf{0}) \\
&\quad + 2^{n(H(U_1,U_2)+\epsilon)} \Pr(A_{1,n}\mathbf{w}_1 = \mathbf{0} \ \wedge \ A_{2,n}\mathbf{w}_2 = \mathbf{0}) \\
&= \epsilon_n + 2^{-(\lceil nR_1 \rceil - n(H(U_1|U_2)+2\epsilon))} + 2^{-(\lceil nR_2 \rceil - n(H(U_2|U_1)+2\epsilon))} \\
&\quad + 2^{-(\lceil nR_1 \rceil + \lceil nR_2 \rceil - n(H(U_1,U_2)+\epsilon))}
\end{aligned}$$

for arbitrary, non-zero $\mathbf{w}^t, \mathbf{w}_1^t, \mathbf{w}_2^t \in \mathbb{F}_2^n$ and some $\epsilon_n \to 0$. Thus if $R_1 > H(U_1|U_2) + 2\epsilon$, $R_2 > H(U_2|U_1) + 2\epsilon$, and $R_1 + R_2 > H(U_1, U_2) + \epsilon$, then $EP_e(A_{1,n}, A_{2,n}) \to 0$ as n grows without bound. □

We next turn to linear channel coding on the two additive multiple access channels shown in Figure 1. The first is the additive multiple access channel with erasures, and the second is the additive multiple access channel with additive noise. The additive channel with interference only (no channel noise) can be viewed as a special case of either of the noisy models where errors or erasures occur with probability zero. Let X_1^n and X_2^n denote the random channel inputs, and use Y^n to denote the corresponding random channel output. Then Y^n equals $X_1^n + X_2^n$ corrupted by erasures in the erasure channel model, and $Y^n = X_1^n + X_2^n + Z^n$ for

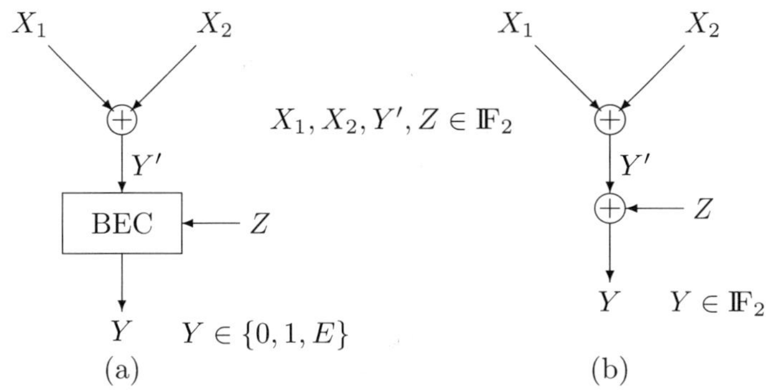

FIGURE 1. Binary additive multiple access channels with (a) erasures and (b) additive noise. In both cases, $Z_1, Z_2, \ldots$ are iid and independent of the channel inputs.

iid additive binary noise Z^n in the additive noise channel model. Both examples use addition over the binary field. All noise is independent of the channel input.

We begin by deriving the multiple access capacities. Special cases of this simple result appear in prior work (see, for example, [**Wol73**]).

LEMMA 5.2. *The multiple access capacities of both the additive multiple access channel with erasures and the additive multiple access channel with additive noise equal the rate region achieved by time-sharing between the points $(C, 0)$ and $(0, C)$, where $C = 1 - q(1)$ for the erasure model and $C = 1 - H(Z)$ for the additive noise model.*

PROOF. The cooperative capacity for each channel equals the corresponding value of C. Since the multiple access capacity without cooperation cannot exceed the cooperative capacity and the time-sharing solution achieves the cooperative capacity, we have the desired result. □

Since time-sharing between two linear codes yields a linear code, all points in the set of achievable rates are achievable by linear multiple access channel codes.

THEOREM 5.3. *Consider a multiple access channel with input alphabets $\mathcal{X}_1 = \mathcal{X}_2 = \mathbb{F}_2$ and output alphabet $\mathcal{Y} = \{0, 1, E\}$. If the channel inputs at time i are $X_{1,i}$ and $X_{2,i}$, then the channel output at time i is the binary sum $X_{1,i} + X_{2,i}$ with probability $q(0)$ and E with probability $q(1)$. Erasures are iid and independent of the channel inputs. Let $\{(B_{1,n}, B_{2,n})\}_{n=1}^{\infty}$ describe a sequence of rate-$(\lambda R, (1-\lambda)R)$ multiple access channel codes. Here*

$$B_{1,n} = \begin{bmatrix} B_{\lambda n} \\ \mathbf{0} \end{bmatrix} \text{ and } B_{2,n} = \begin{bmatrix} \mathbf{0} \\ B_{(1-\lambda)n} \end{bmatrix},$$

where $B_{\lambda n}$ and $B_{(1-\lambda)n}$ are $\lambda n \times \lfloor \lambda n R \rfloor$ and $(1-\lambda)n \times \lfloor (1-\lambda)nR \rfloor$ matrices, respectively, with coefficients chosen iid Bernoulli$(1/2)$. For any $\lambda \in [0, 1]$ and $R < 1 - q(1)$, the given sequence of linear multiple access channel codes gives expected error probability $EP_e(B_{1,n}, B_{2,n}) \to 0$ as $n \to \infty$. Thus all rates (R_1, R_2) with $R_1 + R_2 < 1 - q(1)$ are achievable.

THEOREM 5.4. *Consider a multiple access channel with input-independent, additive noise. Suppose that the input alphabets, output alphabet, and noise alphabet are all equal to the binary field* $\mathbb{F}_2$. *Let noise* $Z_1, Z_2, \ldots$ *be drawn iid according to distribution* $q(z)$. *If the channel inputs at time* i *are* $X_{1,i}$ *and* $X_{2,i}$, *then the channel output at time* i *is* $Y_i = X_{1,i} + X_{2,i} + Z_i$. *Let* $\{(B_{1,n}, B_{2,n}, A_n)\}_{n=1}^{\infty}$ *describe a sequence of rate-*$(\lambda R, (1-\lambda)R)$ *multiple access channel codes. Matrix* A_n *takes form*

$$A_n = \begin{bmatrix} A_{\lambda n} & \mathbf{0} \\ \mathbf{0} & A_{(1-\lambda)n} \end{bmatrix},$$

where $A_{\lambda n}$ *and* $A_{(1-\lambda)n}$ *are* $\lceil \lambda n(1-R) \rceil \times \lambda n$ *and* $\lceil (1-\lambda)n(1-R) \rceil \times (1-\lambda)n$ *matrices, respectively, with entries chosen iid Bernoulli*$(1/2)$. *Matrices* $B_{1,n}$ *and* $B_{2,n}$ *take the forms*

$$B_{1,n} = \begin{bmatrix} B_{\lambda n} \\ \mathbf{0} \end{bmatrix} \text{ and } B_{2,n} = \begin{bmatrix} \mathbf{0} \\ B_{(1-\lambda)n} \end{bmatrix},$$

where $B_{\lambda n}$ *and* $B_{(1-\lambda)n}$ *are the generator matrices corresponding to random parity check matrices* $A_{\lambda n}$ *and* $A_{(1-\lambda)n}$, *respectively. For any* $\lambda \in [0,1]$ *and* $R < 1 - H(Z)$, *the given sequence of linear multiple access channel codes gives expected error probability* $EP_e(B_{1,n}, B_{2,n}, A_n) \to 0$ *as* $n \to \infty$. *Thus all rates* (R_1, R_2) *with* $R_1 + R_2 < 1 - H(Z)$ *are achievable.*

We next tackle the issue of source-channel separation.

THEOREM 5.5. *Given the source of Theorem 5.1 and the channel of Theorem 5.3, if* $H(U_1, U_2) < 1 - q(1)$, *then there exists a sequence of joint source-channel codes with probability of error* $P_e^{(n)} \to 0$. *Conversely, if* $H(U_1, U_2) > 1 - q(1)$, *then the probability of error for any communication system is bounded away from zero. Thus source-channel separation holds for the multiple access erasure channel.*

PROOF. By Theorem 5.1, the Slepian-Wolf region is $R_1 > H(U_1|U_2)$, $R_2 > H(U_2|U_1)$, and $R_1 + R_2 > H(U_1, U_2)$. By Theorem 5.3, the capacity region for the given channel is $R_1 + R_2 > 1 - q(1)$. If $H(U_1, U_2) < 1 - q(1)$, then the regions overlap, and the given source can reliably communicated across the given channel with separate source and channel coding schemes.

Since separation holds for the channel with vector input (X_1, X_2) and scalar output Y, no source pair (U_1, U_2) with $H(U_1, U_2) > 1 - q(1) = I(X_1, X_2; Y)$ can be reliably transmitted across the given communication system. □

THEOREM 5.6. *Given the source of Theorem 5.1 and the channel of Theorem 5.4, if* $H(U_1, U_2) < 1 - H(Z)$, *then there exists a sequence of joint source-channel codes with probability of error* $P_e^{(n)} \to 0$. *Conversely, if* $H(U_1, U_2) > 1 - H(Z)$, *then the probability of error is bounded away from zero. Thus source-channel separation holds for the additive multiple access channel with additive noise.*

PROOF. Parallels the proof of Theorem 5.5. □

We next turn to random linear joint source-channel coding.

THEOREM 5.7. *Consider the source of Theorem 5.1 and the channel of Theorem 5.3. Let* $\{(C_{1,n}, C_{2,n})\}_{n=1}^{\infty}$ *describe a sequence of* $n \times n$ *linear joint source-channel coding encoders with elements chosen iid Bernoulli*$(1/2)$. *Each* $C_{i,n}$ $(i \in \{1,2\})$ *is an* $n \times n$ *matrix with elements chosen iid Bernoulli*$(1/2)$. *If* $H(U_1, U_2) < 1 - q(1)$, *then the expected error probability* $EP_e(C_n) \to 0$ *as* $n \to \infty$.

PROOF. A decoding error occurs if there exists a $\hat{\mathbf{u}}_1 \neq \mathbf{U}_1$ for which $C_{1,n}(\mathbf{U}_1 - \hat{\mathbf{u}}_1) \in \mathcal{E}(Z^n)$, a $\hat{\mathbf{u}}_2 \neq \mathbf{U}_2$ for which $C_{2,n}(\mathbf{U}_2 - \hat{\mathbf{u}}_2) \in \mathcal{E}(Z^n)$, or a $\hat{\mathbf{u}}_1 \neq \mathbf{U}_1$ and $\hat{\mathbf{u}}_2 \neq \mathbf{U}_2$ for which $C_{1,n}(\mathbf{U}_1 - \hat{\mathbf{u}}_1) + C_{2,n}(\mathbf{U}_2 - \hat{\mathbf{u}}_2) \in \mathcal{E}(Z^n)$. Thus

$$
\begin{aligned}
&EP_e^{(n)}(C_{1,n}, C_{2,n}) \\
&= 2\epsilon_n + E\Pr\left(\text{Error} \wedge (U_1^n, U_2^n) \in A_\epsilon^{(n)}(p) \wedge Z^n \in A_\epsilon^{(n)}(q)\right) \\
&\leq 2\epsilon_n + \sum_{(u_1^n, u_2^n) \in A_\epsilon^{(n)}(p)} \sum_{z^n \in A_\epsilon^{(n)}(q)} p(u_1^n, u_2^n) q(z^n) \\
&\quad \cdot \Bigg[\sum_{\hat{u}_1^n \neq u_1^n : (\hat{u}_1^n, u_2^n) \in A_\epsilon^{(n)}(p)} \Pr(C_{1,n}(\mathbf{u}_1 - \hat{\mathbf{u}}_1) \in \mathcal{E}(z^n)) \\
&\quad + \sum_{\hat{u}_2^n \neq u_2^n : (u_1^n, \hat{u}_2^n) \in A_\epsilon^{(n)}(p)} \Pr(C_{2,n}(\mathbf{u}_2 - \hat{\mathbf{u}}_2) \in \mathcal{E}(z^n)) \\
&\quad + \sum_{\hat{u}_1^n \neq u_1^n, \hat{u}_2^n \neq u_2^n : (\hat{u}_1^n, \hat{u}_2^n) \in A_\epsilon^{(n)}(p)} \Pr(C_{1,n}(\mathbf{u}_1 - \hat{\mathbf{u}}_1) + C_{2,n}(\mathbf{u}_2 - \hat{\mathbf{u}}_2) \in \mathcal{E}(z^n)) \Bigg] \\
&\leq 2\epsilon_n + \sum_{(u_1^n, u_2^n) \in A_\epsilon^{(n)}(p)} \sum_{z^n \in A_\epsilon^{(n)}(q)} p(u_1^n, u_2^n) q(z^n) \Big[2^{n(H(U_1|U_2)+\epsilon)} 2^{-n} 2^{n(q(1)+\epsilon')} \\
&\quad + 2^{n(H(U_2|U_1)+\epsilon)} 2^{-n} 2^{n(q(1)+\epsilon')} + 2^{n(H(U_1,U_2)+\epsilon)} 2^{-n} 2^{n(q(1)+\epsilon')} \Big]
\end{aligned}
$$

for some $\epsilon_n \to 0$. Thus the expected error probability decays to zero as n grows without bound provided that $H(U_1, U_2) < 1 - q(1) - \epsilon - \epsilon'$. □

THEOREM 5.8. *Consider the source of Theorem 5.1 and the channel of Theorem 5.4. Let* $\{(C_{1,n}, C_{2,n})\}_{n=1}^\infty$ *describe a sequence of linear joint source-channel codes with elements chosen iid Bernoulli*$(1/2)$. *If* $H(U_1, U_2) < 1 - H(Z)$, *then the expected error probability* $EP_e(C_{1,n}, C_{2,n}) \to 0$ *as* $n \to \infty$.

PROOF. An error occurs if two values of u_1^n are mapped to the same value of x_1^n, two values of u_2^n are mapped to the same value of x_2^n, or if there exist distinct noise vectors that map distinct source vectors to the same channel output. Thus, setting $\mathcal{F}(z^n) = \{\hat{\mathbf{z}} - \mathbf{z} : \hat{\mathbf{z}} \neq \mathbf{z}, \hat{\mathbf{z}}^t \in A_\epsilon^{(n)}(q)\}$ and restricting our attention to typical error sequences, we sum up the error events as: $C_{1,n}(\mathbf{U}_1 - \hat{\mathbf{u}}_1) \in \{\mathbf{0}\} \cup \mathcal{F}(Z^n)$, $C_{2,n}(\mathbf{U}_2 - \hat{\mathbf{u}}_2) \in \{\mathbf{0}\} \cup \mathcal{F}(Z^n)$, and $C_{1,n}(\mathbf{U}_1 - \hat{\mathbf{u}}_1) + C_{2,n}(\mathbf{U}_2 - \hat{\mathbf{u}}_2) \in \mathcal{F}(Z^n)$. From here, the proof parallels the proof of Theorem 5.7. In this case, $|\mathcal{F}(Z^n)| \leq 2^{n(H(Z)+\epsilon)} - 1$, giving

$$
\begin{aligned}
&EP_e^{(n)}(C_{1,n}, C_{2,n}) \\
&\leq 2\epsilon_n + \sum_{(u_1^n, u_2^n) \in A_\epsilon^{(n)}(p)} \sum_{z^n \in A_\epsilon^{(n)}(q)} p(u_1^n, u_2^n) q(z^n) \Big[2^{n(H(U_1|U_2)+\epsilon)} 2^{-n} 2^{n(H(Z)+\epsilon)} \\
&\quad + 2^{n(H(U_2|U_1)+\epsilon)} 2^{-n} 2^{n(H(Z)+\epsilon)} + 2^{n(H(U_1,U_2)+\epsilon)} 2^{-n} 2^{n(H(Z)+\epsilon)} \Big]
\end{aligned}
$$

for some $\epsilon_n \to 0$. Thus the expected error probability decays to zero as n grows without bound if $H(U_1, U_2) < 1 - H(Z) - 2\epsilon$. □

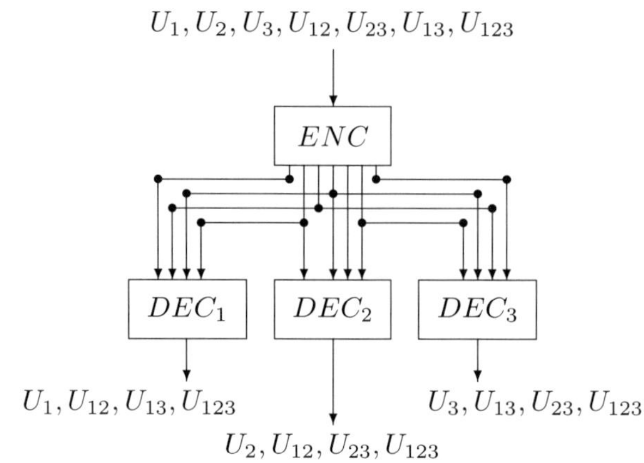

FIGURE 2. A broadcast system source code with three receivers.

6. Broadcast Systems

A broadcast system source code comprises a single encoder and a collection of decoders. Since the case with two receivers has special structure absent from general broadcast system source codes [**ZE99, ZE00**], we focus on the three-receiver system of Figure 2. Samples of source vector $(U_1, U_2, U_3, U_{12}, U_{23}, U_{13}, U_{123})$ are drawn iid from some distribution $p(u_1, u_2, u_3, u_{12}, u_{23}, u_{13}, u_{123})$. The source description contains components of rates R_1, R_2, R_3, R_{12}, R_{23}, R_{13}, and R_{123}. Decoder 1 receives the rate R_1, R_{12}, R_{13}, and R_{123} descriptions and uses them to decode $(U_1, U_{12}, U_{13}, U_{123})$. Decoder 2 receives the rate R_2, R_{12}, R_{23}, and R_{123} descriptions and uses them to decode $(U_2, U_{12}, U_{23}, U_{123})$. Decoder 3 receives the rate R_3, R_{13}, R_{23}, and R_{123} descriptions and uses them to decode $(U_3, U_{13}, U_{23}, U_{123})$. While several receivers decode the common information, each has a different subset of the descriptions with which to decode.

Theorem 6.1 proves an achievable rate region for linear broadcast system source codes. In this case, the linear encoder is a matrix of dimension

$$(\lceil nR_1\rceil + \lceil nR_2\rceil + \lceil nR_3\rceil + \lceil nR_{12}\rceil + \lceil nR_{23}\rceil + \lceil nR_{13}\rceil + \lceil nR_{123}\rceil) \times n.$$

The first $\lceil nR_1\rceil$ bits of the output go to receiver 1 only. The subsequent $\lceil nR_2\rceil$ and $\lceil nR_3\rceil$ bits similarly go to receivers 2 and 3, respectively, and so on. We again use typical set decoding.

THEOREM 6.1. *Let samples of source vector* $(U_1, U_2, U_3, U_{12}, U_{23}, U_{13}, U_{123})$ *be drawn iid according to distribution* $p(u_1, u_2, u_3, u_{12}, u_{23}, u_{13}, u_{123})$ *on* $(\mathbb{F}_2)^7$. *Let* $\{A_n\}_{n=1}^{\infty}$ *be a sequence of rate-*$(R_1, R_2, R_3, R_{12}, R_{23}, R_{13}, R_{123})$ *linear broadcast system source codes with coefficients chosen iid Bernoulli*$(1/2)$. *For any*

$$s \subseteq \{1, 2, 3, 12, 23, 13, 123\},$$

let $u_s = (u_a)_{a\in s}$, *and let* $(nR)_s = \sum_{a\in s}\lceil nR_a\rceil$. *Then for any rates satisfying*

$$\begin{aligned}
(nR)_s &\geq H(U_s|U_{S_1-s}) \quad \forall \quad s \subseteq S_1 = \{1, 12, 13, 123\}, s \neq \phi\\
(nR)_s &\geq H(U_s|U_{S_2-s}) \quad \forall \quad s \subseteq S_2 = \{2, 12, 23, 123\}, s \neq \phi\\
(nR)_s &\geq H(U_s|U_{S_3-s}) \quad \forall \quad s \subseteq S_3 = \{3, 13, 23, 123\}, s \neq \phi
\end{aligned}$$

$\{A_n\}_{n=1}^{\infty}$ *achieves expected error probability* $EP_e(A_n) \to 0$ *as* $n \to \infty$.

PROOF. We break encoder matrix A_n into a collection of $\lceil nR_a \rceil \times n$ submatrices, $a \in \{1, 2, 3, 12, 23, 13, 123\}$, such that

$$A_n^t = \left[A_{1,n}^t A_{2,n}^t A_{3,n}^t A_{12,n}^t A_{23,n}^t A_{13,n}^t A_{123,n}^t\right].$$

Let $EP_e(A_{1*,n})$ denote the expected probability that receiver 1 decodes in error. Receiver 1 errs if it decodes any subset of its desired sources incorrectly. Thus,

$$\begin{aligned} EP_e(A_{1*,n}) &\leq \epsilon_n + \sum_{(u_1^n, u_{12}^n, u_{13}^n, u_{123}^n) \in A_\epsilon^{(n)}} p(u_1^n, u_{12}^n, u_{13}^n, u_{123}^n) \\ &\quad \cdot \sum_{s \subseteq S_1 : s \neq \phi} \sum_{\hat{u}_s^n \neq u_s^n : (\hat{u}_s^n, u_{S_1 - s}^n) \in A_\epsilon^{(n)}} \Pr(A_{s,n}(\mathbf{u}_s - \hat{\mathbf{u}}_s) = \mathbf{0}) \\ &\leq \epsilon_n + \sum_{s \subseteq S_1 : s \neq \phi} 2^{n(H(U_s | U_{S_1 - s}) + 2\epsilon)} 2^{-(nR)_s} \end{aligned}$$

for some $\epsilon_n \to 0$. The arguments for receivers 2 and 3 are similar, and the code error probability is bounded by the sum of the individual decoder error probabilities. □

We next consider two erasure broadcast channel models. In each, a single channel input is sent to receivers 1 and 2. In the first model, the output at receiver 1 is an erasure with probability $q_1(1)$ and the transmitted value with probability $q_1(0)$; likewise, the output at receiver 2 is an erasure with probability $q_2(1)$ and is otherwise received correctly. Without loss of generality, assume that $q_1(1) \leq q_2(1)$. In this model, erasures are assumed to be independent events. In the second model, the erasure probabilities for the two receivers are the same, but the erasures are dependent random variables, with all erasures at the first receiver propagating to the second receiver. By [**CT91**, Theorem 14.6.1], the capacity of the broadcast channel depends only on the conditional marginal distributions $p(y_1|x)$ and $p(y_2|x)$, thus the capacity of the two channels shown and all channels with the same $p(y_1|x)$ and $p(y_2|x)$ (regardless of the statistical dependencies between erasure events Z_1 and Z_2) are identical.[3] Since we consider discrete channels, the degraded broadcast channel converses of [**AK75**] or of [**vdM75**], which allows no or partial common information, are applicable. Note that the elegant and simple converse for degraded BSC broadcast channels of [**Wyn73**], which relies on properties of binary sequences, might be readily extended to our model, albeit without the generality of [**AK75, vdM75**].

Lemma 6.2 proves time-sharing to be optimal for broadcast coding over the given family of channels. Theorem 6.3 is then immediate by the previous linearity of time-sharing argument.

LEMMA 6.2. *Consider a binary erasure channel with output alphabets* $\{0, 1, E\}$ *at each of two receivers. The erasure sequences* $Z_{1,1}, Z_{1,2}, \ldots$ *and* $Z_{2,1}, Z_{2,2}, \ldots$ *are drawn iid according to distributions* $q_1(z_1)$ *and* $q_2(z_2)$*, respectively, where* $Z_{i,j} = 1$ *denotes an erasure event at receiver* i *at time* j*. The channel noise is independent of the channel input. The joint distribution* $q(z_1, z_2)$ *may be any distribution with the given marginals. The capacity region for sending independent information to the two receivers is described by*

$$\frac{R_1}{1 - q_1(1)} + \frac{R_2}{1 - q_2(1)} \leq 1.$$

[3] All channel models considered here assume Z_1 and Z_2 are independent of the channel input.

If independent rates (R_1, R_2) *are achievable and* $R_0 < R_2$*, then* $(R_1', R_2', R_{12}') = (R_1, R_2 - R_0, R_0)$ *is achievable with common information rate* R_{12}' *and independent information rates* R_1' *and* R_2'.

PROOF. By [**CT91**, Theorems 14.6.1 and 14.6.2], the capacity of the given channel is the convex hull of the closure of all (R_1, R_2) satisfying $R_2 \leq I(W; Y_2)$ and $R_1 \leq I(X; Y_1|W)$ for some joint distribution $p(w)p(x|w)p(y_1|x)p(y_2|y_1)$. Auxiliary random variable W has alphabet size 2, and $p(y_2|y_1)$ is derived from the physically degraded channel model. By a symmetry argument, the optimal W is a uniform binary random variable with $p(x|w) = 1 - \beta$ if $x = w$ and $p(x|w) = \beta$ otherwise. Thus

$$\begin{aligned} R_1 &\leq I(X; Y_1|W) = (1 - q_1(1))H(\beta) \\ R_2 &\leq I(W; Y_2) = (1 - q_2(1))(1 - H(\beta)). \end{aligned}$$

Varying $H(\beta)$ from 0 to 1 gives the independent message result. The common information result comes from [**CT91**, Theorem14.6.4]. □

THEOREM 6.3. *Consider the channel from Lemma 6.2. Let* $\{B_n\}_{n=1}^{\infty}$ *describe a sequence of linear channel codes for the broadcast channel, where*

$$B_n = \begin{bmatrix} B_{\lambda n} & \mathbf{0} \\ \mathbf{0} & B_{(1-\lambda)n} \end{bmatrix}$$

Each $B_{\lambda n}$ *has elements chosen iid Bernoulli*$(1/2)$. *If* $R_1/(1 - q_1(1)) + R_2/(1 - q_2(1)) < 1$*, then the expected error probability* $EP_e(B_n) \to 0$ *as* $n \to \infty$.

For the additive noise broadcast channel model, linear codes can do at least as well as the time-sharing bound, but that bound is not the optimal solution [**CT91**].

7. Input-Dependent Noise

By assuming that the channel noise is independent of the channel input, the theorems of the previous section rule out asymmetrical channels like the Z-channel. Unfortunately, the above techniques do not extend to the case where the noise random variable is dependent on the channel input. In the case of the single-transmitter, single-receiver channel, source-channel separation holds in general but fails for linear codes. In the case of the additive multiple access channel with additive noise, separation fails more generally, as shown next. The same phenomena may be observed in erasure channels.

THEOREM 7.1. *Consider a multiple access channel where the input alphabets* $\mathcal{X}_1$ *and* $\mathcal{X}_2$*, output alphabet* $\mathcal{Y}$*, and noise alphabet* $\mathcal{Z}$ *are all equal to the binary field* $\mathbb{F}_2$. *Let* $Z_1, Z_2, \ldots$ *be the noise random process, and use* $X_{1,i}$ *and* $X_{2,i}$ *to describe the channel inputs at time* i. *The channel output at time* i *is* $Y_i = X_{1,i} + X_{2,i} + Z_i$. *Separation fails when* Z_i *and* $(X_{1,i}, X_{2,i})$ *are statistically dependent random variables.*

PROOF. The maximal rate attainable in separate source and channel coding is bounded by the multiple access channel capacity's bound on the sum rate

$$R_1 + R_2 \leq \max_{P_1, P_2} I(X_1, X_2; Y),$$

where P_1 and P_2 are the marginal probability mass functions of X_1 and X_2, respectively. The cooperative capacity of the network provides the alternative bound

$$R_1 + R_2 \leq \max_{P_{12}} I(X_1, X_2; Y).$$

Separation fails when $\max_{P_1,P_2} I(X_1, X_2; Y) < \max_{P_{12}} I(X_1, X_2; Y)$, since the cooperative capacity is achievable through joint coding for the source with $p(u_1, u_2)$ equal to the capacity-achieving value of P_{12}.

For all $i, j \in \{0, 1\}$, let $\Pr(Z = 1|X_1 = i, X_2 = j) = q_{ij} = 1 - \bar{q}_{ij}$. For the multiple access capacity, let $p_i = \Pr(X_i = 1) = 1 - \bar{p}_i$. Then

$$\begin{aligned}\max_{P_1,P_2} I(X_1, X_2; Y) &= \max_{p_1,p_2}[H(\bar{p}_1\bar{p}_2\bar{q}_{00} + \bar{p}_1 p_2 q_{01} + p_1\bar{p}_2 q_{10} + p_1 p_2\bar{q}_{11}) \\ &\quad -\bar{p}_1\bar{p}_2 H(q_{00}) - \bar{p}_1 p_2 H(q_{01}) - p_1\bar{p}_2 H(q_{10}) - p_1 p_2 H(q_{11})].\end{aligned}$$

For the cooperative capacity, let $\Pr(X_1 = i, X_2 = j) = p_{ij}$, where $p_{11} = 1 - p_{00} - p_{01} - p_{10}$. Then we similarly find

$$\begin{aligned}\max_{P_{12}} I(X_1, X_2; Y) &= \max_{p_{00},p_{01},p_{10},p_{11}} [H(Y) - H(Y|X_1, X_2)] \\ &= \max_{p_{00},p_{01},p_{10},p_{11}} [H(p_{00}\bar{q}_{00} + p_{01}q_{01} + p_{10}q_{10} + p_{11}\bar{q}_{11}) \\ &\quad -p_{00}H(q_{00}) - p_{01}H(q_{01}) - p_{10}H(q_{10}) - p_{11}H(q_{11})].\end{aligned}$$

The two equations are not equal in general. For example, let $q_{00} = 0$ and $q_{11} = 1$ while $q_{01} = q_{10} = \frac{1}{2}$. Then $\max_{P_1P_2} I(X_1, X_2; Y) = 0.5$ while $\max_{P_{12}} I(X_1, X_2; Y) = 1$. (The maxima occur at $p_1 = p_2 = \frac{1}{2}$ and $p_{00} = p_{11} = \frac{1}{2}$, respectively.) Separation fails in this example since the source pair (U_1, U_2) with $\Pr(U_0 = 0, U_1 = 0) = \Pr(U_0 = 1, U_1 = 1) = \frac{1}{2}$ can be reliably transmitted across the given channel, despite the fact that the achievable rate region for Slepian-Wolf source coding and the capacity region for the given channel do not overlap. (Slepian-Wolf source coding requires a rate $R_1 + R_2 \geq 1$ while the multiple access capacity region extends only as far as $R_1 + R_2 \leq 0.5$.) □

8. The Case for End-to-End Coding

The preceding sections treat the topics of source and channel coding using the tools of linear network coding, bringing previously disparate areas into a common framework. We end by demonstrating that this unification is not only useful in its combination of tasks once treated entirely separately but is in fact crucial to achieving optimal, reliable communication.

Traditional routing techniques rely entirely on repeat and forward strategies for getting a source from its point of origin to its desired destination. The network coding literature demonstrates the failure of that approach in achieving the optimal performance for some simple multi-cast examples [**ACLY00**]. We next demonstrate the failure of the network coding model.

The common network coding model assumes that all sources are independent and all links are noiseless. Implicit in the given model is the assumption that source and channel coding are performed separately from network coding at the edges of the network, so that the internal nodes need only pass along the information to the appropriate receivers. We next demonstrate that source-network separation and channel-network separation both fail. That is, there exist networks for which network coding and source coding must be performed jointly in order to achieve the optimal performance. Likewise, there exist networks for which network coding

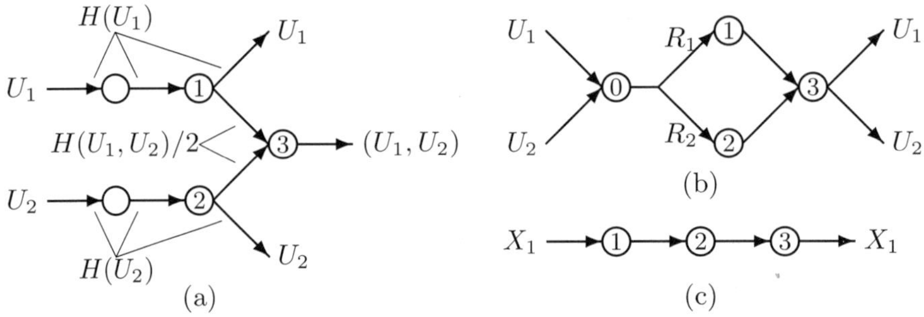

FIGURE 3. Networks for which (a) separation of source and network coding and (b) separation of channel and network coding fail. (c) A network for which decoding at intermediate nodes is required for optimal coding.

and channel coding must be performed jointly in order to achieve the optimal performance. We use a sequence of simple examples to prove these results.

EXAMPLE 8.1. The network of Figure 3(a) comprises two transmitters and three receivers. Receiver nodes 1, 2, and 3 wish to receive U_1, U_2 and (U_1, U_2), respectively. Sources (U_1, U_2) are dependent random variables, with $H(U_1) = H(U_2)$ and $H(U_1, U_2) < H(U_1) + H(U_2)$. All network links are lossless, and the capacities are noted in the figure. Achieving reliable communication in this example requires the descriptions received by nodes 1 and 2 to be dependent random variables and requires sources U_1 and U_2 to be re-compressed at nodes 1 and 2, respectively. Thus separation of source coding and network coding fails.

EXAMPLE 8.2. In the network shown in Figure 3(b), the channel between node 0 and nodes 1 and 2 is a broadcast erasure channel with independent erasures of probabilities $q_1(1) = q_2(1) = q$. The channel between nodes 1 and 2 and node 3 is a multiple access channel without interference. The network coding approach requires labeling each link with its corresponding link capacity. If R_1 and R_2 are the capacities of the edges to receivers 1 and 2, then $R_1 + R_2$ must be less than $1 - q$ by Theorem 6.3. The links from node 1 to node 3 and from node 2 to node 3 are both lossless, with capacity 1 bit per channel use. Optimal network coding on the given channel gives a maximal rate of $1 - q$ from the encoder to the decoder. We contrast with the above separated channel and network coding approach an end-to-end coding strategy. In this case, we do not force zero error probability between node 0 and nodes 1 and 2 but instead simply forward the information received by those nodes to the decoder. The capacity of the resulting code is $1 - q^2$ since receiver 3 suffers an erasure only if both node 1 and node 2 receive erasures.

Example 8.2 illustrates the failure of separate channel and network coding schemes and also reminds us that while codes for canonical network elements can be strung together to achieve codes for more complicated networks, the resulting solutions are not optimal in general. Example 8.2 demonstrates that sometimes decoding at intermediate nodes of the network yields suboptimal performance. Example 8.3 teaches the opposite lesson.

EXAMPLE 8.3. In the channel of Figure 3(c), the links (1,2) and (2,3) are independent erasure channels with erasure probabilities $q_1(1)$ and $q_2(1)$, respectively.

If we do not decode at the intermediate node, then the maximal achievable rate from node 1 to node 3 is $(1-q_1(1))(1-q_2(1))$. Decoding at node 2 yields maximal achievable rate $\min\{1-q_1(1), 1-q_2(1)\} > (1-q_1(1))(1-q_2(1))$.

The failure of separation in Examples 8.1 and 8.2 and the contrasting lessons regarding decoding at intermediate nodes demonstrated by Examples 8.2 and 8.3 make the case for the need for end-to-end coding in network environments. The success of the linear coding technique in network coding, source coding, and channel coding suggests that a unified approach that obviates the need for separate routing, compression, and error correction codes may be within reach. In contrast, the failure of separation across canonical network systems seems to present a far greater challenge to optimal code design for networks.

References

[ACLY00] R. Ahlswede, N. Cai, S.-Y. R. Li, and R. W. Yeung, "Network information flow", *IEEE Trans. Inform. Theory*, vol. 46, no. 4, 2000, pp. 1204–1216.

[Ahl71] R. Ahlswede, "Multi-way communication channels", in *Proc. 2nd. Int'l Symp. Information Theory*, Tsahkadsor, Armenian S.S.R., Prague, Publishing House of the Hungarian Academy of Sciences, 1971, pp. 23–52.

[AK75] R. Ahlswede and J. Körner, "Source coding with side information and a converse for degraded broadcast channels", *IEEE Trans. Inform. Theory*, vol. 21, no. 6, 1975, pp. 629–637.

[Anc77] T. Ancheta, Jr., "Bounds and techniques for linear source coding", *IEEE Trans. Inform. Theory*, vol. 24, no. 2, 1977, p. 276.

[Ber73] P. Bergmans, "Coding theorems for broadcast channels with degraded components", *IEEE Trans. Inform. Theory*, vol. 19, no. 2, 1973, pp. 197–207.

[Csi82] I. Csiszár, "Linear codes for sources and source networks: Error exponents", *IEEE Trans. Inform. Theory*, vol. 28, 1982, pp. 585–592.

[CT91] T.M. Cover and J.A. Thomas, *Elements of information theory*, Wiley, 1991.

[CW79] S.-C. Chang and E. J. Weldon, Jr., "Coding for t-user multiple access channels", *IEEE Trans. Inform. Theory*, vol. 25, no. 6, 1979, pp. 684–691.

[Eli56] P. Elias, "Coding for two noisy channels", in *Proc. Third London Symposium on Information Theory*, London, Academic Press, 1956, pp. 61–74.

[Fel98] G.M. Fel'dman, "The Skitovich–Darmois theorem for discrete periodic Abelian groups", *Theory of Probability and Its Applications*, vol. 42, no. 4, 1998, pp. 611–617.

[Gal62] R.G. Gallager, "Low density parity check codes", *IRE Trans. Inform. Theory*, vol. 8, 1962, pp. 21–28.

[Gal74] R.G. Gallager, "Capacity and coding for degraded broadcast channels", *Probl. Peredach. Inform.*, vol. 10, 1974, pp. 3–14.

[HKM+03] T. Ho, R. Koetter, M. Médard, D. Karger, and M. Effros, "The benefits of coding over routing in a randomized setting", in *Proc. IEEE Int'l Symposium on Information Theory*, Yokohama, Japan, June 2003, p. 442.

[JCJ03] S. Jaggi, P. A. Chou, and K. Jain, "Low complexity algebraic multicast network codes", in *Proc. IEEE Int'l Symposium on Information Theory*, Yokohama, Japan, June 2003, p. 368.

[KM02] R. Koetter and M. Médard, "Beyond routing: an algebraic approach to network coding", in *Proc. INFOCOM 2002*, vol. 1, 2002, pp. 122–130.

[Lia72] H. Liao, "Multiple access channels", Ph. D. Dissertation, Department of Electrical Engineering, University of Hawaii, Honolulu, 1972.

[Mac99] D.J.C. MacKay, "Good error-correcting codes based on very sparse matrices", *IEEE Trans. Inform. Theory*, vol. 45, no. 2, 1999, pp. 399–431.

[PR99] S. S. Pradhan and K. Ramchandran, "Distributed source coding using syndromes (DISCUS) design and construction", in *Proc. Data Compression Conference*, Snowbird, Utah, Mar. 1999, pp. 158–167.

[PR00a] S.S. Pradhan and K. Ramchandran, "Distributed source coding: symmetric rates and applications to sensor networks", in *Proc. Data Compression Conference*, Snowbird, Utah, Mar. 2000, pp. 363–372.

[PR00b] S. S. Pradhan and K. Ramchandran, "Group-theoretic construction and analysis of generalized coset codes for symmetric/asymmetric distributed source coding", in *Proc. Conf. on Information Sciences and Systems*, Princeton, NJ, Mar. 2000.

[PR03] S. S. Pradhan and K. Ramchandran, "Distributed source coding using syndromes (DISCUS): design and construction", *IEEE Trans. Inform. Theory*, vol. 49, no. 3, 2003, pp. 626–643.

[PS95] G. Poltyrev and J. Snyders, "Linear codes for the sum mod-2 multiple-access channel with restricted access", *IEEE Trans. Inform. Theory*, vol. 41, no. 3, 1995, pp. 794–799.

[RPK00] K. Ramchandran, S. S. Pradhan, and R. Koetter, "A constructive framework for distributed source coding with symmetric rates", in *Proc. IEEE Int'l Symposium on Information Theory*, Sorrento, Italy, June 2000.

[SET03] P. Sanders, S. Egner, and L. Tolhuizen, "Polynomial time algorithms for network information flow", in *Proc. of the 15th ACM Symposium on Parallelism in Algorithms and Architectures*, 2003, To appear.

[SPR02] D. Schonberg, S. S. Pradhan, and K. Ramchandran, "LDPC codes can approach the Slepian Wolf bound for general binary sources", in *Proc. Allerton Conference on Communication, Control, and Computing*, Monticello, IL, Oct. 2002.

[SW73] D. Slepian and J. K. Wolf, "Noiseless coding of correlated information sources", *IEEE Trans. Inform. Theory*, vol. 19, 1973, pp. 471–480.

[Uye01] T. Uyematsu, "An algebraic construction of codes for Slepian-Wolf source networks", *IEEE Trans. Inform. Theory*, vol. 47, no. 7, 2001, pp. 3082–3088.

[vdM75] E.C. van der Meulen, "Random coding theorems for the general discrete memoryless broadcast channel", *IEEE Trans. Inform. Theory*, vol. 21, no. 2, 1975, pp. 180–190.

[Wol73] J. K. Wolf, "Multiple user communication", National Telemetry Conference (Atlanta, Georgia), 1973.

[Wyn73] A. D. Wyner, "A theorem on the entropy of certain binary sequences and applications – II", *IEEE Trans. Inform. Theory*, vol. 19, 1973, pp. 772–777.

[ZE99] Q. Zhao and M. Effros, "Broadcast system source codes: a new paradigm for data compression", *Conf. Record, Thirty-Third Asilomar Conference on Signals, Systems and Computers*, Pacific Grove, CA, vol. 1, Oct. 1999, pp. 337–341.

[ZE00] Q. Zhao and M. Effros, "Lossless and lossy broadcast system source codes: theoretical limits, optimal design, and empirical performance", in *Proc. Data Compression Conference*, Snowbird, Utah, Mar. 2000, pp. 63–72.

M. Effros and B. Hassibi: Department of Electrical Engineering, 136-93, California Institute of Technology, Pasadena, CA 91125.

E-mail address: `effros@caltech.edu, hassibi@systems.caltech.edu`

M. Médard, T. Ho, and S. Ray: Laboratory for Information and Decision Systems (LIDS), Massachusetts Institute of Technology, Cambridge, MA 02139

E-mail address: `medard@mit.edu, trace@mit.edu, sray@mit.edu`

D. Karger: Computer Science and Artificial Intelligence Laboratory (CSAIL), Massachusetts Institute of Technology, Cambridge, MA 02139

E-mail address: `karger@mit.edu`

R. Koetter: Coordinated Science Laboratory, University of Illinois at Urbana-Champaign, Urbana, IL 61801

E-mail address: `koetter@uiuc.edu`

DIMACS Series in Discrete Mathematics
and Theoretical Computer Science
Volume **66**, 2004

On Source-Channel Communication in Networks

Michael Gastpar

ABSTRACT. The separation theorem provides a general solution to the point-to-point lossy source-channel communication problem by equating the rate-distortion function of the source with the capacity-cost function of the channel. It is well-known that this principle does not extend to networks in general. Recently, a different perspective on the point-to-point source-channel communication problem has been proposed, based on insight about the optimality of uncoded transmission [**11**]. In this paper, that perspective is extended to networks, leading to optimality results for certain network topologies, including single-source broadcast and multi-access with dependent sources (inspired by sensor network scenarios). These optimality results suggest that it can be substantially suboptimal to implement a network communication scheme by separate source and channel coding. This is also investigated in terms of *scaling laws* that govern the performance as the number of nodes in the network becomes large. As a case in point, for a particular Gaussian sensor network scenario, it can be shown that at fixed sensor power, the minimum achievable distortion for a separation-based approach behaves like $1/\log M$, while the actual minimum achievable distortion behaves like $1/M$, where M is the number of sensor nodes.

1. Introduction

When a (stationary, ergodic) source is transmitted across a (stationary, ergodic) channel in a lossy fashion, the separation theorem [**20**, Thm. 21] (and its extensions in [**6, 13, 21**]) establishes that the smallest achievable distortion can be attained by separating the coding scheme into two parts: a source compression stage, and a channel coding stage. The two stages are linked by abstract discrete *messages* (bits). The source code represents the source in the best way (with respect to the distortion measure) by such discrete messages. The channel code guarantees that the messages are delivered without error.

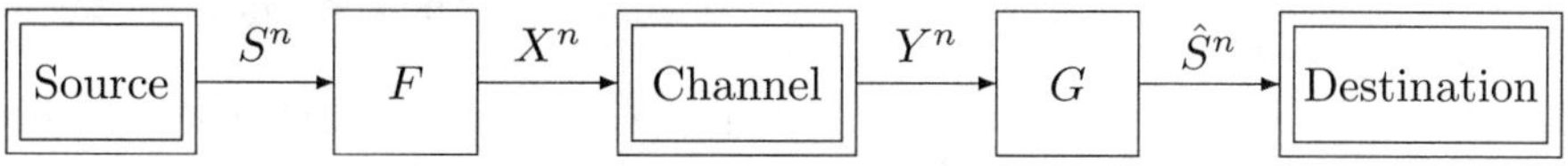

FIGURE 1. Point-to-point source-channel communication.

Key words and phrases. sensor networks, separation theorem, source coding, channel coding, cut-set bound, bit.

When a source network is transmitted across a channel network in a lossy fashion, it is well known that source and channel coding cannot generally be separated from each other without sacrificing optimality. Few results are known (see also the remark in [**4**, p. 282]), including certain separation theorems for very simple network topologies such as the case when the sources are independent, see e.g. [**7**]. It appears that separate source and channel coding is an inefficient perspective to analyze the performance in source-channel networks. This point is explained in more detail below in Section 2.

In this paper, we exploit an alternative perspective on the point-to-point source-channel communication problem [**11**]. This alternative perspective permits to determine the optimal performance achievable in certain network topologies.

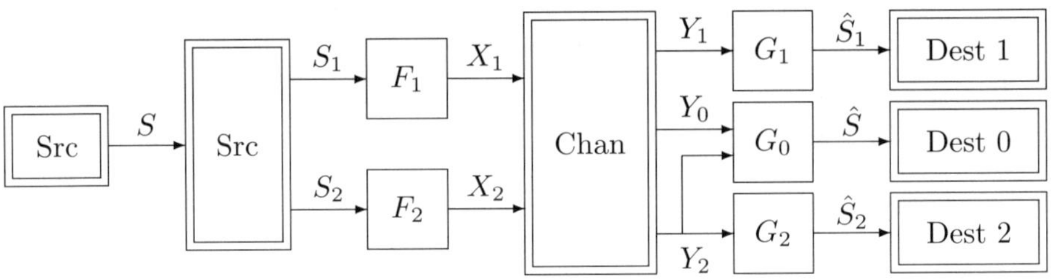

FIGURE 2. A simple source-channel communication network.

1.1. Problem Statement: Cost versus Distortion. A source-channel communication network is the combination of a source network with a channel network. Figure 2 shows a very simple source-channel network. Throughout this paper, we assume that the source distributions are memoryless, that the involved channel networks are also memoryless (in the sense of [**14**]), and that no feedback links are available.[1] Specifying such a source-channel network requires the following four items (see also the definition on p. 281, and the remark on p. 282 in [**4**]):

1. The (joint) probability distribution of the involved sources, and the (joint) conditional probability distribution of all the channel outputs given all the channel inputs. For the example of Figure 2, these are $p(s, s_1, s_2)$ on the source side, and $p(y_0, y_1, y_2|x_1, x_2)$ on the channel side. As illustrated by the figure, some sources may be *hidden*: They cannot be directly observed, but need to be reconstructed.
2. The network topology, which determines, for each encoder, the sources it can access, and the channel inputs it can influence, and for each decoder, which channel outputs it can access, and which destinations it can serve. For the example of Figure 2, this is determined by the connections drawn in the figure.
3. The input cost functions for the channel network inputs. For the example of Figure 2, these are cost functions involving x_1 and x_2.
4. For each destination, it must be specified what it wishes to reconstruct about the sources, and with respect to what distortion measure.

[1]The exclusion of feedback links is not of fundamental importance when under the memoryless assumption, but in order to concentrate on the heart of the matter, we exclude it from our present considerations.

The source-channel communication problem studied in this paper is the trade-off between the cost of transmission and the incurred overall distortion. The cost is assumed to have the shape of an expectation. For the point-to-point setup of Figure 1, the cost is

$$P = \lim_{n\to\infty} \frac{1}{n} E\rho(X^n), \tag{1.1}$$

where X^n denotes a sequence of n channel input symbols. The distortion also takes the shape of an expectation,

$$D = \lim_{n\to\infty} \frac{1}{n} Ed(S^n, \hat{S}^n). \tag{1.2}$$

The goal of the source-channel communication system is to attain an optimal cost-distortion trade-off (P, D), where optimal is understood: over all communication systems, irrespective of their complexity (i.e., irrespective of the coding block length n).[2] In the network case, a cost-distortion trade-off is characterized by all involved distortions $D_1, D_2, \ldots$ and all involved costs $P_1, P_2, \ldots$. This is made more explicit in the next section.

2. Source-Channel Separation in Networks

2.1. Capacity and Rate-distortion. In order to address the issues of capacity and rate-distortion for networks, we have to separately define source networks and channel networks. A source network is specified, by analogy to the arguments in Section 1.1, by the following three items:

1. The (joint) probability distribution of the involved sources.
2. The network topology specifies, for each encoder, the sources it can access, and for each decoder, the encoded bit streams it can access.
3. The distortion measures specify, for each decoder, which sources it should reconstruct, and with respect to what distortion measure.

For such a source network, the rate-distortion region $\mathcal{R}(D_1, D_2, \ldots)$ is the set of all rate tuples $(R_1, R_2, \ldots, R_M)$ for which there exist encoders that permit the decoders to reconstruct the sources at the required fidelity. A similar definition of a source network is given in [**4**, p.237], where it is called a *multiple source.* Notice that a source network according to our definition may also include *hidden* sources, i.e., sources that are not accessible to any encoder, but have to be reconstructed nevertheless. One example of such a network is shown in Figure 2; another example is the CEO problem [**2**]. We will discuss this setup in more detail below in Section 4.2.

A channel network is specified by the following three items:

1. The (joint) conditional probability distribution of all the channel outputs given all the channel inputs.
2. The network topology, which determines, for each encoder, the sources it can access, and the channel inputs it can influence, and for each decoder, which channel outputs it can access, and which destinations it can serve.
3. The input cost functions for the channel network inputs.

[2] This should be understood by analogy to the notion of the *optimum performance theoretically achievable* (OPTA), see [**1**, p. 156] and the *limit of the minimum transmission ratio* (LMTR), see [**4**, p. 129, middle].

The capacity-cost region $\mathcal{C}(P_1, P_2, \ldots)$ is the set of all rate tuples $(R_1, R_2, \ldots, R_M)$ at which a vanishingly small error probability can be achieved in the usual information-theoretic sense.

The combination of the achievability of $\mathcal{R}(D_1, D_2, \ldots)$ with the achievability of $\mathcal{C}(P_1, P_2, \ldots)$ leads to the following lemma about *achievable* cost-distortion tuples:

LEMMA 2.1. *If*

$$\mathcal{R}(D_1, D_2, \ldots) \cap \mathcal{C}(P_1, P_2, \ldots) \neq \emptyset, \tag{2.1}$$

then the cost-distortion tuple $(P_1, P_2, \ldots, D_1, D_2, \ldots)$ *is achievable.*

It is well known that while this lemma describes an interesting set of achievable cost-distortion tuples, it does *not* describe all of them. In other words, the converse does not hold: a cost-distortion tuple $(P_1, P_2, \ldots, D_1, D_2, \ldots)$ may be achievable even if it does not satisfy the condition of Lemma 2.1.

2.2. Multiple Access with Dependent Sources. To the best of our knowledge, the first example of a source-channel network for which separate source and channel code designs lead to suboptimal performance appeared in [**3**]. It addresses the multiple access scenario when the involved sources are dependent. We quote it as follows:

EXAMPLE 2.2. Consider the source-channel network illustrated in Figure 3: Two (correlated) binary sources S_1 and S_2 are to be transmitted over a multiple access channel. The joint distribution of S_1 and S_2 is that the event $(X_1 = 1, X_2 = 0)$ never occurs; the other three events are equally likely, i.e., they occur with probability $\frac{1}{3}$ each. To encode this source in a lossless way, a total rate of $R_1 + R_2 = \log_2 3 = 1.585$ bits is required at least. The channel takes binary inputs, and its output is the (real) sum of the inputs. It can be shown that its capacity region is contained in the triangle $0 \leq R_1 + R_2 \leq 1.5$.

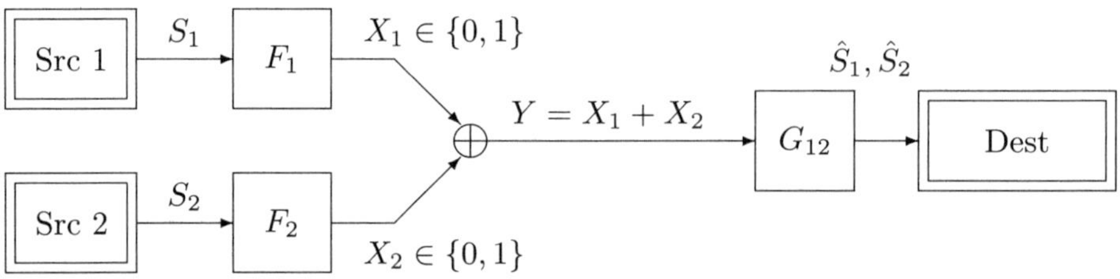

FIGURE 3. Multiple-access with correlated sources.

Hence, the rate region for the source does not intersect the capacity region of the channel, leading one to suspect that it is not possible to transmit these two sources across this multiple access channel without incurring distortion: Certainly, Lemma 2.1 does not establish the achievability of this operating point. However, if the two encoders are simply the identity maps, then it is easy to see that perfect reconstruction is achieved: the sum of S_1 and S_2, together with their (skewed) distribution, uniquely identifies both S_1 and S_2.

It is relatively easy to locate the problem with the separation paradigm in this example: The capacity region for the multi-access channel was computed supposing *independent* sources. Clearly, as explained in [**3**], if the sources can be dependent, the capacity region is generally larger. This is precisely what happens in this example. If, in the definition of the capacity region, we allow for arbitrarily dependent channel inputs, then the separation theorem applies again, and the problem pointed out by the above example does not arise. This is not at all surprising: allowing for arbitrarily dependent sources turns the problem effectively into a point-to-point problem. Yet, the gist of this example is subtler than one might think at this point of the discussion: the two channel inputs *cannot* be arbitrarily dependent since they have to be generated by separate encoders. The dependence of the channel inputs is determined by the dependence of the underlying sources.[3]

This example is primarily a challenge to the definition of the capacity region for a network: Rather than assuming the channel inputs to be independent, to calculate a more meaningful "capacity" for the source-channel network problem, one should allow the channel inputs to be dependent, but only as dependent as the underlying sources. Unfortunately, this more appropriate capacity calculation seems to be a very difficult problem: the best known results have been published in 1980 in [**3**].

Irrespective of the problem of actually calculating the full region, is such a redefined capacity sufficient to solve the general source-channel network communication problem? The fundamental principle behind source/channel separation is to convert the source into *discrete messages*, and to transmit these messages in a reliable fashion across the channel. The separation theorem asserts that irrespective of the distortion measure of interest, such a strategy is sufficient to achieve optimal performance in the point-to-point case. Is it also sufficient to achieve optimal performance in the network case?

For Example 2.2, since there is no distortion measure involved in the first place, such a strategy does achieve optimal performance. Hence, while the above example is interesting, it may not convince the reader of the shortcomings of the separation paradigm in a network context: one might suspect that it is sufficient to redefine the notions of capacity and (possibly) rate-distortion regions.

However, the next section provides an example that illustrates the strict suboptimality of sending discrete messages in a reliable fashion, i.e., the suboptimality of any strategy that separates source from channel coding.

2.3. Gaussian Single-source Broadcast. The second challenge to the separation paradigm is a simple extension to a well-known example: Gaussian single-source broadcast.

EXAMPLE 2.3. Consider the simple source-channel network illustrated in Figure 4: An independent and identically distributed (iid), discrete-time Gaussian source S of mean zero and variance P is to be transmitted across a Gaussian two-user broadcast channel with power constraint P and with noise variances $\sigma_1^2 < \sigma_2^2$. Denote the capacities of the two underlying point-to-point channels by $C_1 = 1/2 \log_2(1 + P/\sigma_1^2)$ and $C_2 = 1/2 \log_2(1 + P/\sigma_2^2)$. We want $D_2 = D_{\mathcal{N}}(C_2)$.

[3] Note that in the separation-based scheme, the optimal source coding is the Slepian-Wolf code, and the outputs of this coding stage are approximately *independent* (see e.g. the related remark in [**24**], after Lemma 3.) It is therefore tempting to guess that usual capacity-achieving channel codes are sufficient to achieve optimal performance. This is *not* true: removing the dependence between the sources is not generally a good idea since this dependence may be fit to the channel (as it is the case in this example), and once it is removed, it cannot be brought in again since the encoders must be separate.

What is the smallest achievable D_1? First, suppose we use a separation-based de-

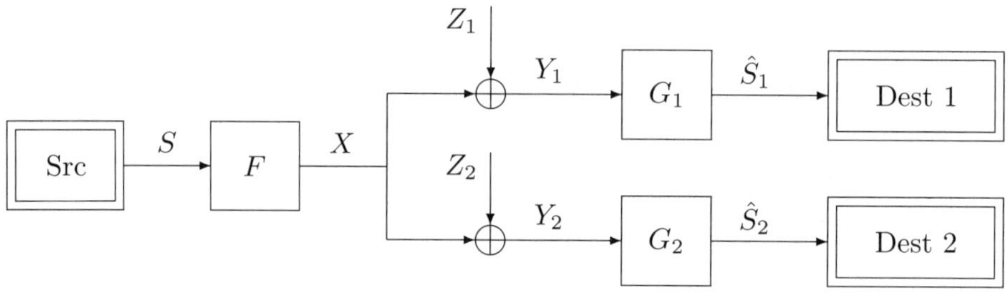

FIGURE 4. Single-source broadcast.

sign. In order to satisfy the constraint on D_2, we have to use a capacity-achieving code of rate C_2 to send to user 2 (the worse user). Can we superimpose another code for user 1? The answer is no: any superposition would be noise for user 2, and hence compromise D_2. Since the broadcast channel at hand is degraded, user 1 can also decode the codewords destined for user 2, hence the smallest D_1 that can be achieved with this scheme is $D_1 = D_2 = D_{\mathcal{N}}(C_2)$. However, it is quickly verified for this example that simply sending S without further coding achieves the distortions $D_1^* = D_{\mathcal{N}}(C_1)$ and $D_2^* = D_{\mathcal{N}}(C_2)$. In other words, the cost-distortion tuple (P, D_1^*, D_2^*) does not satisfy the relationship (2.1), yet it is achievable.

This example efficiently proves that there is no source-channel separation for networks: it is strictly suboptimal in general to send discrete messages in a reliable fashion across the channel part of the network.

3. Cut-set Arguments for Source-Channel Networks

It is well-known that the extension of the separation theorem to networks (as in Lemma 2.1) does not capture the best achievable performance in general. Therefore, our next goal is to derive upper bounds on the achievable performance. In this section, we consider a simple general way of doing this. Bounds are obtained by partitioning the network into two sets, and applying two-terminal results to these two sets. This is similar in spirit to the general upper bounds on the capacity region of a network presented in [**5**, Thm. 14.10.1].

It turns out that under certain circumstances, some of these upper bounds are achievable, thus specifying the *optimal* cost-distortion trade-offs. For a given network topology and cut, the probability distributions, channel input cost functions and distortion measures for which optimality can be established in this fashion could be called *tight sets*, and their significance is illustrated in Section 4.

3.1. Cut-set Outer Bounds for Source-Channel Networks. Bounds on the performance achievable in a source-channel network can be obtained by idealizing the source-channel network as a point-to-point source-channel communication system. Certainly, the optimum performance achievable in any of these idealizations cannot be inferior to the performance achievable in the source-channel network in question.

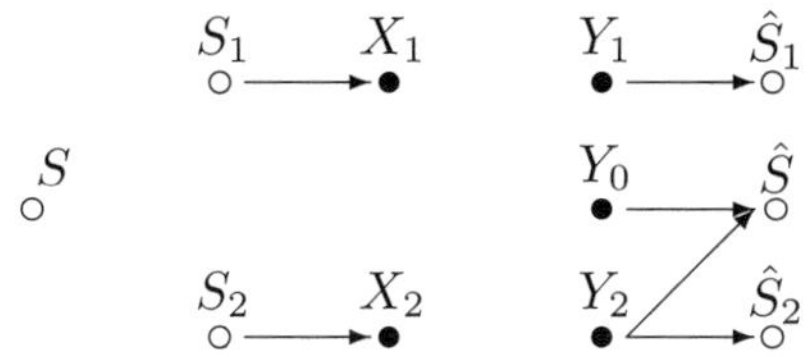

FIGURE 5. Schematic representation of the network of Figure 2.

General network topologies can be idealized as point-to-point communication systems in many different ways. In this paper, we propose the following graphical representation of a source-channel network: We denote source and destination points by empty bullets, and channel inputs and outputs by full bullets. Coding device relationships are represented by a directed edge. For the simple source-channel network of Figure 2, this leads to the graphical representation shown in Figure 5.

In order to find bounds on the achievable cost-distortion trade-offs, the network shown schematically in Figure 5 is now partitioned into two sets. Each set may contain source, channel input, channel output, and reconstruction nodes. We denote these sets by $\mathcal{T}$ and $\mathcal{T}^c$. Examples of such cuts are shown in Figures 6 and 7. The bounds are obtained by associating, with each cut, a point-to-point communication system. Without loss of generality, we take $\mathcal{T}$ to be the transmitting side in the corresponding point-to-point communication system, and $\mathcal{T}^c$ the receiving side. For the transmitting side, we have to identify the source set, denoted by $\mathcal{T}_s$, and the available channel inputs, denoted by $\mathcal{T}_t$. By analogy, for the receiving side, we have to identify the available channel outputs $\mathcal{T}_r^c$.

Before stating a general result, consider the following two examples:

EXAMPLE 3.1. For the cut shown in Figure 6, we find

$$\mathcal{T}_s = \{S, S_1, S_2\}, \ \ \mathcal{T}_t = \{X_1, X_2\}, \text{ and } \mathcal{T}_r^c = \{Y_0, Y_1, Y_2\}. \tag{3.1}$$

Obviously, the cost-distortion tuples (P_1, P_2, D, D_1, D_2) achievable in the network topology of Figure 2 must satisfy

$$R_{(S,S_1,S_2)}(D, D_1, D_2) \ \ \leq \ \ C_{(X_1,X_2)\to(Y_0,Y_1,Y_2)}(P_1, P_2), \tag{3.2}$$

where $R_{(S,S_1,S_2)}(D, D_1, D_2)$ denotes the rate-distortion function of the (vector) source (S, S_1, S_2) with respect to multiple distortion constraints D, D_1, D_2, and $C_{(X_1,X_2)\to(Y_0,Y_1,Y_2)}(P_1, P_2)$ the capacity of the (vector) channel with input (X_1, X_2), output (Y_0, Y_1, Y_2), and multiple cost constraints P_1, P_2. For short, we will denote the set of distortion constraints associated with a certain cut $\mathcal{T}$ by $D_{\mathcal{T}}$, and the set of power constraints by $P_{\mathcal{T}}$. Using this, the above bound is written, for short, as

$$R_{\mathcal{T}_s}(D_{\mathcal{T}}) \ \ \leq \ \ C_{\mathcal{T}_t \to \mathcal{T}_r^c}(P_{\mathcal{T}}). \tag{3.3}$$

To evaluate this condition, it is necessary to determine the rate-distortion and capacity-cost function under *multiple* distortion and cost constraints, respectively. The solution to this problem is well-known, see Appendix A.

EXAMPLE 3.2. For general partitions of the network, the situation is somewhat more involved. We illustrate this by the aid of the example shown in Figure 7. The source set is easily determined: both S_1 and $\hat{S}_1$ reside on the transmitting side $\mathcal{T}$,

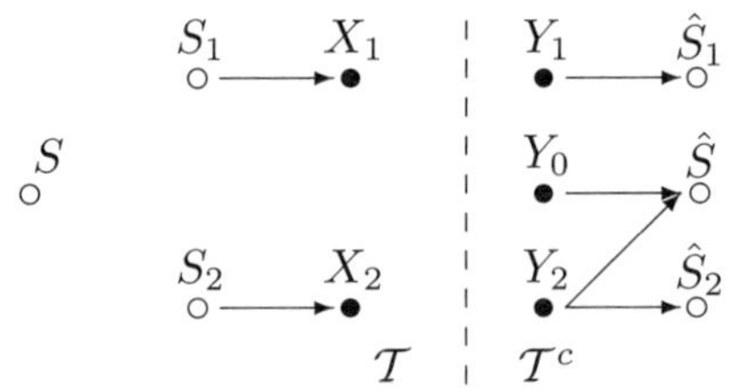

FIGURE 6

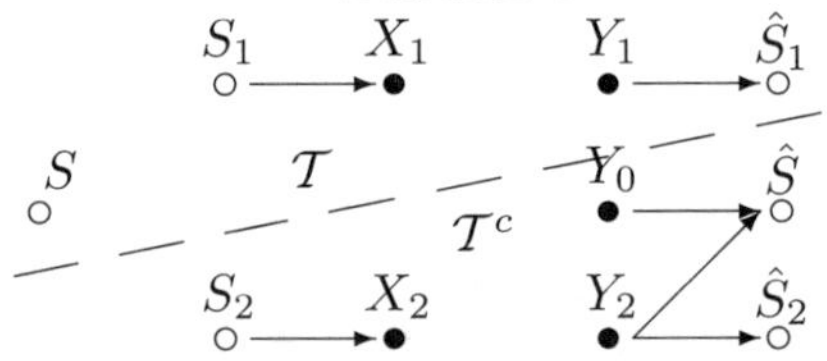

FIGURE 7

hence, in the idealized point-to-point communication system, S_1 does not play the role of a source that needs to be transmitted across the cut. Similarly, both S_2 and $\hat{S}_2$ reside on the receiving side $\mathcal{T}^c$. Hence, only S is to be communicated,

$$\mathcal{T}_s = \{S\}. \tag{3.4}$$

However, there are two choices to associate a role to S_2: it can be seen either as part of the receiving set $\mathcal{T}_r^c$, or as part of the side information set, which we denote by $\mathcal{T}_s^c$. If S_2 is seen as part of the receiving set, then the remaining sets have to be chosen as

$$\mathcal{T}_t = \{S, S_1, X_1\}, \quad \text{and} \quad \mathcal{T}_r^c = \{S_2, Y_0, Y_2\}. \tag{3.5}$$

If S_2 is seen as side information, then the remaining sets have to be chosen as

$$\mathcal{T}_t = \{X_1\}, \mathcal{T}_r^c = \{Y_0, Y_2\}, \quad \text{and} \quad \mathcal{T}_s^c = \{S_2\} \tag{3.6}$$

Moreover, for the cut at hand, the receiving side can transmit as well,

$$\mathcal{T}_t^c = \{X_2\}, \tag{3.7}$$

and there is a (noisy) feedback available to the transmitting side in the shape of Y_1.

As Example 3.2 illustrates, bounds *beyond* those of Example 3.1 can be obtained by not simply cutting the channel network, but also the source network. As we will illustrate in Section 4.2, this can lead to strictly tighter bounds. However, if the source network is cut, and hence, some sources belong to the receiving set $\mathcal{T}^c$, issues of side information must be discussed. Also, if the channel network is cut as in Figure 7, some channel outputs may belong to the transmitting set $\mathcal{T}$, essentially providing a feedback link. Therefore, it remains to determine the optimal cost-distortion trade-offs for a point-to-point communication system with *feedback* and *side information.*

1. The (point-to-point) source-channel communication problem with *feedback* has been studied (for the memoryless case) in [**15**] (see also the discussion in [**7, 10**]). In line with the result that feedback cannot increase the capacity

of a memoryless channel, it is found that feedback does not alter the set of achievable cost-distortion trade-offs. In our bounds, we may therefore omit feedback as long as the networks are memoryless.

2. The (point-to-point) source-channel communication problem with *side information* appears in [**7**, Ch.1]. It can be shown that the optimal cost-distortion trade-offs if the decoder has side information about the source are characterized by the Wyner-Ziv rate-distortion function and the capacity of the channel. A more general solution for the scenario where the encoder also has side information about the channel has been studied independently in [**17**].

EXAMPLE 3.3 (Example 3.2, continued). Hence, for the cut shown in Figure 7, we find the following two bounds:

$$R_S(D) \leq C_{(S,S_1,X_1)\to(S_2,Y_0,Y_2)|X_2}(P_1) \tag{3.8}$$

$$R^{WZ}_{S|S_2}(D) \leq C_{X_1\to(Y_0,Y_2)|X_2}(P_1) \tag{3.9}$$

where $C_{(S,S_1,X_1)\to(S_2,Y_0,Y_2)|X_2}(P_1)$ denotes the capacity of a (vector) channel with input (S, S_1, X_1) and output (S_2, Y_0, Y_2), i.e.,

$$C_{(S,S_1,X_1)\to(S_2,Y_0,Y_2)|X_2}(P_1) = \max I(S, S_1, X_1; S_2, Y_0, Y_2|X_2), \tag{3.10}$$

where the maximum is over probability distributions $p(s, s_1, x_1, x_2)$ that satisfy the cost constraint. Moreover, $R^{WZ}_{S|S_2}(\cdot)$ denotes the Wyner-Ziv rate-distortion function of S with respect to S_2 [**24, 23**]. Note that it cannot generally be decided which one of the two bounds is tighter.

In extension of these examples, one can generally cut a source-channel network into two parts, and idealize the resulting structure as a point-to-point communication system, potentially involving side information and/or feedback. This insight leads to the following statement:

THEOREM 3.4. *If the cost-distortion tuple $(P_1, \ldots, D_1, \ldots)$ is achievable, then it satisfies, for every partition $\mathcal{T}$ of the source-channel network, and every valid assignment of sets $\mathcal{T}_s$, $\mathcal{T}_t$, $\mathcal{T}_r^c$, $\mathcal{T}_t^c$, and $\mathcal{T}_s^c$,*

$$R^{WZ}_{\mathcal{T}_s|\mathcal{T}_s^c}(D_{\mathcal{T}}) \leq C_{\mathcal{T}_t\to\mathcal{T}_r^c|\mathcal{T}_t^c}(P_{\mathcal{T}}) \tag{3.11}$$

where $D_{\mathcal{T}}$ denotes the distortion constraints for all source-destination pairs separated by the cut $\mathcal{T}$, and $P_{\mathcal{T}}$ denotes the cost constraints for all channel inputs at the cut $\mathcal{T}$.

A precise characterization of *valid assignments* is in preparation [**8**]; the key requirement is that all involved sources and channel inputs and outputs must appear in order to obtain a valid bound. For example, for an assignment to be valid, the set $\mathcal{T}_s \cup \mathcal{T}_t$ must contain all the sources that belong to $\mathcal{T}$. The proof of this theorem is straightforward by considering the corresponding idealizations of the underlying network as point-to-point communication systems (potentially involving side information and/or feedback), and using the well-known optimality results for these point-to-point scenarios. More detailed arguments are in preparation [**8**].

REMARK 3.5. The rate-distortion and capacity-cost functions that appear in Equation (3.11) have potentially multiple cost and distortion constraints. This issue is discussed in Appendix A.

REMARK 3.6. There is a slight asymmetry to this theorem: In Equation (3.11), the left hand side is a Wyner-Ziv rate-distortion function [**24, 23**], and it is therefore tempting to guess that on the right, there should be a Gel'fand-Pinsker capacity-cost function [**9**]. This could be made into a valid bound, too: the side information at the encoder would be the channel outputs on the transmitting side, denoted by $\mathcal{T}_r$. For the example of Figure 7, $\mathcal{T}_r = \{Y_1\}$. However, this side information arrives *causally* and is influenced by the channel inputs. Hence, we can obtain a sharper bound by considering it as *feedback*, rather than side information. For the purpose of this exposition, we assumed for simplicity that the considered network is memoryless, and hence, feedback does not alter the bound. Therefore, $\mathcal{T}_r$ can be omitted entirely from the arguments in this case. Note that this asymmetry is witness to the fact that source sequences are thought of as *unclocked* (leading to side information), while channel sequences are *clocked* (leading to feedback), see [**16**].

3.2. Sufficient Conditions for Optimality. It is well known (see the illustrations discussed in Sections 2.2 and 2.3) that source-channel separation does not lead to optimal performance in general network situations. As a corollary to the outer bounds derived in the previous section, the following simple sufficient condition for optimality can be formulated.

COROLLARY 3.7. *For a coding scheme* $(F_1, \ldots, G_1, \ldots)$, *if there exists a set of cuts* $\mathcal{T}_1, \mathcal{T}_2, \ldots, \mathcal{T}_J$ *with the property that every source-destination pair of interest is separated by at least one of the cuts in the set, and for every cut in the set, there exists a valid assignment of sets* $\mathcal{T}_s$, $\mathcal{T}_t$, $\mathcal{T}_r^c$, $\mathcal{T}_t^c$, *and* $\mathcal{T}_s^c$, *such that*

$$R^{WZ}_{\mathcal{T}_s|\mathcal{T}_s^c}(D_{\mathcal{T}}) = C_{\mathcal{T}_t \to \mathcal{T}_r^c|\mathcal{T}_t^c}(P_{\mathcal{T}}), \tag{3.12}$$

or, equivalently, for arbitrary constants ρ_0 *and* $c_1, c_2 > 0$ *and a function* $d_0(s_{\mathcal{T}}, s_{\mathcal{T}^c})$,

$$\rho(x_{\mathcal{T}}, x_{\mathcal{T}^c}) = c_1 D\left(p_{Y_{\mathcal{T}}|x_{\mathcal{T}^c}, x_{\mathcal{T}}} || p_{Y_{\mathcal{T}}|x_{\mathcal{T}^c}}\right) + \rho_0, \tag{3.13}$$

$$d(s_{\mathcal{T}}, \hat{s}_{\mathcal{T}}, s_{\mathcal{T}^c}) = -c_2 \log_2 p(s_{\mathcal{T}}|\hat{s}_{\mathcal{T}}, s_{\mathcal{T}^c}) + d_0(s_{\mathcal{T}}, s_{\mathcal{T}^c}) \tag{3.14}$$

$$I(S_{\mathcal{T}}; Y_{\mathcal{T}^c}|S_{\mathcal{T}^c}) = I(X_{\mathcal{T}}; Y_{\mathcal{T}^c}|X_{\mathcal{T}^c}) \tag{3.15}$$

then the coding scheme performs optimally.[4]

The proof of the sufficiency of (3.12) follows directly from Theorem 3.4. The equivalent characterization given by (3.13)-(3.15) follows along the lines of [**11**] (and its extension to side information in [**19**]).

It is clear that in general network situations, the conditions of this corollary cannot be met. However, there are cases of network topologies and sets of cuts $\mathcal{T}_1, \mathcal{T}_2, \ldots, \mathcal{T}_J$ for which probability distributions, cost functions, and distortion measures can be found that satisfy Corollary 3.7. We will refer to this as the *tight set* of that cut:

DEFINITION 3.8 (tight set). For a fixed network topology and a fixed set of cuts, define the *tight set* to be the set of probability distributions, cost functions, and distortion measures, such that the conditions of Corollary 3.7 can be achieved.

According to this definition, a given network topology generally has many tight sets, one for each possible set of cuts. Tight sets are of interest in the analysis of scenarios for which optimality according to Corollary 3.7 cannot be achieved. In

[4]There are some technical conditions for (3.12) and (3.13)-(3.15), respectively, to be sufficient conditions for the optimality of a point-to-point communication system. See the discussion in [**11**].

such cases, one can still determine the tight set *closest* to the actual probability distributions, cost functions, and distortion measures, and design a coding scheme that *approaches* the optimality conditions for that particular tight set. This can lead to near-optimum performance, as illustrated in Remark 4.9 below.

In the next section, we present examples of topologies and corresponding cuts that have interesting (non-trivial) tight sets. A more detailed consideration of topologies, cuts, and their tight sets is in preparation [**8**].

4. Optimal Performance for Particular Network Topologies

In the remainder of this paper, we present examples of topologies and corresponding cuts for which the tight set is *interesting* in the sense that it contains non-trivial elements. This is relevant for two reasons: On the one hand, for those cases, the optimal performance can be determined (and achieved). On the other hand, as we illustrate, for networks that are *close* to the tight set, good (but not provably optimal) communication strategies can be supplied. These strategies are *good* in the sense that they considerably outperform any separation-based strategy in the considered cases.

4.1. Single-Source Broadcast Topology. The source-channel network topology shown in Figure 8 could be called *single-source broadcast*: a single source is broadcast to multiple destinations. There is one cost P as in (1.1), and M distortions D_m of the form (1.2), one for each output $\hat{S}_m$, $m = 1, \ldots, M$. What are the optimal cost-distortion tuples $(P, D_1, D_2, \ldots, D_M)$?

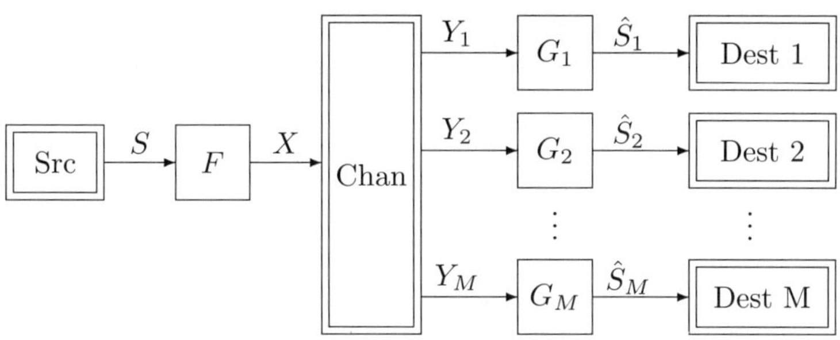

FIGURE 8. The single-source broadcast topology considered in this paper.

A partial answer can be obtained by considering different cuts in the topology shown in Figure 8, and by applying Corollary 3.7. Two natural cuts are shown in Figures 9 and 10. It is intuitive that the cut shown in Figure 9 does not have an interesting tight set: Generally, the capacity $C_{X \to (Y_1, Y_2, \ldots, Y_M)}$ appearing in the corresponding bound (Theorem 3.4) is much too optimistic. The cut illustrated in Figure 10, on the other hand, has an interesting tight set. More precisely, consider along with the cut of Figure 10 the corresponding cut for each of the remaining $M-1$ destinations, i.e., $\mathcal{T}^c = \{Y_m, \hat{S}_m\}$, for $m = 1, 2, \ldots, M$. They induce the following incarnation of Corollary 3.7.

COROLLARY 4.1. *If the coding system* $(F, G_1, G_2, \ldots, G_M)$ *satisfies, for each* $m \in \{1, \ldots, M\}$,

$$R_S(D_m) = C_{X \to Y_m}(P), \tag{4.1}$$

or, equivalently,

$$\rho(x) = c_1^{(m)} D(p_{Y|X}^{(m)}(\cdot|x)||p_Y(\cdot)) + \rho_0^{(m)}, \tag{4.2}$$

$$d^{(m)}(s, \hat{s}_m) = -c_2^{(m)} \log_2 p^{(m)}(s|\hat{s}_m) + d_0^{(m)}(s), \tag{4.3}$$

$$I(S; \hat{S}_m) = I(X; Y_m), \tag{4.4}$$

then it performs optimally.

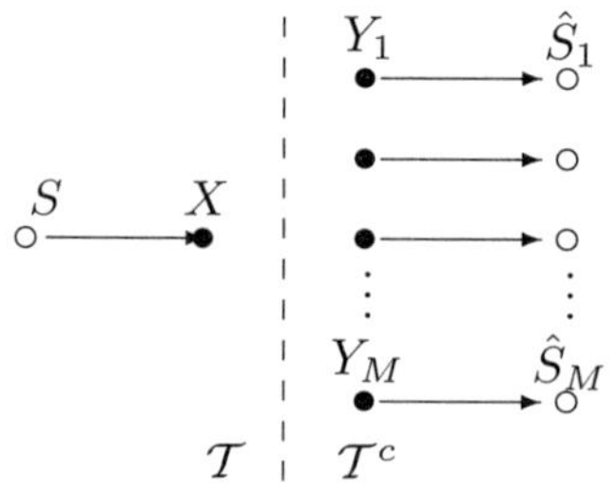

FIGURE 9

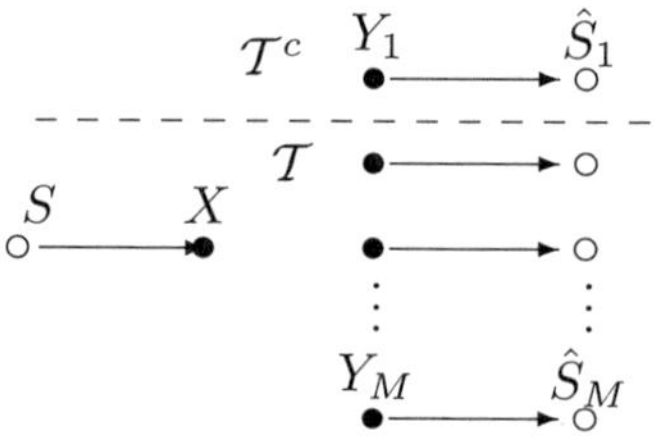

FIGURE 10

Gaussian Scenario. The set of source-channel networks that satisfy Corollary 4.1 is non-empty: One example of a situation where there exists a coding scheme that satisfies the conditions of Corollary 4.1 was discussed in Section 2.3. More generally, the following holds:

THEOREM 4.2. *For the Gaussian example, i.e., $p(s) \sim \mathcal{N}(0, \sigma_S^2)$, $p(y_i|x) \sim \mathcal{N}(x, \sigma_i^2)$, there exists a coding scheme that achieves the conditions of Corollary 4.1 with equality, i.e., it performs optimally.*

PROOF. The converse follows immediately from Corollary 4.1. The achievability is proved by considering uncoded transmission, see [**7**] for further details. □

REMARK 4.3. (scaling laws, and the suboptimality of separate source and channel coding) As explained in the discussion of Section 2.3, separate source and channel coding is strictly sub-optimal in all non-trivial cases. To illustrate this, let us consider the difference in sum distortion between the optimal scheme and separate source/channel coding. Consider thus the network shown in Figure 4 with M branches (instead of 2), and suppose that all the noise variances are strictly larger than zero and strictly smaller than infinity. Moreover, suppose that no more than a fraction αM, for some $\alpha < 1$, of the noise variances are equal. Then, the difference

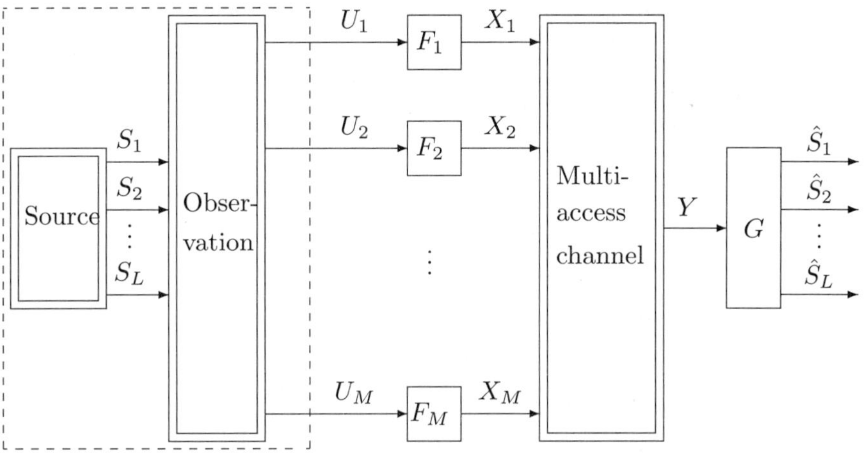

FIGURE 11. The multiple access topology considered in this paper.

between the minimal sum distortion $D_{sum,opt}$ and the sum distortion achieved by separate source and channel coding $D_{sum,sep}$ behaves like

$$D_{sum,opt} - D_{sum,sep} \quad \sim \quad M. \tag{4.5}$$

Note that since the distortion at each destination is bounded by the source variance, linear scaling behavior (as achieved by the separation-based scheme) is the worst possible scaling behavior.

Beyond the Gaussian Scenario. Corollary 4.1 also permits to construct other examples, and reveals the structure of a situation for which optimality can be achieved: the marginal distributions of the M channels in the broadcast scenario must all induce the same Kullback-Leibler divergence in Corollary 3.7 (up to shifts and scales), since there is only one cost function $\rho(x)$ in the single-source topology. The distortion functions, on the other hand, can always be picked according to Corollary 4.1.

4.2. Multiple Access Topology.

The source-channel network topology shown in Figure 11 is a multiple access scenario, modeling for example a sensor network topology. The schematic representation of the network of Figure 11 is shown in Figures 12 and 13, using the shorthand $S = (S_1, S_2, \ldots, S_L)$. One intuitive cut for this network is shown in Figure 12. Again, the tight set of this cut is of limited interest because the corresponding capacity bound in Theorem 3.4 is loose. The cut shown in Figure 13 leads to more interesting results, as we illustrate in the sequel. Corollary 3.7 provides the following optimality condition for the cut of Figure 13:

COROLLARY 4.4. *If the coding system $F_1, F_2, \ldots, F_M, G$ satisfies*

$$R_S(D) \quad = \quad C_{S \to (U_1, \ldots, U_M)}, \tag{4.6}$$

or, equivalently,

$$d(s, \hat{s}) \quad = \quad -c_2 \log_2 p(s|\hat{s}) + d_0(s) \tag{4.7}$$

$$I(S; U_1 U_2 \ldots U_M) \quad = \quad I(S; \hat{S}), \tag{4.8}$$

then it performs optimally.

REMARK 4.5. Note that there is no cost constraint for the cut in Figure 13. This fact can be elegantly exploited to simplify (3.13)-(3.15): there is no condition involving $\rho(\cdot)$. The remaining conditions are (4.7) and (4.8).

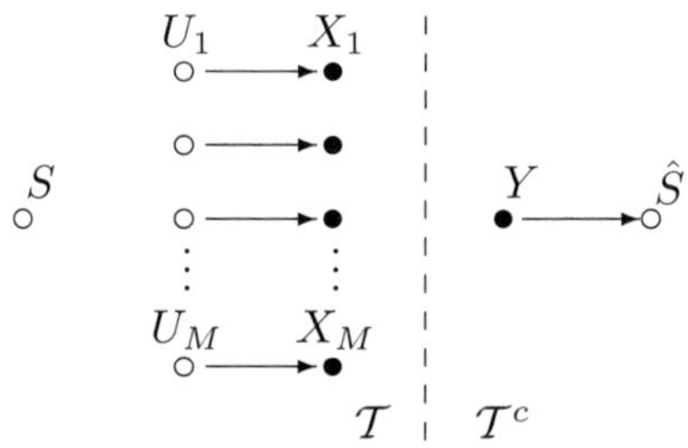

FIGURE 12

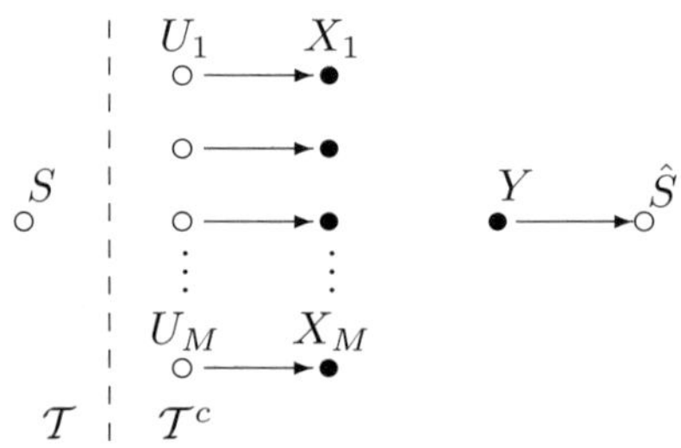

FIGURE 13

REMARK 4.6. There are many more bounds corresponding to the cut shown in Figure 13 since each of the sources $U_1, \ldots, U_M$ can alternatively be seen as side information. Suppose all of them are considered side information. Then, Theorem 3.4 provides the bound

$$R^{WZ}_{S|U_1,\ldots,U_M}(D) \leq 0, \tag{4.9}$$

which is a trivial insight since $U_1, \ldots, U_M$ are, in fact, the only knowledge available about S.

Gaussian Scenario. Figure 14 shows a concrete example of a topology according to Figure 11 for which optimality according to Corollary 4.4 can be achieved, at least asymptotically as the number of (sensor) nodes tends to infinity. We assume S to be a sequence of independent and identically distributed (iid) Gaussian random variables of mean zero and variance σ_S^2, and each of the W_k ("measurement noises") is also iid Gaussian of mean zero and variance σ^2. We also assume the measurement noises to be independent of each other. The constraint on the signals transmitted by the sensors is a sum power constraint $\sum_{k=1}^{M} \lim_{n\to\infty} \frac{1}{n} E\left[\|X_k^n\|^2\right] \leq MP$. The final destination receives

$$Y = \sum_{k=1}^{M} X_k + Z, \tag{4.10}$$

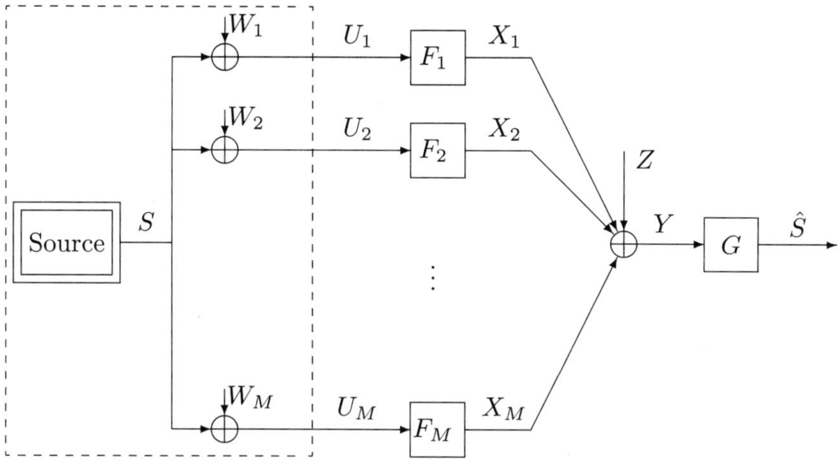

FIGURE 14. The Gaussian example.

where Z is iid Gaussian noise of variance σ_Z^2. The distortion measure in this example is the mean-squared error, measured between sequences S^n and $\hat{S}^n$, as in (1.2).

THEOREM 4.7. *For the Gaussian example, there is a coding scheme that satisfies the cost constraint and*

$$|s-\hat{s}|^2 = -\log_2 p(s|\hat{s}) \tag{4.11}$$

$$\lim_{M\to\infty} I(S;U_1U_2\ldots U_M) - I(S;\hat{S}) = 0. \tag{4.12}$$

That is, it is asymptotically optimal.

The proof of this theorem is given in Appendix B.1.

REMARK 4.8. (scaling laws, and the suboptimality of separate source and channel coding) It can be shown that the corresponding distortion satisfies, as a function of M,

$$\lim_{M\to\infty} MD(M) = 1. \tag{4.13}$$

This is shown as a byproduct of the proof (see Equation (B.4)), and is explained in more detail in [**12**]. An alternative strategy is for each node to encode its observation into bits (using the principles of distributed compression), and to transmit these bits across the multiple-access channel in a reliable fashion. This strategy is in the spirit of the separation theorem, and its performance is bounded by Lemma 2.1. In order to apply this lemma, the key difficulty is to determine the rate-distortion region for the source network (the contents of the dashed box in Figure 14) and the capacity region for the channel network. The source network is also known as the Gaussian CEO problem [**2, 22, 18**], and the channel network is a simple Gaussian multiple access channel, but with potentially dependent messages (see the discussion in Section 2.2). For both problems, only partial results are known, but they are sufficient to establish that for a fixed channel input constraint MP, the distortion satisfies

$$\lim_{M\to\infty} (\log M)D(M) = 1. \tag{4.14}$$

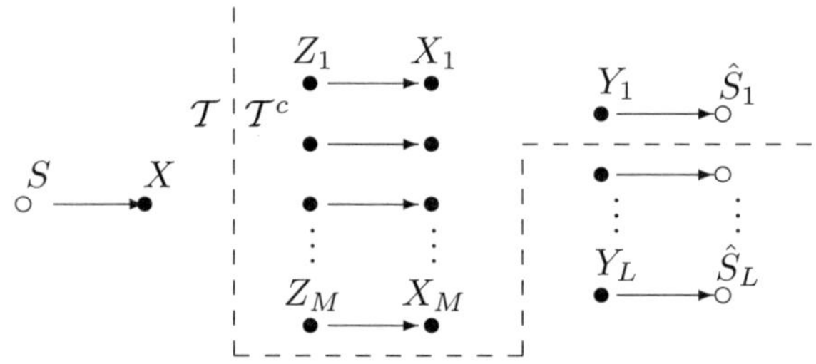

FIGURE 15. A single-source broadcast scenario with relays.

This illustrates that the shortcomings of applying the separation paradigm to source-channel networks may be considerable: the distortion at large M is exponentially larger (as a function of M).

REMARK 4.9 (coding paradigms). For finite M, the conditions of Corollary 4.4 cannot be met with equality, and the optimal performance is unknown to date. However, the comparison of (4.13) with (4.14) reveals immediately that even for moderate M, the coding strategy used to prove Theorem 4.7 *considerably* outperforms any separation-based scheme. Hence, in this example, designing a code that attempts to approach the conditions of Corollary 4.4 is a much more promising strategy than source/channel separation. This suggests an alternative coding paradigm for source-channel networks. This is discussed in more detail in [**12**].

Beyond the Gaussian Scenario. Condition (4.8) of Corollary 4.4 is difficult to meet with equality in many interesting situations: if the multiple access section introduces independent noise, then it is clear that the two mutual information expressions in (4.8) will not generally be equal. However, as the number M of (sensor) nodes increases, the effect of this additive noise disappears. This is true independent of the distribution of that noise. Once Condition (4.8) is satisfied, the distortion measure can be chosen according to (4.7) and optimal performance results. For example, let the (measurement) noises W_k in Figure 14 have arbitrary distribution. This will generally induce a distortion measure *different* from the mean-squared error. However, as the number M of sensors tends to infinity (and under appropriate technical conditions), the distribution of the *sum* of the measurement noises tends to the Gaussian by the central limit theorem. This lets the distortion measure go to the mean-squared error (which can be established along the lines of the proof given in Appendix B.1). This is explained in more detail in [**12**].

4.3. Broadcast Topology with Relays. As a third example, consider the *combination* of single-source broadcast with relays, as illustrated schematically in Figure 15. A cut with an interesting tight set is also shown: Using a combination of arguments similar to the ones leading to Theorems 4.2 and 4.7, it can be shown that as $M \to \infty$, the tight set includes the case where the source is Gaussian, all the channels are standard additive white Gaussian, and the distortion measure is the mean-squared error. Further details will be presented in [**8**].

5. Conclusions

With the advent of sensor networks, it is important to study the behavior of networks that involve both sources and channels, and where the goal is *lossy* transmission of information: The destinations typically want to get the best estimate of the sources, to within a certain fidelity criterion (i.e., distortion measure). For the point-to-point case, this problem has a very elegant solution in the shape of the source-channel separation theorem [**20**, Thm. 21]. No comparably elegant solution for the corresponding network problem has been found to date, and in fact, the optimal achievable performance for general network situations is unknown. It seems that the capacity of the involved channel network, and the rate-distortion region of the involved source network, even if they were known, are quantities of limited interest in the determination of the optimal achievable performance.

This paper studies a simple upper bounding technique for the optimal achievable performance, along with the conditions under which these (generally rather loose) upper bounds are indeed achievable. The investigated technique considers *cuts* (or partitions) of the network, and introduces the notion of the *tight set* for a cut through a network: the set of probability distributions, channel input constraints, and distortion measures, for which the upper bound determined by the particular cut can indeed be achieved. This notion is illustrated by three examples. For all these examples, it is shown that a strategy that separates source from channel coding performs suboptimally in a strong sense: it has a different *scaling behavior* (as the number of nodes in the network grows). For this reason, our arguments may lead to a relevant alternative coding paradigm for source-channel networks.

The nature of information. The separation theorem ensures that information can be righteously thought of as *bits* in the point-to-point case. However, the fact the separation theorem does not extend to networks (and, in fact, can lead to severely suboptimal performance) suggests that bits are *not* the right intuition to understand information in a source-channel network context. The approach presented in this paper may lead to an alternative understanding in terms of *matched measures*.

Acknowledgments

This work is an extension of joint work of the author with Prof. Martin Vetterli (EPFL). The author would also like to acknowledge fruitful discussions with Dr. Gerhard Kramer (Bell Labs) and Prof. Emre Telatar (EPFL), and would like to thank the organizers for this inspiring workshop on network information theory.

Appendix A. Rate-distortion and Capacity-cost with multiple constraints

To apply Theorem 3.4, the ingredients of Equation (3.11) need to be studied in more detail. On the left hand side of the inequality appears the rate-distortion function of a source with respect to multiple distortion measures (and potentially with side information at the decoder). For the scalar case without side information, this appears (without explicit proof) in [**4**, p. 134]. The extension of their result to the vector case is straightforward (at least in the case of discrete, finite alphabets). Combining these arguments with the arguments of Wyner and Ziv [**24, 23**] leads to the following lemma:

LEMMA A.1. *The Wyner-Ziv rate-distortion function for the source S_1 and the side information S_2 is given by*

$$R^{WZ}_{S_1|S_2}(D_1, D_2, \ldots) = \min I(W; S_1) - I(W; S_2) \tag{A.1}$$

where the minimum is over all conditional distributions $p(w|s_1)$ for which there exists a decoder such that for each distortion constraint,

$$Ed(S_1, g_i(W, S_2)) \leq D_i. \tag{A.2}$$

The evaluation of the right hand side of Equation (3.11) requires the computation of the capacity of a vector point-to-point channel with multiple cost constraints. For the scalar case, this appears, also without explicit proof, in [**4**, p. 117]. We quote their statement in the following lemma.

LEMMA A.2. *The capacity of the channel with input X and output Y subject to the cost constraints $E\rho_i(X) \leq P_i$ is given by*

$$C_{X\to Y}(P_1, P_2, \ldots) = \max I(X; Y) \tag{A.3}$$

where the maximum is over all conditional distributions $p(x)$ that satisfy all the cost constraints.

Appendix B. Proofs

B.1. Proof of Theorem 4.7.

PROOF. The converse is given by Corollary 4.4.

The proof of the achievability requires the consideration of a suitable coding strategy. Suppose the sensors apply uncoded transmission. More precisely, sensor k scales $U_k[n]$ to meet its power constraint P,

$$X_k[n] = \sqrt{\frac{P}{\sigma_S^2 + \sigma_W^2}} U_k[n]. \tag{B.1}$$

Recalling that $U_k[n] = S[n] + W_k[n]$, the received signal for the uncoded strategy is

$$Y[n] = \sqrt{\frac{P}{\sigma_S^2 + \sigma_W^2}} \left(MS[n] + \sum_{k=1}^{M} W_k[n] \right) + Z[n]. \tag{B.2}$$

It remains to specify the decoder. Since the encoding operation is memoryless, the optimum decoder (or estimator) G is also memoryless: there is no benefit from considering multiple symbols jointly. The optimum decoder G is then simply the minimum mean-squared error estimator of $S[n]$, given by the standard formula:

$$\hat{S}[n] = \frac{E[SY]}{E[Y^2]} Y[n] = \frac{\sqrt{\frac{P}{\sigma_S^2+\sigma_W^2}} M\sigma_S^2}{\frac{P}{\sigma_S^2+\sigma_W^2}(M^2\sigma_S^2 + M\sigma_W^2) + \sigma_Z^2} Y[n]. \tag{B.3}$$

We can directly evaluate the distortion,

$$\begin{aligned} D_1(MP) &= E|S[n]-\hat{S}[n]|^2 \\ &= \sigma_S^2 - \frac{\frac{P}{\sigma_S^2+\sigma_W^2}M^2\sigma_S^4}{\frac{P}{\sigma_S^2+\sigma_W^2}(M^2\sigma_S^2+M\sigma_W^2)+\sigma_Z^2} \\ &= \frac{\sigma_S^2\sigma_W^2}{\frac{M^2}{M+(\sigma_Z^2/\sigma_W^2)(\sigma_S^2+\sigma_W^2)/P}\sigma_S^2+\sigma_W^2}. \end{aligned} \tag{B.4}$$

We now establish that the suggested coding scheme indeed satisfied conditions (4.7) and (4.8) for the Gaussian example. Consider first condition (4.7). Since $S[n]$ and $\hat{S}[n]$ are jointly Gaussian, we can write $S[n]$ in terms of $\hat{S}[n]$ as follows:

$$S[n] = \frac{E\left[S\hat{S}\right]}{E\left[\hat{S}^2\right]}\hat{S}[n]+W'[n], \tag{B.5}$$

where $W'[n]$ is additive white Gaussian noise. Since $\hat{S}$ is the minimum mean-squared error estimate of S, we find that $E[S\hat{S}]/E[\hat{S}^2]=1$, and hence $S[n]=\hat{S}[n]+W'[n]$. This immediately reveals that $P(s|\hat{s})$ is given by the distribution of $W'[n]$. Since it is Gaussian, we find

$$-\log_2 P(s|\hat{s}) = d_1(s-\hat{s})^2+d_0(s), \tag{B.6}$$

i.e., mean-squared error distortion. The variance of the noise $W'[n]$ is irrelevant for this argument; it only influences the constant d_1. This means that condition (4.7) is satisfied by the Gaussian example (for any M).

For condition (4.8) in our Gaussian example, equality is only achieved asymptotically as the number of sensors tends to infinity. We now analyze this in detail. From (B.3), $\hat{S}$ can be rewritten as

$$\hat{S}[n] = \frac{\frac{P}{\sigma_S^2+\sigma_W^2}M\sigma_S^2}{\frac{P}{\sigma_S^2+\sigma_W^2}(M^2\sigma_S^2+M\sigma_W^2)+\sigma_Z^2}\left(MS[n]+\sum_{i=1}^{M}W_k[n]+\sqrt{\frac{\sigma_S^2+\sigma_W^2}{P}}Z[n]\right).$$

The mutual information expression can be written out as

$$\begin{aligned} I(S;U_1,U_2,\ldots,U_M) &= I(S;\hat{S},U_1,U_2,\ldots,U_M) \\ &= I(S;\hat{S})+I(S;U_1,U_2,\ldots,U_M|\hat{S}). \end{aligned} \tag{B.7}$$

Hence, the difference between the mutual information expressions in (4.8) can be calculated as

$$\begin{aligned} I(S;U_1,U_2,\ldots,U_M)-I(S;\hat{S}) &= I(S;U_1,U_2,\ldots,U_M|\hat{S}) \\ &= h(S|\hat{S})-h(S|U_1,U_2,\ldots,U_M,\hat{S}) \\ &= h(S|\hat{S})-h(S|U_1,U_2,\ldots,U_M) \\ &= h(S|\hat{S})-h(S|U_1+U_2+\ldots+U_M) \end{aligned} \tag{B.8}$$

To make notation somewhat more compact, we define $U=U_1+U_2+\ldots+U_M$, and we replace $\hat{S}$ by a scaled version $\hat{S}'=MS[n]+\sum_{k=1}^{M}W_k[n]+\sqrt{(\sigma_S^2+\sigma_W^2)/P}Z[n]$. Clearly,

$$h(S|\hat{S})-h(S|U_1+U_2+\ldots+U_M) = h(S|\hat{S}')-h(S|U). \tag{B.9}$$

Finally, we use the shorthand

$$\beta = \frac{\sigma_S^2 + \sigma_W^2}{P} \frac{\sigma_Z^2}{\sigma_W^2}. \tag{B.10}$$

Denote by $\Sigma_{V_1,\ldots,V_K}$ the covariance matrix of the random vector $(V_1, \ldots, V_K)$. We find

$$\Sigma_{\hat{S}',S,U} = \begin{pmatrix} M^2\sigma_S^2 + (M+\beta)\sigma_W^2 & M\sigma_S^2 & M^2\sigma_S^2 + M\sigma_W^2 \\ M\sigma_S^2 & \sigma_S^2 & M\sigma_S^2 \\ M^2\sigma_S^2 + M\sigma_W^2 & M\sigma_S^2 & M^2\sigma_S^2 + M\sigma_W^2 \end{pmatrix}, \tag{B.11}$$

which permits to determine easily the required mutual information expression, as follows:

$$\begin{aligned} I(S; U_1, U_2, \ldots, U_M) - I(S; \hat{S}) &= I(S; U_1, U_2, \ldots, U_M | \hat{S}) \\ &= h(S|\hat{S}') - h(S|U) \\ &= h(S, \hat{S}') - h(\hat{S}') - h(S, U) + h(U) \\ &= \log_2 \frac{\det \Sigma_{S,\hat{S}} \det \Sigma_U}{\det \Sigma_{\hat{S}} \det \Sigma_{S,U}} \\ &= \log_2 \frac{(M+\beta)\sigma_S^2\sigma_W^2(M^2\sigma_S^2 + M\sigma_W^2)}{(M^2\sigma_S^2 + (M+\beta)\sigma_W^2)M\sigma_S^2\sigma_W^2} \\ &= \log_2 \frac{(M+\beta)(M^2\sigma_S^2 + M\sigma_W^2)}{M(M^2\sigma_S^2 + (M+\beta)\sigma_W^2)}. \end{aligned} \tag{B.12}$$

This converges to zero as

$$\begin{aligned} I(S; U_1, U_2, \ldots, U_M) - I(S; \hat{S}) &= \log_2 \left(1 + \frac{\beta}{M}\right) \\ &= \frac{\beta/\ln 2}{M} - \frac{\beta^2/\ln 2}{M^2} + \frac{\beta^3/\ln 2}{M^3} - \ldots + \ldots, \end{aligned} \tag{B.13}$$

which is the standard series expansion of the logarithm. In other words, the limit in condition (4.12) converges like $1/M$. □

References

[1] T. Berger, *Rate distortion theory: A mathematical basis for data compression*, Prentice-Hall, Englewood Cliffs, NJ, 1971.
[2] T. Berger, Z. Zhang, and H. Viswanathan, "The CEO problem", *IEEE Trans. Inform. Theory*, vol. IT–42, 1996, pp. 887–902.
[3] T. M. Cover, A. A. El Gamal and M. Salehi, "Multiple access channels with arbitrarily correlated sources", *IEEE Trans. Inform. Theory*, vol. 26, no. 6, 1980, pp. 648–657.
[4] I. Csiszár and J. Körner, *Information theory: Coding theory for discrete memoryless systems*, Academic Press, New York, 1981.
[5] T. M. Cover and J. A. Thomas, *Elements of information theory*, Wiley, New York, 1991.
[6] R. L. Dobrushin, "General formulation of Shannon's basic theorems of information theory", *AMS Transl.*, vol. 33, 1963, pp. 323–438.
[7] M. Gastpar, *To code or not to code*, Ph.D. thesis, Ecole Polytechnique Fédérale (EPFL), Lausanne, Switzerland, 2002.
[8] M. Gastpar, "Cut-set bounds for source-channel networks", in preparation.
[9] S. Gel'fand and M. Pinsker, "Coding for channel with random parameters", *Problems of Control and Information Theory*, vol. 9, 1980, pp. 19–31.
[10] M. Gastpar and B. Rimoldi, "Source-channel communication with feedback", *Proc 2002 IEEE Information Theory Workshop*, Paris, France, Apr. 2003, invited paper.

[11] M. Gastpar, B. Rimoldi and M. Vetterli, "To code, or not to code: Lossy source-channel communication revisited", *IEEE Trans. Inform. Theory*, vol. 49, no. 5, 2003, pp. 1147–1158.

[12] M. Gastpar and M. Vetterli, "Source-channel communication in sensor networks", in *Proc. 2nd International Workshop on Information Processing in Sensor Networks (IPSN'03)*, Leonidas J. Guibas and Feng Zhao, eds., Lecture Notes in Computer Science, Springer, New York, NY, Apr. 2003, pp. 162–177.

[13] A. N. Kolmogorov, "On the Shannon theory of information in the case of continuous signals", *IEEE Trans. Inform. Theory*, vol. IT–2, 1956, 102–108.

[14] G. Kramer, "Capacity results for the discrete memoryless network", *IEEE Trans. Inform. Theory*, vol. 49, no. 1, 2003, pp. 4–21.

[15] J. L. Massey, "Causality, feedback and directed information", in *Proc. 1990 Int'l Symp. Inform. Theory and Its Applications (ISITA'90)*, Hawaii, U.S.A., Nov. 1990, pp. 303–305.

[16] J. L. Massey, "Network information theory: Some tentative definitions", DIMACS Workshop on Network Information Theory, Mar. 2003.

[17] N. Merhav and S. Shamai, "On joint source-channel coding for the Wyner-Ziv source and the Gel'fand-Pinsker channel", *IEEE Trans. Inform. Theory*, submitted in 2002.

[18] Y. Oohama, "The rate-distortion function for the quadratic Gaussian CEO problem", *IEEE Trans. Inform. Theory*, vol. IT–44, no. 3, 1998, pp. 1057–1070.

[19] S. S. Pradhan, J. Chou and K. Ramchandran, "Duality between source coding and channel coding and its extension to the side information case", *IEEE Trans. Inform. Theory*, vol. IT–49, no. 5, 2003, pp. 1181–1209.

[20] C. E. Shannon, "A mathematical theory of communication", *Bell Sys. Tech. Journal*, vol. 27, 1948, pp. 379–423, pp. 623–656.

[21] C. E. Shannon, "Coding theorems for a discrete source with a fidelity criterion", *IRE Nat'l Conv. Rec.*, Mar. 1959, pp. 142–163.

[22] H. Viswanathan and T. Berger, "The quadratic Gaussian CEO problem", *IEEE Trans. Inform. Theory*, vol. IT–43, no. 5, pp. 1549–1559, 1997.

[23] A. D. Wyner, "The rate-distortion function for source coding with side information at the decoder-II: General sources", *Information and Control*, vol. 38, pp. 60–80, 1978.

[24] A. D. Wyner and J. Ziv, "The rate-distortion function for source coding with side information at the receiver", *IEEE Trans. Inform. Theory*, no. IT–22, pp. 1–11, 1976.

Department of EECS, University of California, Berkeley, CA 94720-1770, U.S.A.
E-mail address: gastpar@eecs.berkeley.edu

DIMACS Series in Discrete Mathematics
and Theoretical Computer Science
Volume **66**, 2004

Duality in Multi-user Source and Channel Coding

S. Sandeep Pradhan and Kannan Ramchandran

ABSTRACT. In this paper we address duality between source coding and channel coding and consider extensions of this concept to the case of source and channel coding with side information and to the case of multi-input-multi-output (MIMO) source and channel coding with one-sided collaboration. In the side information case, using this duality, we are able to extend the no rate-loss result of Wyner-Ziv from the Gaussian case to more general distributions. Our notion of duality in this paper is in a functional sense, where the optimal encoder mapping for a MIMO source coding problem becomes identical to the optimal decoder mapping for the dual MIMO channel coding problem, and vice versa. For ease of illustration we give the formulation only for two-input-two-output systems, which can be easily extended to the MIMO case. We present the precise mathematical conditions under which these encoder-decoder mappings are swappable in the two dual MIMO problems, identifying the key roles played by the source distortion and channel cost measures respectively in the MIMO source and channel coding problems in capturing this duality.

1. Introduction

Classical source coding under a distortion constraint and channel coding under a channel cost constraint have long been considered as information-theoretic duals[1] of each other starting from Shannon's landmark paper in 1959 [**3**]. In the source coding (rate-distortion) problem, the goal is to find, for a given source distribution, the conditional distribution between the input source alphabet and the output reconstruction alphabet that minimizes the mutual information [**4**] between the input source and the output reconstruction subject to a target distortion constraint corresponding to a given distortion measure. In the channel coding (capacity-cost) problem, the goal is to find, for a given channel input-output conditional distribution, the channel input distribution that maximizes the mutual information between input and output subject to a target channel cost (or power) constraint corresponding to a channel cost measure.

Cover and Thomas [**4**] point out that these two problems are information-theoretic duals of each other. This duality has also been exploited in the formulation of numerical optimization algorithms for the channel capacity and rate-distortion

---

Key words and phrases. functional duality, source coding, channel coding, side information.

The work was supported in part by NSF ITR grant CCR-0219735, and DARPA Sensor Information Technology Office under the Sensorwebs project F30602-00-2-0538.

[1]This should not be confused for Lagrangian duality in optimization theory [**2**].

problems using the Blahut-Arimoto algorithm [**5**]. In [**4**] (see Sec 13.5 in [**4**]), a packing versus covering interpretation of duality in Gaussian source and channel coding has been formulated to illustrate this duality. Indeed, some of the solutions to practical source coding (respectively channel coding) have been inspired by solutions to channel coding (source coding): e.g., trellis-coded quantization [**6, 7**] in source coding has been inspired by trellis-coded modulation [**8, 7**] in channel coding, and shaping of constellation points [**9**] in channel coding has been inspired by constraining of entropy of quantization points [**10**] in source coding. In [**7**] a duality between quantization and modulation has been analyzed.

In this tutorial paper, we provide a summary of our work [**22, 23, 24**] on functional duality in multi-user source coding and channel coding problems. Specifically, Section 2 and 3 contain a summary of [**24**] and Section 4 contains a summary of [**23**]. As a first step towards this goal, we first address the more classical duality between source and channel coding with the objective of providing a mathematical characterization of their *functional* duality. To be specific, given an optimal source (respectively channel) coding scheme, given by the encoder and decoder, we detail the conditions under which such a scheme is a functional dual to a channel (source) coding scheme, given by the encoder and decoder, in the sense that the optimal encoder mapping for one problem is functionally identical to the optimal decoder mapping for the other problem. We show in the sequel that this functional duality is enabled through appropriate choices of measures and constraints for the dual source (or channel) coding problem. Our inspiration for this formulation is derived from recent work by Gastpar et al. on measure-matching for uncoded communications [**12**].

We then extend this duality to the case of coding with side information, where we study the duality between source coding with side information (SCSI) at the decoder, and channel coding with side information (CCSI) at the encoder. These problems have attracted considerable attention in recent times due to a large class of relevant applications related to both problems. In this paper, we explore the information-theoretic duality between these two problems, and provide a mathematical characterization of the conditions under which they become functional duals, i.e. the encoder for one problem is exchangeable for the decoder of the other.

As an example, we will show that the problem of encoding a memoryless Gaussian source with correlated Gaussian side-information available at the decoder studied by Wyner and Ziv in [**1**] is a functional dual to the Gaussian watermarking problem studied in [**15, 16**], related to the problem of "writing on dirty paper" considered by Costa in [**19**]. Recently, Costa's result [**19**] has been generalized from the case of Gaussian side information to more arbitrary distributions in [**20, 21**]. By invoking our duality concepts, we are able to find a similar generalization of the result of Wyner-Ziv [**1**] relating to no rate-loss for source coding with side information from Gaussian to more arbitrary distributions. Rate-loss refers to the performance loss due to the presence of side information at only one end (decoder only in source coding and encoder only in channel coding) rather than at both ends. A goal of this paper is to inspire the practical dual use of functional blocks for the two problems, building on our preliminary work in [**22**]. It is illuminating to note that both problems have recently inspired promising constructive frameworks based on coset codes that are underpinned by the relevant information-theoretic concepts, e.g. [**27, 16, 22, 28, 21**] for the channel coding problem, and [**29, 30**] for the source coding problem.

Study of this functional duality serves two important purposes: (i) it provides new insights into these problems from the different perspectives of source and channel coding, and allows for cross-leveraging of advances in the individual fields; (ii) more importantly, it provides a basis for sharing efficient constructions of the encoder and decoder functions in the two problems, e.g., through the use of structured algebraic codes, turbo-like codes, trellis-based codes, etc.

Finally, we extend this notion of functional duality to more instances of MIMO source and channel coding problems. We study various MIMO structures admitting different scenarios of collaboration among multi-terminal inputs and/or outputs[2]. The collaboration scenarios we consider involve those where *either* the multi-terminal encoders *or* the multi-terminal decoders can collaborate, i.e. be joint, but not both[3]. Under this one-sided collaboration abstraction, we address four problems of interest in source and channel coding: 1) distributed source coding, 2) broadcast channel coding 3) multiple description source coding with no excess sum-rate, and 4) multiple access channel coding with independent message sets. In 1) and 4), the decoders collaborate, whereas in 2) and 3), the encoders collaborate. These four problems have been studied in the literature extensively. In this paper we point out that for a given distributed source coding problem, under certain cases, we can obtain a specific dual broadcast channel coding problem and vice versa. Similarly, for a given multiple description coding problem, we can find a specific dual multiple access channel coding problem and vice versa.

We note that the functional duality characterized through distributional relationships presented in this paper can be further extended to involve duality in codebooks similar to that considered in Section 2.2 of [**32**]. For channel coding, we need codebooks with probability of error $P_e \approx 0$ and for source coding we need codebooks with probability of error $P_e \approx 1$. In other words, it was shown in [**32**] that an arbitrary channel code (with the additional property of being maximal) designed for a given channel with probability of error close to 1 can be directly used as a source code for the dual source coding problem where the resulting probability that a source word is not reconstructed within the appropriate distortion is close to 0. Thus, for a pair of dual source coding and channel coding problems, the number of codewords in the source codebook is slightly larger than that in the channel codebook. The probability of error of the channel codebook can be driven to zero (where the "fans" [**4**] of nearby codewords hardly overlap) and that for the source codebook can be driven to one (where the "fans" of nearby codewords always overlap). The paper is organized as follows. In Section 2 we study the functional duality in conventional source and channel coding. We extend this notion to the case of source and channel coding with side information in Section 3. Section 4 consider the duality in MIMO source and channel coding. Section 5 concludes the paper.

2. Duality between conventional source and channel coding

Traditionally, the conventional source and channel coding [**4**] problems have been considered as information-theoretic duals of each other. Shannon in his 1959 paper [**3**] on rate-distortion theory stated (italicized for emphasis) "...*duality between the properties of a source with a distortion measure and those of a channel.*

[2]To keep the exposition simple, in this paper we describe only two-input-two-output systems.

[3]The case of collaboration at both ends degenerates to point-to-point MIMO systems.

This duality is enhanced if we consider channels in which there is a cost associated with the different input letters..". In this section we obtain a precise characterization of functional duality between conventional source and channel coding and then extend this notion for source and channel coding with side information. In other words, for a given source coding problem, we obtain a channel coding problem, where the roles of encoder and decoder are functionally exchangeable and the input/output joint distribution is the same with some renaming of variables. For a given source, the rate-distortion function [**4**] denoted by $R(D)$ is the minimum rate of information required to represent it with a distortion constraint D. Similarly, for a given channel, the capacity-cost function [**4**] denoted by $C(W)$ is the maximum rate of information that can be reliably transmitted with a cost constraint W.

We would like to emphasize that the notion of duality pervades the literature starting from Shannon in 1959. To study these concepts in one framework, let us state a correspondence between the variables involved in the two coding problems.

$$\text{source coding}\left\{\begin{array}{lcl}\text{source input} & X \longleftrightarrow Y & \text{channel output}\\ \text{source reconstruction} & \hat{X} \longleftrightarrow X & \text{channel input}\end{array}\right\}\text{channel coding} \tag{2.1}$$

To avoid confusion, we stick to the conventional notation of source coding and use the same for channel coding. Let us now recall two facts which have been recently studied in [**12**] in a totally different context of optimality of uncoded transmission. It was shown in [**12**] that for a given source and a channel, there exist distortion and cost measures such that uncoded transmission is optimal. The essential concepts are presented in the following form for completeness. We denote the given distribution by $\bar{p}(\cdot)$ and the distribution which optimizes the given objective function by $p^*(\cdot)$.
Fact 1 [**12**]: For a conventional channel coding problem with a channel $\bar{p}(x|\hat{x})$, input and output alphabets $\hat{\mathcal{X}}$ and $\mathcal{X}$ respectively, given a channel input distribution $p^*(\hat{x})$, $\exists$ a cost measure $\omega : \hat{\mathcal{X}} \rightarrow \mathbb{R}^+$ and a cost constraint W such that

$$p^*(\hat{x}) = \arg\max_{p(\hat{x}):(X|\hat{X})\sim\bar{p}(x|\hat{x}),E\omega(\hat{X})\leq W} I(X;\hat{X}), \tag{2.2}$$

where the cost measure and cost constraint are given respectively by

$$\omega(\hat{x}) = c_1 D\left(\bar{p}(\cdot|\hat{x})\|p^*(x)\right) + \theta \text{ and } W = E_{p^*(\hat{x})}\left[\omega(\hat{X})\right], \tag{2.3}$$

$D(\cdot\|\cdot)$ is information divergence [**4**], $c_1 > 0$, θ are arbitrary constants, $p^*(x) = \sum_{\hat{x}} \bar{p}(x|\hat{x})p^*(\hat{x})$. Note that this divergence could be infinite.
Fact 2 [**12**]: For a conventional source coding problem, with a source $\bar{p}(x)$, input and reconstruction alphabets $\mathcal{X}$, $\hat{\mathcal{X}}$ respectively, given a conditional distribution $p^*(\hat{x}|x)$, $\exists$ a distortion measure $d : \mathcal{X} \times \hat{\mathcal{X}} \rightarrow \mathbb{R}^+$, and a distortion constraint D such that

$$p^*(\hat{x}|x) = \arg\min_{p(\hat{x}|x):X\sim\bar{p}(x),Ed(X,\hat{X})\leq D} I(X;\hat{X}), \tag{2.4}$$

where the distortion measure and distortion constraint are given respectively by

$$d(x,\hat{x}) = -c_2 \log p^*(x|\hat{x}) + d_0(x) \text{ and } D = E_{\bar{p}(x)p^*(\hat{x}|x)}\left[d(X,\hat{X})\right], \tag{2.5}$$

$c_2 > 0$ and $d_0(x)$ are arbitrary, $p^*(x|\hat{x}) = \frac{\bar{p}(x)p^*(\hat{x}|x)}{\sum_x \bar{p}(x)p^*(\hat{x}|x)}$.

In other words, any input distribution is optimal for any channel provided one is allowed to pick the channel cost measure. Similarly, any conditional distribution is optimal for any source, provided one is allowed to pick the source distortion measure. It should be noted that (as suggested in [**12**]), in Fact 1, the cost measure given in (2.3) is unique (modulo affine transformation) if $\forall\ \hat{x} \in \hat{\mathcal{X}},\ p^*(\hat{x}) > 0$, where as in Fact 2, the distortion measure as given in (2.5) is unique (modulo affine transformation). See [**12**] for details and other examples.

Remark 1: In Fact 1, for a range of cost measures ω, the channel input distribution $p^*(\hat{x})$ maximizes $I(X;\hat{X})$. This cost measure has a nice interpretation in some interesting cases such as Gaussian and binary symmetric channels. Similarly, in Fact 2, the conditional distribution $p^*(\hat{x}|x)$ minimizes $I(X;\hat{X})$ for a range of distortion measures.

Using this, we have the following theorem which connects the source and channel coding problems.

Theorem 1a: For a source coding problem, with a given source $\bar{p}(x)$, input and reconstruction alphabets $\mathcal{X}$ and $\hat{\mathcal{X}}$ respectively, a distortion measure $d : \mathcal{X} \times \hat{\mathcal{X}} \to \mathbb{R}^+$, and a distortion constraint D, let the conditional distribution achieving rate-distortion optimality $R(D)$ be given by:

$$p^*(\hat{x}|x) \triangleq \arg\min_{p(\hat{x}|x): X\sim\bar{p}(x), Ed(X,\hat{X})\leq D} I(X;\hat{X}), \tag{2.6}$$

inducing the following distributions:

$$p^*(x|\hat{x}) \triangleq \frac{p^*(\hat{x}|x)\bar{p}(x)}{\sum_x \bar{p}(x)p^*(\hat{x}|x)}, \quad p^*(\hat{x}) \triangleq \sum_x \bar{p}(x)p^*(\hat{x}|x). \tag{2.7}$$

Then $\exists$ a *dual* channel coding problem for the channel $p^*(x|\hat{x})$, having input and output alphabets $\hat{\mathcal{X}}$ and $\mathcal{X}$ respectively, a cost measure $\omega : \hat{\mathcal{X}} \to \mathbb{R}^+$, and a cost constraint W, such that:

- the rate-distortion bound $R(D)$ is equal to the capacity-cost bound $C(W)$, i.e.,

$$\min_{\substack{p(\hat{x}|x):\ X\sim\bar{p}(x)\\ Ed(X,\hat{X})\leq D}} I(X;\hat{X}) = \max_{\substack{p(\hat{x}):\ (X|\hat{X})\sim p^*(x|\hat{x})\\ E\omega(\hat{X})\leq W}} I(X;\hat{X}); \tag{2.8}$$

- the channel input distribution given by $p^*(\hat{x})$ achieves capacity-cost optimality, i.e.,

$$p^*(\hat{x}) = \arg\max_{p(\hat{x}):X|\hat{X}\sim p^*(x|\hat{x}), E\omega(\hat{X})\leq W} I(X;\hat{X}), \tag{2.9}$$

where the cost measure and cost constraint are given respectively by:

$$\omega(\hat{x}) \triangleq c_1 D\left(p^*(x|\hat{x}) \| \bar{p}(x)\right) + \theta, \quad W \triangleq E_{p^*(\hat{x})}(\omega(\hat{X})), \tag{2.10}$$

for arbitrary $c_1 > 0$ and θ.

Proof: Omitted.

A similar result can be obtained for a given channel coding problem. This is Theorem 1b which will not be presented here due to lack of space. Using the forward part of Shannon's source and channel coding theorems, for a pair of dual problems, the random codebooks are constructed using the same distribution, $p^*(\hat{x})$ and the jointly typical encoding and decoding (done respectively in source and channel coding) are the same in the sense of finding a codeword from the codebook which is jointly typical (in the sense of $p^*(x,\hat{x}) \triangleq \bar{p}(x)p^*(\hat{x}|x)$ or $p^*(x,\hat{x}) \triangleq p^*(\hat{x})\bar{p}(x|\hat{x})$)

FIGURE 1. (a) For a given source coding problem with source $\bar{p}(x)$, the dual channel coding problem is defined in a reverse order. (b) For a given channel coding problem with channel $\bar{p}(x|\hat{x})$, the dual source coding problem is defined in a reverse order.

with the observed L-length sequence (coming from the same distribution $\bar{p}(x)$) of source input and channel output respectively. Thus the distribution $p^*(\hat{x}|x)$ characterizing the function of the encoder of source coding also characterizes the function of the decoder in the dual channel coding. Thus the encoder of the one is functionally identical to the decoder of the other and vice versa. This is also illustrated in Fig. 1.

Using the forward part [**4**] of Shannon's [4] source and channel coding theorems, in the limit of large block-length, a rate-distortion optimal encoder of the former is functionally identical to a capacity-cost optimal decoder of the latter and vice versa in the sense of Theorem 1a and 1b. The results given by Theorem 1a and 1b can also be stated as follows: given a joint distribution $p(x, \hat{x})$, there exists a pair of dual source coding (with source distribution $p(x)$ induced from $p(x, \hat{x})$) and channel coding (with channel distribution $p(x|\hat{x})$ induced from $p(x, \hat{x})$) problems whose optimizations induce this joint distribution on the source and reconstruction alphabets and on the channel output and channel input alphabets respectively.

Let us consider the following example as an illustration of duality.

Example 1: *Source coding*[5] (see Fig. 2(a)): the source is Gaussian with mean 0 and variance σ^2, i.e., $\bar{p}(x) = \mathcal{N}(0, \sigma^2)$, with a quadratic (squared error) distortion measure, $d : \mathcal{X} \times \hat{\mathcal{X}} \to \mathbb{R}^+$ which is given by $d(x, \hat{x}) = (x - \hat{x})^2$, and a distortion constraint D. The optimal conditional distribution [**4**] satisfying (2.6) is of the form $\hat{X} = \mu X + q$, where $p(q) = \mathcal{N}(0, \frac{D(\sigma^2 - D)}{\sigma^2})$ and $\mu = \frac{\sigma^2 - D}{\sigma^2}$, i.e., $p^*(\hat{x}|x) = \mathcal{N}\left(\frac{\sigma^2 - D}{\sigma^2}x, \frac{D(\sigma^2 - D)}{\sigma^2}\right)$. The induced distributions are given by $X = \hat{X} + Z$, where $p(Z) = \mathcal{N}(0, D)$, i.e., $p^*(x|\hat{x}) = \mathcal{N}(\hat{x}, D)$ and $p^*(\hat{x}) = \mathcal{N}(0, \sigma^2 - D)$. Note that $D < \sigma^2$.

Channel coding dual (see Fig. 2(b)): given the additive memoryless Gaussian noise channel as given above, $X = \hat{X} + Z$, i.e., $p^*(x|\hat{x}) = \mathcal{N}(\hat{x}, D)$, and a cost measure $\omega : \hat{\mathcal{X}} \to \mathbb{R}^+$, a cost constraint W; the channel input distribution obtained from the above source coding problem, given by $p^*(\hat{x}) = \mathcal{N}(0, \sigma^2 - D)$ maximizes $I(X; \hat{X})$ over all $p(\hat{x})$ such that $E(\omega(\hat{X})) \le W$, where using Theorem 1a,

$$\omega(\hat{x}) = [c_1 D(p^*(x|\hat{x}) \| \bar{p}(x)) + \theta] = \hat{x}^2 \tag{2.11}$$

for an appropriate choice of parameters: $c_1 = 2\sigma^2$, $\quad \theta = c_1 \left[\frac{1}{2} - \log\sqrt{\frac{\sigma^2}{D}} - \frac{D}{2\sigma^2}\right]$, and the cost constraint is $W = \sigma^2 - D$. This cost measure, $\omega(\hat{x})$ corresponds to

[4]Recall that in the limit of large block-length, in source coding, the rate-distortion bound $R(D)$ is approached from above, while in channel coding, the capacity-cost bound $C(W)$ is approached from below.

[5]With a slight abuse of notation, we denote a Gaussian random variable X with mean μ and variance σ^2 as either $X \sim \mathcal{N}(\mu, \sigma^2)$ or $p(x) = \mathcal{N}(\mu, \sigma^2)$.

the traditional average power constraint on the channel input. Note from Fig. 2 that the roles of the encoder and the decoder of these dual problems are exactly reversed. The test channel in the source coding problem becomes the channel in the dual channel coding problem. It is also interesting to note that we could have started with this channel coding problem and obtained the above source coding problem as its dual by noting that $d(x, \hat{x})$ can be put in the form (given in (2.5)), $-c_2 \log p^*(x|\hat{x}) + d_0(x)$, where $c_2 = 2D$, $d_0(x) = -D\log(2\pi D)$.

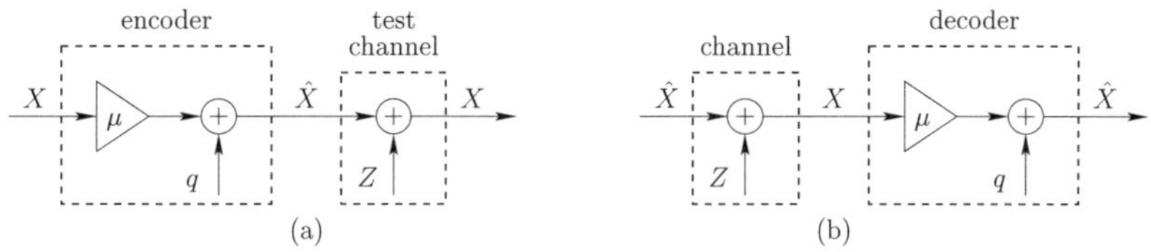

FIGURE 2. (a) Gaussian Source coding: $\bar{p}(x) = \mathcal{N}(0, \sigma^2)$, $\mu = \frac{\sigma^2 - D}{\sigma^2}$, $p(q) = \mathcal{N}(0, \frac{D(\sigma^2 - D)}{\sigma^2})$, $p(Z) = \mathcal{N}(0, D)$. The effect of encoding on X is characterized as $\mu X + q$. Test channel gives the relation between $\hat{X}$ and X. (b) Channel coding dual with the same joint distribution. The decoding is depicted as one of recovering $\hat{X}$ from X.

3. Duality between source and channel coding with side information

3.1. Review of SCSI and CCSI. Consider the problem [1] of rate-distortion optimal lossy encoding of a source X with the side information S available (losslessly) at the decoder as shown in Fig. 3. X and S are correlated random variables

FIGURE 3. Source encoding with side information at the decoder. The encoder transmits at a rate greater than or equal to R bits/ source sample.

with joint distribution $\bar{p}(x, s)$, such that the sequence pair $\{X_k, S_k\}_{k=1}^{\infty}$ denotes independent realizations of the given random variables. Let the alphabets of X and S be $\mathcal{X}, \mathcal{S}$ respectively. The encoding and decoding are done in blocks of length L. The encoder is a mapping: $\mathcal{X}^L \longrightarrow \{1, 2, \ldots, 2^{LR}\}$, and the decoder is a mapping $\{1, 2, \ldots, 2^{LR}\} \times \mathcal{S}^L \longrightarrow \hat{\mathcal{X}}^L$ where $\hat{\mathcal{X}}$ is the reconstruction alphabet and the distortion criterion is given by $E\left[\frac{1}{L}\sum_{k=1}^{L} d(X_k, \hat{X}_k, S_k)\right]$, where $d : \mathcal{X} \times \hat{\mathcal{X}} \times \mathcal{S} \longrightarrow \mathbb{R}^+$ is the per-letter additive distortion measure[6] and $E(\cdot)$ is the expectation

[6]Although $d : \mathcal{X} \times \hat{\mathcal{X}} \rightarrow \mathbb{R}^+$ is typically considered in the literature, the extension to a more general d which includes S is straightforward. It can be interpreted as the distortion between x and $\hat{x}$ when the outcome of the side information is s. This is necessary for a precise formulation of duality between source and channel coding with side information. A similar generalization of cost measure is considered for the case of channel coding with side information.

operator and R is the rate of transmission.
Fact 3 [**1**]: The rate-distortion function for this setup, $R^*(D)$, is given by

$$R^*(D) = \min_{p(u|x),p(\hat{x}|u,s)} \left[I(U;X) - I(U;S)\right], \tag{3.1}$$

such that $S \to X \to U$, and $X \to (U,S) \to \hat{X}$ form a Markov chain and $E\left[d(X,\hat{X},S)\right] \leq D$, where U is an auxiliary random variable with alphabet $\mathcal{U}$. These are the natural Markov chains associated with the definition of the problem.

Now the rate-distortion function $R_{x|s}(D)$ when both the encoder and the decoder have access to the side information is given by:

$$R_{x|s}(D) = \min_{p(\hat{x}|x,s)} I(X;\hat{X}|S), \tag{3.2}$$

such that $E[d(X,\hat{X},S)] \leq D$.

Channel coding with side information [**11, 27, 19**] about the channel at the encoder is shown schematically in Fig. 4. The encoder wishes to communicate over

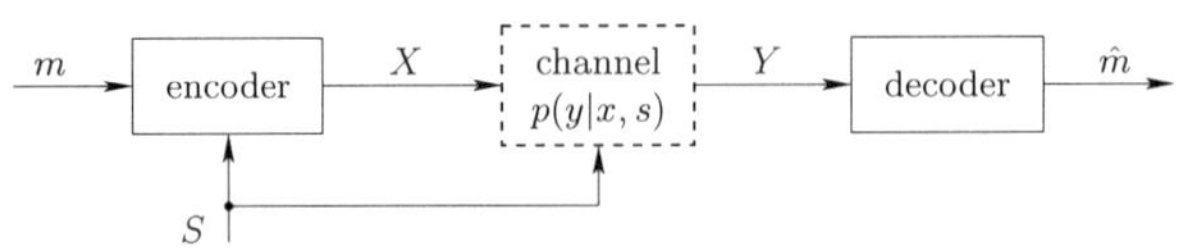

FIGURE 4. Channel coding with side information: the encoder has access to side information S about the channel; m represents the message, and X and Y are the input and the output of the channel respectively.

a channel given by the conditional distribution $\bar{p}(y|x,s)$, where Y is the channel output, X is the channel input which the encoder can control and S, the side information with a given distribution $\bar{p}(s)$, is the second channel input which the encoder cannot control but can only observe, and has alphabet $\mathcal{S}$. Note that the encoder can observe the side information in a non-causal way. Further, there is a cost measure $\omega : \mathcal{X} \times \mathcal{S} \to \mathbb{R}^+$. This can be interpreted as the cost of transmitting x when the side information outcome is s. The encoder is a mapping:$\{1, 2, \ldots, 2^{LC}\} \times \mathcal{S}^L \longrightarrow \mathcal{X}^L$, and the decoder is a mapping: $\mathcal{Y}^L \longrightarrow \{1, 2, \ldots, 2^{LC}\}$, where C is the rate of transmission.
Fact 4 : The capacity $C^*(W)$, for a cost constraint W, of this channel coding setup is given by

$$C^*(W) = \max_{p(u|s),p(x|u,s)} \left[I(U;Y) - I(U;S)\right], \tag{3.3}$$

such that $Y \to (X,S) \to U$, and $Y \to (U,S) \to X$ form a Markov chain and $E[\omega(X,S)] \leq W$, where U is an auxiliary random variable with alphabet $\mathcal{U}$. These are the natural Markov chains associated with the definition of the problem. We want to point out that the original formulation of [**11**] was extended to the case with general cost measures in [**15, 26**].

Now the capacity of the system $C_{y|s}(W)$, when both the encoder and the decoder have access to the side information is given by:

$$C_{y|s}(W) = \max_{p(x|s)} I(X;Y|S), \tag{3.4}$$

such that $E[\omega(X,S)] \leq W$.

Before we go further, first let us state a correspondence between the variables used in the definition of SCSI and CCSI.

$$\text{(3.5)}\qquad \text{SCSI}\left\{\begin{array}{ccc} \text{source input} & X\longleftrightarrow Y & \text{channel output} \\ \text{side information} & S\longleftrightarrow S & \text{side information} \\ \text{auxiliary variable} & U\longleftrightarrow U & \text{auxiliary variable} \\ \text{source reconstruction} & \hat{X}\longleftrightarrow X & \text{channel input} \end{array}\right\}\text{CCSI}$$

We follow the notation of SCSI and use the same for CCSI. Using this correspondence, we can compare the expressions for the rate-distortion functions and the capacity-cost functions of SCSI and CCSI.

3.2. Duality between source and channel coding with common side information. Let us consider a similar formulation of duality for source and channel coding with common side information present at both the encoder and the decoder (denoted by SCSIB and CCSIB respectively, where the appended "B" stands for "both"). This is a straightforward extension of the treatment of the previous section to the case where we condition on the common side information. The motivation for addressing this extension is that this is a necessary step that will serve as a bridge to establishing the duality between SCSI and CCSI. Another motivation is to establish the need for the generalized notion of cost and distortion measures. The following lemmas extend the ideas given in Facts 1 and 2 to this case in a straightforward way and are presented here for completeness.

Lemma 1a: For CCSIB, with a given channel $\bar{p}(x|\hat{x},s)$, side information $\bar{p}(s)$, input, side information and output alphabets $\hat{\mathcal{X}}$, $\mathcal{S}$ and $\mathcal{X}$ respectively, given a conditional channel input distribution $p^*(\hat{x}|s)$, $\exists$ a cost measure $\omega : \hat{\mathcal{X}} \times \mathcal{S} \to \mathbb{R}^+$ and a cost constraint W such that

$$\text{(3.6)}\qquad p^*(\hat{x}|s) = \arg\max_{p(\hat{x}|s)} I(X;\hat{X}|S)$$

under the constraints $(X|\hat{X},S) \sim \bar{p}(x|\hat{x},s)$, $S \sim \bar{p}(s)$ and $E\omega(\hat{X},S) \leq W$, where

$$\text{(3.7)}\qquad \omega(\hat{x},s) = c_1 D\left(\bar{p}(x|\hat{x},s)\|p^*(x|s)\right) + \theta(s), \text{ and } W = E_{\bar{p}(s)p^*(\hat{x}|s)}(\omega(\hat{X},S)),$$

with $c_1 > 0$ and $\theta(s)$ being arbitrary and $p^*(x|s) = \sum_{\hat{x}} p^*(\hat{x}|s)\bar{p}(x|\hat{x},s)$ from standard Bayes' rule.

Proof: Omitted.

Lemma 1b: For SCSIB, with a given source $\bar{p}(x|s)$, side information $\bar{p}(s)$, input, side information and reconstruction alphabets $\mathcal{X}$, $\mathcal{S}$, and $\hat{\mathcal{X}}$ respectively, given a conditional distribution, $p^*(\hat{x}|x,s)$, $\exists$ a distortion measure, $d : \mathcal{X} \times \hat{\mathcal{X}} \times \mathcal{S} \to \mathbb{R}^+$ and a distortion constraint D such that

$$\text{(3.8)}\qquad p^*(\hat{x}|x,s) = \arg\min_{p(\hat{x}|x,s)} I(X;\hat{X}|S)$$

under the constraints $(X|S) \sim \bar{p}(x|s)$, $S \sim \bar{p}(s)$, and $Ed(X,\hat{X},S) \leq D$, where

(3.9)

$$d(x,\hat{x},s) = -c_2 \log p^*(x|\hat{x},s) + d_0(x,s), \text{ and } D = E_{\bar{p}(x|s)\bar{p}(s)p^*(\hat{x}|x,s)}(d(X,\hat{X},S)),$$

with $c_2 > 0$ and $d_0(x,s)$ being arbitrary, and $p^*(x|\hat{x},s) = \frac{\bar{p}(x|s)p^*(\hat{x}|x,s)}{\sum_x \bar{p}(x|s)p^*(\hat{x}|x,s)}$, $p^*(\hat{x}|s) = \sum_x \bar{p}(x|s)p^*(\hat{x}|x,s)$, from standard Bayes' rule.

As noted earlier, with the more general distortion and cost measures, we are able to extend the concepts of Facts 1 and 2 to the case when a common side information is present at both the encoder and the decoder. Let $\mathcal{S}' = \{s \in \mathcal{S} | p(s) > 0\}$. We use this notation for the rest of this paper. The cost measure as given by (3.7) can be shown to be unique modulo affine transformation if $\forall s \in \mathcal{S}'$, $\hat{x} \in \hat{\mathcal{X}}$, $p^*(\hat{x}|s) > 0$. The distortion measure as given by (3.9) is unique modulo affine transformation. We will give an example of a Gaussian source to illustrate the behavior of these measures. We now connect these two coding problems using the following theorem (which is an extension of Theorem 1a), which says that for a given SCSIB, we can associate a dual CCSIB having the same joint distribution.

Theorem 2a: For a SCSIB, with a given source $\bar{p}(x|s)$, side information $\bar{p}(s)$, input, side information and reconstruction alphabets $\mathcal{X}$, $\mathcal{S}$ and $\hat{\mathcal{X}}$ respectively, a distortion measure $d : \mathcal{X} \times \hat{\mathcal{X}} \times \mathcal{S} \to \mathbb{R}^+$, and a distortion constraint D, let the conditional distribution achieving the rate-distortion optimality $R_{x|s}(D)$ be given by:

$$p^*(\hat{x}|x,s) \triangleq \arg\min_{p(\hat{x}|x,s):(X|S)\sim\bar{p}(x|s),S\sim\bar{p}(s),Ed(X,\hat{X},S)\leq D} I(X;\hat{X}|S), \tag{3.10}$$

inducing the following distributions:

$$p^*(x|\hat{x},s) \triangleq \frac{p^*(\hat{x}|x,s)\bar{p}(x|s)}{\sum_x \bar{p}(x|s)p^*(\hat{x}|x,s)}, \quad p^*(\hat{x}|s) \triangleq \sum_x \bar{p}(x|s)p^*(\hat{x}|x,s). \tag{3.11}$$

Then $\exists$ a *dual* CCSIB for the channel $p^*(x|\hat{x},s)$, having side information $\bar{p}(s)$, input, side information and output alphabets $\hat{\mathcal{X}}$, $\mathcal{S}$ and $\mathcal{X}$ respectively, a cost measure $\omega : \hat{\mathcal{X}} \times \mathcal{S} \to \mathbb{R}^+$ and a cost constraint W, such that:

- the rate-distortion bound with side information $R_{x|s}(D)$ is equal to the capacity-cost bound[7] with side information $C_{x|s}(W)$, i.e.,

$$\min_{p(\hat{x}|x,s):\left\{\begin{array}{c}(X|S)\sim\bar{p}(x|s)\\ S\sim\bar{p}(s)\\ Ed(X,\hat{X},S)\leq D\end{array}\right\}} I(X;\hat{X}|S) = \max_{p(\hat{x}|s):\left\{\begin{array}{c}(X|\hat{X},S)\sim p^*(x|\hat{x},s)\\ S\sim\bar{p}(s)\\ E\omega(\hat{X},S)\leq W\end{array}\right\}} I(X;\hat{X}|S) \tag{3.12}$$

- the channel input distribution given by $p^*(\hat{x}|s)$ achieves capacity-cost optimality, i.e.,

$$p^*(\hat{x}|s) = \arg\max_{p(\hat{x}|s):(X|\hat{X},S)\sim p^*(x|\hat{x},s),S\sim\bar{p}(s),E\omega(\hat{X},S)\leq W} I(X;\hat{X}|S), \tag{3.13}$$

where the cost measure and cost constraint are given respectively by

$$\omega(\hat{x},s) \triangleq c_1 D\left(p^*(x|\hat{x},s)\|\bar{p}(x|s)\right) + \theta(s), \quad W \triangleq E_{\bar{p}(s)p^*(\hat{x}|s)}(\omega(\hat{X},S)), \tag{3.14}$$

for arbitrary $c_1 > 0$ and $\theta(s)$.

Proof: Omitted.

A similar result holds true for the case of CCSIB which is an extension of Theorem 1b. It essentially says that for a given CCSIB problem, there exists a dual SCSIB problem with an optimal distortion measure. We are not presenting this here. Further, using the forward part of the coding theorems [**31**], we see that the random conditional codebooks are constructed with the conditional distribution $p^*(\hat{x}|s)$ corresponding to the given outcome of the side information. The jointly typical encoding and decoding in SCSIB and CCSIB respectively are identical.

---

[7] $C_{x|s}(W)$ denotes the capacity of CCSIB using (3.4) and (2.1).

Uniqueness of duals: Similar to the conventional source coding and channel coding problems, it can be seen that (under the condition that $\forall s \in \mathcal{S}', \hat{x} \in \hat{\mathcal{X}}$, $p^*(\hat{x}|s) > 0$), modulo affine transformations, we have a unique association of a distortion measure and a cost measure for a given joint distribution $p^*(x, \hat{x}, s)$, induced from the uniqueness condition stated following Lemma 1a and 1b. In other words, under this condition, we have a unique pair of SCSIB and CCSIB problems which are associated under duality for a given joint distribution $p^*(x, \hat{x}, s)$.

3.3. Duality between SCSI and CCSI. The duality between SCSI and CCSI has been studied in [**22, 25, 26**]. In this section, we formulate the notion of functional duality for the SCSI and CCSI similar to the one developed in the previous sections.

3.3.1. *Duality formulation.* In SCSI, the objective function is $[I(U;X)–I(U;S)]$ which is minimized over $p(u|x)$ and $p(\hat{x}|u, s)$, where U is an auxiliary random variable, under the following condition: $S \to X \to U$, and $X \to (U, S) \to \hat{X}$. Suppose the objective function $[I(U; X)-I(U; S)]$ is optimized by $\{p^*(u|x), p^*(\hat{x}|u, s)\}$. This with the Markov chains completely determines the joint distribution $p^*(x, s, \hat{x}, u) = \bar{p}(s)\bar{p}(x|s)p^*(u|x)p^*(\hat{x}|u, s)$, thus fixing all conditional distributions including $p^*(u|s)$. In CCSI, the objective function is $[I(U; X) - I(U; S)]$, which is maximized over $p(u|s)$ and $p(\hat{x}|u, s)$, where U is an auxiliary random variable, the following condition: $X \to (\hat{X}, S) \to U$, and $X \to (U, S) \to \hat{X}$. Suppose the objective function is optimized by $\{p^*(u|s), p^*(\hat{x}|u, s)\}$. This, with the Markov chains completely determines the joint distribution $p^*(x, s, \hat{x}, u) = \bar{p}(s)p^*(u|s)p^*(\hat{x}|u, s)\bar{p}(x|\hat{x}, s)$, thus fixing all the conditional distributions including $p^*(u|x)$.

In order for general duality between the CCSI and SCSI problems, we have to reconcile the fact that these two problems come with different Markov chain conditions in their very definition. Thus for a general SCSI problem, the distribution minimizing $[I(U; X) - I(U; S)]$ cannot be used for any CCSI problem unless $X \to (\hat{X}, S) \to U$ is satisfied, which is a necessary initial condition for the latter. Therefore, unless the optimizing joint distribution $p^*(x, s, \hat{x}, u)$ satisfies *all the three* Markov chains, there can be no duality. However, there exists a theoretically significant subset of these problems (including the important Gaussian case), where these Markov chains are satisfied, and we do have a functional duality. We have the following theorems characterizing this.

Theorem 3a: For a SCSI, with a given source $\bar{p}(x|s)$, side information $\bar{p}(s)$, input, side information and reconstruction alphabets $\mathcal{X}, \mathcal{S}$ and $\hat{\mathcal{X}}$ respectively, a distortion measure $d : \mathcal{X} \times \hat{\mathcal{X}} \times \mathcal{S} \to \mathbb{R}^+$, and a distortion constraint D, let the conditional distribution achieving the rate-distortion optimality $R^*(D)$ be given by:

(3.15)
$$\begin{Bmatrix} p^*(u|x), \\ p^*(\hat{x}|u, s) \end{Bmatrix} \triangleq \operatorname*{argmin}_{\substack{p(u|x), \\ p(\hat{x}|u, s)}} \; I(U; X) - I(U; S) : \left\{ \begin{matrix} (X|S) \sim \bar{p}(x|s), Ed(X, \hat{X}, S) \leq D \\ S \sim \bar{p}(s), (S \to X \to U), (X \to (U, S) \to \hat{X}) \end{matrix} \right\}$$

inducing the following distributions: $p^*(x, s, \hat{x}, u) \triangleq \bar{p}(s)\bar{p}(x|s)p^*(u|x)p^*(\hat{x}|u, s)$, where we have $p^*(x|\hat{x}, s) \triangleq \frac{\sum_u p^*(x,s,\hat{x},u)}{\sum_{u,x} p^*(x,s,\hat{x},u)}$, $p^*(u|s) \triangleq \frac{\sum_{x,\hat{x}} p^*(x,s,\hat{x},u)}{\bar{p}(s)}$, and $p^*(\hat{x}|s) \triangleq \frac{\sum_{u,x} p^*(x,s,\hat{x},u)}{\bar{p}(s)}$. If $p^*(x, s, \hat{x}, u)$ is such that $X \to (\hat{X}, S) \to U$, then $\exists$ a dual CCSI, for the channel $p^*(x|\hat{x}, s)$, having side information $\bar{p}(s)$, input, side information and output alphabets $\hat{\mathcal{X}}$, $\mathcal{S}$ and $\mathcal{X}$ respectively, a cost measure $\omega : \hat{\mathcal{X}} \times \mathcal{S} \to \mathbb{R}^+$ and a cost constraint W, such that:

- the rate-distortion bound with side information $R^*(D)$ is equal to the capacity-cost bound with side information $C^*(W)$, i.e.,

(3.16)
$$\min_{\substack{p(u|x),\\ p(\hat{x}|u,s)}} : \left\{ \begin{array}{c} I(U;X) - I(U;S) \\ (X|S) \sim \bar{p}(x|s) \\ S \sim \bar{p}(s) \\ Ed(X,\hat{X},S) \leq D \\ S \to X \to U \\ X \to (U,S) \to \hat{X} \end{array} \right\} = \max_{\substack{p(u|s),\\ p(\hat{x}|u,s)}} : \left\{ \begin{array}{c} I(U;X) - I(U;S); \\ (X|\hat{X},S) \sim p^*(x|\hat{x},s) \\ S \sim \bar{p}(s) \\ E\omega(\hat{X},S) \leq W \\ X \to (\hat{X},S) \to U \\ X \to (U,S) \to \hat{X} \end{array} \right\}$$

- the conditional distributions $p^*(u|s)$, $p^*(\hat{x}|u,s)$ achieve capacity-cost optimality, i.e.,

(3.17)
$$\left\{ \begin{array}{c} p^*(u|s), \\ p^*(\hat{x}|u,s) \end{array} \right\} = \underset{\substack{p(u|s)\\ p(\hat{x}|u,s)}}{\operatorname{argmax}} : \left\{ \begin{array}{c} (X|\hat{X},S) \sim p^*(x|\hat{x},s), E\omega(\hat{X},S) \leq W, S \sim \bar{p}(s) \\ (X \to (\hat{X},S) \to U), (X \to (U,S) \to \hat{X}) \end{array} \right\} I(U;X) - I(U;S),$$

where the cost measure and cost constraint are given respectively by

$$\omega(\hat{x},s) \triangleq c_1 D\left(p^*(x|\hat{x},s) \| \bar{p}(x|s)\right) + \theta(s), \quad W \triangleq E_{\bar{p}(s)p^*(\hat{x}|s)}(\omega(\hat{X},S)), \tag{3.18}$$

for arbitrary $c_1 > 0$ and $\theta(s)$.

Proof: Omitted.

Remark 2: A similar result can be obtained for a given CCSI problem. In Theorem 3a, the property of the dual CCSI, given by (3.16), implies that the minimum of $[I(U;X) - I(U;S)]$ with respect to $p(u|x)$ and $p(\hat{x}|u,s)$ under one set of constraints is equal to the maximum of the same objective function $[I(U;X) - I(U;S)]$ with respect to $p(u|s)$ and $p(\hat{x}|u,s)$ under another set of constraints. Further, the property as given by (3.17) implies that the solution to the dual CCSI is exactly the distributions $p^*(u|s)$ and $p^*(\hat{x}|u,s)$ induced from the solution to the given SCSI, provided we are careful about our choice of channel cost measure as given in (3.18). A similar result holds true for the case of a given CCSI problem.

We want to emphasize that unlike conventional source and channel coding or SCSIB and CCSIB, in SCSI and CCSI, we have duality only under the condition as given in Theorem 3. At this point, we do not have any general characterization of the distributions of the source, the channel or the side information, the distortion measures and the cost measures for which this condition holds. In the following, we consider an important generalization of the result of Wyner-Ziv [**1**] relating to no rate-loss for SCSI from Gaussian to more arbitrary distributions. We have obtained this generalization as a dual to the recent generalization of Costa's result to arbitrary side information, obtained in [**20, 21**].

3.3.2. *Generalization of Gaussian case of Wyner and Ziv with no rate-loss.* Recently, in [**20, 21**], a generalization of the "dirty paper" result of Costa [**19**] was considered, where no rate-loss was shown to hold even if the channel side information is not Gaussian (the channel noise has to be Gaussian). That is, for the CCSI problem with $X = S + \hat{X} + Z$ (see correspondence in (3.5)), where Z is i.i.d. Gaussian, there is no capacity loss over the corresponding CCSIB problem where S is known at both ends, with S being arbitrary. By the above duality, we are now in a position to correspondingly generalize the Wyner-Ziv result (with no rate-loss) for the Gaussian source characterized by $X = S + V$ (where X, S, V are all Gaussian) to the more general case where V is Gaussian but X and S are otherwise arbitrary (but related by $X = S+V$): this follows directly from the above duality, and is a direct example of how generalization of a result in one problem leads to a corresponding impact in the dual problem. This important generalization is presented as a corollary in the following. While the SCSI claim of this corollary can be obtained "from first principles" similar to [**20, 21**], it is far more insightful and elegant to deduce this using the duality concepts developed in Theorem 3.

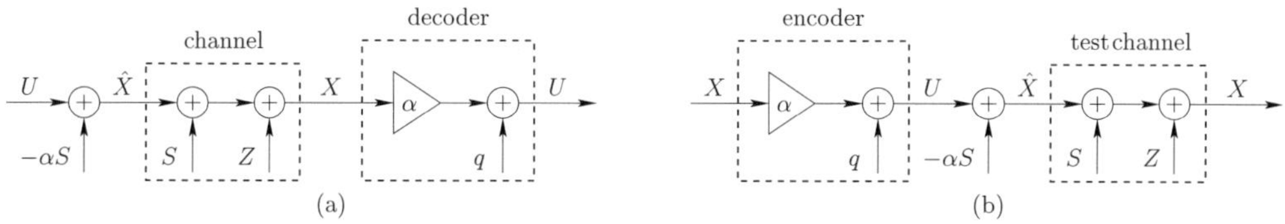

FIGURE 5. Duality: $\alpha = (N - D)/N$, $p(q) \sim \mathcal{N}\left(0, \frac{D(N-D)}{N}\right)$ and $p(Z) = \mathcal{N}(0, D)$ The side information S has arbitrary but fixed distribution. (a) CCSI: the cost measure is $\omega(\hat{x}, s) = \hat{x}^2$. The joint distribution is represented in this form. The decoding operation is depicted as one of recovering U from X. (b) SCSI: the distortion measure is $d(x, \hat{x}, s) = (x - \hat{x} - s)^2$. The joint distribution is represented in this form. The effect of encoding is illustrated as $\alpha X + q$.

CCSI [**20, 21**] (see Fig. 5(a)): Let the channel be additive white Gaussian, given by $X = \hat{X} + S + Z$, with $p(Z) = \mathcal{N}(0, D)$, i.e., $\bar{p}(x|\hat{x}, s) = \mathcal{N}(\hat{x} + s, D)$ for some $D > 0$ and let the side information, given by $\bar{p}(s)$ be *arbitrary*, and let the cost measure be quadratic: $\omega(\hat{x}, s) = \hat{x}^2$ and let $W = N - D$ for some[8] $N > D$. Let $\alpha = \frac{N-D}{N}$ as before. It was shown in [**20, 21**] that $C^*(N - D) = \frac{1}{2}\log\frac{N}{D}$ (no rate-loss) and that the optimizer given by the distribution, $U = \hat{X} + \alpha S$, i.e., $p^*(u|s) = \mathcal{N}(\alpha s, (N - D))$ and the distribution $p^*(\hat{x}|u, s)$ characterizing the channel input, $\hat{X} = U - \alpha S$ induce the relation between U and X as given by $U = \alpha X + q$, where $p(q) = \mathcal{N}(0, \frac{D(N-D)}{N})$, i.e., $p^*(u|x) = \mathcal{N}\left(\alpha x, \frac{D(N-D)}{N}\right)$.

Note that α is equal to the coefficient in the MMSE estimate of $\hat{X}$ from $\hat{X} + Z$. We now provide an interpretation for the joint distribution depicted in Fig. 5(a). Note that the channel input $\hat{X}$ is statistically independent of side information S, i.e., $p^*(\hat{x}|s) = \mathcal{N}(0, N - D)$. Further, it can be verified that the joint distribution satisfies the Markov chain $S \to X \to U$ (necessary condition for finding the dual SCSI). The channel output X is related to the side information S in the following way: $X = S + V$, where $p(V) = \mathcal{N}(0, N)$, i.e., $p^*(x|s) = \mathcal{N}(s, N)$.

Corollary 1: For the above CCSI, we can associate a dual SCSI (see Fig. 5(b)) given as follows: the conditional source X is characterized by $X = S + V$, where $p(V) = \mathcal{N}(0, N)$, i.e., $p^*(x|s) = \mathcal{N}(s, N)$ and the side information $\bar{p}(s)$ is chosen

[8]Using the correspondence as given in (3.5) and renaming $P = N - D$, $N = D$, we get the notation for CCSI conventionally used in the literature.

as above (chosen arbitrarily in CCSI). The conditional distribution given by the above CCSI, $U = \alpha X + q$, i.e., $p^*(u|x) = \mathcal{N}(\alpha x, \frac{D(N-D)}{N})$ and $p^*(\hat{x}|u,s)$ given by $\hat{X} = U - \alpha S$ minimize $[I(U;X) - I(U;S)]$, such that $S \to X \to U$ and $X \to (U,S) \to \hat{X}$ and $E(d(X,\hat{X},S)) \leq D$, which implies $R^*(D) = C^*(N-D)$. The distortion measure is given by

$$d(x,\hat{x},s) = -c_2 \log \bar{p}(x|\hat{x},s) + d_0(x,s) = (x - \hat{x} - s)^2 \tag{3.19}$$

by choosing $c_2 = 2D$ and $d_0(x,s) = -D\log(2\pi D)$ with distortion constraint D.

The reconstruction $\hat{X} = U - \alpha S$ is the MMSE estimate of $(X-S)$ from U and S. Note that in both the problems there is no rate loss compared to the corresponding CCSIB and SCSIB even though $\bar{p}(s)$ is chosen arbitrarily. This CCSI with the given quadratic cost measure is the problem of transmission over a Gaussian channel with known interference similar to the one considered by Costa [**19**]. Thus, its dual is the SCSI with the decoder wishing to reconstruct $(X-S)$ under a mean squared error constraint.

4. MIMO source and channel coding

4.1. Review of rate-distortion functions and capacity-cost functions. In this section we briefly define the four problems. A word about the notation: for the source coding problems, we denote $\mathbf{X}$ as the vector source and $\hat{\mathbf{X}}$ as the vector reconstruction, whereas in channel coding we denote $\mathbf{X}$ as the vector channel output with $\hat{\mathbf{X}}$ denoting the vector channel input. The components of $\mathbf{X}$ are X_1 and X_2, and similarly those of $\hat{\mathbf{X}}$ are $\hat{X}_1$ and $\hat{X}_2$. In the source coding problems, we interchangeably use 1) $\hat{X}_i$ for $i = 1,2$ as different reconstructions of the pair $\hat{X}_1$ and $\hat{X}_2$; or 2) $\hat{X}_i$ as a reconstruction of X_i alone. This will be evident from the distortion measure of the particular problem. In all these problems we use a single distortion/cost measure and optimize sum-rate of representation/transmission. More general cases are studied in [**33**].

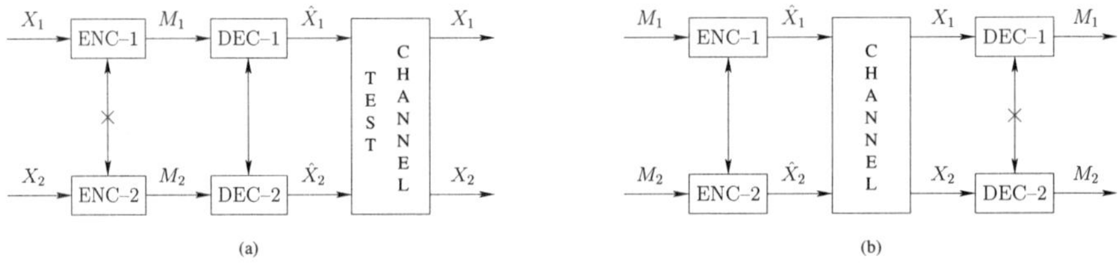

FIGURE 6. (a) Distributed source coding (b) Broadcast channel coding

1. Distributed source coding [**34**]: (see Fig. 1(a)) Let X_1 and X_2 be two correlated memoryless sources with a given joint distribution $\bar{p}(X_1, X_2)$, and with alphabets $\mathcal{X}_1$ and $\mathcal{X}_2$ respectively. The encoder associated with each of these sources wishes to represent its corresponding source using an index sequence. The encoders do not communicate with each other. The joint decoder having access to these two index sequences, wishes to get a joint estimate of the sources. Let $d : \mathcal{X}_1 \times \mathcal{X}_2 \times \hat{\mathcal{X}}_1 \times \hat{\mathcal{X}}_2 \to \mathbb{R}^+$ denote the joint distortion measure, where $\hat{\mathcal{X}}_1$ and $\hat{\mathcal{X}}_2$ denote the reconstruction alphabets. The encoders are given by: $\mathcal{X}_i^L \to \{1,2,\ldots,2^{R_i L}\}$ for $i = 1,2$, and the decoder is given by $\{1,2,\ldots,2^{R_1 L}\} \times \{1,2,\ldots,2^{R_2 L}\} \to \hat{\mathcal{X}}_1^L \times \hat{\mathcal{X}}_2^L$.

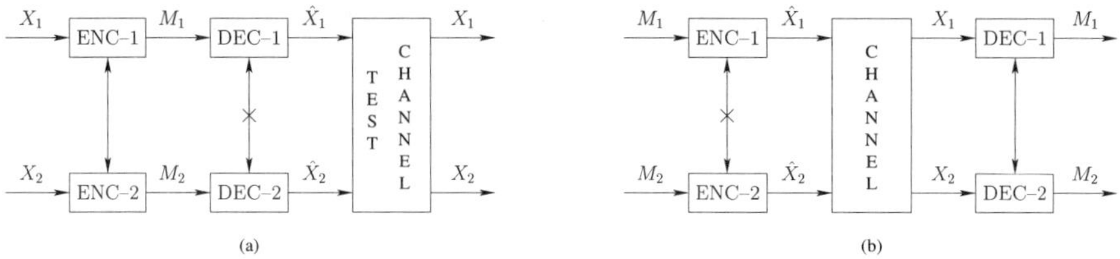

FIGURE 7. (a) Multiple description source coding (b) Multiple access channel coding

For this problem only an achievable rate region is known. An achievable [**34**] sum rate $R_1 + R_2$ for a distortion constraint D, for this problem is given by

$$R_{DS}(D) = \min_{p(u_1,u_2|x_1,x_2),p(\hat{x}_1,\hat{x}_2|u_1,u_2)} [I(X_1;U_1) + I(X_2;U_2) - I(U_1;U_2)] \tag{4.1}$$

such that $U_2 \to X_2 \to X_1 \to U_1$, and $(X_1, X_2) \to (U_1, U_2) \to (\hat{X}_1, \hat{X}_2)$ form a Markov chain, and $Ed(X_1, X_2, \hat{X}_1, \hat{X}_2) \leq D$, where U_1 and U_2 are auxiliary random variables with alphabets $\mathcal{U}_1$ and $\mathcal{U}_2$ respectively. *Examples of the distortion function*: 1) reconstruction of the sum of X_1 and X_2, $(x_1 + x_2 - \hat{x}_1 - \hat{x}_2)^2$; 2) sum distortion of X_1 and X_2, $(x_1 - \hat{x}_1)^2 + (x_2 - \hat{x}_2)^2$.

2. Broadcast channel coding [**17, 18**]: (see Fig. 1(b)) Consider a general broadcast channel with a given conditional distribution $\bar{p}(X_1, X_2|\hat{X}_1, \hat{X}_2)$, with $\hat{\mathcal{X}}_i$ as input alphabet and $\mathcal{X}_i$ as output alphabet for $i = 1, 2$. The joint encoder wishes to simultaneously communicate with two receivers with rates R_1 and R_2. There is a joint cost measure associated with this channel: $w : \hat{\mathcal{X}}_1 \times \hat{\mathcal{X}}_2 \to \mathbb{R}^+$. The encoder is a mapping $\{1, 2, \ldots, 2^{R_1 L}\} \times \{1, 2, \ldots, 2^{R_2 L}\} \to \hat{\mathcal{X}}_1^L \times \hat{\mathcal{X}}_2^L$. The decoders are given by: $\mathcal{X}_i^L \to \{1, 2, \ldots, 2^{R_i L}\}$ for $i = 1, 2$. For this problem, only an achievable rate region is known. An achievable [**18**] sum rate $R_1 + R_2$ for a cost constraint of W is given by

$$C_{BC}(W) = \max_{p(u_1,u_2),p(\hat{x}_1,\hat{x}_2|u_1,u_2)} [I(X_1;U_1) + I(X_2;U_2) - I(U_1;U_2)] \tag{4.2}$$

such that $(U_1, U_2) \to (\hat{X}_1, \hat{X}_2) \to (X_1, X_2)$ and $(X_1, X_2) \to (U_1, U_2) \to (\hat{X}_1, \hat{X}_2)$ form a Markov chain, and $Ew(\hat{X}_1, \hat{X}_2) \leq W$, where U_1 and U_2 are auxiliary random variables with alphabets $\mathcal{U}_1$ and $\mathcal{U}_2$ respectively. *Examples of the cost function*: 1) sum power, $(\hat{x}_1^2 + \hat{x}_2^2)$; 2) power of sum of X_1 and X_2, $(\hat{x}_1 + \hat{x}_2)^2$.

3. Multiple Description source Coding with no excess sum-rate [**35, 36**]: (see Fig. 2(a)) Here we have two correlated sources X_1 and X_2 with a given joint distribution $\bar{p}(X_1, X_2)$ with alphabets $\mathcal{X}_1$ and $\mathcal{X}_2$. The joint encoder wishes to represent these sources using two descriptions to be sent to two receivers. The receivers do not communicate with each other. The encoder is a mapping: $\mathcal{X}_1 \times \mathcal{X}_2 \to \{1, 2, \ldots, 2^{R_1 L}\} \times \{1, 2, \ldots, 2^{R_2 L}\}$. R_i denotes the rate of the ith description. The ith decoder is given by the mapping: $\{1, 2, \ldots, 2^{R_i L}\} \to \hat{\mathcal{X}}_i^L$, and let $d : \mathcal{X}_1 \times \mathcal{X}_2 \times \hat{\mathcal{X}}_1 \times \hat{\mathcal{X}}_2 \to \mathbb{R}^+$ denote the joint distortion measure[9], where $\hat{\mathcal{X}}_1$ and $\hat{\mathcal{X}}_2$ denote

[9]In this paper for a precise notion of duality, we consider a slightly different version (with a single distortion measure) of the multiple description coding than that studied in the literature (with three distortion measure). In the latter, three distortion measures are associated with different subsets of descriptions received. The former is a subset of the latter in the following sense: the reconstruction $\hat{X}_0$ for the reception of all descriptions is a function of the reconstructions

the reconstruction alphabets. The sum-rate-distortion function [**36**] for a distortion constraint D for this problem is given by

$$R_{MD}(D) = \min_{p(\hat{x}_1,\hat{x}_2|x_1,x_2)} I(X_1, X_2; \hat{X}_1, \hat{X}_2) \tag{4.3}$$

such that $\hat{X}_1, \hat{X}_2$ are independent and $Ed(X_1, X_2, \hat{X}_1, \hat{X}_2) \leq D$.

4. Multiple access channel coding with independent message sets [**37, 38**]: (see Fig. 2(b)) Consider a multiple access channel with a given conditional distribution $\bar{p}(X_1, X_2, |\hat{X}_1, \hat{X}_2)$. Two non-collaborating encoders wish to transmit messages to a joint decoder with rates R_1, R_2. The ith encoder is given by the mapping: $\{1, 2, \ldots, 2^{R_i L}\} \rightarrow \hat{\mathcal{X}}_i^L$. The joint decoder is given by $\mathcal{X}_1 \times \mathcal{X}_2 \rightarrow \{1, 2, \ldots, 2^{R_1 L}\} \times \{1, 2, \ldots, 2^{R_2 L}\}$. There is a joint cost function associated with this channel: $w : \hat{\mathcal{X}}_1 \times \hat{\mathcal{X}}_2 \rightarrow \mathbb{R}^+$. The sum capacity-cost function [**37**] is given by

$$C_{MA}(W) = \max_{p(\hat{x}_1,\hat{x}_2)} I(X_1, X_2; \hat{X}_1, \hat{X}_2) \tag{4.4}$$

such that $\hat{X}_1, \hat{X}_2$ are independent and $Ew \leq W$.

4.2. Duality results. Now we give a formulation of duality between these MIMO source and channel coding problems with limited collaboration. Note that although the rate region for general multiple description coding and general multiple access channel coding have been shown to be tight, similar converses for the general case for distributed source coding and broadcast channel coding are still not available. This duality deals only with the available single-letter characterization of rate regions. In the sequel we show that for a given distributed source coding problem, under certain conditions, we can associate a dual broadcast channel coding problem where both problems induce the same joint distribution of variables with suitable correspondence.

Similarly, for a given broadcast channel coding problem, under certain conditions, we can associate a specific dual distributed source coding problem. In a pair of dual problems, the encoder of the one is functionally identical to the decoder of the latter and vice versa. Similarly, we can obtain a duality formulation between multiple description coding with no excess sum-rate and multiple access channel with independent message sets. These results are stated as the following theorems.

Theorem 4a: For a given distributed source coding problem with a given source $\bar{p}(X_1, X_2)$, and alphabets $\mathcal{X}_i$ and reconstruction alphabets $\hat{\mathcal{X}}_i$ for $i = 1, 2$, a distortion measure $d : \mathcal{X}_1 \times \mathcal{X}_2 \times \hat{\mathcal{X}}_1 \times \hat{\mathcal{X}}_2 \rightarrow \mathbb{R}^+$, a distortion constraint D, let the conditional distributions satisfying the optimality condition of (4.1) be given by $p^*(u_1, u_2, |x_1, x_2)$ and $p^*(\hat{x}_1, \hat{x}_2|u_1, u_2)$, inducing the joint distribution given by $p^*(x_1, x_2, u_1, u_2, \hat{x}_1, \hat{x}_2) = \bar{p}(x_1, x_2)\ p^*(u_1, u_2|x_1, x_2)\ p^*(\hat{x}_1, \hat{x}_2|u_1, u_2)$. Let

$$p^*(u_1, u_2) = \sum_{x_1,x_2,\hat{x}_1,\hat{x}_2} p^*(x_1, x_2, u_1, u_2, \hat{x}_1, \hat{x}_2),$$

$$p^*(x_1, x_2|\hat{x}_1, \hat{x}_2) = \frac{\sum_{u_1,u_2} p^*(x_1, x_2, u_1, u_2, \hat{x}_1, \hat{x}_2)}{\sum_{u_1,u_2,x_1,x_2} p^*(x_1, x_2, u_1, u_2, \hat{x}_1, \hat{x}_2)}.$$

$\hat{X}_1$, $\hat{X}_2$ corresponding to the reception of individual descriptions. The single distortion measure $d(x_1, x_2, \hat{x}_1, \hat{x}_2)$ is able to capture this function.

If $p^*(x_1, x_2, u_1, u_2, \hat{x}_1, \hat{x}_2)$ satisfies $(U_1, U_2) \rightarrow (\hat{X}_1, \hat{X}_2) \rightarrow (X_1, X_2)$, then $\exists$ a dual broadcast channel coding problem for the channel $p^*(x_1, x_2|\hat{x}_1, \hat{x}_2)$, with input alphabets $\hat{\mathcal{X}}_i$ and output alphabets $\mathcal{X}_i$, a cost measure $w : \hat{\mathcal{X}}_1 \times \hat{\mathcal{X}}_2 \rightarrow \mathbb{R}^+$, and a cost constraint W such that

- achievable rate bound $R_{DS}(D) = C_{BC}(W)$, i.e.,

(4.5)
$$\min I(X_1; U_1) + I(X_2; U_2) - I(U_1; U_2) = \max I(X_1; U_1) + I(X_2; U_2) - I(U_1; U_2)$$

  where the minimization is over $p(u_1, u_2|x_1, x_2)$ and $p(\hat{x}_1, \hat{x}_2|u_1, u_2)$ with source distribution $\bar{p}(x_1, x_2)$ held fixed such that $Ed \leq D$, $U_2 \rightarrow X_2 \rightarrow X_1 \rightarrow U_1$ and $(X_1, X_2) \rightarrow (U_1, U_2) \rightarrow (\hat{X}_1, \hat{X}_2)$; and the maximization is carried out over $p(u_1, u_2)$ and $p(\hat{x}_1, \hat{x}_2|u_1, u_2)$ with channel conditional distribution $p^*(x_1, x_2|\hat{x}_1, \hat{x}_2)$ held fixed such that $Ew \leq W$, $(U_1, U_2) \rightarrow (\hat{X}_1, \hat{X}_2) \rightarrow (X_1, X_2)$, and $(X_1, X_2) \rightarrow (U_1, U_2) \rightarrow (\hat{X}_1, \hat{X}_2)$,
- the distributions $p^*(u_1, u_2)$ and $p^*(\hat{x}_1, \hat{x}_2|u_1, u_2)$ induced from the first optimization achieve this maximization,

provided the cost measure and the cost constraint are chosen such that

$$w(\hat{x}_1, \hat{x}_2) = c_1 D(p^*(x_1, x_2|\hat{x}_1, \hat{x}_2)||\bar{p}(x_1, x_2)) + \theta, \tag{4.6}$$

and $W = E_{p^*(\hat{x}_1, \hat{x}_2)}[w(\hat{x}_1, \hat{x}_2)]$, for arbitrary $c_1 > 0$ and θ.

Similarly, for a given broadcast channel coding problem, if the optimizing distribution satisfies the Markov chain necessary for the distributed source coding problem, then we can find a dual distributed source coding problem. Due to lack of space, we illustrate this with the following example. Note that the encoder of the first problem is functionally identical to that of the decoder of the latter and vice versa. Further, the optimal random codebooks are constructed using the distributions $p^*(u_1)$ and $p^*(u_2)$.

Example 2: Consider a two-input-two-output broadcast channel $\mathbf{X} = H\hat{\mathbf{X}} + \mathbf{N}$, where $\mathbf{N}$ is a zero-mean Gaussian vector with identity matrix I as the covariance matrix, where H is a matrix. The cost measure is sum-power: $w(\hat{x}_1, \hat{x}_2) = (\hat{x}_1^2 + \hat{x}_2^2)$, and $W = 2P$ for some $P > 0$. It was shown in [**39**] that the sum-rate as given by (4.2) for this channel is tight using Sato's bound, which says that the capacity of a broadcast channel depends only on the marginals $\bar{p}(x_i|\hat{x}_1, \hat{x}_2)$ for $i = 1, 2$. It was shown that by carefully varying the covariance matrix of the noise in the channel while keeping the marginals (ones on the diagonals) the same, the capacity of this channel if the receivers were to cooperate can be made exactly equal to that given by (4.2). Let Σ_n be this least favorable noise covariance matrix (see [**39, 40**]). Then it can be shown that the induced joint distribution does indeed satisfy $U_1 \rightarrow X_1 \rightarrow X_2 \rightarrow U_2$. The covariance matrix of the channel output is $(H\Sigma_{\hat{x}}H^T + \Sigma_n)$, where $\Sigma_{\hat{x}}$ is the optimum input distribution. In other words, if the noise covariance matrix of the given broadcast channel is changed to Σ_n, then we can define its dual distributed source coding problem with jointly Gaussian source with zero-mean and covariance matrix $(H\Sigma_{\hat{x}}H^T + \Sigma_n)$, and a quadratic distortion measure of the form $(\mathbf{x} - H\hat{\mathbf{x}})^T \Sigma_n^{-1} (\mathbf{x} - H\hat{\mathbf{x}})$.

Theorem 5a: Given a multiple description coding problem with no excess sum-rate, with a given source $\bar{p}(X_1, X_2)$, with alphabets $\mathcal{X}_i$ and reconstruction alphabets $\hat{\mathcal{X}}_i$ for $i = 1, 2$, a distortion measure $d : \mathcal{X}_1 \times \mathcal{X}_2 \times \hat{\mathcal{X}}_1 \times \hat{\mathcal{X}}_2 \rightarrow \mathbb{R}^+$, a distortion constraint D, let the conditional distributions satisfying the optimality condition of (4.3) be given by $p^*(\hat{x}_1, \hat{x}_2|x_1, x_2)$, inducing the joint distribution given by $p^*(x_1, x_2, \hat{x}_1, \hat{x}_2) = \bar{p}(x_1, x_2)p^*(\hat{x}_1, \hat{x}_2|x_1, x_2)$. Let $p^*(\hat{x}_1, \hat{x}_2) = \sum_{x_1, x_2} p^*(x_1, x_2, \hat{x}_1, \hat{x}_2)$, and $p^*(x_1, x_2|\hat{x}_1, \hat{x}_2) = \frac{p^*(x_1, x_2, \hat{x}_1, \hat{x}_2)}{p^*(\hat{x}_1, \hat{x}_2)}$. Then $\exists$ a dual multiple access channel coding problem with independent message sets for the channel $p^*(x_1, x_2|\hat{x}_1, \hat{x}_2)$, with input and output alphabets $\hat{\mathcal{X}}_i$ and $\mathcal{X}_i$ for $i = 1, 2$ respectively, a cost measure $w : \hat{\mathcal{X}}_1 \times \hat{\mathcal{X}}_2 \to \mathbb{R}^+$, a cost constraint W, such that

- the sum rate-distortion bound $R_{MD}(D)$ is equal to the sum capacity-cost bound $C_{MA}(W)$, i.e.,

$$\min\ I(X_1, X_2; \hat{X}_1, \hat{X}_2) = \max\ I(X_1, X_2; \hat{X}_1, \hat{X}_2),$$

  where the minimization is carried out over $p(\hat{x}_1, \hat{x}_2|x_1, x_2)$ such that $Ed \leq D$, and $\hat{X}_1$ and $\hat{X}_2$ are independent, with source distribution $\bar{p}(x_1, x_2)$ held fixed; and the maximization is carried out over $p(\hat{x}_1, \hat{x}_2)$ such that $Ew \leq W$, and $\hat{X}_1$ and $\hat{X}_2$ independent, with channel conditional distribution $p^*(x_1, x_2|\hat{x}_1, \hat{x}_2)$ held fixed.
- the distribution $p^*(\hat{x}_1, \hat{x}_2)$ induced from the first optimization achieves this maximization,

provided the cost measure and cost constraint for this problem are chosen such that

$$w(\hat{x}_1, \hat{x}_2) = c_1 D(p^*(x_1, x_2|\hat{x}_1, \hat{x}_2)||\bar{p}(x_1, x_2)) + \theta, \tag{4.7}$$

and $W = E_{p^*(\hat{x}_1, \hat{x}_2)}[w(\hat{x}_1, \hat{x}_2)]$, for arbitrary $c_1 > 0$ and θ.

As in Theorem 1, here too for a pair of dual problems, the encoder of one is functionally identical to the decoder of the other and vice versa. Further, for a given multiple access channel coding problem with independent messages we can associate a specific dual multiple description problem with no excess sum rate. This is illustrated by the following example. The optimal random codebooks are constructed from the distribution $p^*(u_1)$ and $p^*(u_2)$.

Example 3: Given a two-input-two-output multiple access channel coding problem with channel given by: $\mathbf{X} = H\hat{\mathbf{X}} + \mathbf{N}$, where $\mathbf{N}$ is a zero-mean Gaussian vector with identity matrix I as the covariance matrix, where H is a matrix. The cost measure is sum-power: $w(\hat{x}_1, \hat{x}_2) = (\hat{x}_1^2 + \hat{x}_2^2)$, and $W = 2P$ for some P. For simplicity let the rows of H be $[1, \alpha]$ and $[\alpha, 1]$ for some $\alpha > 0$. The optimization of the sum rate yields $C_{MA}(2P) = \frac{1}{2}\log\left[(P(1 + \alpha^2) + 1)^2 - 4\alpha^2 P^2\right]$. This results in the covariance matrix of the channel output being $P(HH^T) + I$. Each encoder transmits at power P. Its dual multiple description coding problem will have a Gaussian vector source with zero mean and covariance matrix given by $P(HH^T) + I$, which is the same as that of the channel output of the given multiple access problem. The appropriate distortion measure is quadratic and is given by $d(\mathbf{x}, \hat{\mathbf{x}}) = (\mathbf{x} - H\hat{\mathbf{x}})^T(\mathbf{x} - H\hat{\mathbf{x}})$.

5. Conclusions

We have considered a mathematical formulation of duality between conventional source and channel coding, and extended it to the case with side information, and MIMO case with one-sided collaboration. Our notion of duality is in the functional sense, i.e. where the encoder/decoder functional mappings can be exactly swapped in the dual problems. We have given several examples for illustration. By using this concept we have obtained a generalization of the Wyner-Ziv result relating to no rate-loss in source coding with side information (with respect to the side information being available at both ends) from Gaussian to arbitrary distributions. A key observation that follows from our duality treatment is that contrary to popular opinion, duality does not equate to no rate-loss in coding with side information. The main motivation for understanding the duality between these two important problems is to enable efficient constructions of the encoder and the decoder based on the framework of structured codes. Our goal is to inspire dual constructions for these two problems that can leverage this functional encoder-decoder duality, and allow progress made in one field to apply naturally to the other as well. This would have an impact on a wide range of emerging applications including sensor networks, data hiding, broadcast and multi-antenna communication systems. Further, other properties of these problems along the lines of [**41, 42**], and the topic of MIMO joint source-channel coding will be addressed as a part of the future work.

Acknowledgments

We would like to thank Jim Chou, Prof. Thomas Cover, Prof. David Tse, Prakash Ishwar, Phillip Chou, Prof. Michael Gastpar and Vinay Vaishampayan for inspiring discussions and comments regarding the paper. We also would like to thank the anonymous reviewers for their critical, encouraging, interesting and inspiring comments which helped to improve the quality of the paper.

References

[1] A. D. Wyner and J. Ziv, "The rate-distortion function for source coding with side information at the decoder," *IEEE Trans. Inform. Theory*, vol. IT-22, pp. 1–10, Jan. 1976.
[2] D. P. Bertsekas, *Nonlinear Programming*. Athena Scientific, 1999.
[3] C. E. Shannon, "Coding theorems for a discrete source with a fidelity criterion," *In IRE Nat. Conv. Rec.*, vol. Part 4, pp. 142–163, 1959.
[4] T. M. Cover and J. A. Thomas, *Elements of information theory*. New York: Wiley, 1991.
[5] R. E. Blahut, "Computation of channel capacity and rate-distortion functions," *IEEE Trans. Inform. Theory*, vol. IT-18, pp. 460–473, July 1972.
[6] M. W. Marcellin and T. R. Fischer, "Trellis coded quantization of memoryless and Gauss-Markov sources," *IEEE Trans. Commun.*, vol. 38, pp. 82–93, Jan. 1990.
[7] M. V. Eyuboglu and G. D. Forney, "Lattice and trellis quantization with lattice and trellis-bounded codebooks- High rate theory for memoryless sources," *IEEE Trans. Inform. Theory*, vol. 39, pp. 46–59, Jan. 1993.
[8] G. Ungerboeck, "Channel coding with multilevel/phase signals," *IEEE Trans. Inform. Theory*, vol. IT-28, pp. 55–67, Jan. 1982.
[9] R. Laroia, N. Farvardin, and S. A. Tretter, "On optimal shaping of multidimensional constellations," *IEEE Trans. Inform. Theory*, vol. IT-40, pp. 1044–1056, July 1994.
[10] R. Laroia and N. Farvardin, "A structured fixed-rate vector quantizer derived from a variable length scalar quantizer- part I: Memoryless sources," *IEEE Trans. Inform. Theory*, vol. IT-39, pp. 851–867, May 1993.
[11] S. Gel'fand and M. Pinsker, "Coding for channel with random parameters," *Problems of Control and Information Theory*, vol. 9, pp. 19–31, 1980.
[12] M. Gastpar, B. Rimoldi, and M. Vetterli, "To code or not to code," *Proc. IEEE Int'l Symposium on Inform. Theory (ISIT), Sorrento, Italy*, June 2000. (also appeared in IEEE Trans. Inform. Theory, pp. 1147-1158, May 2003)
[13] T. Berger, "Multiterminal source coding," *in The information theory approach to communication, (CISM Courses and Lecture Notes No. 229), G. Longo, Ed., Wien and New York: Springer-Verlag.*, 1977.
[14] S. Shamai, S. Verdu, and R. Zamir, "Systematic lossy source/channel coding," *IEEE Trans. Inform. Theory*, vol. 44, pp. 564–579, Mar. 1998.
[15] J. A. O'Sullivan, P. Moulin, and J. M. Ettinger, "Information theoretic analysis of steganography," *Proc. Int. Symp. on information Theory (ISIT), Cambridge, MA*, August 1998. (also appeared in IEEE Trans. Inform. Theory, pp. 563-593, March 2003)

[16] B. Chen and G. W. Wornell, "An information-theoretic approach to the design of robust digital watermarking systems," *Proc. Int. Conf. on Acoustics, Speech and Signal Processing (ICASSP)*, March 1999. (also appeared in IEEE Trans. Inform. theory, 1423-1443, May 2001)

[17] T. M. Cover, "Broadcast channels", *IEEE Trans. Inform. Theory*, vol. IT-18, pp. 2–14, Jan. 1972.

[18] K. Marton, "A coding theorem for the discrete memoryless broadcast channel," *IEEE Trans. Inform. Theory*, vol. IT-25, pp. 306–311, May 1979.

[19] M. Costa, "Writing on dirty paper," *IEEE Trans. Inform. Theory*, vol. 29, pp. 439–441, May 1983.

[20] A. Cohen and A. Lapidoth, "The Gaussian watermarking game" *IEEE Trans. Inform. Theory*, vol. 48, pp. 1639-1667, June 2002.

[21] U. Erez, S. Shamai, and R. Zamir, "Capacity and lattice-strategies for cancelling known interference," in *ISITA 2000, Honalulu, Hawaii*, Nov. 2000.

[22] J. Chou, S. S. Pradhan, and K. Ramchandran, "On the duality between distributed source coding and data hiding," *Proc. of 33rd Asilomar Conf. on Signals, Systems and Computers*, Nov. 1999.

[23] S. S. Pradhan and K. Ramchandran, "On functional duality in MIMO source and channel coding problems having one-sided collaboration", *Proc. IEEE Information theory workshop*, Bangalore, India, Oct. 2002.

[24] S. S. Pradhan, J. Chou, and K. Ramchandran, "Duality between source coding and channel coding and its extension to the side information case", *IEEE Trans. Inform. theory*, vol. 49, pp. 1181-1203, May 2003.

[25] M. Chiang and T. M. Cover, "Unified duality between channal capacity and rate distortion with side information," in *Proc. Int. Symp. on Inform. Theory (ISIT) 2001*, Washington D.C., June 2001. (also appeared in IEEE Trans. Inform. Theory, pp. 1629-1638, June 2002.

[26] R. Barron, B. Chen, and G. W. Wornell, "The duality between information embedding and source coding with side information and some applications," *IEEE Trans. Inform. theory*, vol. 49, pp 1159-1180, May 2003.

[27] C. Heegard and A. El Gamal, "On the capacity of computer memory with defects," *IEEE Trans. Inform. Theory*, vol. 29, pp. 731–739, Sept. 1983.

[28] M. Kesal, M. K. Mihcak, R. Kotter, and P. Moulin, "Iteratively decodable codes for watermarking applications," *Proc. 2nd Int. symp. on Turbo codes and related topics*, Brest, France, Sept. 2000.

[29] R. Zamir and S. Shamai, "Nested linear/ lattice codes for Wyner-Ziv encoding," in *IEEE Inform. Theory Workshop*, Killarney, Ireland, 1998. (also appeared in IEEE Trans. Inform. Theory, pp. 1250-1276, June 2002)

[30] S. S. Pradhan and K. Ramchandran, "Distributed source coding using syndromes (DISCUS) : Design and construction," *Proc. IEEE Data Compression Conf., Snowbird, UT*, March 1999. (also appeared in IEEE Trans. Inform. Theory, pp. 626-643, March 2003)

[31] R. M. Gray, "A new class of lower bounds to information rates of stationary sources via conditional rate-distortion functions," *IEEE Trans. Inform. Theory*, vol. IT-19, pp. 480–489, July 1973.

[32] I. Csiszar and J. Korner, *Information Theory: Coding Theorems for Discrete memoryless sources.* Academic Press, New York, 1981.

[33] S. S. Pradhan, and K. Ramchandran, "Duality in MIMO source and channel coding" *In preparation*, 2002.

[34] T. Berger, "Multiterminal Source Coding," *Information Theory Approach to Communication, (CISM Courses and Lecture Notes No. 229)*, G. Longo, Ed., Wien and New York: Springer-Verlag, 1977.

[35] A. El Gamal and T. M. Cover, "Achievable Rates for Multiple Descriptions," *IEEE Trans. Inform. Theory*, vol. 28, pp. 851–857, Nov. 1982.

[36] R. Ahlswede, "The rate-distortion region for multiple descriptions without excess rate," *IEEE Trans. Inform. Theory*, vol. IT-31, pp. 721–726, Nov. 1985.

[37] R. Ahlswede, "Multiway communication channels," *Proc. 2nd Int. Symp. Inform. Theory, Tsahkadsor, Armenian S. S. R., Publishing house of Hungarian Academy of sciences*, pp. 23–52, 1971.

[38] R. Ahlswede, "An elementary proof of the strong converse theorem for the multiple-access channel," *J. Comb. Inform. Syst. Sci.*, vol. 7, pp. 216–230, 1982.

[39] G. Caire and S. Shamai, "On achievable rates in a multi-antenna Gaussian broadcast channel," in *Proc. Int'l Symp. on Inform. Theory*, Washington D.C., June 2001.
[40] W. Yu and J. Cioffi, "Sum capacity of a Gaussian vector broadcast channel," in *Proc. Int'l Symp. on Inform. Theory*, Lausanne, Switzerland, July 2002.
[41] N. Jindal, S. Vishwanath, and A. Goldsmith, "On the duality of multiple-access and broadcast channels," *Proc. Allerton Conf. on Commn., Computing, and Control*, Oct. 2001.
[42] D. N. C. Tse, and P. Viswanath, "Downlink-Uplink duality and effective bandwidth," *Proc. Int'l Symp. on Inform. Theory,* Lausanne, Switzerland, July 2002.

Department of EECS, University of Michigan, Ann Arbor, Michigan, MI 48109
E-mail address: pradhanv@eecs.umich.edu

Department of EECS, University of California, Berkeley, California, CA 94720
E-mail address: kannanr@eecs.umich.edu

Part IV

Coding

DIMACS Series in Discrete Mathematics
and Theoretical Computer Science
Volume **66**, 2004

Noiseless Data Compression with Low-Density Parity-Check Codes

Giuseppe Caire, Shlomo Shamai, and Sergio Verdú

ABSTRACT. This paper presents a new approach to universal noiseless compression based on error correcting codes. The scheme is based on the concatenation of the Burrows-Wheeler block sorting transform (BWT) with the syndrome former of a Low-Density Parity-Check (LDPC) code. The proposed scheme has linear encoding and decoding times and uses a new closed-loop iterative doping algorithm that works in conjunction with belief-propagation decoding. Unlike the leading data compression methods our method is resilient against errors, and lends itself to joint source-channel encoding/decoding; furthermore it offers very competitive data compression performance.

1. Introduction

Lossless data compression algorithms find numerous applications in information technology. To name some of the major ones:

- packing utilities (such as `gzip`) in operating systems such as Windows, Linux and Unix;
- modem standards such as V.32bis and V.42bis;
- fax standards such as CCITT;
- the back-end of lossy compression algorithms such as JPEG and MPEG;
- compression of headers of TCP/IP packets in wireless networks.

Indeed, the field of lossless data compression has achieved a state of maturity, with algorithms that admit fast (linear-complexity) implementations and achieve asymptotically the fundamental information theoretic limits.

However, emerging high-speed wireless data transmission systems send their payloads uncompressed. The main reasons for the failure of the state-of-the-art in wireless data networks to take into account source redundancy in those applications are:

- Lack of resilience of data compressors to transmission errors.
- Packetized transmission/recording often means that the compression output length is only relevant up to an integer multiple of a given packet length.

1991 *Mathematics Subject Classification.* Primary 68P30, 94A29; Secondary 94A45, 62B10.
Key words and phrases. Noiseless Data Compression, Universal algorithms, Error Correcting Codes, Source Coding, Sources with Memory, Block Sorting Transform.

- The regime for which the algorithms exhibit efficient performance requires much longer packet lengths than those typically used in modern high-speed wireless applications.

We propose a new approach to lossless data compression based on error correcting codes and the block-sorting transform. This approach turns out to be quite competitive with existing algorithms even in the purely lossless data compression setting, particularly for relatively short lengths (of the order of kilobits) of interest in packet wireless transmission.

Section 2 explains the role of linear channel codes in noiseless and almost-noiseless source coding. Section 3 shows how to use LDPC codes and the belief propagation algorithm for compressing and decompressing binary and nonbinary sources. Important gains in performance are possible by devising schemes that take into account that, unlike the noisy channel setting, here the encoder has access to all the information available to the decoder. Section 4 shows several ways to capitalize on this possibility and in particular it describes our closed-loop iterative doping scheme. The challenge of how to adapt the schemes for memoryless compression to general sources with memory is addressed in Section 6. This is solved by the dovetailing of the Block Sorting transform with LDPC encoding and the belief-propagation algorithm. Section 7 describes how to make the overall scheme universal and shows some experimental comparisons with state-of-the-art data compression algorithms.

2. Linear Channel Codes in Data Compression

The Shannon-MacMillan theorem [**Sha48, McM53**] states that for stationary ergodic sources and all $\delta > 0$ there exist fixed-length n-to-m compression codes of any rate m/n exceeding the entropy rate plus δ with vanishing block error probability as the blocklength goes to infinity. While almost-lossless fixed-length data compression occupies a prominent place in information theory it has had no impact in the development of data compression algorithms. However, *linear* error correction codes for additive-noise discrete memoryless channels can be used as the basis for almost-lossless data compressors for memoryless sources because of the following analogy.

A linear fixed-length data compressor is characterized by an $m \times n$ matrix $\mathbf{H}$ which simply maps $\mathbf{s}$, the source n-vector, to the compressed m-vector[1] $\mathbf{Hs}$. The maximum-likelihood decoder selects $g_{\mathbf{H}}(\mathbf{Hs})$, the most likely source vector $\mathbf{u}$ that satisfies $\mathbf{Hu} = \mathbf{Hs}$. Note that the encoder can recognize if the source vector will be decompressed successfully by simply checking whether $g_{\mathbf{H}}(\mathbf{Hs}) = \mathbf{s}$. If this is not the case, it can output an error message, or it can try a different (possibly with larger m) encoding matrix.

On the other hand, consider an additive-noise[2] discrete channel $\mathbf{y} = \mathbf{x} + \mathbf{u}$ driven by a linear channel code with parity check matrix $\mathbf{H}$. Since every valid codeword satisfies $\mathbf{Hx} = \mathbf{0}$, it is easy to see that the maximum-likelihood decoder selects the codeword $\mathbf{y} - g_{\mathbf{H}}(\mathbf{Hy})$, i. e. it selects the most likely noise realization among those that lead to the same *syndrome* $\mathbf{Hy}$. Thus, the problems of almost-noiseless fixed-length data compression and almost noiseless coding of an

[1]The arithmetic is in the finite field on which the source is defined.

[2]The sum is that of the finite field on which the noise and channel inputs and outputs are defined.

$$
\begin{bmatrix}
\mathrm{k} & \mathrm{p} & & \mathrm{q} & \mathrm{t} & \mathrm{e} & \mathrm{z} & \mathrm{i} & \mathrm{p} & \mathrm{j} & \mathrm{p} & \mathrm{h} & \mathrm{u} & \mathrm{t} \\
\mathrm{s} & \mathrm{g} & \mathrm{l} & \mathrm{k} & \mathrm{c} & & \mathrm{l} & \mathrm{u} & & \mathrm{e} & \mathrm{m} & \mathrm{b} & \mathrm{n} & \mathrm{e} \\
\mathrm{c} & & \mathrm{w} & \mathrm{f} & \mathrm{o} & \mathrm{y} & \mathrm{x} & \mathrm{b} & \mathrm{a} & \mathrm{x} & \mathrm{v} & \mathrm{l} & \mathrm{s} & \mathrm{j} \\
\mathrm{g} & \mathrm{o} & \mathrm{j} & \mathrm{f} & \mathrm{s} & \mathrm{i} & \mathrm{e} & & \mathrm{j} & \mathrm{w} & \mathrm{b} & \mathrm{a} & \mathrm{o} & \mathrm{y} \\
\mathrm{c} & \mathrm{r} & \mathrm{t} & \mathrm{o} & \mathrm{x} & \mathrm{d} & \mathrm{h} & \mathrm{k} & \mathrm{e} & \mathrm{x} & \mathrm{o} & \mathrm{h} & \mathrm{h} & \mathrm{r} \\
\mathrm{f} & \mathrm{w} & \mathrm{q} & \mathrm{c} & \mathrm{y} & \mathrm{i} & & \mathrm{g} & \mathrm{g} & \mathrm{s} & \mathrm{u} & \mathrm{z} & \mathrm{y} & \mathrm{t} \\
\mathrm{l} & \mathrm{t} & \mathrm{o} & \mathrm{e} & \mathrm{q} & \mathrm{v} & \mathrm{j} & \mathrm{m} & \mathrm{n} & \mathrm{r} & \mathrm{k} & \mathrm{x} & \mathrm{i} & \mathrm{k} \\
\mathrm{j} & & & \mathrm{e} & \mathrm{g} & \mathrm{l} & \mathrm{a} & \mathrm{k} & \mathrm{u} & \mathrm{m} & & \mathrm{e} & \mathrm{u} & \mathrm{x} \\
\mathrm{i} & \mathrm{f} & \mathrm{e} & \mathrm{m} & \mathrm{x} & \mathrm{h} & \mathrm{y} & \mathrm{o} & \mathrm{e} & \mathrm{t} & \mathrm{b} & & \mathrm{f} & \mathrm{s} \\
\mathrm{s} & \mathrm{u} & \mathrm{o} & \mathrm{k} & \mathrm{r} & \mathrm{c} & & \mathrm{t} & \mathrm{j} & \mathrm{w} & \mathrm{k} & \mathrm{q} & \mathrm{t} & \mathrm{c}
\end{bmatrix}
\begin{bmatrix}
\mathrm{c} \\ \mathrm{l} \\ \mathrm{a} \\ \mathrm{u} \\ \mathrm{d} \\ \mathrm{e} \\ ~ \\ \mathrm{s} \\ \mathrm{h} \\ \mathrm{a} \\ \mathrm{n} \\ \mathrm{n} \\ \mathrm{o} \\ \mathrm{n}
\end{bmatrix}
=
\begin{bmatrix}
\mathrm{p} \\ \mathrm{g} \\ \mathrm{o} \\ \mathrm{l} \\ \mathrm{p} \\ \mathrm{m} \\ \mathrm{u} \\ \mathrm{s} \\ ~ \\ \mathrm{h}
\end{bmatrix}
$$

FIGURE 1. Example of linear data compression in GF(27)

additive-noise discrete channel whose noise has the same statistics as the source are strongly related. Indeed since the maximum-likelihood channel decoder selects the wrong codeword if and only if $g_{\mathbf{H}}(\mathbf{Hu}) \neq \mathbf{u}$, the block error rate achieved by the corresponding maximum-likelihood decoders are identical. This strongly suggests using the parity-check matrix of a channel code as the source encoding matrix. One of the (neglected) consequences of this powerful equivalence relates to the construction of optimum n-to-m source codes, which are well-known to be those that assign a unique codeword to each of the n-sequences with the largest probabilities. For memoryless sources, this can be accomplished for certain (m, n) by using the parity-check matrix of *perfect* codes[3]. To see this (in the binary case) note that using the parity-check matrix of a perfect linear code of radius e, all the sourcewords with weight $0, 1, \ldots, e$ are mapped to distinct codewords. Otherwise, when the code is used for the binary channel there would be different error patterns of weight less than or equal e leading to the same syndrome. For example, in the binary case, we can obtain optimum 7-to-3 and 23-to-11 source codes by using the Hamming and Golay codes respectively. Figure 2 compares the probability that an optimal (Hamming) 7-to-3 source code is successful for a Bernoulli source with bias p with the probability that a Huffman (minimum average length) code operating on 7-tuples outputs a string with no more than 3 bits.

Unfortunately, the foregoing analogy between linear source codes and linear parity-check channel codes seems to have been all but neglected in the literature and we can find few instances in which error correcting codes have been used as data compressors. Dealing with source sequences known to have a limited Hamming weight, Weiss [**Wei62**] noted that since the 2^{n-k} cosets of an e-correcting (n, k) binary linear code can be represented by their unique codewords having weight less than or equal to e, the binary input n-string can be encoded with $n - k$ bits that label the coset it leads. The decompressor is simply the mapping that identifies each coset with its leader. The fact that this is equivalent to computing the

---

[3]A perfect code is one where Hamming spheres of a fixed radius around the codewords fill the complete space of n-tuples without overlap (e.g. [**McE02**]) .

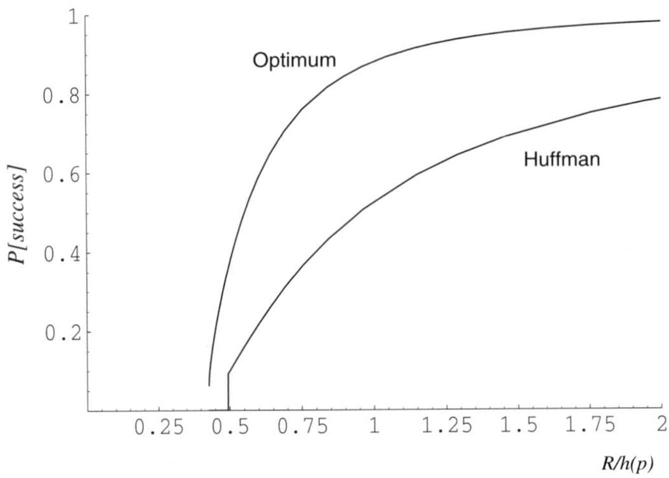

FIGURE 2. 7-to-3 encoding of a biased coin.

syndrome that would result if the source sequence were the channel output was explicitly recognized by Allard and Bridgewater [**AB72**]. Both [**AB72**] and Fung et al [**FTS73**] remove Weiss' bounded weight restriction and come up with variable-to-fixed-length schemes where zeros are appended prior to syndrome formation so that the resulting syndrome is correctable. Also in the setting of binary memoryless sources, Ancheta [**Anc76**] considered fixed-to-fixed linear source codes based on syndrome formation of a few BCH codes. Since the only sources the approach in [**Wei62, AB72, FTS73, Anc76**] was designed to handle were memoryless sources (essentially biased coins) and since the practical error correcting codes known at that time did not offer rates close to channel capacity, that line of research rapidly came to a close with the advent of Lempel-Ziv coding. Also limited to memoryless binary sources is another, more recent, approach [**GFZ02**] in which the source is encoded by a Turbo code whose systematic outputs as well as a portion of the non-systematic bits are discarded; and decompression is carried out by a Turbo decoder that uses knowledge of the source bias. Germane to this line of research is the use of Turbo and LDPC codes [**BM01, GFZ01, Mur02, LXG02**] for Slepian-Wolf coding of correlated memoryless sources as specific embodiments of the approach proposed in [**Wyn74**].

The restriction for a fixed-length source code to be linear is known not to incur any loss of asymptotic optimality for memoryless sources. This can be shown through a standard random coding argument [**CK81**], which is essentially the same used in [**Eli55**] for the optimality of random channel codes. The idea is that, using random codebooks, the intersection of the coset represented by the syndrome formed with the source sequence and the set of typical sequences has one and only one element with high probability as the blocklength goes to infinity. We have extended this result (without recourse to typicality) to completely general sources (with memory and nonstationarity):

THEOREM 2.1. [**CSV**] *If the source has sup-entropy rate*[4] $\bar{H}$, $\frac{m}{n} > \bar{H} + \delta$, *the encoding matrix entries are independent, equiprobable on the alphabet, then the average (over the ensemble of matrices and source realizations) block error probability* $\to 0$ *as* $n \to \infty$

For general linear codes, syndrome forming (source encoding) has quadratic complexity in the blocklength and maximum-likelihood decoding has exponential complexity in the blocklength. These complexities compare unfavorably with the linear encoding/decoding complexities achieved by Lempel-Ziv coding. To address that shortcoming we consider a specific class of error-correction codes in the next section.

3. LDPC Data Compression for Memoryless Sources

By definition, the parity-check matrix $\mathbf{H}$ of a low-density parity-check code is a sparse matrix with a number of nonzero entries growing linearly with the blocklength, and, thus, the linear source compressor that uses $\mathbf{H}$ has linear complexity in the blocklength. Note that this is in contrast to the encoding of LDPC codes for channel encoding as the multiplication by the generator matrix is far less straightforward, requiring the application of the technique in [**RU01b**] to achieve nearly linear complexity.

The sparseness of $\mathbf{H}$ does not imply that a polynomially-complex maximum-likelihood decoder exists. For LDPCs the suboptimal iterative technique known as *Belief-Propagation* (BP) decoding has proved to yield very good results on a variety of memoryless channels. The BP decoders used in channel decoding of binary symmetric channels [**Gal63, RU01a**] operate with the channel outputs rather than with the syndrome vector. However, counterparts to those algorithms that give an approximation to the syndrome-decoding function $g_{\mathbf{H}}$ can easily be derived. In these algorithms, the compressed data is not present at the variable nodes (which represent the uncompressed bits) but at the check nodes, since in the source-coding case, each parity-check equation has a value given by the compressed data. For simplicity and concreteness we specify the algorithm in the binary memoryless case with nonstationary probabilities (which will be relevant in Section 6). Fix the realization of the input to the decoder, $\mathbf{z}$. The set of checknodes in which the bitnode $k \in \{1, \dots n\}$ participates is denoted by $\mathcal{A}_k \subset \{1, \dots m\}$, and the set of bitnodes which are connected to checknode $j \in \{1, \dots m\}$ is denoted by $\mathcal{B}_j \subset \{1, \dots n\}$. With the a priori probability that the kth source symbol equal to 1 denoted by p_k, define the a priori source log-ratios

$$\mathcal{L}_k = \log \frac{1 - p_k}{p_k}, \quad k \in \{1, \dots n\}, \tag{3.1}$$

and the isomorphism $\phi : GF(2) \mapsto \{-1, +1\}$, where $\phi(0) = +1$ and $\phi(1) = -1$. For each iteration $t = 1, 2, \dots$, the algorithm computes the value of the bitnodes

$$\widehat{x}_k = \phi^{-1}\left(\operatorname{sign}\left\{\mathcal{L}_k + \sum_{j \in \mathcal{A}_k} \mu_{j \to k}^{(t)}\right\}\right)$$

by updating the messages sent by the checknodes to their neighboring bitnodes and by the bitnodes to their neighboring checknodes, denoted respectively by $\mu_{j \to k}^{(t)}$ and

[4]See [**HV93**] for the definition of sup-entropy rate.

by $\nu_{k\to j}^{(t)}$, according to the message-passing rules

$$\nu_{k\to j}^{(t)} = \mathcal{L}_k + \sum_{j'\in\mathcal{A}_k-\{j\}} \mu_{j'\to k}^{(t-1)} \tag{3.2}$$

and

$$\mu_{j\to k}^{(t)} = 2\phi(z_j)\tanh^{-1}\left(\prod_{k'\in\mathcal{B}_j-\{k\}} \tanh\left(\frac{\nu_{k'\to j}^{(t)}}{2}\right)\right) \tag{3.3}$$

with the initialization $\mu_{j\to k}^{(0)} = 0$ for all $j \in \{1, \ldots, m\}$. At each iteration, the parity-check equations

$$\sum_{k\in\mathcal{B}_j} \widehat{x}_k = z_k, \quad j = 1, \ldots, m$$

are evaluated. If they are all satisfied, the BP algorithm stops. If after a maximum number of allowed iterations some parity-check equations are not satisfied, a block-error is declared.

In the q-ary case, the BP algorithm is more cumbersome since the distributions are no longer succinctly represented by a scalar. However, a linear-time BP algorithm akin to the one in [**DM98**] can be given [**CSV**] Using the FFT in GF(q), the computational complexity per iteration is $O(E\mathsf{q}\log\mathsf{q})$ if E is equal to the number of nonzero entries in $\mathbf{H}$.

We have shown [**CSV**] that the same pointwise correspondence between channel decoding and source decoding stated for the ML decoder in Section 2 holds also for the BP decoder: the sets of source sequences and noise sequences that lead to errors of the respective BP decoders are identical. This equivalence has important consequences in the design of the LDPC matrix for data compression. Consider an arbitrary LDPC ensemble with BSC-threshold $p^\star$. In the standard terminology, this means that as the blocklength goes to infinity, the bit error rate achieved by BP averaged over the ensemble vanishes for every BSC with crossover probability less than $p^\star$, but not higher. Similarly, we can define the Bernoulli-source threshold of an arbitrary LDPC ensemble for fixed-length data compression, as the supremum of the source biases for which the bit error rate achieved by BP averaged over the ensemble vanishes as the blocklength goes to infinity. Because of the equivalence in performance of the corresponding BP decoders, for a given ensemble the BSC-threshold is equal to the Bernoulli-source threshold. It follows that optimal LDPC ensembles for the BSC yield immediately optimal LDPC ensembles for source coding of biased coins.

To end this section, we present an alternative to the foregoing approach to fixed-length data compression based on error correcting codes for an additive-noise discrete memoryless channel. This alternative approach uses erasure channel coding/decoding designed for the conventional stationary erasure channel. At the compressor, first we apply the n-binary string produced by the source to a rate-R erasure channel encoder. Then, we discard the systematic part and the remaining $n(\frac{1}{R} - 1)$ bits are passed through an interleaver; the compressed m-binary string is given by the uppermost $1 - p$ fraction of the interleaver outputs. The other interleaver outputs are also discarded (Figure 3). Thus,

$$\frac{m}{n} = (1-p)(\frac{1}{R} - 1).$$

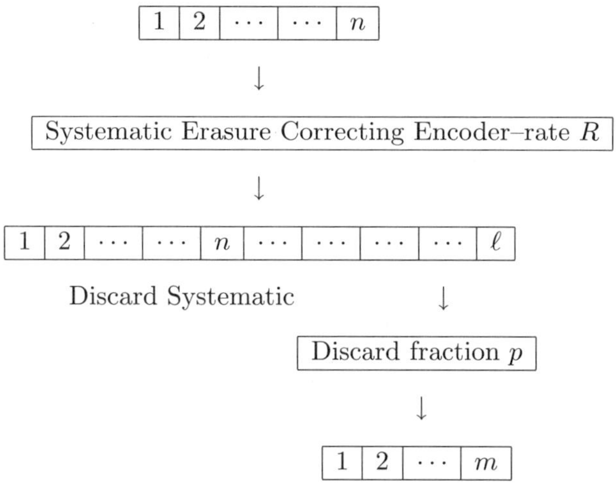

FIGURE 3. Data compression with erasure correcting codes.

There is some freedom in the choice of p and R, respecting the constraint:

$$(1-p)(\frac{1}{R}-1) \approx H + \delta.$$

or equivalently,

$$R \approx \frac{1-p}{1-p+H+\delta}.$$

The data decompressor first appends to the compressed sequence a string of $m\frac{p}{1-p}$ erasures,then it deinterleaves (using the inverse interleaver used at the compressor), it appends n erasures (the missing systematic part), and it feeds the whole string of m bits and $n((\frac{1}{R}-1)p+1)$ erasures (a total of n/R symbols) to the erasure decoder which takes into account the a priori probabilities of the source as follows: Now there are n/R variable nodes, which from top to bottom consist of

- n erasures corresponding to bits whose a priori probabilities are equal to $P_{s_1}(1), \dots P_{s_n}(1)$;
- $mp/(1-p)$ erasures corresponding to bits which are approximated as being equiprobable
- m nonerased bits.

The iterations proceed using the BP algorithm described above once we do the following preprocessing. For each of the $(1/R-1)n$ check nodes, we assign a value to check node i given by the sum of all the information bits contained in the nonerased subset of variable nodes connected to that check node. Now, discard all nonerased variable nodes and their connections. All the remaining variable nodes correspond to erasures; n of them have the a priori probabilities of the source and their loglikelihood updates proceed exactly as in (3.2). For the $mp/(1-p)$ remaining erasure variable nodes, (3.2) also applies but with the first term equal to 0 (corresponding to 1/2 prior probabilities). The methods in Sections 4,6,7 are described in the context of the error-correcting approach but apply verbatim to the erasure-correcting approach.

4. Decoding at the Encoder

In contrast to channel decoding, in noiseless data compression, the source encoder has the same information available to the decoder. Thus, not only it can check whether the original sourceword will be correctly decompressed but it has the luxury of running a mirror image of the decoder iterations.

There are several ways in which this capability can be taken advantage of in order to counter the inherent inefficiencies incurred by the use of LDPC codes and the suboptimal BP decoder.

First note that the "almost noiseless" fixed-to-fixed compression algorithm can be easily adapted to zero-error variable-to-fixed or fixed-to-variable operation by tuning the input/output length in the compression to guarantee decoding success. For example, it is possible to successively generate parity-check equations until successful decoding is achieved. To that end, the use of raptor codes [**Sho03**] is more natural than LDPC codes as shown in [**CSSV**].

In general, the encoder can try several parity-check matrices (with equal or different rates) from a library known at the decoder until success is achieved. A header identifying the actual matrix sent is part of the compressed sequence.

Symbol Doping, i.e. informing the decoder about sure bits, which are treated by the decoder as perfectly known (i.e., having infinite reliability) is another strategy that accelerates convergence and improves the block error probability. It can be done in open-loop mode [5] where the location of the doped symbols is pre-agreed or in closed-loop mode depending on the evolution of the algorithm. However, it would be very costly to need to identify the location of each bit to be doped. A much better alternative is our *Closed-Loop Iterative Doping Algorithm* which dopes the bit that most needs it, i.e. the one with the lowest reliability. The algorithm generates one doped bit per iteration as follows.

1) Initialization: $\mu^{(0)}_{j\to k} = 0$ for all $j \in \{1, \dots, m\}$.

2) Repeat the following steps for $t = 1, 2, \dots$ (iteration count) until successful decoding is reached:

- For all bitnodes $k = 1, \dots, n$ compute

$$\nu_k^{(t)} = \mathcal{L}_k + \sum_{j \in \mathcal{A}_k} \mu^{(t-1)}_{j\to k}$$

  and find the node that achieves the lowest reliability:

$$\widehat{k} = \arg \min_{k=1,\dots,n} \{|\nu_k^{(t)}|\},$$

- Least-reliable symbol doping: Feed the symbol $x_{\widehat{k}}$ directly to the decoder and let

$$\mathcal{L}_{\widehat{k}} = \begin{cases} +\infty & \text{if } x_{\widehat{k}} = 0 \\ -\infty & \text{if } x_{\widehat{k}} = 1 \end{cases}$$

- Bitnode update (3.2) and Checknode update (3.3).

Some qualitative properties of the Iterative Doping Algorithm are:

1. Because of reliability sorting, the position of doped symbols need not be explicitly communicated to the decoder. Hence, the cost of doping is the (random) number of iterations necessary to achieve successful decoding.
2. The algorithm never dopes twice the same symbol.

---

[5] Traditional doping (e.g. [**tB00**]) follows that paradigm.

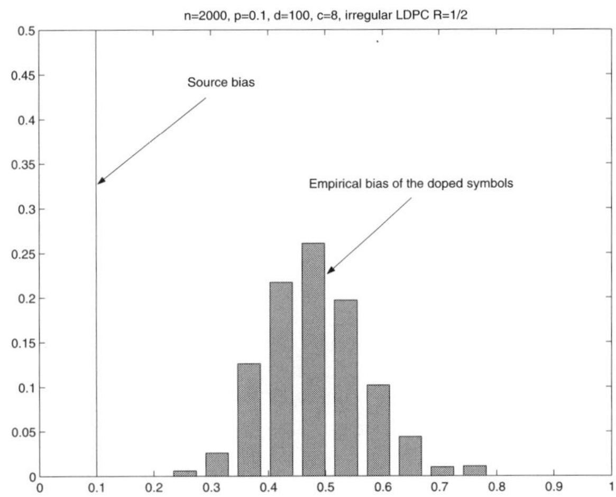

FIGURE 4. Empirical Distribution of the bits generated by the Closed-Loop Iterative Doping Algorithm.

3. Doping the symbol with least reliability is an efficient strategy. In practice this is done only if the reliability is below a certain threshold, in which case the doped bits (conditioned on the knowledge accumulated up until their reception by the decompressor) are approximately fair coin flips. Figure 4 contrasts the distribution of the source (a very biased coin) with the empirical distribution of the bits generated by the Closed-Loop Iterative Doping Algorithm, which is very close to fair-coin flips. In that experiment, the empirical entropy of the doped bits is above 0.95 bits with probability around 0.92. While at the very beginning the lowest-reliability bit has the same bias as the source, after the first iterations it quickly drops below the threshold. Figure 5 illustrates the typical evolution of the average and minimum reliability of the source bits as a function of the BP iterations.

The closed-loop iterative doping algorithm can either be used in fixed-length mode with a prefixed number of doping bits or in zero-error variable-length mode, where the number of doped bits is dictated by the source realization. The mean and variance of the number of doped symbols can be reduced by using a library of several parity-check matrices, [6] by applying the above algorithm to each matrix, choosing the one that achieves successful decoding with the smallest length, and indicating the label of the best matrix to the decoder. Note that doping need not take place at every iteration. In fact, a tradeoff exists between decompression time and encoding efficiency which can be controlled by the doping schedule. Furthermore the doping schedule can also be "closed-loop", controlled by the instantaneous values of the reliabilities computed by the BP algorithm. Although explained in conjunction with the error-correcting approach, the iterative doping algorithm can also be applied to the erasure-correcting approach to data compression explained in Section 3. Figure 6 shows the distribution (complementary cumulative distribution function) of the achieved compression for several schemes operating on a biased coin for biases p

[6]Even after the BP algorithm has converged, there exists the (extremely unlikely) possibility that the chosen codeword is erroneous. In that event the compressor can choose another parity-check matrix (e.g. the identity) to ensure strictly zero-error decompression.

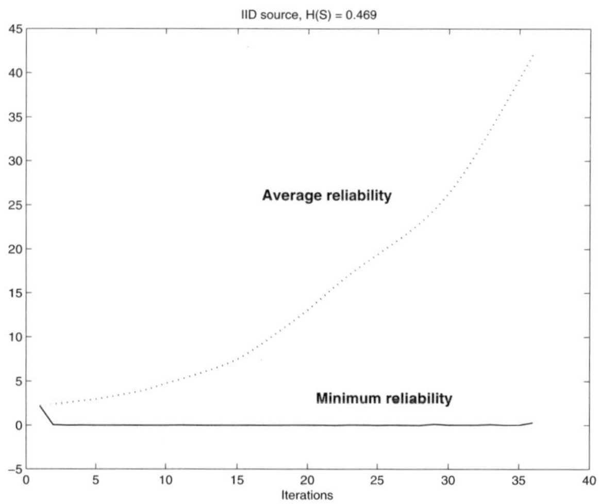

FIGURE 5. Typical evolution of the minimum and average reliability of the BP decoder.

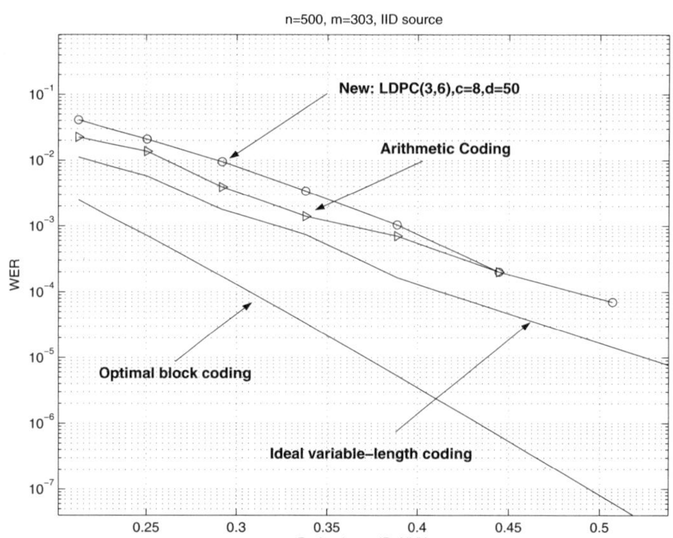

FIGURE 6. Block error rate of 500-to-303 source codes for a biased coin.

ranging from 0.11 to 0.08. Since the code rate is $R = 303/500$, this translates into normalized redundancies $(R - h(p))/h(p)$ ranging from 0.21 to 0.51, where $h(p)$ is the binary entropy function. Note that by means of the distribution of redundancies it is possible to compare fixed-length and variable-length schemes on an equal footing: for a variable-length scheme the "WER" in Figure 6 is simply the probability of the set of source realizations that cannot be encoded with the corresponding redundancy.

The schemes shown in Figure 6 are:

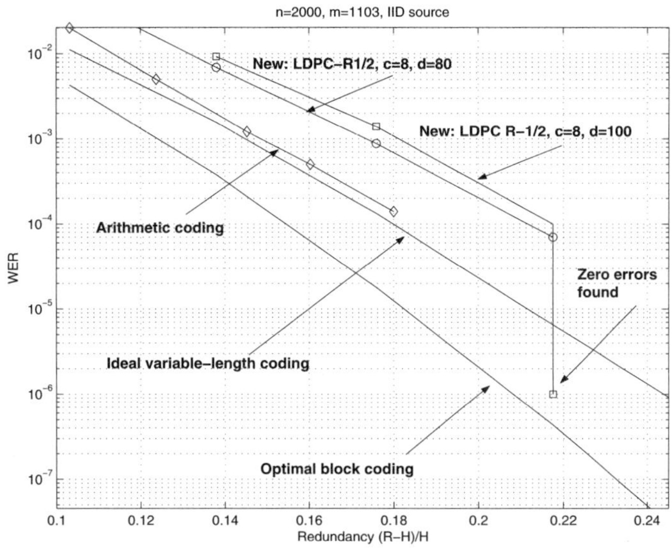

FIGURE 7. Block error rate of 2000-to-1103 source codes for a biased coin.

- *Optimal block coding*: optimal code that assigns a distinct codeword to the most probable 2^{303} source realizations.
- *"Ideal" variable-length coding* (or Information Spectrum (cf. [**HV93**]): where the 'length' of the codeword assigned to $x_1, \dots x_n$ is equal to

$$-\log_2 P_{X_1,\dots X_n}(x_1, \dots, x_n).$$

- *Arithmetic Coding:* Nonuniversal, source exactly known.
- *New code:* with a library of 8 (3,6) regular LDPCs, and 50 closed-loop iterative doped bits.

Figure 7 shows the results of an analogous experiment with a longer blocklength and a library of 8 rate-$\frac{1}{2}$ irregular LDPCs drawn at random from the ensemble designed for the BSC in [**Urb02**]. We show the effect of varying the number of bits allocated to doping from 80 to 100. At the point marked at 10^{-6} no errors were detected in 10,000 trials.

The main benefit accrued by the new scheme over arithmetic coding is much higher resilience to errors at the cost of a small decrease in performance efficiency. Figure 8 illustrates the very different resilience of arithmetic coding and the new scheme against channel erasures. It should be noted that in neither case we take any countermeasures against the channel erasures. In [**CSV04**], we report on source/channel schemes derived from the basic scheme of this paper which exhibit much more robustness against channel noise. A source block of 3000 biased coin flips is compressed into a block of 1500 syndrome bits, 200 doping bits and 3 bits identifying the LDPC. The syndrome bits are decompressed by the conventional BP algorithm with the only difference that a subset of the check nodes are now missing due to the channel erasures. As we vary the coin bias from 0.1 to 0.08, we observe an 'error floor' in Figure 8 which is dominated by the fact that the 203 doping and code library bits are sent completely unprotected. The abscissa in Figure 8 is a normalized measure of the distance from the fundamental limit that

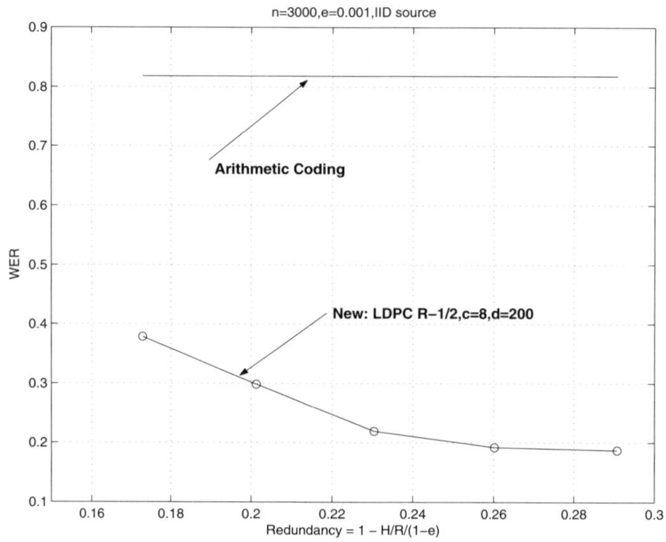

FIGURE 8. Block error rate of a 3000-to-1703 source code and arithmetic coding for a biased coin and a channel with erasure probability equal to $e = 0.001$

would be achievable for asymptotically long blocklengths, namely $\frac{h(p)}{1-e}$ where e is the channel erasure probability.

5. Non-binary Sources: Multilevel Compression Codes

In this section we propose an approach based on multilevel coding and multistage successive decoding to handle q-ary sources, where $\mathsf{q} = 2^L$. In the realm of channel coding, multilevel coding and successive decoding is a well-known technique to construct efficient codes for high-order modulations, see for example [**WFH99**] and more recently [**CS02**] with application to LDPC-coded modulation.

Although as we mentioned in previous sections, both the encoders and decoders can be generalized to the nonbinary case, there are at least two obstacles for the practical application of our method to general q-ary sources:

1. The design of q-ary LDPC ensembles for an arbitrary q-ary additive noise channel $\mathbf{y} = \mathbf{x} + \mathbf{z}$, where addition is in GF(q), or in the ring $\mathbb{Z}_{\mathsf{q}}$, and $\mathbf{z}$ obeys an arbitrary q distribution is still not mature even in the simplest case where $\mathbf{z}$ is i.i.d. See [**DM98, SF02**].
2. The FFT-based q-ary BP decoder mentioned in Section 3 has linear complexity in the source blocklength, but grows as $O(\mathsf{q} \log \mathsf{q})$ with the alphabet size.

By restricting the source alphabet to have cardinality equal to a power of two (e.g., $\mathsf{q} = 2^7$ in ASCII), we are able to use efficiently standard LDPC binary codes and achieve an overall complexity $O(n \log \mathsf{q})$.

For the sake of simplicity, we outline the proposed multilevel approach to data compression for an i.i.d. source in the non-universal setting (i.e., assuming that the source statistics is perfectly known to both the encoder and decoder). The methods in Sections 4,6,7 apply to this multilevel approach also.

Let X be an i.i.d. source $\sim P_X$, defined over an alphabet $\mathcal{X}$ of cardinality 2^L. Define an arbitrary one-to-one binary labeling of the source alphabet $\mu : \mathcal{X} \to \mathrm{GF}(2)^L$, such that $\mu(x) = (b_1, \ldots, b_L)$ is the binary label corresponding to x, for all $x \in \mathcal{X}$. The mapping μ and the source probability assignment P_X induce a probability assignment $P_{B_1,\ldots,B_L}(b_1, \ldots, b_L)$ over $\mathrm{GF}(2^L)$ such that $P_{B_1,\ldots,B_L}(\mu(x)) = P_X(x)$. Without loss of generality, consider the binary random variables B_ℓ in the natural order $\ell = 1, \ldots, L$. We have

$$\begin{aligned} H(X) &= H(B_1, \ldots, B_L) \\ &= \sum_{\ell=1}^{L} H(B_\ell | B_1, \ldots, B_{\ell-1}) \end{aligned} \tag{5.1}$$

From the above decomposition, we see that each *level* ℓ can be thought as a binary piecewise i.i.d. source having up to $2^{\ell-1}$ segments and entropy $H(B_\ell|B_1, \ldots, B_{\ell-1})$. Each segment corresponds to a different value of the conditioning variables $(B_1, \ldots, B_{\ell-1})$. The conditional probability of $B_\ell = 1$ given $(B_1, \ldots, B_{\ell-1}) = (b_1, \ldots, b_{\ell-1})$ is given by

$$p_\ell(b_1, \ldots, b_{\ell-1}) \triangleq \frac{\sum_{(b_{\ell+1},\ldots,b_L)\in\{0,1\}^{L-\ell}} P_{B_1,\ldots,B_L}(b_1, \ldots, b_{\ell-1}, 1, b_{\ell+1}, \ldots, b_L)}{\sum_{(b_\ell,\ldots,b_L)\in\{0,1\}^{L-\ell+1}} P_{B_1,\ldots,B_L}(b_1, \ldots, b_L)} \tag{5.2}$$

Therefore, the foregoing discussion on the compression of binary piecewise i.i.d. sources can be applied to each level ℓ. The only difference is that now the segments for the binary source at level ℓ are defined by the realizations of the previous levels $1, \ldots, \ell - 1$, i.e., encoding and decoding must be performed in a successive fashion.

The multilevel coding algorithm is briefly summarized as follows: we assume that the source distribution P_X is known, therefore, also the conditional marginal probabilities $p_\ell(b_1, \ldots, b_{\ell-1})$ defined in (5.2) and the corresponding ℓ-level entropies $H_\ell \triangleq H(B_\ell|B_1, \ldots, B_{\ell-1})$ are known. Then, we select L LDPC ensembles such that the ℓ-th ensemble has rate R_ℓ larger than, but close to, H_ℓ. In practice, we can optimize each ℓ-th LDPC ensemble for a BSC with parameter $p_\ell = h^{-1}(H_\ell)$. For each ℓ-th ensemble, we construct c parity-check matrices $\{\mathbf{H}_{\ell,i} : i = 1, \ldots, c\}$.

Let $\mathbf{s}$ denote the q-ary source sequence of length n to be compressed and, for each level ℓ, let $\mathbf{b}_\ell = (b_{\ell,1}, \ldots, b_{\ell,n})$ denote the binary sequence obtained by projecting the binary representation of $\mathbf{s}$ onto its ℓ-level binary component. For levels $\ell = 1, 2, \ldots, L$, we produce the binary encoded sequences $\mathbf{z}_\ell$ successively, by applying the LDPC compression method described before, based on the library of parity-check matrices $\{\mathbf{H}_{\ell,i} : i = 1, \ldots, c\}$ and the CLID algorithm. As anticipated above, the ℓ-th level encoder/decoder depends on the realization of the binary sequences at levels $1, \ldots, \ell - 1$ since it makes use of the conditional statistics of $\mathbf{b}_\ell$ given $\mathbf{b}_1, \ldots, \mathbf{b}_{\ell-1}$. This conditioning is incorporated into the BP decoder by using the sequence of conditional probability log-ratios

$$\mathcal{L}_k = \log \frac{1 - p_\ell(b_{1,k}, \ldots, b_{\ell-1,k})}{p_\ell(b_{1,k}, \ldots, b_{\ell-1,k})}$$

for $k = 1, \ldots, n$. Notice that at each level ℓ the symbols $b_{1,k}, \ldots, b_{\ell-1,k}$ are known at the decoder due to successive decoding. In the lossless setting there is no error propagation between the levels.

In the realm of channel coding, multilevel coding and successive decoding is a well-known technique to construct efficient codes for high-order modulations, see for example [**WFH99**] and more recently [**CS02**] with application to LDPC-coded modulation. In the realm of lossy image coding, the multilevel coding idea is reminiscent of the so-called "bit-plane coding" (e.g., see [**TM**]), where a sequence of L-bit integer samples output by some transform coder is partitioned into L binary sequences called "bit-planes". Each ℓ-th sequence is formed by the ℓ-th most significant bits of the original samples, and it is separately compressed by adaptive arithmetic coding.

The resulting encoded binary sequence corresponding to $\mathbf{s}$ is given by the concatenation of all syndromes $\mathbf{z}_\ell$ and corresponding doping symbols, for $\ell = 1, \ldots, L$. Successive encoding and decoding complexity scales linearly with the number of levels, i.e., logarithmically with the alphabet size, as anticipated above.

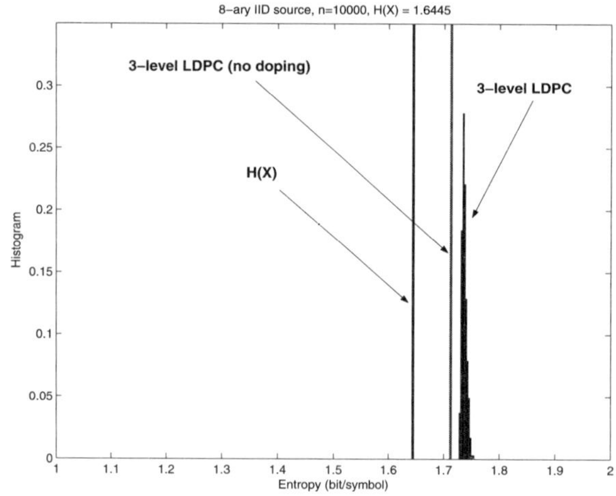

FIGURE 9. Histogram of compression rates with multilevel scheme.

Figure 9 shows the compression rate histogram achieved by the proposed scheme for a 8-ary source ($L = 3$ levels). The source has entropy $H(X) = 1.6445$, and probability distribution

$$P_X = [0.5666, 0.2833, 0.0850, 0.0028, 0.0028, 0.0283, 0.0028, 0.0283]$$

Encoding the 8 letters by the binary representation $000, 001, \ldots, 111$ (level 1 is the least-significant bit), we obtain the level entropies $H_1 = 0.9274, H_2 = 0.5233$ and $H_3 = 0.1938$. We chose LDPC ensembles with slightly conservative rates equal to $R_1 = 0.95, R_2 = 0.55$ and $R_3 = 0.22$, and for each ensemble we used 8 independently generated parity-check matrices. Figure 9 shows the distribution of the achieved coding rates. The vertical line labelled "3-level LDPC (no doping)" corresponds to the compression rate of the above scheme due exclusively to the LDPC encoding in the absence of doping (and thus achieving nonzero block error rate), with the same LDPC codes used in the histogram shown with doping. Notice that the largest contribution to redundancy is due to the conservative choice of the LDPC coding rates, and the Closed Loop Iterative Doping adds a small variable fraction to the overall redundancy. Also, notice that thanks to the iterative doping each level achieves zero decoding error probability. Hence, no catastrophic error propagation between the levels occurs.

6. Sources with Memory

In Sections 3, 4 and 5 we have limited our discussion to encoding memoryless nonstationary sources. However we know from Theorem 2.1 that linear codes can be used to approach the entropy rate of the source even if it has memory. However, the direct application of a syndrome former to a source with memory faces a serious hurdle: it is very cumbersome to design an optimum or near-optimum decoder that takes the source statistics into account. As we saw, it is easy to incorporate the knowledge about the source marginals in the BP decoding algorithm. However, for sources with memory the marginals alone do not suffice for efficient data compression. While the incorporation of Markov structure is in principle possible at the BP decoder by enlarging the Tanner graph, the complexity grows very rapidly with the source memory. In addition it would be futile to search for encoders as a function of the memory structure of the source. We next describe a design approach that enables the use of the BP (marginal based) decoding algorithm in Section 3 while taking full advantage of the source memory.

We propose to use a one-to-one transformation, called the block-sorting transform or Burrows-Wheeler transform (BWT) [**BW94**] which performs the following operation: after adding a special End-of-file symbol, it generates all cyclic shifts of the given data string and sorts them lexicographically. The last column of the resulting matrix is the BWT output from which the original data string can be recovered.

Note that the BWT performs no compression. Fashionable BWT-based universal data compression algorithms (e.g. *bzip*) have been proposed which are quite competitive with the Lempel-Ziv algorithm. To understand how this is accomplished, it is best to consider the statistical properties of the output of the BWT. It is shown in [**EVKV02**] that the output of the BWT (as the blocklength grows) is asymptotically piecewise i.i.d. For stationary ergodic tree sources the length, location, and distribution of the i.i.d. segments depend on the statistics of the source. The universal BWT-based methods for data compression all hinge on the idea of compression for a memoryless source with an adaptive procedure which learns implicitly the local distribution of the piecewise i.i.d. segments, while forgetting the effect of distant symbols.

Our approach is to let the BWT be the front-end. Then we apply the output of the BWT to the LDPC parity-check matrix, as explained in Section 3 for memoryless nonstationary sources.[7] The decompressor consists of the BP decoder, making use of the prior probabilities p_i. The locations of the transitions between the segments exhibit some deviation from there expected values which can be explicitly communicated to the decoder. Once the string has been decompressed we apply the inverse BWT to recover the original string. Figure 10 shows a block diagram of the nonuniversal version of the compression/decompression scheme.

The proof of optimality of the scheme for stationary ergodic sources using capacity-approaching channel codes uses the tools developed in [**EVKV02**].

[7] It is sometimes advantageous to set a threshold H_{th} reasonably close to 1 bit/symbol and feed directly to the output the symbols on segments whose entropy exceeds H_{th}.

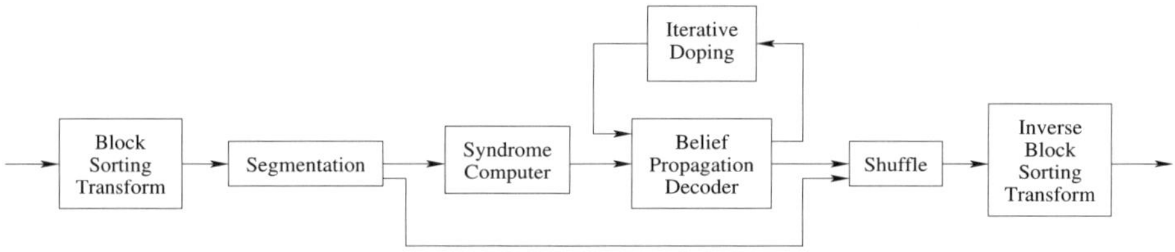

FIGURE 10. Compression/Decompression Scheme: Nonuniversal Version

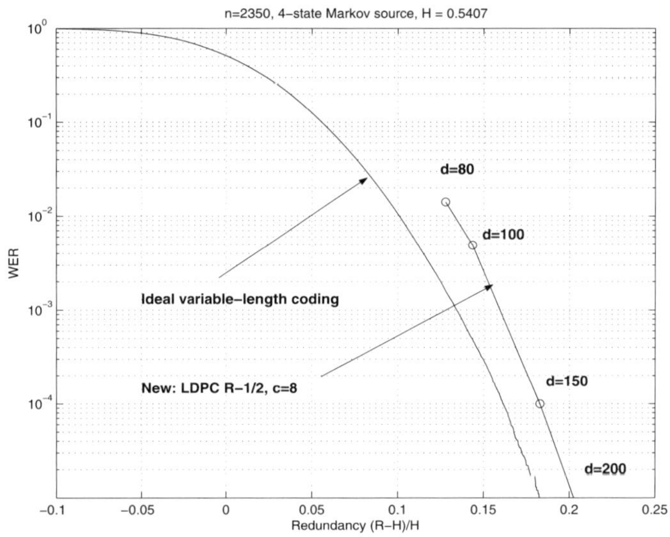

FIGURE 11. Block error rate of a 2350-to-(1350+d) source code for a four-state Markov chain.

As in the case of memoryless sources, the computational complexities of both compression and decompression grow linearly with the data size.

Figure 11 shows the results obtained with a 4-state Markov chain with conditional biases equal to $(0.1, 0.6, 0.4, 0.9)$ leading to an entropy rate of 0.5407 bits per symbol. The coding scheme does not code 350 of the source symbols (corresponding to the segments at the output of the BWT with highest entropy). Varying the number of symbols allocated to closed-loop iterative doping (which now operates in fixed-length mode) yields different rate values. Again, the degree of approximation to the ideal coding curve is rather encouraging.

Our basic scheme can be adapted to Slepian-Wolf coding of correlated stationary ergodic sources for which the fundamental limits were proved in [**Cov75**]. Note that the constructive approaches for Slepian-Wolf coding proposed so far in the literature [**BM01, GFZ01, Mur02, LXG02**] are limited to memoryless sources. Suppose that the sources are correlated according to $\mathbf{s}_1 = \mathbf{s}_2 + \mathbf{u}$ where $\mathbf{u}$ is a Markov process independent of the stationary ergodic process $\mathbf{s}_2$. To approach the point in the Slepian-Wolf-Cover region given by the entropy rate of source 2 and the conditional entropy rate of source 1 given source 2, we may use the BWT-BP-based approach explained above to encode and decode source 2, and then run a BP to recover $\mathbf{s}_1$ on a Tanner graph that incorporates not only the parity-check matrix of the encoder applied to source 1 but the Markov graphical model of $\mathbf{u}$. Note that in this case, no BWT of source 1 is carried out at the expense of higher complexity at the decoder.

7. Universal Scheme

No knowledge of the source is required by the BWT. However, we need a robust LDPC design procedure that yields ensembles of codes that perform close to capacity for nonstationary memoryless channels. Since the capacity-achieving distribution is the same (equiprobable) regardless of the noise distribution, Shannon theory (e.g. [**CK81**]) guarantees that without knowledge of the channel sequence at the encoder it is possible to attain the channel capacity (average of the maximal single-letter mutual informations) with the same random coding construction that achieves the capacity of the stationary channel.

In our universal implementation, the encoder estimates the piecewise constant first-order distribution at the output of the BWT, uses it to select a parity-check matrix rate, and communicates a rough piecewise approximation of the estimated distributions to the decoder using a number of symbols that is a small fraction of the total compressed sequence. After each iteration, the BP decoder refines its estimates of individual probabilities on a segment-by-segment basis by weighing the impact of each tentative decision with the current reliability information. Naturally, such procedures are quite easy to adapt to prior knowledge that may exist from the encoding of the previous data blocks. Moreover, the encoder can monitor the statistics from block to block. When it sees that there is a large change in statistics it can alert the decoder to the segments that are most affected, or even back off in rate.

If the encoder knew that the source is Markov source with S states, then it could detect the segment transitions (or boundary points) T_i just by looking at the first $M = \log_2 S$ columns of the BWT array. In this case, each probability p_i can be estimated by the empirical frequency of ones in the i-th segment. If the source memory is not known a priori, then all memories $M = 0, 1, \ldots$, up to some maximum D can be considered, and the corresponding empirical frequencies can be obtained hierarchically, on a tree. In fact, due to the lexicographic ordering of the BWT, segments corresponding to states $(s, 0)$ and $(s, 1)$ of a memory $M+1$ model can be merged into state s of a memory M model, and the empirical frequency of ones in state s segment can be computed recursively by

$$\begin{aligned} n_1(s) &= n_1(s0) + n_1(s1) \\ n(s) &= n(s0) + n(s1) \end{aligned} \tag{7.1}$$

where $n_1(s)$ and $n(s)$ denote the number of ones and the segment length in segment s (e.g. [**BB**]).

A coarse description of the segmentation and associated probabilities p_i is supplied to the iterative decoder. As outlined above, the decoder may be given the option of refining this statistical description iteratively. The discrete set of possible sources $\mathcal{S}$ communicated to the decompressor corresponds to all possible quantized probabilities and quantized transition points, for all possible source memories. We denote the quantized parameters of a particular instance of the source model by

$\theta \in \mathcal{S}$. We wish to encode the transition points and the probabilities p_i by using

$$L_n(\theta) = \frac{S(\theta)}{2} \log_2 n + O(1) \text{ bits} \tag{7.2}$$

where $S(\theta)$ is the number of states in the model θ. Apart from the value of the constant term, this is the best possible redundancy to encode the source model, according to the minimum description length (MDL) principle [**Ris84**].

A simple heuristic method approaching this lower bound is the following. For each given memory M, let the exact transition points of the segments identified by the first M columns of the BWT array be denoted by $T_i(M)$, for $i = 1, \ldots, 2^M - 1$. We can write

$$T_i(M) = \kappa_i \sqrt{n} + \zeta_i$$

where $\zeta_i = T_i(\theta)$ modulo $\sqrt{n}$ and $\kappa_i = \lfloor T_i(M)/\sqrt{n} \rfloor$. Then, we quantize the remainder ζ_i by using b_1 bits. Hence, the location of the transition point $T_i(M)$ is known up to a maximum error of $\sqrt{n}2^{-b_1}$. We let $\widehat{T}_i(M)$ denote the quantized value corresponding to $T_i(M)$. Notice that after quantization some of the originally distinct transition points might have been quantized to the same value, i.e., some segments after quantization have disappeared from the resulting source model. Let $\{\widehat{T}_j(\theta) : j = 1, \ldots, S(\theta) - 1\}$, denote the set of *distinct* transition points after quantization, where $S(\theta)$ denotes the number of states in the source model θ. Notice that, by construction, $S(\theta) \leq 2^M$. Let p_j denote the empirical frequency of ones in the j-th segment identified by the transition points $\{\widehat{T}_j(\theta)\}$. We use b_2 bits to encode the log-ratios $\mathcal{L}_j(\theta) = \log(1-p_j)/p_j$. The decoder will apply the (quantized) log-ratio $\mathcal{L}_j(\theta)$ on the positions of segment j.

Clearly, each κ_i can be encoded by $\frac{1}{2}\log_2 n$, therefore the description length for the model θ is

$$L_n(\theta) = (S(\theta) - 1)(\frac{1}{2}\log_2 n + b_2) + S(\theta) b_1$$

which is compliant with the MDL principle (7.2).

The degrees of freedom available to the encoder are the model to be described $\theta \in \mathcal{S}$ and the ensemble of LDPC matrices to be chosen. For every matrix the scheme is the variable-length version explained in Section 6 using the closed-loop iterative doping algorithm.

We consider a collection of Q LDPC ensembles (defined by the left and right degree distributions (λ_q, ρ_q) for $q = 1, \ldots, Q$) of rates $0 < R_1 < \ldots < R_Q < 1$, and, for each q-th ensemble, a set of c parity-check matrices

$$\mathcal{H}_q = \left\{\mathbf{H}_{i,q} \in \{0,1\}^{m_q \times n} \ : \ i = 1, \ldots, c\right\} \tag{7.3}$$

such that $m_q/n = 1 - R_q$ and each matrix $\mathbf{H}_{i,q}$ is independently and randomly generated over the ensemble (λ_q, ρ_q). Then, in order to encode $\mathbf{x}$, the proposed scheme finds the model $\theta \in \mathcal{S}$ and the set of parity-check matrices $\mathcal{H}_q$ that minimize the overall output length, i.e., it finds

$$(\widehat{q}, \widehat{\theta}) = \arg \min_{q,\theta} \{L_n(\theta) + M_n(q, \theta, \mathbf{x})\} \tag{7.4}$$

with $M_n(q, \theta, \mathbf{x})$ equal to the output length of the basic LDPC compression scheme using $\mathcal{H}_q$ and θ at the decoder when applied to sourceword $\mathbf{x}$. It then encodes the source model $\widehat{\theta}$ using $L_n(\widehat{\theta})$ bits, and the sourceword $\mathbf{x}$ with the basic LDPC compression scheme using the parity-check matrices in $\mathcal{H}_{\widehat{q}}$.

It is problematic to evaluate $M_n(q, \theta, \mathbf{x})$, as this would require the application of the Closed-loop Iterative Doping Algorithm to $\mathbf{x}$, for all parity-check matrices $\{\mathcal{H}_q : q = 1, \ldots, Q\}$ and all models $\theta \in \mathcal{S}$. However, we make the following observation. Let $\widehat{H}_\theta(\mathbf{x})$ be the empirical entropy of $\mathbf{x}$ according to the probability model θ. Then, if $R_q > 1 - \widehat{H}_\theta(\mathbf{x})$, the number of doping bits $d(\mathbf{x})$ is very large. On the contrary, if $R_q < 1 - \widehat{H}_\theta(\mathbf{x})$, $d(\mathbf{x})$ is very small with respect to n. Hence, we shall use the heuristic approximation:

$$M_n(q, \theta, \mathbf{x}) = m_{q(\theta)} \tag{7.5}$$

where

$$q(\theta) = \max\{1 \leq q \leq Q : R_q < 1 - \widehat{H}_\theta(\mathbf{x})\}.$$

In other words, we choose the LDPC ensemble with largest rate not above the *normalized information density* of the deterministically time-varying BSC determined by θ with noise realization $\mathbf{x}$.

As explained in [**BB**], the BWT and the recursive segment determination can be obtained with complexity linear in n by using suffix-trees methods. This makes the overall complexity of our algorithm linear with n, although the (constant with n) complexity due to BP is large with respect to other universal linear complexity algorithms based on sequential arithmetic coding.

We compare the performance of the proposed data compression algorithm with the standard compression software `gzip` (based on the Lempel-Ziv algorithm) and `bzip` (based on postprocessing the BWT output using Move-to-Front runlength coding and adaptive arithmetic coding).

Figure 12 shows the histogram of the normalized output lengths obtained from 2000 independent trials for a four-state binary Markov source with entropy rate 0.4935 bit/symbols, for the new scheme, `gzip` and `bzip`, for blocklength $n = 10,000$. We used $b_2 = 8$ quantization bits for the log-ratios, $b_1 = 3$ quantization bits for the transition points and a collection of LDPC ensembles with rates equally spaced from 0.005 to 0.0995. For each ensemble, $c = 8$ parity-check matrices were randomly generated.

Instead of testing a given source, our last experiment considers an ensemble of randomly generated binary Markov sources with number of states equally likely to be 1, 2, 4, 8 and 16 (i.e., with memory equal to 0, 1, 2, 3 and 4). The Markov source ensemble is obtained by generating independently the memory length, and then conditional distributions are also generated randomly with a distribution that puts more weight on values either close to 0 or to 1. The ensemble is restricted to produce sources with entropy ranging from 0.05 to 0.75 bits per symbol. Figures 13 and 14 examine histograms of the normalized redundancy (difference between the compression rate and the empirical entropy of the source) for our universal scheme, `gzip` and `bzip` for blocklengths equal to 3,000 and 10,000 respectively. For the latter case, the memory of the Markov source can be up to 5. For our scheme the parameters b_1 and b_2 that govern the quantization coarseness in the description of the segmentation are adapted using the Minimum Description Length principle described above.

We see that as blocklength increases all schemes tend to become more efficient, but the new scheme (which requires linear compression and decompression

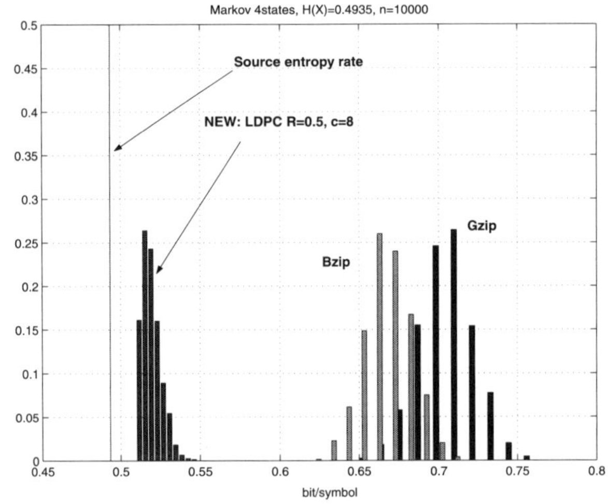

FIGURE 12. Histogram of normalized output lengths for the LDPC compressor, `gzip` and `bzip` for a Markov source with entropy = 0.4935 bit/symbol.

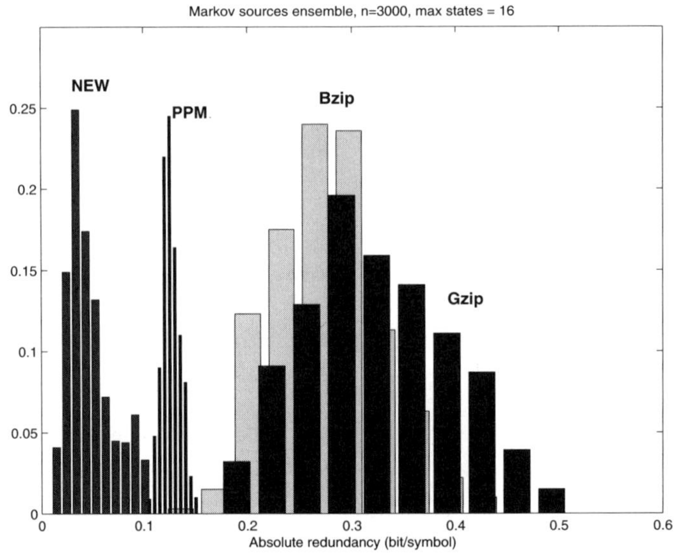

FIGURE 13. Random ensemble of Markov sources: redundancies for the new universal compressor, PPM, `bzip` and `gzip` with source blocklength equal to 3,000.

complexity) maintains an edge even with respect to the PPM scheme which requires quadratic computational complexity. The resilience against errors and the application of this approach to joint source-channel coding are treated in [**CSV04**].

Acknowledgment

Thanks to Mr. H. Cai for his help with the simulations of `bzip`, `gzip` and `PPM`.

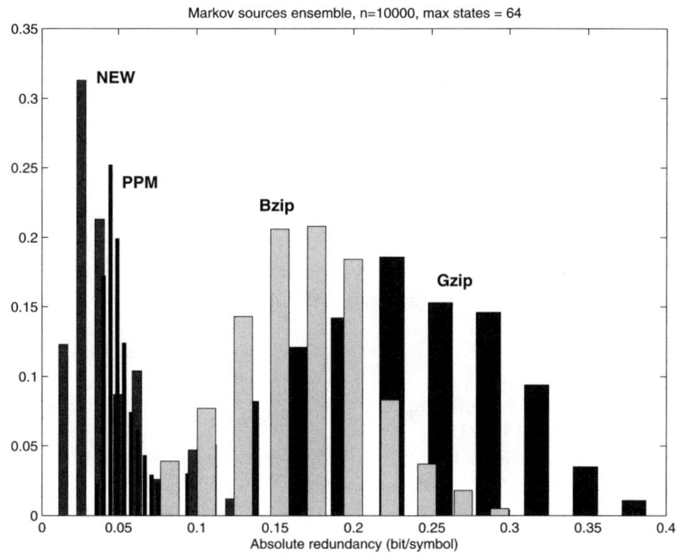

FIGURE 14. Random ensemble of Markov sources: redundancies for the new universal compressor, PPM, `bzip` and `gzip` with source blocklength equal to 10,000.

References

[AB72] P. E. Allard and A. W. Bridgewater, "A source encoding technique using algebraic codes", in *Proc. 1972 Canadian Computer Conf.*, June 1972, pp. 201–213.

[Anc76] T. Ancheta, "Syndrome source coding and it universal generalization", *IEEE Trans. Inform. Theory*, vol. 22, no. 4, July 1976, pp. 432–436.

[BB] D. Baron and Y. Bresler, "A work-efficient parallel two-pass MDL context tree algorithm for universal source coding", submitted for publication.

[BM01] J. Bajcsy and P. Mitran, "Coding for the Slepian-Wolf problem with Turbo codes", in *Proc. 2001 IEEE Globecom*, 2001, pp. 1400–1404.

[BW94] M. Burrows and D. J. Wheeler, "A block-sorting lossless data compression algorithm", Tech. Rep. SRC 124, May 1994.

[CK81] I. Csiszar and J. Korner, *Information theory: Coding theorems for discrete memoryless systems*, Academic, New York, 1981.

[Cov75] T. M. Cover, "A proof of the data compression theorem of Slepian and Wolf for ergodic sources", *IEEE Trans. Inform. Theory*, vol. IT-22, 1975, pp. 226–228.

[CS02] G. Caire and S. Shamai, "Writing on dirty tape with LDPC codes", DIMACS Workshop on Sig. Proc. for Wireless Transmission, Rutgers University, NJ, USA, Oct. 2002.

[CSSV] G. Caire, S. Shamai, A. Shokrollahi, and S. Verdú, "Fountain codes for data compression", in preparation.

[CSV] G. Caire, S. Shamai, and S. Verdú, "Data compression with error correction codes", in preparation.

[CSV04] G. Caire, S. Shamai, and S. Verdú, "Almost-noiseless joint source-channel coding-decoding of sources with memory", in *Proc. 5th International ITG Conference on Source and Channel Coding*, Jan 14-16, 2004.

[DM98] M. C. Davey and D. MacKay, "Low density parity check codes over GF(q)", *IEEE Commun. Letters*, vol. 2, June 1998, pp. 165–167.

[Eli55] P. Elias, "Coding for noisy channels", IRE Convention record, vol. 4, 1955, pp. 37–46.

[EVKV02] M. Effros, K. Visweswariah, S. Kulkarni, and S. Verdú, "Universal lossless source coding with the Burrows-Wheeler transform", *IEEE Trans. Inform. Theory*, vol. 48, no. 5, May 2002, pp. 1061–1081.

[FTS73] K. C. Fung, S. Tavares and J. M. Stein, "A comparison of data compression schemes using block codes", *Conf. Rec. IEEE Int Electrical and Electronics Conf.*, Oct. 1973, pp. 60–61.

[Gal63] R. G. Gallager, *Low-density parity-check codes*, MIT Press, 1963.

[GFZ01] J. Garcia-Frias and Y. Zhao, "Compression of correlated binary sources using Turbo codes", *IEEE Commun. Letters*, vol. 5, Oct. 2001, pp. 417–419.

[GFZ02] J. Garcia-Frias and Y. Zhao, "Compression of binary memoryless sources using punctured Turbo codes", *IEEE Commun. Letters*, vol. 6, Sept. 2002, pp. 394–396.

[HV93] T. S. Han and S. Verdú, "Approximation theory of output statistics", *IEEE Trans. Inform. Theory*, vol. 39, May 1993, pp. 752–772.

[LXG02] A. D. Liveris, Z. Xiong and C. N. Georghiades, "Compression of binary sources with side information at the decoder using LDPC codes", *IEEE Commun. Letters*, vol. 6, no. 10, Oct. 2002, pp. 440–442.

[McE02] R.J. McEliece, *The theory of information and coding*, 2nd edition, Cambridge University Press, Cambridge, U. K., 2002.

[McM53] B. McMillan, "The basic theorems of information theory", *Ann. Math. Statist.*, vol. 24, June 1953, pp. 196–219.

[Mur02] T. Murayama, "Statistical mechanics of the data compression theorem", *J. Phys. A: Math. Gen.*, vol. 35, 2002, L95–L100.

[Ris84] J. Rissanen, "Universal coding, information prediction and estimation", *IEEE Trans. Inform. Theory*, vol. 30, no. 4, July 1984, pp. 629–636.

[RU01a] T. J. Richardson and R. L. Urbanke, "The capacity of low-density parity-check codes under message-passing decoding", *IEEE Trans. Inform. Theory*, vol. 47, Feb. 2001, pp. 599–618.

[RU01b] T. J. Richardson and R. L. Urbanke, "Efficient encoding of low-density parity-check codes", *IEEE Trans. Inform. Theory*, vol. 47, Feb. 2001, pp. 638–656.

[SF02] D. Sridhara and T. E. Fuja, "Low density parity check codes over groups and rings", in *Proc. 2002 IEEE Inform. Theory Workshop*, Oct. 2002, pp. 163–166.

[Sha48] C. E. Shannon, "A mathematical theory of communication", *Bell Sys. Tech. J.*, vol. 27, Jul.-Oct. 1948, pp. 379–423, pp. 623–656.

[Sho03] A. Shokrollahi, "Raptor codes", preprint, 2003.

[tB00] S. ten Brink, "Designing iterative decoding with the extrinistic information transfer chart", *AEU. Int. J. Electron. Commun.*, vol. 34, no. 6, 2000, pp. 389–398.

[TM] D. S. Taubman and M. W. Marcellin, "JPEG2000: standard for interactive imaging".

[Urb02] R. Urbanke, *http://lthcwww.epfl.ch/research/ldpcopt/*, 2002.

[Wei62] E. Weiss, "Compression and coding", *IRE Trans. Inform. Theory*, Apr. 1962, pp. 256–257.

[WFH99] U. Wachsmann, R. Fisher, and J. Huber, "Multilevel codes: theoretical concepts and practical design rules", *IEEE Trans. Inform. Theory*, vol. 45, no. 5, 1999, pp. 1361–1391.

[Wyn74] A. D. Wyner, "Recent results in the Shannon theory", *IEEE Trans. Inform. Theory*, vol. IT-20, Jan. 1974.

Institut Eurecom, Sophia Antipolis, France
E-mail address: giuseppe.caire@eurecom.fr

Technion, Haifa, Israel
E-mail address: sshlomo@ee.technion.ac.il

Princeton University
E-mail address: verdu@princeton.edu

DIMACS Series in Discrete Mathematics
and Theoretical Computer Science
Volume **66**, 2004

Diversity Embedding in Multiple Antenna Communications

Suhas N. Diggavi, Naofal Al-Dhahir, and A.R. Calderbank

ABSTRACT. Rate and diversity impose a fundamental trade-off in space-time coding. High-rate space-time codes come at a cost of lower diversity, and high reliability (diversity) implies a lower rate. In this paper we propose a different point of view where we design high-rate space-time codes that have a high-diversity code embedded within them. This allows a form of communication where the high-rate code opportunistically takes advantage of good channel realizations whereas the embedded high-diversity code ensures that at least part of the information is received reliably. Therefore this is equivalent to multiple users transmitting information, sharing a common resource (power) and requiring different levels of diversity (error probability). We explore this point of view with design issues, along with some preliminary progress on code constructions and information-theoretic considerations.

1. Introduction

Space-time codes provide a tool to make reliable high-data rate wireless communications a reality. In [**21, 12**], it was shown that multiple transmit antennas can provide high rate communications. In [**20**], a different point of view was explored where the emphasis was on providing reliability in the form of error probability. Here, correlation of signals across the different transmit antennas was introduced to provide higher reliability albeit at the cost of transmission rate.

These two points-of-view can be combined by observing that there exists a trade-off between rate and reliability (diversity). This was explored in the context of finite-rate (fixed alphabet size) codes in [**20**] and in the context of information theoretic rate growths in [**24**]. Both of these results show that to achieve a high transmission rate, one might need to sacrifice reliability (diversity) and vice-versa. Therefore, the main question addressed by most researchers has been how to design transmission techniques that achieve a particular point on this trade-off. For example, the emphasis in the coding literature has been the design of maximal-diversity codes, *i.e.* one extremal point in this trade-off. In [**21, 12, 15**], the point of view taken is that of obtaining the maximal rate without consideration to reliability. There are also examples where a different point in the trade-off is achieved using codes designed for this case (see for example, [**10**]).

S. N. Diggavi is the contact author. This work was presented in part in the DIMACS workshop on Network Information Theory, March 2003.

The natural question to ask is whether there exists a strategy that combines high-rate communications with high-reliability (diversity). The main idea in this paper is to propose the design of codes that achieve a high-rate, but have embedded within them a high-diversity (lower-rate) code. Clearly the overall code will still be governed by the rate-diversity trade-off, but the idea is to ensure the reliability (diversity) of at least part of the total information. A simple way to achieve this would be to time division multiplex (TDM) between codes that attain different rate-diversity points. In this paper, we explore code constructions that cannot be achieved by such simple switching strategies.

One way to view this transmission technique is from the point of view of compound channels [**8**]. Here, the information is transmitted over a channel that is unknown to the transmitter (and receiver). The strategy then is to ensure that information is decodable by the worst channel. In fact, the capacity could be strictly smaller since the transmitter needs to have a single code that is universally good for the entire class of channels [**8**]. Therefore, this is a conservative strategy, in that the transmission is robust to the worst channel, and cannot utilize the opportunity to transmit at a higher rate if a good channel is available. In [**6**], Cover proposed a broadcast strategy for transmission over compound channels. Here the idea was to superpose codewords such that the achievable rate could be strictly better than the above conservative strategy if a more benign channel is available. However, the disadvantage is that the minimum rate is smaller than that of the conservative strategy. The quasi-static fading wireless channel, where the coding is over one fading interval, is a non-ergodic channel that fits the compound channel problem. Given a random choice of channel fading values, the Shannon capacity over a class of Rayleigh fading channels is zero [**16**]. However, one can transmit at a positive rate for given outage probabilities [**16, 21, 12**]. Therefore, most transmission schemes are designed for a particular rate at a given outage probability. One exception is a broadcast strategy proposed for single-antenna fading channels which was explored in [**2, 3**], where superposition coding was used to obtain a continuum of rate and outage probabilities. In the single-antenna Rayleigh-fading case, the class of channels could be considered degraded versions of each other, depending on the received signal-to-noise ratio (SNR). The multiple-antenna channel presents a different problem where the class of channels are not degraded versions (see for example [**23**] and references therein). Moreover, it provides additional degrees of freedom that can be exploited to increase the rate and/or diversity [**21, 12, 20, 24**]. In this paper we utilize these additional degrees of freedom in order to design embedded codes. Independently, Shamai [**18**] has recently presented some extensions of the broadcast approach of single-antenna channels of [**2**] to multiple antenna channels.

The idea of unequal error protection (UEP) for information symbols has a long and rich history (see for example [**17**] and references therein). Most of the codes for UEP are designed for the Euclidean distance metric encountered in the Gaussian channel [**5**]. Another way to interpret our code-design idea is from the viewpoint of unequal error protection with the diversity metric suitable for fading channels [**20**].

The final motivation in such a design is from a networking point-of-view. Since the channel is unknown at the transmitter, such an embedding strategy makes opportunistic use of the channel. If a good channel realization is available, then we do not need significant redundancy to achieve a particular error rate target and therefore can achieve a higher information rate. This is in contrast to a strategy based on incremental redundancy codes [**14, 22**] where a low redundancy code is first sent and if an error is found then the parity symbols are sent upon feedback. In our strategy, the transmitted codebook has an embedded high-diversity code and therefore eliminates the re-transmission of parity symbols. Moreover, the rate increment is obtained without feedback about received information.

This paper is organized as follows. In Section 2, we introduce the notation used in the paper and also provide some of the background needed on space-time code design criteria as well as information-theoretic considerations. Section 3 introduces in detail the objectives of our transmission strategy and the code design criteria. We present some code constructions in Section 4 and prove some properties associated with them. The information-theoretic issues with such an embedding strategy are explored in Section 5. A numerical example in Section 6 shows the performance of one of the codes of Section 4. We conclude the paper with a brief discussion of several open issues.

2. Preliminaries

Our focus in this paper is on the quasi-static flat–fading channel where we transmit information coded over M_t transmit antennas and have M_r antennas at the receiver. Furthermore, the assumption is that the transmitter has no channel state information, whereas the receiver is able to perfectly track the channel (a common assumption, see for example [**2, 20**]). The code is designed over T transmission symbols and the received signal after demodulation and sampling can be written as

$$\mathbf{Y} = \mathbf{H}\mathbf{X} + \mathbf{Z}, \tag{2.1}$$

where $\mathbf{Y} = [\mathbf{y}(0), \ldots, \mathbf{y}(T-1)] \in \mathbb{C}^{M_r \times T}$ is the received sequence, $\mathbf{H} \in \mathbb{C}^{M_r \times M_t}$ is the quasi-static channel fading matrix, $\mathbf{X} = [\mathbf{x}(0), \ldots, \mathbf{x}(T-1)] \in \mathbb{C}^{M_t \times T}$ is the space-time coded transmission sequence with transmit power constraint P, and $\mathbf{Z} = [\mathbf{z}(0), \ldots, \mathbf{z}(T-1)] \in \mathbb{C}^{M_r \times T}$ is assumed to be additive white Gaussian noise with variance σ^2.

The coding scheme is limited to one quasi-static transmission block. Similar arguments can be made if we are allowed to code across only a *finite* number of quasi-static transmission blocks [**16**]. This allows us to view the channel in (2.1) as a non-ergodic channel since the performance is determined by single randomly chosen channel fading matrix $\mathbf{H}$.

In this context we define the notion of diversity order [**20**] as follows.

DEFINITION 2.1. *A coding scheme which has an average error probability* $\bar{P}_e(\mathrm{SNR})$ *as a function of* SNR *that behaves as*

$$\lim_{\mathrm{SNR}\to\infty} \frac{\log(\bar{P}_e(\mathrm{SNR}))}{\log(\mathrm{SNR})} = -d \tag{2.2}$$

is said to have a diversity order of d.

In words, a scheme with diversity order d has an error probability at high SNR behaving as $\bar{P}_e(\mathrm{SNR}) \approx \mathrm{SNR}^{-d}$.

2.1. Code Design Criteria. For codes designed for a finite (and fixed) rate, one can bound the error probability by using *pairwise error probability* (PEP) between two candidate codewords. This leads to the now well-known rank criterion for determining the diversity order of a space-time code [**20, 13**]. Consider a codeword sequence $\mathbf{X} = [\mathbf{x}^T(0), \ldots, \mathbf{x}^T(T-1)]$ as defined in (2.1), where $\mathbf{x}(k) = [\mathbf{x}_1(k), \ldots, \mathbf{x}_{M_t}(k)]^T$. The PEP between two codewords $\mathbf{x}$ and $\mathbf{e}$ can be determined by the codeword difference matrix $\mathbf{B}(\mathbf{x}, \mathbf{e})$ [**20, 13**], where

$$\mathbf{B}(\mathbf{x},\mathbf{e}) = \begin{pmatrix} \mathbf{x}_1(0)-\mathbf{e}_1(0) & \ldots & \mathbf{x}_1(T-1)-\mathbf{e}_1(T-1) \\ \vdots & \vdots & \vdots \\ \mathbf{x}_{M_t}(0)-\mathbf{e}_{M_t}(0) & \ldots & \mathbf{x}_{M_t}(T-1)-\mathbf{e}_{M_t}(T-1) \end{pmatrix}.$$

For fixed rate codebook $\mathcal{C}$, the pairwise error probability between two distinct codewords $\mathbf{x}$ and $\mathbf{e}$ is given by[1] [**20**]

$$P_e(\text{SNR}, \mathbf{x} \longrightarrow \mathbf{e}) \doteq \text{SNR}^{-M_r \text{rank}(\mathbf{B}(\mathbf{x},\mathbf{e}))}. \tag{2.3}$$

Since we are dealing with a fixed rate codebook, by using the simple union bound argument, it can be shown that the diversity order is given by [**20**]

$$d = M_r \min_{\mathbf{x} \neq \mathbf{e} \in \mathcal{C}} rank(\mathbf{B}(\mathbf{x},\mathbf{e}))\ . \tag{2.4}$$

The error probability is determined by *both* the coding gain and the diversity order. Hence, the code design criterion prescribed in [**20**] is to design the codebook $\mathcal{C}$ so that the minimal rank of the codeword difference matrix corresponds to the required diversity order and the minimal determinant gives the corresponding coding gain. In this paper the focus is on the diversity order only, and we define corresponding criteria for embedded codebooks.

2.2. Rate vs Diversity. A natural question that arises is how many codewords can we have which allow us to attain a certain diversity order. For a flat Rayleigh fading channel, this has been examined in [**20**] where the following result was obtained.

THEOREM 2.2. *(Tarokh* et al *1998) If we use a constellation of size 2^b and the diversity order of the system is qM_r, then the rate R that can be achieved is bounded as*

$$R \leq \frac{1}{T} \log\left[A_{2^{bT}}(M_t, q)\right], \tag{2.5}$$

where $A_{2^{bT}}(M_t, q)$ is the maximum size of a code of length M_t with minimum Hamming distance q defined over an alphabet size 2^{bT}.

The discussion in Section 2.1 and Theorem 2.2 is suitable for fixed-rate (finite-alphabet) codebooks. Another point-of-view explored in [**24**], allows the rate of the codebook to increase with SNR. This viewpoint is motivated because the capacity of the multiple-antenna channel grows with SNR behaving as $\min(M_r, M_t)\log(\text{SNR})$ [**12, 24, 11**], at high SNR even for finite M_r, M_t. Therefore, [**24**] defines a multiplexing gain of a transmission scheme as follows.

[1]We use the notation $\doteq$ to denote exponential equality [**7**], *i.e.*, $g(\text{SNR}) \doteq \text{SNR}^a$ means that $\lim_{\text{SNR}\to\infty} \frac{\log g(\text{SNR})}{\log \text{SNR}} = a$. Moreover, if $g(\text{SNR}) \doteq f(\text{SNR})$, it means that, $\lim_{\text{SNR}\to\infty} \frac{\log g(\text{SNR})}{\log \text{SNR}} = \lim_{\text{SNR}\to\infty} \frac{\log f(\text{SNR})}{\log \text{SNR}}$.

FIGURE 1. Embedded codebook

DEFINITION 2.3. *A coding scheme which has a transmission rate of* $R(\text{SNR})$ *as a function of* SNR *is said to have a multiplexing gain* r *if*

$$\lim_{\text{SNR}\to\infty} \frac{R(\text{SNR})}{\log(\text{SNR})} = r. \tag{2.6}$$

Therefore, the system has a rate of $r\log(\text{SNR})$ at high SNR. The main result in [**24**] states that

THEOREM 2.4. *(Zheng and Tse 2002) For* $T > M_t + M_r - 1$*, and* $K = \min(M_t, M_r)$*, the optimal trade-off curve* $d^*(r)$ *is given by the piece-wise linear function connecting points in* $(k, d^*(k)), k = 0, \ldots, K$ *where*

$$d^*(k) = (M_r - k)(M_t - k). \tag{2.7}$$

Therefore, both Theorems 2.2 and 2.4 show the tension between achieving high-rate and high-diversity. The question addressed in this paper is whether we can design codes with high-rate which contain within them a code which has high-diversity.

3. Diversity Embedding

The codebook structure proposed in this paper takes two information streams (see Figure 1) and outputs the transmitted sequence $\{\mathbf{x}(k)\}$. The objective is to ensure that each information stream gets the designed rate and diversity levels. In this section, we describe this approach and criteria in further detail, with specific code constructions given in Section 4.

3.1. Opportunistic Communication. The basic idea is to design a codebook which allows many levels of diversity for information streams. In particular we focus on two levels of diversity, but this procedure can be easily generalized to more levels. We design the transmitted information stream $\{\mathbf{x}(k)\}$ to depend on two information streams $\{\mathbf{a}(k)\}$ and $\{\mathbf{b}(k)\}$. Let $\mathcal{A}$ denote the message set from the first information stream and $\mathcal{B}$ denote that from the second information stream. The rates for the two message sets are, respectively, $R(\mathcal{A})$ and $R(\mathcal{B})$. The decoder jointly decodes the two message sets and we can define two error probabilities, $\bar{P}_e(\mathcal{A})$ and $\bar{P}_e(\mathcal{B})$ which denote the average error probabilities for message sets $\mathcal{A}$ and $\mathcal{B}$, respectively. We design the code such that a certain tuple (R_a, D_a, R_b, D_b) of rates and diversities are achievable, where $R_a = R(\mathcal{A}) = \frac{\log(|\mathcal{A}|)}{T}$, $R_b = R(\mathcal{B}) = \frac{\log(|\mathcal{B}|)}{T}$ and analogous to definition 2.1,

$$D_a = \lim_{\text{SNR}\to\infty} \frac{\log \bar{P}_e(\mathcal{A})}{\log(\text{SNR})}, \quad D_b = \lim_{\text{SNR}\to\infty} \frac{\log \bar{P}_e(\mathcal{B})}{\log(\text{SNR})}. \tag{3.1}$$

Hence, if we examine the joint codebook, $\mathcal{C} = \{\mathcal{A}, \mathcal{B}\}$, the total rate is $R = R_a + R_b$ and the diversity is $D = \min(D_a, D_b)$. Therefore, in a baseline comparison with a single-layer codebook, the rate-diversity operating point is $(R_a + R_b, \min(D_a, D_b))$. If (R, D^*) is the optimal single-layer rate-diversity point predicted by Theorems 2.2 and 2.4, then we would like $D_a > D^*$ implying that $D_b \leq D^*$. This means that a rate $(R_a + R_b, \min(D_a, D_b))$, has a high-diversity message set $\mathcal{A}$ embedded within it. The main focus of this paper is to construct codes with this property and also to explore some characteristics of such codes. As mentioned earlier, a simple switching (TDM) strategy between codebooks designed for different rate-diversity levels could produce such a construction. However, in Section 4 we explore codes that cannot be constructed by simple switching strategies.

The reason why embedded diversity codes allow a form of opportunistic communication is that we can design the total rate $R_a + R_b$ to be large, and design D_a to be large as well. Note that there would be natural bounds on the achievable tuple (R_a, D_a, R_b, D_b), and we briefly explore this question in Section 5. This implies that we cannot get arbitrary combinations of the rate tuples. The opportunism arises because if the channel realization $\mathbf{H}$ is good, in that the channel matrix is far from singular, then the high total rate allows us to send a large amount of information through such a clear channel without knowing a-priori the channel realization at the transmitter. However, if the channel realization is not good, the embedded high-diversity message set $\mathcal{A}$ might still be decodable.

3.2. Code Design Criteria. We examine code design criteria for finite alphabet (fixed-rate) codes. The transmitted sequence $\{\mathbf{x}(k)\}$ can be divided into codeword clusters as shown in Figure 2, where the codeword clusters shown correspond to all $\{\mathbf{x}(k)\}$ arising due to a particular message $\mathbf{a} \in \mathcal{A}$. The joint decoding of the two message sets yields candidate clusters and elements within the clusters. Given a desired tuple (R_a, D_a, R_b, D_b), we need to design message sets $\mathcal{A}, \mathcal{B}$ with size $2^{R_a T}$ and $2^{R_b T}$, respectively, to have the following properties. For message set $\mathcal{A}$, we want to design the code such that the pairwise error probability behaves as SNR^{-D_a}. Similarly for message set $\mathcal{B}$, we want to achieve diversity order of D_b. The code design criterion ensures that both these constraints are satisfied.

Let us examine a maximum-likelihood decoder jointly on the message sets $\mathcal{A}, \mathcal{B}$. Denote transmitted sequences as $\{\mathbf{x}_{\mathbf{a},\mathbf{b}}(k)\}$, with the subscripts denoting that the sequence arose due to messages $\mathbf{a} \in \mathcal{A}, \mathbf{b} \in \mathcal{B}$ as shown in Figure 1. Using (2.1) the maximum likelihood decoding metric when the channel state information is available at the receiver is given by,

$$(3.2) \qquad \left(\hat{\mathbf{a}}, \hat{\mathbf{b}}\right) = \arg \min_{\mathbf{a} \in \mathcal{A}, \mathbf{b} \in \mathcal{B}} ||\mathbf{Y} - \mathbf{H}\mathbf{X}_{\mathbf{a},\mathbf{b}}||^2.$$

Therefore using (2.3) we can write the pairwise error probability on the joint message set as,

$$(3.3) \qquad P_e(\text{SNR}, \{\mathbf{a}, \mathbf{b}\} \longrightarrow \{\hat{\mathbf{a}}, \hat{\mathbf{b}}\}) \doteq \text{SNR}^{-M_r \text{rank}(\mathbf{B}(\mathbf{X}_{\mathbf{a},\mathbf{b}}, \mathbf{X}_{\hat{\mathbf{a}},\hat{\mathbf{b}}}))}.$$

The pairwise error probability between two codewords in the message set $\mathcal{A}$ is given by,

$$(3.4) \qquad P_e(\text{SNR}, \mathbf{a} \longrightarrow \hat{\mathbf{a}}) \doteq \text{SNR}^{-M_r \min_{\mathbf{b}_1, \mathbf{b}_2 \in \mathcal{B}} \text{rank}(\mathbf{B}(\mathbf{X}_{\mathbf{a},\mathbf{b}_1}, \mathbf{X}_{\hat{\mathbf{a}},\mathbf{b}_2}))}.$$

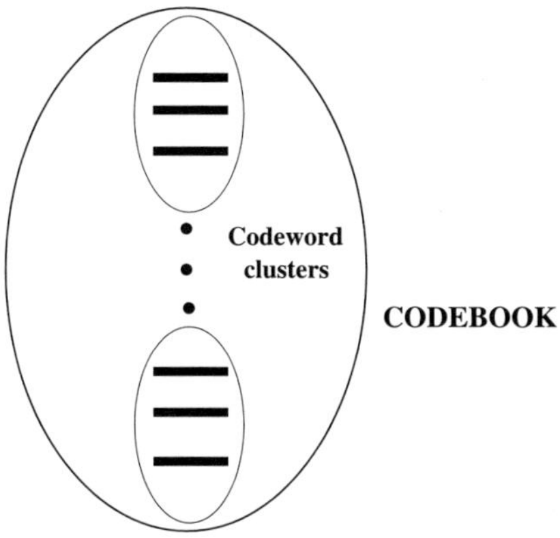

FIGURE 2. Codeword Clusters

Since we are dealing with fixed rate codebooks, by using a simple union bound argument we can write the diversity d_a for message set $\mathcal{A}$ as,

$$d_a = M_r \min_{\mathbf{a}_1 \neq \mathbf{a}_2 \in \mathcal{A}} \min_{\mathbf{b}_1, \mathbf{b}_2 \in \mathcal{B}} rank(\mathbf{B}(\mathbf{x}_{\mathbf{a}_1,\mathbf{b}_1}, \mathbf{x}_{\mathbf{a}_2,\mathbf{b}_2})) \tag{3.5}$$

Hence for the design constraint to be met, we need

$$\min_{\mathbf{a}_1 \neq \mathbf{a}_2 \in \mathcal{A}} \min_{\mathbf{b}_1, \mathbf{b}_2 \in \mathcal{B}} rank(\mathbf{B}(\mathbf{x}_{\mathbf{a}_1,\mathbf{b}_1}, \mathbf{x}_{\mathbf{a}_2,\mathbf{b}_2})) \geq D_a/M_r \tag{3.6}$$

In an identical manner, we can show for the message set $\mathcal{B}$, we need the following to hold.

$$\min_{\mathbf{b}_1 \neq \mathbf{b}_2 \in \mathcal{B}} \min_{\mathbf{a}_1, \mathbf{a}_2 \in \mathcal{A}} rank(\mathbf{B}(\mathbf{x}_{\mathbf{a}_1,\mathbf{b}_1}, \mathbf{x}_{\mathbf{a}_2,\mathbf{b}_2})) \geq D_b/M_r. \tag{3.7}$$

Basically, (3.6) implies that if we choose to transmit a particular message $\mathbf{a} \in \mathcal{A}$, regardless of which message is chosen in message set $\mathcal{B}$, we are ensured a diversity level of D_a for this message set. A similar argument will hold for message set $\mathcal{B}$.

Note that this criterion focuses *only* on the diversity level achieved by the code design. In general, the error probability depends *both* on the diversity order defined in Definition 2.1 as well as a coding gain [**20**]. The coding gain could be an important issue especially in low to moderate SNR regimes. Also, the code design criterion is suitable only for fixed rate codebooks. When one needs to design codebooks whose rates grow with SNR [**24**], alternative code design criteria could be formulated.

3.3. Challenges. There are several challenges in designing codes that meet the criteria prescribed in Section 3.2. The first obvious challenge is to design codes that can guarantee the desired tuple (R_a, D_a, R_b, D_b). The second challenge arises due to decoding complexity. In principle, we need to jointly decode both message sets $\mathcal{A}, \mathcal{B}$, and since the design is to have a high total rate $(R_a + R_b)$, the joint decoding could be quite expensive. Finally, the question arises on whether the designs are extremal, in that they achieve a point on the boundary of the achievable tuples. This requires the characterization of the achievable tuples in a manner similar to Theorems 2.2 and 2.4 which was done for the case of a single layer of transmission.

There are several natural approaches that one can attempt. The first guess would be a multilevel transmission technique similar to that done for Gaussian channels [**5**]. In this case, the idea would be based on set-partitioning multi-dimensional signal sets which are *not* necessarily generated as a product of partitions from lower-dimensional signal sets. This can be accomplished as follows. In order to illustrate the partitioning, we take the example of 4PSK signal sets. Given that M_t 4PSK signals are to be transmitted, we need to partition the $M_t \times$ 4PSK signal into a partition chain. Therefore, there are 4^{M_t} signal points in the original signal set. We partition this into $2M_t$ levels, with the lth level containing 2^l disjoint subsets, where we have denoted the original signal set with level $l = 0$. We choose a partition chain, $S_0|S_1|\ldots|S_r$ where $r \leq 2M_t$. Then, codes $\{\mathcal{C}_i\}_{i=1}^r$ are used to choose elements from the partition chain. The advantage is that multi-stage decoding could be employed to reduce the decoding complexity. The main disadvantage is that like all trellis codes, the complexity is still quite large.

In [**10**] and references therein, several approaches based on constellation rotation are used to guarantee diversity. These methods are based on codes that are linear over the complex field and have the advantage of being decodable using a sphere decoder [**9**] which has an average complexity that could be polynomial in the rate and therefore is attractive for decoding high-rate codes. However, in all approaches using rotated codes, there is a significant increase in the transmitted alphabet size (constellation expansion) which we attempt to avoid. But the restriction to codes that are linear in the complex field is attractive and we study such designs in Section 4. Our designs do *not* expand the transmitted alphabet size.

4. Code Constructions

In this Section we restrict our attention to code designs that are linear over the complex field in order to be able to decode them efficiently using a sphere decoder [**9**]. In Section 4.1 we describe some general properties of the code constructions. Some specific constructions along with their properties are given in Section 4.2.

4.1. Additive Codewords Model. We examine code designs that are additive, in that the transmitted signal is such that

$$\mathbf{X}_{\mathbf{a},\mathbf{b}} = \mathbf{X}_{\mathbf{a}} + \mathbf{X}_{\mathbf{b}}. \tag{4.1}$$

This allows the composite code to be linear in the complex field as well. Given the design criterion in (3.5), it is clear that to ensure that the message set $\mathcal{A}$ gets a diversity level of D_a, a necessary (but *not* sufficient) condition is that

$$\min_{\mathbf{a}_1 \neq \mathbf{a}_2 \in \mathcal{A}} rank(\mathbf{X}_{\mathbf{a}_1} - \mathbf{X}_{\mathbf{a}_2}) \geq D_a/M_r, \tag{4.2}$$

due to the linearity of the code in (4.1). The code design should be such that any perturbation of $\mathbf{x}_a$ due to message set $\mathcal{B}$ does not disturb this rank property.

We can now apply the code design criterion developed in Section 3.2 to the additive codewords model. For illustration, consider the case where we want $D_a = M_r M_t$, *i.e.* maximal diversity. Then we clearly need $(\mathbf{X}_{\mathbf{a}_1} - \mathbf{X}_{\mathbf{a}_2})$ to have full rank for $\mathbf{a}_1 \neq \mathbf{a}_2$. We also need to ensure that $(\mathbf{X}_{\mathbf{a}_1} - \mathbf{X}_{\mathbf{a}_2}) + (\mathbf{X}_{\mathbf{b}_1} - \mathbf{X}_{\mathbf{b}_2})$ is still full rank for *any* $\mathbf{b}_1, \mathbf{b}_2 \in \mathcal{B}$. This translates to the condition

$$\nexists \mathbf{v} \in \mathbb{C}^{1\times M_t} \text{ such that } \mathbf{v}(\mathbf{X}_{\mathbf{b}_1} - \mathbf{X}_{\mathbf{b}_2})(\mathbf{X}_{\mathbf{a}_1} - \mathbf{X}_{\mathbf{a}_2})^\dagger = -\mathbf{v}, \quad \forall \mathbf{b}_1, \mathbf{b}_2 \in \mathcal{B}, \mathbf{a}_1 \neq \mathbf{a}_2 \in \mathcal{A} \tag{4.3}$$

where[2] $(\mathbf{Q})^{\dagger} = \mathbf{Q}^*(\mathbf{Q}\mathbf{Q}^*)^{-1}$ denotes the pseudo-inverse of a matrix. In cases of a square design, this translates to a question about existence of certain eigenvalues of the matrix defined in (4.3). Also, for square designs, the condition in (4.3) can equivalently be stated in terms of the right eigenvector in $\mathbb{C}^{M_t}$. The condition in (4.3) allows us to eliminate designs that perturb the full rank design for message set $\mathcal{A}$.

In general, the additive codeword model is amenable to computationally simpler lattice decoding strategies, such as the sphere decoder [**9**]. Moreover, rank conditions may be easier to verify under these constraints. These reasons motivate us to examine constructions based on this model.

4.2. Code Examples. In this section we provide four code constructions that illustrate the design trade-off involved in diversity-embedded codes. We restrict our attention to examples with $M_t = 4$. We also start with a baseline code derived from the rate-$\frac{3}{4}$ orthogonal design based on Octonions [**19, 4**]. In all these examples, there are no restrictions on which constellations $\mathcal{S}$ are used to transmit codeword $\mathbf{X}_{\mathbf{a},\mathbf{b}}$. Therefore the proofs of diversity order are based on symbols from a complex field and do not use properties of specific constellations.

Example 1: Here $\mathcal{A}$ comes from the message set $\{a(0), a(1), a(2)\} \in \mathcal{S}$ and $\mathcal{B}$ comes from $b(0) \in \mathcal{S}$. This implies that $R_a = \frac{3}{4} \log |\mathcal{S}|$, and $R_b = \frac{1}{4} \log |\mathcal{S}|$.

$$(4.4) \qquad \mathbf{X}_{\mathbf{a},\mathbf{b}} = \mathbf{X}_{\mathbf{a}} + \mathbf{X}_{\mathbf{b}} = \begin{bmatrix} a(0) & a(1) & a(2) & b(0) \\ -a^*(1) & a^*(0) & 0 & a(2) \\ -a^*(2) & 0 & a^*(0) & -a(1) \\ 0 & -a^*(2) & a^*(1) & a(0) \end{bmatrix}.$$

This code can be shown to achieve full diversity of $4M_r$ for the message set $\mathcal{A}$ and diversity M_r for message set $\mathcal{B}$. The proof of this is simple and we illustrate it in order to demonstrate how the criterion in (3.5) can be applied. Let us denote $\tilde{\mathbf{a}} = \mathbf{a}_1 - \mathbf{a}_2$ and $\tilde{\mathbf{b}} = \mathbf{b}_1 - \mathbf{b}_2$. Since this is a square design, and $\mathbf{X}_{\mathbf{a}}$ is a unitary matrix, the condition given in (4.3) translates to

$$(4.5) \qquad \nexists \mathbf{v} \text{ such that for } \tilde{\mathbf{a}} \neq \mathbf{0} \quad \mathbf{X}_{\tilde{\mathbf{b}}}\mathbf{X}^*_{\tilde{\mathbf{a}}}\mathbf{v} = -||\tilde{\mathbf{a}}||^2\mathbf{v},$$

for all $\tilde{\mathbf{b}}$, where $||\tilde{\mathbf{a}}||^2 = |a(0)|^2 + |a(1)|^2 + |a(2)|^2 \neq 0$. The condition in (4.5) means that $\mathbf{X}_{\tilde{\mathbf{b}}}\mathbf{X}^*_{\tilde{\mathbf{a}}}$ should not have a negative real eigenvalue. It can easily be shown that for this design all the eigenvalues of this matrix are zero and hence the condition is met. At first glance, this design might seem uninteresting since we know that according to Theorem 2.2 (see [**20**]) there exist codes with rate $\log |\mathcal{S}|$ and diversity $M_r M_t$. However, we do not know of codes linear in the complex field, which are not designed for specific signal constellations, and have *no* constellation expansion, with such a property.

■

Example 2: Here $\mathcal{A}$ comes from the message set $\{a(0), a(1)\} \in \mathcal{S}$ and $\mathcal{B}$ comes from $\{b(0), b(1), b(2), b(3)\} \in \mathcal{S}$. This implies that $R_a = \frac{1}{2} \log |\mathcal{S}|$, and $R_b = \log |\mathcal{S}|$,

[2]For a matrix $\mathbf{X}$, we use the notation X^* to denote the Hermetian transpose of the matrix, which for scalars is just complex conjugation.

leading to a total rate of $R_a + R_b = \frac{3}{2}\log|\mathcal{S}|$.

$$\text{(4.6)}\qquad \mathbf{X_{a,b}} = \mathbf{X_a} + \mathbf{X_b} = \begin{bmatrix} a(0) & a(1) & 0 & 0 \\ -a^*(1) & a^*(0) & 0 & 0 \\ b(0) & b(1) & a^*(0) & -a(1) \\ b(2) & b(3) & a^*(1) & a(0) \end{bmatrix}.$$

This code can be shown to achieve full diversity of $4M_r$ for the message set $\mathcal{A}$ and diversity M_r for message set $\mathcal{B}$. Therefore, this example achieves the tuple, $(\frac{1}{2}\log|\mathcal{S}|, 4M_r, \log|\mathcal{S}|, M_r)$. The proof of this claim is quite simple and follows a similar argument as in Example 1. In this example the total rate is $\frac{3}{2}\log|\mathcal{S}|$, with a composite diversity of M_r, however it has a code of maximal diversity and rate $\frac{1}{2}\log|\mathcal{S}|$ embedded within it. Another question is whether such a code can be constructed by a TDM strategy. This is not possible for the following reason. A full-diversity code needs to occupy at least M_t symbols, and hence for a square design $T = M_t$. This implies that we cannot construct a switching scheme that has a full diversity code and has a rate beyond $\log|\mathcal{S}|$.

■

Example 3: Here $\mathcal{A}$ comes from the message set $\{a(0), a(1)\} \in \mathcal{S}$ and $\mathcal{B}$ comes from $\{b(0), b(1), b(2), b(3)\} \in \mathcal{S}$. This implies that $R_a = \frac{1}{2}\log|\mathcal{S}|$, and $R_b = \log|\mathcal{S}|$, identical to Example 2.

$$\text{(4.7)}\qquad \mathbf{X_{a,b}} = \mathbf{X_a} + \mathbf{X_b} = \begin{bmatrix} a(0) & a(1) & b(2) & b(3) \\ -a^*(1) & a^*(0) & b^*(3) & -b^*(2) \\ b(0) & b(1) & a^*(0) & -a(1) \\ -b^*(1) & b(0) & a^*(1) & a(0) \end{bmatrix}.$$

This code can be shown to achieve diversity of $3M_r$ for the message set $\mathcal{A}$ and diversity $2M_r$ for message set $\mathcal{B}$. Therefore, this example achieves the tuple, $(\frac{1}{2}\log|\mathcal{S}|, 3M_r, \log|\mathcal{S}|, 2M_r)$. The proof of this involves a set closely related to the quaternions (used in the Alamouti code [**1**]). For $a(0), a(1) \in \mathbb{C}$, define the following sets

$$\text{(4.8)}\qquad \mathcal{Q} = \begin{bmatrix} a(0) & a(1) \\ -a^*(1) & a^*(0) \end{bmatrix}, \quad \tilde{\mathcal{Q}} = \begin{bmatrix} a(0) & a(1) \\ a^*(1) & -a^*(0) \end{bmatrix}.$$

The set $\mathcal{Q}$ is a multiplicative group (called the quaternionic group [**4**]), and $\tilde{\mathcal{Q}}$ is *not* a multiplicative group. However, it has the following properties

$$\text{(4.9)}\qquad \begin{aligned} \mathbf{F} \in \tilde{\mathcal{Q}}, &\quad \mathbf{F}^{-1} \in \tilde{\mathcal{Q}} \\ \mathbf{E}, \mathbf{F} \in \tilde{\mathcal{Q}}, &\quad \mathbf{EF} \in \mathcal{Q}, \\ \mathbf{E} \in \mathcal{Q}, \mathbf{F} \in \tilde{\mathcal{Q}}, &\quad \mathbf{EF} \in \tilde{\mathcal{Q}} \\ \mathbf{E} \in \tilde{\mathcal{Q}}, \mathbf{F} \in \mathcal{Q}, &\quad \mathbf{EF} \in \tilde{\mathcal{Q}}. \end{aligned}$$

Let us index elements of the sets $\mathbf{E} \in \mathcal{Q}$ and $\mathbf{F} \in \tilde{\mathcal{Q}}$ in terms of the indeterminates $\{u, v\}$ as $\mathbf{E}[u, v]$ and $\mathbf{F}[u, v]$. Using this notation, we can rewrite the code in (4.7) as,

$$\text{(4.10)}\qquad \mathbf{X_{a,b}} = \mathbf{X_a} + \mathbf{X_b} = \begin{bmatrix} \mathbf{E}[a(0), a(1)] & \mathbf{F}[b(2), b(3)] \\ \mathbf{E}[b(0), b(1)] & \mathbf{E}[a^*(0), -a(1)] \end{bmatrix},$$

where $\mathbf{E} \in \mathcal{Q}$ and $\mathbf{F} \in \tilde{\mathcal{Q}}$. Given two distinct candidate message sets $\{\mathbf{a}_1, \mathbf{b}_1\}$ and $\{\mathbf{a}_2, \mathbf{b}_2\}$, let us denote $\tilde{\mathbf{a}} = \mathbf{a}_1 - \mathbf{a}_2$ and $\tilde{\mathbf{b}} = \mathbf{b}_1 - \mathbf{b}_2$. To show that $D_a = 3M_r$, we need to show that if $\tilde{\mathbf{a}} \neq \mathbf{0}$, then $\min_{\tilde{\mathbf{a}}\neq \mathbf{0}} \min_{\tilde{\mathbf{b}}} \operatorname{rank}(\mathbf{X}_{\tilde{\mathbf{a}},\tilde{\mathbf{b}}}) = 3$. By choosing $\tilde{b}(0) = \tilde{a}(0), \tilde{b}(1) = \tilde{a}(1)$ and $\tilde{b}(2) = \tilde{a}^*(0), \tilde{b}(3) = -\tilde{a}(1)$, we get $\det(\mathbf{X}_{\tilde{\mathbf{a}},\tilde{\mathbf{b}}}) = 0$, and hence the diversity for message set $\mathcal{A}$ is at most $3M_r$, *i.e.* $D_a \leq 3M_r$. But, the matrix $\begin{bmatrix} \mathbf{E}[\tilde{a}(0), \tilde{a}(1)] \\ \mathbf{E}[\tilde{b}(0), \tilde{b}(1)] \end{bmatrix}$ for $\mathbf{E} \in \mathcal{Q}$, has orthogonal columns and therefore has full column rank (*i.e.* rank of 2). This shows that $D_a \geq 2M_r$. We show that $D_a = 3M_r$ by contradiction. Let us assume that $D_a = 2M_r$, i.e., there exists $\tilde{\mathbf{a}} \neq \mathbf{0}, \tilde{\mathbf{b}}$ such that $\operatorname{rank}(\mathbf{X}_{\tilde{\mathbf{a}},\tilde{\mathbf{b}}}) = 2$. When either $\mathbf{E}[\tilde{b}(0), \tilde{b}(1)] = \mathbf{0}$ or when $\mathbf{F}[\tilde{b}(2), \tilde{b}(3)] = \mathbf{0}$, one can easily see that this cannot happen. Suppose it is true for $\mathbf{E}[\tilde{b}(0), \tilde{b}(1)] \neq \mathbf{0}$ and $\mathbf{F}[\tilde{b}(2), \tilde{b}(3)] \neq \mathbf{0}$. This implies that there exists $\Gamma \in \mathbb{C}^{2\times 2}$ such that,

$$\begin{bmatrix} \mathbf{E}[\tilde{a}(0), \tilde{a}(1)] \\ \mathbf{E}[\tilde{b}(0), \tilde{b}(1)] \end{bmatrix} = \begin{bmatrix} \mathbf{F}[\tilde{b}(2), \tilde{b}(3)] \\ \mathbf{E}^*[\tilde{a}^*(0), -\tilde{a}(1)] \end{bmatrix} \Gamma. \tag{4.11}$$

Hence this implies that

$$\mathbf{E}[\tilde{b}(0), \tilde{b}(1)] = \mathbf{E}^*[\tilde{a}^*(0), -\tilde{a}(1)]\mathbf{F}^{-1}[\tilde{b}(2), \tilde{b}(3)]\mathbf{E}[\tilde{a}(0), \tilde{a}(1)],$$

which cannot happen due to properties in (4.9) resulting in the contradiction. Hence this shows that $D_a = 3M_r$. Due to the orthogonality of columns of $\begin{bmatrix} \mathbf{E}[\tilde{a}(0), \tilde{a}(1)] \\ \mathbf{E}[\tilde{b}(0), \tilde{b}(1)] \end{bmatrix}$ and those in $\begin{bmatrix} \mathbf{F}[\tilde{b}(2), \tilde{b}(3)] \\ \mathbf{E}^*[\tilde{a}^*(0), -\tilde{a}(1)] \end{bmatrix}$ it is clear that $D_b = 2M_r$.

The contrast with Example 2 is that although the rates for each layer are identical, here we achieve a higher diversity for the message set $\mathcal{B}$ but at the cost of a lower diversity for the message set $\mathcal{A}$. In this example as well, we cannot construct a TDM code that achieves this. If we need a code of diversity 3, it needs to occupy at least 3 time symbols. Hence for block size $T = M_t = 4$, we are left with 1 symbol in which to obtain diversity two and rate $\log |\mathcal{S}|$, which is clearly not possible.

■

The next example illustrates the case of a non-square design.

Example 4: In this example, $M_t = 4$ and the block size is $T = 5$ symbols, giving rise to a non-square code matrix design. Here $\mathcal{A}$ comes from the message set $\{a(0), a(1)\} \in \mathcal{S}$ and $\mathcal{B}$ comes from $\{b(0), b(1), b(2), b(3)\} \in \mathcal{S}$. This implies that $R_a = \frac{2}{5}\log|\mathcal{S}|$, and $R_b = \frac{4}{5}\log|\mathcal{S}|$, leading to a total rate of $R_a + R_b = \frac{6}{5}\log|\mathcal{S}|$.

$$\mathbf{X}_{\mathbf{a},\mathbf{b}} = \mathbf{X}_{\mathbf{a}} + \mathbf{X}_{\mathbf{b}} = \begin{bmatrix} a(0) & -a^*(1) & b(0) & b(2) & -b^*(3) \\ a(1) & a^*(0) & b(1) & b(3) & b^*(2) \\ 0 & 0 & a^*(0) & a^*(1) & -b^*(1) \\ 0 & 0 & -a(1) & a(0) & b^*(0) \end{bmatrix}. \tag{4.12}$$

This code can be shown to achieve diversity of $4M_r$ for the message set $\mathcal{A}$ and diversity $2M_r$ for message set $\mathcal{B}$. Therefore, this example achieves the tuple, $(\frac{2}{5}\log|\mathcal{S}|, 4M_r, \frac{4}{5}\log|\mathcal{S}|, 2M_r)$. Given the construction from Example 2, we can easily prove that for $\tilde{\mathbf{a}} \neq \mathbf{0}$, $\operatorname{rank}(\mathbf{X}_{\tilde{\mathbf{a}},\tilde{\mathbf{b}}}) = 4$, and hence for message set $\mathcal{A}$ we get a diversity order of $4M_r$. To prove the claimed diversity order for message set $\mathcal{B}$, we need to show the following

$$\min_{\substack{\tilde{\mathbf{a}} \\ \tilde{\mathbf{b}}\neq \mathbf{0}}} \operatorname{rank}(\mathbf{X}_{\tilde{\mathbf{a}},\tilde{\mathbf{b}}}) = 2. \tag{4.13}$$

Clearly, for $\tilde{a}(0) = \tilde{a}(1) = \tilde{b}(0) = \tilde{b}(1) = 0$, $\text{rank}(\mathbf{X}_{\tilde{\mathbf{a}},\tilde{\mathbf{b}}}) = 2$ and hence the minimal rank is at most 2. We prove the result by contradiction. Suppose there exists $\tilde{\mathbf{a}}$ and $\tilde{\mathbf{b}} \neq \mathbf{0}$ such that $\text{rank}(\mathbf{X}_{\tilde{\mathbf{a}},\tilde{\mathbf{b}}}) = 1$. This implies that for such a choice, all the rows are multiples of one another, i.e.,

$$\begin{bmatrix} \tilde{a}(0) \\ -\tilde{a}^*(1) \\ \tilde{b}(0) \\ \tilde{b}(2) \\ -\tilde{b}^*(3) \end{bmatrix} = \alpha \begin{bmatrix} \tilde{a}(1) \\ \tilde{a}^*(0) \\ \tilde{b}(1) \\ \tilde{b}(3) \\ \tilde{b}^*(2) \end{bmatrix}, \quad \begin{bmatrix} 0 \\ 0 \\ \tilde{a}^*(0) \\ \tilde{a}^*(1) \\ -\tilde{b}^*(1) \end{bmatrix} = \beta \begin{bmatrix} 0 \\ 0 \\ -\tilde{a}(1) \\ \tilde{a}(0) \\ \tilde{b}^*(0) \end{bmatrix}, \quad \begin{bmatrix} \tilde{a}(1) \\ \tilde{a}^*(0) \\ \tilde{b}(1) \\ \tilde{b}(3) \\ \tilde{b}^*(2) \end{bmatrix} = \gamma \begin{bmatrix} 0 \\ 0 \\ \tilde{a}^*(0) \\ \tilde{a}^*(1) \\ -\tilde{b}^*(1) \end{bmatrix}$$

For the above to be true, we would need $\tilde{a}(0) = 0 = \tilde{a}(1)$ and $\tilde{b}(0) = \tilde{b}(1) = \tilde{b}(2) = \tilde{b}(3) = 0$, which results in a contradiction. Hence we get the result claimed in (4.13), giving $D_b = 2M_r$.

This code also cannot be constructed using a switching strategy. A full-diversity code needs to occupy at least M_t symbols, and hence the message set $\mathcal{A}$ needs to occupy $M_t = 4$ symbols. Hence for block size $T = 5$, we are left with 1 symbol in which to obtain diversity two and rate $\frac{4}{5} \log |\mathcal{S}|$, which is clearly not possible. ■

5. Achievable rates

In this section we study a characterization of the achievable tuples (R_a, D_a, R_b, D_b). There can be two types of characterizations, one based on fixed-rate (finite alphabet) codes which resemble the characterization of Theorem 2.2 [**20**], and the other a rate-growth characterization akin to Theorem 2.4 [**24**]. We present a characterization based on rate-growth in this section with the caveat that the rate growths investigated here are different from the fixed rate values given code constructions of Section 4.

5.1. Characterization. In the rate growth characterization, identical to Definition 2.3, we can define two multiplexing gains r_a, r_b for message sets $\mathcal{A}$ and $\mathcal{B}$, respectively. Therefore, the tuple in this case would be (r_a, D_a, r_b, D_b) which would be a different characterization from the tuple examined in a fixed-rate case. We also assume that the codeword length is large enough to make average error probability equivalent to the outage probability[3]. Therefore, the information-theoretic characterization consists of finding the outage probabilities associated with rate growths of r_a, r_b in the message sets $\mathcal{A}, \mathcal{B}$.

5.2. Achievable Region. Since different error probability behaviour (diversity order) for the two information streams is desired, we want to analyze the individual error probabilities induced by a coding and decoding strategy. Given a joint codebook $\mathbf{X}_{\mathbf{a},\mathbf{b}}$, indexed by the information from message sets $\mathcal{A}, \mathcal{B}$, and a joint decoding scheme $\mathcal{D}$, we want to characterize the individual error probabilities on the message sets $\mathcal{A}$ and $\mathcal{B}$. More precisely, if the decoder outputs $\{\hat{\mathbf{a}}, \hat{\mathbf{b}}\}$, and the transmitted information is $\{\mathbf{a}, \mathbf{b}\}$, we want to characterize,

$$\mathbb{P}_e(\mathcal{A}) = \text{Prob}\left\{\{\hat{\mathbf{a}}, \hat{\mathbf{b}}\} : \hat{\mathbf{a}} \neq \mathbf{a}\right\}, \quad \mathbb{P}_e(\mathcal{B}) = \text{Prob}\left\{\{\hat{\mathbf{a}}, \hat{\mathbf{b}}\} : \hat{\mathbf{b}} \neq \mathbf{b}\right\}. \tag{5.1}$$

[3] An alternate interpretation is that the diversity can be shown to be equivalent to the outage probability in the SNR exponent similar to that in [**24**].

In examining these error probabilities in terms of diversity order, we are interested in the high SNR regime. Instead of directly examining the error probabilities, we examine the outage behaviour of the codes with the understanding that this will closely reflect the error probability behaviour [**24**]. For different diversity orders desired of the message sets $\mathcal{A}$ and $\mathcal{B}$, the general characterization of the individual outage behaviour is a difficult problem. Given this, we take a simpler approach by examining a particular codebook design and decoding strategy.

We examine the additive codeword model introduced in Section 4.1, and define the power distribution between the two message sets. We generate a random codebook $\mathbf{X_{a,b}} = \mathbf{X_a} + \mathbf{X_b}$ where both $\mathbf{X_a}$ and $\mathbf{X_b}$ are generated from i.i.d. Gaussian codebooks with average powers P_a, P_b. Given the total power constraint P, the power allocation needs to satisfy $P_a + P_b \leq P$. We use a successive decoding strategy, where $\mathbf{X_a}$ is decoded considering $\mathbf{X_b}$ as part of the noise. Then the decoded $\hat{\mathbf{X}}_\mathbf{a}$ is subtracted from the received signal $\mathbf{Y}$, and $\mathbf{X_b}$ is decoded. Note that such a decoding strategy from a diversity order perspective may not be optimal, but is perhaps the simplest case to analyze. Given this coding and decoding strategy, one can write the individual outage probabilities $\mathbb{P}_{out}^{(\mathcal{A})}(\text{SNR}), \mathbb{P}_{out}^{(\mathcal{B})}(\text{SNR})$ as follows.

$$
\begin{aligned}
\text{(5.2)} \qquad \mathbb{P}_{out}^{(\mathcal{A})}(\text{SNR}) &= \text{Prob}\left\{\mathbf{H} : \log \frac{|\mathbf{I} + \text{SNR}\mathbf{H}\mathbf{H}^*|}{|\mathbf{I} + \text{SNR}_b\mathbf{H}\mathbf{H}^*|} < R_a\right\} \\
\tilde{\mathbb{P}}^{(\mathcal{B})}(\text{SNR}) &= \text{Prob}\left\{\mathbf{H} : \log |\mathbf{I} + \text{SNR}_b\mathbf{H}\mathbf{H}^*| < R_b\right\} \\
\mathbb{P}_{out}^{(\mathcal{B})}(\text{SNR}) &= \max\left\{\mathbb{P}_{out}^{(\mathcal{A})}(\text{SNR}), \tilde{\mathbb{P}}^{(\mathcal{B})}(\text{SNR})\right\},
\end{aligned}
$$

where $\text{SNR} = \frac{P}{\sigma^2}$, $\text{SNR}_b = \frac{P_b}{\sigma^2}$, and $|\mathbf{A}|$ denotes the determinant of the matrix $\mathbf{A}$. Note that the average achievable rate is given by,

$$
\text{(5.3)} \qquad R(SNR) = (1 - \mathbb{P}_{out}^{(\mathcal{A})}(\text{SNR}))R_a + (1 - \mathbb{P}_{out}^{(\mathcal{B})}(\text{SNR}))R_b,
$$

which could be another criterion to optimize. We design the power allocation to the message sets $\mathcal{A}, \mathcal{B}$ respectively be such that $\frac{P_a}{P_b} = (P/\sigma^2)^\beta = \text{SNR}^\beta$, $\beta \in [0, 1]$. Then, at high SNR, we have $\text{SNR}_a \doteq \text{SNR}$, $\text{SNR}_b \doteq \text{SNR}^{1-\beta}$.

Then, for a given β, in a manner similar to [**24**], we can characterize $\mathbb{P}_{out}^{(\mathcal{A})}(\text{SNR})$ and $\tilde{\mathbb{P}}^{(\mathcal{B})}(\text{SNR})$, as

$$
\text{(5.4)} \qquad \mathbb{P}_{out}^{(\mathcal{A})}(\text{SNR}) \doteq \text{SNR}^{-\tilde{d}_a}, \ \tilde{\mathbb{P}}^{(\mathcal{B})}(\text{SNR}) \doteq \text{SNR}^{-\tilde{d}_b},
$$

where

$$
\begin{aligned}
\text{(5.5)} \qquad \tilde{d}_a &= \inf_{\alpha \in \mathcal{F}_a} \sum_{i=1}^{\min(M_t, M_r)} \left[|M_t - M_r| + 2i - 1\right] \alpha_i \\
\tilde{d}_b &= \inf_{\alpha \in \mathcal{F}_b} \sum_{i=1}^{\min(M_t, M_r)} \left[|M_t - M_r| + 2i - 1\right] \alpha_i,
\end{aligned}
$$

and

$$\mathcal{F}_a = \{\alpha_1 \geq \alpha_2 \ldots \geq \alpha_{\min(M_t,M_r)} \geq 0 : \sum_{i=1}^{\min(M_t,M_r)} (1-\alpha_i)^+ - \sum_{i=1}^{\min(M_t,M_r)} (1-\beta-\alpha_i)^+ < r_a\} \tag{5.6}$$

$$\mathcal{F}_b = \{\alpha_1 \geq \alpha_2 \ldots \geq \alpha_{\min(M_t,M_r)} \geq 0 : \sum_{i=1}^{\min(M_t,M_r)} (1-\beta-\alpha_i)^+ < r_b\},$$

where $(\cdot)^+ = \max(\cdot, 0)$. Since successive decoding is employed, the diversity levels achieved for the given β are given by $D_a(\beta) = \tilde{d}_a$ and $D_b(\beta) = \min(\tilde{d}_a, \tilde{d}_b)$, and the decoding order would matter. Therefore, the achievable tuple using this particular coding and decoding strategy is parameterized by β. This characterization is quite straightforward and for specific cases (such as $M_t = M_r = 2$) one can obtain explicit solutions to (5.5). However, this may not be a tight characterization of the achievable region since successive decoding may not be the right approach for diversity considerations, and the chosen power allocation strategy might not be optimal.

In more detail, for $M_t = 2 = M_r$, one can demonstrate that we can achieve the following rate tuple.

$$\begin{array}{rcl} \text{If } r_a \in (0,1), D_a & < & 1+3(1-r_a) \\ \text{If } r_a \in (1,2), D_a & < & 2-r_a \\ \text{If } r_a \in (0,1), \text{and } (r_a+r_b) \in (0,1) & & \\ D_b & < & 4(1-r_a)-3r_b = D^*(r_a+r_b)-r_a \\ \text{If } r_a \in (0,1), \text{and } (r_a+r_b) \in (1,2) & & \\ D_b & < & 2-r_a-(r_a+r_b) = D^*(r_a+r_b)-r_a \\ \text{If } r_a \in (1,2), D_b & = & 0, \end{array} \tag{5.7}$$

where $D^*(r)$ denotes the optimal diversity order for a multiplexing gain of r as given in [**24**]. Therefore, atleast for the case of $M_t = M_r = 2$, one obtains a tuple (r_a, D_a, r_b, D_b) such that (r_a, D_a) lies on the optimal rate-diversity trade-off curve specified in [**24**] and (r_a+r_b, D_b) loses diversity order of exactly r_a over the optimal. Note that since we cannot dominate the "single-layer" rate-diversity tradeoff, we have a natural outer-bound for the rate tuple.

$$\begin{array}{rcl} D_a & < & D^*(r_a) \\ D_b & < & D^*(r_b) \\ \min(D_a, D_b) & < & D^*(r_a+r_b). \end{array} \tag{5.8}$$

Therefore, the best we could have hoped for when $M_t = 2 = M_r$ is for (r_a+r_b, D_b) to lie on the optimal rate-diversity curve as specified in [**24**]. However, we are below it by an amount of r_a. It is unclear if this is due to the particular coding/decoding scheme used or if the "single-layer" outer bound is not achievable.

There might be a technique based on recent results on the multiple-antenna broadcast channel (see for example [**23**] among others) allowing us to employ a precoding strategy that is different from just superposition coding. The difference

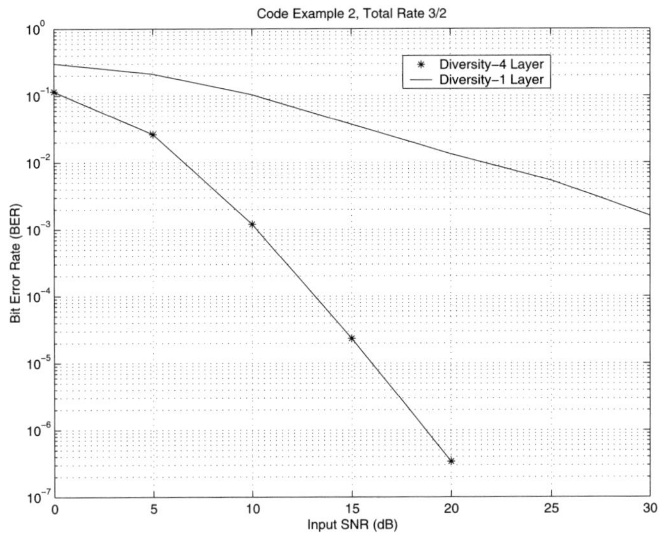

FIGURE 3. Error performance of Embedded code in Example 2

in our case from the equivalent broadcast channel considered there is that the channel is necessarily unknown at the transmitter for us, whereas it is assumed to be known in their case. However, we are currently investigating coding strategies that go beyond superposition coding to improve the inner bound.

6. Numerical Example

To illustrate the diversity-embedding property of the codes in Section IV, consider code example 2. Figure 3 depicts the bit error rate for the two information layers where the slopes of the 2 curves are markedly different indicating different diversity levels. We assume BPSK modulation (for simplicity), a Rayleigh flat-fading channel, and maximum likelihood decoding. At a BER of 10^{-2}, one layer can be decoded under much worse channel conditions than the other layer (about 15 dB less SNR). Another view point is the following : at given channel conditions (say an SNR of 15 dB), one layer can include information with more stringent reliability requirements (e.g. real-time data or video) than the other layer (e.g. voice or non-real-time data) and the 2 layers can still be decoded successfully meeting their individual QoS requirements.

7. Discussion

In this paper we introduced the idea of diversity embedded space-time codes in which a high-rate space-time code is designed to have a (lower-rate) high-diversity code embedded within it. The main idea was to opportunistically use a quasi-static channel realization without knowing it at the transmitter. The constructions given were better than simple time-sharing and we also explored an information-theoretic characterization of the achievable tuples. There are several open questions including characterization of the achievable region, extremal code constructions and practical performance under complexity constraints. We hope that this work is a first step towards understanding these issues.

Acknowledgements

We gratefully acknowledge several stimulating discussions with Vinay Vaishampayan and constructive comments from an anonymous reviewer.

References

[1] S.M. Alamouti, "A simple transmit diversity technique for wireless communications", *IEEE Journal on Sel. Areas in Commun.*, vol. 16, no. 8, pp. 1451–1458, Oct. 1998.

[2] E. Biglieri, J. Proakis and S. Shamai, "Fading channels: Information-Theoretic and Communications aspects", *IEEE Trans. Inform. Theory*, vol. 44, no. 6, pp. 2619–2692, Oct. 1998.

[3] S. Shamai (Shitz), "A broadcast strategy for the Gaussian slowly fading channel", in *IEEE Int'l Symp. on Inform. Theory*, Ulm, Germany, p 150, June 1997.

[4] A. R. Calderbank and A. F. Naguib, "Orthogonal designs and third generation wireless communication" in J. W. P. Hirschfeld, editor, *Surveys in Combinatorics 2001, London Mathematical Society Lecture Note Series #288*, pp. 75–107. Cambridge Univ. Press, 2001.

[5] A R. Calderbank and N. Seshadri, "Multilevel codes for Unequal Error Protection", *IEEE Trans. Inform. Theory*, vol. 39, no. 4, pp. 1234–1248, July 1993.

[6] T.M. Cover, "Broadcast channels", *IEEE Trans. Inform. Theory*, vol. 18, pp. –14, Jan. 1972.

[7] T.M. Cover and J.A. Thomas, *Elements of Information Theory*, John Wiley and Sons, Inc., New York, 1991.

[8] I. Csiszar and J. Korner, "*Information Theory: Coding theorems for Discrete Memoryless Channels", Academic Press, New York, 1982.*

[9] M.O. Damen, A. Chkeif, and J.-C. Belfiore, Lattice codes decoder for space-time codes, IEEE Commun. Letters, *vol. 4, pp. 161-163, May 2000.*

[10] M.O. Damen, H. El-Gamal, and N. Beaulieu, "On optimal linear space-time constellations", in Int'l Conf. on Commun., *May 2003.*

[11] S.N. Diggavi, "On achievable performance of spatial diversity fading channels" IEEE Trans. Inform. Theory, *vol. 47, no. 1, pp. 308–325, Jan. 2001.*

[12] G.J. Foschini, "Layered space-time architecture for wireless communication in a fading environment when using multi-element antennas", Bell Labs Technical Journal, *1(2), pp. 41–59, Sept. 1996.*

[13] J.-C. Guey, M.P. Fitz, M.R. Bell, and W.-Y. Kuo, "Signal design for transmitter diversity wireless communication systems over Rayleigh fading channels", IEEE Trans. Commun., *vol. 47, no. 4, pp. 527–537, Apr. 1999.*

[14] J. Hagenauer. "Rate Compatable Punctured Convolutional Codes (RCPC codes) and their applications", IEEE Trans. Commun., *vol. 36, no. 4, pp. 389–400, Apr. 1988.*

[15] B. Hassibi and B. Hochwald, "High-Rate Codes That Are Linear in Space and Time", IEEE Trans. Inform. Theory, *pp. 1804–1824, July 2002.*

[16] L H. Ozarow, S Shamai, and A. D. Wyner, "Information theoretic considerations for cellular mobile radio", IEEE Trans. on Vehicular Technology, *vol. 43, no. 2, pp. 359–378, May 1994.*

[17] A. Seeger, Hierarchical Channel Coding for Digital Video Broadcasting, *PhD thesis, Technical University of Munich, Munich, Germany, 1999.*

[18] S. Shamai (Shitz) and A. Steiner, "Single user broadcasting in a MIMO channel", in Proc. Inform. Theory Workshop, *Paris, France, pp 38–41, Apr. 2003.*

[19] V. Tarokh, H. Jafarkhani, and A.R. Calderbank, "Space-Time Block Codes from Orthogonal Designs", IEEE Trans. Inform. Theory, *pp. 1456–1467, July 1999.*

[20] V. Tarokh, N. Seshadri, and A.R. Calderbank, "Space-time codes for high data rate wireless communications: Performance criterion and code construction", IEEE Trans. Inform. Theory, *vol. 44, no. 2, pp. 744–765, Mar. 1998.*

[21] E. Telatar, "Capacity of multi-antenna Gaussian channels", European Trans. on Telecommunications, *vol. 10, no. 6, pp. 585–596, Nov.-Dec. 1999.*

[22] R. van Nobelen, N. Seshadri, J. Whitehead, and S. Timiri, "An adaptive radio link protocol with enhanced data rates for GSM evolution", IEEE Personal Communications*, vol. 6, no. 1, Feb. 1999.*

[23] W. Yu. Competition and Cooperation in Multiuser Communication Environments*, PhD thesis, Stanford University, Stanford, CA., 2002.*

[24] L. Zheng and D.N.C. Tse, "Diversity and multiplexing: A fundamental tradeoff in multiple antenna channels", IEEE Trans. Inform. Theory*, vol. 49, no. 5, pp. 1073–1096, May 2003.*

AT&T SHANNON LABS, 180, PARK AVE, BLDG 103, FLORHAM PARK, NEW JERSEY, NJ 07932, USA.

Current address: School of Computer and Communication Sciences, Laboratory of Information and Communication Systems (LICOS), Swiss Federal Institute of Technology (EPFL), EPFL-IC-ISC-LICOS, Bldg, PSE A, Lausanne, Switzerland, CH 1015.

E-mail address: `suhas.diggavi@epfl.ch`

DEPARTMENT OF ELECTRICAL ENGINEERING UNIVERSITY OF TEXAS AT DALLAS, RICHARDSON, TX 75083 USA.

E-mail address: `aldhahir@utdallas.edu`

PROGRAM IN APPLIED AND COMPUTATIONAL MATHEMATICS, PRINCETON UNIVERSITY, PRINCETON, NEW JERSEY, USA.

E-mail address: `calderbank@math.princeton.edu`

DIMACS Series in Discrete Mathematics
and Theoretical Computer Science
Volume **66**, 2004

Cooperative Communication in Wireless Systems

Elza Erkip, Andrew Sendonaris, Andrej Stefanov, and Behnaam Aazhang

ABSTRACT. The broadcast nature of wireless communications suggests that a source signal transmitted towards the destination can be "overheard" at neighboring nodes. Cooperative communication refers to processing of this overheard information at the surrounding nodes and retransmission towards the destination to create spatial diversity, thereby to obtain higher throughput and reliability. In this paper we describe information theoretic models suitable for cooperation, study achievable rate regions and outage probabilities, and describe channel coding techniques that allow us to exploit the diversity advantages of cooperation.

1. Introduction

Ad-hoc wireless networks are based on multi-hop communications, where the information from the source to the destination is relayed via other mobiles. An ad-hoc network does not have a fixed infrastructure, so this relaying operation is essential in order to overcome the path loss incurred over large distances. Multi-hop ideas are also utilized in cellular and wireless LAN systems to provide higher quality of service, power savings and extended coverage.

Information theory of multi-hop communication dates back to the relay channel model, which contains a source, a destination and a relay whose goal is to facilitate information transfer from the source to the destination. The relay channel was introduced by Van der Meulen [**23**] and investigated extensively by Cover and El Gamal [**3**]. Cover and El Gamal provided a number of relaying strategies, found achievable regions and provided upper bounds to the capacity of a general relay channel. They also provided an expression for the capacity of the degraded relay channel, in which the communication channel between the source and the relay is physically better than the source-destination link. The capacity of the general relay channel is still unknown. Motivated by the recent interest in multi-hop, a number of recent papers investigate the use of multiple relays. Some relevant references include [**7, 8, 9, 15, 18, 19, 26**].

Even though the information theoretic model allows for the destination to listen to both the source and the relay, in most multi-hop systems the destination only processes the signal coming from the relay. This is justified in a wireless channel

Key words and phrases. Multi-access communication, fading channels, diversity.
The first author was supported in part by NSF Grant No. CAREER-0093163.

where path loss has the dominant effect. Since the source is generally further away from the destination than the relay, the received signal at the destination due to the source would be much weaker than the relay signal. However, when fading is also taken into account, this scheme would incur considerable loss, especially in diversity, compared to one in which the destination processes both signals. Hence one can use multi-hop not just to overcome path loss, but also to provide diversity.

Motivated by the above observation, cooperative communication involves two main ideas: (i) Use relays (or multi-hop) to provide spatial diversity in a fading environment, (ii) Envision a collaborative scheme where the relay also has its own information to send so both terminals help one another to communicate by acting as relays for each other (called "partners").

One can think of a cooperative system as a virtual antenna array, where each antenna in the array corresponds to one of the partners. The partners can overhear each other's transmissions though the wireless medium, process this information and re-transmit to collaborate. This provides extra observations of the source signals at the destinations, the observations which are dispersed in space and usually discarded by current implementations of cellular, wireless LAN or ad-hoc systems. However, since the elements of this array are not co-located and are connected via noisy, fading links, it is not clear a priori how much the benefits of this cooperation would be. Our goal in this paper is to argue that the benefits, in terms of achievable data rates, diversity and error performance, are significant. In our discussion, we briefly describe some of our prior and ongoing work along with relevant literature, and provide directions for future research. We first provide an information theoretic model to describe the cooperative system, a set of achievable rates and an outage probability analysis. Then we talk about how one can design and analyze channel codes that can exploit the predicted benefits of a cooperative system.

2. Information Theoretic Model and Analysis

For ease of exposure, we consider a cooperative system consisting of two source terminals denoted by T_1 and T_2. These terminals could communicate with a common destination (such as a cooperative system in cellular) or more generally could have separate destinations. Even though the cooperative concept is equally applicable to both cases, we will constrain ourselves to the common destination case for the analysis. Our model is illustrated in Figure 1. Mathematically we have the discrete-time model

$$Y_0 = K_{10}X_1 + K_{20}X_2 + Z_0 \qquad (2.1)$$

$$Y_1 = K_{21}X_2 + Z_1 \qquad (2.2)$$

$$Y_2 = K_{12}X_1 + Z_2 \qquad (2.3)$$

where Y_0 denotes the signal received at the common destination, Y_1 and Y_2 denote the overheard signals at each of the partners and X_1 and X_2 represent the signals transmitted by terminal 1 and 2 respectively at a particular time instant t. The noise terms Z_0, Z_1 and Z_2 are independent from each other and have iid complex Gaussian samples in time with variances σ_i^2, $i = 0, 1, 2$ respectively. We assume a flat fading Rayleigh channel with complex Gaussian channel gains K_{ij}. The gains K_{10}, K_{20} and K_{12} are independent as they correspond to different links. In general, the relationship between K_{12} and K_{21} depends on how the partners access the channel. We will assume that the channel between two partners is reciprocal

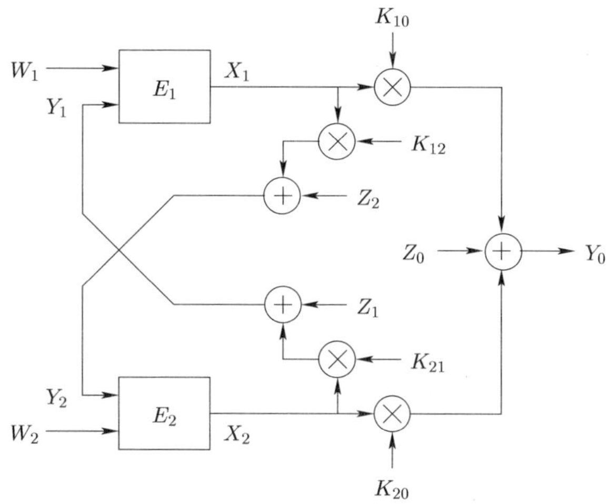

FIGURE 1. Block diagram of a fading Gaussian cooperative channel

leading to $K_{12} = K_{21}$. However, this assumption is not necessary for our results and can be relaxed. For the achievable rate region, we use the notion of ergodic capacity, so we do not make any assumptions about the time variations of the channel except that they form an ergodic random process. When we consider outage probabilities and frame error rates corresponding to particular channel codes, we will assume that the channel varies slowly and is constant during the communication session.

We allow for both partners to transmit and receive at the same time and we assume that each terminal can perform perfect echo cancelation. As illustrated in equations (2.2) and (2.3) this leads to Y_1 (Y_2) having no contribution from X_1 (X_2). We also assume that both terminals are synchronized. Even though these assumptions may not hold in a practical system, they are quite common in the information theory literature and they allow us to investigate the fundamental benefits of cooperation. We will argue in Section 3 that even when we relax some of these assumptions, cooperative communication still provides considerable improvement over non-cooperative systems.

All of the receivers have perfect channel state information, that is they can exactly measure the channel gain of the incoming signals. For the achievable rate region and outage probability analysis in this section, we also assume that there is some partial channel state information at transmitters in the form of the phase of the complex channel gains K_{10} and K_{20}. This allows the partners to form signals that coherently combine at the destination. We relax this assumption in Section 3.

2.1. Achievable Rate Region. This section summarizes some of our results from [**20, 21**]. We provide an achievable rate region for the two-user cooperative model above. We make the observation that this model is contained in the multiple access channel with generalized feedback which was analyzed for discrete memoryless and Gaussian channels in [**2, 24**]. The achievability results will make use of the signal structure of [**24**]. Our main contribution will be to illustrate the potential diversity and throughput benefits of cooperation in a wireless network with varying link qualities.

In general, causality of the system suggests that $X_{1,t}$ the signal transmitted by T_1 at time t can only depend on the message of T_1, W_1 and what T_1 has "overheard" so far, $(Y_{1,1}, \dots, Y_{1,t-1})$. However, we will use a more restricted signaling strategy based on superposition block Markov encoding [**4**], a technique which has been successfully used in multi-user systems involving feedback or some form of an inter-user link. We envision transmission for B blocks, each of length n. Both B and n are assumed to be large. In fact, for the achievable rate region, n has to be large enough to observe different fading levels so that ergodic capacity is the right notion to use. In each block, both terminals transmit a new message. The transmitted signal from T_1 in block j depends on $W_1(j)$, the message in that block and $(\mathbf{Y}_1(1), \dots, \mathbf{Y}_1(j-1))$, all the signals received up to and including block $j-1$. Note that $\mathbf{Y}_1(i)$ denotes n observations of the output signal in block i. The destination uses backward decoding [**25, 27**], that is starts decoding from the last block and moves one by one to the first.

We next state the achievable region for the cooperative channel, and provide a sketch of the proof which illustrates the signal structure. We then provide comparisons with the non-cooperative capacity region.

THEOREM 2.1. *An achievable rate region for the cooperative system given in (2.1)-(2.3) is the closure of the convex hull of all rate pairs* (R_1, R_2) *such that* $R_1 = R_{10} + R_{12}$ *and* $R_2 = R_{20} + R_{21}$ *with*

$$R_{12} < E\left\{C\left(\frac{|K_{12}|^2 P_{12}}{|K_{12}|^2 P_{10} + \sigma_1^2}\right)\right\} \tag{2.4}$$

$$R_{21} < E\left\{C\left(\frac{|K_{21}|^2 P_{21}}{|K_{21}|^2 P_{20} + \sigma_2^2}\right)\right\} \tag{2.5}$$

$$R_{10} < E\left\{C\left(\frac{|K_{10}|^2 P_{10}}{\sigma_0^2}\right)\right\} \tag{2.6}$$

$$R_{20} < E\left\{C\left(\frac{|K_{20}|^2 P_{20}}{\sigma_0^2}\right)\right\} \tag{2.7}$$

$$R_{10} + R_{20} < E\left\{C\left(\frac{|K_{10}|^2 P_{10} + |K_{20}|^2 P_{20}}{\sigma_0^2}\right)\right\} \tag{2.8}$$

(2.9)

$$R_{10} + R_{20} + R_{12} + R_{21} < E\left\{C\left(\frac{|K_{10}|^2 P_1 + |K_{20}|^2 P_2 + 2|K_{10}||K_{20}|\sqrt{P_{U1} P_{U2}}}{\sigma_0^2}\right)\right\},$$

for some power assignment satisfying $P_1 = P_{10} + P_{12} + P_{U1}$, $P_2 = P_{20} + P_{21} + P_{U2}$. *The function* $C(x) = \frac{1}{2}\log(1+x)$ *is the capacity of an additive white Gaussian noise channel with signal to noise ratio* x *and* E *denotes expectation with respect to the fading parameters* K_{ij}.

PROOF. The proof follows [**24**]. Here we sketch it briefly to illustrate the signal structure and decoding scheme.

In the cooperative system, unlike the degraded relay channel, one cannot ensure the partner will always be able to receive more information than the destination. Hence for every block j, T_1 divides its information $W_1(j)$ into two parts, one to be relayed through the partner ($W_{12}(j)$ at rate R_{12}), the other to be transmitted directly to the destination ($W_{10}(j)$ at rate R_{10}). The transmitted signal X_1 consists of three parts X_{10}, used to send W_{10}, X_{12} used to send W_{12}, and U_1 which ensures cooperation. The respective powers allocated to these signal components are P_{10}, P_{12} and P_{U1}. We have

$$\mathbf{X}_{10}(j) = \sqrt{P_{10}}\tilde{\mathbf{X}}_{10}(W_{10}(j), W_{12}(j-1), W_{21}(j-1)) \tag{2.10}$$

$$\mathbf{X}_{12}(j) = \sqrt{P_{12}}\tilde{\mathbf{X}}_{12}(W_{12}(j), W_{12}(j-1), W_{21}(j-1)) \tag{2.11}$$

$$\mathbf{U}_1(j) = \sqrt{P_{U1}}e^{-j\theta_{10}}\tilde{\mathbf{U}}(W_{12}(j-1), W_{21}(j-1)), \tag{2.12}$$

with $\mathbf{X}_1(j) = \mathbf{X}_{10}(j) + \mathbf{X}_{12}(j) + \mathbf{U}_1(j)$ and $P_1 = P_{10} + P_{12} + P_{U1}$. We assume $K_{10} = |K_{10}|e^{j\theta_{10}}$, hence θ_{10} is the phase of the complex fading between T_1 and the destination. Here $\mathbf{X}_1(j)$ denotes n transmitted symbols for block j. The entries of the random codebooks are generated by choosing $\tilde{\mathbf{X}}_{10}$, $\tilde{\mathbf{X}}_{12}$ and $\tilde{\mathbf{U}}$ independently, all consisting of n iid samples of $\mathcal{N}(0,1)$ distribution. The signal transmitted by T_2, $\mathbf{X}_2(j)$, is generated in a similar fashion. Note that $\tilde{\mathbf{U}}$ is used by both terminals in their codebooks.

We observe that the signal $\mathbf{X}_1(j)$ not only depends on $W_1(j) = (W_{10}(j), W_{12}(j))$, but also on $W_{12}(j-1)$ and $W_{21}(j-1)$. Obviously, T_1 knows $W_{12}(j-1)$. We will also ensure that R_{21}, the rate of transmission for W_{21}, is chosen so that W_{21} can be perfectly recovered at T_1. Therefore at block j $(W_{12}(j-1), W_{21}(j-1))$ will be known at both terminals and can be used to form the basis for cooperation.

In order to find out the conditions on R_{12} (R_{21}) for perfect recovery of W_{12} (W_{21}) at the partner, we first look at block 1. We assume $(W_{12}(0), W_{21}(0)) = (0,0)$. Terminal 2 receives $\mathbf{Y}_2(1) = (Y_{2,1}(1), Y_{2,2}(1), \ldots, Y_{2,n}(1))$ where $Y_{2,t}(1)$ is given by equation (2.3) for all $t = 1, \ldots, n$. The signal $\mathbf{X}_1(1)$ depends on $W_{12}(0)$ and $W_{21}(0)$ both of which are known, $W_{12}(1)$ which T_2 is interested in, and $W_{10}(1)$ which T_2 will not attempt to find out. Using the representation in equations (2.10)-(2.12), we observe that $\mathbf{U}_1(1)$ is known and hence can be canceled, $\mathbf{X}_{10}(j)$ will be treated as noise and $\mathbf{X}_{12}(1)$ will be decoded at terminal 2. Assuming the fading is ergodic over the block length n, provided that

$$R_{12} < \mathrm{E}\left\{C\left(\frac{|K_{12}|^2 P_{12}}{|K_{12}|^2 P_{10} + \sigma_1^2}\right)\right\},$$

terminal 2 can estimate $W_{12}(1)$ with arbitrarily low probability of error. Note that this condition is given by equation (2.4) of Theorem 2.1. Based on equation (2.5) we can make similar arguments for perfect recovery of $W_{21}(1)$ at T_1. Moving sequentially from block $j-1$ to block j, $j = 2, \ldots, n$ we can ensure that at the beginning of block j, both partners know $(W_{12}(j-1), W_{21}(j-1))$.

We now illustrate how equations (2.6)-(2.9) lead to reliable transmission of W_{10}, W_{12}, W_{20} and W_{21} to the destination. The decoding starts from the last block [**25, 27**] in which no new information is transmitted. Therefore we can set

$$(W_{10}(B), W_{12}(B), W_{20}(B), W_{21}(B)) = (0,0,0,0).$$

Although this reduces the overall information rate by the factor $(B-1)/B$, the rate loss is negligible for large B. In this block the destination wishes to decode $W_{12}(B-1)$ and $W_{21}(B-1)$. Since $W_{10}(B), W_{12}(B), W_{20}(B), W_{21}(B)$ are known, the condition

$$R_{12} + R_{21} < \mathrm{E}\left\{C\left(\frac{|K_{10}|^2 P_1 + |K_{20}|^2 P_2 + 2|K_{10}||K_{20}|\sqrt{P_{U1}P_{U2}}}{\sigma_0^2}\right)\right\} \tag{2.13}$$

is sufficient for reliable reproduction. The factor $\sqrt{P_{U1}P_{U2}}$ results from the coherent addition of the cooperative signals U_1 and U_2.

Moving into block $B-1$, the destination now has to decode $(W_{10}(B-1), W_{20}(B-1), W_{12}(B-2), W_{21}(B-2))$. Following multiuser achievability results in [**5**] and using [**6, 1**] to replace all the bounds on the rates by their expected values where expectation is over the fading amplitudes, sufficient conditions on R_{10}, R_{20}, R_{12} and R_{21} for asymptotically error free transmission are given by equations (2.6)-(2.9) and (2.13).

Dependency of all the signal components (namely X_{10}, X_{12}, U_1, X_{20}, X_{21} and U_2) on the cooperation information $(W_{12}(B-2), W_{21}(B-2))$ leads to equations (2.9) and (2.13). Since (2.13) is dominated by (2.9) it will be omitted in the final formulation. The destination then proceeds backwards in the same manner until all the blocks are decoded.

By considering different power assignments P_{10}, P_{12}, P_{U1} (and respective powers for T_2) satisfying the total power constraint and time-sharing among different strategies, we obtain the achievable region stated in Theorem 2.1. □

In order to illustrate potential benefits of a cooperative system, we draw the achievable rate region for the proposed cooperative strategy of Theorem 2.1, together with the capacity region of the non-cooperative system in Figure 2. The non-cooperative case corresponds to the usual Gaussian fading multiple access channel. We also include the "ideal" cooperative scenario in which the inter-user channel is perfect. This represents the capacity of a two-antenna system with total power $P_1 + P_2$ and channel phase information at the transmitter. We assume both terminals have the same power constraint and the quality of the channel between each terminal to the destination (represented as the mean of the fading levels K_{10} and K_{20}) is the same. We illustrate the achievable rate region of Theorem 2.1 for various qualities of the inter-user channel, with higher mean of K_{12} corresponding to a better channel. We observe that even when the inter-user channel has similar or worse quality than the user-destination channel, cooperation results in a larger rate region. As the quality of the inter-user channel improves, the achievable rate region greatly increases and gets closer to the ideal multi-antenna system.

Performance of the suggested cooperative system for an asymmetric scenario is shown in Figure 3. The fading for T_1 has higher mean than T_2. This, for example could occur if T_1 is closer to the destination. We observe that cooperation continues to increase the set of achievable rates. Even though the user with severe fading (lower fading mean) benefits more from cooperation, the equal rate $(R_1 = R_2)$ and the maximum rate sum point $(R_1 + R_2)$ is increased considerably with cooperation. This suggests that depending on the system requirements (such as maximizing fairness or the total throughput) even the good user can benefit from cooperation. Section 3 will provide further examples on the symmetric and asymmetric cooperative systems.

We note that relay channel corresponds to $R_1 = 0$ or $R_2 = 0$. Hence in Figures 2 and 3, the points at which any rate curve intersects the x or the y-axis give achievable rates for the corresponding relay channel. Since the cooperative curve is above the line joining $R_1 = 0$ and $R_2 = 0$ points, we argue that cooperation performs better than time sharing between the two relays.

2.2. Probability of Outage. While the ergodic capacity region, or the set of achievable rates, tell us about the long term average throughputs, outage probability [**17**] shows us the robustness of the system to the variations in the channel. In order to calculate the outage probability of the cooperative system, we assume that

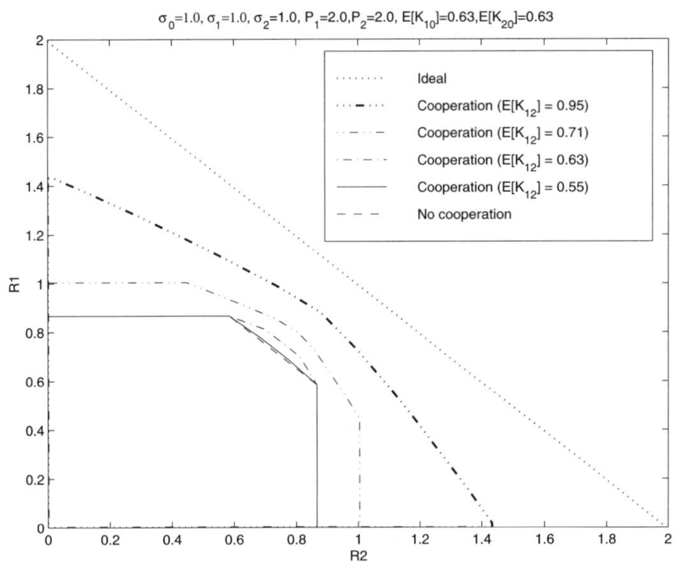

FIGURE 2. Achievable rate region for two-user cooperation. Both users have similar average quality links towards the destination.

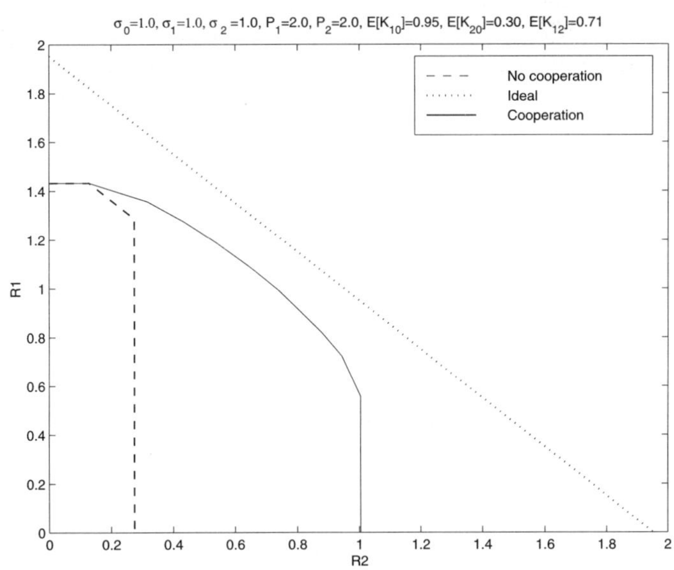

FIGURE 3. Achievable rate region for two-user cooperation. Users have different average quality links towards the destination.

the fading is slow and remains constant for the duration of B blocks. In that case, the achievable rate region depends on the current values of the fading levels K_{ij} and is random. Assuming the transmit signal structure and the decoding scheme in the proof of Theorem 2.1, equations (2.4)-(2.9) without the expectations lead to an achievable rate region. To illustrate the improvement in outage probability with cooperation, we consider a symmetric system as in Figure 2 and focus on the largest equal rate operating point $R_1 = R_2 = R_{max}$ that can be sustained by cooperation. Note that R_{max} is random and depends on the fading levels of all the links involved. The outage probability $P_{out} = P(R_{max} < r)$ tells us the probability of a cooperative system being able to sustain an equal operating rate of r for both users.

In Figure 4 we show the outage probability of the cooperative scheme as a function of the operating rate r. For comparison, we also plot the equal rate outage probabilities of a non-cooperative (multi-access) system and an ideal system where the inter-user channel is error free. We observe that the outage probability for the cooperation scheme is smaller than that of no cooperation. This is true despite the fact that the increase in achievable rate due to cooperation is moderate for the scenario depicted in Figure 4, as can be seen from Figure 2 ($\mathrm{E}[K_{12}] = 0.63$). Hence even in cases when it does not significantly increase achievable rates, cooperative communication is still able to increase robustness against channel variations. This is due to increased spatial diversity of the system; with cooperation, partners are able to utilize each other's links towards the destination in case their own links fail. To illustrate this further, Figure 5 shows the equal rate outage probability as a function of the user signal to noise ratio (SNR) for a fixed rate $r = 0.18$. We observe that the cooperation curve falls steeper than no cooperation and is parallel to the ideal case. Since the slope of this curve for high SNR illustrates the level of diversity, we can conclude that cooperation provides diversity equivalent to that of a two-antenna array. Comparison with a worse inter-user channel ($\mathrm{E}[K_{12}] = 0.45$) shows that the diversity gains are still present. However now the coding gain is less, that is the outage curve exhibits a shift to the right. We of course expect the performance to depend on the inter-user channel quality. This will be illustrated further in Section 3.

3. Coding for Cooperative Systems

In this section we illustrate how cooperation continues to provide substantial performance gains over a non-cooperating wireless system when we incorporate some practical constraints. We will review some recent literature and describe some of our ongoing work on channel coding for cooperation.

In order to model a more practical system, we have to change some of the assumptions of Section 2. In Section 2 we had allowed both nodes to listen to each other's transmissions and transmit their own information at the same time. Even though this is standard in information theory literature, in practice a wireless device cannot perform perfect echo-cancelation, hence it cannot simultaneously transmit and receive. To incorporate this constraint, we assume that the terminals transmit and receive at different times. Also, in order to have a simple receiver which does not employ multiuser decoding, we assume the terminals have an orthogonal multiple accessing scheme. As an example we consider time division among nodes, that is when there is no cooperation, each terminal has a separate time slot consisting of N uses of the channel as in Figure 6(a). When they cooperate, as shown in Figure 6(b), each terminal divides its time slot into two equal parts. In the first $N/2$ channel uses, the terminal that owns the time slot transmits a signal. This signal is received by both the partner and the destination. The second $N/2$ channel uses are reserved

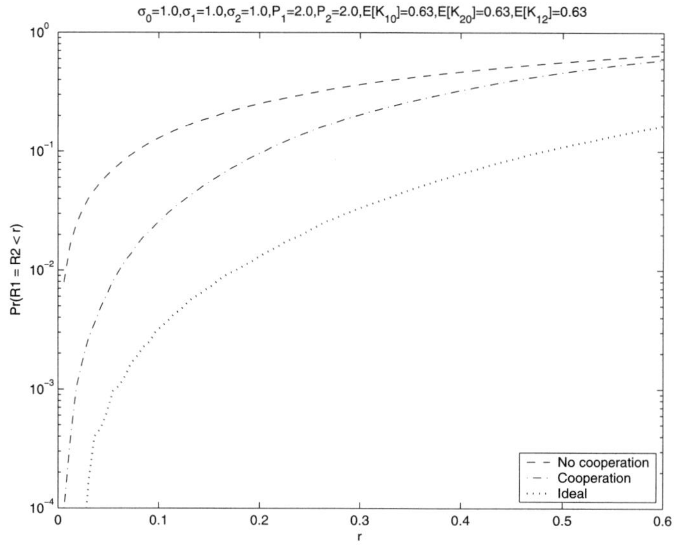

FIGURE 4. Probability of outage versus common rate r for two-user cooperative system. Both users have similar average quality links towards the destination.

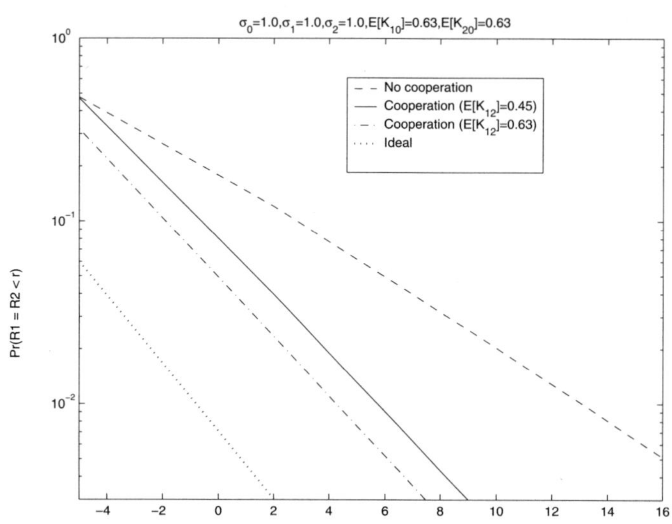

FIGURE 5. Probability of outage versus signal to noise ratio for two-user cooperative system. Both users have similar average quality links towards the destination. The common operating rate is $r = 0.18$.

for cooperation. We will describe a number of different cooperative strategies the partner can utilize below.

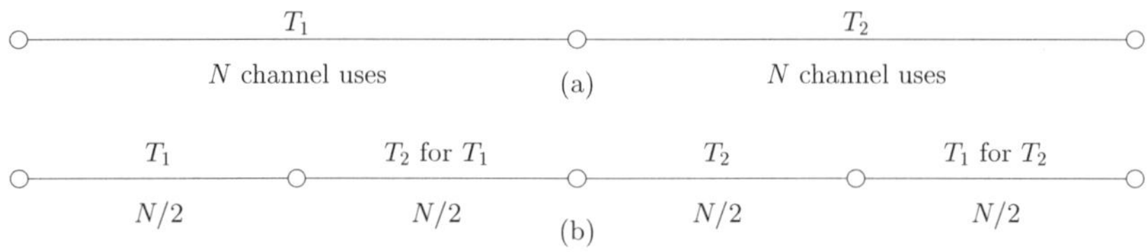

FIGURE 6. Cooperation through time division. (a) Non-cooperative orthogonal transmissions, (b) Cooperative scheme.

Another assumption we relax from Section 2 is the channel phase knowledge at the transmitters. The accurate knowledge of the phase may be hard to obtain in practice, so we assume that the transmitters do not have any knowledge about the fading amplitudes except for their statistics. As before, we assume that receivers have perfect channel state information. We will observe that even with the above set of assumptions cooperation continues to provide substantial performance gains.

The above cooperation scheme through time division was first suggested in [**13, 14**] which also provided a number strategies for cooperation. All the links were assumed to be slowly fading, hence the proper information theoretic measure is the outage probability. The emphasis was on the diversity, the large signal-to-noise ratio (SNR) exponent of 1/SNR in the outage probability, of the suggested cooperative strategies.

Amplify-and-forward and adaptive decode-and-forward are two cooperative strategies investigated in [**13, 14**] that result in full (in this case two level) diversity. In the amplify-and-forward scheme, the partner simply scales its received signal to satisfy its own power constraint and re-transmits to cooperate. The destination combines the first $N/2$ symbols coming from the original terminal with the $N/2$ forwarded symbols from the partner. For the adaptive decode-and-forward strategy, the partner attempts to decode the original information based on the signal it receives. As long as the inter-user channel has a received SNR high enough to support the desired rate, there is no outage and Shannon-type perfect decoding is possible. In that case, the partner re-encodes the information and transmits in the remaining $N/2$ symbols where N is large. Otherwise, the original terminal simply repeats the same codeword in the second half of its time slot. Note that both of the protocols described involve some kind of repetition at the partner. However, we know from channel coding techniques that there are more effective ways of designing codes. Coding gain as well as diversity is important in the performance of a channel code.

For cooperative channel coding, we will work with finite block lengths N and focus on designing and analyzing codes suitable for cooperation. We follow the time division scheme in Figure 6. We assume slow or quasi-static fading, that is each link has a constant fading level for N symbols. Our protocol is similar to the adaptive-decode-and forward of [**13, 14**] and that of [**11**]. We make use of the cyclic redundancy check (CRC) commonly used for error detection in wireless communication systems. Excluding the CRC, in a non-cooperative system each terminal sends N coded bits per frame. In order to cooperate, T_1 multiplexes these N bits properly and only sends half of its coded bits. If the original channel code had rate R, this corresponds to an effective coding rate of $2R$. These bits are

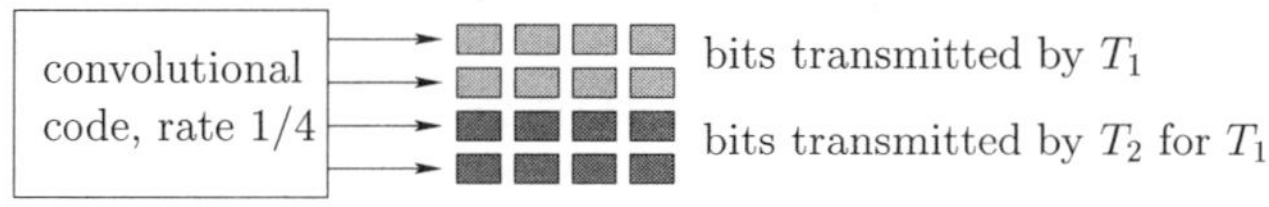

FIGURE 7. An example of the bit mapping for cooperation for a rate 1/4 convolutional code

received by both the destination and the partner. The partner, T_2, decodes these $N/2$ bits and detects whether there are any errors using the CRC. If the partner has the correct information, it re-encodes and sends the *additional* $N/2$ coded bits T_1 did not transmit. This is illustrated in Figure 7 for a convolutional code of rate 1/4. Otherwise, T_1 is informed and it continues its transmission of the remaining $N/2$ coded bits. The destination waits until the end of the frame and combines both $N/2$ observations to decode the information bit stream. Assuming the destination estimates the current fading level every $N/2$ bits, there is no need to notify it as to whether the partner received the information correctly or not. Then T_1 and T_2 change roles, so T_2 acts as the source while T_1 relays the information.

Note that in the suggested cooperative coding scheme, when the partner cannot decode correctly, T_1 suffers no loss from the non-cooperative case. This feature is not present in the adaptive decode-and-forward protocol, as it forces the source to repeat information rather than designing the "best" codebook for the whole N uses of the channel.

From the perspective of the destination, when partner decodes correctly, the first $N/2$ coded bits observe a fading amplitude of K_{10}, the second $N/2$ bits an independent fading amplitude K_{20}. Hence the overall effect at the destination is that of block fading, with two fading blocks. Based on this observation, we argue that codes designed for block fading channels (such as those in [**12**]) are suitable for cooperation. However, the cooperative systems impose additional constraints. In order to cooperate often, that is for the partner to correctly decode, the first half of the coded bits (or the punctured code) should form a good code in the quasi-static inter-partner channel. Also, when the cooperation does not take place, all the coded bits face the same fading level, so the code must be good for quasi-static channel as well as the cooperative block fading channel. We will provide an example of such a code in Section 3.2, more can be found in [**22**].

We note here that Hunter and Nosratinia [**11**] suggested the use of rate compatible punctured convolutional (RCPC) codes [**10**] for cooperation. However, RCPC codes were not designed with diversity schemes or block fading channels in mind. We think that the block fading framework allows us to work with a richer family of codes and also enables us to provide a performance analysis illustrating the diversity and coding gains of cooperative coding. Also, by starting from a good code in the inter-user channel and adding additional parity bits to get a cooperative block fading code, we can in fact improve the performance over a good code (say a code designed for a block fading channel) punctured to be used in the inter-user channel. Hence we think *overlaying* a code with additional parity bits is more suitable than puncturing a code to be used in the inter-user channel. More details on this can be found in [**22**]. The overlay ideas can also be used to take into account the cases in which source and partner divide up the N bits unequally as suggested in [**11**].

In the next subsection, we analyze the diversity achieved by user cooperation by studying upper bounds on the frame error rates of cooperative codes. We then provide some simulations illustrating the suggested diversity and coding gains.

3.1. Performance Analysis of Cooperative Codes. In order to find bounds on the performance of cooperative codes, we will focus on the frame error probability of the cooperative coding scheme described above. We concentrate on T_1 and let P_f^C denote the overall frame error rate of a channel code when used for cooperation. We also let P_f^{in} denote the frame error probability of the portion of the code used in the inter-user channel (corresponding to block length $N/2$), P_f^{QS} denote the frame error probability over the quasi-static channel of T_1 to destination (corresponding to a block length of N) and P_f^{BF} denote the frame error probability over the cooperative block fading channel (first $N/2$ coded bits face T_1-destination link, second $N/2$ bits face T_2-destination link). We can then write

$$P_f^C = (1 - P_f^{in})P_f^{BF} + P_f^{in} P_f^{QS}.$$

We can upper bound P_f^C as

$$P_f^C \leq P_f^{BF} + P_f^{in} P_f^{QS}. \tag{3.1}$$

We now investigate each of the terms in this upper bound. Let SNR_1 denote the average (averaged over the Rayleigh fading) received signal–to–noise ratio at the destination corresponding to the transmission from T_1. The value for SNR_1 depends on P_1, σ_0^2 and $E[K_{10}]$. Similarly, let SNR_2 denote the average received signal–to–noise ratio at the destination corresponding to the transmission from T_2 and SNR_{in} denote the average received signal–to–noise ratio at partner (T_2) corresponding to the transmission from T_1.

Note that in the cooperative block fading channel, the first block observes an average signal–to–noise ratio of SNR_1 while the second block has SNR_2. Even though this is different than the usual block fading model in which all blocks have the same average SNR, the pairwise error probability can be derived in a form similar to [**12**]. Hence, utilizing the pairwise error probability expression for the block Rayleigh fading channel and the union upper bound on the frame error probability, we have

$$P_f^{BF} \leq \sum_{\boldsymbol{c}} \sum_{\boldsymbol{e} \neq \boldsymbol{c}} \frac{1}{\Xi^2(\boldsymbol{c},\boldsymbol{e})\,(\text{SNR}_1/4)^{\mathcal{I}_{d_1^2}}\,(\text{SNR}_2/4)^{\mathcal{I}_{d_2^2}}} \tag{3.2}$$

In order to define the terms in the above expression, we first define the code Euclidian distances. Let us consider two codewords $\boldsymbol{c} = (c_1, \dots, c_N)$ and $\boldsymbol{e} = (e_1, \dots, e_N)$ each consisting of N bits. The distance $d_i^2(\boldsymbol{c},\boldsymbol{e}) = \sum_{n=1}^{N/2} |c_{n+(i-1)N/2} - e_{n+(i-1)N/2}|^2$, $i = 1, 2$, denotes the squared Euclidean distance among first and second $N/2$ bits of the two codewords respectively. Note that for the cooperative block fading channel, these two parts of the codewords face independent fading. The term $\Xi^2(\boldsymbol{c},\boldsymbol{e})$ denotes the product of the non–zero squared Euclidean distances $d_1^2(\boldsymbol{c},\boldsymbol{e})$ and $d_2^2(\boldsymbol{c},\boldsymbol{e})$ and $\mathcal{I}$ denotes the indicator function.

For the quasi-static frame error probability P_f^{QS} of the T_1-destination channel, the relevant distance term is $\Psi^2(\boldsymbol{c},\boldsymbol{e}) = d_1^2(\boldsymbol{c},\boldsymbol{e}) + d_2^2(\boldsymbol{c},\boldsymbol{e})$ and it denotes the squared

Euclidean distance between the two entire codewords $\boldsymbol{c}$ and $\boldsymbol{e}$. This gives us the upper bound

$$P_f^{QS} \leq \sum_{\boldsymbol{c}} \sum_{\boldsymbol{e} \neq \boldsymbol{c}} \frac{1}{\Psi^2(\boldsymbol{c}, \boldsymbol{e}) \mathrm{SNR}_1/4} \tag{3.3}$$

The inter-user channel is also quasi-static, but it only utilizes the first $N/2$ coded bits. Hence,

$$P_f^{in} \leq \sum_{\boldsymbol{c}} \sum_{\boldsymbol{e} \neq \boldsymbol{c}} \frac{1}{\Phi^2(\boldsymbol{c}, \boldsymbol{e}) \mathrm{SNR}_{in}/4} \tag{3.4}$$

where $\Phi^2(\boldsymbol{c}, \boldsymbol{e}) = d_1^2(\boldsymbol{c}, \boldsymbol{e})$.

Using equations (3.2)-(3.4) in the upper bound of (3.1), we can bound the cooperative coding frame error probability as

$$\begin{aligned} P_f^C \leq & \left(\sum_{\boldsymbol{c}} \sum_{\boldsymbol{e} \neq \boldsymbol{c}} \frac{1}{\Xi^2(\boldsymbol{c}, \boldsymbol{e}) \left(\mathrm{SNR}_1/4\right)^{\mathcal{I}_{d_1^2}} \left(\mathrm{SNR}_2/4\right)^{\mathcal{I}_{d_2^2}}} \right) \\ & + \left(\sum_{\boldsymbol{c}} \sum_{\boldsymbol{e} \neq \boldsymbol{c}} \frac{1}{\Phi^2(\boldsymbol{c}, \boldsymbol{e}) \mathrm{SNR}_{in}/4} \right) \left(\sum_{\boldsymbol{c}} \sum_{\boldsymbol{e} \neq \boldsymbol{c}} \frac{1}{\Psi^2(\boldsymbol{c}, \boldsymbol{e}) \mathrm{SNR}_1/4} \right). \end{aligned} \tag{3.5}$$

We envision cooperative systems to act as virtual antenna arrays and provide us with additional spatial diversity. However, this depends crucially on the quality of the inter-user channel. We now investigate two extreme scenarios for the inter-user channel quality to study the potential gains of cooperation.

Case I: Good Inter–User Channel. First, we consider the performance when the inter–user channel is very good. If the inter–user channel has very high average signal–to–noise ratio, $\mathrm{SNR}_{\mathrm{in}}$, then P_f^{in} will be very small and the equation (3.1) is dominated by P_f^{BF}. Therefore we have $P_f^C \approx P_f^{BF}$ and full second order diversity is obtained. This is of course, expected. When the inter-user channel is almost perfect, cooperative communication (using time division) corresponds to a regular block fading channel.

Case II: Poor Inter–User Channel. In this case, we assume that the inter–user channel has poor quality, that is P_f^{in} is high. We note that for high signal–to–noise ratios, block fading error probability P_f^{BF} will be lower than that of P_f^{QS} as it provides two level diversity. Hence the upper bound on P_f^C is dominated by the term $P_f^{in} P_f^{QS}$. Therefore,

$$P_f^C \leq \left(\sum_{\boldsymbol{c}} \sum_{\boldsymbol{e} \neq \boldsymbol{c}} \frac{1}{\mathrm{SNR}_{in}/4} \frac{1}{\Phi^2(\boldsymbol{c}, \boldsymbol{e})} \right) \left(\sum_{\boldsymbol{c}} \sum_{\boldsymbol{e} \neq \boldsymbol{c}} \frac{1}{\mathrm{SNR}_1/4} \frac{1}{\Psi^2(\boldsymbol{c}, \boldsymbol{e})} \right). \tag{3.6}$$

As the inter–user channel quality is low, we can assume that for the range of transmit powers of interest, the received inter–user channel average signal–to–noise ratio SNR_{in} is at most equal to some value C_{in}. Then the tightest upper bound for P_f^C is obtained for $\mathrm{SNR}_{in} \approx C_{in}$. For high signal–to–noise ratios in T_1-destination channel, this results in the approximation P_f^C,

$$P_f^C \approx \frac{1}{C_{in}} \left(\frac{1}{\mathrm{SNR}_1/4} \right) \frac{1}{\min_{\boldsymbol{c}, \boldsymbol{e}} \left\{ \Phi^2(\boldsymbol{c}, \boldsymbol{e}) \Psi^2(\boldsymbol{c}, \boldsymbol{e}) \right\}} \tag{3.7}$$

Hence the minimum product distance $\min_{\boldsymbol{c},\boldsymbol{e}} \left\{\Phi^2(\boldsymbol{c},\boldsymbol{e})\Psi^2(\boldsymbol{c},\boldsymbol{e})\right\}$ dominates the performance at large values of the signal–to–noise ratio SNR_1.

We observe that when the inter-user channel quality is very poor, the diversity of the cooperative system is one and is limited by the diversity of the quasi-static T_1-destination link. However, despite the limited diversity, there is still some coding gain with respect to the non–cooperative transmission, as indicated by the squared Euclidean distance product in equation (3.7). In the next section we illustrate via simulations that this coding gain enables the cooperative scheme to outperform non-cooperative communication even when the inter-user link is very noisy and severely faded. For more moderate inter-user channel qualities, the performance of cooperative coding substantially improves, and provides diversity as well as coding gains.

3.2. Simulation Results. In this section we present the performance of the proposed cooperative coding scheme via simulations to illustrate the potential benefits. As discussed above, we assume a Rayleigh slow fading channel. Hence, we use the quasi–static model, where the fading coefficients remain the same for the duration of the entire frame for each user. Note, however that the users observe independently faded channels. As an illustrative example, we use a constraint length $K = 4$ convolutional code with generator polynomials (13,15,15,17) in octal notation and BPSK modulation [**12**]. This is an appealing solution due to the widespread use of convolutional codes and the simple maximum likelihood decoding algorithm [**16**]. The extensions to higher order modulations are also possible [**12**].

The way in which the transmission of bits is organized in order to form a cooperative code is illustrated in Figure 7 for the rate 1/4 convolutional code. As discussed, we would like to have the best convolutional code operating in the quasi–static inter–user channel and user–destination channel. The rate 1/2, (15,17) code provides the best performance in the quasi-static inter–user channel [**16**]. When partner fails to decode and the original terminal continues with transmission, the rate 1/4, (13,15,15,17) code provides the best performance in the quasi–static user–destination channel [**16**]. When cooperation indeed takes place, the same rate 1/4 code, also provides full diversity and excellent coding gain over the cooperative block fading channel [**12**]. Hence, with proper multiplexing of the coded bits, T_1 first transmits the bits corresponding to the (15,17) generator polynomials. Terminal 2 receives this transmission, decodes the information bits, and then re–encodes them using the (13,15) generator polynomials. Note that in the case when T_2 cannot successfully decode the transmission from T_1, T_1 transmits the rest of the coded bits, corresponding to the (13,15) generator polynomials, by itself.

Similar to the situations analyzed in Figures 2 and 3, we consider both a symmetric scenario, in which terminals have similar quality links towards the destination, and an asymmetric scenario. We will also investigate the effect of inter-user channel quality on the performance of the suggested cooperative scheme thereby confirming the intuitions gained in Section 3.1.

In the symmetric scenario, both terminals have channels of similar quality, as represented by equal average signal–to–noise ratios SNR_1 and SNR_2, to the destination. We demonstrate the performance of the (13,15,15,17) code in terms of the frame error rate (FER) versus this common signal-to-noise ratio. Similar results could also be obtained in terms of the bit error rate. We compare the frame error rates of single user scheme (non-cooperative), cooperative with perfect inter-user channel ("ideal"), and cooperative with various inter-user quality channels (represented by inter-user FER of 0.01, 0.1 and 0.5). Our results are summarized in Figure 8(a).

We observe that the suggested cooperative coding scheme with perfect inter–user channel provides a performance improvement of about 4 dB at FER of 10^{-1} and about 10 dB at FER of 10^{-2} with respect to the non–cooperative, single user transmission. As the inter-user channel quality degrades, or the inter-user FER increases, the performance gracefully degrades from the perfect inter-user channel case, and approaches to that of single–user transmission. For low inter-user FER (0.01), the performance is very close to the perfect inter-user channel. Also, slope of the FER curves for high SNR suggest that cooperation for low inter-user frame error rates can indeed achieve full second order diversity as suggested by Section 3.1. When the inter-user link has poor quality (FER=0.5) the diversity is limited to one. Nevertheless, as predicted in Section 3.1, there is still some coding gain with respect to the non–cooperative transmission, which results in performance improvements. We would like to note that the FER trends of cooperative coding, as a function of the inter-partner link quality, are similar to those of the achievable rate region and outage probability studied in Section 2.

We next focus on the asymmetric scenario, which happens when, say, SNR_1 is much larger than SNR_2. We consider this case by fixing one of the terminal's channel to the destination at a relatively high average signal to noise ratio. We then vary the quality of the other terminal's channel to the destination and observe the performance of both cooperating users.

For the rate 1/4, (13,15,15,17) convolutional code, we fix SNR_1 at 15 dB, which results in a frame error rate of about 10^{-2} in the non–cooperative case. The inter–user channel frame error rate is 0.5 which corresponds to a poor inter-user channel. We vary the average signal–to–noise ratio of T_2 and plot the cooperative and non-cooperative FER's of both terminals as a function of SNR_2 in Figure 8(b). We observe that with cooperation, T_1 achieves the frame error rate of 10^{-2} when the signal–to–noise ratio of T_2 is only about -4 dB. At higher signal–to–noise ratios cooperative performance for T_1 is better than in the non–cooperative case. Terminal 2 also improves its performance by about 3 dB with respect to the non–cooperative case for all the signal–to–noise ratios investigated. Hence cooperation benefits *both* users even in an asymmetric case and poor inter-user channel.

We would like to compare this asymmetric situation with that of Figure 3. In Figure 3 we had observed that even though the maximum rate of the good user does not improve by much, the set of achievable rates increase considerably for an asymmetric cooperative scenario. For the coding scheme discussed above, the gains are even more dramatic, even when the inter-user has a high FER of 0.5 the good also user benefits from cooperation.

4. Conclusions

In a cooperative communication system two or more active users in a network share their information and jointly transmit their messages, either at the different times or simultaneously, to obtain greater reliability and efficiency than they could obtain individually. In this paper we consider a simple two-user cooperative system to illustrate the benefits. We provide both an information theoretic and a coding

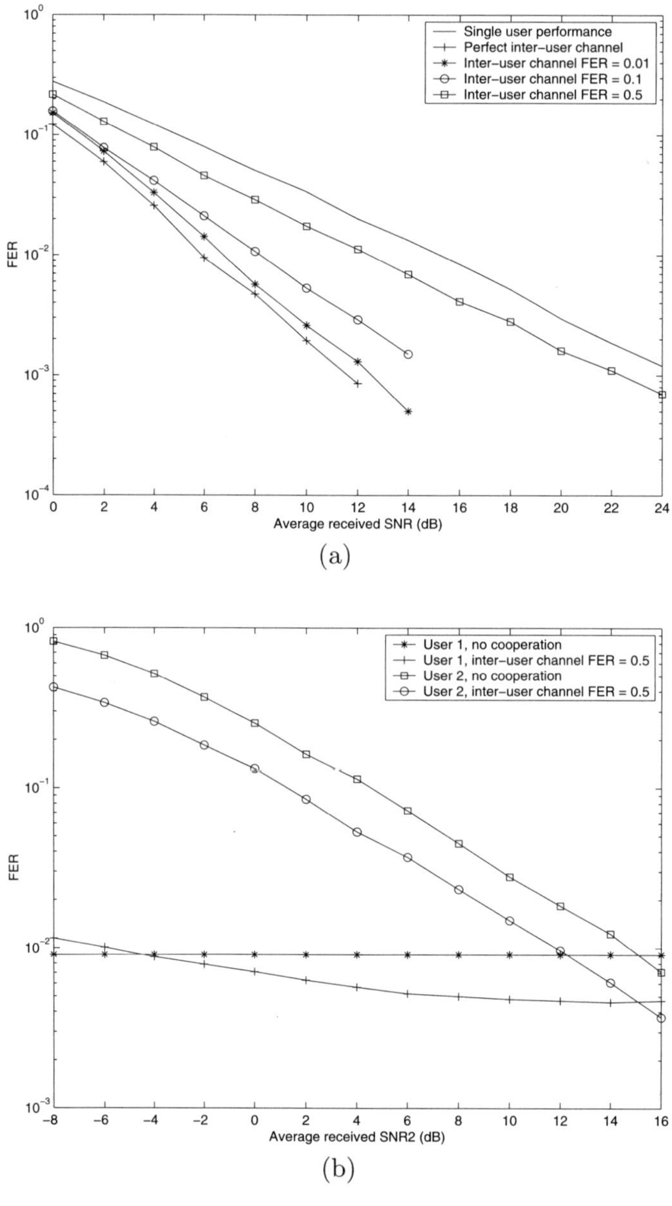

FIGURE 8. Two user coded cooperation for different inter-user channel qualities: (a) symmetric, (b) asymmetric users. (13,15,15,17) convolutional codes, quasi-static fading.

perspective to cooperation. Our achievable rate region and coding protocol illustrate few of the many possible schemes of collaboration among wireless terminals, yet the benefits of cooperation are clear. Through cooperation both terminals are able to simultaneously increase their throughputs and reliabilities even when they are connected via low quality links, or when one terminal has a much better link then the other. Cooperation enables the terminals to make use of each other's antennas, an extra spatial dimension which is typically not utilized.

Throughout this paper we assumed the partners are fixed and we focused on possible ways of cooperating. In order to successfully use the cooperative principles in a wireless network, one has to be able to choose a good partner. Our ongoing work investigates how partner choice should be made and what the geometry of cooperation is. We are also investigating the added diversity benefits as the number of partners increase, and how one can design and analyze cooperative space-time codes when terminals have multiple antennas.

Acknowledgments

The authors would like to thank Zinan Lin for help in generating Figure 8.

References

[1] E. Biglieri, J. Proakis and S. Shamai, "Fading channels: Information theoretic and communications aspects", *IEEE Trans. Inform. Theory*, vol. 44, pp. 2619–2692, Oct. 1998.

[2] A. Carleial, "Multiple-access channels with different generalized feedback signals", *IEEE Trans. Inform. Theory*, vol. 28, pp. 841–850, Nov. 1982.

[3] T.M. Cover and A. El Gamal, "Capacity theorems for the relay channel", *IEEE Trans. Inform. Theory*, vol. 25, pp. 572–584, Sept. 1979.

[4] T. Cover and C. Leung, "An achievable rate region for the multiple-access channel with feedback", *IEEE Trans. Inform. Theory*, vol. 27, pp. 292–298, May 1981.

[5] T.M. Cover and J.A. Thomas, *Elements of Inform. Theory*, John Wiley & Sons, 1991.

[6] R. Gallager, "An inequality on the capacity region of multiaccess fading channels", in *Communications and Cryptography–Two Sides of One Tapestry*, pp. 129–139, Kluwer, 1994.

[7] M. Gastpar, G. Kramer and P. Gupta, "The multiple-relay channel: Coding and antenna-clustering capacity", in *Proc. IEEE Int'l Symposium on Inform. Theory*, Lausanne, Switzerland, July 2002.

[8] M. Gastpar and M. Vetterli, "On the capacity of wireless networks: The relay case", in *Proc. IEEE Infocom*, New York, June 2002.

[9] P. Gupta and P. R. Kumar, "Towards an information theory of large networks: An achievable rate region", *IEEE Trans. Inform. Theory* vol. 49, pp. 1877–1894, Aug. 2003.

[10] J. Hagenauer, "Rate-compatible punctured convolutional codes (RCPC codes) and their applications", *IEEE Trans. Commun.*, vol. 36, pp. 389–400, Apr. 1988.

[11] T. Hunter and A. Nosratinia. "Cooperation diversity through coding", in *Proc. IEEE Int'l Symposium Inform. Theory*, Lausanne, Switzerland, July 2002.

[12] R. Knopp and P. A. Humblet. "On coding for block fading channels", *IEEE Trans. Inform. Theory*, vol. 46, pp. 189–205, Jan. 2000.

[13] J. N. Laneman, G. W. Wornell, and D. N. C. Tse, "An efficient protocol for realizing cooperative diversity in wireless networks", in *Proc. IEEE Int'l Symposium Inform. Theory*, Washington D.C., June 2001.

[14] J. N. Laneman, D.N.C. Tse and G. W. Wornell. "Cooperative diversity in wireless networks: Efficient protocols and outage behaviour", accepted *IEEE Trans. Inform. Theory.*

[15] J. N. Laneman and G. W. Wornell, "Distributed space-time coded protocols for exploiting cooperative diversity in wireless networks", *IEEE Trans. Inform. Theory*, vol 49, pp. 2415–2425, Oct. 2003.

[16] S. Lin and D.J. Costello, *Error Control Coding: Fundamentals and Applications.*, Prentice-Hall, 1983.

[17] L. Ozarow, S. Shamai and A. Wyner, "Information theoretic considerations for cellular mobile radio", *IEEE Trans. Vehicular Technology*, vol. 43, pp. 359–377, May 1994.

[18] A. Reznik, S. Kulkarni and S. Verdu, "Capacity and optimal resource allocation in the degraded Gaussian relay channel with multiple relays", in *Proc. 40th Annual Allerton Conference on Communication, Control, and Computing*, Allerton Conf., Monticello, IL, Oct. 2002.

[19] B. Schein and R. Gallager, "The Gaussian parallel relay network", in *Proc. IEEE Int'l Symposium on Inform. Theory*, Sorrento, Italy, June 2000.

[20] A. Sendonaris, E. Erkip and B. Aazhang, "Increasing uplink capacity via user cooperation diversity" in *Proc. IEEE Int'l Symposium on Inform. Theory*, Boston, Aug. 1998.

[21] A. Sendonaris, E. Erkip and B. Aazhang, "User cooperation diversity–Part I: System description" *IEEE Trans. Commun.*, vol. 51, pp. 1927–1938, Nov. 2003.

[22] A. Stefanov and E. Erkip, "Cooperative coding for wireless networks", under review.

[23] E.C. van der Meulen. "Three-terminal communication channels", *Advances in Applied Probability*, vol. 3, pp. 120–154, 1971.

[24] F. M. J. Willems, E. C. van der Meulen and J. P. M. Schalkwijk, "Achievable rate region for the multiple access channel with generalized feedback", in *Annual Allerton Conference on Communication, Control, and Computing*, 1983.

[25] F. Willems and E. van der Meulen, "The discrete memoryless multiple-access channel with cribbing encoders", *IEEE Trans. Inform. Theory*, vol. 31, pp. 313–327, May 1985.

[26] L. Xie and P. R. Kumar, "A network information theory for wireless communication: Scaling laws and optimal operation", submitted to *IEEE Trans. Inform. Theory.*

[27] C. Zeng, F. Kuhlmann, and A. Buzo, "Achievability proof of some multiuser channel coding theorems using backward decoding", *IEEE Trans. Inform. Theory*, vol. IT–35, pp. 1160–1165, Nov. 1989.

Department of Electrical and Computer Engineering, Polytechnic University, Five Metrotech Center, Brooklyn, NY 11201

E-mail address: `elza@poly.edu`

Qualcomm Inc., Campbell, CA

E-mail address: `sendos@qualcomm.com`

Department of Electrical and Computer Engineering, Polytechnic University, Five Metrotech Center, Brooklyn, NY 11201

E-mail address: `stefanov@poly.edu`

Department of Electrical and Computer Engineering, Rice University, Houston, TX 77005

E-mail address: `aaz@rice.edu`

DIMACS Series in Discrete Mathematics
and Theoretical Computer Science
Volume **66**, 2004

Hybrid ARQ with Random Transmission Assignments

Emina Soljanin, Ruoheng Liu, and Predrag Spasojevic

ABSTRACT. In mobile packet data and voice networks, a special coding scheme, known as the incremental redundancy hybrid ARQ (IR HARQ), achieves higher throughput efficiency than ordinary turbo codes by adapting its error correcting code redundancy to fluctuating channel conditions characteristic for this application. An IR HARQ protocol operates as follows. Initially, the information bits are encoded by a "mother" code and a selected number of parity bits are transmitted. If a retransmission is requested, only additional selected parity bits are transmitted. At the receiving end, the additional parity bits are combined with the previously received bits, allowing for an increase in the error correction capacity. This procedure is repeated after each subsequent retransmission request until the entire codeword of the mother code is transmitted. A number of important issues such as error rate performance after each transmission on time varying channels, and rate and power control are difficult to analyze in a network employing a particular HARQ scheme, *i.e.*, a given mother code and given selection of bits for each transmission. By relaxing only the latter constraint, namely, by allowing random selection of the bits for each transmission, we provide very good estimates of error rates allowing us to address to a certain extent the rate and power control problem.

1. Introduction

In conventional *a*utomatic *r*epeat re*q*uest (ARQ) schemes, frame errors are examined at the receiving end by an error detecting (usually cyclic redundancy check (CRC)) code. If a frame passes the CRC, the receiving end sends an acknowledgement (ACK) of successful transmission to the receiver. If a frame does not pass the CRC, the receiving end sends a negative acknowledgement (NAK), requesting retransmission. User data and its CRC bits may be additionally protected by an error correcting code which increases the probability of successful transmission. Such ARQ schemes which combine the ARQ principle with error control coding are known as *h*ybrid ARQ schemes.

The standard measure of ARQ protocol efficiency is *throughput*, defined as the average number of user data bits accepted at the receiving end in the time required for transmission of a single bit. Therefore the level of redundancy of the error correcting code employed in an HARQ scheme has two opposing effects on the scheme

Key words and phrases. Hybrid ARQ, random puncturing, turbo code ensembles.
Ruoheng Liu was supported in part by the NSF Grant #CCR-0205362.

efficiency, namely, with increased redundancy the probability of successful transmission increases but the percentage of user data in the frame decreases. Usually, a fixed rate code which is well suited to the channel characteristics and throughput requirements is selected.

In applications with fluctuating channel conditions within a range of signal-to-noise ratios (SNRs), such as mobile and satellite packet data transmission, the so called *incremental redundancy* (IR) HARQ schemes exhibit higher throughput efficiency by adapting their error correcting code redundancy to different channel conditions. An IR HARQ protocol operates as illustrated by the example in Fig. 1. At the transmitter, the information and CRC bits are encoded by a systematic

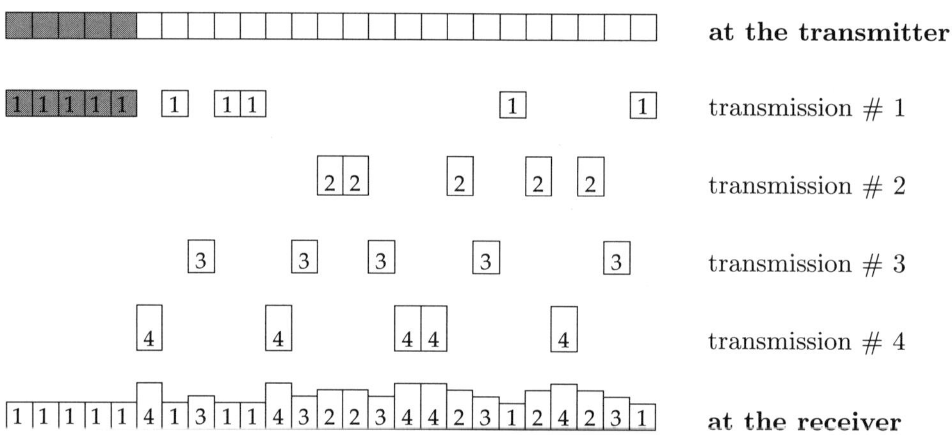

FIGURE 1. Incremental redundancy HARQ protocol.

"mother" code. In Fig. 1, the codeword at the transmitter is represented by a string of 25 boxes. The first 5 (gray in the figure) correspond to the systematic bits. Initially, only the systematic part of the codeword and a selected number of parity bits are transmitted (transmission #1 in the figure). The selected parity bits together with the systematic bits form a codeword of a punctured mother code. Decoding of this code is performed at the receiving end. If a retransmission is requested, the transmitter sends additional parity bits possibly under different channel conditions or at different power (depicted as taller boxes in transmission #2 in the figure). Decoding is again attempted at the receiving end, where the new parity bits are combined with those previously received. The procedure is repeated after each subsequent retransmission request until all the parity bits of the mother code are transmitted.

First ideas for systems combining error correction and ARQ date back to the work of Wozencraft and Horstein in 1960 [**1**], [**2**]. A historic overview of further development of such techniques, now known as hybrid ARQ, can be found in [**3**]. Recent interest in the scheme comes from the quest for reliable and efficient transmission under fluctuating conditions in wireless networks. An information-theoretic analysis of some HARQ protocols, concerning throughput and average delay for block-fading Gaussian collision channels have been reported in [**4**]–[**7**]. Another line of recent work on HARQ is concerned with the mother code and its puncturing. Given the number of parity bits which are at each stage omitted form the mother code (*i.e.*, punctured and not transmitted), their identity is determined by a *puncturing pattern*. The throughput of HARQ schemes is strongly affected by the power of the mother code used in the system and the family of codes obtained by puncturing. Thus recently proposed HARQ schemes use powerful turbo codes, and design of puncturing patterns is an important issue [**8**]–[**16**].

We here have two goals motivated directly by questions in practice. The first is to evaluate the error rate performance after each transmission, which is equivalent to evaluating performance of punctured turbo codes on time varying channels. The second is to show how one should go about choosing the signal power and the number of bits for transmission j after a failed transmission $j-1$. To approach and solve both problems, we introduce the idea of random transmission assignments of the mother code bits, which is related to our previous work on randomly punctured turbo codes [**20**], [**21**].

2. Channel Model and Performance of the Mother Code

2.1. Time-Invariant Channel. We first consider a binary input memoryless channel with output alphabet Ω and transition probabilities $W(y|0)$ and $W(y|1)$, $y \in \Omega$. Performance of turbo codes on such channels has been widely studied by various techniques; particularly successful are those based on density evolution [**17**] and EXIT charts [**18**]. For our analysis of the mother turbo code and IR HARQ scheme performance on time-varying channels (described in the following section), it is especially convenient to use the coding theorems for turbo code ensembles established recently by Jin and McEliece in [**19**]. We briefly review their results below.

When a codeword $\boldsymbol{x} \in \mathcal{C} \subseteq \{0,1\}^n$ has been transmitted, the probability that the maximum likelihood (ML) detector finds codeword $\boldsymbol{x'}$ at Hamming distance h from $\boldsymbol{x}$ more likely can be bounded as follows:

$$P_e(\boldsymbol{x}, \boldsymbol{x'}) \leq \gamma^h, \tag{2.1}$$

where γ is the *Bhattacharyya noise parameter* defined as

$$\gamma = \sum_{y \in \Omega} \sqrt{W(y|x=0)W(y|x=1)} \tag{2.2}$$

if Ω is discrete and as

$$\gamma = \int_{\Omega} \sqrt{W(y|x=0)W(y|x=1)}\, dy$$

if Ω is a measurable subset of $\mathcal{R}$.

For an (n,k) binary linear code $\mathcal{C}$ with the weight enumerator A_h (*i.e.*, A_h codewords of weight h), we have the well known *union-Bhattacharyya bound* on the ML decoder word error probability

$$P_W^{\mathcal{C}} \leq \sum_{h=1}^{n} A_h \gamma^h.$$

To derive their coding theorems, Jin and McEliece use the union-Bhattacharyya bound on the ML decoder word error probability averaged over the set of all turbo codes with identical component codes but different interleavers.

Suppose that the mother turbo code consists of L pseudorandom interleavers, and L recursive convolutional encoders. There are $k!$ possible choices for each interleaver. Consequently, for a given set of L recursive convolutional encoders, there are $(k!)^L$ different (n,k) turbo codes, corresponding to all different interleavers. We denote this *set* by $\mathcal{C}^{(n)}$. By the mother turbo code *ensemble* $[\mathcal{C}]$, we will mean a *sequence* of turbo code sets $\{\mathcal{C}^{(n)}\}$ with a common rate. We are interested in asymptotic performance of $\mathcal{C}^{(n)}$ when $n \to \infty$.

For a turbo code ensemble $[\mathcal{C}]$, the average number of codewords of weight h in $\mathcal{C}^{(n)}$ is denoted by $\overline{A}_h^{[\mathcal{C}](n)}$. The bound on the ML decoder word error probability averaged over the ensemble is obtained by averaging the (additive) union bound:

$$\overline{P}_W^{[\mathcal{C}]} \leq \sum_{h=1}^{n} \overline{A}_h^{[\mathcal{C}](n)} \gamma^h. \tag{2.3}$$

To further analyze this expression, we write

$$\overline{P}_W^{[\mathcal{C}]} \leq \sum_{h=1}^{n} \overline{A}_h^{[\mathcal{C}](n)} \gamma^h \leq \sum_{h=1}^{D_n} \overline{A}_h^{[\mathcal{C}](n)} + \sum_{h=D_n+1}^{n} \overline{A}_h^{[\mathcal{C}](n)} \gamma^h, \tag{2.4}$$

where D_n is a sequence of numbers such that

$$D_n \to \infty \text{ and } \frac{D_n}{n^\epsilon} \to 0 \ \forall \epsilon > 0. \tag{2.5}$$

The average number of codewords of weight $h > D_n$ in the ensemble $[\mathcal{C}]$ can be bounded in terms of the ensemble *noise threshold* defined as follows [**19**]:

$$c_0^{[\mathcal{C}]} = \limsup_{n\to\infty} \max_{D_n < h \leq n} \frac{\log \overline{A}_h^{[\mathcal{C}](n)}}{h}.$$

It was shown in [**19**] that for a turbo code ensemble $[\mathcal{C}]$ with the number of component codes $L \geq 2$, the ensemble noise threshold $c_0^{[\mathcal{C}]}$ is a finite positive number. Therefore, we have

$$\overline{A}_h^{[\mathcal{C}](n)} \leq_n \exp\big(h c_0^{[\mathcal{C}]}\big), \qquad D_n < h \leq n, \tag{2.6}$$

where $\leq_n$ means that the inequality holds for large enough n. By using the inequality (2.6), we see that on a binary-input memoryless channel whose Bhattacharyya parameter $\gamma < \exp(-c_0^{[\mathcal{C}]})$, the second term of the right-hand-side of the bound (2.4) goes to zero as n increases. The analysis of the first term of (2.4) is related to the analysis of the minimum distance of turbo codes [**22**]–[**26**]. For turbo codes with $L > 2$ interleaver branches, Kahale and Urbanke proved that the minimum distance of a turbo code with a random interleaver is at least $\Omega(n^{1-2/L})$ with high probability [**22**]. For this case, it was shown in [**19**] that we have the so-called *interleaver gain:*

$$\overline{P}_W^{[\mathcal{C}](n)} = O(n^{-L+2+\epsilon}) \quad \text{for any } \epsilon > 0. \tag{2.7}$$

For turbo codes with $L = 2$ interleaver branches, Breiling in [**23**] proved that the minimum distance of turbo codes is upper bounded by $O(\log n)$, and three groups of authors in [**24, 25, 26**] showed that, for some specially constructed interleavers, the minimum distance of turbo codes grows as $O(\log n)$. Thus, for an ensemble of two-branch turbo codes with "good" interleavers, we have

$$\lim_{n\to\infty} \sum_{h=1}^{D_n} \overline{A}_h^{[\mathcal{C}](n)} = 0$$

when $D_n <_n \text{const} \cdot \log n$. It follows that for both $L > 2$ with random interleavers and $L = 2$ with specially designed interleavers, we have

$$\lim_{n\to\infty} \overline{P}_W^{[\mathcal{C}](n)} = 0 \tag{2.8}$$

when $\gamma < \exp(-c_0^{[\mathcal{C}]})$.

2.2. Time-Varying Channel. We again consider a DMC with the binary input alphabet $\{0,1\}$ and output alphabet $\mathcal{Y}$, but this time we assume that the channel varies during the transmission of a single codeword, namely, channel transition probabilities at time i are $W_i(b|0)$ and $W_i(b|1)$, $b \in \mathcal{Y}$. When codeword $\boldsymbol{x} \in \{0,1\}^n$ has been transmitted, the probability that the maximum likelihood (ML) detector finds codeword $\boldsymbol{x'} \in \{0,1\}^n$ more likely can be bounded as follows:

$$P_e(\boldsymbol{x},\boldsymbol{x'}) \le \sum_{\boldsymbol{y}\in\mathcal{Y}^n} \sqrt{W^n(\boldsymbol{y}|\boldsymbol{x})W^n(\boldsymbol{y}|\boldsymbol{x'})},$$

where we denote

$$W^n(\boldsymbol{y}|\boldsymbol{x}) = \prod_{i=1}^n W_i(y_i|x_i).$$

It is easy to see that

$$\begin{aligned} P_e(\boldsymbol{x},\boldsymbol{x'}) &\le \sum_{\boldsymbol{y}\in\mathcal{Y}^n} \sqrt{W^n(\boldsymbol{y}|\boldsymbol{x})W^n(\boldsymbol{y}|\boldsymbol{x'})}\Big] \\ &= \prod_{i=1}^n \Big(\sum_{b\in\mathcal{Y}} \sqrt{W_i(b|x_i)W_i(b|x_i')}\Big). \end{aligned} \tag{2.9}$$

Note that when $x_i = x_i'$, the corresponding factor $\sum_{b\in\mathcal{Y}} \sqrt{W_i(b|x_i)W_i(b|x_i')}$ in the product (2.9) equals 1 and can be omitted. When $x_i \ne x_i'$, the corresponding factor $\sum_{b\in\mathcal{Y}} \sqrt{W_i(b|x_i)W_i(b|x_i')}$ equals to the Bhattacharyya noise parameter γ_i of the channel at time i-th:

$$\gamma_i = \sum_{b\in\mathcal{Y}} \sqrt{W_i(b|0)W_i(b|1)}$$

Therefore, the bound (2.9) can be written as

$$P_e(\boldsymbol{x},\boldsymbol{x'}) \le \prod_{i:\, x_i\ne x_i'} \gamma_i. \tag{2.10}$$

Note that when all γ_i have the same value γ (time-invariant channel case), the above bound reduces to the well known γ^h bound (2.1), where h is the Hamming distance between $\boldsymbol{x}$ and $\boldsymbol{x'}$.

We now assume that the codewords of the mother code are transmitted in m transmissions, and the decoding is performed after the last transmission has been received. This will help us to later analyze an IR HARQ protocol with at most m transmissions. Let $\mathcal{I} = \{1,\ldots,n\}$ denote the set indexing the bit positions in a codeword. For the m transmissions, set $\mathcal{I}$ is partitioned in m subsets $\mathcal{I}(j)$, for $1 \le j \le m$. During the j-th transmission, only bits at positions i where $i \in \mathcal{I}(j)$ are transmitted. We assume that the channel is slowly time-varying, namely that $W_i(y|0)$ and $W_i(y|1)$ remain constant for all bits at positions i taking part in the same transmission. Consequently, the Bhattacharyya noise parameter for transmission j depends only on j:

$$\gamma_i = \gamma(j) \text{ for all } i \in \mathcal{I}(j).$$

Let $h_j = d_H(\boldsymbol{x}, \boldsymbol{x}', \mathcal{I}(j))$ denote the Hamming distance between sequences $\boldsymbol{x}$ and $\boldsymbol{x}'$ over the index set $\mathcal{I}(j)$. The bound (2.10) can be written as

$$P_e(\boldsymbol{x}, \boldsymbol{x}') \leq \prod_{j=1}^{m} \gamma(j)^{h_j}, \qquad h_j = d_H(\boldsymbol{x}, \boldsymbol{x}', \mathcal{I}(j)).$$

In the case of only two transmissions, we have

$$P_e(\boldsymbol{x}, \boldsymbol{x}') \leq \gamma(1)^{d_H(\boldsymbol{x}, \boldsymbol{x}', \mathcal{I}(1))} \cdot \gamma(2)^{d_H(\boldsymbol{x}, \boldsymbol{x}', \mathcal{I}(2))} = \gamma(1)^{h_1} \gamma(2)^{h-h_1},$$

where h is the Hamming distance between $\boldsymbol{x}$ and $\boldsymbol{x}'$.

Let $A_{h_1 \ldots h_m}$ denote the number of codewords with weight h_j over the index set $\mathcal{I}(j)$, for $1 \leq j \leq m$. The union bound on the ML decoder word error probability is given by

$$P_W \leq \sum_{h_1=1}^{|\mathcal{I}(1)|} \cdots \sum_{h_m=1}^{|\mathcal{I}(m)|} A_{h_1 \ldots h_m} \prod_{j=1}^{m} \gamma(j)^{h_j}. \tag{2.11}$$

Further direct analysis of this expression seems formidable, even in the case of only two transmissions for which we have

$$\begin{aligned} P_W &\leq \sum_{h_1=1}^{|\mathcal{I}(1)|} \sum_{h_2=1}^{|\mathcal{I}(2)|} A_{h_1 h_2} \gamma(1)^{h_1} \gamma(2)^{h_2} \\ &= \sum_{h=1}^{n} \sum_{h_1=1}^{|\mathcal{I}(1)|} A_{h_1\, h-h_1} \gamma(1)^{h_1} \gamma(2)^{h-h_2}. \end{aligned}$$

We thus resort to finding the expected performance over all possible transmission assignments where a bit of a mother code is assigned to transmission j with probability α_j, $\alpha_j > 0$, $\sum_j \alpha_j = 1$. The expected (and asymptotic as $n \to \infty$) number of bits assigned to transmission j equals to $\alpha_j n$. In the place of (2.11), we derive an expression for the expected word error probability to which the results of [**19**] can be directly applied.

2.3. Random Transmission Assignment. We will assume that a bit of a mother code is assigned to transmission j with probability α_j, $\alpha_j > 0$, $\sum_j \alpha_j = 1$. Such scheme can actually be implemented as follows:

1. For each bit position i, $i = 1, 2, \ldots, n$, generate a number θ_i independently and uniformly at random over $[0, 1)$.
2. Compute m numbers λ_j as follows:

$$\lambda_j = 1 - \sum_{i=1}^{j} \alpha_i \text{ for } 1 \leq j \leq m.$$

   Note that $0 = \lambda_m < \lambda_{m-1} < \cdots < \lambda_2 < \lambda_1 < 1$.
3. Make the transmission assignment for each bit i, $i = 1, 2, \ldots, n$, as follows:
   (a) if $\theta_i \geq \lambda_1$, assign bit i to transmission 1, otherwise
   (b) if $\lambda_j \leq \theta_i < \lambda_{j-1}$, for some j s.t. $2 \leq j \leq m$, assign bit i to transmission j.

We are interested in the expected performance of the mother code under the above probabilistic model. If each bit of a codeword with Hamming weight h is randomly assigned to transmission j with probability α_j, then the probability that the sub-word corresponding to the j-th transmission has weight h_j for $1 \leq j \leq m$ is given by

$$\binom{h}{h_1}\binom{h-h_1}{h_2}\cdots\binom{h-h_1-\cdots-h_{m-1}}{h_m}\alpha_1^{h_1}\alpha_2^{h_2}\cdots\alpha_m^{h_m}. \tag{2.12}$$

Therefore, for a given codeword with Hamming weight h, the expected value of $A_{h_1,\ldots,h_m}$ is given by

$$\overline{A}_{h_1,\ldots,h_m} = A_h\binom{h}{h_1}\binom{h-h_1}{h_2}\cdots\binom{h-h_1-\cdots-h_{m-1}}{h_m}\alpha_1^{h_1}\alpha_2^{h_2}\cdots\alpha_m^{h_m},$$

and consequently, the expected value of the union bound (2.11) is

$$\begin{aligned}\overline{P}_W \leq & \sum_{h_i\geq 0;\sum h_i\leq n} \overline{A}_{h_1,\ldots,h_m}\gamma(1)^{h_1}\gamma(2)^{h_2}\cdots\gamma(m)^{h_m}\\ =&\sum_h A_h\Big\{\sum_{\sum h_i=h}\binom{h}{h_1}\binom{h-h_1}{h_2}\cdots\binom{h-h_1-\cdots-h_{m-1}}{h_m}\prod_{j=1}^m\big(\gamma(j)\alpha_j\big)^{h_j}\Big\}\\ =&\sum_h A_h\Big(\sum_{j=1}^m\gamma(j)\alpha_j\Big)^h.\end{aligned}$$

We define the average Bhattacharyya noise parameter seen by the mother code as

$$\overline{\gamma} = \sum_{j=1}^m \gamma(j)\alpha_j. \tag{2.13}$$

Then, we have

$$\overline{P}_W^{[\mathcal{C}]} \leq \sum_{h=1}^n \overline{A}_h^{[\mathcal{C}](n)}\overline{\gamma}^h. \tag{2.14}$$

Following the results of [**19**], if

$$\overline{\gamma} < \exp(-c_0^{[\mathcal{C}]}), \tag{2.15}$$

we have $\lim_{n\to\infty}\overline{P}_W^{[\mathcal{C}](n)} = 0$.

3. A Random Transmission Assignment IR HARQ Scheme

We consider an IR HARQ scheme with at most m transmissions where a bit is assigned to transmission j with probability α_j. Transmission j takes place if transmission $j-1$ fails. The rates α_j may be predetermined (*e.g.*, specified by a standard) or determined based on current network conditions. In both cases, we are interested in evaluating performance after j transmissions, $1 \leq j \leq m$. In the latter case, we are interested in determining α_j to achieve some required performance.

The random transmission assignment for an incremental redundancy HARQ protocol can be implemented by an "on-the-fly" dynamic version of the algorithm described in the beginning of Sec. 2.3:

Before the IR HARQ protocol starts:

1. For each bit position i, $i = 1, 2, \ldots, n$, generate a number θ_i independently and uniformly at random over $[0, 1)$.
2. Compute λ_1 as $\lambda_1 = 1 - \alpha_1$.
3. If $\theta_i \geq \lambda_1$, assign bit i to transmission 1.

If transmission $j - 1$ fails for $2 \leq j < m$:

1. Determine α_j, if it was not predetermined.
2. Compute λ_j as $\lambda_j = \lambda_{j-1} - \alpha_j$.
3. If $\lambda_j \leq \theta_i < \lambda_{j-1}$, assign bit i to transmission j.

If transmission $m - 1$ fails:

transmit all remaining bits.

We denote by $\overline{\gamma}(j)$ the average Bhattacharyya noise parameter seen by the mother code after j-th channel transmission. For $j < m$, not all bits of the mother code are transmitted. A bit is punctured (*i.e.*, not transmitted) with probability $(1 - \alpha_1 - \cdots - \alpha_j)$. To be able to use the results of Sec. 2.3, we will assume that the punctured bits are transmitted over a really bad channel, *i.e.*, a channel with $\gamma(j+1) = 1$. This assumption allows us to compute $\overline{\gamma}(j)$ as

$$\overline{\gamma}(j) = \alpha_1 \cdot \gamma(1) + \cdots + \alpha_j \cdot \gamma(j) + (1 - \alpha_1 - \cdots - \alpha_j) \cdot 1.$$

This equation holds for $1 \leq j < m$ and for $j = m$ as well since the last term becomes equal to 0. Note that $\gamma(m) = \overline{\gamma}$, where $\overline{\gamma}$ is defined by (2.13).

In this paper, by evaluating performance after transmission j, we will mean computing $\overline{\gamma}(j)$. Recall that the knowledge of $\overline{\gamma}(j)$ allows only the computation of upper bounds on the average error probability of the turbo code ensembles. However, it has been conjectured in [**19**], based on experimental evidence, that those upper bounds are asymptotically close to the best possible, and that probability of error of an ensemble exhibits a threshold behavior, *i.e.*, either approaches zero or goes to 1 as $n \to \infty$. For the same reasons, we will require that $\overline{\gamma}(j) < \exp(-c_0^{[\mathcal{C}]})$, which in turn implies $\lim_{n\to\infty} \overline{P}_W^{[\mathcal{C}](n)} = 0$.

3.1. First Transmission and Punctured Turbo Code Ensembles. If a bit is assigned to the first transmission with probability α_1, the transmitter receives on the average $\alpha_1 \cdot n$ bits of the mother code over the channel with Bhattacharyya noise parameter $\gamma(1)$. Parameter $\gamma(1)$ is determined by the current channel model and level of noise, which depend on the speed of the mobile and other conditions in a wireless network, and by the signal power which is chosen by the transmitter. The remaining $(1 - \alpha_1) \cdot n$ bits of the mother code are not transmitted. As mentioned above, we can equivalently assume that they are transmitted over a really bad channel, *i.e.*, a channel with $\gamma(2) = 1$. This assumption allows us to compute $\overline{\gamma}(1)$, the average Bhattacharyya noise parameter after the first transmission, as

$$\overline{\gamma}(1) = \alpha_1 \cdot \gamma(1) + (1 - \alpha_1) \cdot 1.$$

Our goal is to guarantee $\lim_{n\to\infty} \overline{P}_W^{[\mathcal{C}](n)} = 0$, and we have seen that can be done by choosing α_1 or $\gamma(1)$ or both so that $\overline{\gamma}(1) < \exp(-c_0^{[\mathcal{C}]})$, *i.e.*,

$$\alpha_1 \cdot \gamma(1) + (1 - \alpha_1) \cdot 1 < \exp(-c_0^{[\mathcal{C}]}). \tag{3.1}$$

Condition (3.1) can be written in a form which clearly shows the tradeoff between the rate of the first transmission code and the signal power:

$$\alpha_1(1-\gamma(1)) > 1-\exp(-c_0^{[\mathcal{C}]})$$

To satisfy this lower bound on the product of α_1 and $1-\gamma(1)$, the transmitter can either increase the code redundancy α_1 or increase the signal power which results in a decrease of $\gamma(1)$ and increase of $1-\gamma(1)$. An increase in redundancy results in the lower throughput of the user while an increase in the power results in a higher interference level experienced by other users in the network. Since $\gamma(1)$ is positive, there is a minimal redundancy requirement:

$$\alpha_1 > 1-\exp(-c_0^{[\mathcal{C}]}). \tag{3.2}$$

In the case of predetermined α_1, the required signal power is specified by

$$\gamma(1) < \frac{\exp\left(-c_0^{[\mathcal{C}]}\right)-(1-\alpha_1)}{\alpha_1}. \tag{3.3}$$

It is interesting to compare the above results with those obtained by the authors in [**20**], where randomly punctured turbo codes were studied. We briefly present the connection. The general structure of a punctured turbo code is shown in Fig. 2. The puncturing device punctures each codeword symbol independently

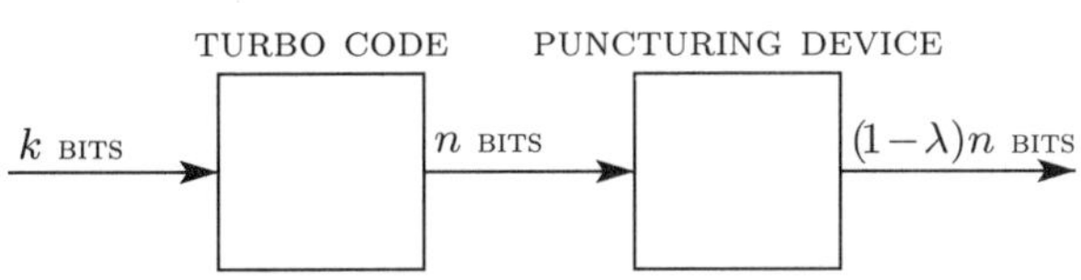

FIGURE 2. Punctured turbo codes. The puncturing device punctures each bit independently with probability λ. The expected number of remaining bits equals $(1-\lambda)n$.

with probability λ. Therefore, if an (n,k) rate R code is punctured, the expected number of punctured bits equals λn and the resulting code expected rate, as well as the asymptotic rate when $n\to\infty$, equals $R/(1-\lambda)$. For each mother code in the set $\mathcal{C}^{(n)}$, we will have a set of 2^n punctured codes corresponding to the 2^n possible puncturing patterns. Each code in this set appears with the probability determined by the puncturing pattern. The set of codes obtained by puncturing all codes in the set $\mathcal{C}^{(n)}$ is denoted $\mathcal{C}_P^{(n)}$. By the punctured code turbo code *ensemble* $[\mathcal{C}_P]$, we will mean a *sequence* of randomly punctured turbo code sets $\{\mathcal{C}_P^{(n)}\}$.

In [**20**], we analyzed the expected error rate performance of the punctured codes by bounding their expected weight enumerators. If a codeword of weight d enters a puncturing device, the codeword at the output will have a weight h with probability $\binom{d}{h}(1-\lambda)^h\lambda^{d-h}$. Since on the average $\overline{A}_d^{[\mathcal{C}](n)}$ codewords of weight d enter the puncturing device, the expected number of punctured codewords of weight h is given by

$$\overline{A}_h^{[\mathcal{C}_p](n)} = \sum_{d\geq h}\overline{A}_d^{[\mathcal{C}](n)}\binom{d}{h}\lambda^{d-h}(1-\lambda)^h. \tag{3.4}$$

By applying the bound (2.6) on $\overline{A}_h^{[\mathcal{C}_P](n)}$ in the above expression and using the Chernoff bound, we showed in [**20**] that if the codeword symbols of a turbo code ensemble $[\mathcal{C}]$ with a finite noise threshold $c_0^{[\mathcal{C}]}$ are punctured with probability λ satisfying

$$\log \lambda < -c_0^{[\mathcal{C}]}, \tag{3.5}$$

then there exists a finite *noise threshold for the punctured code ensemble* $c_0^{[\mathcal{C}_P]}$ such that

$$c_0^{[\mathcal{C}_P]} \leq \log \left[\frac{1-\lambda}{\exp\left(-c_0^{[\mathcal{C}]}\right) - \lambda} \right] \tag{3.6}$$

and

$$\overline{A}_h^{[\mathcal{C}_P](n)} \leq_n \exp\left(h c_0^{[\mathcal{C}_P]}\right), \qquad D_n < h \leq n. \tag{3.7}$$

Similarly as in [**19**], by using the inequality (3.7), in the bound (2.3), it can be shown (see [**20**] for details) that for a turbo code ensemble $[\mathcal{C}]$ with $L \geq 2$ component encoders, punctured at rate λ and a binary-input memoryless channel whose Bhattacharyya parameter satisfies

$$\gamma < \exp(-c_0^{[\mathcal{C}_P]}), \tag{3.8}$$

we have

$$\lim_{n \to \infty} \overline{P}_W^{[\mathcal{C}_P](n)} = 0. \tag{3.9}$$

Here λ satisfies (3.5) and $c_0^{[\mathcal{C}_P]}$ satisfies (3.6). Now, we can compare these results with those obtained by the random transmission assignment approach in the beginning of the section. Note that since $\lambda = 1 - \alpha_1$, condition (3.2) is equivalent to (3.5), and condition (3.8) together with (3.6) is equivalent to (3.3).

3.2. Subsequent Transmissions. We now assume that the decoding after transmission $j-1$ failed. On the average $n\alpha_j$ bits will participate in the j-th transmission, and the remaining $(1 - \alpha_1 - \cdots - \alpha_j) \cdot n$ bits of the mother code will not be transmitted. We again assume that they are transmitted over a really bad channel, *i.e.*, a channel with $\gamma(j+1) = 1$, and compute $\overline{\gamma}(j)$, the average Bhattacharyya noise parameter after the j-th transmission, as

$$\overline{\gamma}(j) = \alpha_1 \cdot \gamma(1) + \cdots + \alpha_j \cdot \gamma(j) + (1 - \alpha_1 - \cdots - \alpha_j) \cdot 1.$$

Again, our goal is to guarantee $\lim_{n\to\infty} \overline{P}_W^{[\mathcal{C}](n)} = 0$, and we have seen that can be done by choosing α_j or $\gamma(j)$ or both so that

$$\overline{\gamma}(j) < \exp(-c_0^{[\mathcal{C}]}). \tag{3.10}$$

Condition (3.10) can be written in a form which clearly show the tradeoff between the rate of the j-th transmission code and the signal power:

$$\alpha_j(1 - \gamma(j)) > 1 - \exp(-c_0^{[\mathcal{C}]}) - \sum_{i=1}^{j-1} \alpha(i)(1 - \gamma(i)).$$

Similar conclusions as those of the analysis for the first transmission hold: to satisfy the above lower bound on the product of α_j and $1 - \gamma(j)$, the transmitter can either increase the code redundancy α_1 or increase the signal power which results in a decrease of $\gamma(j)$ and increase of $1 - \gamma(j)$. An increase in redundancy results in the lower throughput of the user while an increase in the power results in a higher interference level experienced by other users in the network. Since $\gamma(j)$ is positive, there is a minimum redundancy requirement:

$$\alpha_j > 1 - \exp(-c_0^{[\mathcal{C}]}) - \sum_{i=1}^{j-1} \alpha(i)(1-\gamma(i)).$$

In the case of predetermined α_j, the required signal power is specified by

$$\gamma(j) < \frac{\exp\left(-c_0^{[\mathcal{C}]}\right) - (1-\alpha_j) - \sum_{i=1}^{j-1} \alpha(i)(1-\gamma(i))}{\alpha_j}.$$

4. An Example

Here we study an example $R = 1/3$ turbo code specified by the 1xEV-DV wireless standard as a mother code. The turbo encoder consists of $L = 2$ recursive convolutional encoders with rates $R_1 = 1/2$ and $R_2 = 1$ connected in parallel through an "S-random" interleaver. The component code transfer functions are

$$G_1(D) = \left[1, \frac{1+D+D^3}{1+D^2+D^3}\right] \text{ and } G_2(D) = \left[\frac{1+D+D^3}{1+D^2+D^3}\right].$$

For an IR HARQ scheme, the bits of the mother code are assigned randomly to 15 transmissions so that the rates of the resulting punctured codes are

$$1,\ 0.95,\ 0.9,\ 0.85, \ldots, 0.4,\ 0.35,\ \frac{1}{3}.$$

Note that the rate of the punctured mother code after transmission j is given by $R_p(j) = R/\sum_{i=1}^{j} \alpha_i$. Thus we can compute transmission rates α_i corresponding to the above set of punctured code rates. The assignment of bits to transmissions is implemented as described in Sec. 3.

We determined the throughput and the average FER performance of this IR HARQ scheme by simulation. The simulations were done for the standard interleaver lengths of $k = 384$ and 3840, and BPSK over an AWGN channel for a range of E_s/N_0. The average throughput performance for this HARQ scheme is plotted in Fig. 3. We can see that, for a range of puncturing rates, random puncturing delivered codes whose performance ensured that the throughput be in the region between the cutoff rate and the capacity. After a certain rate the performance of the punctured codes leaves this region. The analysis presented in this paper shows how to estimate this point. We next show that for this particular example, the estimate is in a very good agreement with the numerical value observed in the simulation.

We have computed the average weight enumerator $\overline{A}_d^{[\mathcal{C}](n)}$ of the mother codes in the set $\mathcal{C}^{(n)}$ by applying the technique of [**27**] for code length $n = 1152$ and code rate $R = 1/3$, and obtained

$$c_0^{[\mathcal{C}](n)} = \max_{D_n < d \le n} \frac{\log \overline{A}_d^{[\mathcal{C}](n)}}{d} = 0.5198.$$

Since $c_0^{[\mathcal{C}]} >_n c_0^{[\mathcal{C}](n)}$, the minimal redundancy requirement (3.2) for the first transmission gives

$$\alpha_1 > 0.4054 \text{ and thus } R_p = \frac{R}{\alpha_1} < 0.822. \tag{4.1}$$

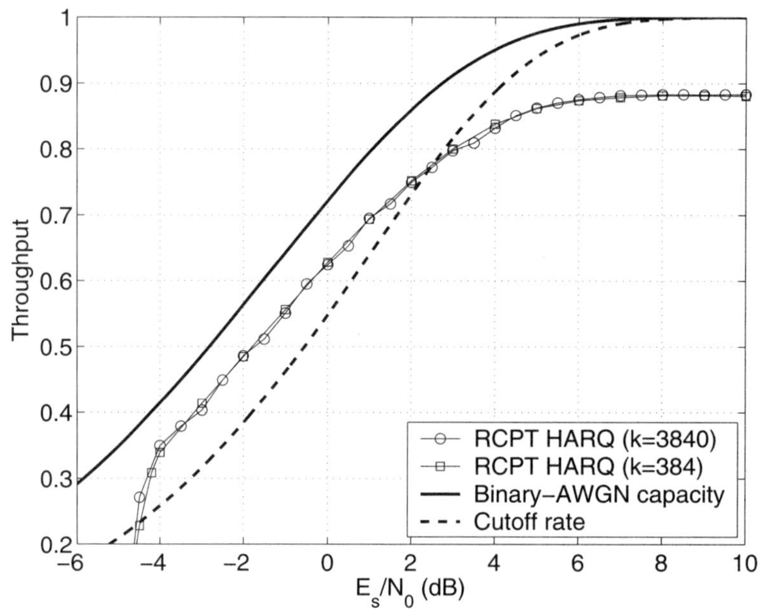

FIGURE 3. Average throughput performance of an BPSK IR HARQ scheme on AWGN channel for two interleaver lengths.

Although our results give only a necessary condition on the minimal α_1, the simulation results of Fig. 3 show that an abrupt loss in performance occurs roughly for the code rate of 0.82.

Fig. 4 compares the average FER performance of the punctured turbo codes with rates 0.7, 0.8 and 0.9 and interleaver lengths $k = 384$ and 3840. Condition (3.2) on the minimal punctured code redundancy, $\alpha_1 > 1 - \exp(-c_0^{[\mathcal{C}]})$, implies that the punctured code rates below $R/\alpha_1 < 0.82$ are necessary to guarantee $\overline{\gamma}(1) < \exp(-c_0^{[\mathcal{C}]})$. From Fig. 4, we see that when rates are 0.7 and 0.8, the FER of the $k = 3840$ code drops noticeably faster to 10^{-3} than that of the $k = 384$ code. We also see that, when the rate is 0.9, the FERs of both the $k = 384$ and the $k = 3840$ codes do not go below 0.1.

5. Conclusions

Because of their good performance, HARQ schemes are included in current proposals for wireless data/voice networks. A number of important issues such as error rate performance after each transmission and rate and power control are difficult to analyze in a network employing a particular HARQ scheme, *i.e.*, a given mother code and given selection of bits for each transmission. We here addressed two issues motivated directly by questions in practice. The first was to evaluate the error rate performance after each transmission, which is equivalent to evaluating performance of punctured turbo codes on time varying channels. The second was to show how one should go about choosing the signal power and the number of bits for transmission j after a failed transmission $j-1$. To approach and solve both problems, we introduced the idea of random transmission assignments of the mother

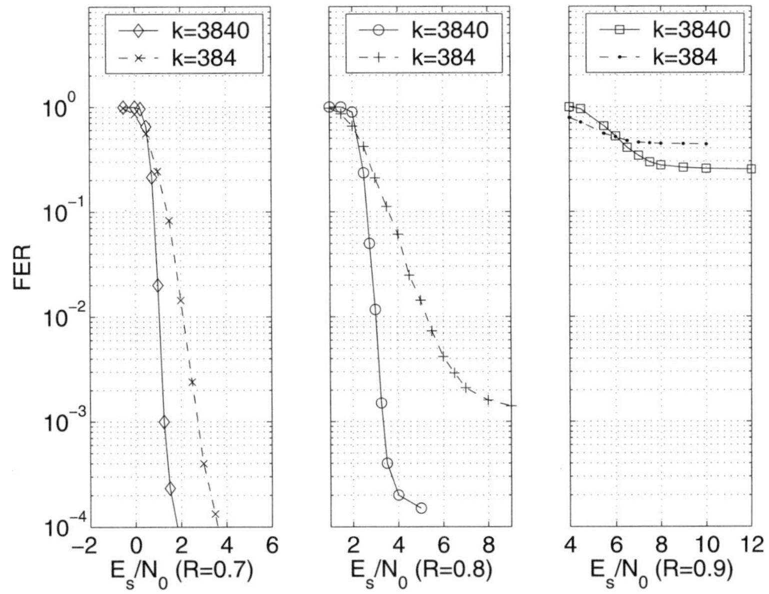

FIGURE 4. Average FER performance of punctured turbo codes on an AWGN channel for two interleaver lengths $k = 384$ and 3840. The mother turbo code has rate 1/3, and the punctured codes have rates 0.7, 0.8, and 0.9.

code bits. Although theoretical results we obtained are mainly upper bounds and necessary conditions, simulation results show that they can be very useful tools for predicting end evaluating performance of practical schemes.

Acknowledgments

The authors would like to thank A. Ashikhmin, J. Kim, S. Ramakrishna, P. Whiting, and A. van Wijngaarden for many discussions on practical HARQ schemes, and to Gerhard Kramer for his comments on an earlier version of the paper.

References

[1] J. M. Wozencraft and M. Horstein, "Digitalized communication over two-way channels," presented at the Fourth London Symp. Inform. Theory, London, UK, Sept. 1960.

[2] J. M. Wozencraft and M. Horstein, "Coding for two-way channels," Tech. Rep. 383, Res. Lab. Electron., MIT, Cambridge, MA, Jan. 1961.

[3] D. J. Costello, Jr., J. Hagenauer, H. Imai, and S. B. Wicker, "Applications of Error-Control Coding,", *IEEE Trans. Inform. Theory,* Vol. 44, pp. 2531–2560, Oct. 1998.

[4] G. Caire and D. Tuninetti, "ARQ protocols for the Gaussian collision channel," *IEEE Trans. Inform. Theory,* Vol. 47, pp. 1971–1988, July 2001.

[5] D. Tuninetti and G. Caire, "The optimal throughput of some wireless multiaccess systems," *IEEE Trans. Inform. Theory,* Oct. 2002.

[6] C.-F. Leanderson and G. Caire, "The performance of incremental redundancy schemes based on convolutional codes in the block-fading Gaussian collision channel," submitted to *IEEE Trans. Wireless Comm.,* Dec. 2001, available at `www.eurecom.fr/~caire`.

[7] S. Sesia, G. Caire and G. Vivier, "Incremental redundancy Hybrid ARQ schemes based on low-density parity-check codes," submitted to *IEEE Trans. Commununications,* Feb. 2003, available at `www.eurecom.fr/~caire`.

[8] D. N. Rowitch, L. B. Milstein, "On the performance of hybrid FEC/ARQ systems using rate compatible punctured turbo (RCPT) codes," *IEEE Transactions on Communications*, Vol. 48 Issue: 6, pp. 948 959, June 2000.

[9] R. Mantha and F. Kschischang, "A Capacity–approaching hybrid ARQ scheme using turbo codes," *1999 IEEE Global Telecommunication Conference (GLOBECOM'99)*pp. 2341–2345.

[10] P. Jung, J. Plechinger, M. Doetsch, and F. M. Berens, "A pragmatic approach to rate compatible punctured turbo-codes for mobile radio applications," in Proc. 6th Int. Conf. on Advances in Commun. and Control, Corfu, Greece, June 1997.

[11] K. R. Narayanan and G. L. Stuber, "A novel ARQ technique using the turbo coding principle," *IEEE Communication Letters*, vol. 1, pp. 49-51, Mar. 1997.

[12] J. Li and H. Imai, "Performance of hybrid-ARQ protocols with rate compatible turbo codes," in Proc. 1997 Int. Symp. on Turbo Codes, Brest, France, pp. 188 191, Sept. 1997.

[13] O. F. Acikel and W. E. Ryan, "Punctured Turbo Codes for BPSK/QPSK Channels," *IEEE Trans. Communications*, vol. 47, No. 9, pp. 1315-1323, Sept. 1999.

[14] A. S. Barbulescu And , S. S. Pietrobon, "Rate compatible turbo-codes," *IEEE Electronics Letters*, vol. 31, pp. 535-536, Mar. 1995.

[15] J. Hagenauer, "Rate compatible punctured convolutional codes (RCPC Codes) and their application," *IEEE Trans. Communications*, vol.36, pp. 384-400, Apr. 1988.

[16] D. N. Rowitch and L. B. Milstein, "Rate compatible punctured turbo (RCPT) codes in a hybrid FEC/ARQ system," in Proc. Communications Theory Mini-Conf. of GLOBECOM'97, Phoenix, AZ, pp. 55 59, Nov. 1997.

[17] T. Richardson, A. Shokrollahi, and R. Urbanke, "Tresholds for turbo codes," *Proc. IEEE Int. Symp., Inform. Theory*, Sorrento, Italy, June 2000, pp. 317.

[18] S. ten Brink, "Convergence of iterative decoding," *Electron. Lett.*, vol. 35, no. 10, pp. 806–808, May 1999.

[19] H. Jin and R. J. McEliece, "Coding Theorems for Turbo Code Ensembles," *IEEE Trans. on Information Theory*, Vol. 48, pp. 1451–1461, June 2002.

[20] R. Liu, P. Spasojevic and E. Soljanin, "Punctured turbo code ensembles," *Proc. 2003 IEEE Inform. Theory Workshop*, Paris, France, March 31–April 4, 2003.

[21] R. Liu, P. Spasojevic and E. Soljanin, "On the role of puncturing in hybrid ARQ schemes," *Proc. 2003 IEEE Int. Symp. Inform. Theory (ISIT 2003)*, Yokohama, Japan, June 29–July 4, 2003.

[22] N. Kahale and R. Urbanke, "On the minimum distance of parallel and serially concatenated codes," *Proc. 1998 IEEE Int. Symp. Inform. Theory (ISIT 1998)*, Cambridge, MA, USA, Aug. 16–21, 1998, p. 31.

[23] M. Breiling, "A logarithmic upper bound on the minimum distance of turbo codes," *submitted to IEEE Trans. Inform. Theory,* April 2001, available at `www.lnt.de/~breiling`.

[24] D. Truhachev, M. Lentmaier, and K. Sh. Zigangirov, "Some Results Concerning Design and Decoding of Turbo-Codes," *Probl. Peredach. Inform.,* vol. 37, no. 3, July–Sept. 2001.

[25] L. Bazzi, M. Mahdian and D. Spielman, "The minimum distance of turbo-like codes," *submitted to IEEE Trans. Inform. Theory,* May 2003, available at `http://www-math.mit.edu/~spielman`.

[26] G. Zemor and J. Boutros, "Interleavers for turbo codes that yield a minimum distance growing with blocklength," presented at *DIMACS Workshop on Algebraic Coding Theory and Information Theory,* Dec. 2003.

[27] D. Divsalar and F. Pollara, "Weight distributions for turbo codes using random and nonrandom Permutations," *JPL TDA Progress Report* 42-122, pp. 56–65, Aug. 1995.

Emina Soljanin: Bell Labs, Lucent, 600 Mountain Av., Murray Hill NJ 07974
E-mail address: `emina@lucent.com`

Ruoheng Liu: ECE Department, Rutgers University, Piscataway NJ 08854
E-mail address: `liurh@winlab.rutgers.edu`

Predrag Spasojevic: ECE Department, Rutgers University, Piscataway NJ 08854
E-mail address: `spasojev@winlab.rutgers.edu`

DIMACS Series in Discrete Mathematics
and Theoretical Computer Science
Volume **66**, 2004

An Information-Theoretic Approach to Bit-Stuffing for Network Protocols

Jack Keil Wolf

In the X.25 protocol, bit-stuffing has been used to prevent 6 consecutive 1's from occurring in the data sequence. By interchanging the roles of 0's and 1's, the X.25 constraint is an example of a type of run-length-limited constrained binary sequence called a (0,5) sequence. This, in turn, is a special case of a binary (d, k) constrained sequence which is used in almost all digital storage systems and in many communication systems. Thus in what follows, we consider the more general case of these (d, k) sequences which are defined next.

For d and k nonnegative integers with $0 < d < k$, binary (d, k) sequences have the property that at least d and at most k 0's occur between adjacent 1's. More specifically, for $d > 0$ and finite k, the sequences are produced by the edge labels when taking tours of the graph shown in Figure 1.

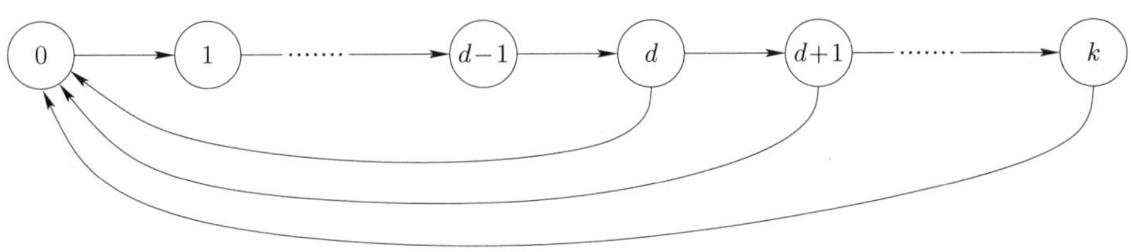

FIGURE 1. Graph for (d, k) codes

In this paper we will investigate the code rates which can be achieved with bit-stuffing and compare these rates with the Shannon capacity. We will use as our constraint binary (d, k) codes, although our technique applies to a much wider class of codes. We will begin with traditional bit-stuffing on unmodified data which gives rates strictly less than capacity. Then we show how bit-stuffing can be modified to yield rates equal to capacity for some values of d and k. Finally we show how bit-stuffing can be further modified to yield rates equal to capacity for all values of d and k.

This work was supported in part by the Center for Magnetic Recording Research and by the National Science Foundation.

For any value of d and k ($0 < d < k$), one can use bit-stuffing to convert an arbitrary data sequence into a sequence that satisfies the (d, k) constraint. A loose statement of an algorithm for accomplishing this conversion is as follows:

- Stuff d 0's after every 1. (Skip this step if $d = 0$.)
- Stuff a 1 after every occurrence of k 0's. (Skip this step if k is infinite.)
- Otherwise insert a binary data digit.

It is easy to follow this algorithm by referring to the appropriate graph that describes the constraint. Since the most complicated case is when $d > 0$ and k is finite, we show the graph for this case (Fig. 2) in which the stuffed bits are underlined and the data bits are not underlined.

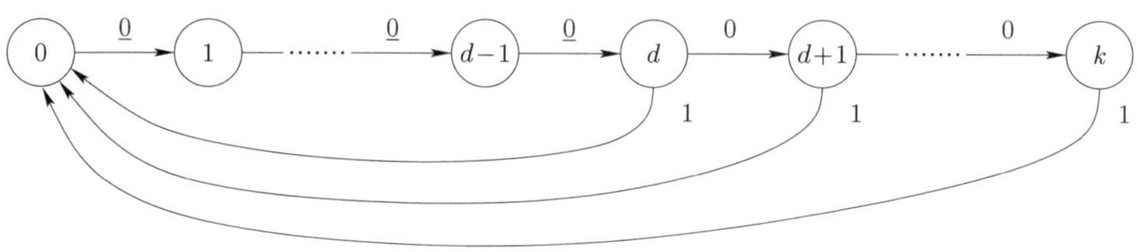

FIGURE 2. Bit-stuffing for $d > 0$ and finite k.

The code rate for bit-stuffing is the average number of data symbols per coded symbol. The code rate here is computed for i.i.d. binary data with equally likely 0's and 1's. The Shannon capacity of a (d, k) constrained sequence is the maximum code rate of any encoder-decoder that satisfies the constraint. Therefore the code rate for bit-stuffing is less than or equal to the Shannon capacity of the constraint.

If one uses bit-stuffing on uncoded data, except for the trivial case of $(d = 0, k = \infty)$, the code rate always is strictly less than the Shannon capacity. The code rate again is computed for i.i.d. binary data with equally likely 0 s and 1 s. By a modification to bit-stuffing, using a device called a distribution transformer to be defined in the next paragraph, we can improve the code rate.

A distribution transformer is a device that converts the binary data sequence into an i.i.d. binary sequence that is p-biased for $0 < p < 1$. The probability of a 1 in this biased stream is equal to p. The distribution transformer can be implemented by a source decoder for a p-biased stream. The conversion occurs at a rate penalty $h(p)$, where

$$h(p) = -plog(p) - (1-p)log(1-p).$$

When a distribution transformer has been used with bit-stuffing, we can choose p to maximize the average code rate and sometimes the resulting average code rate is equal to the Shannon capacity.

As shown by Bender and Wolf [**BW93**], after optimizing p, the code rate can be made equal to the Shannon capacity for two cases: $(d, d+1)$ and (d, ∞), sequences for every $d > 0$. However, even after choosing the optimum value of p, the code rate is strictly less than the Shannon capacity for all other values of d and k. Figure 3 shows the relative rate of (d, k) codes (the average rate normalized by the Shannon capacity) versus k for fixed values of d ($d = 0, 1, 2, 3, 4, 5$). The legend is of the form (d, k, c) where the last symbol "c" refers to a charge constraint. In this case, there is no charge constraint so that c is equal to infinity (which prints as an 8 and should be ignored). It should be noted that for all values of d, the relative rate is 1 for $k = d + 1$ and for k equal to infinity.

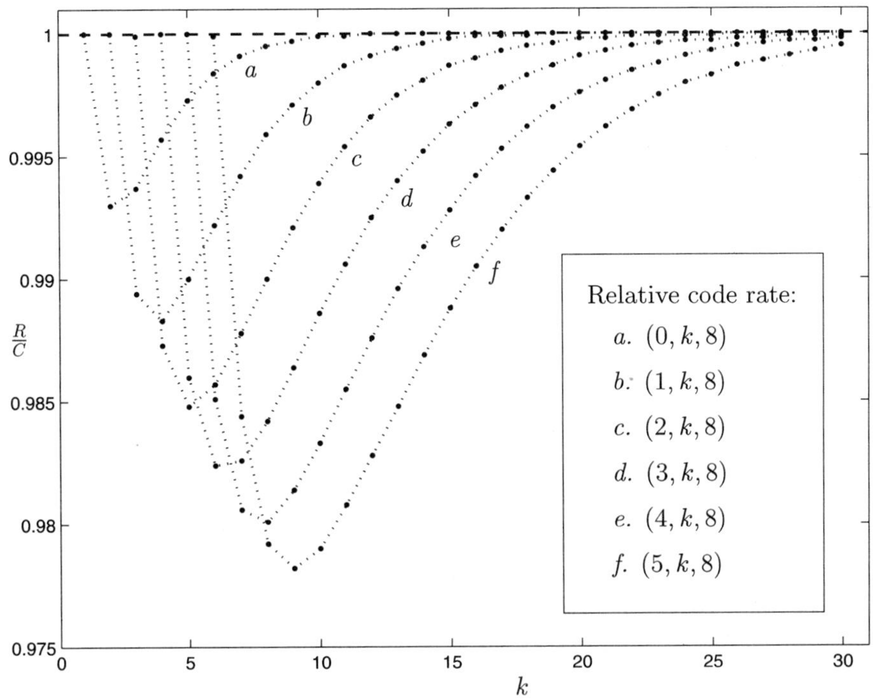

FIGURE 3. Relative rate $\frac{R}{C}$ for (d, k) codes versus k for $d = \{0, 1, 2, 3, 4, 5\}$.

We now show how with a further modification of bit-stuffing, we can make the average rate of (d, k) codes equal to the Shannon capacity for all values of d and k. To do this we introduce the notion of multiple distribution transformers.

Sequences that achieve the Shannon capacity in a constraint graph induce probabilities on the edges of the graph. These sequences are referred to as maxentropic sequences. For finite k, the Shannon capacity is achieved when the edges of the constraint graph are assigned the probabilities as indicated in Figure 4. Here the parameter λ is given by the equation $\lambda = 2^{C(d,k)}$.

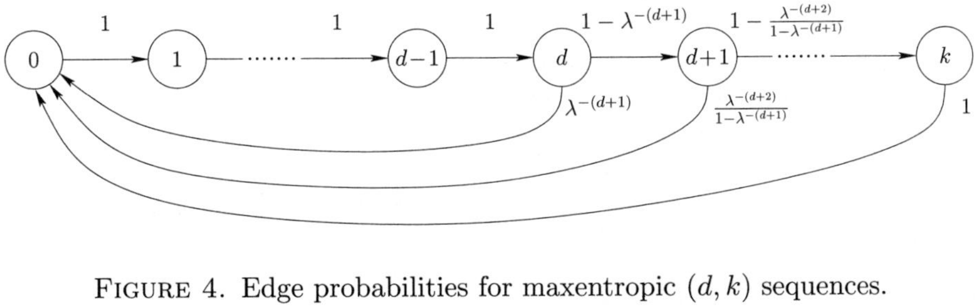

FIGURE 4. Edge probabilities for maxentropic (d, k) sequences.

We now come to the main result of this paper. We first illustrate this result for the specific example of a (1,3) constraint. The maxentropic edge probabilities for the graph of the (1,3) code are shown in Figure 5. Note that in Figure 5 there are two states (the middle states) with two exiting edges per state while the other states (the states at the two ends) have only one exiting edge per state. The leftmost of the middle states has a probability of 0.4655 on its exiting edge corresponding to a data 1. The rightmost of these two middle states has a probability of 0.5943 on its exiting edge corresponding to a data 1.

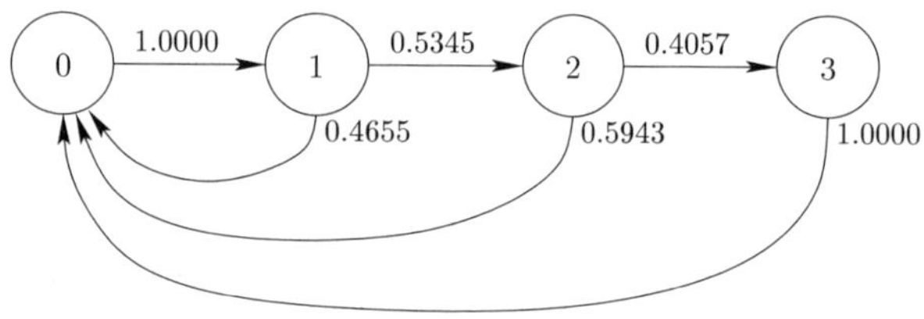

FIGURE 5. Edge probabilities for a maxentropic (1,3) code.

We will now describe how bit-stuffing can be used in conjunction with two distribution transformers to form (1,3) sequences at an average rate equal to the Shannon capacity. We first take our equally probable i.i.d. data sequence and break it up into two sequences, one of which is input to a distribution transformer with parameter $p = 0.4655$ and the other of which is input to a distribution transformer with parameter $p = 0.5943$.

Encoding is best understood by reference to Figure 5. Whenever we are in the leftmost end state we stuff a 0 while whenever we are in the rightmost end state we stuff a 1. Whenever we are in the leftmost middle state we take a biased output from the distribution transformer with bias $p = 0.4655$ and whenever we are in the rightmost middle state we take a biased output from the distribution transformer with bias $p = 0.5943$. Movement on the graph is dictated by the values of the symbols where a 1 takes us back to the leftmost end state and a 0 moves us to the right in the graph. The fact that the average rate is equal to the Shannon capacity follows directly from the fact that the edge probabilities on the graph correspond to the edge probabilities of maxentropic sequences satisfying the constraint.

The percentage of equally likely i.i.d. data symbols that are input to each distribution transformer is governed by the steady state probabilities of the states corresponding to these transformers.

We now turn to the general case of (d, k) codes for arbitrary d and k ($k < \infty$) and show how to use bit-stuffing in conjunction with $(n-k)$ distribution transformers in order to encode at an average rate equal to the Shannon capacity. The graph for such constraints have $(n - k)$ middle states with two branches exiting each of these states. To encode we would now use $(n - k)$ distribution transformers with the biases chosen to correspond to the edge probabilities of these middle states. The encoder is shown in Figure 6.

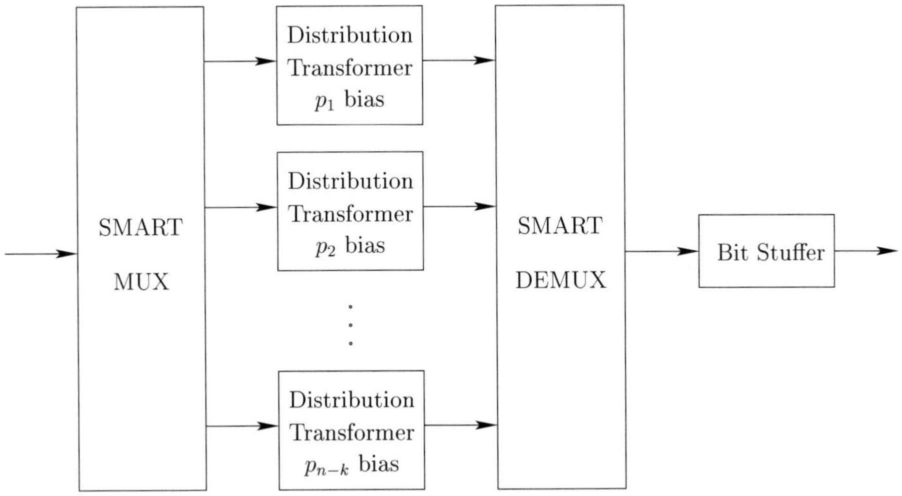

FIGURE 6. Bit-stuffing with multiple transformers.

Although the technique for using bit-stuffing with multiple distribution transformers to obtain codes with average rate equal to the Shannon capacity was explained for the case of (d, k) codes, this approach applies to a much wider variety of systems.

References

[BW93] P.E. Bender and J.K. Wolf, "A Universal Algorithm for Generating Optimal and Nearly Optimal Run-Length Limited, Charge-Constrained Binary Sequences", in *Proc. 1993 Int'l Symp. Inform. Theory*, San Antonio, Texas, Jan. 17–22, 1993, p. 6.

J. K. WOLF IS WITH THE UNIVERSITY OF CALIFORNIA-SAN DIEGO, ELECTRICAL AND COMPUTER ENGINEERING DEPARTMENT AND THE CENTER FOR MAGNETIC RECORDING RESEARCH.

E-mail address: `jwolf@ucsd.edu`

Titles in This Series

66 **Piyush Gupta, Gerhard Kramer, and Adriaan J. van Wijngaarden, Editors,** Advances in Network Information Theory

65 **Santosh S. Vempala,** The Random Projection Method

64 **Melvyn B. Nathanson, Editor,** Unusual Applications of Number Theory

63 **J. Nešetřil and P. Winkler, Editors,** Graphs, Morphisms and Statistical Physics

62 **Gerard J. Foschini and Sergio Verdú, Editors,** Multiantenna Channels: Capacity, Coding and Signal Processing

61 **M. F. Janowitz, F.-J. Lapointe, F. R. McMorris, B. Mirkin, and F. S. Roberts, Editors,** Bioconsensus

60 **Saugata Basu and Laureano Gonzalez-Vega, Editors,** Algorithmic and Quantitative Real Algebraic Geometry

59 **Michael H. Goldwasser, David S. Johnson, and Catherine C. McGeoch, Editors,** Data Structures, Near Neighbor Searches, and Methodology: Fifth and Sixth DIMACS Implementation Challenges

58 **Simon Thomas, Editor,** Set Theory: The Hajnal Conference

57 **Eugene C. Freuder and Richard J. Wallace, Editors,** Constraint Programming and Large Scale Discrete Optimization

56 **Alexander Barg and Simon Litsyn, Editors,** Codes and Association Schemes

55 **Ding-Zhu Du, Panos M. Pardalos, and Jie Wang, Editors,** Discrete Mathematical Problems with Medical Applications

54 **Erik Winfree and David K. Gifford, Editors,** DNA Based Computers V

53 **Nathaniel Dean, D. Frank Hsu, and R. Ravi, Editors,** Robust Communication Networks: Interconnection and Survivability

52 **Sanguthevar Rajasekaran, Panos Pardalos, and D. Frank Hsu, Editors,** Mobile Networks and Computing

51 **Pierre Hansen, Patrick Fowler, and Maolin Zheng, Editors,** Discrete Mathematical Chemistry

50 **James M. Abello and Jeffrey Scott Vitter, Editors,** External Memory Algorithms

49 **Ronald L. Graham, Jan Kratochvíl, Jaroslav Nešetřil, and Fred S. Roberts, Editors,** Contemporary Trends in Discrete Mathematics

48 **Harvey Rubin and David Harlan Wood, Editors,** DNA Based Computers III

47 **Martin Farach-Colton, Fred S. Roberts, Martin Vingron, and Michael Waterman, Editors,** Mathematical Support for Molecular Biology

46 **Peng-Jun Wan, Ding-Zhu Du, and Panos M. Pardalos, Editors,** Multichannel Optical Networks: Theory and Practice

45 **Marios Mavronicolas, Michael Merritt, and Nir Shavit, Editors,** Networks in Distributed Computing

44 **Laura F. Landweber and Eric B. Baum, Editors,** DNA Based Computers II

43 **Panos Pardalos, Sanguthevar Rajasekaran, and José Rolim, Editors,** Randomization Methods in Algorithm Design

42 **Ding-Zhu Du and Frank K. Hwang, Editors,** Advances in Switching Networks

41 **David Aldous and James Propp, Editors,** Microsurveys in Discrete Probability

40 **Panos M. Pardalos and Dingzhu Du, Editors,** Network Design: Connectivity and Facilities Location

39 **Paul W. Beame and Samuel R Buss, Editors,** Proof Complexity and Feasible Arithmetics

38 **Rebecca N. Wright and Peter G. Neumann, Editors,** Network Threats

37 **Boris Mirkin, F. R. McMorris, Fred S. Roberts, and Andrey Rzhetsky, Editors,** Mathematical Hierarchies and Biology

36 **Joseph G. Rosenstein, Deborah S. Franzblau, and Fred S. Roberts, Editors,** Discrete Mathematics in the Schools

35 **Dingzhu Du, Jun Gu, and Panos M. Pardalos, Editors,** Satisfiability Problem: Theory and Applications

34 **Nathaniel Dean, Editor,** African Americans in Mathematics

33 **Ravi B. Boppana and James F. Lynch, Editors,** Logic and Random Structures

32 **Jean-Charles Grégoire, Gerard J. Holzmann, and Doron A. Peled, Editors,** The SPIN Verification System

31 **Neil Immerman and Phokion G. Kolaitis, Editors,** Descriptive Complexity and Finite Models

30 **Sandeep N. Bhatt, Editor,** Parallel Algorithms: Third DIMACS Implementation Challenge

29 **Doron A. Peled, Vaughan R. Pratt, and Gerard J. Holzmann, Editors,** Partial Order Methods in Verification

28 **Larry Finkelstein and William M. Kantor, Editors,** Groups and Computation II

27 **Richard J. Lipton and Eric B. Baum, Editors,** DNA Based Computers

26 **David S. Johnson and Michael A. Trick, Editors,** Cliques, Coloring, and Satisfiability: Second DIMACS Implementation Challenge

25 **Gilbert Baumslag, David Epstein, Robert Gilman, Hamish Short, and Charles Sims, Editors,** Geometric and Computational Perspectives on Infinite Groups

24 **Louis J. Billera, Curtis Greene, Rodica Simion, and Richard P. Stanley, Editors,** Formal Power Series and Algebraic Combinatorics/Séries Formelles et Combinatoire Algébrique, 1994

23 **Panos M. Pardalos, David I. Shalloway, and Guoliang Xue, Editors,** Global Minimization of Nonconvex Energy Functions: Molecular Conformation and Protein Folding

22 **Panos M. Pardalos, Mauricio G. C. Resende, and K. G. Ramakrishnan, Editors,** Parallel Processing of Discrete Optimization Problems

21 **D. Frank Hsu, Arnold L. Rosenberg, and Dominique Sotteau, Editors,** Interconnection Networks and Mapping and Scheduling Parallel Computations

20 **William Cook, László Lovász, and Paul Seymour, Editors,** Combinatorial Optimization

19 **Ingemar J. Cox, Pierre Hansen, and Bela Julesz, Editors,** Partitioning Data Sets

18 **Guy E. Blelloch, K. Mani Chandy, and Suresh Jagannathan, Editors,** Specification of Parallel Algorithms

17 **Eric Sven Ristad, Editor,** Language Computations

16 **Panos M. Pardalos and Henry Wolkowicz, Editors,** Quadratic Assignment and Related Problems

15 **Nathaniel Dean and Gregory E. Shannon, Editors,** Computational Support for Discrete Mathematics

14 **Robert Calderbank, G. David Forney, Jr., and Nader Moayeri, Editors,** Coding and Quantization: DIMACS/IEEE Workshop

13 **Jin-Yi Cai, Editor,** Advances in Computational Complexity Theory

12 **David S. Johnson and Catherine C. McGeoch, Editors,** Network Flows and Matching: First DIMACS Implementation Challenge

11 **Larry Finkelstein and William M. Kantor, Editors,** Groups and Computation

10 **Joel Friedman, Editor,** Expanding Graphs

For a complete list of titles in this series, visit the AMS Bookstore at **www.ams.org/bookstore/**.